FUNDAMENTALS OF COMPUTERS

Seventh Edition

V. RAJARAM
Emeritus Professor
Supercomputer Education and Research Centre
Indian Institute of Science, Bangalore

NEEHARIKA ADABALA
Chief Architect
CybULab Private Limited
Bangalore

PHI Learning Private Limited
Delhi-110092
2026

In fond memory of ***Shri Asoke K. Ghosh*** *(October 1942 – February 2024), Founder Chairman and Managing Director of PHI Learning, whose vision endlessly inspires.*

The Legacy Continues . . . .

Published by Pushpita Ghosh, PHI Learning Private Limited, Rimjhim House, 111, Patparganj Industrial Estate, Delhi-110092 and Printed by Glorious Printer, Delhi-110092.

₹650.00

FUNDAMENTALS OF COMPUTERS, Seventh Edition
V. Rajaraman and Neeharika Adabala

ISBN-978-93-5443-961-2 (Print Book)
ISBN-978-93-5443-919-3 (e-Book)

Contents

In memory of
my uncle *Dr. P.S. Viswanathan*
and
my aunt *Srimati Sitalakshmi*

—V. Rajaraman

Preface

A student must understand how a computer functions in addition to knowing how to program it. The primary objective of this book is to explain to beginners how a computer works. Computer salesmen and advertisers tend to use numerous obscure technical terms to impress customers. Very often, such jargon overwhelms many managers and computer users because they do not understand it; hence, another objective of this book is to explain in simple language what many of these terms mean. The hardware and software components of a computer are crucial for its functioning, and thus, both aspects are explained in this book.

This book is intended as a text for a course on 'Fundamentals of Computers' to be taught concurrently with programming courses. It would, therefore, be useful for the first course in computers taught to undergraduate computer science and computer engineering students, as well as postgraduate courses in computer applications (BCA and MCA). Rapid advances in computer technology have made it imperative for *all engineers* to understand the hardware features of computers, in addition to knowing how to program them in a high-level language. A core course is being introduced in undergraduate engineering curricula on the fundamentals of computers, and this book would be appropriate for this course. Given the extensive use of computers in business and industry, students in management schools require a course on computers, and this book would be suitable for such a course. There is a trend to introduce computer science as a subject in B.Sc. courses; again, this book can be used as a text for this course.

Besides its use as a text, this book would provide managers, engineers, and scientists a basic introduction to the hardware and software of computers. This knowledge is essential for appreciating the power and limitations of computers, as well as for selecting appropriate applications and hardware.

This book has evolved from a set of notes the first author used in various courses, thus these are classroom-tested. These notes have been used for concurrent reading in short intensive programming courses, in computer appreciation courses for managers and engineers, and undergraduate programmes for engineers.

The first six editions of this book received excellent response from the readers and were highly acclaimed. Numerous suggestions were also received from the readers. This seventh edition has been written by extensively revising the sixth edition along with a co-author. However, the basic structure of the book has been retained. All chapters were thoroughly reviewed. Several chapters were rewritten to reflect advances. A new chapter on the 'Basics of Artificial Intelligence' has been added in the present edition to reflect the emerging importance of this subject.

Chapter 1 explains the concept of computer algorithms, computer structure, and programming languages. Chapter 2 describes how various types of data are represented and stored in a computer. Chapter 3 describes several devices used to input data and programs to computers and the devices used to write the results of computation. Chapter 4 analyzes the properties of storage devices used to fabricate computer memories. It also describes the structure of different types of memories. In Chapter 5, the logical structure of a processor (also known as the *Central Processing Unit*) of a computer is presented. A small hypothetical computer is used to explain the basic ideas in the design of processors. Chapter 6 discusses how binary arithmetic operations are carried out by a computer. Chapter 7 presents Boolean algebra and its applications in the design of arithmetic and logic circuits. Chapter 8 covers how I-O units, the memory, and the processor are interconnected and the methods used to reduce the effects of speed mismatch between these units.

Chapters 9 and 10 are mainly concerned with the software of computers. Chapter 9 introduces the need for high-level languages for computers and briefly describes a number of popular programming languages. Chapter 10 presents the important concept of operating systems. It explains how various units are coordinated and how their functioning overlaps, using software aids. This chapter has been extensively revised.

Chapter 11 deals with microcomputers. Given the rapid growth of microcomputer applications, we have devoted a full chapter to this topic and explained the logical structure of microprocessors, the architecture of microcomputers, and their applications. Recently, smart cards and radio frequency identification tags have been extensively used. Both these devices use embedded microprocessors. Thus, a new section has been introduced to describe these. Chapter 12 explains how computers are classified as tablet, laptop (or notebook) computers, PCs, servers, mainframes, distributed and parallel computers, and as first, second, third, and fourth-generation machines.

The last four chapters are recent topics not usually found in most 'first books' on computers. Chapter 13 describes Computer Networks. It includes Local Area Networks (LANs), Internetworking using TCP/IP protocol, Intranets and Virtual Private Networks. Chapter 14 deals with analog and digital communications. In this chapter, various physical media used in computer communications are introduced. Specifically both wired and wireless communications are discussed. As mobile communication and smartphones have proliferated, we have described 4G and 5G mobile communication systems. We have also described new wireless systems such as WiMAX and WiGig. Chapter 15 is new and introduces recent advances in the input/output of computers. We describe graphical user interfaces (GUI) and how the extra computational load resulting from graphics is supported by the use of Graphics Processing Units (GPUs). We illustrate the recent trends towards more natural/intuitive interfaces to computers by describing 3D displays, multi-touch, gesture, and speech interaction systems. We also present advanced interface technologies, including haptic devices and brain-computer interfaces. Chapter 16 describes multimedia systems. All modern computers process not only numbers and text but also pictures (graphics), audio, and video. Various file formats for compressed graphics are described. We discuss in this chapter how to acquire and store audio and video data. Specifically, we have explained MP3 compression for audio and MPEG compression of video. Computer technology is rapidly changing. Besides rapid improvements in processors and memory, communication speed is also increasing enormously. This has led to new methods of using computers by means of the Internet infrastructure. Peer to Peer, Volunteer, Grid, and Cloud computing are rapidly growing. These environments have become very important. Of late, Artificial Intelligence and its applications have become important. We decided to add a chapter on the Basics of AI.

The level of discussion of topics in this book is elementary, emphasizing major ideas rather than providing in-depth discussion. The book concludes with a glossary of over 350 technical terms used in the book.

The presentation in this book is aimed at self-study. Each chapter begins with learning goals and ends with an extended summary and a large number of review questions.

We would like to express our heartfelt thanks to our colleagues Professor Anurag Kumar, Professor P.C.P. Bhatt, Prof. Venkat Arun, Dr. Siddharth Aravindan, and Prof. M.R.N. Murthy for reading parts of this book and giving valuable suggestions which enabled us to improve this book.

We would like to thank Ms. Pushpita Ghosh and her entire team at PHI Learning for their unstinting support in publishing this book. Finally, the first author would like to express his affectionate appreciation to his wife Dharma for the critical reading of the book, editing it, and her dedicated support in writing this book.

V. RAJARAMAN
NEEHARIKA ADABALA

1 Computer Basics

LEARNING GOALS

After reading this chapter, you should be able to:

- Explain what is an algorithm.
- Describe the major parts of a computer required to carry out algorithms.
- Explain the main characteristics of computers.
- Explain why programs are stored in the memory of a computer.
- Show how problems are solved by computers.

Computers now have a profound impact on every sphere of human activity and have brought many changes in industry, government, education, medicine, scientific research, law, social sciences, and even in arts such as music and painting. They help us to perform daily tasks, enable communication, assist in professional work, and entertain, among other applications.

The daily tasks they perform are:

- Assisting in bus, airline, and railway reservation.
- Shopping online for books, music, mobile phones, and various consumer-goods.
- Searching for information using search engines like–Google, Bing, DuckDuckGo, and Ask.com.
- Accessing encyclopedias such as Wikipedia available on the World Wide Web.
- Writing essays or creating documents using word processors.
- Getting answers to questions using chatbots like ChatGPT, Gemini, and Copilot.

Communication assistance they provide includes:

- Sending emails using mail apps such as Gmail, Hotmail, and Yahoo!

- Chatting with friends using applications such as Facebook, X, WhatsApp, and Zoom (for video conferencing).

Professional assistance they provide includes:

- Assisting aerospace engineers with flight simulation and training pilots.
- Helping accountants with applications such as spreadsheet programs.
- Aiding doctors in diagnosing diseases using medical images such as CAT scans.
- Assisting meteorologists in weather forecasting.
- Assisting government registrars by storing and retrieving data on land records.

Entertainment tasks they perform include:

- Composing and playing music.
- Creating animated movies.
- Playing video games, chess, and card games.

The areas of applications of computers are confined only by limitations on human creativity and imagination. Any task that can be carried out systematically, using a precise step-by-step method, can be performed by a computer. Every educated person today should be familiar with various features of computers their strengths, weaknesses, and their internal structure to choose a suitable computer and use it effectively. The main objective of this book is to explain these aspects of computers in a simple language.

1.1 ALGORITHMS

To solve a problem using a computer, it is necessary to develop a detailed and precise step-by-step solution method. Step-by-step methods for solving problems are not new or peculiar to computers. They have been used for a long time in almost all walks of life. One such method, taken from a popular magazine, is presented as Example 1.1.

Example 1.1 Recipe for Making Potato Bondas

Ingredients

Potatoes 250 grams, chopped onions 3 (small), finely chopped green chillies 5, gram flour 100 grams, oil for frying, water for the batter, salt 2 teaspoons.

Method

Step 1: Boil potatoes till cooked, peel and mash them until they are soft.
Step 2: Mix fried onions, green chillies, and salt with the mashed potatoes.
Step 3: Take little portions of the mixture and make small balls.
Step 4: Mix gram flour, water, and a little salt and beat well till a smooth and creamy batter is obtained.
Step 5: Dip the potato balls in the batter. Take out and deep fry in oil on a low fire.
Step 6: Take out when the balls are fried to a golden brown colour.

Result

A dozen potato bondas ready to be served hot with tomato sauce.

The recipe given above has the following properties:

1. It begins with a list of ingredients, which we may call the *inputs.*
2. A *sequence of instructions* is given to process the inputs.
3. As a result of carrying out the instructions, some *outputs* (namely, potato bondas) are obtained.

The instructions given to process the inputs are, however, *not precise*. They are ambiguous. For example, in Step 4, we are instructed to 'beat well till a smooth and creamy batter is obtained'. The interpretation of 'smooth and creamy' can vary from person to person. Owing to such imprecise instructions, different persons following the same recipe with the same inputs (ingredients) may produce potato bondas that vary in size, shape, and taste!

We will now examine another step-by-step procedure (again taken from a popular magazine).

Example 1.2 A Procedure to Knit a Sweater

Materials required

Needles No. 12:2, Wool 4 ply: 9 balls.

Method

Step 1: Cast on 133 stitches.
Step 2: Repeat Steps 3 and 4, 11 times.
Step 3: Knit 2, * Purl 1, Knit 1, Repeat from * to last stitch, Knit 1.
Step 4: Knit 1, * Purl 1, Knit 1, Repeat from * to End.

....

....

(Similar Steps)

Result

A sweater.

The above example illustrates the following points:

1. This procedure has inputs and a set of steps to process the inputs to produce an output.
2. The procedure is more precise and unambiguous than the recipe for potato bondas. There is very little chance of misinterpretation.
3. The number of different instructions used in the procedure is very few. If one knows how to knit, purl, cast stitches on and off needles, and count, then they can knit any sweater.
4. By a proper permutation and combination of this elementary set of instructions, one can create an infinite number of patterns for sweaters. For example, if Step 3 is made 'Knit 1, * Knit 1, Purl 2, Repeat from * to last stitch', the sweater's pattern will be very different.

The preciseness of the instructions combined with their limited variety makes it possible to design a machine that can knit automatically. A forerunner of the modern computer was a loom built by Jacquard, a French engineer in 1801, which could be 'programmed' to create numerous patterns. The program consisted of cards with specific patterns of holes that controlled the loom.

We have illustrated two simple step-by-step methods of solving problems. We will now explain when a step-by-step method can be called an *algorithm.*

The origin of the word algorithm is not known. It is, however, generally accepted among mathematicians that it comes from the name of a famous Arab mathematician Abu Jafar Mohammed ibn Musa al-Khwarizmi (*circa* 825) (literally meaning father of Jafar Mohammed, son of Moses, native of al-Khwarizm), who wrote the celebrated book *Kitab al-jabr wal-muqabla (Rules of Restoration and Reduction).* The last part of his name al-Khwarizmi was corrupted as *"algorithm"*. An algorithm may be defined as a finite sequence of instructions (to solve a problem) which has the following five basic characteristics:

1. An algorithm begins with instruction(s) to accept *inputs.* These *inputs* are processed by the subsequent sequence of instructions in the algorithm.
2. The *sequence of instructions* specified in the algorithm must be precise and unambiguous. In other words, the instructions must not be vague. It must also be possible to carry them out. For example, the instruction 'Go to hell' is precise, but cannot be carried out.
3. Each *instruction* must be sufficiently *basic* such that it can, in principle, be carried out by a person with paper and pencil.
4. The total *time* to carry out all the steps in the algorithm must be *finite*. As algorithms may contain instructions to repeat a group of instructions, this requirement implies that the number of repetitions must be *finite.*
5. An algorithm must produce one or more *outputs* (namely, the result of processing the inputs).

Based on the above definition, observe that the recipe of Example 1.1 does not qualify as an algorithm as it is not precise. The knitting pattern, on the other hand, does qualify.

We will now write a step-by-step procedure to solve a data processing job. The problem is to find the average number of vowels occurring in a short passage.

Example 1.3 Procedure to Find the Average Number of Vowels in a Passage

Step 1: Let Number of characters = 0
Step 2: Let Number of vowels = 0
Step 3: Repeat Steps 4, 5, 6 and 7 until no more characters are left in the passage.
Step 4: Read one character from the passage.
Step 5: Add 1 to Number of characters.
Step 6: If the character is any one of the letters A, E, I, O, U, a, e, i, o, u, add 1 to Number of vowels.
Step 7: Move to the next character.
Remark: Step 8 is reached only when no more characters are left in the passage. If any character is left, go back to Step 4.
Step 8: Average Number of vowels = $\frac{\text{Number of vowels}}{\text{Number of characters}}$
Step 9: Write Average Number of vowels, Number of characters.
Step 10: Stop.

This step-by-step procedure qualifies as an algorithm for the following reasons:

(i) It has an input, namely, the passage to be examined.
(ii) The sequence of instructions is precisely specified and not ambiguous.
(iii) Each instruction is basic and can be carried out by a person using paper and pencil.
(iv) The total number of instructions carried out is finite.
(v) The procedure terminates when the end of the passage is reached.
(vi) It has outputs, namely, the average number of vowels and the number of characters.

1.2 SIMPLE MODEL OF A COMPUTER

If a machine is to be built to carry out the algorithm of Example 1.3, it should have the following features:

(i) It should be able to read a text consisting of a series of characters.
(ii) It should be able to interpret each instruction in the algorithm and carry it out.
(iii) It should be able to add and divide.
(iv) It should be able to compare a character read from the passage with the letters A, E, I, O, U, a, e, i, o, u and if it matches any of these characters, add 1 to the number of vowels.
(v) It should be able to store (or remember) computed values.
(vi) It should be able to write (or output) the answers obtained.
(vii) If the steps in the algorithm are to be carried out *automatically* without human intervention, the entire algorithm must be *stored* for reference. As the algorithm is also repetitive, that is, a set of steps are carried out again and again until a condition is satisfied, it is necessary to have all the steps in the algorithm stored in a storage unit.

A computing machine designed to carry out algorithms for processing data has the configuration of Figure 1.1. In Figure 1.1, it is seen that an *input unit* is provided to read the algorithm and the data to be processed by the algorithm. The *memory unit* stores the algorithm and computed values. The *processing unit* interprets the instructions and carries them out. It can perform arithmetic operations, character manipulation operations, and logical operations. The *output unit* prints or displays computed results. In some computers input and output are combined such as the touch screens in tablet computers and smart phones.

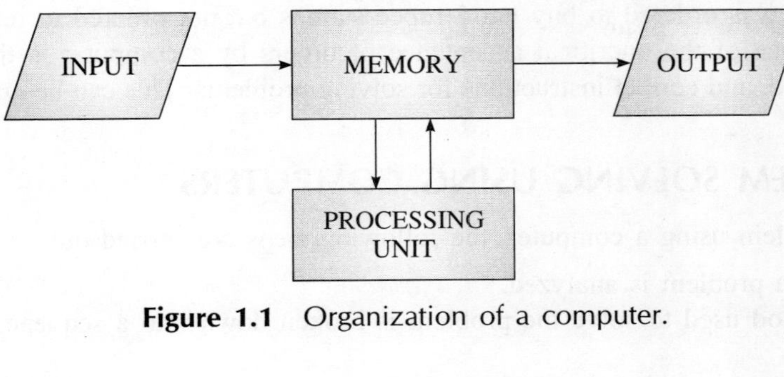

Figure 1.1 Organization of a computer.

In Example 1.2, it was seen that it is possible to develop an enormous number of unique patterns by permuting and combining a few basic types of instructions. The same principle is used in building computers. Thus, by using a computer's processing unit which can interpret and execute as few as 10 different operations, it is possible to perform a large variety of data processing tasks.

1.3 CHARACTERISTICS OF COMPUTERS

The interesting features of a computer are:

1. Computers are built to carry out a small variety of instructions. It is not necessary to have more than about 100 distinct instructions even for a very powerful machine.
2. Instructions are very simple, for example, add, subtract, read a character, write a character, store a character, compare numbers, characters, etc.
3. Most instructions are carried out in less than a millionth of a second.
4. Instructions are carried out obediently with no questions asked.
5. Instructions are carried out correctly.

A computer may thus be imagined as a servant who would carry out instructions, precisely, obediently, uncritically, at a very high speed, and without exhibiting any emotions. As human beings, we use judgement based on experience, often on subjective and emotional considerations. Such value judgements often depend on what we call sound 'common sense'. In contrast, a computer exhibits no emotions and has no common sense. An algorithm may be written for a computer to compose music based on rules of composition. The computer, however, cannot judge the quality of the resultant music or enjoy it. It must be clearly understood that computers are machines that can be programmed to follow instructions; they don't have their own priorities and judgements. Computers are machines that can help us in many ways, but they do not pose a threat to us.

Being obedient without exercising 'common sense' can be very frustrating and unproductive. This is illustrated by the experience of a Colonel who sent his obedient assistant to a post office with the order 'Go to the Post Office and buy ten 5 rupee stamps'. The assistant went with the money to the post office and did not return for a long time. The Colonel got worried and went in search of him to the post office and found him standing there with the stamps in his hand. When the Colonel became angry and asked him why he was standing there, pat came the reply that he was ordered to buy ten 5 rupee stamps but not ordered to return with them!

A consequence of the uncritical acceptance of orders by a computer is the need to give extensive, detailed, and correct instructions for solving problems. This can be quite challenging.

1.4 PROBLEM SOLVING USING COMPUTERS

To solve a problem using a computer, the following steps are carried out:

1. The given problem is analyzed.
2. The method used to solve the problem is broken down into a sequence of elementary tasks.

3. Based on this analysis, an algorithm is formulated to solve the problem. The algorithm should be precise, concise, and unambiguous. Based on our discussions, we realize that algorithm formulation is difficult and time-consuming.
4. The algorithm is then expressed using a precise notation, known as a **computer programming language**. A well-written algorithm, when expressed in this notation, becomes a **computer program**.
5. The computer program is fed to the computer and stored in its memory.
6. The computer's processing unit retrieves an instruction of the program from the memory, interprets it, and executes it. Normally there would be one or more instructions to output the result(s) of computation.
7. When all the instructions in a program are interpreted and executed and a stop instruction is found, the computer halts.

We will now consider an example of formulating a computer algorithm and writing a computer program corresponding to the algorithm.

Example 1.4 Finding the Highest Marks in a Class

Find out the highest marks obtained in an examination and the roll number of the student obtaining the highest marks. For simplicity, it is assumed that only one student obtains the highest marks.

Input

We first decide the format in which the marks would be presented. We assume that each student's paper will have a roll number and total marks obtained by the student.

Method

Having decided on the data format, we formulate the steps needed in a procedure to pick the highest marks.

Step 1: Read the first student's paper and note down the roll number and the marks. This is the highest marks found so far.

Step 2: Repeat Steps 3 and 4 until no more papers are left.

Step 3: Read the next student's paper. Compare the marks in this paper with the highest marks found so far.

Step 4: If the marks read in Step 3 is greater than the highest marks noted, then erase that and replace it with the marks read in Step 3 and replace the roll number noted down earlier with this new roll number. Else do nothing.

Remarks: When no more papers are left we go to Step 5. Until then Steps 3 and 4 are repeated.

Step 5: Print the roll number and the maximum marks noted.

1.4.1 Flowchart

Having obtained an algorithm for solving the problem, we express the algorithm in a pictorial form called a *flowchart*. The flowchart is primarily used as an aid in formulating and understanding algorithms. The sequencing of instructions and repetition of groups of instructions may be quickly seen by inspecting a flowchart. The flowchart for the algorithm of Example 1.4 is shown in Figure 1.2.

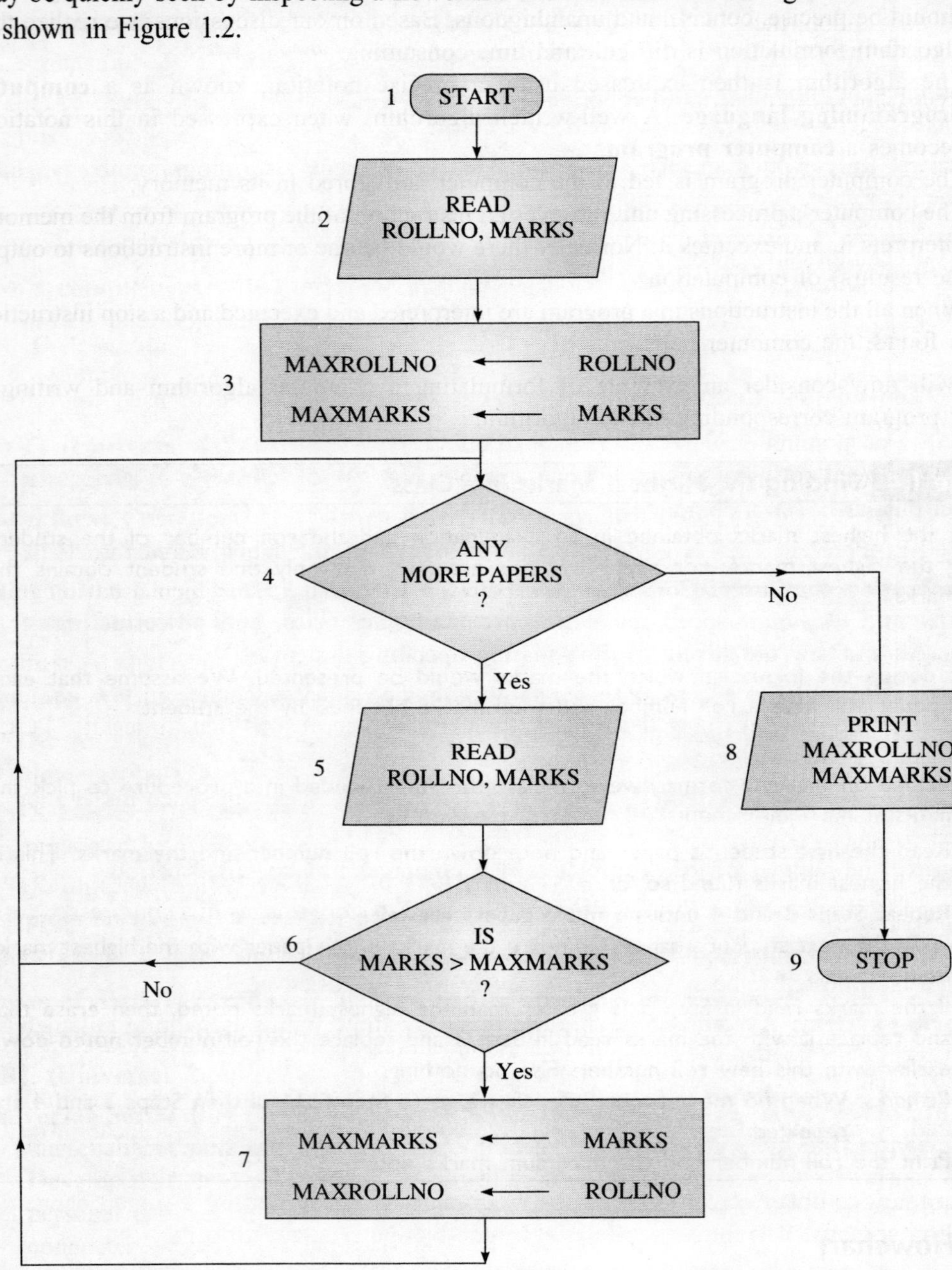

Figure 1.2 A flowchart giving the method for picking the highest marks.

For easy visual recognition, a standard convention is used in drawing flowcharts. In this standard convention, the following shapes are used for various blocks in a flowchart:

(i) Rectangles with rounded ends are used to indicate START and STOP.
(ii) Parallelograms are used to represent input and output operations.
(iii) Diamond-shaped boxes are used to indicate questions asked or conditions tested, based on whose answers appropriate exits are taken by a procedure. The exits from the diamond-shaped box are labelled with the answers to the questions.
(iv) Rectangles are used to indicate any processing operation such as storage and arithmetic.

1.4.2 Program

The next step is to express the flowchart in a more precise and concise notation called a *programming language.* A computer program corresponding to the flowchart of Figure 1.2 written in a programming language called FORTRAN 90 is given below:

A reader need not worry if he or she does not fully understand the notation used to express the algorithm. It is given only to show the reader what a program looks like.

```
PROGRAM max_marks
    IMPLICIT NONE
    INTEGER: roll_no, marks, max_roll_no, max_marks
        READ*, roll_no, marks
        max_marks = marks
        max_roll_no = roll_no
    DO
        READ*, roll_no, marks
        IF (roll_no == 0) EXIT! roll_no = 0 indicates no more papers
        IF (marks > max_marks)
            max_marks = marks
            max_roll_no = roll_no
        ENDIF
    END DO
    PRINT *, max_marks, max_roll_no
END PROGRAM max_marks
```

The above program is a straightforward translation of the flowchart. It uses a precise notation which should be learnt by a programmer.

1.4.3 Working of a Computer

We learnt how to obtain an algorithm and a program to solve the given problem (Example 1.4). We will now learn how the algorithm is executed by a computer. The model of the computer shown in Figure 1.1 will be used for illustration.

We will assume that the flowchart of Figure 1.2 is read by the input unit and stored in the computer's memory. (Strictly speaking, a program, and *not* a flowchart, is read and stored in a computer's memory. We use the flowchart, instead of the program, only because the reader may not know a programming language.) The data to be processed, namely, the roll number and marks, are written in a file in the order in which they would be used by the flowchart, and read by an input unit and stored in the computer's memory (see Figure 1.3).

The processing unit of the computer reads from the memory the first block in the flowchart, which says 'START'. This instruction gets all the units in the computer ready. After this, the processing unit retrieves from the memory the next instruction given in the flowchart (block 2 in Figure 1.2) which states:

READ ROLLNO, MARKS

This command is interpreted as 'Read the first number from the data file at the input unit. Name a location in memory as ROLLNO. Clear it and store in it the number read. Similarly, store the second number from the datafile in a memory location named 'MARKS'. Figure 1.3(b) illustrates this.

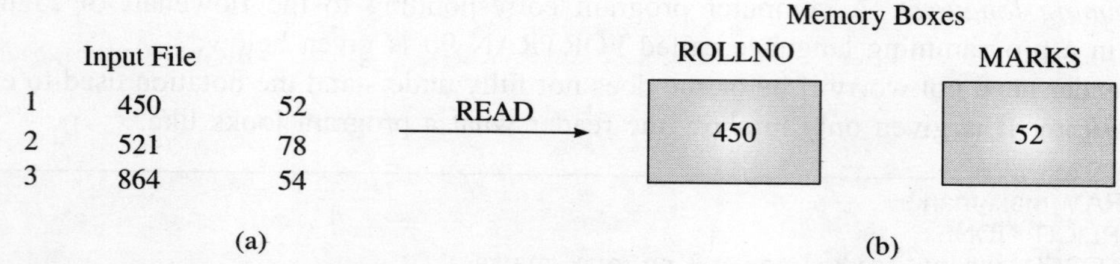

Figure 1.3 Input data file and the result of executing the first READ instruction.

The next block (block 3, Figure 1.2) is now taken up for execution. It is interpreted as:

"generate a variable name MAXROLLNO which clears a memory location and labels it MAXROLLNO". Copy into it the contents of the memory location named ROLLNO. Clear another memory location and label it MAXMARKS. Copy into it the contents of location named MARKS'. Figure 1.4 illustrates this.

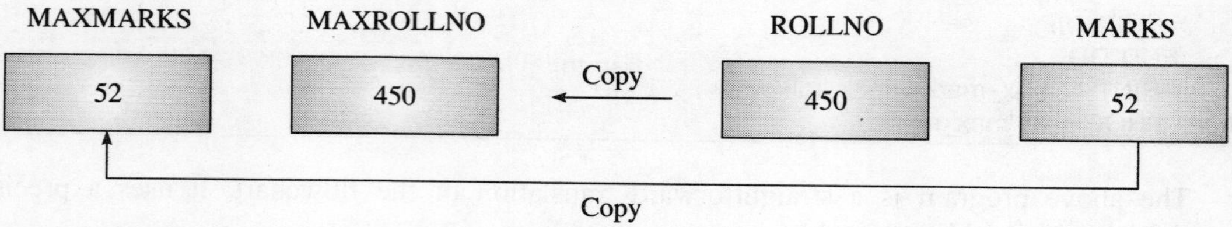

Figure 1.4 Status of memory locations after executing instructions in block 3 of the flowchart shown in Figure 1.2.

Following the flowchart, the next block (block 4) asks the question: 'Any more papers?' This is interpreted by the processing unit and it checks whether there are any more data in the input file at the input unit. Data 2 and 3 (Figure 1.3a) would still be there and the answer to the question is 'Yes'. The path labelled 'Yes' is thus followed and block 5 in the flowchart is taken up for execution. It states:

READ ROLLNO, MARKS

It is interpreted as before and the numbers in the input file (Figure 1.3), are read and the values in it are stored in boxes ROLLNO and MARKS *after erasing* their earlier contents. After executing this instruction, the contents of memory locations will be as shown in Figure 1.5.

Figure 1.5 Status of memory locations after executing instructions in block 4 and block 5 of Figure 1.2.

Next, block 6 in the flowchart is reached in which the question 'Is MARKS > MAXMARKS?' is asked. This is interpreted as 'Is the number stored in the memory location labelled MARKS greater than the number stored in MAXMARKS?' Referring to Figure 1.5, we see that the number stored in MARKS, namely, 78, is greater than that stored in MAXMARKS, namely, 52. Thus, the path labelled 'Yes' is followed and block 7 is reached, which instructs that the contents of memory location MAXMARKS should be replaced by the contents of MARKS and the contents of MAXROLLNO by the contents of ROLLNO. The status of values stored in memory locations at the end of this step is shown in Figure 1.6.

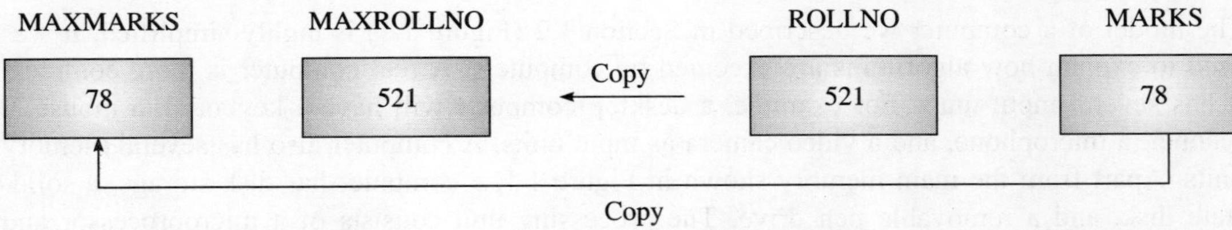

Figure 1.6 Status of memory locations after executing instructions in blocks 6 and 7 of Figure 1.2.

The path leading out of block 7 in the flowchart leads back to block 4 of the chart. Executing block 4, we see that data are still left in the input file. Executing block 5, the numbers 864 and 54 are read into ROLLNO and MARKS, respectively (Figure 1.7). Executing block 6, we see that 54 stored in MARKS is less than 78 stored in MAXMARKS. Thus, the 'No' path is taken out of block 6 and we reach block 4.

Figure 1.7 Status of memory locations after the last record in the input is read.

When block 4 is executed, we see that no more data is left in the input file. Thus, execution of block 4 gives 'NO' as the answer and we reach block 8 of the flowchart.

The instruction in block 8 commands that the contents of locations MAXROLLNO and MAXMARKS are to be printed by the output unit. Thus, the numbers 521 and 78 are printed. After doing this, the instruction in block 9 is reached which stops computation.

1.4.4 Stored Program Concept

The computer model used in this section was first proposed in 1945 by John Von Neumann, a chemical engineer turned computer scientist. The major contribution of Von Neumann is the idea of storing a program and the data to be processed in the same memory. Storing a program in memory is essential if a series of instructions is to be repetitively carried out. For instance, in Example 1.4, after Steps 3 and 4 are carried out, the algorithm returns to the previous Step 3 if more data are left in the input file. The previous step cannot be carried out unless it is 'stored' and is available for reference in the memory.

Storing a program in memory also makes the operation of computers *automatic*. Unlike a calculator where one has to press buttons after each operation is carried out, the instructions stored in the memory of a computer are taken one by one automatically to the processing unit, interpreted, and executed without human intervention.

1.4.5 Hardware and Software

The model of a computer we described in Section 1.2 (Figure 1.1) is highly simplified. It was used to explain how algorithms are executed by computers. A real computer is more complex. It has several input units. For example, a desktop computer will have a keyboard, a mouse, a scanner, a microphone, and a video camera as input units. A computer also has several memory units. Apart from the main memory shown in Figure 1.1, a computer has disk storage, a solid-state disk, and a removable pen drive. The processing unit consists of a microprocessor and several support chips. The computer also has many output units. The most common output units are a video monitor, a printer, and a speaker.

The block diagram of a computer shown in Fig, 1.1 is that of a 'stand-alone' computer. Nowadays, an isolated single computer is rare. A computer has a Network Interface Card (NIC) which connects it to other computers. A computer also has a unit called a *modem* or a wireless router that connects it to the Internet—a worldwide network of computers. A computer not connected to the Internet cannot use applications such as email, Facebook, Google, X etc.

The units of a computer we described above constitute what is known as *hardware*. A computer is useless unless it has several ready-made programs to enable easy use of the hardware. This is provided by *software*. The most important software required to use a computer is known as an Operating System (OS). An OS coordinates the activities of various parts of a computer, namely, the CPU, the Input-Output units, and the memory. It optimizes the use of the resources of a computer. Some commonly used OSs are Windows by Microsoft, macOS for Apple computers, Linux (an open-source OS), and Android used in smartphones. Besides the OS, it is also essential for a computer to have a set of application programs. The most important application programs consist of a word processor, a program to send/receive email, one that systematically organizes and assists in retrieving data, and a program to access the World Wide Web called a browser. In the following chapters, we will describe some of these application programs.

SUMMARY

We summarize now the main points presented in this chapter:

1. To solve a problem using a computer, it is necessary to develop an algorithm.
2. An algorithm is a finite sequence of instructions. Each instruction is precise, unambiguous, and capable of being carried out by a machine in a finite time. Most algorithms have inputs and outputs.
3. A computer is a machine that executes an algorithm written to process data fed into it and produces the required results.
4. An algorithm is expressed in a graphical form known as a flowchart. A flowchart is mainly used to aid understanding of algorithms.
5. A programming language is a precise notation used to express algorithms. An algorithm expressed in a programming language is called a computer program.
6. A computer is designed using four basic units to enable it to process data. It has an *input unit* that accepts the data and the program to process the data. It stores these in a *memory unit.* The program retrieved from the memory unit is interpreted and executed by a *processing unit.* The computed results are stored in memory and displayed or printed using an *output unit.*
7. Storing a program in memory is essential to formulate concise, repetitive algorithms and for automatic program execution.
8. The main characteristics of a computer are its speed, accuracy, versatility to perform a variety of tasks, automatic program execution without human intervention, and capacity to carry out repetitive jobs routinely any number of times.
9. Nowadays, no computer is isolated. Computers are connected to other computers using a network interface card and to the Internet using a modem or a wireless router.

REVIEW QUESTIONS

1.1 Pick out a recipe from a popular magazine and express it in a step-by-step procedure.

1.2 Explain why a procedure given for a recipe in a cookbook may not be termed an algorithm.

1.3 What is the basic difference between a procedure given for knitting a sweater and a recipe?

1.4 Explain the term algorithm.

1.5 What is a programming language?

1.6 What is a computer program?

1.7 Draw a block diagram of a computer. Explain the function of each of the blocks.

1.8 Example 1.4 is a procedure to find the highest marks obtained in a class. Modify it to find the lowest marks obtained.

1.9 Modify the procedure of Example 1.4 to find the average marks of a class.

1.10 Obtain a flowchart corresponding to the algorithm of Exercise 1.9. Using the model of a computer presented in this chapter, explain how a computer will find the average marks.

1.11 In obtaining the algorithm for Example 1.4, it is assumed that the maximum mark is obtained by only one student. How would you modify the algorithm to find out the roll numbers of all the students who obtain the maximum marks?
Hint: Assume that we can re-read the input data file.

1.12 Draw a flowchart corresponding to the algorithm of Example 1.3 given in the text.

1.13 Explain how the flowchart obtained in Exercise 1.12 will be executed by a computer using the model of a computer.

1.14 Formulate an algorithm to find the average number of occurrences of each of the letters Q, X, Y, Z in an English passage.

1.15 Obtain an algorithm to find the average number of letters in each sentence in an English passage.

1.16 Explain in what ways are real computers different from the abstract model of a computer given in Figure 1.1.

1.17 Explain the terms hardware and software. What is an operating system? Why is it necessary to use a computer?

1.18 What are application programs? Give some examples of application programs.

1.19 What is a Network Interface Card? What is its use?

1.20 How is a computer connected to the Internet? Why should a computer be connected to the Internet?

2 Data Representation

LEARNING GOALS

After reading this chapter, you should be able to:

- Explain why binary numbers are used in computers.
- Describe how characters are represented in computers.
- Show how integers and numbers with fractional parts are represented in computers for storage and processing.
- Convert decimal numbers to binary and hexadecimal numbers and vice versa.

To explain how data is processed by a computer, we should first understand the form in which data is stored in its memory. In this chapter, we shall see how data is transformed or coded to facilitate its storage and processing.

Five types of data are stored and processed by computers. They are:

1. Text, which consists of strings of characters
2. Numbers
3. Audio, namely, speech and music
4. Pictures—monochrome and colour
5. Video, which is a sequence of pictures such as a movie or an animation. Usually, video data is accompanied by a soundtrack which is synchronized with pictures.

Of these, text and numbers are simple data types which were the dominant types used till recently. Other data types constitute multimedia data. In this chapter, we will discuss only text and numbers. In Chapter 16, we will discuss other data types and their representation.

Textual data consists of strings of characters. Characters include letters and special symbols. For example, a computer may be programmed to read a list of names, sort them alphabetically, and print the sorted list. A list of names, such as SIVA, RAMA, and KRISHNA, read by an input unit would be stored in memory, sorted by the program alphabetically, and printed as the list KRISHNA, RAMA, SIVA. The data processed in this case are *strings of characters,* the strings being SIVA, RAMA, and KRISHNA.

The other data type includes decimal numbers, such as 1234, 48.5, etc. Numbers are processed using arithmetic operations, such as addition, subtraction, multiplication, and division. In this case, we assign *values* to numbers, and processing them results in new values.

The characters and numbers fed to a computer, and the output from the computer, must be usable by people. For this, symbols used by a natural language (e.g., English letters) and decimal digits are appropriate. These constitute the *external data representation.* On the other hand, the representation of data inside a computer must match the technology used by the computer to store and process data. Thus, we should first determine the most appropriate *internal representation of data* and then specify unique transformation rules to convert the external representation to the internal representation and vice versa.

2.1 REPRESENTATION OF CHARACTERS IN COMPUTERS

Physical devices used to store and process data in computers are *two-state* devices. A switch, for example, is a two-state device; it can be either ON or OFF. Data on a magnetic surface is recorded reliably when the surface is magnetized in either one of two opposite directions. The two states in this case are the magnetic field aligned from left to right (S→N) and that aligned from right to left (N←S). Electronic devices such as transistors used in computers function most reliably when operated as switches, that is, either in a conducting mode or in a non-conducting mode. Thus, all data stored and processed in computers are transformed or coded as strings of two symbols, one symbol to represent each state. The two symbols normally used are 0 and 1. These are known as *bits,* an abbreviation for *bi*nary digi*ts.*

There are four unique combinations of two bits, namely:

00   01   10   11

There are $2 \times 2 \times 2 = 8$ unique combinations or strings of 3 bits each and they are:

000   001   010   011   100   101   110   111

Each unique string of bits may be used to represent or code a symbol. To code the 26 capital or upper-case letters of English, at least 26 unique strings of bits are needed. With 4 bits, there are only 16 ($2 \times 2 \times 2 \times 2 = 16$) unique strings of 4 bits, and thus 4 bits are not sufficient. Five bits, however, are sufficient as 32 ($2 \times 2 \times 2 \times 2 \times 2 = 32$) strings of 5 bits each can be formed. Twenty-six out of these 32 strings of 5 bits may be picked to code the 26 capital letters as illustrated in Table 2.1.

Data processing using computers requires processing not only the 26 upper-case English letters but also the 26 lower-case English letters, 10 digits, and around 32 other characters, such as punctuation marks, arithmetic operator symbols, and parentheses. Thus, the total number of characters to be coded is $26 + 26 + 10 + 32 = 94$. With strings of 6 bits each, it is possible

Table 2.1 Illustrating the coding of the capital English letters

Bit string	*Letter*	*Bit string*	*Letter*
0 0 0 0 0	A	1 0 0 0 0	Q
0 0 0 0 1	B	1 0 0 0 1	R
0 0 0 1 0	C	1 0 0 1 0	S
0 0 0 1 1	D	1 0 0 1 1	T
0 0 1 0 0	E	1 0 1 0 0	U
0 0 1 0 1	F	1 0 1 0 1	V
0 0 1 1 0	G	1 0 1 1 0	W
0 0 1 1 1	H	1 0 1 1 1	X
0 1 0 0 0	I	1 1 0 0 0	Y
0 1 0 0 1	J	1 1 0 0 1	Z
0 1 0 1 0	K	1 1 0 1 0	Not used
0 1 0 1 1	L	1 1 0 1 1	
0 1 1 0 0	M	1 1 1 0 0	
0 1 1 0 1	N	1 1 1 0 1	
0 1 1 1 0	O	1 1 1 1 0	
0 1 1 1 1	P	1 1 1 1 1	

to code only $2^6 = 64$ characters. Thus, 6 bits are insufficient for coding these 94 characters. If we use strings of 7 bits each, we will have $2^7 = 128$ unique 7-bit strings and can code up to 128 characters. Strings of 7 bits each are therefore sufficient to code 94 characters.

The coding of characters has been standardized to facilitate the exchange of recorded data between computers. The most popular standard is known as ASCII (*A*merican *S*tandard *C*ode for *I*nformation *I*nterchange). This uses 7 bits to code each character. Besides codes for characters, in this standard, codes are defined to convey information, such as the end of line, end of page, etc., to the computer. These codes are said to be *control characters* that are not printable. Table 2.2 gives the ASCII code for printable and *non-printable* (control) characters. Columns 1 and 2 are non-printable codes. The entry CR, for example, indicates carriage return (or end of line) control character. The most significant bits of the code are given in Table 2.2 as the column headings and the least significant bits of the code are the row headings. Thus the code for A, for example, is identified from the table by finding the column and the row bits. The column gives bits 100 as bits $b_6\ b_5\ b_4$ and the row gives bits 0001 for $b_3\ b_2\ b_1\ b_0$.

Thus, the code for A is:

b_6	b_5	b_4	b_3	b_2	b_1	b_0
1	0	0	0	0	0	1

The internal coded representation of the string RAMA J is:

1010010	1000001	1001101	1000001	0100000	1001010
R	A	M	A	SPACE	J

Observe that the blank between RAMA and J also needs a code. This code is essential to leave a blank between RAMA and J when the string is printed.

In addition to ASCII, another code known as ISCII (Indian Script Code for Information Interchange) has been standardized by the Indian Standards Organization. The full description of this code is available in the document IS: 13194:1991 published by the Indian Standards Organization. It is an 8-bit code that allows English and Indian script alphabets to be used simultaneously. It retains the standard ASCII code for English. It extends Table 2.2 by adding six more columns 1010, 1011, 1100, 1101, 1110, and 1111 (observe that Table 2.2 as shown has columns from 000 to 111 only). With this addition, it is possible to define 96 more characters. A common code for all Indian languages is feasible as all Indian scripts have a common origin from the *Brahmi* script. The phonetic nature of Indian languages is used to design the keyboard. All consonants have an implicit vowel. For example, क = क् + अ. Thus, a consonant such as कि is split into क् + इ. Using this idea, the consonants and vowels are separated. Two character codes are, therefore, needed for a consonant.

Table 2.2 ASCII code for characters

Least significant bits of code	*Most significant bits $b_6 b_5 b_4$*							
$b_3\ b_2\ b_1\ b_0$	000	001	010	011	100	101	110	111
0 0 0 0	NUL	DLE	SPACE	0	@	P		p
0 0 0 1	SOH	DC1	!	1	A	Q	a	q
0 0 1 0	STX	DC2	"	2	B	R	b	r
0 0 1 1	ETX	DC3	#	3	C	S	c	s
0 1 0 0	EOT	DC4	$	4	D	T	d	t
0 1 0 1	ENQ	NAK	%	5	E	U	e	u
0 1 1 0	ACK	SYN	&	6	F	V	f	v
0 1 1 1	BEL	ETB	’	7	G	W	g	w
1 0 0 0	BS	CAN	(	8	H	X	h	x
1 0 0 1	HT	EM	)	9	I	Y	i	y
1 0 1 0	LF	SUB	*	:	J	Z	j	z
1 0 1 1	VT	ESC	+	;	K	[	k	{
1 1 0 0	FF	FS	,	<	L	\	l	|
1 1 0 1	CR	GS	–	=	M	]	m	}
1 1 1 0	SO	RS	.	>	N	Λ	n	~
1 1 1 1	SI	US	/	?	O	—	o	DEL

A string of bits that represents a character is known as a *byte.* Characters coded in ISCII need 8 bits for each character. Thus, a byte, in this case, is a string of 8 bits. A character coded in ASCII will need only 7 bits.

The need to accommodate characters of languages other than English was foreseen while designing ASCII and thus 8 bits were specified to represent characters. A *byte* is commonly understood as a string of 8 bits. The International Standards Organization standardized an 8-bit code (ISO 646) for Latin scripts used in Europe in addition to English letters. This was widely used in Europe. The ASCII code is a proper subset of this code.

It was realized in the early 1990s that the US/Europe-centric coding of characters needed revision. A group of professionals which included computer scientists, linguists, and scholars from disciplines such as mathematics, music, etc. was formed to design a character coding scheme that could be used universally for all languages of the world including Chinese, Japanese, Korean, Urdu, Arabic, and Hebrew. In 1991, the group proposed a standard called *Unicode* which was a 16-bit code. This is called Unicode 1.0 now. The primary idea of Unicode is to separate the coding of characters from their graphical representation called *glyphs.* For example, the letter A may be printed in several fonts. This is not the concern of Unicode whose only function is to assign a unique number for every character in every language of the World. Unicode evolved with time as computers became an essential tool for all disciplines. With the advent of the Internet, the interchange of information internationally and the need to mix various languages and symbols such as those used in mathematics, chemistry, and music became necessary. Thus, Unicode was modified to accommodate not only all living languages but also symbols of various types, including ancient hieroglyphics such as Indus script. As of 2024, the latest Unicode version is Unicode 15.1 and it has been standardized by the International Standards Organization as ISO/IEC 10646. Unicode 15.1 is a 32-bit code. In theory, it can encode 2^{32} (over a billion) characters. However, it currently defines 149813 characters. It has left several optional codes for future use for symbols/characters one may invent to use in areas such as dance choreography.

Unicode 15.1 supports three encoding forms called *Unicode Transformation Format (UTF)* for practical use. (Using 32 bits for each character is wasteful). They are: UTF-8, UTF-16, and UTF-32. UTF-8 codes are the same as ASCII codes for the first 128 characters to ensure backward compatibility. UTF-16 supports all living languages and defines 2^{16} codes. This covers most practical requirements including mathematics symbols. This is called the *basic multilingual plane*. UTF-8 and UTF-16 have also been approved by the World Wide Web Consortium for character coding of Web documents.

2.2 REPRESENTATION OF INTEGERS

In the last section, we saw how characters and strings of characters are represented internally in a computer. Decimal digits are also considered as characters and codes are assigned to them. These codes for digits are primarily used when digits are used merely as symbols with no 'value' assigned to them. They are called *binary-coded decimal* characters. For example, the string KA05M438 is the registration number of a car, which has both letters and digits. In this string, the digits have no 'value' in a conventional sense. Thus, we can use ASCII code to represent this string of characters.

If we want to store decimal numbers in a computer and perform arithmetic operations using them, the representation must have a *value* assigned to the numbers. To do this, we *convert* a decimal number to another number that uses only the symbols '0' and '1' and has a value equal to that of the given decimal number.

Consider, for example, the decimal number 4903. The value of each digit in this number is determined by the following:

(i) *Digit* itself
(ii) *Position* of the digit in the number
(iii) *Base* or *radix* of the number system

The base of a number system is defined as the number of distinct symbols used to represent numbers in the system. The decimal system uses the ten symbols 0, 1, 2, 3, 4, 5, 6, 7, 8, and 9 and its base is thus ten.

Given a decimal integer, we assign it a value by first assigning weights to each digit position. The weights are unity for the rightmost digit and ten, hundred, thousand, and so on for successive digits to its left.

We multiply each digit by its weight and add all products to obtain the value of the number. The value of the decimal number 4903 is calculated as:

4×10^3	+	9×10^2	+	0×10^1	+	3×10^0	
4000	+	900	+	0	+	3	= 4903
Thousands position		Hundreds position		Tens position		Units position	

The notation used to express numbers described above is known as the *positional system.*

If a number system has only two symbols, then its *base* is 2. Such a system is known as a ***binary*** system. The two symbols used in the system, namely, 0 and 1, are binary digits or ***bits.*** Numbers in this system are strings of bits. A binary number is shown below:

1 0 1 0 1

↓ ↓

Most significant bit — Least significant bit

The rightmost bit is called the *least significant bit* and the leftmost bit is the *most significant bit.* The weights assigned to bits in this system are powers of 2, namely, $2^0 = 1$, $2^1 = 2$, $2^2 = 4$, etc. To find the decimal value of a binary number, we multiply its least significant bit by the weight 1, the next bit to its left by 2, and so on. Thus, the decimal value of the binary number 10101 is calculated as shown below:

1		0		1		0		1	
1×2^4	+	0×2^3	+	1×2^2	+	0×2^1	+	1×2^0	
16	+	0	+	4	+	0	+	1	= 21

As another example, the binary number 10010101 is converted to its decimal equivalent as shown below:

$$(1 \times 2^7) + (0 \times 2^6) + (0 \times 2^5) + (1 \times 2^4) + (0 \times 2^3) + (1 \times 2^2) + (0 \times 2^1) + (1 \times 2^0) = 149$$

Counting in the binary system is similar to that in decimal. In decimal, we start from 0, add a 1, obtain 1, and continue adding 1 successively till we reach 9. As the base of the system is ten, there are no further symbols. Thus, when we add 1 to 9, we count 10. The 1 becomes the *carry* to the tens position in the decimal system. Similarly, we count 100 after reaching 99.

Counting in a binary system is similar. In the binary system of enumeration, 0 + 1 = 1 and 1 + 1 = 10. Thus, counting in the binary system of enumeration proceeds as follows:

0, 1, 10, 11, 100, 101, 110, 111, 1000, 1001, ...

Table 2.3 shows the binary counting sequence. Observe that we require 3 bits to represent decimal numbers from 0 to 7 and 4 bits to represent 8 and 9. Thus, on the average, $\frac{8 \times 3 + 2 \times 4}{10} = 3.2$ binary digits are required to represent a decimal digit. What we mean by the statement: 'a decimal digit is represented on the average by 3.2 bits' is that if we convert a large number of decimal numbers and obtain their binary equivalents, the number of bits in each binary equivalent would be approximately 3.2 times the number of digits in the corresponding decimal number.

Table 2.3 Binary counting sequence

Binary number	*Decimal equivalent*	*Binary number*	*Decimal equivalent*
0	0	1001	9
1	1	1010	10
10	2	1011	11
11	3	1100	12
100	4	1101	13
101	5	1110	14
110	6	1111	15
111	7	10000	16
1000	8	10001	17

Just like powers of 10 are important in the decimal system of enumeration, powers of 2 are important in the binary system. We give in Table 2.4 powers of 2 and their decimal values. The abbreviation K in Table 2.4 stands for 1024, which is approximately 1000, a *kilo*.

Table 2.4 Powers of 2

Power of 2	*Decimal value*	*Abbreviation*	*Power of 2*	*Decimal value*	*Abbreviation*
2^0	1		2^{11}	2048	2K
2^1	2		2^{12}	4096	4K
2^2	4		2^{13}	8192	8K
2^3	8		2^{14}	16384	16K
2^4	16		2^{15}	32768	32K
2^5	32		2^{16}	65536	64K
2^6	64		2^{17}	131072	128K
2^7	128		2^{18}	262144	256K
2^8	256		2^{19}	524288	512K
2^9	512		2^{20}	1048576	1M
2^{10}	1024	1K	2^{30}	1073741824	1G

Thus, the notation 16K means 16 × 1024 = 16,384. The abbreviation M (mega) stands for 1024 × 1024 = 1,048,576. The abbreviation G (giga) is used to represent 1024 × 1024 × 1024, which is nearly a billion, T (tera) to represent 1024 × 1024 × 1024 × 1024 = 2^{40}, larger than a trillion, and P (peta) to represent 1024 × 1024 × 1024 × 1024 × 1024 = 2^{50}, larger than a quadrillion! With the need to represent even larger numbers, a unit called E (exa) to represent $1024 \times 1024 \times 1024 \times 1024 \times 1024 \times 1024 = 2^{60}$ has recently appeared. In the MKS units, K is used to represent a kilo, which is equal to 1000. To distinguish between 1024 and 1000, sometimes the notation Ki is used to represent 1024 and K to represent 1000. Similarly, Mi is used to represent 2^{20}, Gi for 2^{30}, Ti for 2^{40}, etc. This notation is not universally used.

2.3 REPRESENTATION OF FRACTIONS

So far we have considered decimal and binary integers. Decimal fractions are interpreted as follows:

$$0.235 = 2 \times 10^{-1} + 3 \times 10^{-2} + 5 \times 10^{-3}$$

0.235	= 2 × 10⁻¹ +	3 × 10⁻² +	5 × 10⁻³
↑	↑	↑	↑
Decimal point	One-tenth position	One-hundredth position	One-thousandth position

Observe that negative powers of 10 are used as weights to multiply the digits in the fractional part of the number.

A binary fraction is represented by a string of 1s and 0s on the right of a binary point. The bits are multiplied by negative powers of 2 to obtain the decimal value of the binary fraction as shown below:

$$0.1011 = 1 \times 2^{-1} + 0 \times 2^{-2} + 1 \times 2^{-3} + 1 \times 2^{-4}$$

(↑ Binary point)

$$= \frac{1}{2} + 0 + \frac{1}{8} + \frac{1}{16}$$

$$= \frac{11}{16} = 0.6875 \text{ (in decimal)}$$

We give below some more examples of binary numbers and their decimal equivalents:

(i) $(111011.101)_2 = 1 \times 2^5 + 1 \times 2^4 + 1 \times 2^3 + 0 \times 2^2 + 1 \times 2^1 + 1 \times 2^0 + 1 \times 2^{-1} + 0 \times 2^{-2} + 1 \times 2^{-3}$

$$= 32 + 16 + 8 + 2 + 1 + \frac{1}{2} + \frac{1}{8}$$

$$= (59.625)_{10}$$

(ii) $(11000.0011)_2 = 1 \times 2^4 + 1 \times 2^3 + 0 \times 2^2 + 0 \times 2^1 + 0 \times 2^0 + 0 \times 2^{-1} + 0 \times 2^{-2} + 1 \times 2^{-3} + 1 \times 2^{-4}$

$$= 16 + 8 + \frac{1}{8} + \frac{1}{16}$$

$$= (24.1875)_{10}$$

Note that we have used the subscript 2 to indicate that the number is binary and the subscript 10 to indicate that the number is decimal. This notation to represent the base of a number is useful to prevent misinterpretation of numbers.

2.4 HEXADECIMAL REPRESENTATION OF NUMBERS

The average number of bits needed to represent a decimal digit is 3.2, as pointed out in Section 2.2. Thus, the binary equivalent of a 10-digit number will be approximately 32 bits long. It is difficult to write such long strings of 1s and 0s and convert them to equivalent decimal numbers without making mistakes. The *hexadecimal* system, which uses 16 as the base, is a convenient notation to express binary numbers. This system, by definition, uses 16 symbols, namely, 0, 1, 2, 3, 4, 5, 6, 7, 8, 9, A, B, C, D, E, F. Note that the symbols A, B, etc. now represent numbers. As 16 is a power of 2, that is, 2^4, there is a one-to-one correspondence between a hexadecimal digit and its binary equivalent. We need 4 bits to represent a hexadecimal digit. Table 2.5 gives a table of hexadecimal digits and their binary and decimal equivalents.

Table 2.5 Binary hexadecimal and decimal equivalents

Binary number	*Hexadecimal equivalent*	*Decimal equivalent*	*Binary number*	*Hexadecimal equivalent*	*Decimal equivalent*
0000	0	0	1000	8	8
0001	1	1	1001	9	9
0010	2	2	1010	A	10
0011	3	3	1011	B	11
0100	4	4	1100	C	12
0101	5	5	1101	D	13
0110	6	6	1110	E	14
0111	7	7	1111	F	15

A binary number can be quickly converted to its hexadecimal equivalent by grouping successive 4 bits of the binary number starting with the least significant bit and replacing each 4-bit group with its hexadecimal equivalent as shown in Table 2.5. Example 2.1 illustrates this process.

Example 2.1

(i) Binary number	0111	1100	1101	1110	0011	
Hexadecimal equivalent:	7	C	D	E	3	
(ii) Binary number	0001	0001	1111	0000 •	0010	1100
Hexadecimal equivalent:	1	1	F	0 •	2	C

Observe that in (ii) of Example 2.1, groups are formed from right to left (i.e., from the least significant bit to the most significant bit) for the integer part of the number and from left to right (i.e., from the most significant to the least significant bit) for the fractional part of the number. If the number of bits in the integer part is not a multiple of 4, we insert *leading* 0s, as leading 0s have no significance for the integer part. If the number of bits in the fractional part is not a multiple of 4, then we introduce *trailing* 0s, as trailing 0s have no significance in the fractional part.

Conversion from hexadecimal to decimal system is simple. It uses the fact that the base of the hexadecimal system is 16. We give below two examples of hexadecimal to decimal conversion.

Example 2.2

(i) $(D6C1)_{16} = D \times 16^3 + 6 \times 16^2 + C \times 16^1 + 1 \times 16^0$

$$= 13 \times 16^3 + 6 \times 16^2 + 12 \times 16 + 1 \times 16^0$$
$$= 53248 + 1536 + 192 + 1$$
$$= (54977)_{10}$$

(ii) $(F9A \cdot BC3)_{16} = F \times 16^2 + 9 \times 16^1 + A \times 16^0 + B \times 16^{-1} + C \times 16^{-2} + 3 \times 16^{-3}$

$$= (15 \times 256) + (9 \times 16) + (10 \times 1) + 11/16 + 12/256 + 3/4096$$
$$= 3840 + 144 + 10 + 11/16 + 12/256 + 3/4096$$
$$= (3994.7351074)_{10}$$

2.5 DECIMAL TO BINARY CONVERSION

As mentioned at the beginning of this chapter, external to the computer we use decimal numbers, whereas internally we use binary representation. We thus have to convert decimal to binary. The method of converting a decimal integer to its binary equivalent is based on the fact that any decimal integer may be expressed as a sum of powers of 2:

$$d = (23)_{10} = (1 \times 2^4) + (0 \times 2^3) + (1 \times 2^2) + (1 \times 2^1) + (1 \times 2^0)$$
$$= (10111)_2$$

The easiest way to find the coefficients of the powers of 2 is to divide the given number by 2 and the successive quotients by 2. The division is terminated when a quotient becomes zero. The binary equivalent of the decimal number is given by the sequence of remainders obtained during division. The least significant bit of the binary number is the first remainder obtained and its most significant bit is the last remainder. The procedure is illustrated below:

Example 2.3

(i) Find the binary equivalent of $(23)_{10}$

		Remainder	
2	23		
2	11	1	⟶ Least significant bit
2	5	1	
2	2	1	
2	1	0	
	0	1	⟶ Most significant bit

Thus, the binary equivalent is $(10111)_2$.

(ii) Find the binary equivalent of 36

Divisor	Quotient	*Remainder*	
2	36		
2	18	0	⟶ Least significant bit
2	9	0	
2	4	1	
2	2	0	
2	1	0	
	0	1	⟶ Most significant bit

$(36)_{10} = (100100)_2$

Decimal to hexadecimal conversion is similar. In this case, 16 is used as the divisor instead of 2. Example 2.4 illustrates decimal to hexadecimal conversion.

Example 2.4

(i) Find the hexadecimal equivalent of $(23)_{10}$

Divisor	Quotient	*Remainder*	
16	23		
16	1	7	⟶ Least significant hex-digit
	0	1	⟶ Most significant hex-digit

$(23)_{10} = (17)_{16} = 1 \times 16 + 7 \times 16^0 = (23)_{10}$

(ii) Find the hexadecimal equivalent of $(41819)_{10}$

Divisor	Quotient	*Decimal remainders*	*Decimal remainders*	
16	41819			
16	2613	11	B	⟶ Least significant hex-digit
16	163	5	5	
16	10	3	3	
	0	10	A	⟶ Most significant hex-digit

$(41819)_{10} = (A35B)_{16}$

Decimal fractions may also be converted to binary. The method is based on observing that a decimal fraction is expressed as a sum of negative powers of 2. Successive multiplication of the fraction by 2 would give the coefficients of the negative powers of 2.

It is clear from Example 2.5 that if we multiply a decimal fraction by 2, the integer part of the answer will be the most significant bit of the binary fraction. The fractional part of the answer is multiplied by 2 to obtain the next significant bit of the binary fraction. The procedure is continued till the fractional part of the product is 0. The method is illustrated next in Example 2.6.

Example 2.5

$$\begin{aligned}
(0.8125)_{10} &= 0.5 + 0.25 + 0.0625 \\
&= 1 \times 2^{-1} + 1 \times 2^{-2} + 0 \times 2^{-3} + 1 \times 2^{-4} \\
2 \times 0.8125 &= 1 + (1 \times 2^{-1} + 0 \times 2^{-2} + 1 \times 2^{-3}) \\
&= 1 + 0.625 \\
2 \times 0.625 &= 2\ (1 \times 2^{-1} + 0 \times 2^{-2} + 1 \times 2^{-3}) \\
&= 1 + (0 \times 2^{-1} + 1 \times 2^{-2}) \\
&= 1 + 0.25 \\
2 \times 0.25 &= 2\ (0 \times 2^{-1} + 1 \times 2^{-2}) \\
&= 0 + 0.5 \\
2 \times 0.5 &= 2 \times 2^{-1} \\
&= 1
\end{aligned}$$

Thus, $(0.8125)_{10} = (0.1101)_2$

Example 2.6

(i) Find the binary equivalent of $(0.5625)_{10}$

Product	*Integer part of product*	
$0.5625 \times 2 = 1.125$	1	⟶ Most significant bit
$0.1250 \times 2 = 0.25$	0	
$0.2500 \times 2 = 0.5$	0	
$0.5 \times 2 = 1.0$	1	⟶ Least significant bit

$(0.5625)_{10} = (0.1001)_2$

(ii) Find the binary equivalent of 0.3

	Product	*Integer part of product*	
0.3×2	0.6	0	⟶ Most significant bit
0.6×2	1.2	1	
0.2×2	0.4	0	
0.4×2	0.8	0	
0.8×2	1.6	1	
0.6×2	1.2	1	Recurs beyond this point as 1001

Thus, $(0.3)_{10} = (0.01001(1001))_2$

Example 2.6 shows that the binary fraction equivalent of a terminating decimal fraction may not terminate.

Converting decimal fractions to hexadecimal fractions is similar. In this case, we multiply the decimal fraction by 16.

Example 2.7

(i) Find the hexadecimal equivalent of $(0.5625)_{10}$

Product	*Integer part*
$0.5625 \times 16 = 9.0000$	9

Thus, $(0.5625)_{10} = (0.9)_{16}$

(ii) Find the hexadecimal equivalent of $(0.3)_{10}$

	Product	*Integer part of product*	*Hex-digit*	
0.3×16	4.8	4	4	
0.8×16	12.8	12	C	
0.8×16	12.8	12	C	Recurs beyond this point

Thus, $(0.3)_{10} = (0.4CCC\ldots)_{16}$

2.6 ERROR DETECTING CODES

Errors may occur in recording data on magnetic surfaces due to bad spots on the surface. Errors may also be caused by electrical disturbances during data transmissions between units. It is thus necessary to devise methods to detect such errors. The main principle used for detecting errors in coded data is the introduction of extra bits in the code to aid error detection. A common method is to append a bit called *parity check bit* to each character code. A parity check bit is appended to the 7 bits of the code of each character in such a way that the total number of 1s in each character code is *even.* For instance, the ASCII code of the letter E is 1000101. The number of 1s in this string is odd. A parity check bit 1 is appended to this string to obtain a code that is now 8 bits long and has an even number of 1s. If the ASCII code of a character has an even number of 1s in it, then the parity check bit appended is 0. For example, the ASCII code of A is 1000001 and its code with an appended parity check bit is 10000010. All characters now have 8-bit codes, including the parity check bit. Whenever a character is read from storage or received from a remote location, the number of 1s in its code is counted. It has to be even. If it is odd, then at least one bit is wrong. A *single* error in any of the 8 bits of the code will definitely be detected. Two errors cannot be detected by this scheme as the total number of 1s in the code will remain even after 2 bits change. As the probability of more than one error occurring is very small, this scheme is commonly accepted as adequate.

Instead of appending a parity check bit which makes the total number of 1s in the code even, one may choose to append a parity check bit which makes the total number of 1s in the code odd. Such a parity check bit is known as an *odd parity check* bit. This scheme also facilitates the detection of a single error in a code.

Codes have also been devised which use more than one check bit to not only detect but also correct errors. These are called *error-correcting codes.* We will not discuss these codes in this book.

SUMMARY

1. As the physical devices used to store and process data in computers are two-state devices, it is necessary to transform or code all data using only two symbols.
2. The two symbols used are, by convention, the digits 0 and 1. These are called 'binary digits' or 'bits' in short.
3. The number of unique strings possible in a code with 2 bits in each string is 4. These strings are 00, 01, 10 and 11. In general, the number of unique strings with n bits in each string is 2^n. Each string in this set may be used to code or represent one character. There are 128 unique strings with 7 bits each.
4. The American Standards Institution has evolved a standard code to represent characters to be stored and processed by computers. This code, called ASCII, uses 7 bits to represent each character. The ASCII code defines codes for English letters (capital and small), decimal digits, and 32 special characters, as well as codes for several symbols used to control the operation of a computer. The symbols used for control are non-printable.
5. A string of 8 bits used to represent a character is known as a *byte*. A new character code capable of representing characters used by any language of the world including emojis is called Unicode. The latest version, Unicode 15.1, uses 32 bits and can in theory represent over a billion characters. However, the standard has defined 149,813 characters. In practice the codes UTF-8 and UTF-16 that conform to Unicode coding but use 8 or 16 bits are used. UTF-8 is compatible with ASCII. UTF-16 can represent all living languages of the world and is approved by the World Wide Web consortium.
6. Decimal numbers are coded depending on how they are to be processed by the computer. If they are used merely as symbols without attached values, such numbers (e.g., motor car registration numbers, pin codes, telephone numbers, etc.) are *coded* using the ASCII code. If values are to be assigned to decimal numbers and if they are used as operands in arithmetic operations, they are *converted* to equivalent binary numbers.
7. Binary numbers are formed using the positional notation. Powers of 2 are used as weights in the binary number system. A binary number 10111, for example, has a decimal *value* $= 1 \times 2^4 + 0 \times 2^3 + 1 \times 2^2 + 1 \times 2^1 + 1 \times 2^0 = 23$.
8. A decimal number is converted into an equivalent binary number by dividing the number by 2 and storing the remainder as the least significant bit of the binary number. The quotient is divided by 2 and the remainder becomes the next bit of the binary number. This procedure is continued till the quotient becomes 0. The binary equivalent of 9, for example, is 1001.

9. High-valued binary numbers will be represented by a long sequence of 0s and 1s. A more concise representation is obtained using the hexadecimal notation. The base of the hexadecimal system is 16 and the symbols used in this system are 0, 1, 2, 3, 4, 5, 6, 7, 8, 9, A, B, C, D, E, F. Strings of 4 bits have an exact equivalent hexadecimal value. This facilitates the conversion of binary numbers to hexadecimal numbers. For example, the binary number 101 1101 1011 1110 0011 0100 is equal to the hexadecimal number 5DBE34.
10. Decimal fractions may be converted to binary fractions.
11. Errors may occur while recording and reading data or when data is transmitted from one unit to another in a computer. Detection of a single error in the code for a character is possible by introducing an extra bit in its code. This bit, known as the parity check bit, is appended to the code. This bit is chosen so that the total number of 1s in the new code is even. If a single bit is incorrectly read, written, or transmitted, then the total number of 1s in the corrupted code would become odd, thereby indicating an error.

REVIEW QUESTIONS

2.1 What is the meaning of the term 'external representation' of data?

2.2 What are the considerations that govern the selection of a representation for storing and processing data in a computer?

2.3 Why are the binary digits used to code data to be stored in a computer?

2.4 How many unique strings are there with 6 bits in each string?

2.5 If the capital English letters, digits, and 16 special characters are to be coded as strings of bits, how many bits will be required for each string?

2.6 What is ASCII code?

2.7 How many bits per character does ASCII code use?

2.8 Why are characters that are not printable assigned codes in ASCII?

2.9 Define a byte.

2.10 What is ISCII?

2.11 What is Unicode? What is the advantage of using Unicode?

2.12 What is UTF-8 code? What is its relation to Unicode?

2.13 What is the UTF-16 code? In what way is it superior to UTF-8?

2.14 Under what circumstances are decimal digits coded using ASCII?

2.15 Under what circumstances are decimal numbers converted into binary numbers?

2.16 What is the difference between the bits used in a code such as ASCII and those used in binary numbers?

2.17 Find the decimal values of the following binary numbers: 1011010, 0101111, 111111, and 100001.

2.18 What are the binary equivalents of the decimal numbers 7, 20, 31, and 64?

2.19 In the octal number system, the symbols used are 0, 1, 2, 3, 4, 5, 6, and 7. What is the base of the system?

2.20 What is the binary equivalent of the octal number 723?

2.21 What is the octal equivalent of the binary number 10001010101?

2.22 What are the decimal equivalents of the following binary fractions: 0.01101, 0.11010, 0.00011?

2.23 What are the binary equivalents of the following decimal fractions: 0.7625, 0.8, 0.245?

2.24 What is the decimal equivalent of the octal fraction 0.647?

2.25 What is the octal equivalent of the decimal fraction 0.789?

2.26 What is the advantage of using hexadecimal numbers?

2.27 Convert the following binary numbers to hexadecimal: 100101010101, 0101110111101, 1011000001.

2.28 What are the decimal values of the hexadecimal numbers found in the previous question?

2.29 Convert the following binary numbers to hexadecimal and then to decimal:

1000100101.1101011, 101001011111.0010001

2.30 Convert the following decimal numbers to hexadecimal:

285.48, 3452.645, 678920.45

2.31 What is the purpose of using a parity check bit?

2.32 Write down the ASCII codes for H, T, and 7. Add an even parity check bit to each code. Explain how a single error will be detected in each code.

3 Input/Output Units

LEARNING GOALS

After reading this chapter, you should be able to:

- List devices available to input and output numeric and textual data, explain how they work and know their relative advantages and disadvantages.
- Select an output device appropriate for a given task.
- Distinguish between hard copy and soft copy devices which are used to input and output data.

In the previous chapter, we discussed methods to convert textual and numeric data to a set of bits for storage in a computer's memory. Data to be processed by a computer are not limited to text and numbers. As we pointed out in the previous chapter, modern computers process various types of data. They may be pictures (e.g., digital photographs), audio (e.g., speech or music), or video (e.g., a movie). They may also be signals from sensors such as temperature sensors or data sent by other computers. To process these data, we have to acquire them, convert them to a binary form (often called *machine readable form*), and store them in the memory of a computer. The device(s) used to acquire data are known as *input unit(s)*. There is a large variety of input units depending on the type of data to be read.

The data read using an input unit is stored in the computer's memory and processed. After processing, it is sent to an *output unit* when commanded by a program. The output unit converts the internal representation of data into a form that can be used as required by the application. The output may, therefore, be one of several types. For example, it may be a text (e.g., a word-processed essay), a table of numbers, a picture, audio (speech, music), a video (e.g., a movie), a command to an instrument, or data to be sent to another computer. Thus, there are a variety of output units depending on the nature of the output.

Figure 3.1 illustrates the various types of inputs and outputs that we encounter nowadays. Observe that we have divided inputs/outputs into HUMAN and MACHINE. By HUMAN we mean input units used by humans and output units to be used by humans. By MACHINE we mean inputs generated by computers/sensors and outputs meant for computers/sensors. From the above discussion, it is clear that there is a large variety of input and output units in a computer system. New input and output units are also invented periodically. It is not feasible to describe all of them in this book. In this chapter, we will describe some currently used units for input/output of textual and numeric data. Units used to input/output other data types will be described later, where appropriate, in this book.

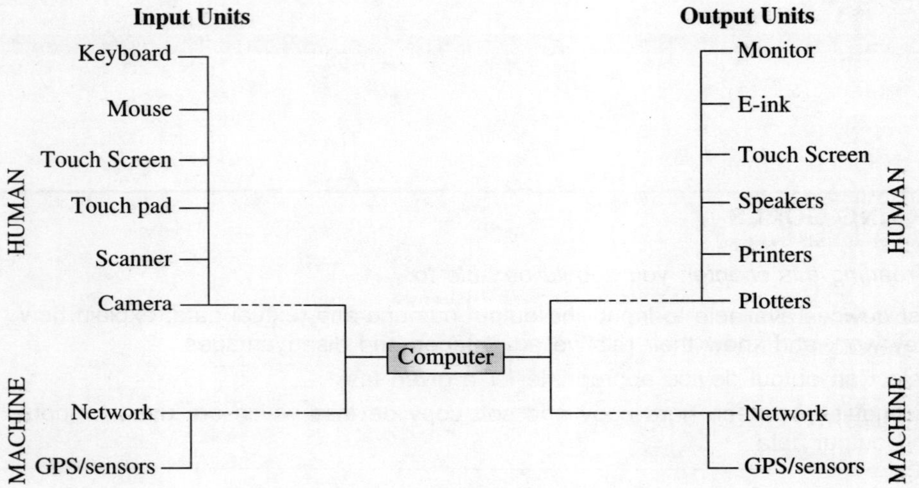

Figure 3.1 Input/output of computers.

3.1 TRADITIONAL COMPUTER INPUT/OUTPUT UNITS

The input and output units of a computer are normally abbreviated as I/O units. Some of them are general-purpose, that is, they are used by almost all computers. The most commonly used unit of this type is the keyboard of a desktop or a laptop computer. (Tablet computers use touch screens on which 'virtual keyboards' are used.) Special purpose units are magnetic ink character readers, optical mark readers, scanners, and bar code readers.

3.1.1 Keyboard

The most common input unit is a keyboard used for manual data entry. This keyboard has been standardized for use in all types of computers, such as a PC, a workstation, or a notebook computer. It is also called a 'QWERTY' keyboard as these are the first six letters in the third row from the top of most keyboards. The arrangement of letters in a keyboard was standardized for mechanical typewriters in the last century but has continued as most typists are used to it and there is unwillingness to change. A keyboard consists of the following major categories of keys:

1. *Letter keys:* These are the 26 letters of the English alphabet arranged as in (now obsolete) mechanical typewriters.
2. *Digit keys:* There are two sets of digit keys: one on the second row from the top of the keyboard and the other is a numeric keypad at the bottom right which allows quick entry of numbers with the fingers of one hand.
3. *Special character keys:* These are characters such as < >? / { } [ ] ( ) . , ; " \ ! @ # $ % ^ & * – + = —. Most of these are printed when the shift key in the keyboard is pressed down and the key on which it is written is pressed. For example, when the shift key and the key with digit 2 in the second row from the top are pressed together, @ is printed.
4. *Non-printable control keys:* These are used for backspacing, going to the next line, tabulation, moving the cursor up or down, inserting, deleting characters, etc. There is also a *space bar* at the bottom to leave a space.
5. *Function keys:* These are labelled F1, F2, to F15. When one of these keys is pressed, a program corresponding to it (stored in the computer) is invoked.

When a key is pressed, the corresponding character is displayed on a display unit (also called a monitor) connected to it, which we describe in the following section.

3.1.2 Display Unit

A display unit (also known as a monitor) consists of a video screen. When a key of an associated keyboard is pressed, the corresponding character is displayed on the screen. Simultaneously, a cursor moves to the position where the next character will be input. A *cursor* is a small vertical line, or an underline, which can be moved horizontally or vertically to indicate the position of a character.

A display unit is classified as an *output unit* as it displays the computed results. The data typed using a keyboard is immediately displayed on the screen of the display unit. This visual feedback is essential for a person using the keyboard to verify that the correct key is pressed. When a key on the keyboard is pressed, the corresponding character is displayed on the screen and an appropriately coded series of electrical pulses are sent to the computer's memory. If a wrong key is pressed, the operator can backspace and retype the correct character. Some 'intelligent' display units have built into them computing power and extra storage, allowing sophisticated editing of data before they are sent to the computer. They may also be programmed to display a blank form with appropriate prompts to facilitate data entry.

Till a few years ago, the technology used for most display units was cathode ray tubes. They are now hardly used as they are bulky and consume too much power. Currently, the most common technology used is a Liquid Crystal Display (LCD) which is also known as a *flat panel display*. We will describe it in the next section.

3.1.3 Computer Mouse

A mouse is a hand-held device fitted with one or more buttons and shaped to sit conveniently under one's palm. The name mouse probably came as a wire connecting it to a display unit that looks like a tail and the shape of the device resembles a mouse. A mouse is a *locator* that is used to move a pointing arrow or a cursor around the display screen to locate a desired point on the screen. Currently, the most commonly used mouse is the *optical mouse*. This mouse has light-emitting diodes to illuminate a flat surface (such as a tabletop) on which the mouse is moved. An optical sensor senses the relative motion of the mouse as it is moved on the table. The motion is processed by a powerful special-purpose image chip which translates the mouse's motion on the surface to the movement of a pointer on the display screen. A mouse is normally connected by a wire to the computer. Nowadays wireless mice are available. A wireless mouse transmits its motion to the display screen using radio waves and is convenient to use. Clicking the left/right buttons of the mouse initiates actions that are performed by the computer connected to the display unit.

3.2 OTHER INPUT TECHNOLOGIES

3.2.1 Touch Pad

A Touch Pad (also called a Track Pad) is a pointing device similar to a mouse. It is used in laptop computers. It is a small pad situated below the keyboard. Pressing or tapping its left bottom corner mimics a left click and pressing its right bottom corner a right click of a mouse button. The pad incorporates a capacitance. If a finger is placed on the pad, the capacitance at that point changes as our body acts as ground. The change in capacitance of the pad touched by the finger is translated to a pointer position on the display screen. The pointer is thus moved by moving the finger. You cannot use a pencil or a stylus instead of a finger in this type of touchpad as they are insulators and the capacitance of the pad will not change when it is touched with these. Resistive pads have been designed in which the resistance of the pad where it is touched changes. These pads use a pencil or a stylus. Resistive pads are cheaper than capacitive touch pads but not as accurate.

3.2.2 Touch Screen

In desktop computers, a mouse is used to point an icon on the screen and clicked to invoke a program. Hand-held computers, known as tablet computers, are now becoming popular. They do not have a separate keyboard. The keyboard is displayed on the screen of the display and by touching with a finger a virtual key, code corresponding to it is input. Icons are displayed on the screen and when an icon is touched, a program corresponding to it is invoked. These are called *touchscreen displays*. The principle of operation of a touch screen is similar to that of a touchpad. The position of an icon or a letter/digit touched on the screen is sensed to send the correct input to the processor of the computer connected to it. The position is sensed by printing on a liquid crystal display a set of transparent electrodes parallel to the *X*-axis. An insulator is stuck over this grid. A grid of transparent electrodes parallel to *the Y*-axis is printed over this. This creates a grid of capacitors on the screen. The value of the capacitance changes when the screen is touched because the human body is a conductor. The *X–Y* coordinates of the point on the screen that is touched is thus sensed. This coordinate is used to identify the icon or the virtual key. Just as in a touchpad, this system will not work if a pencil or a stylus is used instead of a finger or if you wear gloves as these will not conduct electricity and the capacitor value will not change. Touch screens are also used by smartphones.

There is another technology used in touch screens. It is called a resistive screen. In this case, a conductor is printed over the screen. When it is touched with a stylus, the resistance changes and this is used to detect the position where it is touched. It is not very accurate and is used in cheaper devices. One advantage of the resistive touch screen is that it can be touched with a stylus or a gloved finger.

Some more specialized input technologies are occasionally used. These are briefly described in what follows.

3.2.3 Magnetic Ink Character Recognition (MICR)

In this technology, human-readable characters are printed on documents (such as cheques) using a special magnetic ink. A magnetic ink character reader can recognize such characters. In a cheque, for instance, the cheque number and branch code are pre-printed at the bottom using magnetic ink. The amount written in the cheque is entered later by a clerk using a machine that prints the amount with magnetic ink. The cheque itself can now be read using a special input unit that can recognize magnetic ink characters. This method eliminates the need to enter data manually from cheques. Besides saving time, this method ensures the accuracy of data entry.

Figure 3.2 illustrates magnetic ink character fonts.

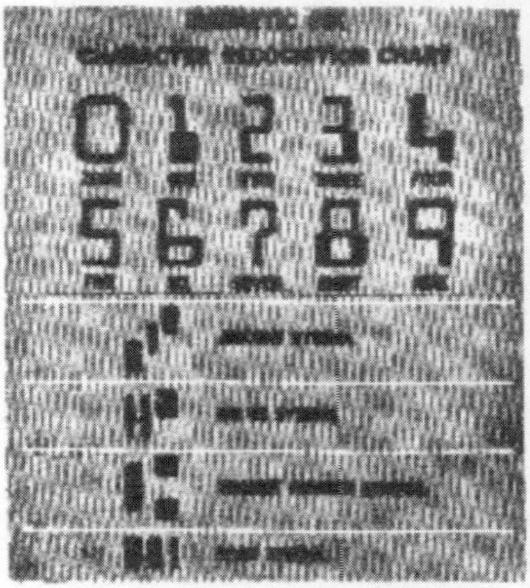

Figure 3.2 Photograph of magnetic ink characters.

3.2.4 Optical Mark Reading and Recognition (OMR)

In this technology, special pre-printed forms are designed with boxes that can be marked with a dark pencil or ink. Each box is annotated distinctly so that the user clearly understands his response when he darkens a box. Such a document is read by a document reader which transcribes the marks into electrical pulses which are transmitted to the computer.

These documents are applicable in areas where responses are one out of a small number of alternatives and the volume of data to be processed is large. Thus, they are used for:

(i) Marking objective-type answer papers in examinations with a huge number of candidates.
(ii) Market surveys, population surveys, etc., where responses can be restricted to one or more out of a few possibilities.
(iii) Order forms containing a small choice of items.
(iv) Time sheets of factory employees where start and stop times may be marked.

The advantage of this technology is that data is entered at its source and no further manual transcription is required. This minimizes data entry errors. The main disadvantage is the need for accurate alignment of printing on forms and the need for good quality expensive paper. The form cannot be redesigned frequently because any change will require reprinting of the form, which is costly.

3.2.5 Flatbed Scanner

A flatbed scanner has the following parts:

1. An optical system consisting of a light beam, lens, and mirrors.
2. An array of solid-state 'electronic eyes', technically known as a CCD (Charge Coupled Device) array, which senses light and gives an electrical output, whose value depends on the intensity of the light.
3. An electronic circuit that converts the electrical output given by the array of 'electronic eyes' to a set of bits that are stored in the memory of a computer.

The scanner has a flat glass surface over which the document to be scanned is placed, with the printed side facing the glass as in a Xerox copier. The paper is pressed down with a cover. A light source focuses light on an entire line as a thin beam. This is called a *scan line*. Light is reflected from the paper along the scan line. Wherever there is a dark spot (corresponding to a printed character), no light is reflected, and wherever there is no print, that is, it is white, bright light is reflected. This is illustrated in Figure 3.3. The reflected light is gathered by a row of 'electronic eyes', that is, a row of CCDs. Dark spots that do not reflect light are sensed and stored as 0s and white spots reflect light as 1s by the array of CCDs. In

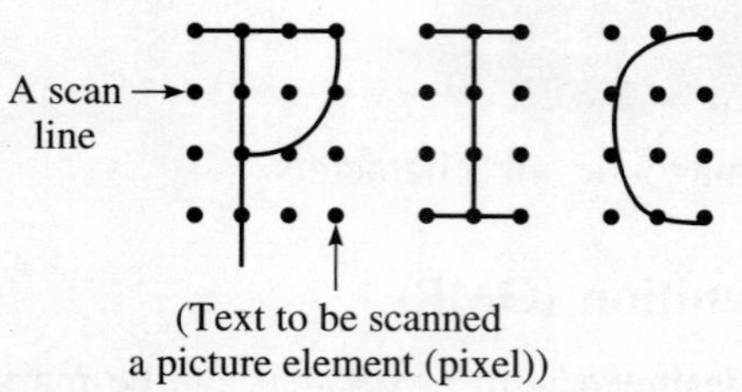

(a)

←P→				←I→			←C→		
0	0	0	0	0	0	0	1	0	0
1	0	1	0	1	0	1	0	1	1
1	0	0	1	1	0	1	0	1	1
1	0	1	1	0	0	0	1	0	0

Y ↑ → X

Bits after scanning
(1 store for a white spot and 0 for a black spot)

(b)

Figure 3.3 Scanning a text.

many scanners, 300 CCDs are arranged per inch on a horizontal line, giving 300 bits per inch resolution. After gathering bits from one scan line, the motor moves the light source to the next scan line, and the black and white parts of this line are converted to 0s and 1s again. The process continues till the entire page is scanned from top to bottom. The number of scan lines in the vertical or *Y*-direction is determined by the mechanical precision of the motor moving the light beam. It is usually double the horizontal resolution. Thus, if the horizontal resolution is 300 bits per inch, there will be 600 scan lines per inch in the vertical direction. It usually takes between 5 and 20 seconds to scan a full page.

Each reflected light beam picked up by the CCD array is called a *picture element* which is abbreviated *as pixel*. Thus, a scanner with 300 CCD elements per inch in the *X*-direction and 600 scan lines per inch in the *Y*-direction will store 300 × 600 = 180,000 pixels per square inch. If the scanned text is printed characters, each pixel is represented by 1 bit, a black being 0 and a white 1. If we scan a document with a text area of 7″ × 9″, the number of bits stored will be 7″ × 300 × 9 × 600 bits = 11.34 Megabits = 1.4175 MB. (In this book, we will use the notation 1 Mb for 1 Megabit, and 1 MB for 1 Megabyte. Similarly, 1 Gb is 1 Gigabit and 1 GB is 1 Gigabyte.) This scanned version of the text is known as a *bit map* form.

If the material being scanned is a picture, the scanned output is a bit map. Normally pictures are not pure black and white but have several shades of grey. Scanners use 8 bits to store each pixel, giving 256 tones of grey. Thus, a 7″ × 9″ picture will require 11.34 MB of storage if stored in bit-mapped form. Nowadays all scanners also scan colour pictures, in which case 24 bits are used per pixel, tripling the storage requirements to 34 MB. Storage space can be reduced by using compression algorithms. There are several algorithms and formats for compressed pictures. A widely used format is called *jpeg* (standardized by the joint photographic experts group). For moderate-quality compressed pictures, it reduces the storage requirement by a factor of 64, and for quality indistinguishable from the original, the compression is by a factor of 2. The storage needed for a moderate quality jpeg compressed (7″ × 9″) colour picture is thus around 0.5 MB. There are other storage formats for pictures called *gif* and *tiff*, which we will describe later.

If the information in the 7″ × 9″ print area is 'pure' text, it can be typed and stored as ASCII coded characters. Assuming 80 characters per line and 24 lines, the number of characters is 1920. This requires a storage space of 1920 bytes if ASCII code is used. Observe that the bit map form requires 750 times the storage space compared to the ASCII-coded form! If we compress the scanned material by a factor of 10 (text cannot be compressed as much as a picture as it has to be readable), the bit map form will still require around 75 times more storage space. Storing a text as a bit map is very inefficient. The question that will naturally occur is: 'Is it possible to convert the bit map form to ASCII form?' The answer is a qualified yes. The conversion from bit map form to ASCII form is done by a software called *Optical Character Recognizer* (or OCR for short) which we will describe in the next section.

3.2.6 Optical Character Recognizer

As we pointed out in the last section, a scanner treats a page of text an image and gives a bit map representation of the page. The main disadvantages of bit map representation are:

- It requires a huge storage space.
- As individual characters are not stored, it is difficult to search the text for character strings.

A software, known as Optical Character Recognition software, has been designed to take a scanned text as input and convert it into its ASCII-coded equivalent. Four broad categories of text need recognition:

1. Printed or typed text using a standard font such as Times Roman 10.
2. Handwritten text using a cursive script, that is, individual letters are connected.
3. Pre-printed forms with blank spaces which are filled by handwriting. The letters are unconnected.
4. A page containing text with mixed fonts, pictures, and tables.

Let us consider each case. In case 1, namely, printed or typed text using a single well-known font, OCR software does an excellent job. It is easy to obtain 99.5% accuracy. Accuracy of even 100% has been reported by some commercial software (see OKI printing solutions—www.bli.com).

In case 2, handwritten texts using cursive handwriting styles differ widely. Thus, recognizing scanned cursive handwriting is difficult and has been a research topic for several years. Now (2025), recognition accuracy is between 80 and 90%. Better accuracy has been obtained in specialized applications where vocabulary is known in advance or inferred from context (e.g., postal address).

At this stage, we need to distinguish between online handwriting recognition and offline recognition (also known as static recognition) using OCR. In online handwriting recognition, a person writes on the screen of a tablet computer with a stylus. The movement of the stylus can be sensed while writing, which is additional information to the recognition system. A user can train the system to recognize his/her handwriting (by trial and error). Such personalized recognition systems perform much better. In some good systems, the recognition accuracy exceeds 99%.

In case 3, namely, pre-printed forms filled by hand using uppercase with unconnected letters, an accuracy of 99.5% has been attained.

In case 4, where old books, newspapers, etc. are scanned, the material will include pictures, tables, equations, etc. It may also be in multiple columns. The fonts will not normally be uniform. They may include boldface, italics, and other non-standard fonts. In such cases, the accuracy depends on the quality of the image, page skew, scanner distortions, type size, font types, etc. In these cases, the accuracy is around 95% to 99% under controlled conditions. It is necessary to proofread and manually correct the errors in the recognized text.

The main principle used by the OCR software is to compare each scanned letter with a sample set stored in the computer and find a match. This matching becomes easy if the font used is known to the OCR software and a uniform font is used. Having found matches for letters, a word is formed by stringing letters found between blank spaces in the text. The word is matched with words stored in a dictionary of words. The nearest matching word from the dictionary is selected. Thus, even if one or two letters in a word are incorrectly recognized, the matching process selects the correct word. All selected words are put together to form the

ASCII coded text which is output. The quality of recognition depends on the size of the stored dictionary and the recognition method. As we said earlier, OCR software today does not give 100% correct outputs. Thus, it is necessary to manually correct errors, if any, in the output text. The number of corrections may be quite small (1 in 100 words) if the software is good.

An operator 'proofreads' the text output by OCR by comparing it with the original scanned text. This is time-consuming but is much faster than retyping an entire page.

3.2.7 Bar Code

In this method, small bars of varying thickness and spacing are printed on packages, badges, tags, etc., which are read by optical readers and converted to electrical pulses. The pattern of bars is unique and standardized in most countries. For example, in Europe, each product is given a unique 13-digit code called *Unique Product Code* (*UPC*) and this is represented in bar code form on every container of the product. This book has a bar code uniquely identifying it at the bottom right-hand corner of the back cover. The bar code is read by a hand-held optical scanner with a set of light-emitting diodes on a flat surface at its bottom. The scanner surface is slowly dragged over the bar code and the light-emitting diodes illuminate the bar code. The reflected light is sensed by sensors and converted to bits and input to a computer's memory. This device is commonly used in retail stores and bookshops.

Two-dimensional codes (2D patterns of dark rectangles) called QR (Quick Response) codes have recently become popular. The code consists of three distinct squares in the top two and the bottom left corner and a smaller square a little inside the bottom right corner (see Figure 3.4). The rest of the square area has numerous tiny squares which encode data. The QR code is read by a digital camera (usually a smartphone camera) and a program (called an App) is used to decode its contents. The content is a binary string which includes error correcting bits. The bits normally encode a vendor's World Wide Web address (i.e., the URL). When the digital camera of a smartphone is pointed at the QR code, it captures the image. The image is aligned with the

Figure 3.4 A quick response code.

squares in the four corners. Free Apps are available for smartphones that interpret the QR code and get the URL. The URL is used to connect the phone to the Internet and access the vendor's website. Even though we have described the current popular use of QR codes, originally, they were invented by Japanese car manufacturers to store detailed information about cars. They were later used in several applications to store larger amounts of data compared to bar codes.

Recently, microchips called Radio Frequency Identification (RFID) tags have been used in some applications to store a large amount of data on items. RFID tags can be read from a distance. We will describe RFID tags in Chapter 11.

3.3 COMPUTER OUTPUT DEVICES

There are three common devices used to output data from a computer. These are flat panel displays, e-ink displays, and printers. Flat panel displays are used in display units described in Section 3.1.2. E-ink displays (also called e-book readers) are recent and are used to download e-books (i.e., computer-readable books). Printers are called *hard copy* devices as the data is written on paper and can be conveniently read by people without using any special gadgets. There is another set of output devices commonly known as *soft copy* devices which store data as bit strings. They can be read and interpreted only by computers. Solid-state memory sticks (called pen drives) are soft copy devices. As these are removable portable devices, the data stored in them can be read by another computer and stored in its memory for processing. We will discuss pen drives in the next chapter on memories. In this section, we will describe flat panel display technology, e-ink technology, and printers.

3.3.1 Flat Panel Display

Till a few years ago, most display units were Cathode Ray Tube (CRT) displays. They are now hardly used as they are bulky and consume too much power. Currently, the most popular display unit is a *Liquid Crystal Display* (*LCD*), which is also known as a flat panel display.

The main principle used by liquid crystal displays is the polarizing property of light. A vertically polarized light beam is blocked by a horizontal polarizing filter. If the filter is slowly rotated from horizontal orientation to vertical orientation, the intensity of the light emerging from the filter gradually increases. The rotation of the polarizing filter is mimicked by the rotation of liquid crystals in LCD.

A liquid crystal display used in computer monitors consists of the following parts (see Figure 3.5a):

1. A light source. Early models used fluorescent tubes as the light source. Current models use light-emitting diodes (LEDs). LEDs are brighter and their power consumption is low.
2. A glass plate next to the light source. The side of the glass plate facing the light source has a transparent film stuck on it. This film is a filter that polarizes light vertically. The other side of the glass plate has fine vertical grooves.
3. Another glass plate that has horizontal grooves on its inner side and a horizontally polarizing filter on its outer side. Liquid crystals are sandwiched between the grooved

sides of the two glass plates. The liquid crystals are called super-twisted nematic crystals (STN). The crystals are normally twisted between vertical and horizontal grooves of the two glass plates.

4. The horizontal and vertical grooves form a grid. Each point of intersection of the grid is a *pixel* (picture element) of the display. A liquid crystal bubble is formed for each pixel (Figure 3.5b).
5. Transparent electrodes (indium tin oxide) are printed on the outside surface of the two glass plates parallel to the grooves forming a grid of electrodes.
6. At each grid intersection point, a Thin Film Transistor (TFT) switch is used to control the rotation of the liquid crystal.

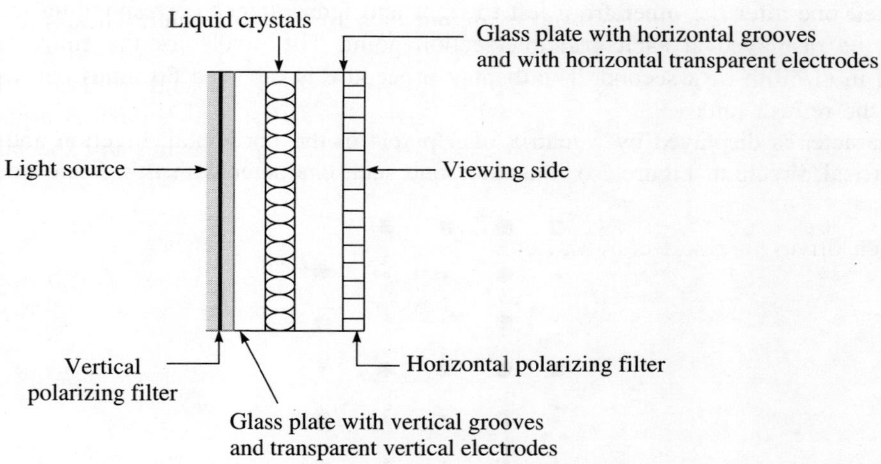

(a) Cross section of liquid crystal display screen side view

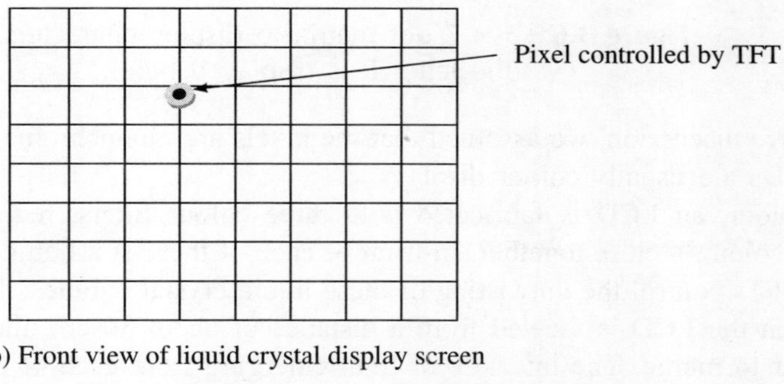

(b) Front view of liquid crystal display screen

Figure 3.5 A liquid crystal display.

When no voltage is applied to the vertical electrodes, the vertically polarized light entering the liquid crystal is twisted by the crystal and when it reaches the horizontally polarized filter, it passes through it. Thus, from the viewing side (Figure 3.5a), light is seen. When a positive Voltage *V* is applied to the vertical electrode and a horizontal electrode is grounded, the TFT generates an electric field that untwists the crystal at the intersection of the two electrodes.

At the highest voltage level, the crystal is completely untwisted. Thus, the vertically polarized light travels with the same polarization through the crystal and is blocked by the horizontally polarized filter on the viewing side and no light is seen. Voltages between *V* and 0 untwist the crystal by varying amounts, thereby modulating the intensity of the light seen from the viewing side. If the voltage *V* is represented by 8 bits, $2^8 = 256$ grey levels of light are perceived. Each intersection point in the grid has a TFT and can be independently controlled.

The pixel values to be displayed are stored in a *graphics memory*. For a screen with 800 vertical electrodes and 600 horizontal electrodes (usually represented as 800 × 600), there will be 1,440,000 bytes (3 bytes/pixel) in the memory. The pixel values are used to control the voltages to be applied to the vertical electrodes of the LCD. Pictures are displayed by selecting and grounding horizontal electrodes sequentially from top to bottom. The vertical electrodes are selected one after the other from left to right and fed voltages corresponding to the pixel values to be displayed at each grid intersection point. The pixels for the entire screen are displayed in (1/60)th of a second. The display procedure is repeated 60 times per second and is called the refresh rate.

A character is displayed by a matrix of *n* pixels in the horizontal direction and *m* pixels in the vertical direction. Figure 3.6 illustrates one such character with $n = 5$ and $m = 7$.

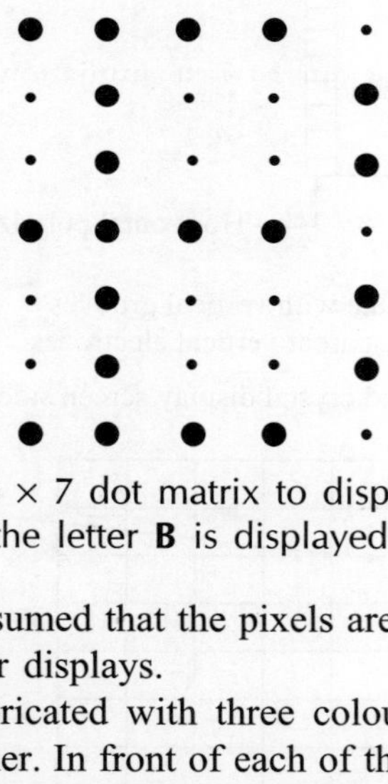

Figure 3.6 5 × 7 dot matrix to display characters. (the letter **B** is displayed here).

In the above discussion, we assumed that the pixels are monochrome with 256 grey levels. Flat panel LCDs are usually colour displays.

To get colour, an LCD is fabricated with three colour filters, red, blue, and green (the three primary colours), close together. In front of each of these is a liquid crystal bubble. Three independent TFTs control the untwisting of these liquid crystal bubbles. The three filters are so close that when the LCD is viewed from a distance of about 30 cm, the colours of the three bubbles appear to merge. The intensity of light emerging from each of these is independently controlled by the voltages applied to the three TFTs. Varying the brightness of each of them changes the colour perceived. If each primary colour has 256 levels of intensity, 256 × 256 × 256 = 1,677,216 colours are perceived.

Apart from colour, the other important characteristic of an LCD is its *resolution*. Resolution is usually given as the number of horizontal pixels × number of vertical pixels. The resolution depends upon the size of the screen. The size is quoted as the length of the diagonal of the screen. The ratio of the length of the screen to the height of the screen is called *the aspect ratio*. It is usually 4:3 in LCDs used in computers. The resolution is continuously increasing with improvements in technology.

Liquid crystal displays have several good qualities, such as the following:

1. They are compact and light. They are less than 2 inches thick.
2. Their power consumption is low. It is primarily the power needed to light the LEDs.
3. The pictures are not distorted as the screen is flat.
4. There is no flickering.
5. It does not use high voltage, unlike the older cathode ray tube displays.

Some of the disadvantages of liquid crystal displays are:

1. The viewing angle is limited. In other words, viewing from a side rather than from the front makes the image not clearly visible. The viewing angle is between 120° and 170°.
2. The number of TFTs used is very large (for an 800 × 600 screen, it is 1,440,000). During the manufacturing process, some of these TFTs are usually damaged. Thus, pixels controlled by these TFTs will be stuck (i.e., bright or dark). Manufacturers allow these to pass. Usually, bad pixels on the screen will be less than 100 and spread out on the screen and will not be perceived.
3. If the time taken to untwist liquid crystals is significant, there will be smearing of the video scene. This will be seen during fast animations.
4. The behaviour of liquid crystals is affected by heat. If the environment is hot, the display misbehaves.

Those interested in technical details of how LCDs work would find a good description with animation at http://electronics.howstuffworks.com/lcd.htm.

3.3.2 E-ink Display

The E-ink display is primarily used to display e-books. This display's main advantage is that it does not consume any power while it displays a page. Only when a new page is to be displayed (i.e., when a page is flipped to a new page), power is consumed. Another advantage is easy readability in bright light. Its reading comfort is almost like that of printed paper. LCDs, on the other hand, strain the eyes of the reader as the screen is refreshed 60 times a second and this affects reading comfort. LCDs are also difficult to read in bright light as they are lit by a light source whose power is limited.

E-ink consists of millions of transparent micro-capsules that encapsulate electrically charged black and white pigment balls. These micro-capsules are sandwiched between a transparent electrode layer which has a grid of electrodes and a supporting layer. When a positive voltage is applied to the electrode layer, the black pigment balls which are negatively charged migrate upwards in the bubble and black dots are seen. A negative voltage applied to the electrode brings the white balls to the top. The grid of electrodes is used to address the capsules and create black and white pixels which make up a text or a picture. The bubbles reflect ambient light. Thus, the display can be read wherever there is adequate light, including bright sunlight. The bubbles remain undisturbed until the voltages applied to the grid of electrodes are changed. Once a page of text is displayed, no power is consumed. Power is required only when the bubbles are rearranged to display another page. In the e-book application, this is a great advantage as power is consumed only when pages are flipped by a reader. Once the rechargeable batteries of an e-book are charged, it need not be recharged for a few days. E-ink is primarily black and white. Colour e-ink readers are now available and their price is coming down. Animation is also not possible in e-books, as the response time of bubbles is slow.

E-ink technology is still evolving and is currently being used primarily in e-book readers. It is expected that foldable e-ink displays will appear soon in the market (see www.techdigest.tv/2012/02/next-gen_colour.html). Currently (2025), three popular e-book readers are Amazon's Kindle, Nook marketed by Barnes and Noble, and Kobo Libra colour. Typical e-book readers are light (around 300 g), easy to hold (19 cm × 13.5 cm), and with (600 × 800) pixel display. Books are downloaded to the reader using Wi-Fi or a mobile telecommunication system. They can also be connected to PCs. E-book readers have a flash memory inside and can store thousands of books. They also incorporate text-to-speech convertors and music players. We give in Table 3.1 a comparison of e-ink readers and flat panel displays.

Table 3.1 Comparing flat panel display and e-ink reader

Flat panel display readers	*E-ink readers*
Full colour	Black and white/color
Harder on eyes	Easy on eyes
Animation possible	No animation (too slow)
Backlit	Needs ambient light
Difficult to read outdoors	Easy to read outdoors
Battery life 10 h	Battery life several weeks
Heavy	Light (1/3rd of LCD's weight)

Those interested in the details of how e-ink technology works can search: Wikipedia for e-ink or how the stuff works e-ink. Wikipedia also has full specifications of the latest e-book readers marketed by several companies.

3.3.3 Printers

Getting *a hard copy* (i.e., printed copy of processed data) on paper is essential in many applications. Printed output is easy to read without any electronic aids. Thus, printers that print documents (both text and pictures) are essential peripherals with any computer, whether it is used in an office or at home. Printers may be classified as *contact printers* or *non-contact printers*. Contact printers may be further classified as *character printers* or *line printers*. Character printers print one character at a time, whereas line printers assemble an entire line and print one line after another. There are a variety of printers available in the market today. The most commonly used and reasonably priced printers are non-contact printers. The two most popular non-contact printers are *inkjet printers* and *laser printers*. Inkjet and laser printers usually print both monochrome and colour. Laser printers are more expensive than inkjet printers. The print quality of laser printers is better than that of inkjet and contact printers.

There are two types of contact printers. They are *dot matrix printers* and *line printers*. Dot matrix printers are not widely used now. They are used only if multiple copies of a document are required. The running cost of dot matrix printers is low. Fast printers which print 132 characters/line and print about 1000 pages a minute are usually line printers and are used only in large computer centres using mainframe computers that print massive documents such as inventory, payroll, dividend cheques, mark sheets of public examinations, etc. In this section, we will first describe how these printers work.

Printing with non-contact printers

Normally, when you want to print a document with figures, tables, etc., you use a word processor and a non-contact printer. A page to be printed appears on the video display. You would like it printed exactly as you see it on the screen. This is known as WYSIWYG (What You See Is What You Get). This is accomplished by software that drives the printers. The steps involved are:

1. You view the page on the display and when you are satisfied, you select a printer that will print it.
2. A program called a printer driver translates the bits corresponding to the documents to another bit map appropriate for the specified printer. This bit map corresponds to characters as well as pictures to be printed. It is transferred to a memory in the printer.
3. A processor in the printer interprets the bit-mapped image and controls the printer head mechanism to print the document and pictures (if any).

3.3.4 Inkjet Printers

An inkjet printer consists of a print head that has several small holes or nozzles. Ink wells hold ink near the nozzles. Individual wells can be heated rapidly (in a few microseconds) by an integrated circuit resistor. When the resistor heats up, the ink near it is ejected through the nozzle and makes dots on paper placed near the head. A high-resolution inkjet printer has around 50 nozzles within a height of 7 mm and can print with a resolution of 300 dots per inch. A fairly complex electronic system selects the nozzles to be heated based on the character to be printed. The printer has enough memory to print an entire page accommodating different fonts. The characters printed on paper are fused in it by moving the paper between two rollers.

Colour inkjet printers use three separate inkjets, one for each of the primary colours, namely, red, green, and blue. By mixing appropriate combinations of these colours, all colours are created. The printing speed of inkjet printers is around 120 characters per second. Pictures can be drawn with inkjet printers besides printing text by storing the bit map of the image in the printer's memory. Inkjet printers are inexpensive. The print cartridge should be replaced when the ink in it is exhausted. The print cartridges are expensive. They may cost almost half the price of the printer! The cheaper the printer, the more expensive the replacement cartridge. Thus, when you buy an inkjet printer, it is wise to ask the price of a replacement cartridge.

3.3.5 Laser Printers

Laser printers are faster than inkjet printers. Low-cost printers print eight pages per minute and are affordable even for home use. They have a resolution of 600–1200 dots per inch, depending on the cost of the printer. The printer prints dots based on 0s and 1s in the bit-mapped image to be printed. The steps followed to print a page are:

1. The bit-mapped image of a page stored in the printer's memory is scanned horizontally from left to right line by line.
2. A laser beam is reflected by a mirror system and moves from left to right along a horizontal line. The reflected beam impinges on the surface of an electrically sensitive cylinder.
3. When a 1 is encountered in the bit map, it turns on the laser beam. Else it is turned off.
4. The dot where the laser beam hits the surface of the cylinder is charged. If there are 600 bits per line, 600 dots are created on the cylinder.
5. The cylinder rotates near a reservoir containing a toner. The toner is attracted to the charged spots on the cylinder and adheres to these spots.
6. A paper is placed below the roller. It is transported across the cylinder as the cylinder rotates.
7. The paper is pressed between the cylinder and a rigid heated plate. The toner sticking to the cylinder is transferred to the paper as the cylinder rotates.

The image transferred to paper is sharp and of high quality as the laser beam is very sharply focused and the spot on the cylinder is not blurred. Laser printers of resolution 1200 bits/inch are available commercially. Colour laser printers are also available, but the per-page cost is over double that of black and white printers.

3.3.6 Dot Matrix Printers

Dot matrix printers are *contact printers*. They are also called *serial printers* as they print one character at a time with a printer head moving across a line. The print head of a dot matrix printer consists of a set of 9–24 pins arranged vertically. Dot matrix printers with 24 pins give a good appearance to printed output and are called *letter-quality printers*. The ASCII code of a character to be printed is sent to the printer electronics. The character code is decoded by the printer electronics which selects a subset of pins on the head to hit a carbon ribbon between the head and a sheet of paper. The head moves from left to right and columns are successively selected to form a character to be printed. Many dot matrix printers are bidirectional, that is, they print from left to right and from right to left when the head returns. This is possible as a buffer stores several lines to be printed. Printing in both directions speeds up printing. The print electronics of dot matrix printers can be modified to print scripts other than English, for example, Devanagari, Tamil, etc. The reduction in the cost of inkjet printers and their better print quality as compared to dot matrix printers have considerably reduced the use of dot matrix printers. However, dot matrix printers are still used to create multiple copies of a document. Further, the recurring cost of printing is low (about a tenth of the cost of an inkjet printer).

As dot matrix printers are contact printers, it is easy to obtain multiple copies by placing carbon sheets between paper sheets. Continuous stationery, that is, fan-fold forms with holes on both sides which are advanced by sprockets on both ends of the printer's carriage are usually used in these printers. However, single sheets of paper of variable width up to 13.5 inches may also be used. Paper quality may be poorer than the ones used in inkjet/laser printers. As the cost of consumables (namely, printer ribbon, paper) is low and print and graphics quality are adequate for most office use, they are preferred by small businesses and government offices. One of their primary disadvantages is that they are noisy compared to inkjet and laser printers and may disturb co-workers in shared offices.

3.3.7 Line Printers

A line printer prints a complete line at a time. Printing speed varies from 200 to 2000 lines per minute with 75–300 characters on a 15-inch line. Six to eight lines per vertical inch are printed. One may buy printers with a variety of character sets. Usually, ASCII character sets are used with English letters. Printers are available in almost all scripts, for example, Japanese, Arabic, Cyrillic (Russian), Hindi, Tamil, Telugu, etc.

Early line printers were of two types: *drum printers* and *chain printers*. Drum printers consisted of a cylindrical drum on whose surface sets of characters to be printed were embossed. Chain printers had a steel band on which the character sets were embossed. Owing to their inflexibility to change fonts and print graphics, these printers have been superseded by what are known as *line matrix printers*. We describe how these printers function in what follows.

Line matrix printer uses a print head consisting of pins which are moved electromechanically to strike a ribbon (usually black) placed between the print head and the paper. Thus, a black dot (or pixel) is printed when one pin strikes the ribbon. A line of characters to be printed is stored in temporary memory and used by appropriate digital electronic circuits to activate the pins to print a line. The paper is then advanced and the next pixel row is printed. As the pixels are printed row by row, the print fonts, the distance between characters on a line, and the lines per inch are adjustable depending on the font type. The main features of this printer are as follows:

- Any one of several fonts can be selected.
- Any one of several scripts besides English can be printed.
- Graphics (i.e., pictures) can be printed.
- Bar codes can be printed.
- By placing carbon paper between sheets of paper (called multipart continuous stationery), several copies can be taken. Normally up to six copies can be printed.
- Ribbons are in cartridges to facilitate easy change. Ribbons can be reused.
- Printer speeds vary from 200 to 2000 lines per minute depending on the font type, language, etc.
- Characters per inch in the horizontal direction range from 5 to 20.
- The distance between lines can be varied by the output program.

Line printers use continuous fan-fold forms of paper rather than single sheets to allow fast printing (several pages per minute). This paper called continuous stationery (as described in the previous subsection) has holes on both sides. The continuous stationery is advanced through the printer using sprockets which use the holes on the sides of the paper for this purpose. There are several widths of continuous stationery available depending on the application. Some forms are pre-printed, such as cheques and examination result sheets. The faster printers use stackers to re-fold and stack the fan-fold continuous stationery as they emerge from the printer.

Line printers are used primarily when large volumes of data are to be printed. Some examples are electoral rolls, payroll, and mark sheets of examinations taken by thousands of students. In several of the above examples, pre-printed continuous stationery is used and several copies are required. In India, a popular brand of line printer is Lipi. Figure 3.7 shows a, line printer.

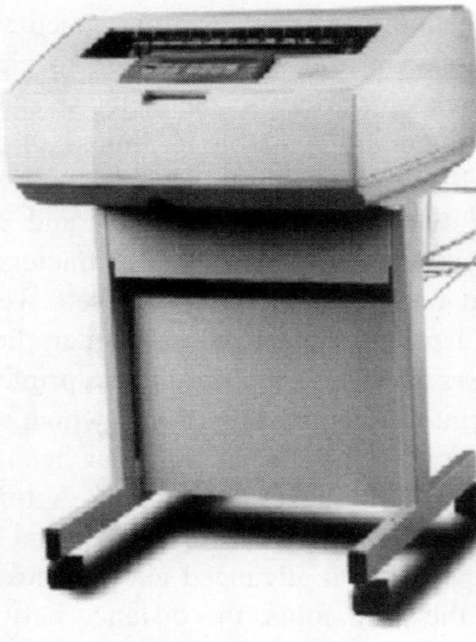

Figure 3.7 Photograph of IBM 6400 line matrix printer (Photo *Courtesy:* International Business Machines Corp.)

3.3.8 Plotters

Even though printers can be used to draw figures, they are unsuitable for drawing engineering drawings, such as building plans, machine parts, circuit diagrams, etc. Thus, special *plotters* to produce good-quality drawings have been designed and are available in the market. There are two types of plotters. One is called a *drum plotter* and the other a *flatbed plotter*.

In a drum plotter, the paper on which the graph is to be drawn is mounted on a rotating drum. A pen that can move linearly, that is, perpendicular to the direction of drum rotation, is mounted on a carriage. The drum can rotate in a clockwise or anticlockwise direction under the control of the plotting instructions sent by the computer. The pen can move left to right or right to left. The pen can also move up or down. The movements of the pen and drum are controlled by the graph plotting program. The program can thus draw various drawings and also annotate them by using the pen to draw characters.

A flatbed plotter has a stationary horizontal plotting surface on which paper is fixed. The pen is mounted on a carriage which can move in X or Y direction. The pen can also be moved up or down. A graph plotting computer program is used to move the pen to trace the desired drawing.

3.4 CHOOSING A PRINTER

As we have already pointed out, a printed output is called a *hard copy* as opposed to a *soft copy*, which is the same material stored in a computer-readable form. The advantage of a soft copy is that a recipient of such a copy can edit it (i.e., change it) easily as it can be read by a computer and processed. It is a disadvantage for the person who created it as it may be duplicated easily at a low cost. We saw that there are many printers available to create hard copies. An important question that will arise when you want to buy a printer is how to select a printer. Should it be an inkjet printer, a laser jet printer, or a dot matrix printer? For selecting a printer, appropriate questions to ask are:

1. What is the application of the printed output? Is the printed copy for rough use? Are multiple copies needed?
2. Will figures/pictures be interspersed with printed lines?
3. Is colour printing required?
4. What is the estimated cost of printing per page?
5. What is the number of pages to be printed per day?

Based on these questions, we give in Table 3.2 a comparison chart. From this chart, we see that if you want to buy an inexpensive printer for your home PC, an inkjet printer is appropriate.

Table 3.2 Comparison of printers

Printer type	*Speed*	*Quality of printing*	*Cost/page*	*Can figures be incorporated?*	*Initial cost*	*Print volume/ capacity*
Line printer	1000 lines per minute up to 132 characters/ line	Medium, no colour printing	Low. Multiple copies can be printed	No, but pie charts, bar charts possible	High	Very high, thousands of pages per day
Dot matrix printer	100 characters/s	Medium, colour printing with special ribbon	Low. Multiple carbon copies can be printed	No, but pie charts, bar charts, etc. possible	Medium	High, several hundred pages per day
Inkjet printer	100 characters/s	Good, 150 dots/cm, colour printers available	High. Replacement print cartridge expensive. Single copy	Yes	Low	Low, less than 25 pages per day
LaserJet printer (low cost home models)	8 pages/min	Good, 300 dots/cm, colour laser printers available	Medium for black and white. Single copy	Yes	Medium	Medium, several hundred pages per day
Laser jet printer (high speed publisher's models)	100 pages/min	Excellent, 600 dots/cm	High Single copy	Yes	High	Very high, several thousand pages per day

Nowadays colour inkjets are quite inexpensive and popular for home use as you can print colour pictures from the Internet or pictures you took with your digital camera. However, replacement print heads of inkjet printers are relatively expensive.

If you want an office printer where the requirement is to send multiple copies to several people, a dot matrix printer is appropriate. The advantage of a dot matrix printer is that its running cost is the lowest of all printers—a few paise per page. If you want a good print quality office printer where hundreds of pages are printed per day, laser jet (low cost) is quite adequate. A publisher who prints books needs a heavy-duty, high-resolution laser printer as the print quality of books should be excellent and the volume of printing will be quite high.

SUMMARY

1. Data to be processed by computers originate as written documents. It is necessary to convert these to a form readable by the computer's input unit.
2. Documents are converted to a machine-readable form by entering data using the keyboard of a personal computer and storing it in memory.
3. The commonly used input unit is the keyboard of video terminals. Besides this, magnetic ink character readers, bar code readers, and optical mark readers are used for specific applications.
4. Flatbed optical scanners are used to convert the printed material to bit maps. If the printed material uses standard fonts, character recognition software is used to convert the bit map files to ASCII files.
5. Hand-written cursive scripts can also be scanned and converted to ASCII with AI-based recognition software.
6. The most common output unit is a flat panel Liquid crystal display which is used by desktop and laptop computers for viewing the results of computation.
7. E-ink displays are used to view text and images, for example, e-books.
8. Hard copies of output are obtained by using printers. There are several types of printers. The most common printer for home use is an inkjet printer. Offices use laser printers. If a larger volume of printing and multiple copies is needed, dot matrix and line printers are used.
9. Graphical output may be obtained using plotters, inkjet, or laser printers. Flat panel display units are also useful to examine graphical outputs.
10. Engineering drawings are drawn using a drum or flatbed plotters.

REVIEW QUESTIONS

3.1 Explain the term 'data in machine-readable form'.

3.2 What is the most common input device used with computers?

3.3 What are the different types of keys in a keyboard? Explain the use of each of these key types.

3.4 What are the function keys in a keyboard?

3.5 What is a flatbed scanner? When is it used?

3.6 What is OCR? Where is it used?

3.7 Where are MICR characters used?

3.8 What is a bar code? Where are bar codes used? What are the advantages of using bar codes? How are bar codes read?

3.9 What is a QR code? Where is it used? How is the QR code read?

3.10 What is the difference between a soft copy and a hard copy?

3.11 Describe briefly the main principle used in liquid crystal displays.

3.12 Describe briefly the main principle used in e-ink displays.

3.13 In what application is liquid crystal display used?

3.14 In what application is the e-ink display used?

3.15 What is the difference between a line printer and a character printer?

3.16 When are line printers used?

3.17 What technology do modern line printers use?

3.18 What is the difference between an impact printer and a non-impact printer? Which is capable of higher speed?

3.19 What is the advantage of an inkjet printer compared to a dot matrix printer? What is its disadvantage?

3.20 What is the difference between a video graphic terminal and a graph plotter?

3.21 What is a computer mouse? Explain how it is used.

3.22 Describe how an e-ink display works. What is its primary application?

3.23 What devices are used to obtain a graphical output from a computer?

3.24 A page has 2000 characters. How many bits are needed to store it in a bit-mapped form? How many bits are needed if it is stored as ASCII?

3.25 What are the major differences between an inkjet printer and a laser printer? For what applications will you use a laser printer?

4 Computer Memory

LEARNING GOALS

After reading this chapter, you should be able to:

- Explain the properties required of a device to be used as a cell in the memory of a computer.
- Describe how memory cells are arranged to create different types of memories.
- Identify the parameters used to specify memory types and their characteristics.
- List various physical devices used to construct memories and their properties.
- Explain how the main memory of a computer is organized.
- Describe how various secondary storage devices such as hard disks, CDROMs, DVDROMs, flash memory, and cartridge tape drives function and their properties.
- Select a storage unit appropriate for a given application.

Memory or storage is required in a computer to store the programs and data. A memory comprises a large number of *cells,* with each cell capable of storing one bit. The cells may be organized as a set of addressable words, each word storing a sequence of bits. In one such organization, the time to store or retrieve a word is independent of the address of the word. This organization, called *Random Access Memory* (RAM), is used as the *main memory* of computers. Another organization arranges cells in a linear sequence to form a *serial access memory*. Cells used to fabricate a random access memory are made (in current technology) with semiconductor flip-flops or capacitors. Cells used in serial access memories of large size (hundreds of gigabytes) are magnetic dipoles on movable magnetizable surfaces. Magnetic surface recording may be organized in different configurations, such as hard disks and tapes. Optical recording with laser beams is used to store data on the surface of a coated disk. Such a serial access memory is CDROM (Compact Disk Read Only Memory). Better optical recording method which recorded data on multiple layers on a disk surface was also designed. This storage device is known as Digital Versatile Disk Read Only Memory (DVDROM). Optical recording devices are becoming obsolete with the advent of high-capacity semiconductor serial storage devices.

Various memory organizations discussed in this chapter can be classified based on their storage capacity, the method of storing and retrieving data, the time needed to store and retrieve data, the cost per bit of storage, and whether it requires a continuous power supply to retain data stored in it. As the speed of data retrieval increases, the cost per cell goes up. In a computer system, a *hierarchy of storage systems* is provided. At the top of the hierarchy is a very high-speed, high-cost, low-capacity memory which requires a continuous supply of power to store data, and at the bottom is a low-speed, low-cost, high-capacity memory which requires no power while it stores data. The speeds and capacities at various levels are chosen so that for a given budget one gets a well-balanced system that meets application requirements.

4.1 MEMORY CELL

A memory cell may be defined as a device that can store a symbol selected from a set of symbols and may be characterized by the following properties:

(i) The number of stable states it can be placed.
(ii) Whether a cell can store a symbol indefinitely even when power is turned off.
(iii) Whether the stored symbol is retained in the cell after it is read or disturbed.
(iv) The time taken to read a symbol from a cell and the time taken to write a new symbol in it.
(v) Whether a symbol, once written, can only be read and not changed.

The number of stable states a cell can be placed in determines the number of distinct symbols it can store. Each stable state may be assigned to represent a symbol. Thus, if a cell can be placed in 10 stable states, each state may be used to represent one symbol and so the cell can store a decimal digit. If a cell can be placed in only two stable states, one stable state represents a 0 and the other a 1. This cell may be used to store a binary digit.

If a symbol can be stored in a cell indefinitely without a continuous energy supply, it is known as a *non-volatile* cell. On the other hand, if the symbol stored in a cell disappears when no energy is supplied, it is known as a *volatile* cell.

Normally, if a symbol is read from a cell its content should not be disturbed. Such a cell is known as one with a *non-destructive* readout. If the symbol is erased, as a consequence of reading, the readout is said to be *destructive.* The time taken to read a symbol from a cell is called *read-time* and the time taken to write a symbol is called *write-time.*

If in a memory cell, a symbol is permanently written and can only be read, then it is known as a *read-only cell.*

4.2 MEMORY ORGANIZATION

Memory cells fabricated using current technology can be placed in either one of two stable states. We call these cells binary cells and each cell can store a binary digit. As stated earlier, one of the two stable states is used to represent the binary 0 and the other the binary 1.

Figure 4.1 shows a storage cell. The cell has an *input data line* on which the symbol to be written is sent to the cell. To write this symbol in the cell, a *write-control signal* is sent to the cell via the write-line. If the content of a cell is to be read, a *read-control signal* is sent on the read-line and the cell's content may be sensed on the *output data line*.

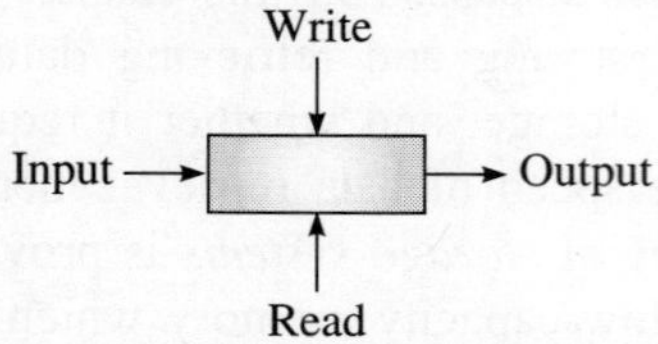

Figure 4.1 A memory cell.

By appropriate variation in the interconnection of binary memory cells, it is possible to organize different types of memories. We will assume that individual cells are non-volatile and reading is non-destructive. The simplest organization of a set of cells is shown in Figure 4.2. In this organization, three cells are interconnected in such a way that the write-control lines of all the cells are connected together. The read-control lines are also connected. The bits to be written in each cell are fed to the appropriate input data lines. When the write-signal is applied to the write-control line, these bits are written in the individual cells. The previous contents in cells are automatically erased when the new data is written. To read the contents of the cells, a read signal is applied to the common read line. The contents of the cells appear on the respective output data lines. The contents of individual cells are not erased by the read operation as reading from these cells is assumed to be non-destructive. This interconnection of cells is called a *register*. The register in Figure 4.2 stores three bits.

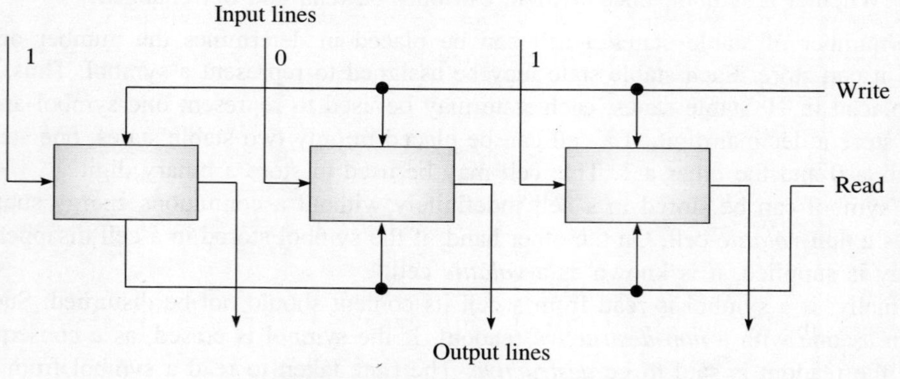

Figure 4.2 A 3-bit register.

A group of registers may be interconnected as shown in Figure 4.3 to form a memory. This memory is said to store four words of three bits each. In this organization, the input data lines of the first bit of all four registers are connected. Similarly, the input data lines of the second bits are connected and those of the third are also connected as shown in Figure 4.3. The output lines of each of the bits of the registers are also connected.

Observe the four write lines, one for each 3-bit register, and four read lines. To write data in this memory, the register in which the data is to be written is selected. If data is to

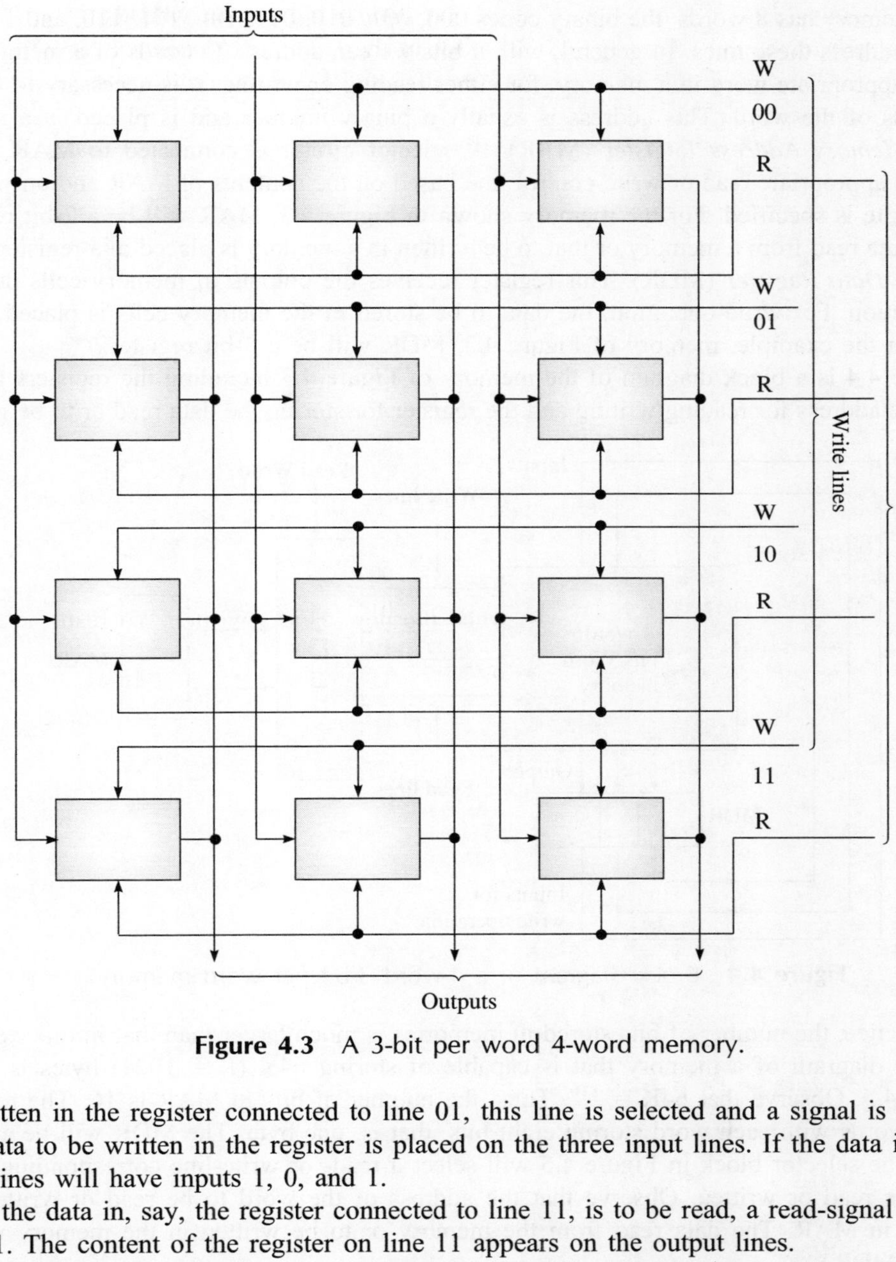

Figure 4.3 A 3-bit per word 4-word memory.

be written in the register connected to line 01, this line is selected and a signal is sent on it. The data to be written in the register is placed on the three input lines. If the data is 101, the three lines will have inputs 1, 0, and 1.

If the data in, say, the register connected to line 11, is to be read, a read-signal is sent on line 11. The content of the register on line 11 appears on the output lines.

Each of the four registers has one read-line and one write-line. At a time, we may either read from or write in a register. Each register in the memory should have a unique identification so that the appropriate register may be selected for writing or reading. In Figure 4.3, each pair of read/write lines corresponding to a register is identified by the binary codes 00, 01, 10 and 11. This memory has 4 words and each word stores 3 bits. The identification code of each register corresponding to a word in the memory is known as its *address*.

If a memory has 8 words, the binary codes 000, 001, 010, 011, 100, 101, 110, and 111 will uniquely address these lines. In general, with *n* bits we can address 2^n words of a memory. To select an appropriate word in a memory, for either reading or writing, it is necessary to specify the address of the word. This address is usually a binary number and is placed in a register called a *Memory Address Register* (MAR). A selector circuit is connected to MAR, which selects the appropriate read or write-control line based on the contents of MAR and on whether read or write is specified. For the memory shown in Figure 4.3, MAR will be a 2-bit register.

The data read from a memory or that to be written in a memory is placed in a register called a *Memory Data Register* (MDR). This register receives the outputs of memory cells during a read operation. For write-operation, the data to be stored in the memory cells is placed in this register. In the example, memory of Figure 4.3, MDR will be a 3-bit register.

Figure 4.4 is a block diagram of the memory of Figure 4.3 including the registers used to specify the address for reading/writing and the register for storing the data read or to be written.

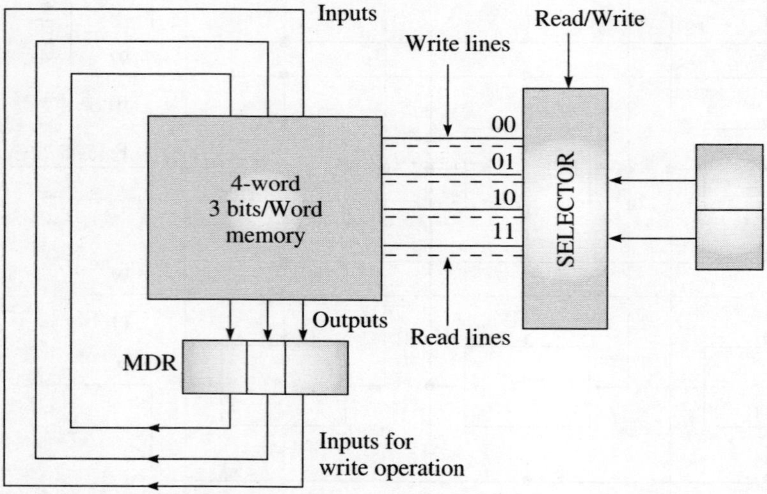

Figure 4.4 Block diagram of a 4-word 3-bit per word memory.

In practice, the number of bits stored in memories is much larger than that in this example. The block diagram of a memory that is capable of storing 64K (K = 1024) bytes is shown in Figure 4.5. Observe that 64K = 2^{16}. Thus, the number of bits in MAR is 16. The memory has 64K words with each word storing eight bits, that is, one byte. The MDR will be an 8-bit register. The selector block in Figure 4.5 will select a read- or write-line corresponding to the word to be read or written. Observe that the address of the word to be read or written will be placed in MAR. The data read from the memory or to be written in the memory will be placed in MDR.

If the number 173 = $(10101101)_2$ = $(AD)_{16}$ is to be written in the memory in address $(1111110101011010)_2$ = $(FD5A)_{16}$, then the number $(AD)_{16}$ is entered in MDR and the address $(FD5A)_{16}$ in MAR. The write-signal is initiated. The number in MDR, namely, $(AD)_{16}$, will be written in location $(FD5A)_{16}$ *replacing* the data in that location. To read the contents of a word whose address is $(AB34)_{16}$, this address $(1010101100110100)_2$ is placed in MAR.

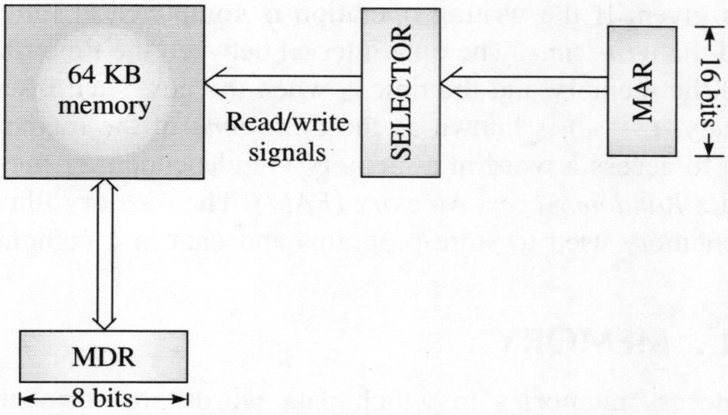

Figure 4.5 Block diagram of a 64 KB memory.

A read-signal is initiated. A copy of the data stored in $(AB34)_{16}$ is retrieved and placed in MDR. If the cells used in the memory are destructive read-out, then the contents in the specified address will be cleared to zero. In this case, whatever is read from the memory would, however, be available in MDR to be written back in the memory.

Assume that at time t_0 the address from which data is to be retrieved is placed in MAR and a read-signal is applied. If at time t_1 the required data is available in MDR, the elapsed time $(t_1 - t_0)$ is known as the *access time* of the memory (Figure 4.6a). The access time is usually slightly larger than the read-time of individual cells in the memory. If data is to be written in the memory, the data is placed in MDR and the address in MAR at time t_2 (see Figure 4.6b)

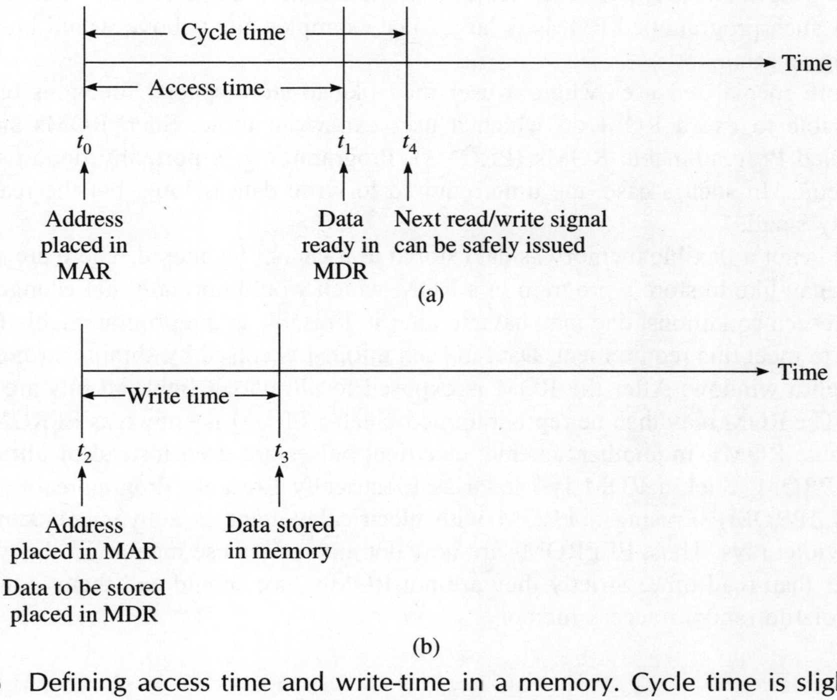

Figure 4.6 Defining access time and write-time in a memory. Cycle time is slightly larger than access time.

and a write-signal is given. If the writing operation is completed at time t_3, then the elapsed time $(t_3 - t_2)$ is called the *write time*. The time interval between the time t_0 at which a read/write command is given to the memory and the time t_4 when the next such instruction can be issued to the memory (namely, $t_4 - t_0$) is known as the *cycle time* of the memory (see Figure 4.6a).

If the time taken to access a word in a memory is independent of the address of the word, the memory is called a *Random Access Memory* (*RAM*). The memory illustrated in this section is RAM. The main memory used to store programs and data in a computer is a RAM.

4.3 READ ONLY MEMORY

There are random access memories in which data words are permanently written during fabrication. A word can later be read from the memory by specifying its address. The contents of the word cannot, however, be altered. Such a memory is called a *Read Only Memory* (*ROM*). Reading from a ROM should be non-destructive. The memory should also be non-volatile. An important application of a ROM is to store tables that do not change, for example, tables of trigonometric functions. Suppose we want to store Sine θ. Then a ROM is fabricated to store the value of Sine θ for various values of θ. To find Sine ϕ for a given ϕ, the value of ϕ is placed in the address register of ROM and a Read-signal is issued. Sine ϕ stored in a word of the ROM is retrieved and put in the MDR of ROM. Another application of ROM is for storing short programs for special applications. For example, a program to control the sequencing of operations of a washing machine may be stored in a ROM and interpreted by the processing unit. A ROM with data written in it during manufacture in a factory is known as a *factory programmed* ROM. Such factory programming is feasible only in cases where the demand for such programmed ROMs is large. The examples cited above would be suitable for factory programming.

For more specialized uses where a user may like to store special functions or programs, it is preferable to use a ROM on which a user can write these. Such ROMs are available and are called Programmable ROMs (PROMs). Programming is normally done using special writing circuits. In such a case, the time required to write data is long, but the read-time will be relatively small.

PROM is not a flexible memory as data stored in it cannot be altered. There are applications where one may like to store a program in a ROM which would normally not change, but under some unforeseen conditions, one may have to alter it. Erasable and reprogrammable ROMs have been made to meet this requirement. Data in such a ROM is erased by shining strong ultraviolet light through a window. After the ROM is exposed to ultraviolet light, all bits are erased and become 0. The ROM may then be reprogrammed. Such a PROM is known as EPROM (Erasable Programmable ROM). In another scheme, electrical pulses are used instead of ultraviolet light to erase a PROM. Such a ROM is known as Electrically Erasable Programmable Read Only Memory (EEPROM). Erasing a PROM with electrical voltage is convenient compared with using ultraviolet rays. Thus, EEPROMs are now dominant. In these memories, the write-time is much larger than read-time. Strictly they are not ROMs—we should call them slow write–fast read non-volatile random access memory.

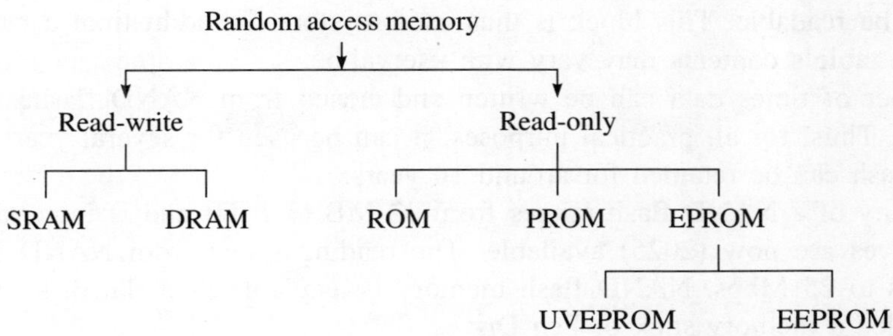

4.3.1 Flash Memory

Flash memory is a variety of EEPROM. It does not use the same technology as the EEPROM discussed in Section 4.3 and has different features. However, it also uses semiconductors, is non-volatile, and is a fast read–slow write device like EEPROM.

There are two types of flash memory: NOR flash and NAND flash. Each of these has different characteristics and different uses. Historically, NOR flash memory was the first one to be invented and was later followed by NAND flash. Currently, NAND flash is more widely used and is variously known as pen drives, memory stick or flash disk. The memory system comes either as a long flat pluggable device (5 cm × 2 cm × 1.5 cm) or as a 3 cm × 3 cm flat disk. They have built-in controller for read/write. The sizes given are indicative and not standard.

NOR flash memory

NOR flash memory is a random access memory similar to EEPROM. We can thus address an individual word or a byte to read. However, we can erase a single byte unlike an EEPROM, where the entire contents are erased. Reading from NOR flash memory is fast, around 10 ns/byte. The erase and write times are about 100 times larger than the read time. A NOR flash is suitable as a replacement for ROM, in which a fixed program can be stored. It can be erased 100,000 times without deterioration in performance. NOR flash manufacturers provide spare blocks in case of write failure and a bad block management system which keeps track of bad blocks in the system and prevents writing new data in those blocks.

NAND flash memory

Unlike NOR flash, NAND flash memory is not a random access memory. It is, however, non-volatile and fast read, slow write memory. A NAND flash is organized as a set of *pages* where each page is typically 512 to 2048 bytes. Besides data bytes, each page is provided with a few bytes (12–16 bytes) to detect and correct errors in the data stored in it. A set of around 32 pages is combined to form a *block*. The minimum accessible unit of data to be read from a NAND flash is a page. Thus, 512 bytes are read (assuming the page size is 512 bytes) at a time. Pages are addressable. Data is erased and written as a block of around 32 pages.

NAND flashes also have several bad blocks when manufactured and some blocks can become bad with use. Thus, manufacturers provide more blocks than what is specified as the capacity of the flash. Bad blocks are marked as non-usable and alternate blocks are provided. While using a NAND flash, the logical organization allows the correction of a single-bit error in 256 bytes. If more errors occur, the data cannot be corrected and is unusable. Block 0 is guaranteed to be readable. This block is thus used to store the address of a bad block table. The bad block table's contents may vary with use.

The number of times data can be written and erased from NAND flashes is typically a million cycles. Thus, for all practical purposes, it can be used for several years. Data written in a NAND flash can be retained for around 10 years.

The capacity of a NAND flash ranges from 32 MB to 1 TB and is increasing each year. 4 TB flash drives are now (2025) available. The reading speed from NAND flashes ranges from 10 Mbps to 25 Mbps. NAND flash memory is available as a flat disk or a stick. It is commonly called a memory stick or Pen Drives.

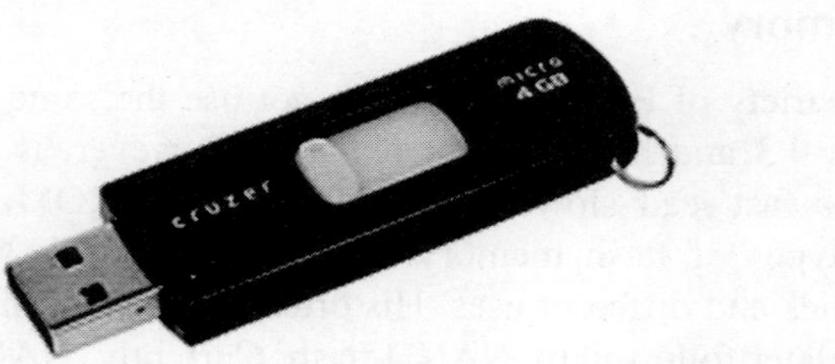

Figure 4.7 Picture of a NAND Flash Memory (Pen Drive)

4.4 SERIAL ACCESS MEMORY

Consider the organization of memory cells shown in Figure 4.8. In this organization, the output of a cell is the input to the next cell. A read-signal places the contents of each of the cells on the respective output lines. A write–signal following this read-signal will store these bits in the respective "next" cells. One read-write pair of signals would thus "shift" the contents of the cells right by one cell position and the bit stored in the rightmost cell will appear on the output line. A sequence of read–write signals will serially shift the contents of the register. After three read–write (namely, shift) signals, the output will be 0. As the bits stored in the cells appear serially (i.e., one after another) at the output, this memory is called a *serial access memory.* The structure shown in Figure 4.8 is known as a *shift register.* If the output of the shift register is connected to its input, each shift signal will circularly shift the contents of the memory. A series of shift signals will keep the contents of the memory circulating.

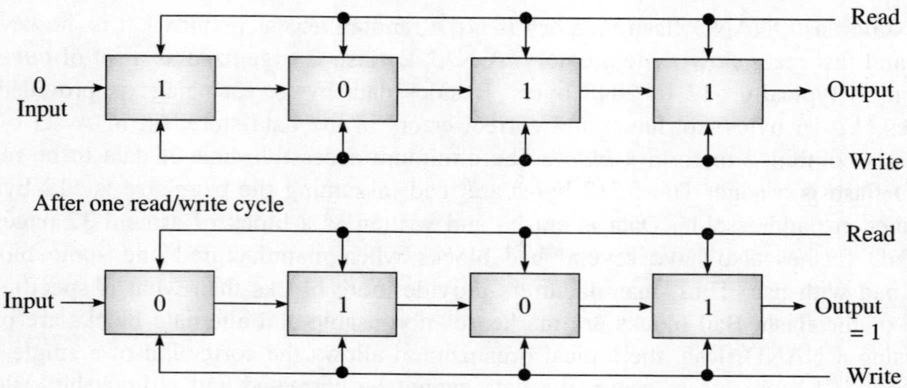

Figure 4.8 A serial access memory.

Another model of memory cells is shown in Figure 4.9a. In this model, one bit is stored in each cell. The *Read-head* reads the content of the cell placed below it and places it on the output line. The cells are moved *physically* from left to right and as each cell appears below the read-head, its content is placed on the output. The bits appear on the output as shown in Figure 4.9b.

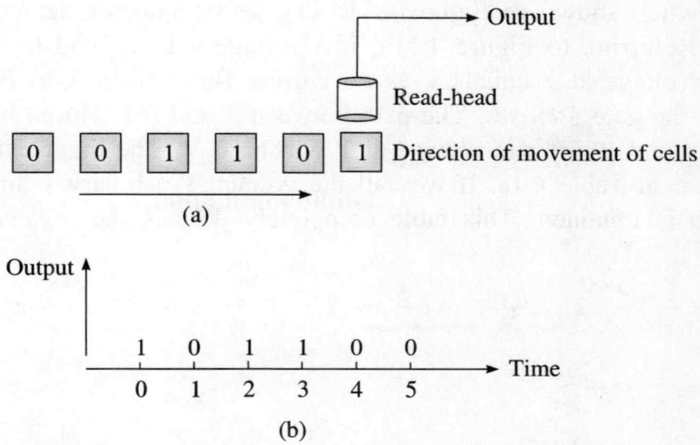

Figure 4.9 Illustration of reading with read-head.

A write-head writes in the cells as shown in Figure 4.10(a). As the cells move below the write-head, the bits fed to the write-head are stored in the cells as shown in Figure 4.10b. This model of serial access memory is appropriate to explain the operation of memories using magnetic surface recording.

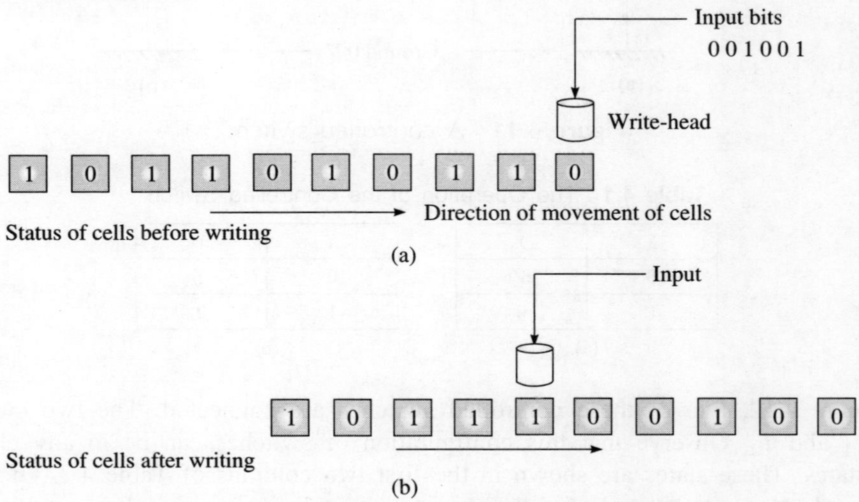

Figure 4.10 Illustration of writing with write-head.

A serial access memory is a non-addressable memory. In other words, sets of bits stored in the memory cannot be selectively retrieved by specifying their locations in the memory. The bits stored can be retrieved only in strict serial order.

4.5 PHYSICAL DEVICES USED TO CONSTRUCT MEMORIES

4.5.1 Semiconductor Flip-flop

Semiconductor devices, magnetic surfaces, and polycarbonate layers on glass platters are used to fabricate memory cells. The device used for making semiconductor memory cells is a semiconductor switch shown in Figure 4.11. The semiconductor device is modelled as a *controlled switch.* Referring to Figure 4.11a, if a voltage 0 is applied to point X, the "gate" g is *open* and the voltage at Y equals V as no current flows from A to B. If a voltage V is applied to point X, the gate g *closes*. The path between Y and B is closed by the gate. As B is connected to the ground (0 V), the voltage at Y will be 0 V. The input-output relationship of this device is shown in Table 4.1a. If we call the voltage V a binary 1 and 0 Volts a binary 0, then Table 4.1b is obtained. This table completely defines the *logical* behaviour of the controlled switch.

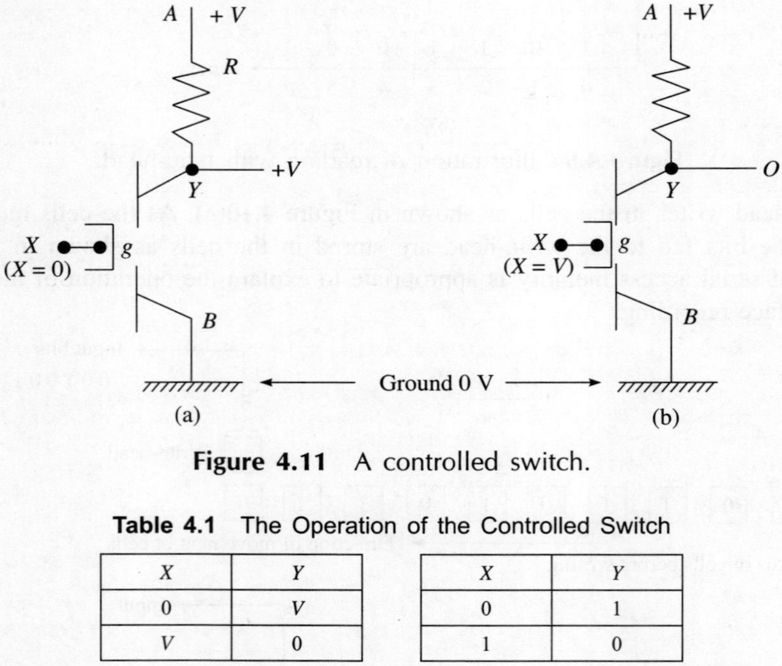

Figure 4.11 A controlled switch.

Table 4.1 The Operation of the Controlled Switch

X	Y
0	V
V	0

(a)

X	Y
0	1
1	0

(b)

In Figure 4.12, two of these controlled switches are connected. The two switches are labelled T_1 and T_2. Observe that this configuration of switches can be in any one of four possible states. These states are shown in the first two columns of Table 4.2. Of these four states, g_1 and g_2 cannot be open together because if g_1 is open, the voltage at Y_1 will be V, which will make X_2 also equal to V and thus close g_2. Similarly, g_1 and g_2 cannot be closed together because if g_1 is closed, Y_1 will be equal to 0, which will make X_2 also equal to 0, thus opening g_2. The state g_1 closed and g_2 open is possible. In this case, Y_1 will be 0 as g_1 is closed and X_2 which is equal to Y_1 will also be 0, which will open g_2. This state is known as a *stable* state as the circuit will continue to remain in this state as long as it is not disturbed by an external voltage. The state g_1 open and g_2 closed is also stable. In this case, g_1 open will make Y_1 equal to V, which in turn makes X_2 go to V, which will close g_2. This circuit which has two stable states can be used as a memory cell. One of the stable states may be used to represent the storage of a binary 1 and the other a binary 0. This circuit is known as a *flip-flop*. Table 4.2 summarizes the above discussion.

Table 4.2 State of flip-flop of Figure 4.12

g_1	g_2	*State*	*Voltage* Y_2	*Bit stored*
Open	Open	Not possible	–	–
Open	Closed	Stable	0	0
Closed	Open	Stable	V	1
Closed	Closed	Not possible	–	–

A flip-flop may be made to store a 1 or a 0 by using an external input voltage. Referring to Figure 4.12, if the input voltage is made V for a short period, the gate g_1 will close. The voltage Y_1 will become 0 and it will open gate g_2. The voltage Y_2 will equal V and the flip-flop will go to the 1 state. If the input voltage is 0 for a short period, g_1 will open and g_2 will close. Y_2 will become 0 and the flip-flop will go to the 0 state. The functioning of this flip-flop with input is summarized in Table 4.3.

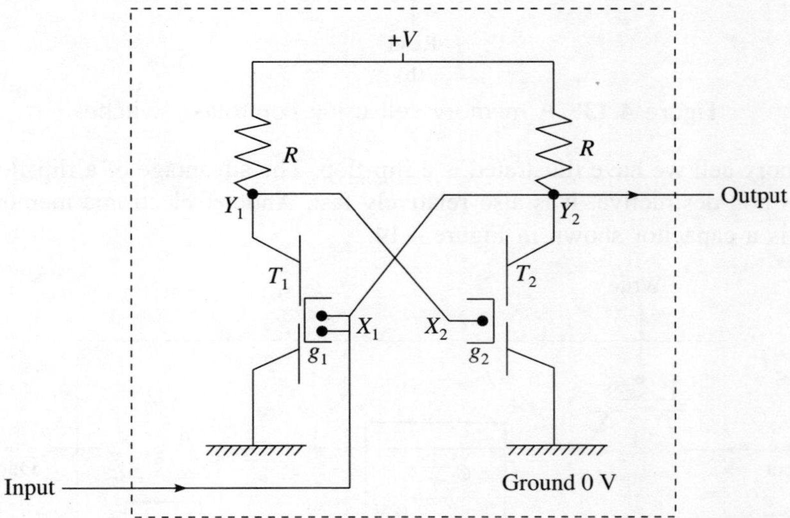

Figure 4.12 Two controlled switches connected as a flip-flop memory cell.

Write and read controls may be introduced by two controlled switches which close the input and output paths as shown in Figure 4.13a. In Figure 4.13b, the memory cell with the controlled switches (shown within dotted lines in Figure 4.13a) is shown as a memory cell of Figure 4.1, which was used in the logical description of Section 4.2.

Table 4.3 Functional characteristics of a flip-flop

Input	*Current state*	*New state*	*Output*
0	0	0	0
0	1	0	0
1	0	1	1
1	1	1	1

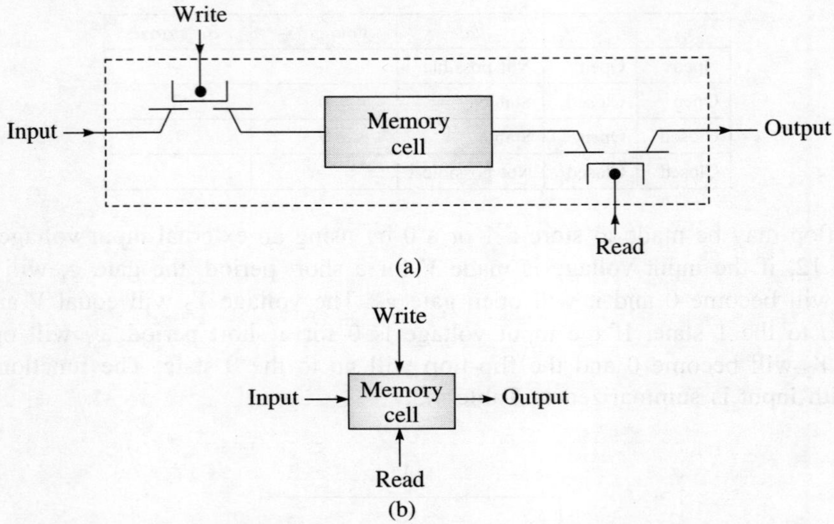

Figure 4.13 A memory cell using controlled switches.

The memory cell we have illustrated is a flip-flop. The advantage of a flip-flop is that read out from it is non-destructive. It is also relatively fast. Another electronic memory cell that is used widely is a capacitor shown in Figure 4.14.

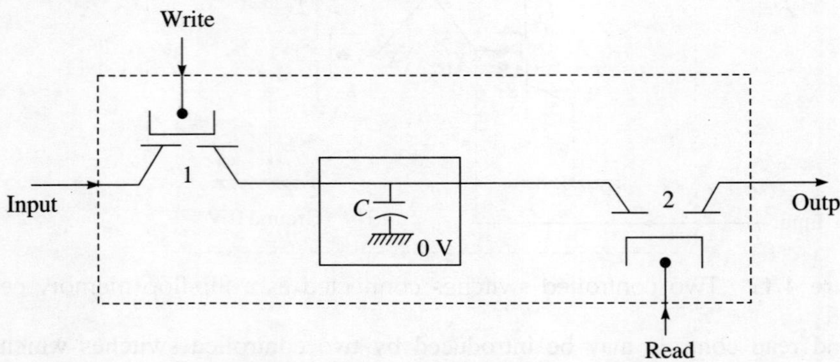

Figure 4.14 A capacitor memory cell.

When a voltage V corresponding to a 1 is applied to the input line and the write switch is closed, C gets charged to voltage V. When a read-signal is applied, switch 2 closes, and a voltage V (which corresponds to a 1) is sensed at the output. If 0 V is applied to the input, the capacitor C does not get charged and the output when read is 0. The major advantages of a capacitor memory cell are: (i) it is inexpensive and (ii) it is compact. Thus, large memories can be built at a reasonable cost. The main memories of most computers use this technology for memories. They are called DRAM (Dynamic Random Access Memory), whereas memories built using flip-flops are called SRAM (Static Random Access Memory). The main disadvantages of capacitors as memory cells are: (i) capacitors tend to discharge gradually. Thus, the contents of all the capacitors in memory require refreshing (i.e., the original values in them should be rewritten) periodically (normally after each read cycle). (ii) The readout is destructive; that is, the capacitor discharges (the content of the memory cell becomes 0 and is lost) after it is read requiring writing after reading. Thus, DRAMs are slower than SRAMs. As they are cheaper, they are widely used as the main memory of computers.

4.5.2 Magnetic Surface Recording

The physical device that realizes the logical memory cell model of Figure 4.8 is a magnetic recording surface. To write data on the surface, a current is passed through a coil wound on an elctromagnetic head. The current generates a magnetic field in the gap in the head. (See Figure 4.15). The field may be in one of two directions, depending on the current's direction in the coil surrounding the electromagnet. A plastic surface coated with a ferromagnetic material is placed below the head. The surface is magnetized in either of two directions, depending on the magnetic field across the recording head. If a portion of the surface is magnetized in the left-to-right direction, it is assumed that a 1 is written. If the surface is magnetized in the right-to-left direction a 0 is assumed to be written.

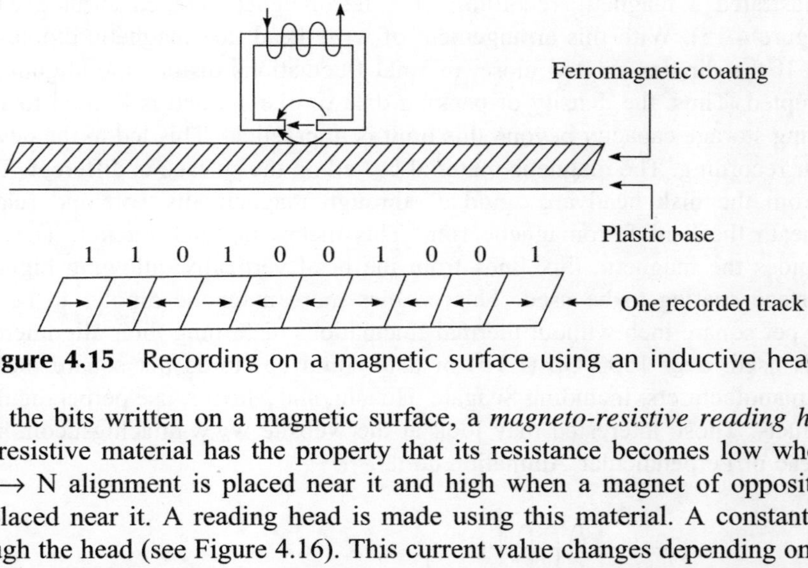

Figure 4.15 Recording on a magnetic surface using an inductive head.

To read the bits written on a magnetic surface, a *magneto-resistive reading head* is used. A magneto-resistive material has the property that its resistance becomes low when a magnet with say S → N alignment is placed near it and high when a magnet of opposite alignment N ← S is placed near it. A reading head is made using this material. A constant current I is passed through the head (see Figure 4.16). This current value changes depending on the polarity of the magnetic spot below the head. When a 1 (S → N alignment) moves below the head, the resistance of the head reduces and consequently, the current through the head increases. When a 0 (N ← S alignment) moves below the head, the head's resistance increases and the head current decreases (see Figure 4.16). The increase or decrease of the head current is detected by a sense amplifier and is interpreted as either a 1 or a 0. Both read and write heads use thin films of the material on a tiny head. The MR head is sensitive and has led to an increased density of packing bits on a magnetic surface. Bit density with MR heads is around 55 Gb/cm^2.

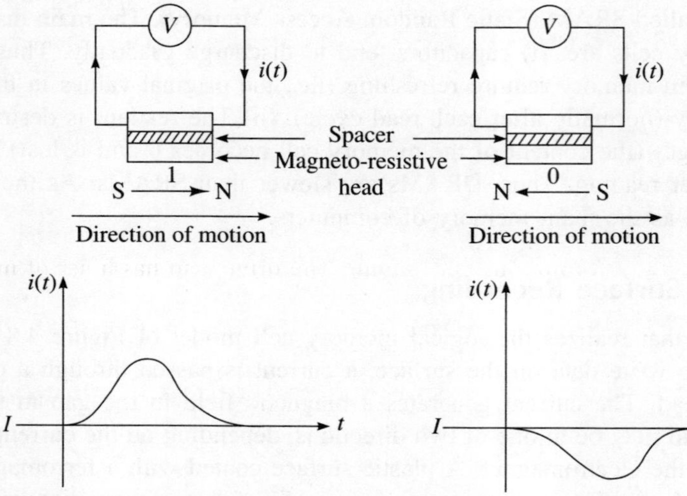

Figure 4.16 Reading bits from a magnetic recording using a magneto-resistive head.

Perpendicular recording

We have illustrated a magnetic recording of a ferromagnetic-coated surface with a plastic base (see Figure 4.15). With this arrangement of write-head, the magnetic dipoles are aligned horizontally. If the dipoles are too close, thermal fluctuations disturb the alignment, and data may be corrupted. Thus, the density of packing data on the surface is limited to 100–200 Gb/cm^2. Increasing storage capacity beyond this limit is impractical. This led to the development of perpendicular recording. The magnetic material coated on the surface is different. The magnetic flux lines from the disk head are "guided" through magnetically soft and relatively thick layer underneath the hard ferromagnetic film. This makes the disk thicker. The magnetically soft layer guides the magnetic flux lines from the head vertically, allowing higher coercivity magnetic surface coating to be used. This enables more magnetic dipoles to be packed (see Figure 4.17) per square inch without thermal fluctuations disturbing their alignment. When this technology is used, over 1000 Gb (1 Tb) of data could be stored per square inch. Currently, several disk manufacturers, including Seagate, Hitachi, and Maxtor, use perpendicular recording in their products. Those interested may look at the website www.hitachigst.com/hdd/research/recording_head/pr/Perpendicular Animation.html.

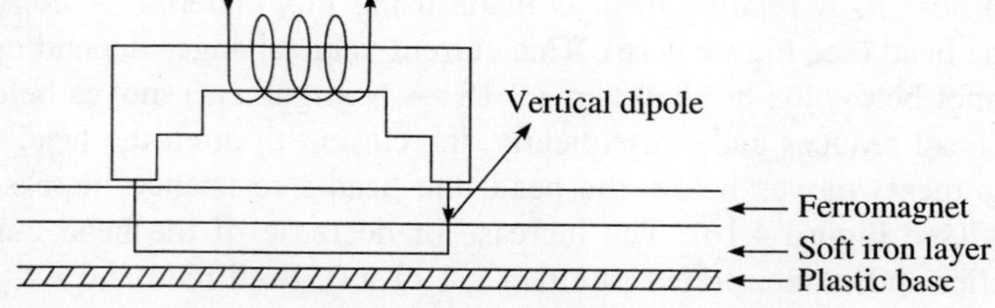

Figure 4.17 Perpendicular recording on magnetic surface.

The two most popular magnetic surface recording devices used currently are hard disk and magnetic tape. Earlier floppy disks made with the flexible magnetic tape material enclosed in an envelope were used for storage. They are now obsolete and not available in the market.

4.6 MAGNETIC HARD DISK

Magnetic disks are smooth metal plates coated on both sides with a thin film of magnetic material. A set of such magnetic plates are fixed to a spindle one below the other to make up a disk pack (Figure 4.18). The disk pack is sealed and mounted on a disk drive. Such a disk drive is known as a Winchester disk drive. The disk drive consists of a motor that rotates the disk pack about its axis at 7200 revolutions per minute. The drive also has a set of magnetic heads mounted on arms. The arm assembly moves in and out in the radial direction (Figure 4.18).

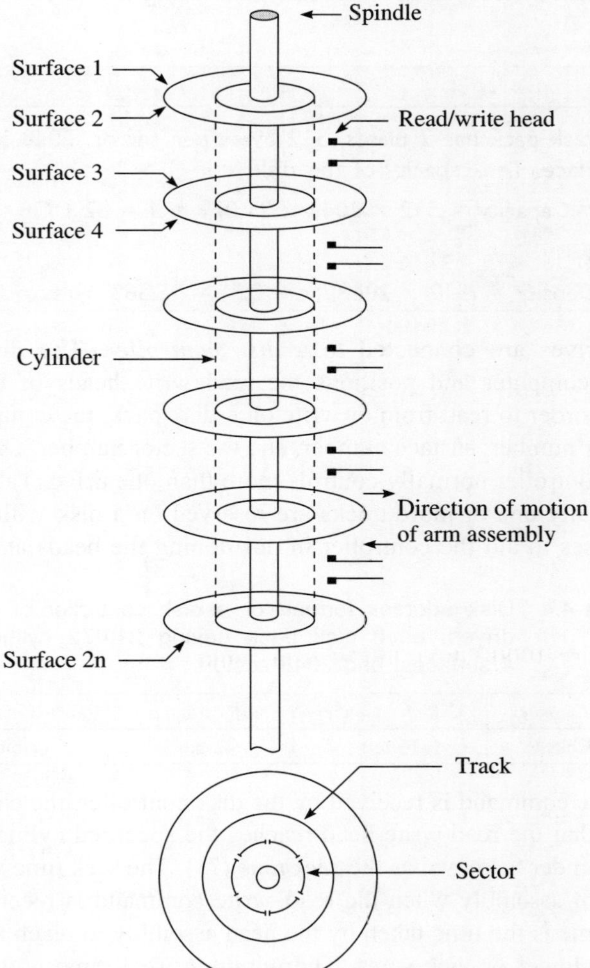

Figure 4.18 A magnetic disk memory.

Data is recorded on the surface of a disk as it rotates about its axis. Thus, data is along circular *tracks* on each disk surface. A set of concentric tracks are recorded on each surface. A set of corresponding tracks in all surfaces of a disk pack is called a *cylinder* (see Figure 4.18). If a disk pack has n plates, there are $2n$ surfaces. Thus, the number of tracks per cylinder is $2n$. A track is divided into sectors. Read and write operations on a disk start at sector boundaries. If the number of bytes to be stored in a sector is less than its capacity, the rest of the sector is padded with the last byte recorded. Assume s bytes are stored per sector, p sectors are there per track, t tracks per surface and m surfaces. Then the capacity of the disk is:

$$\text{Capacity} = s \times p \times t \times m \text{ bytes}$$

If d is the diameter of the disk in inches, the density of recording is:

$$\text{Density} = (s \times p)/(\pi \times d) \text{ bytes/inch}$$

The tracks are packed close to one another. Thus using $\pi \times d$ as the length of a track is appropriate.

Example 4.1

A 3.5 inch diameter disk pack has 2 plates, 512 bytes per sector, 2048 sectors per track, and 21,072 tracks per surface. The capacity of the disk is:

$$\text{Capacity} = 512 \times 2048 \times 21{,}072 \times 4 = 82.3 \text{ GB}$$

The recording density is:

$$\text{Density} = (512 \times 2048)/(\pi \times 3.5) = 95{,}363 \text{ bytes/inch}$$

A set of disk drives are connected to a *disk controller*. The disk controller accepts commands from the computer and positions the read–write heads of the specified disk for reading or writing. In order to read from or write on a disk pack, the computer must specify the drive number, cylinder number, surface number, and the sector number. Drive number should be specified, because a controller normally controls more than one drive. Table 4.4 shows the disk address format. Normally one or more tracks are reserved on a disk with permanent recording to provide timing pulses to aid the controller in positioning the heads at the specified address.

Table 4.4 Disk address format for a disk controller of eight drives, each disk pack having 21,072 cylinders, 4 surfaces, and 2048 sectors

Drive number	*Cylinder number*	*Surface number*	*Sector number*
3 bits	15 bits	2 bits	11 bits

When a read–write command is received by the disk controller, the controller first positions the arm assembly so that the read-write head reaches the specified cylinder. The time taken to reach the specified cylinder is known as the *seek time* (*Ts*). The seek time varies depending upon the position of the arm assembly when the read–write command is received by the controller. The maximum seek time is the time taken by the head assembly to reach the innermost cylinder from the outermost cylinder or vice versa. The minimum seek time is 0 if the head assembly happens to be positioned on the selected cylinder. The average seek time is usually specified and it is of the order of 10 ms.

Once the head assembly is positioned on the specified cylinder, the head corresponding to the specified surface is switched. This switching is electronic and is almost instantaneous. After the head is selected, there is a further delay because the specified, sector has to reach the read-write head. This rotation delay is variable. The average rotational delay equals half the time taken by the disk to rotate once. This time is known as the *latency time* (T_l). For a disk rotating at 7200 rpm, T_l is $\frac{0.5}{7200}$ min = 4.17 ms. The sum of average latency and seek time is known as the average *access time*.

When a sector is reached, the data is read at a speed determined by the speed of rotation of the disk. One full revolution of a 7200 rpm by a disk takes 8.33 ms. In one revolution one track with 2048 sectors, 512 bytes/sector is read. Thus, in 8.33 ms, 2048 × 512 = 1 MB are read, giving a transfer rate of 1 MB/8.33 × 10^{-3} = 120 MB/s. The time needed to read a sector is 4.26 μs. Observe that the time to access a sector

$$= \text{Average seek time} + \text{Average latency time} = 10 + 4.17 = 14.17 \text{ ms}$$

which is about 3300 times the time required to read a sector. The main point is that the time to reach a sector dominates the time to read the stored data. It is thus advantageous to read a number of consecutive sectors into a buffer store once a sector is reached, assuming that consecutive sectors will be required in an application. This is called *disk caching*. Disk cache sizes are between 8 and 64 MB.

All disk drives nowadays have a built-in controller which is normally a microprocessor. The processing power is used to compress data before storing it in a sector. The compression method is called Run Length Encoding (RLE). The idea is to avoid storing long sequences of 1s or 0s if they occur in the data. For example, if a data is 111111111111001, observe a sequence of twelve 1s in it. Instead of storing these, we can compress it to 11001 (12 followed by 1) before storing it and expand it after retrieval. A long sequence of 0s can also be similarly compressed. We have given the basic idea without giving details. In actual practice, we require an indication as to whether the data is compressed or not and also decide when RLE will be effective. It has been found statistically that RLE compression by a factor of 3 is often possible. Compression, besides increasing the disk's capacity, also increases the transfer rate of disks.

Besides moving the head to the correct sector for read–write and initiating read-write, the disk controller also checks whether the data sent from the main memory of the computer is correctly written on the disk. It is done by reading back the data written in the sector using a read-head, which is located next to the write-head. Each byte read is compared with the contents of a buffer register in the controller which contains the byte sent from the main memory for writing. If they do not match, there is an error. The controller also appends a Cyclic Redundancy Code (CRC) byte to the data written in a sector. The CRC byte is obtained by adding all the bytes in a sector and appending the least significant byte of the sum to the data bytes. When data is read back from a sector, the individual bytes read are added and the least significant byte of the sum is compared with the CRC byte read. If they do not match, an error is signalled.

The specifications of some commonly available disk drives in 2025 are given in Table 4.5. Figure 4.19 illustrates the inside view of a disk drive. Disk memory is often called *direct access memory* as the required data can be accessed by giving its address.

Table 4.5 Specifications of some disk drives (2025)

Model	*Capacity*	*Cache (MB)*	*Rotation speed (rpm)*	*Transfer Rate (Internal)*
Seagate Barracuda ST XX Series	16 TB to 24 TB	512	7200	190 MB/s
Western Digital 40EZAZ	4 TB	256	5400	180 MB/s
Seagate Exos X20	20 TB	256	7200	285 MB/s

Figure 4.19 Inside view of a disk drive.

Winchester disks come in many sizes and capacities and with many types of controllers. Normally an interface called SATA (Serial Advanced Technology Attachment) is used to connect it to the computer. A 3.5 inch diameter disk of 1 inch height is the preferred disk for use in desktop computers. Older servers used an interface known as a Small Computer System Interface (SCSI—it is normally pronounced SCUZZY). Larger disks of capacity over 8 TB are used in high-end servers, such as those that store video data or large organizational databases. They normally use a SATA interface. Larger computers such as mainframes use an array of disks in a configuration called RAID (Redundant Array of Inexpensive Disks). They use an extra disk to automatically detect errors and (sometimes) correct them during read operation.

Disk storage technology is progressing rapidly. Capacities go up each year (almost doubling every 15 months) and cost goes down.

4.6.1 Solid State Disks

The primary disadvantages of hard disks are the large latency and seek time to access data due to the mechanical spinning of the disk. Thus, attempts were made to emulate disks using solid-state memory. Two possible alternatives were DRAMs and Flash memories as replacements for hard disks. The major problems with DRAM are that they are volatile and expensive. Flash memories, on the other hand, are non-volatile and cost much lesser than DRAMs. Thus, flash memory-based systems to emulate hard disks are now used, particularly in portable computers.

Their primary advantages are:

- Their access time to a sector is microseconds (around 50 microseconds) rather than milliseconds as they have no rotating mechanical disk.
- The sequential write speed is round 10 GB/s.
- They consume much less power and are suitable for portable battery-operated devices.
- They can withstand extreme environments and mechanical shocks.

Solid state drives consist of three main parts:

1. A small DRAM as a cache to store a directory of block placement and bad block management. Some blocks in NAND flashes have manufacturing defects and also become unreliable with repeated use.
2. An array of NAND flash memory devices that operate in parallel.
3. A microcontroller, to control the device and implement error correcting code and a small battery to back up DRAM when power fails.

Currently (2025) SSDs of up to 128 TB capacity are available. However, they are uneconomical in large sizes as their storage cost per byte is four times that of hard disks. Their primary uses are in two areas:

- As a replacement for hard disks in laptops.
- As a buffer for a larger hard disk drive. The hard disk need not spin all the time as a set of tracks expected to be used immediately may be stored in SSD and used from there eliminating seek and latency delay in hard disks. Hard disks with SSD are called Hybrid disks.

4.7 OPTICAL DISKS

A high-capacity secondary storage is a Laser Disk commonly known as Compact Disk (abbreviated CD). CDs were widely used in the entertainment electronics market where they replaced cassette tapes and long-playing records in the 1990s. The disks were also used for data storage and known as Compact Disk Read Only Memory (CDROM). The CDROM disk, also known as a laser disk, is a shiny metal like disk whose diameter is 5.25 inches (12 cm). It can store around 650 MB (equivalent to 250,000 printed pages).

Data in CDROM is written by creating pits on the disk surface by shining a laser beam. As the disk rotates, the laser beam traces out a continuous spiral. The sharply focused beam creates a circular pit of around 0.8-micrometre diameter wherever a 1 is written and no pit (also called a land) if a zero is written. From a master disk, many copies can be reproduced by stamping a disk.

CDROMs were followed by DVDROMs with 8 GB capacity and Blu-Ray Disks with a capacity of 50 GB. These were popular from 1985 to 2015. Inexpensive Pen drives with a capacity of a few GB emerged around 2015 and CDROMs, DVDROMs, and optical storage media in general became obsolete. In the 1990s CDROMs were used to distribute software. With the emergence of the Internet software distribution by physical media has disappeared. Nowadays customers download software from the vendors' site via the Internet.

4.8 CLOUD STORAGE

Cloud storage is a service where service providers provide customers storage on-demand via their Internet connection. The service provider maintains a large bank of high-capacity disks on computers known as servers. Users primarily use cloud storage to backup data and program files. The access time to files on the cloud depends on the Internet speed between a user's computer and the cloud server. This speed is variable. Many cloud service providers such as Google and Dropbox give users around 10 to 15 GBs of cloud storage free and charge for extra GBs of storage usually as monthly rentals. Vendors assure the security of files. However, as the storage medium is shared by several users, it is advisable to back up sensitive files in one's system. Even though the service providers assure a good quality of service sometimes access to files from the cloud may be slow or unavailable for a few minutes/hours. (In Chapter 17, we will describe cloud computing in detail).

4.9 MAGNETIC TAPE DRIVE

Magnetic tape memories use flexible plastic ribbons coated with magnetic material on which data is recorded. The tape medium on which data is recorded is sealed in a cartridge. Data is recorded on magnetic tapes using magnetic recording heads, similar to the ones used in hard disks. The current technology is called LTO, also known as Ultrium. It is an industry standard that uses a 12.65 mm width, 1035 m long magnetic tape enclosed in a cartridge. A tape recorded using the drive of say IBM can be read by a drive manufactured by HP and vice versa. The LTO standard was evolved in 2000 as LTO-1 and has steadily improved. The standard is adopted by all the major vendors of magnetic tapes. Starting with LTO-4 and LTO-5 standards, 16 magnetic heads are used to write and read along 16 parallel tracks on the tape when the tape moves below these heads. When the end of the tape is reached, the tape reverses direction, the heads move laterally and 16 more tracks are recorded in the opposite direction. This type of recording is called *serpentine* recording. Data can be recorded as is or may be compressed using a standard compression algorithm. Data compression/decompression is done by a built-in hardware unit that uses a lossless compression algorithm. The latest model LTO-9 introduced in 2021 has 32 heads. It stores 18 TB uncompressed and 45 TB compressed. Data can be encrypted. It can be configured as WORM (Write Once Read Many times). This is done to prevent accidental overwriting of important archival data. The maximum read/write speed of LTO-9 is 400 MB/s in uncompressed mode. The tape is usually certified for 1 million passes or 100 full backups and has 30 years shelf-life. One of the major applications of LTO tape is archiving data stored on disks. Normally archival tape storage libraries have thousands of tapes and there is a danger of mix up. Thus, every LTO tape cartridge has a memory chip inside it. This memory can be read by a non-contact reader to identify a cartridge to avoid human errors and prevent mounting a wrong cartridge. A robot controls the stacking and retrieving of cartridges from an archives library maintained by large computer centres. LTO technology is continuously evolving as pointed out earlier. When a new standard is announced it ensures that tapes written using the two earlier standards could be read with the new standard.

Magnetic tapes are used nowadays in computers for the following purposes:

(i) Backing up data stored in disks. It is necessary to regularly save data stored on disk in another medium so that if by accident the data on disk is overwritten or if data gets corrupted due to hardware failure the saved data may be written back on the disk.

(ii) Storing processed data (e.g., files of students' examination results) for future use. This is called *archiving*.

4.10 MEMORY HIERARCHY

So far, we have described several devices used to store data in a computer. You may wonder why there is such a large variety of storage devices. The primary reason is the tradeoff between cost per byte of storage and access time and the secondary reason is whether the storage is volatile or not. A computer system needs all the storage devices described in this chapter in a balanced configuration. The memory system is organized as a hierarchy consisting of many levels. At the top level is a high-speed, low-capacity, volatile memory called a cache and at the bottom is high capacity slow access non-volatile tape storage. Nowadays tape drives are used only by large supercomputer centres and data centres of large companies and banks. Most users depend on cloud storage to back up their data.

In Table 4.6, we have summarized the average capacity of the devices, their access times, and the relative cost per byte of storage. From the table, it is seen that small semiconductor memories using high-speed transistor flip-flops known as *cache memories* are the most expensive as well as the fastest in the set. At the other end, we have tapes and cloud storage with high storage capacity, low-speed serial access, and low cost per byte of storage. In a computer system, it is necessary to use a judicious combination of all these types of storage devices for the best results. The situation is similar to the method used to store files in offices. The most urgent files are kept for immediate attention on the table of a manager. This is analogous to the data stored in a small high-speed memory of a computer, called *cache* memory, which stores the instructions and data to be immediately used. Files that need to be examined on a given day by a manager would be normally kept in an in-tray on the side of the table and can be immediately accessed by the manager. The main semiconductor random access memory of a computer is similar to this. It stores the program currently being executed. Files that do not have to be referred to immediately but which should be within easy reach of the manager are kept in an organized manner in a filing cabinet. The disk storage in a computer is similar to this. It stores programs and data which would be needed soon. It also stores the data that would be required for immediate reference. As it is non-volatile programs and data are periodically backed up on disks. Rarely used files and those that need to be preserved for audit and legal requirements are kept in big index files in the main office away from the manager's room. The magnetic tape storage system and cloud storage fulfill a similar purpose. Finally, legal and reference books are kept in a library. Pen drives fulfill a similar purpose. Duplicate copies of programs and data are stored in Pen drives.

The most appropriate tape for backing up and archiving massive data from a disk today is LTO-9 Ultrium tapes. Software or data distribution is best done from the vendors' websites. The best medium now for storing personal files and retrieving them easily is the pen drive.

Table 4.6 Comparative characteristics of memories

Memory type	*Average Capacity in bytes*	*Technology*	*Average access time*	*Purpose in a computer*	*Relative cost*
Cache L3	8 MB	SRAM	10 ns	Instruction and data needed immediately	10
Main memory	32 GB	DRAM	100 ns	Program and data	1
Disk memory	8 TB	Magnetic. Surface	5 ms	Large data files Large programs overfowing memory	1/100
Solid-state disk	2 TB	Integrated circuit	2 GBps	Same as disk memory	1/10
Flash memory (Pen Drive)	1 TB	Integrated circuit	2 GBps	Storing personal data files	1/1000
Tape Drive (LTO-9)	18 TB	12.65 mm Tape cartridge	NA	Archiving files	1/10000

SUMMARY

1. A memory or storage of a computer is organized using a large number of cells. Each cell stores a binary digit.
2. A memory cell that does not lose the bit stored in it when no power is supplied to the cell is known as a non-volatile cell.
3. The time taken to store a bit in a cell and the time taken to read it are important parameters of a cell.
4. Several cells, with each cell storing a bit, constitute a word. A word is a group of bits that are stored and retrieved as a unit. The main memory system of a computer is organized to store a number of words. A word may store one or more bytes. The length of a word may be specified as "*n* bits per word". The storage capacity of a memory is specified as the number of bytes it can store. Typically, a word has 32 bits.
5. Each word in the main memory of a computer is stored in an addressable location. A Memory Address Register (MAR) stores the address of the location in the memory from where a word is to be retrieved or where a word is to be stored. The data retrieved from the memory or the data to be stored in memory are placed in a memory data register (MDR).
6. To store a word in memory, it is placed in MDR and the address where it is to be stored is entered in MAR, and a write command is given. The time taken to write a word is known as the write time.
7. To retrieve a word from memory the address of the word is placed in MAR and a read command is issued. The retrieved data is placed in MDR by the memory. The time to retrieve data is called the access time of the memory.
8. In a random access memory (RAM), the access time and the write time of a word are independent of the address of the word.
9. A random access memory may be fabricated with permanently stored data that cannot be erased. Such a memory is called a Read Only Memory (ROM).

10. A ROM in which data can be written permanently in the field is known as a programmable ROM (PROM). If it can be erased and reprogrammed, it is known as an erasable programmable ROM (EPROM).

11. A flash memory popularly known as a pen drive, is a type of electrically erasable programmable ROM (EEPROM). Unlike a ROM it is not a random access memory but stores data in blocks of 512 to 2048 bytes which is retrieved as a block.

12. A serial access memory is organized by arranging memory cells in a linear sequence. Data is retrieved or stored in such a memory by a read-write head. Data is presented serially for writing and is retrieved serially during reading.

13. A flip-flop made of semiconductor devices is used to fabricate a memory cell. These memory cells are organized as a random access memory. This memory is called static RAM.

14. A capacitor with associated switches can also be used as a memory cell. In this cell, the data is lost when it is read or with passage of time. It is thus periodically refreshed. Memory made using these cells is called a Dynamic Random Access Memory (DRAM).

15. A bit may be stored on a magnetic surface by magnetizing the surface in either one of two directions. The surface is magnetized using a write-head. A read-head is used to retrieve a stored bit. Currently, perpendicular recording has superseded horizontal surface recording.

16. Magnetic surface recording devices commonly used in computers are hard disks and magnetic tapes.

17. A hard disk consists of several hard platters mounted on a spindle. The platters are coated with magnetic material. Data is organized along tracks on each platter. Each track is divided into sectors. Each sector on the disk has a unique address. Hard disks can store up to 20 TB. Retrieval time is of the order of tens of milliseconds. Hard disks are used in computers to store user program files and data.

18. Solid state disks (SSDs) consist of a set of flash memories as the primary storage medium. As there are no moving parts, its access time is much smaller than hard disk. It consumes less power and is rugged. The cost/byte of SSD is 10 times that of hard disk. The capacity of SSDs (2025) range from 256 MB to 128 TB.

19. CDROM uses a laser beam to record and read data along spiral tracks on a 5.25” disk. A disk can store around 650 MB of data. CDROMs are normally used to store massive text data (such as encyclopedias) which is permanently recorded and read many times. CDROMs that can be written on the users’ premises are called writable CDROMs. They are used as archival stores and for software and data distribution. They are almost obsolete now (2025).

20. Cloud storage is provided by vendors on-demand on the Internet. They are normally banks of hard disks. Up to 15 GB is normally free. It is used to back up files.

21. A magnetic tape is a serial access non-addressable memory. The time taken to store and retrieve data from tapes is slow (of the order of seconds). Tapes are mostly used as a backup storage device and for archiving data.

22. A computer system is organized with a balanced configuration of different types of memories. The main random access memory is used to store the program that is currently executed by the computer. Magnetic disks and SSDs are used to store large data files and program files awaiting execution. Tapes are used to back up the files from the disk. Pen drives are used to backup and archive data. Pen drives are portable.

REVIEW QUESTIONS

4.1 What is the purpose of the main memory in a computer?

4.2 What are the main characteristics of a memory cell?

4.3 What is a non-volatile memory?

4.4 What is the destructive reading of a memory cell? Give an example of a destructive read cell.

4.5 What is a register?

4.6 Draw a block diagram of a memory that has 8 words of 4 bits each.

4.7 What is the size in bits of MAR of a 16 KB memory? Assume that the word size is 1 byte.

4.8 What are the sizes in bits of MAR and MDR of 512 MB, word addressable memory with 16-bit words?

4.9 Define the term "access time" of a memory.

4.10 What is the distinction between the write time of a memory and its access time?

4.11 Define the term "random access memory".

4.12 What is a read-only memory? Is a ROM a random access memory?

4.13 What is flash memory? What are the two types of flash memory? Compare their characteristics.

4.14 What is a serial access memory?

4.15 Explain the operation of a controlled switch.

4.16 Explain the operation of a flip-flop.

4.17 Explain how a capacitor memory cell stores data. Is data stored in such a cell volatile?

4.18 Why do memories use capacitor cells that need refreshing?

4.19 Explain how data is written on and read from magnetic surfaces.

4.20 Explain how data is organized on a hard disk.

4.21 Define the terms "seek time" and "latency time" of a hard disk.

4.22 If a hard disk has 10 surfaces, each surface is 6 inches in diameter, and the density of recording is 60000 bits per linear inch, estimate the number of bits per cylinder of the disk.

4.23 If a hard disk rotates at 7200 rpm and the surface recording density on it is 1 Mbpi, what is the data transfer rate of the disk?

4.24 What is a sector in a hard disk?

4.25 Why do we have a variety of memories in a computer system?

4.26 What is a solid-state disk? What are its applications?

4.27 Compare the features of magnetic hard disks and SSDs.

4.28 What is a CDROM? In what way is it different from a hard disk?

4.29 What are the primary applications of magnetic tape storage?

4.30 What is the capacity of a LTO-9 tape? Is data encryption built-in in LTO tapes?

4.31 Is there a method to uniquely identify tape cartridges before they are mounted on a tape drive? If yes why? How is it done? Why is it necessary?

4.32 What do you understand by the term memory hierarchy? Why is it necessary for a computer Draw a diagram illustrating memory hierarchy giving the fastest memory on top.

5 Processor

LEARNING GOALS

After reading this chapter, you should be able to:

- Describe the logical organization of the Central Processing Unit (CPU) of a computer.
- Explain the structure of machine language instructions and how they are stored and executed.
- Simulate a simple computer.
- Describe the additional features processors need to simplify programming and alleviate the speed mismatch between the main memory and the processor.

The processing unit in a computer interprets instructions given in a program and carries them out. Processors are designed to interpret a specified set of instruction codes. Each instruction code is a string of binary digits. All processors have input/output instructions, arithmetic instructions, logic instructions, branch instructions, and instructions to manipulate characters. The number and type of instructions available differ from processor to processor. In this chapter, we will illustrate the general structure of a processor and show how it interprets and executes instructions.

5.1 STRUCTURE OF INSTRUCTIONS

An instruction to be executed by a processor should specify the following:

1. The task to be carried out by the processor.
2. The address or addresses in memory where the operand or operands would be found.

3. The address in memory where the result is to be stored.
4. The address in memory from where the next instruction to be carried out is to be taken.

For example, suppose an operand stored in address *P* in memory is to be added to one stored in *Q* and the result is to be stored in an address *R*, and the address of the next instruction to be executed is *S*, the instruction would be of the following type:

ADD	*P*	*Q*	*R*	*S*
What task? (Operation code)	Address of the first operand	Address of the second operand	Address of the result	Address where the next instruction would be found

The instruction given above is known as a *four-address instruction.* If a memory has 256 K addresses, each address would be 18 bits long. Four addresses would require 72 bits and in addition, bits are needed for the operation code. The storage required to store a four-address instruction would therefore be quite large. Many instructions would not require all the addresses. Normally in an algorithm, instructions are carried out sequentially, that is, one after another. If an instruction is stored in an address *X*, the next instruction would be stored in the next consecutive address, namely, $X + 1$. Only on rare occasions is the normal sequence violated and the program jumps to a specified address. Thus, the fourth address, *S*, need not be explicitly specified in each instruction. If we remove the fourth address, we get a *three-address instruction.* Three addresses require 54 bits to specify if the memory has 256K addresses. This instruction length is also too long. Again, however, many instructions would not require all three addresses. For example, an instruction to change the sign of a number stored in memory would need only the address of the number. To simplify the design of processors, it would be preferable to have a uniform size for all instructions. If it is decided to use only one address in each instruction, the processor design will be simplified. We would, however, need a register in the processor where an operand may be stored and whose address need not be explicitly specified but will be *implied* in various operations. One such register is known as *the accumulator register.* If a processor has an accumulator, then an instruction to ADD given earlier may be reformulated as a series of three instructions:

1. Clear the accumulator register in the processor and place the first operand from the address *P* in it.
2. Add to the accumulator register the operand stored in *Q* and leave the result in the accumulator.
3. Store the contents of the accumulator in address *R* of memory.

These instructions are summarized as the three single-address instructions shown in Table 5.1. It should be clearly understood while writing a program that when we say ADD *Q*, we do not mean add the number *Q*. We mean add the number *stored in memory in address Q.* The availability of an accumulator in a processor allows intermediate results to be kept in it and subsequently used without unnecessarily storing it in the memory and retrieving it from the memory. As an example, a series of instructions to read a set of numbers, add them and, print the result are given in Table 5.2. Observe that the intermediate results remain in the accumulator and are used subsequently. Observe the column labelled 'instruction address' in the program of Table 5.2. Each instruction in a program is also stored in memory. The address where the first instruction of the above program is stored is X. The second instruction is stored in the next address $X + 1$. Succeeding instructions are stored in successive addresses. The notation C(K) in Table 5.2 means contents of address K in memory. The content of the accumulator is abbreviated as ACC in this table.

Table 5.1 A sequence of single-address instructions

What task? (Operation)	*Address of operand*	*Abbreviated instruction*
Clear the accumulator and place the operand stored in P	P	CLA P
Add operand in Q to it	Q	ADD Q
Store the content of the accumulator in R	R	STO R

Table 5.2 A program to add a set of numbers

Address where instruction is stored in memory	*Operation*	*Operand address*	*Remarks*
X	READ	K	Read $n1$ from the input unit and store it in K
$X + 1$	READ	L	Read $n2$ from the input unit and store it in L
$X + 2$	READ	M	Read $n3$ from the input unit and store it in M
$X + 3$	READ	N	Read $n4$ from the input unit and store it in N
$X + 4$	CLA	K	Move C (K) = $n1$ to the accumulator
$X + 5$	ADD	L	ACC ← ACC + C (L) = $n1 + n2$
$X + 6$	ADD	M	ACC ← ACC + C (M) = $n1 + n2 + n3$
$X + 7$	ADD	N	ACC ← ACC + C (N) = $n1 + n2 + n3 + n4$
$X + 8$	STO	W	C (W) ← ACC = $n1 + n2 + n3 + n4$
$X + 9$	PRINT	W	Print C (W) = $n1 + n2 + n3 + n4$
$X + 10$	HALT		

In a processor, a string of bits is used to code the operations. Addresses are also binary numbers. If a processor has 16 different operations, 4 bits would be needed to represent each operation. If the memory size is 4K words, then 12 bits are required to represent each address. The *format of a typical instruction* is shown in Figure 5.1. Using the operation codes given in Table 5.3, the program of Table 5.2 is shown in Table 5.4. The program is stored beginning from address $(008)_{hex}$. Hexadecimal notation is used for conciseness. The term 'address' used in the preceding discussions refers to the address of an operand. The length of the operand (number of bits in it) is not specified. If we assume that the length of an operand equals the length of an instruction, then the instruction and the operand are said to occupy one *word* in a computer's memory. If the smallest addressable unit in a computer is a word, then such a computer is known as a *word-addressable computer*. A computer in which each byte stored can be addressed individually is known as a *byte-addressable* computer. The program given in Table 5.4 is known as a *machine language program*. Observe that the instructions are stored in the memory beginning from address 008 up to address 012. Data to be processed is also stored in the same memory from address 200 up to 204. It is the responsibility of the machine

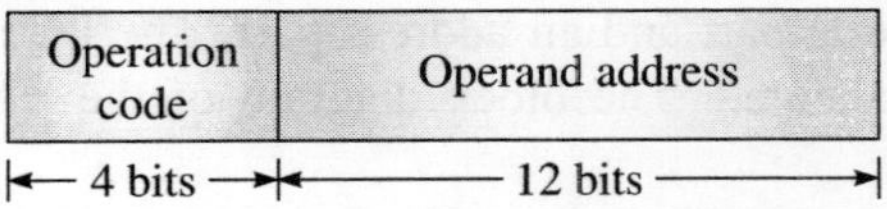

Figure 5.1 Format of a single-address instruction.

Table 5.3 Binary and hexadecimal codes for operations

Operation	*Operation code (in binary)*	*Operation code (in hexadecimal)*
READ	1010	A
CLA	0001	1
ADD	0010	2
STO	0110	6
PRINT	1011	B
HALT	1111	F

Table 5.4 Machine language program corresponding to the program of Table 5.2

Instruction address (hexadecimal)	Instruction		Remarks
	Operation code	*Operand address*	
008	A	200	Read *n*1 and store it in 200
009	A	201	Read *n*2 and store it in 201
00A	A	202	Read *n*3 and store it in 202
00B	A	203	Read *n*4 and store it in 203
00C	1	200	Accumulator ← C (200) = *n*1
00D	2	201	ACC ← ACC + C (201) = *n*1 + *n*2
00E	2	202	ACC ← ACC + C (202) = *n*1 + *n*2 + *n*3
00F	2	203	ACC ← ACC + C (203) = *n*1 + *n*2 + *n*3 + *n*4
010	6	204	C (204) ← ACC = *n*1 + *n*2 + *n*3 + *n*4
011	B	204	Print C (204) = *n*1 + *n*2 + *n*3 + *n*4
012	F		Halt

language programmer to ensure that the program locations and data locations in memory are kept separate and instructions are not accidentally written over data. In the next section, we will examine the logical structure a processor must have to execute machine language programs.

5.2 DESCRIPTION OF A PROCESSOR

In this section, we will describe the processor of a hypothetical computer we name HYPCOM. The reason why we use a hypothetical computer is that it is easy to explain fundamental ideas with a simple model. Real commercial computers are too complex to explain basic concepts to a beginner. The processor of HYPCOM has an accumulator register (ACC). (As stated in Section 4.2, a register is an interconnected set of memory cells, each storing a bit). The other registers in the processor are an *instruction register* (IR) and a *program counter register* (PC). The instruction register is used to store temporarily the instruction being executed. It consists of two parts: an operation code part and an address part. The PC register stores the address of the next instruction to be executed. The block diagram of the HYPCOM processor is shown in Figure 5.2.

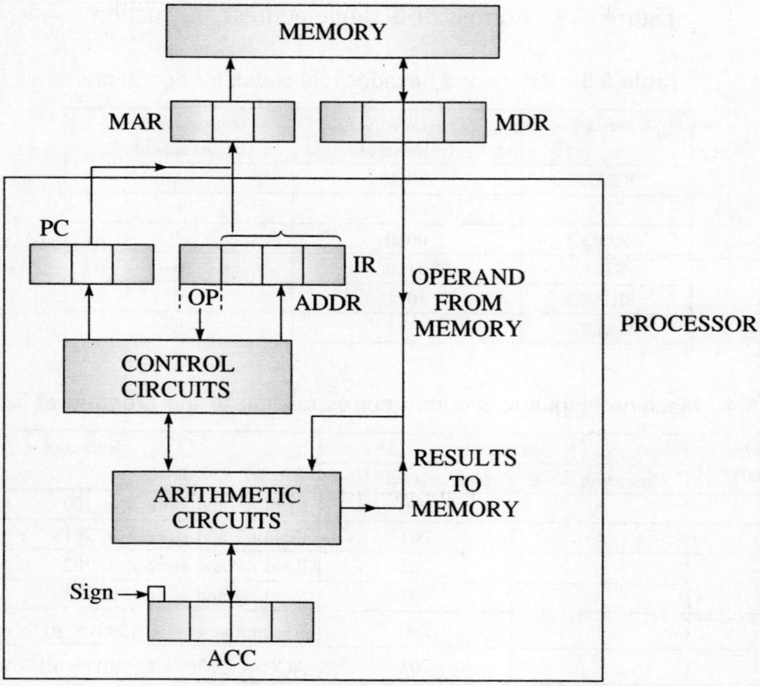

Figure 5.2 Logical structure of HYPCOM processor.

The other specifications of HYPCOM are:

(i) It has a 4K word addressable memory.
(ii) A word of HYPCOM is 16 bits long.
(iii) A word of HYPCOM stores either an instruction or data to be processed.
(iv) It has 15 operation codes.
(v) The instructions are single-address instructions. Four bits are needed to represent 15 operation codes. Twelve bits are needed to address a 4K memory. An instruction is thus 16 bits long.
(vi) It has an input unit which is used to feed both instructions and data. A 16-bit word is read via the input unit and stored in the memory when a READ operation code is executed by the processor.
(vii) It has a printer as its output unit which is used to print a 16-bit word from the memory when a PRINT operation code is executed by the processor.

The operation codes of HYPCOM and what each operation does are given in Table 5.5. The logical structure of HYPCOM is shown in Figure 5.3.

Table 5.5 Operation codes of HYPCOM and their meanings

Operation code (Hexadecimal)	*Mnemonic used*	*Instruction format*	*Meaning*	*Status of registers*
1	CLA	124A	Clear the accumulator and place the contents of the specified memory address in it	OP = 1 ADDR = 24A ACC ← MEM (24A
2	ADD	24BF	Add to the accumulator the contents of the specified address	OP = 2 ADDR = 4BF ACC ← ACC + MEM (4BF)
3	SUB	3AFD	Subtract from the accumulator the contents of the specified address	OP = 3 ADDR = AFD ACC ← ACC – MEM (AFD)
4	MUL	4BAF	Multiply the contents of the accumulator by the contents of the specified address	OP = 4 ADDR = BAF ACC ← ACC × MEM (BAF)
5	DIV	545D	Divide the contents of the accumulator by the contents of the specified address and leave the integer quotient in the accumulator	OP = 5 ADDR = 45D ACC ← ACC/MEM (45D)
6	STO	6AFE	Store the contents of the accumulator in the specified address in the memory	OP = 6 ADDR = AFE MEM (AFE) ← ACC
7	JMP	7653	Take the next instruction from address 653 of the memory	OP = 7 ADDR = 653 PC ← ADDR = 653
8	JNE	8446	Take the next instruction from address 446 if ACC < 0 else take the next instruction from the address given in the PC	OP = 8 ADDR = 446 *if* ACC < 0 *then* PC ← ADDR = 446
9	JZE	9648	Take the next instruction from address 648 if ACC = 0 (ignore the sign of ACC) else the next instruction from the address given in the PC	OP = 9 ADDR = 648 *if* ACC = 0 *then* PC ← ADDR = 648
A	READ	A798	Store in the specified memory address the data read from the input unit	OP = A ADDR = 798 MEM (ADDR) ← Input
B	PRINT	B547	Print the data retrieved from the specified memory address	OP = B ADDR = 547 Print MEM (ADDR)
C	SHR	C008	Shift the contents of ACC (excluding sign) right by 8 bits	OP = C ADDR = 008. Shift ACC right by 8 bits
D	COM	D000	Complement the contents of ACC. Each bit of ACC is replaced by its complement. If a bit is 1, it is made 0 and if it is 0, it is made into 1	OP = D ADDR (None) ACC ← $\overline{\text{ACC}}$ (overscore is complement operator)

(Contd.)

Table 5.5 Operation codes of HYPCOM and their meanings (*Contd.*)

Operation code (Hexadecimal)	*Mnemonic used*	*Instruction format*	*Meaning*	*Status of registers*
E	XOR	EABF	Match each bit of ACC with each bit of the contents of the specified address. If the bits are equal, make the bit of ACC = 0 else make that bit in ACC = 1	OP = E ADDR = ABF ACC ← ACC *XOR* MEM (ABF)
F	HLT	F000	Halt computation	OP = F ADDR (None)

Remarks:
1. MEM (address) is interpreted as contents of the memory in the specified address.
2. ACC ← MEM (address) is interpreted as 'Move into ACC the contents of the specified memory address'.
3. In SHR, the number in the ADDR part is an operand and not interpreted as the address of the operand.

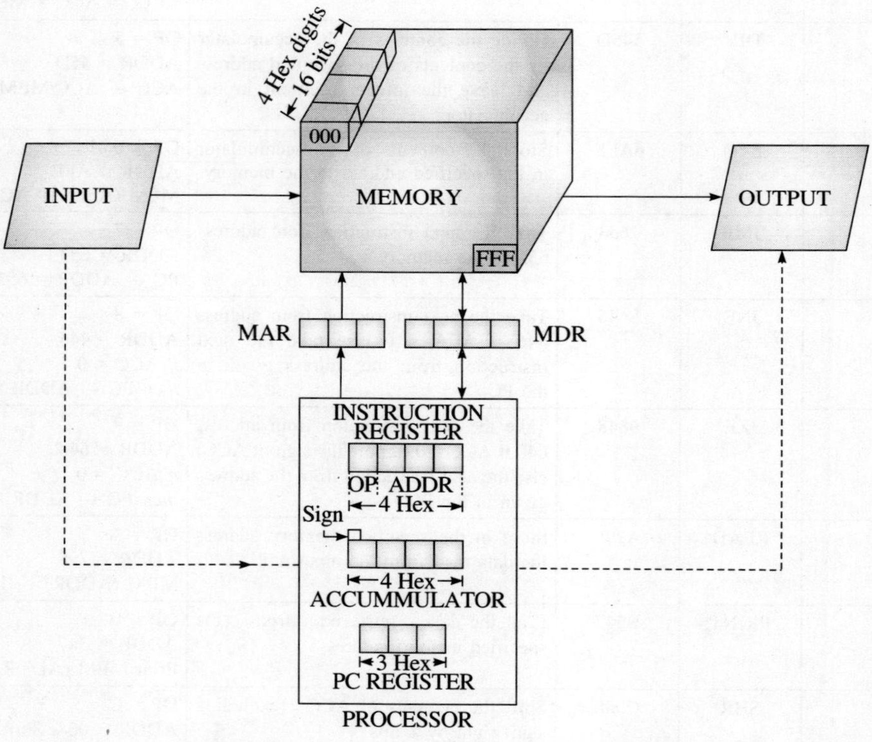

Figure 5.3 Logical structure of HYPCOM.

The operation codes may be grouped as follows:

1. *Data movement operation codes*
   CLA, STO
2. *Arithmetic operation codes*
   ADD, SUB, MUL, DIV

3. Control operation codes
   JMP, JNE, JZE, HLT
4. Input/output operation codes
   READ, PRINT
5. Logical operation codes
   SHR, COM, XOR

The data movement group moves data from the memory to the accumulator and from the accumulator to the memory. The arithmetic group does addition, subtraction, multiplication, and division.

The result of an arithmetic operation is left in the accumulator and must not exceed the capacity of the accumulator. The control group is intended to implement decision boxes in flowcharts. Normal sequential execution of instructions is altered when jump instructions are executed. The input/output group's function is self-evident. The logical group is useful for the operation involving characters. The exclusive-or (XOR) operation is specifically useful to examine whether the contents of two words in memory are identical. Table 5.6 defines the exclusive-or operation between bits. It is seen that if the exclusive-or of corresponding bits of two words give all zeros, then the two words are identical.

Table 5.6 Exclusive-or operator

A	B	A *XOR* B
0	0	0
0	1	1
1	0	1
1	1	0

Word 1	0 1 0 1 1 1 0 0 1 0 1 0 1 1 1 0
Word 2	0 1 0 1 1 1 0 0 1 0 1 0 1 1 1 0
Word 1 *XOR* Word 2	0 0 0 0 0 0 0 0 0 0 0 0 0 0 0 0

5.3 MACHINE LANGUAGE PROGRAM

We will now write a small machine language program for HYPCOM. The program is to compare two numbers *X* and *Y* and output the larger one. The program is given in Table 5.7. In this table, columns 2 and 3 contain the machine instructions. Column 1 gives the address where the instruction is stored. This information is necessary to write the program. For example, in the program shown in Table 5.7, the instruction 8007 stored in address 004 commands that the next instruction to be executed should be taken from the memory address 007 if the content of the accumulator is less than zero. A programmer must know what instruction is stored in address 007.

The last column of Table 5.7 explains what each instruction in the machine language does. This explanation is essential to understand the program.

Table 5.7 A machine language program to find the larger of two numbers

Address where the instruction is stored	*Machine instruction*		*Explanation of instruction*
	Operation code	*Operand address*	
000	A	625	Read from the input unit a number and store it in address 625 MEM (625) ← *X*
001	A	626	Read from the input unit a number and store it in address 626 MEM (626) ← *Y*
002	1	625	ACC ← MEM (625) = *X*
003	3	626	ACC ← *X*-MEM (626) ∴ ACC ← *X* –*Y*
004	8	007	If (*X* – *Y*) < 0 then take the next instruction from address 007; else continue
005	B	625	If (*X* – *Y*) ≥ 0 control comes to this instruction. In this case Print *X*
006	F	000	Halt
007	B	626	If (*X* –*Y*) < 0 control comes here. In this case Print *Y*
008	F	000	Halt

We will now examine step by step how this program is interpreted and executed by HYPCOM's processor.

Step 1: The program is read via the input unit and stored in successive addresses in memory. The first instruction is stored in address 000 of the memory, the second in address 001, etc. The last instruction is stored in address 008. This step is known as *the program loading* phase.

The status of the memory of HYPCOM at the end of loading the program in Table 5.7 is shown in Table 5.8.

Table 5.8 Status of memory after the program is loaded

Memory address	*Contents of address*
000	A625
001	A626
002	1625
003	3626
004	8007
005	B625
006	F000
007	B626
008	F000

Step 2: The address of the first instruction to be executed is entered in the PC register in the processor. As the program is stored starting at address 000, the initial number stored in the PC register is 000.

PC ← 000

Step 3: The instruction from the memory, stored in the address as given by the PC register, is fetched and placed in the instruction register. This is done by the control circuits of the processor by copying the contents of the PC register into the memory address register MAR. The memory circuits then place the contents of the specified address in the memory data register MDR. The contents of MDR are then moved to the instruction register IR. This is summarized below:

MAR ← PC = 000;

MDR ← MEM (PC) = MEM (000) = A625;

IR ← MDR = A625

Step 4: The content of the PC register is incremented by 1 so that the PC register contains the address of the next instruction to be executed.

PC ← PC + 1 = 001

Step 5: The OP code part of the instruction register IR is decoded. Appropriate circuitry in the processor carries out the decoding operation. In the example, the operation code of the instruction in the IR register is A, which is interpreted as 'Read from the input unit a number and store it in the memory at the address specified in the instruction'. Suppose the number 285 is fed to the input unit. This number will be stored at address 625 specified in the instruction. The sequences of events which occur when this instruction is executed are:

MDR ← Input data

MAR ← 625

MEM (MAR) = MEM (625) = MDR = Input data = 285

Step 6: The processor will fetch from the memory the next instruction to be executed. The address in the memory to be accessed is found in the PC register. Thus,

MAR ← PC = 001

MDR ← MEM (PC) = MEM (001) = A626

IR ← MDR = A626

Step 7: The PC register is incremented by 1. Thus, PC ← PC + 1 = 002.

Step 8: The OP code of the instruction is again A. Thus, as in Step 5, a number from the input unit is read and stored in the specified memory address. If the number fed to the input unit is 899, then MEM (626) = 899.

Step 9: The next instruction is fetched from the memory address given in the PC register, namely, 002. Thus,

MAR ← PC = 002

MDR ← MEM (MAR) = MEM (002) = 1625

IR ← MDR = 1625

Step 10: The PC register is incremented by 1. Thus, PC ← PC + 1 = 003.

Step 11: The OP code is 1. When it is decoded, the processor clears the Accumulator and moves into it the contents of the memory address 625. Thus, ACC ← MEM (625) = 285.

Step 12: The next instruction is fetched from Memory (PC), namely, MEM (003). Thus, IR ← MEM (003) = 3626

Step 13: The PC register is incremented by 1. Thus, PC ← PC + 1 = 004.

Step 14: The OP code is 3. When decoded the processor subtracts from the Accumulator the contents of MEM (626). Thus,

ACC ← ACC – MEM (626) = 285 – 899 = – 614

Step 15: The next instruction is fetched from the memory address given by the PC register, namely, 004. Thus,

IR ← MEM (004) = 8007

Step 16: The PC register is incremented by 1. Thus, PC ← PC + 1 = 005.

Step 17: The OP code is 8. When decoded the processor checks the contents of ACC. It finds that the number stored in ACC is less than 0. It thus replaces the contents of the PC register by the address part of the instruction in IR. Thus,

PC ← 007

Step 18: The next instruction is fetched from the memory address given by the PC register, namely, 007. Thus,

IR ← MEM (007) = B626

Step 19: The PC register is incremented by 1. Thus, PC ← PC + 1 = 008.

Step 20: The OP code in the IR register is B. The processor decodes this code. This code is to print the contents of the specified address. Thus, the content of the memory address 626 is sent to the printer. As MEM (626) = 899, this number is printed.

Step 21: The next instruction is fetched from the memory address given by the PC register, namely, 008. Thus,

IR ← MEM (008) = F000

Step 22: The PC register is incremented by 1. Thus, PC ← PC + 1 = 009.

Step 23: The OP code in the IR register is F. The processor decodes this code. This code is to halt the execution of the program.

We see from the above example that a computer (HYPCOM) does the following to execute a program:

1. The program is stored in the computer's memory from a specified address. Instructions are stored in successive addresses.
2. The starting address of the program is placed in the PC register.
3. The instruction from the memory address as specified in the PC register is fetched and placed in the instruction register IR.
4. The PC register is incremented by 1.
5. The operation code in the IR register is decoded by the control circuits of the processor.
6. If the specified operation requires an operand to be fetched from the memory, it is done.

7. The operation is carried out.
8. Steps 3 to 7 are repeated until a halt instruction is executed.

5.4 ALGORITHM TO SIMULATE THE HYPOTHETICAL COMPUTER

In the last section, we have shown step by step how a machine language program for HYPCOM is executed. We give as Algorithm 5.1 the entire operation of loading a program in memory and its execution. In this algorithm, we have used MAR to represent the memory address register and MDR to represent the memory data register.

Algorithm 5.1

Phase 1: *Loading the program into the memory.*
{Initialize the PC register to the starting address of the program to be stored in the memory}
PC ← 0; {The starting address is assumed to be 0.}
{The statements between *repeat* and *until* are repeated until all the instructions are stored in the memory}
repeat
Read an instruction from the input unit and place it in MDR;
Store the contents of MDR in the memory at the address specified in the PC register.
MAR ← PC; MEM (PC) ← MDR;
PC ← PC + 1
until the end of the program;
Phase 2: *In this phase, the program stored in the memory is executed.*
{Initialize the PC register to the address of the first instruction in the program} PC ← 0;
{The statements between *repeat* and *until* are repeatedly performed until a HALT instruction (OP code = F) is encountered}
repeat
IR ← MEM (PC)
{The most significant 4 bits of the IR register is the OP code. The next 12 bits specify the operand address in the memory}
OP = IR [16..13]; ADDR = IR [12..1];
PC ← PC + 1; {PC is incremented to specify the address from where the next instruction is to be retrieved}
Decode the OP code and perform the actions specified.
OP = 1: ACC ← MEM (ADDR);
OP = 2: ACC ← ACC + MEM (ADDR);
OP = 3: ACC ← ACC – MEM (ADDR);
OP = 4: ACC ← ACC × MEM (ADDR);
OP = 5: ACC ← ACC/MEM (ADDR); {Division stores the quotient in ACC}
OP = 6: MEM (ADDR) ← ACC;
OP = 7: PC ← ADDR;
OP = 8: *if* ACC < 0 *then* PC ← ADDR;
OP = 9: *if* ACC = 0 *then* PC ← ADDR;

OP = A: MEM (ADDR) ← Input;
OP = B: Output ← MEM (ADDR);
OP = C: Shift ACC *right* by ADDR bits;
OP = D: ACC ← $\overline{\text{ACC}}$ {Bitwise complement ACC}
OP = E: ACC ← ACC *XOR* MEM (ADDR);
OP = F: {HALT};
until (OP = F);
End of Algorithm 5.1.

We will now write another machine language program for HYPCOM. This program will illustrate the formation of a loop.

Example 5.1

Problem: A program is to be written to find the heaviest student in a class of students.
A procedure for solution:

Step 1: Note the weight of each student in the class on a slip.
Step 2: When all the weights are noted down, put a slip at the end with an entry of 0. This slip will indicate the end of data on the weights of students. As 0 cannot be a weight, it is a logical number to choose as the end of data.
Step 3: Read the weight in the first slip and call it the Heaviest. This is logical because if there is only one student in the class, that student is the heaviest.
Step 4: Read the next slip.
Step 5: If the number in this slip = 0, it indicates that there are no more slips. Thus, go to Step 8. Otherwise continue.
Step 6: If weight read > Heaviest, then Heaviest ← weight read; otherwise retain Heaviest as it is.
Step 7: Go back to Step 4.
Step 8: Output weight stored in Heaviest.

The above procedure is formulated as the machine language program of Table 5.9.

In this machine language program, we allocate address 500 to store the weight read and address 501 to store the heaviest weight. The comments in the remarks column of Table 5.9 explain the machine language program.

The reader is urged to go through this program using the HYPCOM simulation algorithm and understand in detail how HYPCOM would load and execute the instructions of the machine language program.

In this section, we examined the logical structure of a simple hypothetical computer. Processors of real computers are more powerful. There is usually a large variety of operation codes. Operation codes are implemented to reduce programming effort and enable computers to perform a variety of jobs. For example, operation codes to facilitate carrying out program loops and to perform operations on arrays of numbers and strings of characters are usually implemented. Besides more operation codes, the processor is designed with more registers and several methods of addressing the memory. We will enhance HYPCOM and introduce some added features in the next section.

Table 5.9 A HYPCOM machine language program to find the heaviest student in a class

Memory address where the instruction is stored	*Instruction*		*Remarks*
	Operation code	*Operand address*	
000	A	501	Read the first weight and store it in address 501 as the heaviest
001	A	500	Read the next weight and store it in address 500
002	1	500	ACC ← MEM (500) Move the weight read to the accumulator
003	9	009	ACC = 0 indicates the end of weights. If ACC = 0, take the next instruction from 009 which outputs the heaviest stored in MEM (501) else continue
004	3	501	ACC ← ACC – MEM (501)
005	8	001	IF ACC < 0, then it means MEM (501) is larger than MEM(500).Thus, MEM(501) is not changed. The program loops back to read the next weight. Else the next instruction is executed
006	1	500	If MEM(500) is larger, move it to MEM(501).
007	6	501	This is done in two instructions at 006 and 007
008	7	001	The program loops back to read the next weight
009	B	501	Output MEM (501) which has the heaviest weight is stored in it
00A	F	000	Halt

5.5 ENHANCING HYPCOM

HYPCOM has only 15 instructions. It also has only five registers, namely, an instruction register, a program counter register (PC), an accumulator, a memory address register (MAR), and a memory data register (MDR). The main objective of introducing a basic processor was to explain in simple terms how a processor works. Real processors have many more instructions. They also have more registers in the processing unit and other useful features, such as modifying addresses referred to by instructions. These features are introduced in processors with two basic objectives. The first is to simplify programming by introducing several well-chosen machine instructions. The second objective is to reduce the delay in fetching data/instructions from the memory to the processor and data from the I/O units to the memory and vice versa. In real computers, the main memory is 100 times slower than the processor, and I/O units are 1000 times slower than the main memory.

We will illustrate with an example how programs may be simplified by enhancing the features available in HYPCOM. Suppose it is required to add nine components of a vector AI and print the sum. A simple algorithm to do this is given below:

```
S ← 0
for i = 1 to 9 do
   begin Read ai; S ← S + ai end; Write S;
Stop.
```

Using the instructions currently available in HYPCOM, a program to implement this algorithm is given in Table 5.10. Observe that the first three instructions in this program read the constants 0, 9, and 1 using the input unit. As the input unit is slow, it would be desirable to have an instruction to store these constants in registers in the processor. Later in this section, we will introduce this feature in HYPCOM. In the program of Table 5.10, the instructions in the memory addresses from 003 to 011 implement the *for* loop. Observe the instructions in the memory addresses 007, 008, and 009. The instruction in 007 stores in the accumulator the content of 003, which is an *instruction*. Instruction 008 subtracts 1 from it, and the new value is stored back in 003 by instruction 009. Thus, the next time the instruction in 003 is retrieved, it will be A108, and will be interpreted as 'read a number from the input unit and store it in the memory address 108'. Thus, a_2, the next component of the vector, will be stored in 108. Observe that the *address* part of the instructions stored in locations 003 and 005 of the memory is *modified.* Such *address modification* is essential in operations with vectors. The *for* loop index is used to modify the address. Exit from the *for* loop is implemented by the instructions stored in 00D, 00E, 00F, and 010. This is done explicitly by taking the final value of the index, namely, 9 into the accumulator, subtracting 1 from it, storing it back in the accumulator (instruction stored in 00F), and checking if it has become 0. Two data transfers from the memory to the processor have taken place, which it would be desirable to avoid, knowing the speed mismatch between the processor and the memory. Besides this, the method used in the program of Table 5.10 to modify an address by using an instruction as an operand, subtracting 1 from it, and storing it back is tricky and prone to error.

Table 5.10 A machine language program for HYPCOM to add the components of a vector

Address where the instruction is stored	*Machine instruction*		*Explanation of instruction*
	Operation code	*Operand address*	
000	A	090	Mem(90) ← 0. S initialized to 0 and stored in 90
001	A	091	Mem(91) ← 9. Final index in 91
002	A	092	Mem(92) ← 1. Decrement in 92
003	A	109	Read into Mem(109) a_1
004	1	090	ACC ← Mem(90) = S
005	2	109	ACC ← S + Mem(109) = S + a_1
006	6	090	Mem(090) = S ← S + a_1
007	1	003	ACC ← A109
008	3	092	ACC ← ACC – 1 = A108 (Address modified)
009	6	003	Mem(003) ← A108 (Instruction in 003 changed)
00A	1	005	ACC ← 2109
00B	3	092	ACC ← ACC – 1 = 2108
00C	6	005	Mem(005) ← 2108 (Instruction in 005 changed)
00D	1	091	ACC ← Mem(91)

(Contd.)

Table 5.10 A machine language program for HYPCOM to add the components of a vector (*Contd.*)

Address where the instruction is stored	*Machine instruction*		*Explanation of instruction*
	Operation code	*Operand address*	
00E	3	092	ACC ← ACC − 1 = 9 − 1 = 8
00F	6	091	Mem(091) ← ACC = 8 (Index decremented)
010	9	012	If ACC = 0 go to 012
011	7	003	go to 003 (003 now has A108)
012	B	090	Print Mem(90) = S
013	F	000	Stop

We will now modify HYPCOM, which meets the twin objectives of easing programming and reducing unnecessary data transfer between the I/O devices and the memory, as well as between the processor and the memory. First, we introduce registers in the processor which are useful in storing intermediate results during processing without having to store them in the memory. In HYPCOM only a single accumulator was available to store results of arithmetic operations and this forced the result to be stored in the memory after each arithmetic operation. The registers can also be used to store indices and modify them. Modification of indices in the registers is required in setting up *for* loops and for use as subscripts of vectors. The instruction structure is changed to include, besides the memory address, addresses of two registers—one used as an operand register and the other as an *index register.* Besides this, some additional instructions are needed to use these registers.

The new instruction structure is:

OP	*R*	*X*	*A*
HH	H	H	HHH
(H is a hexadecimal digit)			

The operation code has been expanded to two hexadecimal digits. We can now code up to 256 instructions. The *R* field is the address of a register where operands may be stored and manipulated. The *X* field is the address of a register which would be used as an index register. *A* is normally the address of a location in the memory. It may be interpreted differently based on the OP code. This will be explained in what follows.

The new instructions we introduce are:

1. Store a number given in the *A* field in the specified register.
   For example,

OP	*R*	*X*	*A*
21	2	0	009

   The new OP code 21 means: store the *number* in the address field in the specified register, namely, Reg. 2. This instruction thus stores 9 in Reg. 2. Observe that the address field of the instruction is used as an *operand.* Such an instruction is known as an *immediate* instruction. Instead of reading a number via the input unit, storing it in the memory, and then bringing it into a register in the processor, this instruction stores a number in the address field directly in a register and thus saves time.

2. The immediate instruction is extended to all arithmetic operations. For example, the instruction

OP	*R*	*X*	*A*
22	2	0	004

adds the operand 4 to the content of register 2. The instruction 2330005 subtracts 005 from the content of register 3. Similar instructions are introduced for multiplication and division.

3. It is useful to move the content of a register to the memory and vice versa. For example, the instruction

OP	*R*	*X*	*A*
06	2	0	345

is interpreted as: 'store the content of register 2 in address 345 of the memory'. Observe that we are using a register instead of the accumulator in this modified new instruction. The instruction

OP	*R*	*X*	*A*
01	2	0	468

is interpreted as: 'clear register 2 and load the content of address 468 of the memory in it'. Moving data between registers is also useful. Thus, the instruction

OP	*R*	*X*	*A*
26	2	4	000

is interpreted as: 'move the content of register 4 to register 2'.

4. An instruction using an index register is primarily used to modify the address given in the address field of an instruction and obtain an *effective address* to address a location in the memory. For example, the instruction

OP	*R*	*X*	*A*
01	2	3	468

is interpreted as follows:

Add the content of register 3 specified in the *X* field (index register field) in the instruction to the address 468. The sum is the effective address. Move the content of this effective address in the memory to register 2. Thus, if the content of register 3 is 11, then the effective address would be 468 + 11 = 479. Thus, the content of the address 479 of the memory will be moved to register 2 by this instruction.

Indexing may be used with the instructions add, subtract, multiply and divide. Thus, the instruction

OP	*R*	*X*	*A*
02	3	4	643

means 'Add to the content of register 3 the content of the memory address (643 + the content of register 4). If register 4 has 5 in it, then the content of the memory address 648 will be added to the content of register 3'.

5. One of the main uses of an index register is to facilitate setting up *for*-loops and subscript manipulation of vectors and matrices. Thus, decrementing (subtracting 1) and incrementing (adding 1) to an index register coupled with a test to see if the index has become zero is very useful. For example, the instruction

OP	*R*	*X*	*A*
19	0	2	008

is interpreted as: 'decrement the content of index register 2 by 1 and jump to 008 if the number in the index register is zero, else go to the next instruction in sequence'. The instruction

OP	*R*	*X*	*A*
20	3	2	120

is interpreted as: 'increment the content of index register 2 by 1 and jump to 120 if the number stored in the index register equals the content of register 3'.

Using some of these new instructions, we have rewritten the program of Table 5.10 and given it in Table 5.11. Observe that the program has become shorter and easier to understand. The program will also be executed faster.

Table 5.11 A machine language program using modified HYPCOM with the additional instructions to add the components of a vector

Address of instruction	*Machine instruction*				*Explanation of instruction*
	OP	*R*	*X*	*Address*	
000	21	2	0	009	C(Reg 2) ← 009. Index i in Reg 2
001	21	3	0	000	C(Reg 3) ← 0. Reg 3 used for S
002	A	0	2	100	Mem(100 + Reg (2)) ← input = a_1
003	2	3	2	100	C(Reg 3) ← Mem(100 + Reg (2)) + C(Reg 3) = a_1 + S
004	19	0	2	006	C(Reg 2) ← C(Reg 2) – 1. If C(Reg (2)) = 0 go to 006
005	7	0	0	002	go to 2. (Repeat loop)
006	6	3	0	099	Mem(99) ← C(Reg 3) = S
007	B	0	0	099	Print S
008	F	0	0	000	Stop

Some more important features that we will add to HYPCOM are a *base register* in instruction and a feature known as *indirect addressing*. These are explained in what follows.

Base register

The three hexadecimal digits in the address field of HYPCOM may be used to address 4096 locations. A larger memory may be addressed by increasing the length of the *A* field. However, it is not an acceptable solution as each instruction will become longer. In an instruction using an index register, the contents of the index register are added to the address field of the instruction to create an *effective address*. If the index register stores 8 hexadecimal digits (32 bits), the effective address can be as large as 32 bits, giving an addressable space (number of addressable locations) of 2^{32} = 4 Giga words (1 Giga = 10^9)! This is an enormous address space. Index registers are introduced mainly for subscript manipulation. For address space expansion, another register called a *base register* may be introduced. For example, the HYPCOM instruction structure may be modified as:

OP	*R*	*X*	*B*	*A*
HH	H	H	H	HHH
(H is a hexadecimal digit)				

where the *B* field refers to a register address to be taken as a base register. The effective address is *A* + *C* (Reg *X*) + *C* (Reg *B*).

Besides its use in expanding the addressable memory space, a base register is also useful in *program relocation*. Suppose a program occupies addresses from 008 to 103 in memory, and later it is to be located from 408 to 503. Such relocation is required when more than one program is stored in memory in multiprogramming (we will introduce multiprogramming in Chapter 8). Assume a program is written using Register 8 as the base register with its content 0. If a program changes the content of Register 8 to 400, the program will have all its memory references relocated between 408 and 503.

Indirect addressing

In direct addressing, the address of an operand is given in the *A* field. In indirect addressing, the *A* field specifies the address where one should look to get the address of an operand. It is somewhat like searching for a 'treasure' in an address but not getting the treasure there but another address where you would find the treasure. Thus, if we introduce an instruction in HYPCOM with OP code 31: 'move indirect the content of the memory to the specified register' its effect will be as given below:

	OP	*R*	*X*	*A*
Instruction:	31	2	0	468

Reg 2 ← MEM (MEM(468))
If MEM(468) = 862 then Reg 2 ← MEM(862).

Indirect addressing is very useful in programming access to a table which may be relocated in memory. It is also useful in passing the parameters to a subroutine when it (a subroutine) is called.

In this chapter, we began by describing a small hypothetical computer called HYPCOM with only 15 instructions and a simple instruction structure with only direct memory addressing. We saw that programming such a computer is very tedious. Besides, the computer will be very slow as it has no features to alleviate the speed mismatch between the processor and the main memory. We then introduced features in HYPCOM to ease programming and increase its speed. The new features are:

1. Increase in the number of operation codes
2. Change in the structure of the instruction by introducing addressable registers
3. Index register and base register and their use in address modification
4. Immediate addressing and indirect addressing
5. Performing arithmetic operations using the contents of registers

We will describe the use of some of these features again when we discuss microcomputers.

SUMMARY

1. A processing unit in a computer interprets instructions in a program and carries them out.

2. An instruction in general consists of a part that specifies the operation to be performed and other parts which specify the addresses of operands.

3. A single-address instruction specifies the address of only one operand.

4. In a processor, a string of bits is used to code operations, and another string of bits is used to specify the address.

5. To code *n* operations in binary, we need *x* bits such that $2^x = n$. Similarly, to specify *W* addresses in memory, we need *y* bits such that $2^y = W$. For example, to code 16 operations, we need 4 bits such that $2^4 = 16$. Similarly, to select one address out of 4K addresses in memory, we need 12 bits such that $2^{12} = 4 \times 1024$.

6. An instruction consisting of an operation code and operand address or addresses designed for a specific computer is known as a machine language instruction of that computer.

7. A sequence of machine language instructions to solve a problem is known as a machine language program.

8. Machine language instructions for input/output, data movement, arithmetic, logic and controlling sequencing of operations are available in all computers.

9. A computer's processor has storage registers to store operands and results. It also has a register to store the instruction being executed and a register that stores the address of the next instruction to be executed.

10. Given a problem, it is possible to write a machine language program to solve it. In writing machine language programs, however, one has to pay attention to all details, including the status of all the processor registers, addresses of instructions, and data in memory.

11. A machine language program is executed by a computer in two phases. In the first phase, it reads and stores the program in its memory. After storing the program, it initiates program execution. In the program execution phase, instructions are retrieved from the memory one after another, decoded, and executed.
12. The instruction set of a processor, namely, the group of instructions that it can interpret and execute, is determined by the different application programs to be executed by it. The number and function of registers in the processor are also determined by the nature and size of application programs.
13. Processors are designed with the twin objectives of easing programming and preventing processor-to-memory communication delays.
14. Specific features introduced in a processor to reduce communication with the memory include several general-purpose registers and immediate addressing. In immediate addressing, data is used in the address field of an instruction.
15. Index registers coupled with special instructions facilitate setting up program loops and operations on vectors.
16. Base registers are used to enhance addressable memory space and to facilitate program relocation (required in multiprogramming).
17. Indirect addressing is useful to look up tables and to link subprograms to a main program.

REVIEW QUESTIONS

5.1 What details are to be specified by an instruction to a computer?

5.2 Explain the terms single-address instruction, two-address instruction, three-address instruction and four-address instruction.

5.3 Supposing that a computer has a two-address instruction, what is the most appropriate use of the two addresses?

5.4 Write a small machine language program for a two-address computer to add two numbers and output the sum.

5.5 If a computer has 128 operation codes and a memory capacity of 512 K addresses, how many bits would be required for a two-address instruction?

5.6 Repeat 5.5 for a computer with a single-address instruction.

5.7 Write a machine language program to add six numbers and output the answer. Assume single-address instructions. Use the instruction codes given in Table 5.3.

5.8 Write a machine language program for HYPCOM to find the smallest of three numbers.

5.9 Explain how the operation code for jump (code 7) in HYPCOM is executed.

5.10 What is the purpose of the PC register in HYPCOM?

5.11 If a computer is a single-address computer, word addressed, and has 64 operation codes and 16 K addresses, answer the following questions:

(i) What is the length of the instruction register?
(ii) How many bits are there in the PC register?
(iii) What is the length of the ACC register?

5.12 If the hexadecimal number AF64 is stored in address 456 of HYPCOM and the content of ACC is FA64, what will be the contents of ACC after HYPCOM instruction E456 is executed?

5.13 Repeat 5.12 assuming that the content of address 456 in the memory of HYPCOM is FA64.

5.14 If the content of address 847 of HYPCOM is AB76, what will be stored in 847 after the following HYPCOM instructions are executed?

1847
C008
6847

5.15 If the content of address FA3 of HYPCOM is A457, what will be stored in FA3 after the following instructions are executed?

1FA3
D000
6FA3

5.16 Explain step by step how the program written in Table 5.9 will be loaded in its memory and executed by HYPCOM.

5.17 Given a set of weights of students in a class (in hexadecimal), write a machine language program for HYPCOM to output the average weight of students in the class and the number of students in the class.

5.18 What is the largest positive decimal number that can be stored in the accumulator of HYPCOM?

5.19 Develop the logical structure of a computer, which we will call XYZ-COMP. This computer has the following specifications:

(i) Eight operation codes: load accumulator, store accumulator, add, subtract, halt, jump on negative, read, and output.
(ii) 32 K word memory.
(iii) Instruction and data length equal a word.
(iv) Single-address instruction format.

5.20 Write a simulation algorithm to simulate XYZ-COMP. Use octal numbers (numbers using base 8) in your simulation algorithm.

5.21 Write a machine language program for HYPCOM to add two vectors, each having 8 components.

5.22 Explain the necessity of address modification in the machine language program of review question 5.21.

5.23 Rewrite the program of Exercise 5.21 using the modified HYPCOM presented in Section 5.5.

5.24 Write a machine language program for modified HYPCOM to find the scalar product of two 8-component vectors.

5.25 What is the purpose of immediate addressing?

5.26 What is the purpose of index registers in a processor?

5.27 What is the objective of introducing several general-purpose registers in a processor?

5.28 What instructions are useful in implementing loops?

5.29 What is a base register?

5.30 What is the difference between an index register and a base register?

5.31 What is the primary use of a base register?

5.32 What is 'program relocation'? How is a base register used to relocate programs?

5.33 What is 'indirect addressing'? What is the use of such addressing?

6 Binary Arithmetic

LEARNING GOALS

After reading this chapter, you should be able to:

- Add, subtract, multiply, and divide binary integers.
- Represent negative binary numbers in two's complement form and simplify subtraction.
- Represent real numbers (numbers with fractional parts) using a normalized floating point representation using mantissa and exponent.
- Perform floating point addition, subtraction, multiplication, and division.

In Chapter 2, we learnt that decimal numbers are converted to binary because processors of computers perform arithmetic operations only on binary numbers. We should know how to do binary arithmetic to understand the working of processors. This is the main objective of this chapter.

6.1 BINARY ADDITION

In this section, we will discuss how to add binary numbers. Counting is a form of addition since successive numbers, while counting, are obtained by adding 1. In the decimal system, we start with 0 and by successively adding 1, we reach 9. As the base of the decimal system is 10, there are no further symbols. Thus, after 9 we count 10. The 1 becomes a carry to the tens position in the positional system. In the binary system, the count progresses as follows:

$$0, 1, 10, 11, 100, 101, \ldots$$

To add two binary numbers, we write one below the other with their least significant bits (LSBs) aligned. If the numbers have fractional parts, then the binary points must be aligned.

We start addition from the least significant bit. Assume that *a* and *b* are the two bits to be added. An addition table to add *a* to *b* is given in Table 6.1. The table shows the sum and the carry bits when two bits are added. This table is called a *half-adder* table.

Table 6.1 A half adder table

a	*b*	*Sum*	*Carry*
0	0	0	0
0	1	1	0
1	0	1	0
1	1	0	1

Example 6.1

We give three examples of binary addition which use the half adder table.

Carry	11	01	111.0
Augend	11	101	11.10
Addend	01	001	01.11
	100	110	101.01

We see from these examples that while adding two binary numbers, we may have to add a maximum of three bits. These are the bits of the augend and the addend and the carry bit, if any, from the previous stage of addition. An addition table for these three bits as inputs is given in Table 6.2, which is known as the *full adder table.*

Table 6.2 A binary addition table including carry

Augend bit *a*	*Addend bit* *b*	*Carry from the previous stage*	*Sum* *a* + *b*	*Carry to next stage*
0	0	0	0	0
0	0	1	1	0
0	1	0	1	0
0	1	1	0	1
1	0	0	1	0
1	0	1	0	1
1	1	0	0	1
1	1	1	1	1

6.2 BINARY SUBTRACTION

To subtract, we use a subtraction table (Table 6.3) similar to the one used for addition. In the second row of Table 6.3, note that when we subtract 1 from 0, we have to borrow 1 from the adjacent higher bit position. The process of 'borrowing' and 'borrow propagation' is shown in Example 6.2.

Table 6.3 Half-subtractor table

a	*b*	*Difference*	*Borrow*
0	0	0	0
0	1	1	1
1	0	1	0
1	1	0	0

Example 6.2

We give four examples of binary subtraction.

Borrow	1	11.1	11	11
Minuend	101	10.00	100	110
Subtrahend	011	01.11	001	011
Difference	010	00.01	011	011

Thus, when subtracting bits of the *n*th stage, we should know whether a 1 has been borrowed from that stage by the (n – 1)th stage. Further, apart from finding the difference, we must also determine whether a 1 has to be borrowed from the (n + 1)th stage. A full-subtractor table having the minuend, subtrahend, and the bit borrowed from the *n*th stage as inputs, which gives the difference as well as the borrow to be taken from the (n + 1)th stage, is shown in Table 6.4.

Table 6.4 Full-subtractor table

Inputs			*Outputs*	
a_n Minuend	b_n Subtrahend	*Bit borrowed from the nth stage*	*Difference*	*Borrow to be taken to the* (n + 1)*th stage*
0	0	0	0	0
0	0	1	1	1
0	1	0	1	1
0	1	1	0	1
1	0	0	1	0
1	0	1	0	0
1	1	0	0	0
1	1	1	1	1

6.3 SIGNED NUMBERS

So far, we have used only positive numbers. In practice, we use both positive and negative numbers as operands. In the binary system, we represent the sign of a number using an extra bit at the extreme left of the number. By convention, the symbol 0 is used to represent the + sign and 1 to represent the – sign. For instance, +5 is represented by 0,101 and –7 is represented by 1,111. We have used a comma to separate the sign bit from the number for clarity. When a number is stored in a computer's register, the comma is implied. This method of representation of binary integers is known as sign-magnitude representation.

When we want to subtract *b* from *a*, we look at the magnitudes and the signs of both these numbers. When *a* and *b* have opposite signs, we add their magnitudes and know how to determine the sign of the result. On the other hand, if *a* and *b* have the same sign, we always subtract the smaller magnitude from the larger and once again decide the sign independently. Similarly, when we have to add, depending upon the signs of the numbers, we may end up subtracting or adding their magnitudes, the procedures for which are different.

It would, of course, be more convenient if we could evolve another convention for representing positive and negative numbers which would allow us to use one basic procedure for both addition and subtraction. If the procedure was the same, we could use a single electronic circuit to implement both addition and subtraction. A convention for representing negative numbers that allow this is the *complement representation* of numbers.

We will explain complement representation by first considering the subtraction of decimal numbers. Consider the following examples of subtractions which are given in pairs.

Example 6.3

We give three examples of subtraction using 10's complement:

458	458	894	894	498	498
− 349	+ 650	− 648	+ 351	− 042	+ 957
109	+ 1	246	+ 1	456	+ 1
	1109		1246		1456
	− 1000		− 1000		− 1000
	109		246		456

We subtract a number from another in each of the above pairs by adding what is known as the 10's complement of the decimal number and deleting the overflow digit 1. The 10's complement of a digit x is defined as:

$$10\text{'s complement of } x = (10 - x) = (9 - x) + 1$$

Suppose we want to find $y - x$. We can do the following:

$$y - x = y + (10 - x) - 10 = y + (9 - x) + 1 - 10$$

Observe subtracting 10 is equivalent to deleting the overflow digit 1.

Finding $(9 - x)$ for any digit x is very simple as it can be done by table look-up without subtracting as shown below:

x	0	1	2	3	4	5	6	7	8	9
$9 - x$	9	8	7	6	5	4	3	2	1	0

The same idea is used in binary subtraction. In binary subtraction, we use the addition of *2's complement* of a binary number.

6.4 TWO'S COMPLEMENT REPRESENTATION OF NUMBERS

The 2's complement of a binary number x, which has n bits, is given by $(2^n - x)$. Consider the number +3 whose binary representation is 011. It has three bits. Hence, the 2's complement of +3 is $(2^3 - 3)$, which is 5. The binary representation of 5 is 101. Thus, 101 is the 2's complement of 011.

In a computer, all numbers are represented in a uniform fashion using a fixed number of bits. Thus, for an n-bit machine, the range of numbers it can handle is from 0 to $2^n - 1$. For simplicity, consider a 4-bit machine. Sixteen positive numbers (from 0 to 15) can be represented using these 16 strings of four bits. Now we devise a new scheme of representing negative numbers for this machine using these 16 strings of 4 bits as follows. We use the first seven strings of 4 bits, namely, 0001 to 0111, to represent positive numbers 1 to 7. We use seven of the remaining strings of 4 bits, namely, 1001 to 1111, to represent negative numbers –1 to –7. There are two remaining 4-bit strings, namely, 0000 and 1000. The string 0000 is used to represent the digit 0 and the string 1000 is not used. Thus, we have divided the total range from 0000 to 1111 into two halves and restricted ourselves to the use of numbers having a maximum magnitude of seven. Using this method, we can represent positive and negative numbers using 4 bits as indicated in Figure 6.1. In general, the 2's complement of an n-bit number x is $(2^n - x)$. Of the n bits of the complement representation, $(n - 1)$ bits represent the magnitude, and the most significant bit the sign.

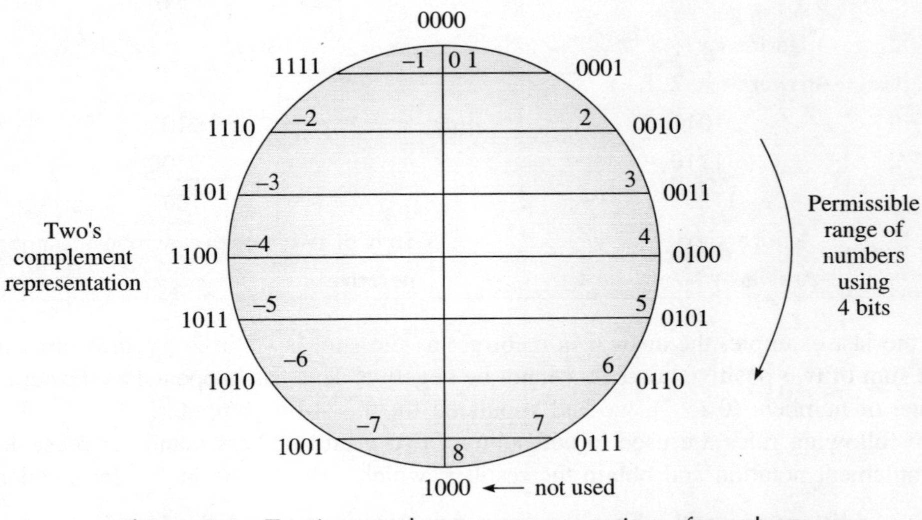

Figure 6.1 Two's complement representation of numbers.

There is a simple procedure to obtain the 2's complement of a binary number. We first complement each bit of the number (i.e., replace 1 by 0 and 0 by 1). Now we add a 1 to the number. For example, consider the number 5 whose binary representation is 0101. Bit complementation yields 1010. Now adding a 1 to this number gives 1011, which is the 2's complement representation for –5.

Yet another method of obtaining the 2's complement of a binary number is to scan the number from right to left and complement all bits appearing *after* the first appearance of a 1. For example, the 2's complement of 0010 is 1110 and that of 0011 is 1101.

6.5 ADDITION/SUBTRACTION OF NUMBERS IN 2'S COMPLEMENT NOTATION

If we represent all negative numbers in 2's complement form, we have the same procedure for addition and subtraction. A number is subtracted by adding its 2's complement. This is illustrated in the following example where the carry, if any, from the most significant bit, during addition, should be ignored. The result has to be interpreted appropriately using the same convention. In other words, if the answer is negative, it will be in 2's complement form.

Example 6.4

Using 2's complement representation, (a) subtract 3 from 5; (b) subtract – 3 from – 5; (c) add – 5 and – 2; and (d) add 5 and 4. It is assumed that the computer is a 4-bit computer.

(a)	5	0101	(b)	–5	1011
	–3	1101		+3	0011
		10010			1110
		Ignore carry			Answer = – 2
		Answer = + 2			
(c)	– 5	1011	(d)	5	0101
	– 2	1110		4	0100
		11001			1001 Incorrect answer
		Ignore carry			Sum of two positive numbers cannot be negative.
		Answer = –7			

In the last example, the answer is incorrect as the sum is –7 in 2's complement notation, and the sum of two positive numbers cannot be negative. This has happened as the sum exceeds the range of numbers (0 to 7), we had stipulated for this 4-bit computer.

The following rules are used to add/subtract two n-bit numbers x and y represented using 2's complement notation and obtain the result z, which will also be in 2's complement form.

(i) **Addition:** If x and y have the same sign (the most significant bits of x and y are the same), add the numbers including the sign bits, and ignore the overflow bit. If the sign bit of z = sign bit of x, declare the answer as correct, otherwise, the answer is not correct and is out of range. If x and y have different signs, add x and y including sign bits. Ignore overflow.

(ii) **Subtraction:** If x and y have the same sign (the most significant bits of x and y are the same), take the 2's complement of y. Add x and y, including their sign bits. Ignore the overflow bit. The result is the answer z. If the sign bits of x and y are different, take the 2's complement of y. Add x and y and ignore the overflow bit (if any). If the sign bit of the sum z = the sign bit of x, the answer is out of range and incorrect. Otherwise, the answer is correct.

6.6 BINARY MULTIPLICATION

Multiplication is nothing but successive addition. Thus, to multiply 5 by 4, we add 5 to itself 4 times. This basic idea is used to implement binary multiplication.

The procedure for multiplying two signed binary numbers depends on the method used to represent negative numbers. If negative numbers are represented in the 2's complement form, multiplication becomes complicated. In this section, we will discuss only the multiplication of numbers in sign-magnitude notation. This is justifiable as numbers in other notations can be converted to this form before multiplication. For special procedures to directly multiply numbers in 2's complement notation, the student may refer to Rajaraman and Radhakrishnan (2008).

Example 6.5

Multiply 1101 by 1011.

Consider the following longhand multiplication method:

Multiplicand	1101
Multiplier	1011
Partial product	1101
	1101
	0000
	1101
Product (Sum of partial product)	10001111

The method used for multiplication is summarized as follows:

Step 1: Examine the least significant bit (LSB) of the multiplier. If it is a 1, copy the multiplicand and call it the first partial product. If the LSB is a zero, enter zero as the first partial product. Preserve (or store) the partial product.

Step 2: Examine the bit to the left of the bit examined last. If it is a 1, go to Step 3. Else, go to Step 4.

Step 3: Add the multiplicand to the previously stored partial product after shifting right the partial product by one bit. This sum becomes the new partial product. Go to Step 5.

Step 4: Get a new partial product by shifting to the right the previous partial product by one bit.

Step 5: Repeat Steps 2 to 4 till all bits in the multiplier have been considered. The final value obtained for the partial product is the final product.

Observe from this 'long-hand' or 'paper and pencil' method of multiplying that we should

(i) Preserve the multiplicand as it is added repeatedly to the partial products.
(ii) Preserve the partial product and shift it.
(iii) Note that the number of bits in each new partial product is one bit more than the previous one. The number of bits in the final product can equal the sum of the number of bits in the multiplier and the multiplicand.
(iv) Note also that after each bit of the multiplier has been used to develop a partial product, it is not used again. It may thus be erased or discarded.

These observations enable us to develop an algorithm for multiplication suitable for implementation in a digital system.

To multiply, we need three registers. Assuming an 'n-bit' multiplier and an 'n-bit' multiplicand, we need two 'n-bit' registers to store the multiplier and the multiplicand and a '$2n$-bit' register to store the final product and the intermediate partial products. Instead of having a separate '$2n$-bit' register for the product, we can append a '$(n + 1)$-bit' register to the left of the 'n-bit' multiplier register to store the partial and the final product. A smaller third register is sufficient if we remember that after each bit of the multiplier is used to develop a partial product, it is discarded. After appending the two registers, the resulting register will be $(2n + 1)$ bits long and sufficient to store the final product. The three registers are shown in Figure 6.2.

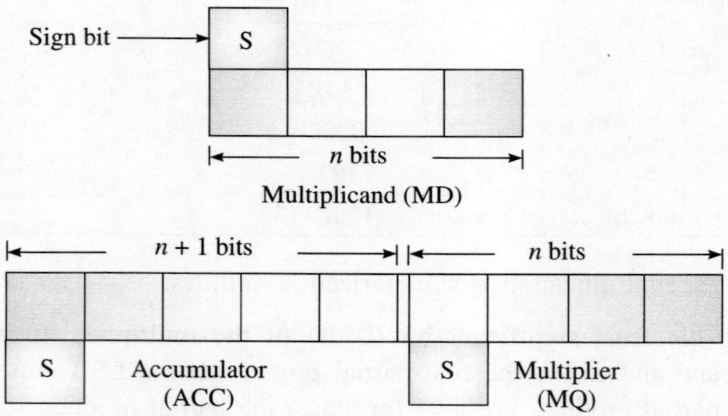

Figure 6.2 Illustration of multiplication using registers (S is sign bit).

We thus implement multiplication using three registers, namely, a multiplicand register which can store n bits, a multiplier–quotient (MQ) register of n bits to store the multiplier (or the quotient during division), and an accumulator in which partial products are added and stored. This register needs $(n + 1)$ bits as the partial sums may be $(n + 1)$ bits long.

The configuration of the registers is shown in Figure 6.2 for $n = 4$.

The accumulator and the MQ register are physically joined so that their contents can be shifted together either to the left or to the right.

Algorithm

Procedure for multiplying two n-bit numbers. Keep the sign bits of all registers undisturbed.

Step 1: Set count = n.

Step 2: Check the least significant bit of MQ. If it is a 1, add the contents of the multiplicand register to the contents of the accumulator. If it is a 0, do not add.

Step 3: Shift right the contents of the accumulator and MQ register together by one bit.

Step 4: Replace count by (count −1).

Step 5: If count = 0 go to Step 6, else go to Step 2.

Step 6: The product will be contained in the accumulator and the MQ register. The most significant bits will be in the accumulator.

Step 7: Set the sign of the product (sign of accumulator contents) negative, if either the sign of the multiplier or the sign of the multiplicand (but not both) is negative. Else, set the sign positive.

6.7 BINARY DIVISION

Binary division may also be implemented by following a procedure similar to that used in longhand division with appropriate modifications. We will discuss in this section a method for dividing numbers represented using the sign-magnitude notation. The method is called the 'restoring method' for division. Another method, called the 'non-restoring method', is also popular but we do not discuss it in this book.

We will illustrate division by the longhand method used for decimal numbers, which can then be extended to binary numbers.

Example 6.6 Longhand Division of Decimal Integers

Consider a three-digit dividend and a three-digit divisor. Let the dividend be 721 and the divisor 025. To divide 721 by 25, we first see if 25 will 'go into' the first digit 7 of the dividend. In other words, we subtract 25 from 7 and see if the answer is negative or positive. In this case, the answer is −18. Thus, 25 does not 'go into' 7. The first digit of the quotient is thus zero. To proceed further, we have to 'restore' the negative answer −18 back to the original dividend. We do this by adding 25 and getting 7 back. The next digit of the dividend, namely 2, is now appended to 7. We now examine whether 25 can go into 72, and if so, how many times: We see that 72 − 25 is positive. Thus, 25 can go into 72 at least once. Next, we try if 2 × 25 can go into 72. As 72 − (2 × 25) is positive, 25 can go into 72 at least twice. We next try 72 − (3 × 25) and see that the answer is −3. Thus, 25 can go into 72 only 2 times. The quotient digit is 2, and we restore the remainder to −3 + 25 = 22. The last digit 1 of the dividend is appended to 22, giving 221. Repeating the same step, namely, finding out how many times 25 will go into 221, we see that it can go 8 times. Thus, the quotient digit is 8. The division ends as no more digits are left in the dividend. The quotient is thus 028 and the remainder is 21. The division process is illustrated below. See (a).

Divisor	Dividend	Quotient	Divisor	Dividend	Quotient
025)	721	(028	11)	1011	(0011
	25			11	
	–18		Borrow ⟶	110	
	25 ⟶	Restoring step	Restore	11	
	72			010	
	75			11	
	–03		Borrow	111	
	25 ⟶	Restoring step	Restore	11	
	221			101	
	225			11	
	–004		No Borrow	101	
	25 ⟶	Restoring step		11	
	21 ⟶	Remainder	No Borrow	10 ⟵	Remainder
	(a)			(b)	

Binary division is similar and, in fact, simpler. It is simpler as we have to check only whether the divisor will go into the dividend or not. The question of how many times the divisor will go into the dividend is irrelevant as the quotient bit can be either 1 or 0. Binary division is illustrated in Example 6.7.

Example 6.7 Longhand Division of Binary Integers

We illustrate longhand division of 1011 by 11 (see (b) in Example 6.6).

The method used in Example 6.6 is expressed as the following step-by-step procedure.

Step 1: Let *y* be the most significant bit of the dividend.
Repeat Steps 2, 3 and 4 *n* times where *n* is the number of bits in the dividend.

Step 2: Subtract the divisor from *y*.

Step 3: If a borrow is generated in subtraction
then set quotient bit to 0 and add the divisor to the remainder
else set quotient bit to 1

Step 4: Append the next significant bit of the dividend to the remainder and call it *y*.

For the longhand division presented above, we see that

(i) The divisor is to be preserved as it is to be successively subtracted from the dividend.

(ii) The dividend bits are used starting from the most significant bit. Once a bit is used to develop a quotient, it is not needed again. The bit to its right is appended to the remainder for developing the next quotient bit.

(iii) As each quotient bit is developed, a corresponding most significant bit of the dividend may be discarded.

We may thus use the same three registers as used for multiplication. The three registers used are again an n-bit register to store the divisor, a $(n + 1)$-bit accumulator in which the dividend is originally stored and from which the divisor is subtracted in each step, and an n-bit quotient register (see Figure 6.2). The accumulator and the MQ register may be again physically joined so that their contents can be shifted together.

6.8 FLOATING POINT REPRESENTATION OF NUMBERS

There are two types of arithmetic operations which are required in computers. These are:

(i) Integer arithmetic
(ii) Real or floating point arithmetic

Integer arithmetic, as the name implies, deals with integer operands, that is, operands without fractional parts. Real arithmetic, on the other hand, uses numbers with fractional parts and is used in most computations.

We saw, in the last chapter, that the memory of computers is organized as an array of words, with each word capable of storing a finite number of bits. In HYPCOM, we had a memory with each word storing 16 bits. One method of representing real numbers in HYPCOM would be by assuming a fixed position for the binary point and storing numbers (after appropriate shifting) with an assumed decimal point, as shown in Figure 6.3.

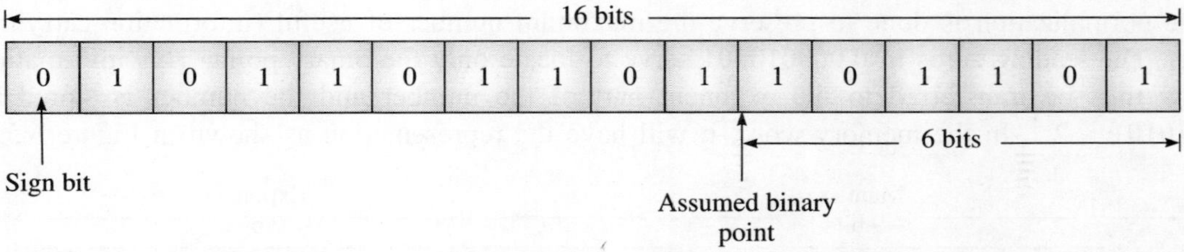

Figure 6.3 A memory location storing +101101101.101101.

If such a convention is used, the maximum and the minimum (in magnitude) numbers that may be stored are:

$$111111111.111111 = (2^9 - 1) \cdot (1 - 2^{-6}) \quad \text{(Maximum)}$$
$$= 511.984375$$
$$000000000.000001 = 2^{-6} = 0.015625 \quad \text{(Minimum)}$$

This range is inadequate in practice, and therefore a different convention for representing real numbers is used. This convention aims at preserving the maximum number of significant digits in a real number and increasing the range of values of real numbers stored. This representation is called the *normalized floating point mode* of representing and storing real numbers. In this mode, a real number is expressed as a combination of a *mantissa* and an *exponent.* The mantissa is made less than 1 and greater than or equal to 0.1, and the exponent is the power of 2 which multiplies the mantissa. For example, the number

$$1011.0101 \times 2^7$$

is represented in this notation as

$$0.10110101 \times 2^{11} = 0.10110101E01011$$

The mantissa is 0.10110101 and the exponent 1011. The number is stored as shown in Figure 6.4.

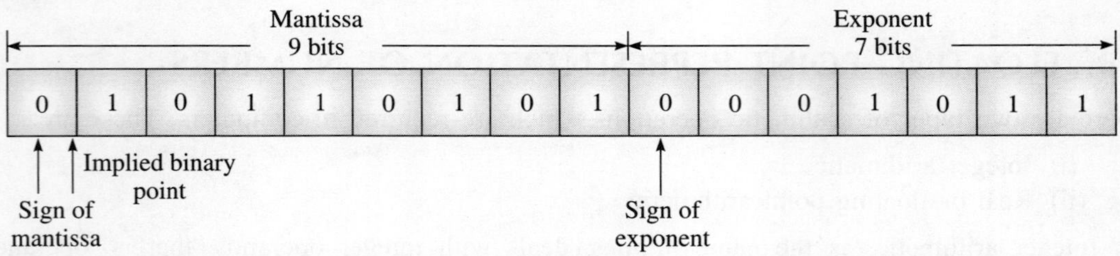

Figure 6.4 Representation of a binary number in normalized floating point mode.

In the representation of Figure 6.4, the 16 bits available in a memory word are arbitrarily divided into two parts. 9 bits are used for the mantissa and 7 bits for the exponent. The mantissa and exponent have their independent signs. While storing numbers, the leading bit in the mantissa is always made non-zero by appropriately shifting it and adjusting the value of the exponent. Thus, the number 0.000010101 would be stored as shown in Figure 6.5. The shifting of the mantissa to the left till its most significant bit is non-zero is called *normalization.* The normalization is done to preserve the maximum number of useful (information-carrying) bits. The leading zeros in 0.000010101 serve to locate only the binary point. This information may thus be transferred to the exponent part of the number and the number is stored as 0.10101×2^{-4}. In the memory word, it will have the representation as shown in Figure 6.5.

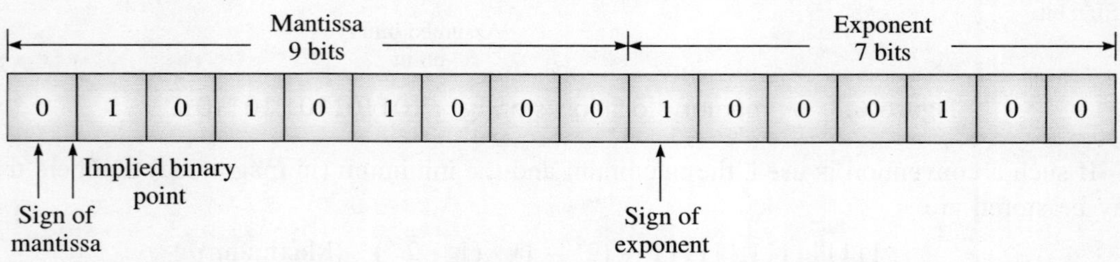

Figure 6.5 Representation of 0.000010101 in normalized floating point mode.

When numbers are stored using this notation, the range of numbers (magnitude) that may be stored will be:

$$\text{(Maximum) } 0.11111111E0111111 = (1-2^{-8}) \times 2^{(2^6-1)}$$

$$\cong 2^{63}$$

$$\text{(Minimum) } 0.10000000E1111111 = (2^{-1}) \times 2^{-(2^6-1)}$$

$$= 2^{-64}$$

This range is much larger than the range from 2^9 to 2^{-6} obtained with the fixed point representation. This increase in range is obtained by sacrificing seven significant bits.

If a 16-bit word is used to store a real number, the number of significant mantissa bits is only 8, which is equivalent to approximately three decimal digits. This is not at all sufficient in practical computation. Thus, if we want to store and compute using real numbers in HYPCOM, we should allot at least two words (32 bits) to each real number. In this case, one possible way of dividing the 32 bits into mantissa and exponent is to allocate 24 bits to the mantissa (including sign) and 8 bits to the exponent and its sign. This will give about 7 decimal digits in the mantissa and an exponent range of $2^{\pm(2^7 - 1)} = 2^{\pm 127} = 10^{\pm 38}$. Incidentally, this format was used for floating point numbers in the IBM Personal Computer. Currently 64-bits are used for floating point numbers.

6.9 ARITHMETIC OPERATIONS WITH NORMALIZED FLOATING POINT NUMBERS

6.9.1 Addition

If two numbers represented in normalized floating point notation are to be added, the exponents of the two numbers must be equal, and the mantissa of the smaller number shifted right by the difference in exponents. This is illustrated by the following examples:

Example 6.8

Add x = = 0.111010010E0101010 to y = 0.110101101E0100101

The difference between the exponents of x and y is 5. The number y is smaller. Thus, y is shifted by 5 bit positions to the right and the mantissas added as shown below:

x = 0.111010010E0101010

y = 0.000001101E0101010

$x + y$ = 0.111011111E0101010

Example 6.9

x = 0.110110111E0110110

y = 0.111011011E0110110

$x + y$ = 1.110010010E0110110

= 0.111001001E0110111

In this addition, the mantissa is made less than 1 after the addition by shifting the mantissa right by 1 bit and adding 1 to the exponent.

6.9.2 Subtraction

Subtraction is performed using complement representation. Once again, the exponents of the two numbers are compared. The number with the smaller exponent is shifted right by the difference in exponents.

Example 6.10

$$x = 0.101010101E0001010$$
$$y = 0.100010110E0000110$$

To find $x - y$.

As the exponent of x is greater than that of y by 4, the mantissa of y is shifted by 4 bit positions to the right before adding its complement to x.

$$y \text{ shifted by 4 bits is } 0.000010001E0001010$$
$$\text{2's complement of } y \text{ is } 0.111101111E0001010$$
$$x = 0.101010101E0001010$$
$$+ \text{ 2's complement of } y = \underline{0.111101111E0001010}$$
$$x - y = 0.101000100E0001010 \text{ (Discard overflow bit)}$$

6.9.3 Multiplication

Two numbers represented in the normalized floating point mode are multiplied by multiplying the mantissas and adding the exponents. After the multiplication of the mantissas, the result mantissa is normalized and exponents adjusted.

Example 6.11

$$x = 0.110101010E0010110$$
$$y = 0.110000000E0000101$$
$$x \times y = 0.100111111E0011011$$

Example 6.12

$$x = 0.101011001E01101101$$
$$y = 0.101000000E01111100$$
$$x \times y = 0.110101111E11101001$$

↓

overflow bit

The exponent is larger than the largest positive exponent that can be stored. This is known as an *overflow condition.*

6.9.4 Division

Two numbers x and y represented in the normalized floating point mode are divided by dividing the mantissa of x by that of y. The exponent of y is subtracted from the exponent of x.

Example 6.13

$$x = 0.100110101E0110010$$
$$y = 0.110011100E0100010$$
$$(x/y) = 0.110000000E0010000$$

In this chapter, we have illustrated the basic methods used in binary arithmetic. Our examples were quite simple to allow students to work out and understand the arithmetic using 'paper and pencil'. In commercial computers, the number of bits used to represent integers and floating point numbers will be at least 32 bits. All recent processors use 64 bits to represent floating point numbers. When 64 bits are used to store floating point numbers, the number of significant digits in the mantissa will be 15 digits. This is called *double precision* floating point number. In early computers, the arithmetic units were built using transistor gates. Currently, with the advent of integrated circuits, single-chip Arithmetic Logic Units (ALUs) are used which implement all the algorithms in hardware. ALUs use complex algorithms to increase the speed of arithmetic. Chips range from those that use 4-bit operands to 64-bit operands. They accept necessary operands and operation codes (add, subtract, multiply, divide, complement, OR, AND, XOR) and give the result as output. There are also chips implementing floating point arithmetic (called FPUs). Modern microprocessors integrate within a single-chip ALU memory and other support circuits. Those interested may refer to Rajaraman and Radhakrishnan (2008).

SUMMARY

1. Addition of binary numbers is simple as there are only two symbols 0 and 1 in the binary system. Addition uses the addition table: $0 + 0 = 0$, $0 + 1 = 1$, $1 + 0 = 1$ and $1 + 1 = 0$ with a carry of 1.
2. Binary subtraction uses the subtraction table:
$0 - 0 = 0$, $1 - 0 = 1$, $1 - 1 = 0$, and $0 - 1 = 1$ with a borrow of 1 to the next bit position.
3. Negative numbers may be represented using either a sign magnitude representation or a complement representation. In the sign magnitude representation, 0 is used to represent + sign and 1 – sign.
4. The complement representation of negative numbers is useful primarily because it simplifies subtraction. The 2's complement of an n-bit binary number x is $(2^n - x)$. To subtract a number y from a number x, the 2's complement of y is added to x and the overflow bit is ignored.
5. Binary multiplication is similar to decimal multiplication. The multiplication table is $0 \times 0 = 0$, $0 \times 1 = 0$, $1 \times 0 = 0$ and $1 \times 1 = 1$.
6. Two binary numbers are multiplied by successive addition of multiplicand to itself after shifting it right if the multiplier bit is 1.
7. Binary division is performed by successive subtraction of the divisor from the dividend and developing the quotient bits.

8. The number of bits in the operands stored and manipulated in computers is finite. To represent numbers with a fractional part (real numbers), we may use a representation with a decimal point at a fixed position or use a mantissa and exponent representation. The representation using a mantissa and an exponent allows a wider range of magnitudes for real numbers and is known as floating point representation.
9. To preserve the maximum number of significant bits, the mantissa is normalized with its leading bit as a 1.
10. Addition and subtraction of floating point numbers are performed by first making the exponents of the two operands equal. The mantissa of the smaller number is shifted right by the difference in exponents. The mantissas are then added or subtracted.
11. In the multiplication of two floating point numbers, the mantissas are multiplied and the exponents are added.
12. In the division of two floating point numbers, the mantissas are divided and the divisor's exponent is subtracted from that of the dividend.

REVIEW QUESTIONS

6.1 Add the following binary numbers:
(i) 1110.1101 + 110101.01101
(ii) 1011011.111 + 1010110.1010
(iii) 110111.11 + 11011101.0101

6.2 Subtract the following binary numbers. Assume that the numbers are represented in sign magnitude notation.
(i) 10101.1010 – 10001.0011
(ii) 11011.011 – 11110.101
(iii) 1001000.001 – 1000011.011

6.3 Subtract the following decimal numbers using 10's complement representation for negative numbers:
(i) 485 – 128
(ii) 684 – 35
(iii) 964 – 988

6.4 Subtract the following binary numbers using 2's complement representation of negative numbers:
(i) 10101 – 10001
(ii) 11011 – 1110
(iii) 100100 – 100011

6.5 Subtract the following binary numbers using 2's complement representation of negative numbers:
(i) 101101.0011 – 100101.0001
(ii) 11011.110 – 101.001
(iii) 10111.1001 – 11000.1101

6.6 Multiply the following binary numbers using longhand multiplication:
(i) 10011 × 1101
(ii) 110.101 × 1011.001
(iii) 1101.101 × 110101.11

6.7 Divide the following binary numbers in longhand:
(i) 1011/011
(ii) 110111/1011
(iii) 110001.110/111.110

6.8 Represent the following numbers using floating point notation. Assume 16-bit word.
(i) 10110.1101
(ii) 1101100.10
(iii) 0.000011011011

6.9 If a word has 32 bits, how many bits would you allocate for mantissa and exponent? Explain your choice.

6.10 Add the following binary numbers using 16-bit floating point representation:
(i) 1011011.110101 + 110101.0101
(ii) 11011.1101 + 1011.10110
(iii) 0.000111 + 111.00111

6.11 Subtract the following binary numbers using a 16-bit floating point representation:
(i) 1011011.1101 – 01110.1101
(ii) 101110.110 – 1110.0011
(iii) 100110.101 – 011.110011

6.12 Multiply the following numbers using a 16-bit floating point representation:
(i) 1011.110 × 1010.110
(ii) 0.11011 × 0.111011
(iii) 1110111.111 × 11011.1101

6.13 Divide the following numbers using a 16-bit floating point representation:
(i) 1011.110/1010.110
(ii) 0.11011/0.111011
(iii) 110111.111/11011.1101

6.14 Repeat Exercise 6.11 using 2's complement representation for negative numbers.

7

Logic Circuits

LEARNING GOALS

After reading this chapter, you should be able to:

- Explain the basic principles of Boolean algebra.
- Use Boolean algebra to design switching circuits.
- Develop truth tables given the requirements of a logic circuit.
- Convert a truth table to an equivalent logic circuit.
- Realize logic circuits using controlled semiconductor switches.
- Explain the basic ideas used to fabricate integrated circuits..

In this chapter, we will first introduce an algebra useful in designing logic circuits of processors. Subsequently, we will use this algebra to design simple logic circuits for logical and arithmetic operations performed by processors.

7.1 INTRODUCTION

George Boole (1815–1864), a logician, developed an algebra, known as *Boolean algebra* to examine a given set of propositions (statements) to check their logical consistency and simplify them by removing redundant statements or clauses. He used symbols to represent simple propositions. Compound propositions were expressed in terms of these symbols and connectives. For example, 'Ram is intelligent *and* he does well in examinations' is a compound proposition consisting of two simple ones connected by the connective AND.

Let the proposition 'Ram is intelligent' be represented by the symbol A and let the symbol B represent the proposition 'Ram does well in examinations'. A symbolic way of representing the whole statement will be *A* AND *B*. Similarly, the proposition 'My friend would give me a box of sweets *or* a greeting card for my birthday' contains the connective OR. Once again, representing the individual propositions by the symbols *C* and *D*, we can write *C* OR *D* to refer to the whole statement.

The use of symbols to represent propositions, connectives, and their truth and falsity led to the name *Symbolic Logic* for this subject.

In 1938, Shannon discovered that a simplified version of Boolean algebra could be used in the analysis and synthesis of telephone switching networks where a large number of electromechanical relays and switches were used. The one-to-one correspondence between symbolic logic, on the one hand, and switching circuits, on the other hand, is explained in the next section.

7.2 SWITCHING CIRCUITS

Consider a switch that is either 'closed' or 'open'. This is similar to the situation in Propositional Calculus, where a proposition is either 'true' or 'false'. In Figure 7.1a, we have two switches *A* and *B* which are normally open. They are connected in series with a battery and a lamp. The lamp will light only when both *A* and *B* are closed. Notice the similarity between this and a compound proposition in which an AND connective is used.

Now consider the arrangement of switches shown in Figure 7.1b where two switches *C* and *D* are connected in parallel. The lamp will light when either *C* or *D* or both are closed. We recognize the similarity between this and the truth of a compound proposition when the OR connective is used. We can now see a one-to-one correspondence between 'closed' and 'true'. Similarly, 'open' corresponds to 'false'. Because of this analogy, we call these switching circuits *logic circuits*.

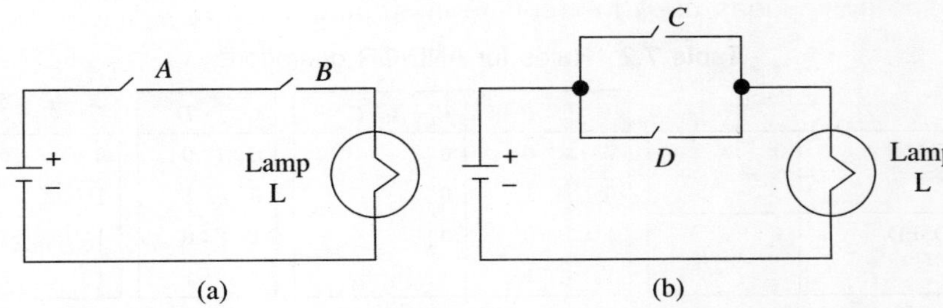

Figure 7.1 (a) Switches in series; (b) switches in parallel.

Thus, we have switches that can be only open or closed and similarly propositions that are either *true* or *false*. In other words, these can be considered as variables that can only assume either one of two values. For convenience, we use the symbols 0 or 1 to represent these values. Remember that 0 and 1 have no arithmetic significance at all. They only have a logical significance because they are symbolic representations of falsehood and truth, respectively. Such variables which can have only two values are called *Boolean variables*. Thus, a Boolean variable *x* is either 1 or 0, that is, either true or false.

We have observed a one-to-one correspondence between series and parallel connections of switches and the connectives AND and OR of propositional calculus. We can consider these connectives as performing operations on Boolean variables. Let us further represent AND by the symbol . and OR by the symbol + so that the condition for lighting the lamp in Figure 7.1(a) can be written as $A \cdot B$, and for Figure 7.1(b) the condition can be expressed as $C + D$.

7.3 AND/OR OPERATIONS

The behaviour of the switching circuits shown in Figures 7.1(a) and 7.1(b) is summarized in Table 7.1.

Table 7.1 Logical nature of switching circuit operation

Switch A	*Switch B*	*Lamp L*	*Switch C*	*Switch D*	*Lamp L*
open	open	OFF	open	open	OFF
open	closed	OFF	open	closed	ON
closed	open	OFF	closed	open	ON
closed	closed	ON	closed	closed	ON

(a) Series connected switches (AND) (b) Parallel connected switches (OR)

Table 7.2(a) shows the use of symbols 0 and 1 to represent the states of switches and lamps. Using this symbol assignment, we construct Tables 7.2(b) and 7.2(c) from Tables 7.1(a) and 7.1(b), respectively.

Now considering the switches as independent Boolean variables, and lamps as dependent variables, Tables 7.2(b) and 7.2(c) form the rules for the AND and OR operations, respectively.

Table 7.2 Rules for AND/OR operations

OPEN OFF	0
CLOSED ON	1

(a) Symbol assignment to states of switch and lamp

A	*B*	$L = A \cdot B$
0	0	0
0	1	0
1	0	0
1	1	1

(b) Rule for AND operation

C	*D*	$L = C + D$
0	0	0
0	1	1
1	0	1
1	1	1

(c) Rule for OR operation

Referring to Table 7.2(b), we note that the rule for AND operation is the same as that of ordinary multiplication. This is a happy coincidence. Although the logical AND operation has nothing to do with the arithmetic operation of multiplication, it enables us to remember the rule without additional effort. Thus, we refer to $A \cdot B$ as a *product* of A and B.

Referring to Table 7.2(c), the coincidence of this table with an addition table is limited only to the first three rows. The last row gives $1 + 1 = 1$, which obviously is not valid for addition in arithmetic. We have to especially remember this and, despite this, for convenience, we refer to $C + D$ as the *sum* of C and D.

Note that the AND and OR operations involve at least two variables, and are called *binary operators*. Obviously, by their repeated use, we can perform these operations on many variables.

Referring to Figure 7.1(a), we note that the order in which the switches A and B are connected in series is not important from the point of view of the circuit operation. In other words, we could interchange the switches A and B and still obtain the same performance. This idea is expressed as $A \cdot B = B \cdot A$. Similarly, we see from Figure 7.1(b), $C + D = D + C$. Thus, we recognize that *commutative law* holds good for the + and · operations. Figure 7.2 illustrates the basis for the *distributive law* of AND operation in Boolean algebra, which gives

$$A \cdot (B + C) = A \cdot B + A \cdot C \tag{7.1}$$

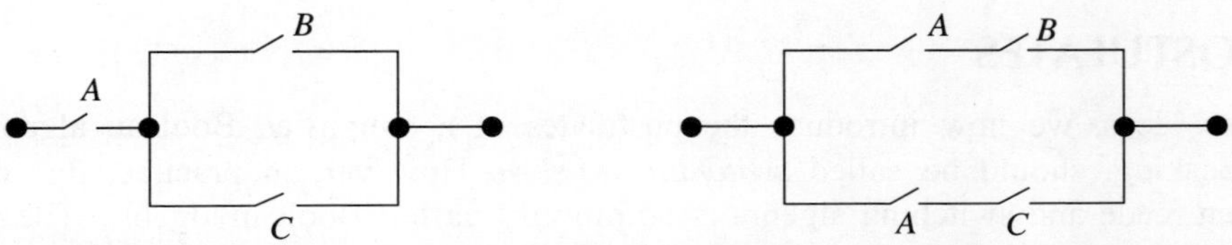

Figure 7.2 Equivalent switch connections illustrating distributive law for AND operation.

Similarly, Figure 7.3 shows how, in Boolean algebra, distributive law holds for OR operation as well. This gives us the interesting equality $A + (B \cdot C) = (A + B) \cdot (A + C)$, which does not apply in the algebra of real numbers we are used to. Boolean algebra does not have operations equivalent to subtraction and division.

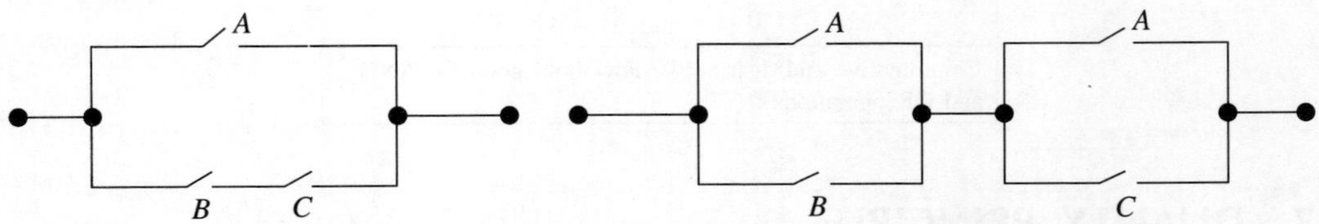

Figure 7.3 Equivalent switch connections illustrating distributive law for OR operation.

7.4 NOT OPERATION

When the proposition 'Ram is intelligent' is *true*, the *negated* proposition 'Ram is *not* intelligent' is *false,* and vice versa. There is an analogous situation in switching circuits. Some electromechanical relays have normally closed contacts. These contacts open when the relays operate. Thus, the normally closed contact represents a negation of the normally open contact of the *same relay.*

Again using symbol assignment, we define the NOT operation as follows. If $A = 0$, NOT A (written as $\overline{A}$ and read as A bar) = 1. Or when $B = 1$, $\overline{B} = 0$. In other words, the process of negation, which is also called complementation, converts the symbolic 0 to a 1 and vice versa, that is, $\overline{0} = 1$ and $\overline{1} = 0$. Note that the NOT operation is performed on a single variable, and hence it is called a *unary operation.* There is no equivalent operation in the algebra of real numbers.

7.5 BOOLEAN FUNCTIONS

We observed that the AND, OR, and NOT operations performed on Boolean variables, in turn, result in Boolean variables. This gives the 'closure' property. As in ordinary algebra, we have the concept of a function of Boolean variables or an expression containing Boolean variables. For example, consider the equation

$$X = A \cdot B + \overline{C} \cdot D + E \cdot F \tag{7.2}$$

Here, the variable X is a function of A, B, C, D, E, and F. This is written as $X = f(A, B, C, D, E, F)$ and the right-hand side of the equation is called an *expression.* The symbols A, B, C, D, E, *and* F are called *literals*.

7.6 POSTULATES

With these ideas, we now introduce the postulates of a simplified Boolean algebra which, strictly speaking, should be called *switching algebra.* However, in practice, this distinction is not often made and switching algebra is commonly called Boolean algebra. The postulates are summarized in Table 7.3. Using these we will now prove some theorems.

Table 7.3 Postulates of switching algebra

Boolean variables are either 1 or 0	
0 + 1 = 1 + 0 = 1	1.0 = 0.1 = 0
1 + 1 = 1	0.0 = 0
0 + 0 = 0	1.1 = 1
$\overline{0} = 1$ and $\overline{1} = 0$	
Commutative and distributive laws hold good for AND and OR operations	

7.7 DUALITY PRINCIPLE

Observe that we have listed some of the postulates in two parts. One part may be obtained from the other if '+' is interchanged with '·' and '0' is interchanged with '1'. This important property is known as the *duality principle.* This principle ensures that if a theorem is proved using the postulates, a dual theorem obtained by interchanging + with · and 0 with 1 automatically holds and need not be proved separately. Thus, in Section 7.8, along with each theorem, the dual theorem is stated without proof.

7.8 THEOREMS

As Boolean algebra deals with variables that can have only two values, it is, in principle, possible to prove every theorem by considering all possible cases. This method of proving theorems is called exhaustive enumeration or *perfect induction*. We will first present some simple theorems. Using the postulates and these simple theorems, we will prove some more theorems that are not so obvious.

Simple Theorems

These are directly implied in the postulates. Thus, these are often considered postulates themselves.

$$0 + X = X \qquad 1 \cdot X = X \tag{7.3}$$

$$X + \overline{X} = 1 \qquad X \cdot \overline{X} = 0 \tag{7.4}$$

Theorem 1(a) $A + A = A$ *1(b)* $A \cdot A = A$

Proof:
When $A = 0$, $0 + 0 = 0 = A$. When $A = 1$, $1 + 1 = 1 = A$.
For both $A = 0$ and 1, $A + A = A$. Thus, the theorem holds.
As we pointed out in Section 7.7, no proof is given for the (b) part of all theorems as they are dual theorems.

Theorem 2(a) $A + 1 = 1$ *2(b)* $A \cdot 0 = 0$

Proof:
When $A = 0$, $0 + 1 = 1$. When $A = 1$, $1 + 1 = 1$.
Thus, $A + 1 = 1$.

Theorem 3(a) $A + A \cdot B = A$ *3(b)* $A \cdot (A + B) = A$

Proof:
$A + A \cdot B = A \cdot 1 + A \cdot B = A \cdot (1 + B) = A \cdot 1 = A.$

Theorem 4 $\overline{\overline{A}} = A$

Proof:
When $A = 0$, $\overline{A} = 1$, $\overline{\overline{A}} = \overline{1} = 0 = A$. When $A = 1$, $\overline{A} = 0$, $\overline{\overline{A}} = \overline{0} = 1 = A$.
Thus, $\overline{\overline{A}} = A$.

Theorem 5(a) $A + (\overline{A} \cdot B) = A + B$ *5(b)* $A \cdot (\overline{A} + B) = A \cdot B$

Proof:
$A + (\overline{A} \cdot B) = (A + \overline{A}) \cdot (A + B)$ (Distributive law)
$= 1 \cdot (A + B) = (A + B)$

Theorem 6(a) $\overline{A + B} = \overline{A} \cdot \overline{B}$ *6(b)* $\overline{A \cdot B} = \overline{A} + \overline{B}$

Proof: Table 7.4 is used to show that the left-hand side is equal to the right-hand side for all values of A and B.

Table 7.4 Proof of Theorem 6(a)

A	B	$A + B$	$\overline{A + B}$	$\overline{A}$	$\overline{B}$	$\overline{A} \cdot \overline{B}$
0	0	0	1	1	1	1
0	1	1	0	1	0	0
1	0	1	0	0	1	0
1	1	1	0	0	0	0

Columns 4 and 7 are identical, and hence the theorem is proved. Theorems 6(a) and 6(b) are important and useful. They are known as *De Morgan's laws.* They can be extended to n variables as given below.

$$\overline{A_1 + A_2 + A_3 + \cdots + A_n} = \overline{A}_1 \cdot \overline{A}_2 \cdot \overline{A}_3 \cdots \overline{A}_n \tag{7.5}$$

$$\overline{A_1 \cdot A_2 \cdot A_3 + \cdots + A_n} = \overline{A}_1 + \overline{A}_2 + \overline{A}_3 + \cdots + \overline{A}_n \tag{7.6}$$

Some important identities of Boolean algebra are collected in Table 7.5. The student should become thoroughly conversant with this table to use the algebra effectively.

Table 7.5 Summary of important identities

Theorems	*Dual theorems*
$A + 0 = A$	$A \cdot 1 = A$
$A + B = B + A$	$A \cdot B = B \cdot A$
$A \cdot (B + C) = A \cdot B + A \cdot C$	$A + (B \cdot C) = (A + B) \cdot (A + C)$
$A + \overline{A} = 1$	$A \cdot \overline{A} = 0$
$A + A = A$	$A \cdot A = A$
$A + 1 = 1$	$A \cdot 0 = 0$
$A + A \cdot B = A$	$A \cdot (A + B) = A$
$\overline{\overline{A}} = A$	
$A + \overline{A} \cdot B = A + B$	$A \cdot (\overline{A} + B) = A \cdot B$
$\overline{A + B} = \overline{A} \cdot \overline{B}$	$\overline{A \cdot B} = \overline{A} + \overline{B}$

7.9 PRECEDENCE OF OPERATORS

To evaluate Boolean expressions, it is necessary to define the precedence of operators. The precedence is as follows:

1. Scan the expression from left to right.
2. First evaluate expressions enclosed in parentheses.
3. Perform all the complement (NOT) operations.
4. Perform all ·(AND) operations next in the order in which they appear.
5. Perform all + (OR) operations last.

Example

Indicate the precedence of operations in the Boolean expression $X \cdot \overline{X} + Y \cdot (\overline{X + Z}) + (X \cdot Z)$.

Solution:

$X \cdot \overline{X} + Y \cdot (\overline{X + Z}) + (X \cdot Z)$

$\overline{X + Z} \quad X \cdot Z$ First scan

$\overline{X} \cdot \overline{Z} \quad X \cdot Z$ Second scan

$0 + Y \cdot \overline{X} \cdot \overline{Z} + X \cdot Z$ Third scan

7.10 VENN DIAGRAM

To fix our ideas of Boolean algebra, a pictorial model known as the Venn diagram is useful. This diagram consists of a rectangle inside which several circles are drawn, one circle for each variable. The region inside the circle belongs to the variable, and the region outside the circle belongs to its complement. Figure 7.4 shows a Venn diagram for two variables X and Y. The Region inside the circle named X represents X and that outside $\overline{X}$. With two intersecting circles X and Y, we have four regions corresponding to $X \cdot Y$, $X\ \overline{Y}$, $\overline{X} \cdot Y$, $\overline{X} \cdot \overline{Y}$, as shown in the figure.

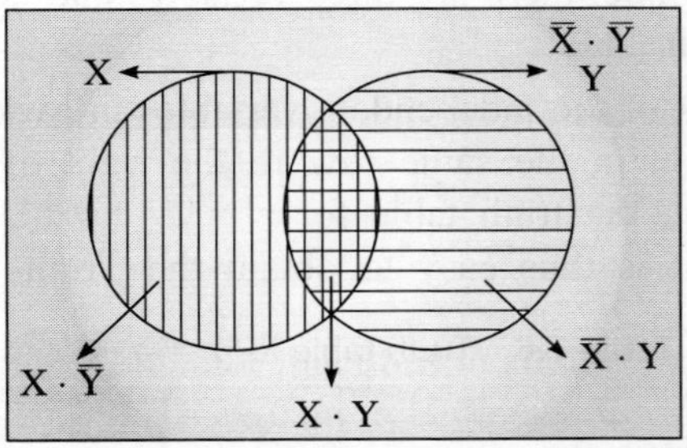

Figure 7.4 Venn diagram for two variables

Venn diagrams may be used to illustrate postulates and theorems of Boolean algebra. Figure 7.5 illustrates the identity $a + b \cdot c = (a + b) \cdot (a + c)$. In Figure 7.5(a), the area covered by the slanted lines corresponds to the expression $a + (b \cdot c)$. In Figure 7.5b area $(a + b)$ is marked by horizontal lines and area $(a + c)$ by vertical lines. The area intersected by the horizontal and vertical lines corresponds to the expression $(a + b) \cdot (a + c)$, and this is identical to the area in Figure 7.5(a). Venn diagrams thus provide an aid to remember or prove the theorems of Boolean algebra.

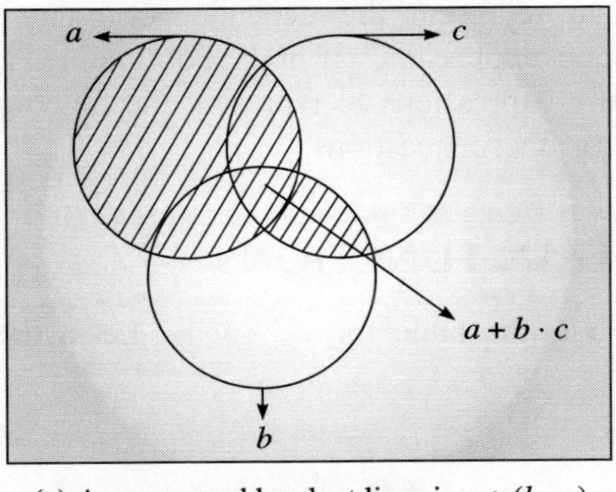

(a) Area covered by slant lines is $a + (b \cdot c)$

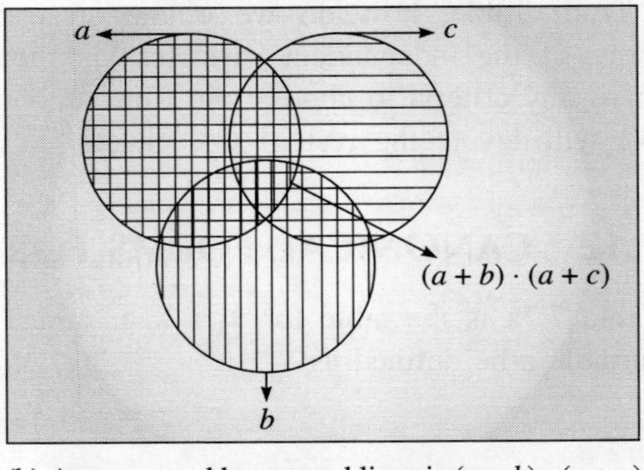

(b) Area covered by crossed lines is $(a + b) \cdot (a + c)$

Figure 7.5 Venn diagram illustrating distributive law for OR operations.

7.11 TRUTH TABLE

Consider a Boolean function $z = f(a, b, c)$. A table which lists the value of the dependent variable z for each set of values of the independent variables a, b, and c is known as a Truth Table.

We will now obtain a Truth Table for $z = \overline{a} + b \cdot c$. To obtain the table, we follow the steps enumerated below:

Step 1: Form a table with one column for each independent variable and one column for the dependent variable. Use a vertical thick line to separate the dependent and independent variables.

Step 2: Assuming that there are n independent variables in the function, start with 00. .0 (n bits) as values of the independent variables and form successive rows (each containing n bits) in the natural binary counting sequence till the count becomes $(2^n - 1)$. In our example, there are three variables and hence eight rows starting from 000 and ending with 111.

Step 3: Substitute the values of the independent variables in each row and enter the evaluated value of the function in the same row to the right of the thick vertical line.

Following this procedure, the truth table for $z = \overline{a} + b \cdot c$ is developed in Table 7.6. Given a Boolean function, it is thus easy to obtain the Truth Table.

Table 7.6 Truth table for $z = \overline{a} + b \cdot c$

a	b	c	z
0	0	0	1
0	0	1	1
0	1	0	1
0	1	1	1
1	0	0	0
1	0	1	0
1	1	0	0
1	1	1	1

In dealing with practical situations, we often face the reverse problem. That is, given a Truth Table, how do we obtain an expression to represent the dependent variable in terms of the independent variables? Is there a unique expression? If it is not unique, are there any criteria to choose one from among the many expressions to represent the function? We will devote the rest of this chapter to answering these questions.

7.12 CANONICAL FORMS FOR BOOLEAN FUNCTIONS

Table 7.7a is the table for $z_1 = \overline{x} \cdot \overline{y}$ and Table 7.7b is the table for $z_2 = x \cdot \overline{y}$. Let a third variable z be defined as

$$z = z_1 + z_2 = \overline{x} \cdot \overline{y} + x \cdot \overline{y} \tag{7.7}$$

Let us form the truth table for z which is given in Table 7.7(c). Note that the column corresponding to z could have been formed by 'ORing' the columns corresponding to z_1 and z_2. Thus, there are two entries of 1 for z (corresponding to the rows xy = 00 and 10), one contributed by z_1 and the other contributed by z_2, respectively.

Table 7.7 Illustrating canonical forms of Boolean functions

x	y	$z_1 = \bar{x} \cdot \bar{y}$
0	0	1
0	1	0
1	0	0
1	1	0

(a)

x	y	$z_2 = x \cdot \bar{y}$
0	0	0
0	1	0
1	0	1
1	1	0

(b)

z_1	z_2	$z = z_1 + z_2$
1	0	1
0	0	0
0	1	1
0	0	0

(c)

Referring to Eq. (7.7), we note the same fact, namely, that z becomes 1 when z_1 becomes 1 or z_2 becomes 1. z_1 assumes the value 1 only when $x = 0$, $y = 0$ for which $z_2 = 0$. Similarly, z_2 becomes 1 only when $x = 1$, $y = 0$ for which $z_1 = 0$. Thus, each term on the right-hand side of Eq. (7.7) assumes a value 1 for one and only one set of values of x and y. Each such set leads to a value 1 in the corresponding row of the truth table for z. Thus, by concentrating on the 1 entries in the truth table, we can form a Boolean expression corresponding to any truth table. The systematic procedure for this is as follows:

Step 1: Inspect the column corresponding to z starting with the top row. Pick the row with an entry 1 for z.

Step 2: One term in the Boolean expression for z is obtained by 'ANDing' all the independent variables in the truth table; the independent variables with 0 entry appear in the complement form and those with 1 entry appear as they are.

Step 3: Repeat steps 1 and 2 till all the 1 entries in z column are exhausted. Obtain the final expression for z by 'ORing' the terms corresponding to the 1 entries in the z column.

We will now apply this procedure to the Truth Table 7.8.

Table 7.8 Truth table of a Boolean function

a	b	c	z
0	0	0	0
0	0	1	1
0	1	0	0
0	1	1	0
1	0	0	1
1	0	1	1
1	1	0	1
1	1	1	1

Step 1: Row 2 of the column corresponding to z is a 1.

Step 2: The term corresponding to this 1 in the Boolean expression for z is $\bar{a} \cdot \bar{b} \cdot c$.

Step 3: Rows 5, 6, 7, 8 have 1 entries for z. The corresponding terms are: $a \cdot \overline{b} \cdot \overline{c}, a \cdot \overline{b} \cdot c$ $a \cdot b \cdot \overline{c}$, and $a \cdot b \cdot c$. Thus,

$$z = \overline{a} \cdot \overline{b} \cdot c + a \cdot \overline{b} \cdot \overline{c} + a \cdot \overline{b} \cdot c + a \cdot b \cdot \overline{c} + a \cdot b \cdot c \tag{7.8}$$

We will take another example of obtaining a Boolean expression corresponding to a truth table. The example is the table for the full adder discussed in Chapter 6. The table is reproduced as Table 7.9. In this table, a_n and b_n are the augend and addend bits and c_n is the carry bit to be added. These are the input variables. The outputs are the sum bit s_n and the carry bit c_{n+1} which is to be taken to the $(n + 1)$th bit position before addition. The Boolean expression for s_n is obtained by inspecting the rows in which $s_n = 1$ and obtaining a Boolean term corresponding to those rows and 'ORing' them. Thus,

$$s_n = \overline{a}_n \cdot \overline{b}_n \cdot c_n + \overline{a}_n \cdot b_n \cdot \overline{c}_n + a_n \cdot \overline{b}_n \cdot \overline{c}_n + a_n \cdot b_n \cdot c_n \tag{7.9}$$

$$c_{n+1} = \overline{a}_n \cdot b_n \cdot c_n + a_n \cdot \overline{b}_n \cdot c_n + a_n \cdot b_n \cdot \overline{c}_n + a_n \cdot b_n \cdot c_n \tag{7.10}$$

Table 7.9 Truth table for a full adder

a_n	b_n	c_n	s_n	c_{n+1}
0	0	0	0	0
0	0	1	1	0
0	1	0	1	0
0	1	1	0	1
1	0	0	1	0
1	0	1	0	1
1	1	0	0	1
1	1	1	1	1

7.13 LOGIC CIRCUITS

The three logical operations AND, OR, and NOT are said to be logically complete, as any Boolean function may be realized using these three operations. The standard symbols given in Figure 7.6 are used to represent the Boolean operations AND, OR, and NOT, respectively. Using these gates, we can realize the expressions for s_n and c_{n+1} given as Eqs. (7.9) and (7.10) as shown in Figure 7.7. This circuit is called a *full adder* circuit. If the three bits to be added are fed to the inputs a_n, b_n, and c_n of the full adder, the sum s_n and carry c_{n+1} appear as output.

Figure 7.6 Standard symbols for logic gates.

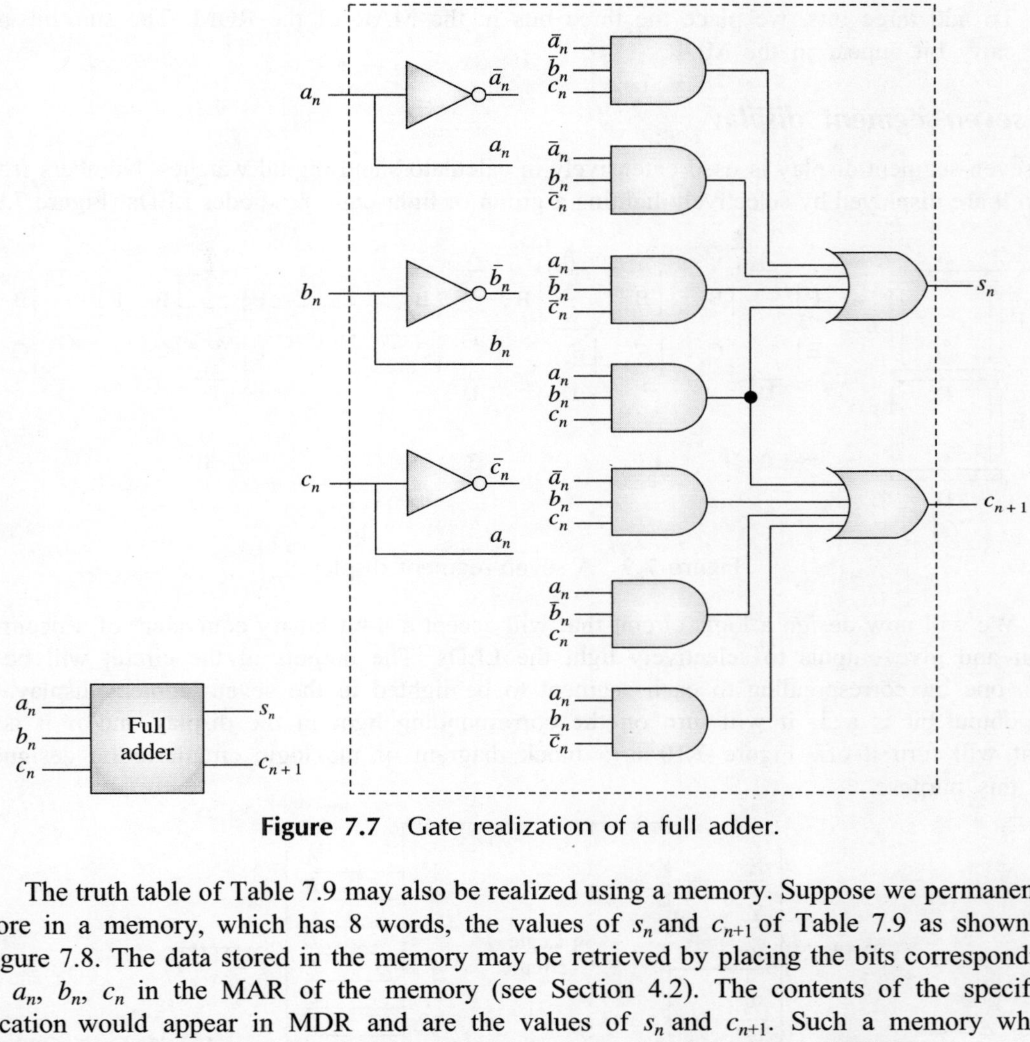

Figure 7.7 Gate realization of a full adder.

The truth table of Table 7.9 may also be realized using a memory. Suppose we permanently store in a memory, which has 8 words, the values of s_n and c_{n+1} of Table 7.9 as shown in Figure 7.8. The data stored in the memory may be retrieved by placing the bits corresponding to a_n, b_n, c_n in the MAR of the memory (see Section 4.2). The contents of the specified location would appear in MDR and are the values of s_n and c_{n+1}. Such a memory where a table may be stored permanently is known as a *read only memory* (ROM).

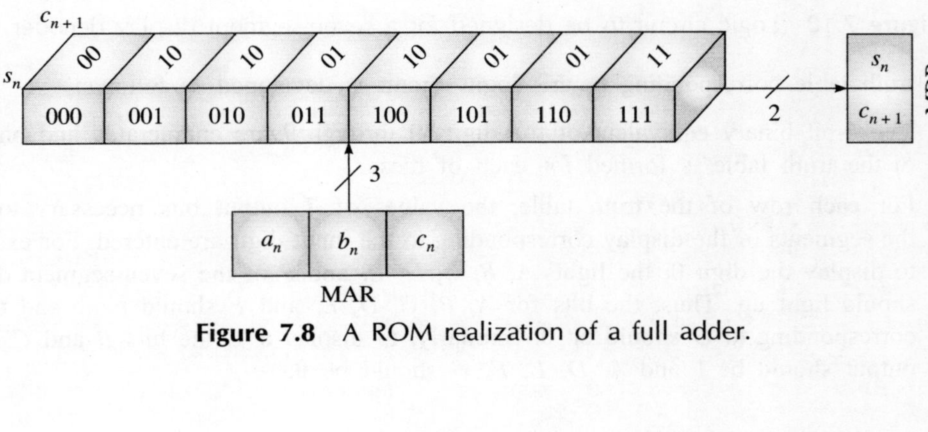

Figure 7.8 A ROM realization of a full adder.

To add three bits, we place the three bits in the MAR of the ROM. The sum bit and the carry bit appear in the MDR.

A seven-segment display

A seven-segment display is used extensively in calculators and digital watches. Numbers from 0 to 9 are displayed by selectively lighting a group of light-emitting diodes LEDs (Figure 7.9).

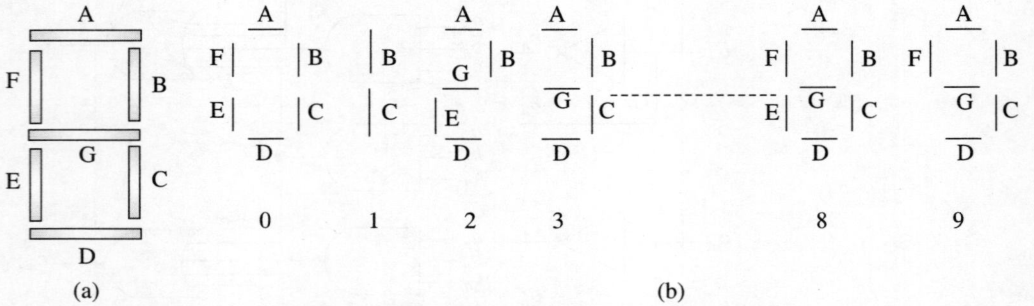

Figure 7.9 A seven-segment display.

We will now design a logic circuit that will accept a 4-bit binary equivalent of a decimal digit and give outputs to selectively light the LEDs. The outputs of the circuit will be 7 bits, one bit corresponding to each segment to be lighted in the seven-segment display. If the output bit is a 1, it will turn on the corresponding light in the display and if it is a 0, it will turn it off. Figure 7.10 is a block diagram of the logic circuit to be designed for this purpose.

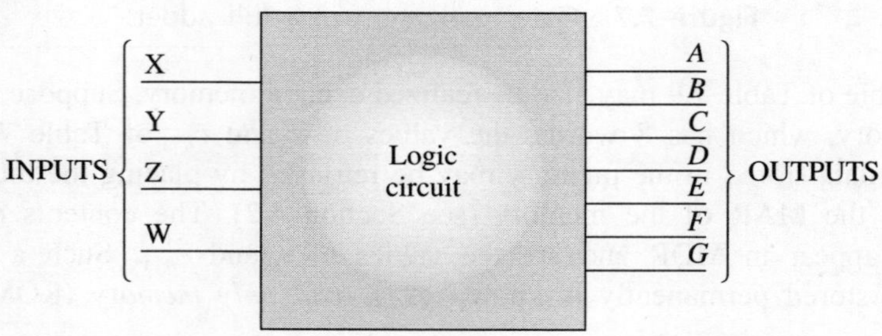

Figure 7.10 Logic circuit to be designed for a seven-segment display decoder.

The truth table corresponding to this logic circuit is developed as follows:

Step 1: The 4-bit binary equivalent of the digits 0 through 9 are enumerated and one row of the truth table is formed for each of these.

Step 2: For each row of the truth table, the values of 7 output bits necessary to light the segments of the display corresponding to the input digit are entered. For example, to display the digit 0, the lights *A*, *B*, *C*, *D*, *E*, and *F* of the seven-segment display should light up. Thus, the bits for *A*, *B*, *C*, *D*, *E*, and *F* should be 1 and the bit corresponding to *G* should be 0. Similarly, to display a 1, the bits *B* and *C* of the output should be 1 and *A*, *D*, *E*, *F*, *G* should be 0.

Step 3: The combinations of input bits 1010, 1011, 1100, 1101, 1110, and 1111 should not occur, as the input is expected to be a single digit. If these inputs occur by mistake, an error indication should be displayed. We will use the letter *E* as an error indication and display it by lighting up segments *A, F, G, E,* and *D.*

The truth table developed is given as Table 7.10.

We can realize a logic circuit using AND, OR, and NOT gates by writing Boolean expressions for *A, B, C, D, E, F, and G* in terms of *X, Y, Z, and W*. For example, the expression for *B* is

$$B = \overline{X} \cdot \overline{Y} \cdot \overline{Z} \cdot \overline{W} + \overline{X} \cdot \overline{Y} \cdot \overline{Z} \cdot W + \overline{X} \cdot \overline{Y} \cdot Z \cdot \overline{W} + \overline{X} \cdot \overline{Y} \cdot Z \cdot W +$$
$$\overline{X} \cdot Y \cdot \overline{Z} \cdot \overline{W} + \overline{X} \cdot Y \cdot Z \cdot W + X \cdot \overline{Y} \cdot \overline{Z} \cdot \overline{W} + X \cdot \overline{Y} \cdot \overline{Z} \cdot W$$

Similar expressions may be obtained for *A, C, D, E, F,* and *G.*

Another method of realizing the seven-segment display is to store the outputs *A, B, C, D, E, F, and G* in a 16-word ROM. The 16 words of the ROM are the 16 rows of the truth table (Table 7.10). The address bits are *X, Y, Z,* and *W* and the contents are the corresponding values of *A, B, C, D, E, F, G* in the truth table. For example, address 0111 corresponding to $X = 0$, $Y = 1$, $Z = 1$, $W = 1$ will store the bits $A = 1$, $B = 1$, $C = 1$, $D = 0$, $E = 0$, $F = 0$ and $G = 0$. To display a digit, its binary values *X, Y, Z,* and *W* are fed to the MAR of the ROM. The output of the ROM, which appears in a 7-bit MDR, lights up the display LEDs.

Table 7.10 Truth table to design seven-segment display

		INPUTS				OUTPUTS						
		X	*Y*	*Z*	*W*	*A*	*B*	*C*	*D*	*E*	*F*	*G*
LEGAL DIGITS	0	0	0	0	0	1	1	1	1	1	1	0
	1	0	0	0	1	0	1	1	0	0	0	0
	2	0	0	1	0	1	1	0	1	1	0	1
	3	0	0	1	1	1	1	1	1	0	0	1
	4	0	1	0	0	0	1	1	0	0	1	1
	5	0	1	0	1	1	0	1	1	0	1	1
	6	0	1	1	0	1	0	1	1	1	1	1
	7	0	1	1	1	1	1	1	0	0	0	0
	8	1	0	0	0	1	1	1	1	1	1	1
	9	1	0	0	1	1	1	1	1	0	1	1
ERROR		1	0	1	0	1	0	0	1	1	1	1
		1	0	1	1	1	0	0	1	1	1	1
		1	1	0	0	1	0	0	1	1	1	1
		1	1	0	1	1	0	0	1	1	1	1
		1	1	1	0	1	0	0	1	1	1	1
		1	1	1	1	1	0	0	1	1	1	1

7.14 PARALLEL AND SERIAL ADDERS

In the last section, we obtained a logic circuit for a full adder. The full adder adds three bits fed to it and produces a sum bit and a carry bit. If we want to add two 15-bit integers, we can use 15 full adders and get a 16-bit answer as shown in Figure 7.11. Such an adder is called a *parallel adder*. As this adder uses one full adder per bit to be added, it is expensive. It is, however, very fast.

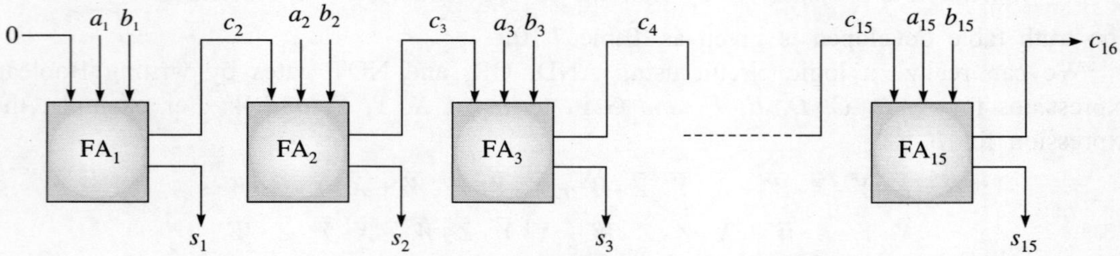

Figure 7.11 A parallel adder to add two 15-bit numbers.

Another method of addition is by using a single full adder and feeding bits to be added one after another to it. Such an adder is called a *serial adder.* A serial adder for 15-bit operands is shown in Figure 7.12. The two operands are stored in two 15-bit shift registers. At time t_1, the two least significant bits are shifted and the full adder adds the two bits. Carry, if any, is stored in the carry flip-flop (see Section 4.4 for a description of a shift register). At time t_2, the two bits a_2 and b_2 of the two operands and the carry bit c_2 (if any) which resulted from adding a_1 and b_1 are shifted to the full adder and added. This sequence is continued, and at interval t_{15} the two bits a_{15} and b_{15} along with carry bit c_{15} are added, producing the sum bit s_{15} and carry bit c_{16}. The sum bits are stored in the sum register. Carry bit c_{16}, if any, will be stored in the carry flip-flop.

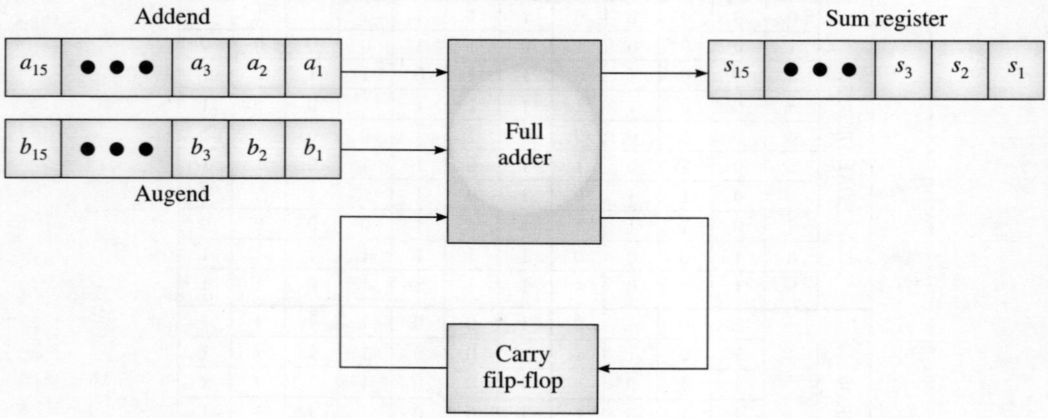

Figure 7.12 A serial adder to add two 15-bit numbers.

7.15 PHYSICAL DEVICES USED TO CONSTRUCT GATES

In Section 4.5.1, we presented a model of a controlled semiconductor switch. We showed how such a switch may be used to construct a storage cell. In this section, we will see how the controlled switch may be used to construct NOT, AND, and OR gates.

For ready reference, we give in Figure 7.13 the model of a controlled switch. If a voltage 0 is applied to point A, the *gate* g opens and the voltage at W equals V as no current will flow from P to Q. If a voltage V is applied at point A, g closes, and consequently, the path PQ closes. The voltage at W becomes 0. The input-output relationship of this device is shown in Table 7.11(a). If we call V a binary 1 and 0 a binary 0, then Table 7.11(b) is obtained. It is clear from this table that the output W is the NOT of A ($W = \overline{A}$). Thus, the controlled switch is a NOT gate.

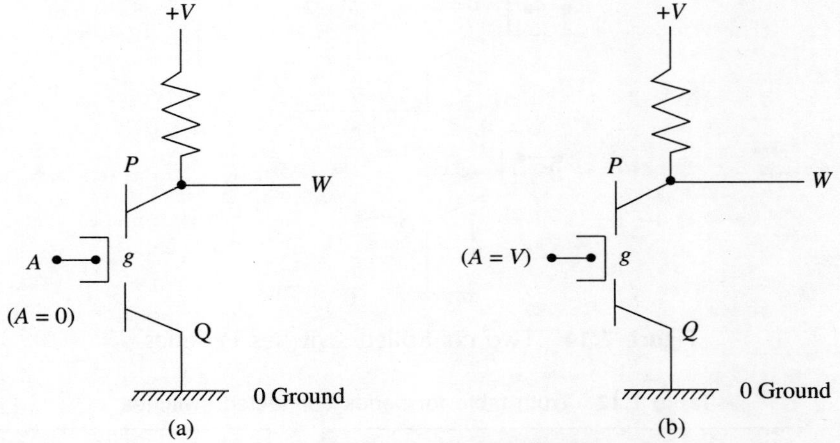

Figure 7.13 A controlled switch.

Table 7.11 Truth table for a controlled switch

A	g	*Path PQ*	W	A	W
0	Open	Open	V	0	1
V	Closed	Closed	0	1	0
				$W = \overline{A}$	
(a)				(b)	

If we connect two controlled switches in series, as shown in Figure 7.14, we obtain Table 7.12(a), which gives the output voltage as a function of the input voltages at A and B. The truth table describing the operation of the switches is given as Table 7.12(b). We see from it that the output W of the gates is given by

$$W = \overline{A \cdot B}$$

This gate is called NAND (NOT of AND) gate. If we connect a NOT gate of Figure 7.13 to the output W, this three-gate circuit will realize the AND operation.

Two controlled switches connected in parallel are shown in Figure 7.15. The operation of this configuration is explained in Table 7.13(a). The truth table corresponding to Table 7.13(a) is given as Table 7.13(b). The output W of this gate is given by

$$W = \overline{A + B}$$

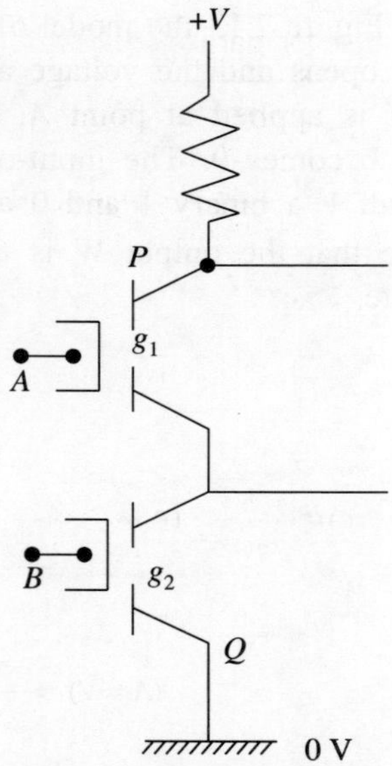

Figure 7.14 Two controlled switches in series.

Table 7.12 Truth table for series connected switches

A	B	g_1	g_2	Path PQ	W
0	0	Open	Open	Open	V
V	0	Closed	Open	Open	V
0	V	Open	Closed	Open	V
V	V	Closed	Closed	Closed	0

(a)

A	B	W	$\bar{W}$
0	0	1	0
1	0	1	0
0	1	1	0
1	1	0	1
$\bar{W} = A \cdot B$ or $W = \overline{A \cdot B}$			

(b)

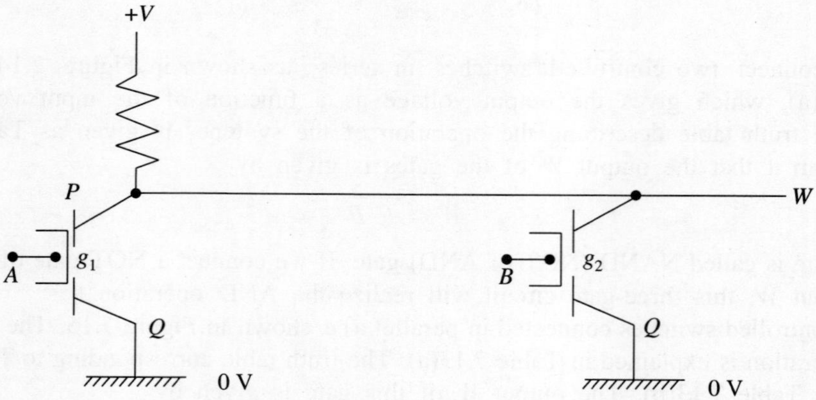

Figure 7.15 Two controlled switches in parallel.

Table 7.13 Truth table for parallel connection of switches

A	B	g_1	g_2	Path PQ	W
0	0	Open	Open	Open	V
0	V	Open	Closed	Closed	0
V	0	Closed	Open	Closed	0
V	V	Closed	Closed	Closed	0

(a)

A	B	W	$\overline{W}$
0	0	1	0
0	1	0	1
1	0	0	1
1	1	0	1

$\overline{W} = A + B$ or $W = \overline{A + B}$

(b)

This gate is called NOR (NOT of OR) gate. If we connect a NOT gate of Figure 7.13 to the output W, this three-gate circuit will realize the OR operation.

It is simple to realize NAND gates with semiconductor devices. It is thus commonly used to design logic circuits. The symbol of a NAND gate is shown in Figure 7.16. It is a 'universal' gate because AND, OR, and NOT operations can all be realized using only the NAND operation. This is given as follows:

NOT realization with NAND

$$\overline{A} = \overline{A \cdot 1} = A \text{ NAND } 1 \text{ (1 is a constant)}$$

AND realization with NAND

$$\overline{\overline{A \cdot B}} = A \cdot B = (A \text{ NAND } B) \text{ NAND } 1$$

OR realization with NAND

$$A + B = \overline{\overline{A} \cdot \overline{B}} \text{ (using De Morgan's Theorem)}$$

$$= (A \text{ NAND } 1) \text{ NAND } (B \text{ NAND } 1)$$

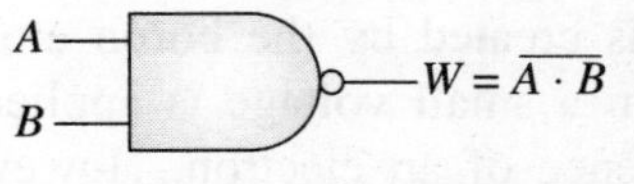

Figure 7.16 A NAND gate.

These realizations are shown in Figure 7.17(a–c), respectively.

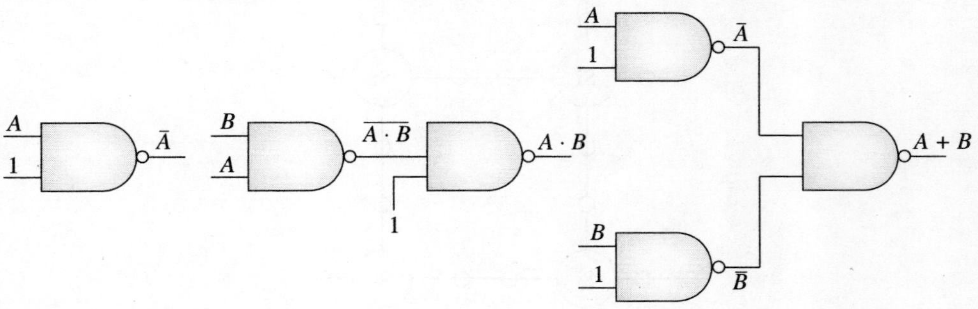

(a) (b) (c)

Figure 7.17 NOT, AND, OR realization with NAND gates.

NOR gates are also universal gates. Several NAND or NOR gates are packaged into an integrated circuit chip and are used to design logic circuits.

7.16 TRANSISTORS

The controlled switch is constructed using an electronic device called a *transistor.* The raw material used in making transistors is *silicon*, a semiconductor. To understand how transistors can be made from silicon, we should first understand the electrical properties of silicon. Metals like copper are good conductors of electricity and they have a large number of free electrons which are free to wander around the material. Insulators such as glass, on the other hand, are poor conductors of electricity as all the electrons in the material are tightly bound to their parent atoms. A large voltage is required to release them from their parents. Semiconductors such as germanium and silicon are neither good conductors nor insulators. They do not have many free electrons but are capable of releasing electrons bound to the atoms with a modest amount of energy.

An atom of silicon has four valence electrons in its outermost shell. In pure silicon crystal, pairs of these electrons are shared with neighbouring atoms so that each atom is surrounded by eight shared electrons in a tight bond. Pure silicon is, therefore, a poor conductor (see Figure 7.18). Semiconductor devices are made by introducing 'minute' amounts of controlled impurity atoms in the crystal (about one in a million atoms). This process is called *doping.* For example, we may dope silicon with phosphorus atoms which have five electrons in their outermost shell. A phosphorous atom can displace a silicon atom in the crystal without disrupting the crystal structure. The extra electron gets detached from its parent in the crystal structure and can be moved around by applying a small voltage. Silicon doped with phosphorous (or any other pentavalent atom) is called an *n-type* semiconductor as it has mobile electrons. If we dope silicon with boron, an element with three electrons in its outermost shell, the resulting crystal structure will have a missing electron in the bonds between neighbours. This deficiency is said to create a *hole.* The hole that is created by the boron atom can also get detached from its parents and become mobile when a small voltage is applied to the material. The hole is not a real particle, but only the absence of an electron. However, a hole can move through the crystal lattice and behave like a positive charge. Silicon doped with boron (or a trivalent atom) is known as a *p-type* semiconductor as it has a mobile positive electric charge.

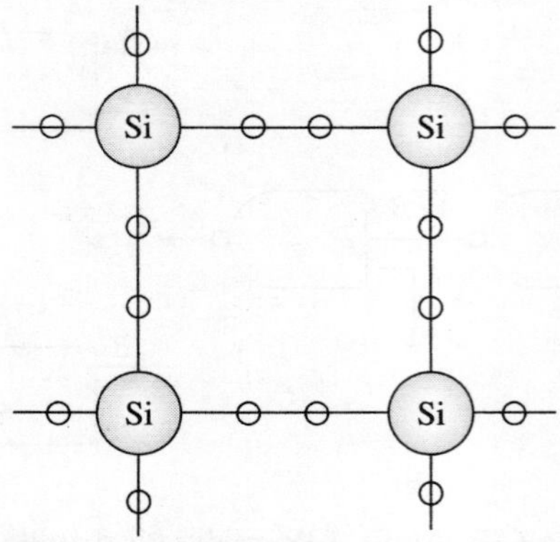

Figure 7.18 Pure silicon crystal.

One type of transistor widely used in digital computers is called Metal–Oxide–Silicon Field Effect Transistor (MOSFET). These terms refer to the three elements employed in its construction. In a typical MOSFET, two areas of *n*-type silicon are embedded on a *p*-type silicon substrate. The two *n*-type areas are connected to metal terminals called the *source* and the *drain*. The surface of the *p*-type substrate is oxidized. The silicon dioxide layer formed on the surface is an insulator and isolates the source and the drain. A layer of metal is deposited on the silicon dioxide layer between the source and the drain. This layer is called the *gate* (see Figure 7.19).

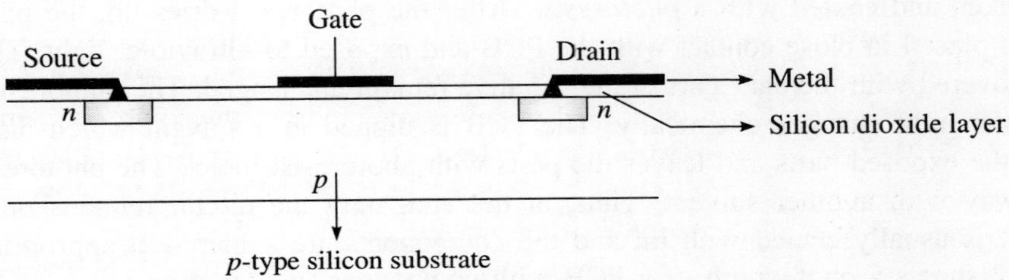

Figure 7.19 A MOSFET.

The transistor is operated by grounding the source and the substrate. A positive voltage is applied to the drain. As the substrate is *p*-type with excess holes (positive charge), no current flows between the substrate and drain. If the gate is grounded, no current can flow from the source to the drain as the intervening layer is *p*-type with excess holes. If a positive voltage is applied to the gate, it repels the holes and attracts the free electrons. Thus, a small layer of electrons forms near the surface. This layer is called an *n*-type channel (Figure 7.20). These electrons are attracted by the positive voltage applied to the drain and thus current flows from the source to the drain. In other words, by applying a positive voltage to the gate, we 'close' the electrical path between the source and the drain. Thus, the MOSFET is a controlled switch.

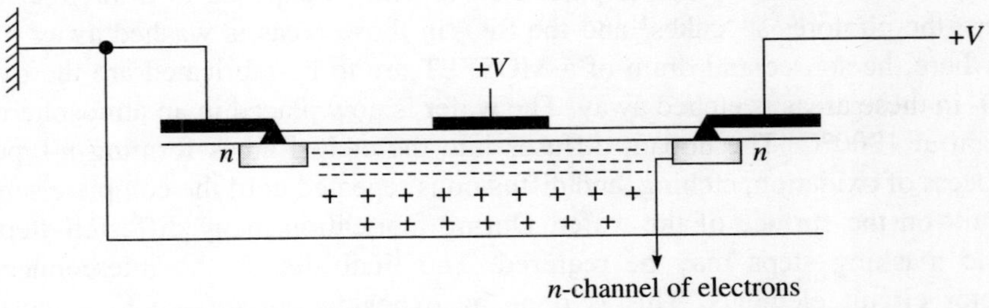

Figure 7.20 Illustration of transistor action.

Dimensions are critical in fabricating MOSFET. The critical dimensions are the thickness of the oxide layer under the gate electrode and the distance separating the source from the drain. The sensitivity of the transistor's response to a gate voltage is inversely related to the thickness of the oxide layer.

7.17 INTEGRATED CIRCUITS

Electronic circuits may be fabricated by using discrete components such as transistors, resistors and capacitors and connecting them with wires. Such circuits are called *discrete circuits.* The invention of Printed Circuit Boards (PCB) represents a major advance in circuit fabrication. To make a PCB, the interconnections among the components are laid out as strips of black lines (see Figure 7.21). This design is photographed and a negative is taken and reduced to a size determined by the size of the PCB. A raw PCB is a sheet of insulator (such as a phenol board or a glass epoxy board) with a thin sheet of copper bonded on one or both of its sides. This board is taken and coated with a *photoresist.* After the photoresist dries up, the photographic negative is placed in close contact with the PCB and exposed to ultraviolet light. The parts of the PCB covered with the dark part of the negative remain unchanged. The photoresist exposed to ultraviolet light changes chemically. The PCB is dipped in a solvent which dissolves the copper in the exposed parts and leaves the parts with photoresist intact. The photoresist is now washed away with another solvent. Thus, at the end, only the circuit remains on the PCB. The circuit is usually coated with tin and the components are soldered at appropriate places. Figure 7.22 shows a photograph of a PCB with components mounted on it.

Integrated circuits are also fabricated using an approach similar to PCB fabrication. The first step is to prepare very pure silicon (impurity less than 1 part in ten million). The silicon is melted in a quartz crucible and the appropriate quantity of dopant (*p* type) is added. A seed crystal is dipped into the molten material and very slowly withdrawn. The molten silicon is drawn into a giant single crystal several centimetres in diameter and more than a metre long. A single crystal is used in order to conform to the model of silicon atoms arranged in layers sharing electrons with four neighbours. The crystal is ground to a truly cylindrical shape. It is then cut with a diamond saw into circular wafers. Integrated circuits (ICs) are built on these wafers. The wafer (about 0.5 mm thick) is ground and polished to a mirror finish.

The *p*-type silicon wafer is next heated to about 1000°C in an atmosphere of oxygen. This oxidizes the surface and a layer of insulating silicon dioxide (SiO_2) is formed. The surface is coated with photoresist and a mask is placed on it. This is exposed to ultraviolet light. In the exposed part, the photoresist 'cakes' and the SiO_2 in those areas is washed away by a solvent. The areas where the source and drain of a MOSFET are to be fabricated are the exposed parts and the SiO_2 in these areas is etched away. The wafer is now placed in an atmosphere containing *n*-type dopant at 1200°C. The dopant diffuses into the etched areas forming *n*-type pockets.

The process of oxidation, etching, and diffusion is repeated until the complete semiconductor circuit is built on the surface of the wafer. During fabrication many diffusion steps and 6–10 photographic masking steps may be required. The final step is the interconnection of the semiconductor circuit elements. This is done by exposing the surface to a metallic vapour such as aluminum. This forms an aluminum layer over the whole surface. This is etched using masking, photoresist coating, and exposure steps, leaving the desired conductor connections intact. Figure 7.23 illustrates the steps for a small section of an IC.

All the above processes are applied to the entire wafer which may contain 100 individual ICs. Each wafer may contain a million transistors. The wafer is now probed and each chip is tested electrically for insulation, etc. The chip is then tested for its functional characteristics using automatic electronic test equipment. Circuits that fail any of the tests are marked with

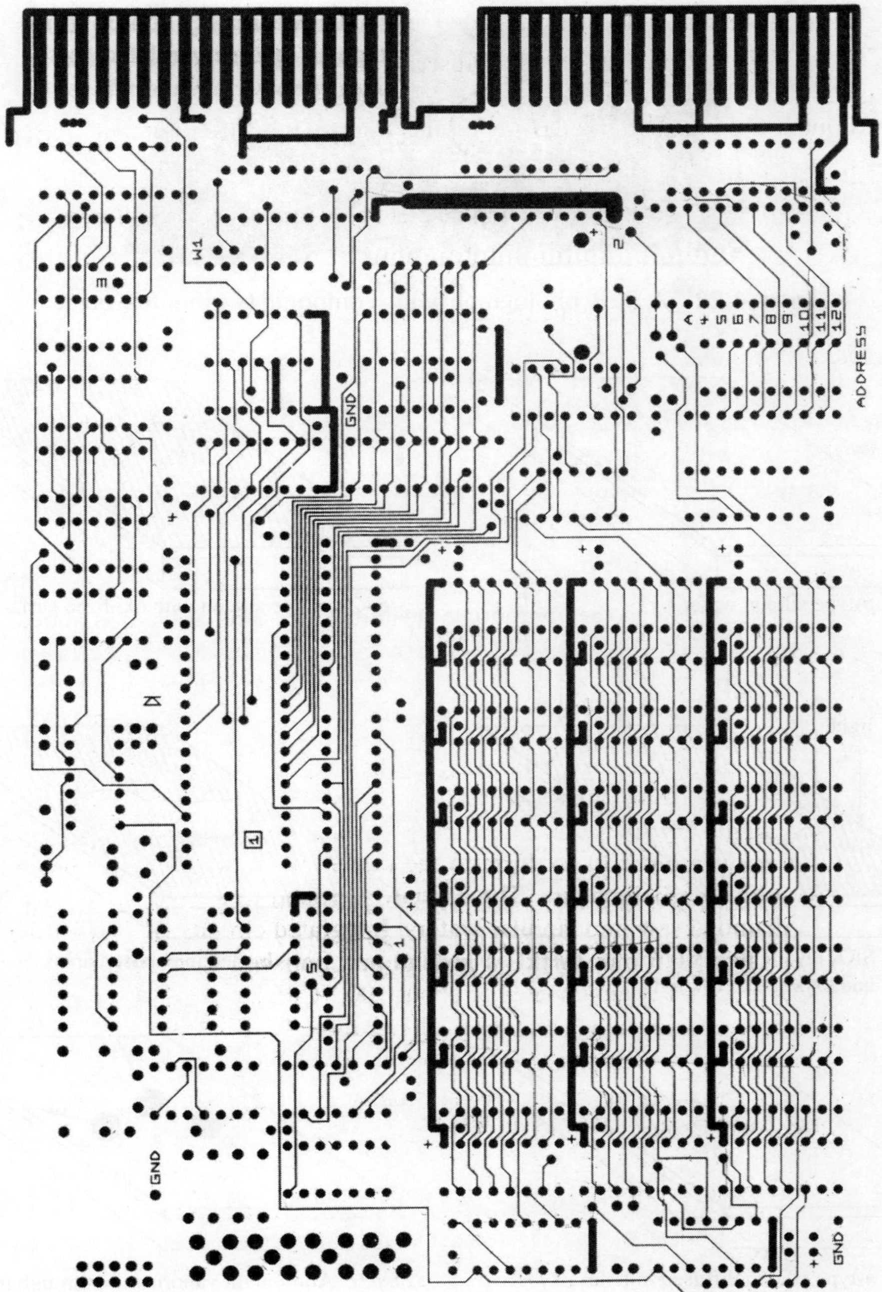

Figure 7.21 Graphics of a portion of a PCB.

Figure 7.22 A PCB photograph with components mounted on it.

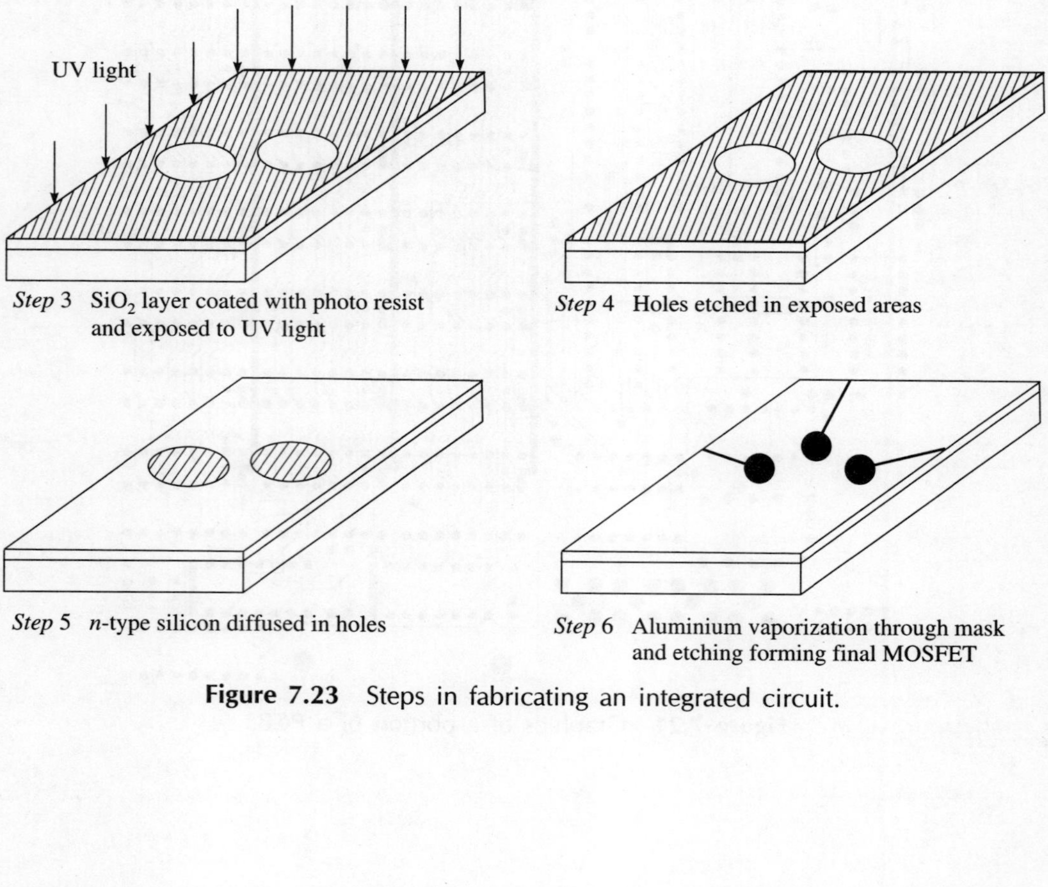

Figure 7.23 Steps in fabricating an integrated circuit.

a spot of ink. Many circuits do fail. As much as 50% may fail but production is automatic and in large quantities low yields are acceptable.

The wafer is scribed with a diamond tool and broken like glass, separating the individual ICs. Each good chip is mounted on a package base and glued down. Connections are made to the external leads in the package by bonding gold wires to the metal 'islands' on the chip boundary. The chip is now encapsulated in a metal, plastic or ceramic can.

The most critical and expensive operation in the fabrication of ICs is the final step in which the leads are connected to the terminals. Thus, the number of terminals for outside connection is kept small. For ICs incorporating 10,000 transistors, the terminals used are only around 30.

ICs are classified as Small-Scale Integrated circuits (SSI), Medium Scale Integrated circuits (MSI), Large-Scale Integrated circuits (LSI), Very Large-Scale Integrated circuits (VLSI) and Ultra Large Integrated circuits (ULSI). The classification is in terms of the number of logic gates in the circuit which in turn determines the complexity of the logical function performed by the IC. An SSI normally has less than 12 gates, an MSI has over 12 and less than 100 gates, an LSI over 100 and less than 10,000 gates, a VLSI has over 10,000 and less than 100,000 gates, and a ULSI has above 100,000 gates in a silicon chip. Currently (2025), microcomputers in a chip with several processors containing billions of gates are being fabricated.

SUMMARY

1. George Boole, a mathematician, developed an algebra known as Boolean algebra. This algebra deals with propositions which are either *true* or *false*. The operators in this algebra are *AND*, *OR*, and *NOT*. These operators are used to combine propositions.
2. Shannon discovered that Boolean algebra can be used to design switching circuits. As computer circuits also use a combination of switches that can be in one of two states, *open* or *closed*, Boolean algebra is useful in designing these circuits.
3. A set of axioms or postulates is first stated in Boolean algebra. These postulates define the valid symbols in this algebra, which are 0 and 1. The valid operators which operate on these two symbols are next defined. These are the AND, OR and NOT operators. The symbols ·, + and – (overbar) are used to represent these operators (Table 7.3).
4. Boolean variables connected with Boolean operators form Boolean expressions. A set of theorems is derived using postulates of Boolean algebra. These are useful for manipulating Boolean expressions (Table 7.5 summarizes the theorems).
5. In order to design a logic circuit, we first list all the *inputs* or independent variables. We then make a table whose rows are all possible combinations of values of input variables. As each input variable can have only one out of two values (0 or 1), the number of distinct combinations of n variables is 2^n. Thus, if there are three independent variables, there will be eight rows in this table. For each input combination, the appropriate values of the dependent or output variables are entered in the table. Such a table is called a *truth table*.
6. Given a truth table, it is possible to obtain closed-form Boolean expressions that relate the output variables to the input variables.

7. Examples of truth tables to describe a full adder and a display decoder are given in Section 7.12.
8. Boolean expressions corresponding to truth tables may be implemented as logic circuits using AND, OR, and NOT gates.
9. Truth Tables may also be implemented using read only memories (ROM). In this implementation, the independent variables in the truth table are the addresses in a ROM. The output bits are stored in the ROM in the corresponding addresses.
10. Controlled semiconductor switches may be used to realize AND, OR, and NOT operations. Thus, these switches may be used to construct logic circuits in processors.
11. NAND (NOT of AND) gate and NOR (NOT of OR) gate are called universal gates as AND, OR, and NOT gates may be realized using them. They are also easy to fabricate as integrated circuits.
12. A commonly used controlled switch is a transistor which is fabricated using silicon. One useful component is the Metal–Oxide–Silicon Field Effect Transistor (MOSFET) used as a switch.
13. A MOSFET consists of a *p*-type silicon substrate on which a source and drain of *n*-type silicon are diffused. The surface of the *p*-type substrate is oxidized, forming an insulator. Over this a metal strip is fabricated between the source and the drain, forming a gate. A small voltage applied to the gate creates an electrical path between the source and the drain (Figures 7.19 and 7.20).
14. An integrated circuit is fabricated on a chip of doped silicon using processes of oxidation, coating with photoresist chemicals, etching, diffusion, metal vaporization, gold bonding of leads, and finally encapsulation.
15. Integrated circuits may be classified as SSI, MSI, LSI, VLSI, and ULSI depending on the number of gates in the chip and the complexity of the logical function performed by it.

REVIEW QUESTIONS

7.1 Why is Boolean algebra relevant in the design of logic circuits of computers?

7.2 State the postulates of Boolean algebra.

7.3 Realize the following Boolean expressions using switches:
(i) $L = A + B \cdot C$
(ii) $M = A \cdot D + B \cdot D + A \cdot C$

7.4 Obtain truth tables for L and M defined in Question 7.3.

7.5 Show that

$$X \cdot Y + X \cdot Z + X \cdot Y \cdot Z = X \cdot Y + X \cdot Z$$

by method of perfect induction.

7.6 Show that $(A + B) \cdot (A + C) = A + B \cdot C$.

7.7 Prove De Morgan's laws for three variables.

7.8 Using theorems of Boolean algebra, prove the following:

(i) $X \cdot Y + X \cdot Z + Y \cdot Z = X \cdot Y + \overline{X} \cdot Y \cdot Z + X \cdot Z$

(ii) $(X \cdot Y) \cdot (\overline{X} \cdot \overline{Z} + Z) \cdot (X \cdot \overline{Z + Y}) = 0$

(iii) $X \cdot \overline{Y} + Y \cdot \overline{Z} + \overline{X} \cdot \overline{Z} = X \cdot \overline{Y} \cdot Z + \overline{Y} \cdot \overline{Z} + Y \cdot \overline{Z} = X \cdot \overline{Y} + \overline{Z}$

7.9 Obtain the truth table for the exclusive OR *(XOR)* operation described by the equation A *XOR* B = $\mathrm{A} \cdot \overline{\mathrm{B}} + \overline{\mathrm{A}} \cdot \mathrm{B}$.

7.10 Prove that (A *XOR* B) *XOR* C = A *XOR* (B *XOR* C).

7.11 Obtain a truth table to design a 3-bit subtractor. The input bits are the subtrahend, minuend and borrow. The output bits are the difference and borrow to next bit. Obtain Boolean expressions for the truth table.

7.12 Realize the 3-bit subtractor using AND, OR, NOT gates.

7.13 Realize the 3-bit subtractor using a ROM.

7.14 Design a logic circuit to multiply two positive numbers, each 2-bit long.

7.15 A comparator is a circuit which compares two numbers *A* and *B* and gives an output 1 if $A \geq B$. Assume *A* and *B* are two-bit positive numbers. Obtain a logic circuit for the comparator. Use NAND gates for realization.

7.16 Design a logic circuit to generate an odd parity bit for hexadecimal digits. Use NOR gates for realization.

7.17 What element is used to fabricate a transistor?

7.18 What is the difference between a conductor, a semiconductor and an insulator?

7.19 What is an *n*-type silicon? What is a *p*-type silicon?

7.20 What do you understand by the acronym MOSFET?

7.21 What is the purpose of gate in MOSFET?

7.22 How is MOSFET useful as a controlled switch?

7.23 What dimensions are critical in MOSFET fabrication?

7.24 Define a discrete circuit.

7.25 What is a PCB?

7.26 Explain how PCB is fabricated.

7.27 Describe the steps followed in fabricating ICs.

7.28 Why is the circuit called IC?

7.29 What are the most critical operations in IC fabrication?

7.30 Differentiate between SSI, MSI, LSI and VLSI.

8 Computer Architecture

LEARNING GOALS

After reading this chapter, you should be able to:

- Describe how the main units of a computer, namely, the processor, the memory, and the I/O units are interconnected.
- Describe how data is read from the I/O units to the main memory and written from the main memory to the I/O units.
- Explain the hardware and software methods used to alleviate the speed mismatch between the processor and the main memory and between the main memory and the I/O units.
- Describe the types of buses used to connect fast and slow I/O units to PCs.
- Describe how recent computers use a General-Purpose Graphics processor to accelerate computing speed.

In previous chapters, we described how the main units of a computer work. In this chapter, we will discuss how these units are interconnected physically and how their functioning is coordinated by appropriate communication among them.

The main difficulty in coordinating the functioning of the units of a computer is the inherent *speed mismatch* between the units. For example, a processor can process a byte in about 0.5 ns, whereas it takes about 15 ns to fetch a byte from the main (DRAM) memory. The processor will be forced to wait for data and unable to work at full speed. The speed mismatch between the main memory and the I/O units is much worse. A fast hard disk reader could read a sector in a few microseconds after a delay of about 5ms for positioning the read head on the desired sector. A Solid-State Disk is much faster—around 5 microseconds to access a byte. Observe that the main memory is about 30 times slower than the processor and I/O units are 1000 times slower than the main memory. The consequences of this speed mismatch can be appreciated by the following analogy. Assume an officer is the "processor", the in-tray on his desk the "main memory" and a filing cabinet in his assistant's office is the "I/O unit", for example, a disk. Assume the officer takes 10 minutes to process a file. As the main memory is 30 times slower than the processor, it will take 10 × 30 = 300 minutes for the officer to fetch the file from the in-tray. As the I/O unit is 1000 times slower than the main memory it will take 1000 × 100 = 100,000 minutes for the assistant to fetch the file from the filing cabinet and put it in the in-tray. Thus for a file that takes 10 minutes to process, the time to fetch it is 300 + 100,000 minutes which is nearly 69 days! This is unacceptable.

Another complication that arises when connecting I/O units to a computer is due to the variety of I/O units used by computers. The speed of manual input from terminals would be at around 1 byte per second, whereas the speed of input from a disk would be at around 1 byte per microsecond. A manual input sends 1 byte at a time, whereas a disk would send a stream of around 500 bytes. Thus, the I/O unit–memory–processor coordination is quite complicated.

One may reduce the speed mismatch problem through system solutions. An important idea is that of buffering. Buffer storage is introduced between the units of a computer to increase the overall system speed and to ease coordination. Ideally one would like each unit to work at its full potential speed and all the units to work simultaneously. This ideal cannot be achieved by hardware only. A software-hardware system solution is needed.

8.1 INTERCONNECTION OF UNITS

We saw in Chapter 4 that the main memory of a computer stores a set of addressed words. Words are retrieved from the main memory by specifying their address. As all data to be processed by a computer are stored in the main memory, the characteristics of the interconnection paths are determined by the main memory. To achieve reasonable speed, all the bits of a word stored in the main memory are transmitted simultaneously. *A set of wires that carries a group of bits simultaneously, that is, in parallel, and has an associated control scheme is known as a bus.* A bus that carries a word to or from the main memory is known as a *data bus.* Its width will equal the word length (in bits) of the main memory. To retrieve a word from the main memory, it is necessary to specify its address. The address is carried by a Memory Address Bus (MAB) whose width equals the number of bits in the MAR of the memory. Thus, if a computer's main memory stores 1G, 32-bit words, the data bus will be 32 bits wide and the address bus 30 bits wide. Besides buses to carry address and data, we also need control signals between the units of a computer. For instance, control signals issued by the processor to the main memory to READ or to WRITE and to the I/O units to START or to STOP are carried by a *control bus.* A *system bus* will thus consist of a data bus, a memory address bus, and a control bus. Figure 8.1 shows the processor–memory interconnection.

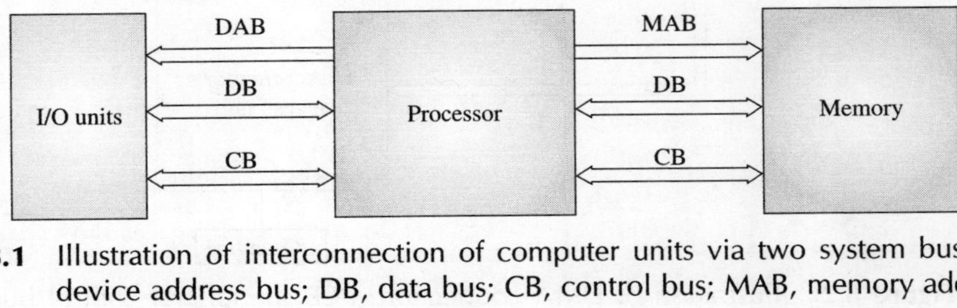

Figure 8.1 Illustration of interconnection of computer units via two system buses. DAB, device address bus; DB, data bus; CB, control bus; MAB, memory address bus.

One method of connecting I/O units to a computer is to connect them to the processor via buses. Usually, three buses are used (see Figure 8.1). These are a data address bus (labelled DAB in Figure 8.1) that specifies the addresses of the I/O units to be accessed by the processor, a Data Bus (DB) that carries a word from the addressed input unit to the processor or carries a word from the processor to the addressed output unit and a Control Bus (CB) that carries commands, such as READ, WRITE, START, SEEK and STOP from the processor to the I/O units. It also conveys the I/O units' status information to the processor. The I/O to processor system bus will thus consist of the I/O device address lines, data lines, and control lines. This interconnection method will require the processor to completely supervise and participate in transferring data from and to I/O units. All data to be input will be taken to a processor register from the input unit and from there to the main memory. Similarly, all data to be output will be taken from a processor register to the specified output unit. Such data transfer to and from the processor to the I/O units is known as *program-controlled data transfer*.

The interconnection of the I/O units, the processor, and the main memory using two independent system buses is known as a *two-bus* interconnection structure.

As pointed out in the previous paragraph, this interconnection structure requires the processor to share its resources during I/O transfer. As I/O units are much slower than the processor, this interconnection method is undesirable. Thus, another interconnection method that minimizes the participation of the processor in I/O transfer is often used. This is also a two-bus structure. One bus connects the processor to the main memory. The other bus, instead of connecting the I/O units to the processor, connects them directly to the main memory. In this structure, the I/O devices are connected to a special interface logic unit known as the *Direct Memory Access* logic (DMA) unit. The processor issues a READ or WRITE command to the DMA logic unit giving it the device address, the address in memory where data read from the input unit is to be stored (or from where data is to be taken to output), and the number of data words to be transferred. This command is accepted by the DMA (Direct Memory Access) unit which now transfers the data. This interconnection structure is shown in Figure 8.2.

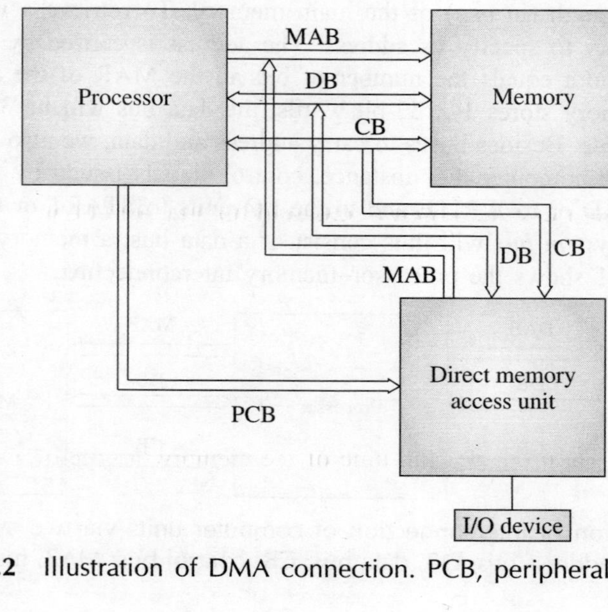

Figure 8.2 Illustration of DMA connection. PCB, peripheral control bus.

Another popular method of interconnecting units (mostly used in early Personal Computers) is by a single bus as shown in Figure 8.3. This is called a *unibus* system. In this case, the bus is shared by three units, namely, the I/O unit, the main memory, and the processor. Data can be transferred only between any two of the three units at a time. If the processor and an I/O unit want to use the bus simultaneously, only one can be granted the bus. This decision is made by a circuit known as a *bus arbitration unit*.

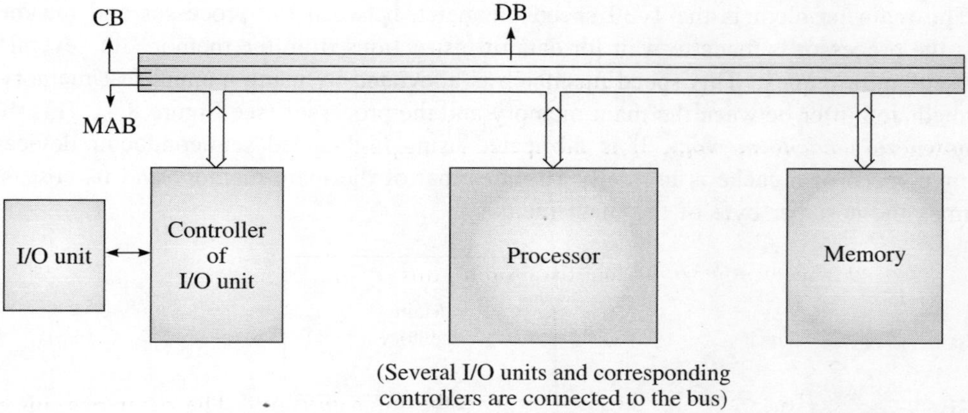

Figure 8.3 A UNIBUS connection of units.

Generally, I/O units are given preference over the processor. This is because I/O units (such as a disk) have moving parts that cannot be stopped suddenly and if the bus is not granted, data may be lost. The main advantage of a single bus system is the ease of addressing I/O units. These units use the same memory address space. This simplifies the programming of I/O units as no special I/O instructions are needed. A READ instruction with an address corresponding to an input device will read data from that device. Besides this advantage, it is easy to add new devices as no new instructions specific to the device would be required.

This single bus is called the *PC system bus* or ISA (Industry Standard Architecture) *bus*. This was sufficient for early slow PCs but has now been superseded. We will discuss this later in this chapter.

8.2 PROCESSOR TO MEMORY COMMUNICATION

The following sequence of events takes place when data is to be moved from the memory to the processor:

Step 1: The processor places in the MAR, the address of the data to be moved.

Step 2: The processor issues a READ command to the memory via the control bus.

Step 3: The memory places the retrieved data in MDR and transfers it via the data bus to the processor. Based on the read time of the memory, a specific number of processor clock intervals are allotted for the completion of this operation. During this period, the processor is forced to wait.

For writing in memory, the steps are similar.

Step 1: The processor places in MAR, the address where data is to be written.

Step 2: The processor transmits the data to be written in the memory via the data bus to MDR.

Step 3: The processor issues a WRITE command to the memory via the control bus.

Step 4: The data in MDR is written in the memory at the address specified in MAR.

The main problem is the 1–30 speed mismatch between the processor and the memory. Thus, the processor is made to wait for data or instructions from the memory for several cycles after sending a request. This speed mismatch is alleviated by using a small fast memory as an intermediate buffer between the main memory and the processor (see Figure 8.4). This memory is known as a *cache memory*. It is fabricated using high-speed semiconductor devices. The effective speed of a cache is normally 10 times that of the main memory and its cost is about 10 times the cost per byte of the main memory.

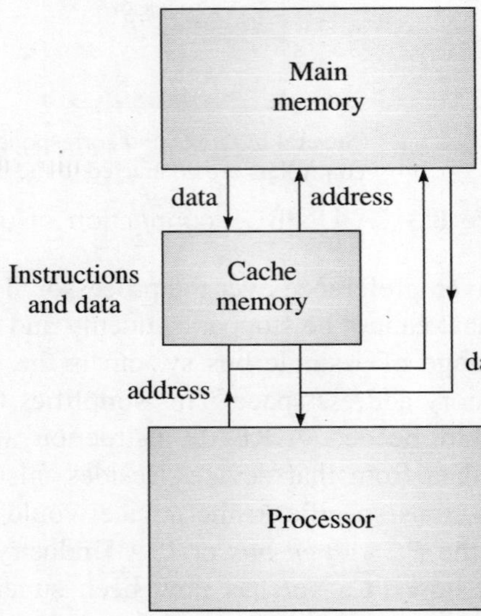

Figure 8.4 Illustration of use of a cache memory.

Most programs execute instructions in the order in which they are written. This is called *spatial locality* of reference to the main memory by instructions in a program. We also find *temporal locality* in programs. In other words, if an instruction is executed, there is a high probability that the same instruction will be executed again very soon. This is true as most programs have several *while* and *for* loops and the instructions in a loop are executed repeatedly. The locality of reference to instructions is upset when branch instructions are encountered. Branch instructions, however, do not occur frequently in well-written programs. Locality of reference to locations in the memory is valid not only for instructions in a program but also for data read by a program (e.g., arrays, records in a file, etc.).

Locality of reference to locations in memory is the main characteristic that makes using a cache memory effective in alleviating the speed mismatch between the main memory and the processor. Many computers are designed with two cache memories: one of them is called an *instruction cache* and the other a *data cache.* They are normally of equal size and small compared to the main memory. Currently, they are around 64MB, whereas main memory sizes are around 16 GB.

A block of instructions is copied into the instruction cache from the main memory. A block of data to be processed by these instructions is copied into the data cache. The processor fetches instructions and data from the respective caches. Thus, fetch time is considerably reduced. When instructions in the caches are exhausted, the next block of instructions/data is copied into these caches from the main memory. This is done automatically by the hardware without any programmer's intervention. If at any time, a jump instruction is encountered by a program and the required instruction is not in the cache, the program fetches the instruction from the main memory. The probability of this occurring is not very high. It is found, in practice, that more than 90% of the time, the instruction and the data needed to execute a program would be available in the caches. Thus, the effective memory speed is increased.

The block of instructions/data fetched from the main memory for storage in the cache is known as *the cache line*. It is normally of the order of 16–64 bytes. With improving technology, it has become feasible to incorporate a small fast memory in the CPU chip itself. Thus, most computers nowadays have a three-level hierarchy of caches. The first two level caches are fabricated as a part of the CPU chip. This is called on-chip caches or *L1 and L2 caches.* The time to access a byte from the L1 cache is normally 3 to 4 CPU clock cycles (less than a nanosecond). L2 caches are larger but slower. As the area of the CPU chip is limited, the sizes of the L1 and L2 caches are small. L1 size is around 256 KB and L2 size is around 2 MB. There are two L1 caches, namely, an *instruction cache* and *a data cache,* of equal size.

The third level cache is outside the CPU chip. This is called *L3 cache*. It uses SRAM which is faster than DRAM used to fabricate the main memory. The access time of the L3 cache is larger than that of the L2 cache. The size of the L3 cache is of the order of 2 MB to 64 MB and the access time is a few nanoseconds. There are normally two L3 caches: one for data and the other for instructions. Blocks of around 64 bytes are brought to the L3 cache from the main memory and from there to the L2 cache. Observe that the L3 cache can be filled while the CPU processes data from the L2 cache.

8.3 I/O DEVICES TO PROCESSOR COMMUNICATION

We learned in Section 8.1 that one way of connecting I/O units (or devices) to a computer is to connect them to the processor using a device address bus, a data bus, and a control bus. Each I/O device in a computer has a *controller* which controls the operation of the device. For example, a disk controller controls the movement of the reading head, positioning of the head, and detection of errors. The controller is connected to the buses via an *interface logic* unit. The interface logic decodes the control commands received from the processor and sends them to the controller. It also buffers the data flow from the device to the processor and vice versa. Figure 8.5 illustrates the details of one interface unit. With this connection of an I/O device to the processor, data from the I/O device is transmitted to the memory through a register in the processor. The sequence of steps followed to transmit data is given below:

Step 1: The processor sends the address of the I/O device from which data is to be read via the device address bus to the device interface and issues a READ command.

Step 2: The device interface logic acknowledges the signal and turns on a 'device busy' flip-flop. No further requests are entertained by the device as long as the busy flip-flop is set.

Step 3: The I/O device reads the data and places it in the data register of the interface. It also sets the data ready flip-flop.

Step 4: The processor continually interrogates the data-ready flip-flop and waits until this flip-flop is set.

Step 5: When the data ready flip-flop is set, the processor reads the data from the interface data register and places it in the appropriate processor register. It sends data received acknowledgment signal to the device interface and resets the device busy flip-flop.

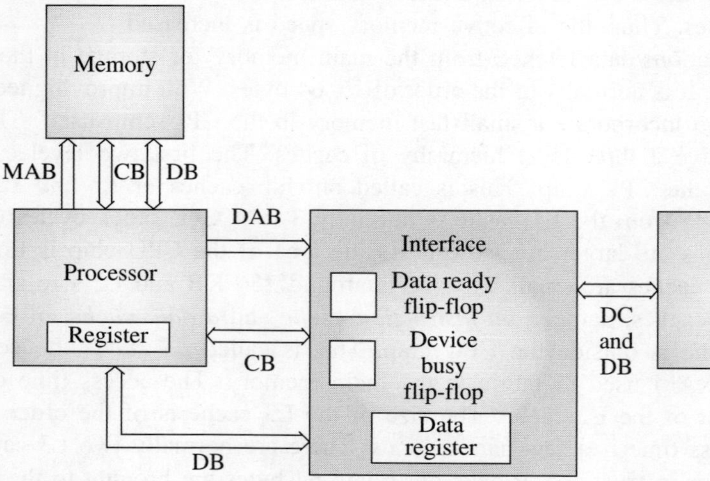

Figure 8.5 Details of processor to I/O communication. MAB, memory address bus; DB, data bus; DAB, device address bus; CB, control bus; DC, device control.

This method of data transfer is called *program-controlled data transfer*. This method forces the processor to wait till the device can read the data and is thus very inefficient as I/O devices are normally 1000 times slower than the processor.

There is another method of data transfer from I/O devices to the processor which is more efficient. In this method, a programmer estimates the time required to read the data from a specified device. The READ command is issued many steps before the data is needed in computation. The processor must have a sufficient number of instructions to be carried out while the interface fills up the data buffer. When the interface buffer is full and is ready to send the data to the processor, the interface sends a signal to the processor informing it that the data is ready. This signal is known as an *interrupt signal*. When the processor receives the interrupt signal, it knows that the data it had asked for is ready. The processor suspends its current job and transfers the data from the interface data register to its register. This method of reading data is called *program-controlled interrupt data transfer*.

The main disadvantage of this method is the need for the processor to suspend and later resume the work it was doing when it was interrupted. If there are many devices in a system for reading and writing, then each device can initiate an interrupt independent of the other. The processor should be able to distinguish among them and attend to each request based on some priority rules. Besides this, a programmer must have a good estimate of the time needed for reading and processing data to avoid keeping the processor idle when the required data is not ready.

We saw in Section 8.1 that a computer's I/O devices may have a direct data path to the memory. If such a connection exists, another data transfer method will be appropriate. This method uses the logic in the direct memory access interface (DMA interface) and eliminates the participation of the processor in data transfer.

The configuration of the computer system with this interconnection structure is shown in Figure 8.6. The DMA interface, in addition to a data buffer register, DMA busy flip-flop, and data ready flip-flop, has a memory address register which gives the location in the main memory where the data is to be stored. If several words are to be transferred from the device to the memory, a count of these words is also stored in a counter in the DMA.

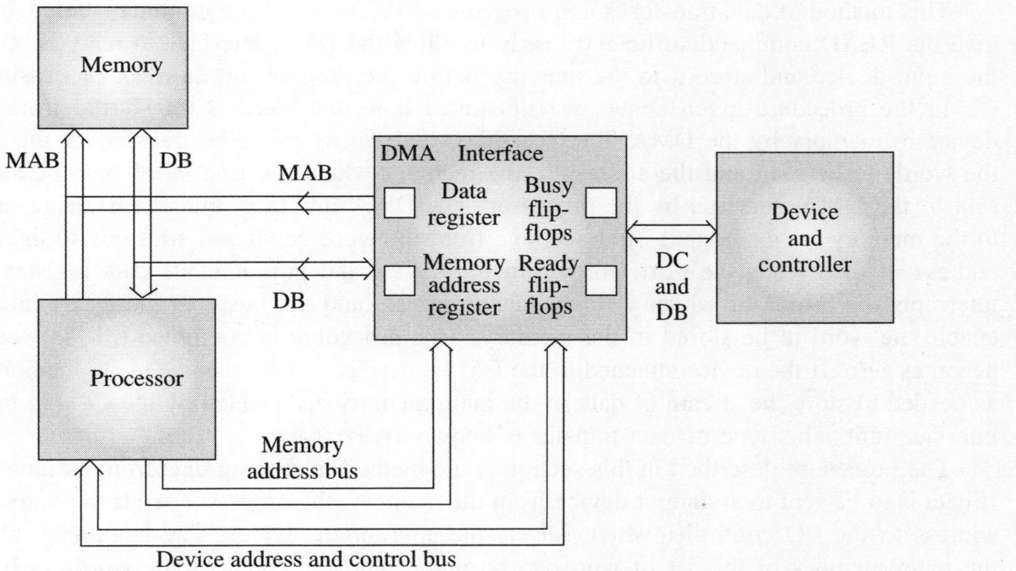

Figure 8.6 Details of direct data transfer from an input device to the memory.

The procedure used to transfer data from an I/O device to the memory using a DMA is as follows:

Step 1: When a READ instruction is encountered by the processor, it sends the device address via the I/O device address bus. This is decoded by the I/O controller, and the DMA interface of the appropriate device is selected. The processor also sends the address in the main memory where the data is to be stored and requests that the data be read.

Step 2: The processor continues with the next instruction in the program. It has no further direct role in data transfer.

Step 3: The DMA unit sets a busy flip-flop, reads the data from the device, and puts it in its data register.

Step 4: When the data has been entered in the data register in the DMA unit, the data-ready flip-flop in the DMA unit is set and an interrupt signal is sent to the processor.

Step 5: The processor completes the instruction it is currently executing. It then yields the memory address and data buses to the DMA interface for one memory cycle. The DMA transfers the data in its data register to the address in the main memory specified in its address register.

This procedure where a memory cycle is taken by the DMA interface unit from the processor to enable it to transfer data to the memory is known as *cycle stealing*. Observe that this entire data transfer procedure is hidden from the programmer and is done by hardware. In other words, the programmer does not need to program this data transfer process. In computer literature, such hardware procedures that are hidden from programmers and *not visible* to them are known as *transparent* to programmers. While the term, 'transparent' may not be the most intuitive choice it is universally used in computer jargon.

This method of data transfer is *non-program-controlled.* The programmer, should, however, give the READ command sufficiently early to allow the DMA interface to read the data from the input device and store it in the memory before the program needs it for processing.

In the procedure given above, we illustrated how one word is transferred from the I/O device to memory by the DMA interface. If several words are to be transferred, the count of the words to be read and the address in the memory where the first word is to be stored are sent to the DMA interface by the processor. The DMA interface, after transferring one word to the memory (as explained), subtracts one from the word count and adds one to the memory address. It then reads the next word from the device and puts it in its data register. It then interrupts the processor which yields a memory cycle and the buses to the DMA interface to enable the word to be stored in the memory. This procedure is continued till the word count becomes zero. If the device attached to the DMA interface is fast, then as many memory cycles as needed to store the stream of data in the main memory are yielded by the CPU to the DMA interface unit. This type of data transfer is known as *burst mode.*

The procedure described in this section is the method of reading data from an input device. If data is to be sent to an output device from the memory, the processor sends the output device address to the I/O controller which selects the appropriate device. The beginning address in the main memory of the set of words to be output and the count of the words to be output are sent to the DMA interface. The DMA interface reads the first word from the memory by cycle stealing and sends it to the device. After the device writes the data, DMA reduces the word count by one, adds one to the memory address, and reads the next word from the memory in a memory cycle stolen from the processor. This continues until all the words are written. Observe that in this case also, the processor proceeds with its work after giving a WRITE command, and the DMA interface writes the data on the specified output device without the direct participation of the processor. The processor's time is not wasted.

To summarize, observe that data transfer from or to I/O devices is faster and more convenient when a DMA interface is used compared to program-controlled data transfer via a processor register. The processor's valuable time is not wasted in DMA transfer. This advantage is gained by providing extra hardware, namely, a DMA interface unit and additional buses. The new buses are the data and the address bus which connect the DMA interface with the memory and the address bus which connects the processor to the DMA interface.

At this stage, you may wonder why the Memory Address Bus and Data Bus are shared by the DMA interface and the processor which forces the processor to yield these buses whenever data is to be transmitted via DMA to the memory. Why should one not provide two separate sets of buses to the memory, one set to the processor and the other set to the DMA, so that the two can work independently? The reason is cost. Fabricating a memory with two independent buses is expensive as logic circuits have to be added to the memory to resolve contention if data sent on the two buses try to write in the same location in the memory. As I/O is slow, the number of times the processor has to yield the buses to the DMA interface maybe once in 100 memory cycles, which will not slow down the processor. Thus, it is not cost-effective to provide two independent sets of buses to the main memory.

8.4 INTERRUPT STRUCTURES

In the previous section, we introduced the idea of sending/receiving data from I/O devices to the memory by program-controlled interrupt transfer. We will expand on this concept in the current section.

An interrupt signal is sent by an I/O interface to a processor when the I/O is ready to send or receive data to or from the main memory. The processor completes the instruction it is processing and acknowledges the interrupt signal. It then stores the information needed to resume the program it was executing and jumps to another program called an *interrupt service routine* to cater to the I/O read/write request.

The interrupt servicing may be compared to what a homemaker does when she is interrupted by the telephone ringing while boiling milk in the kitchen. She turns off the flame, closes the pan with a lid, and rushes to pick up the phone. After attending to the call, she returns to the kitchen, removes the lid from the pan, and turns on the flame to resume what she was doing.

An interrupt servicing procedure consists of the following steps:

Step 1: An interrupt signal is received by the processor.

Step 2: The processor completes the present instruction being executed.

Step 3: The processor stores the content of the program counter and other registers in the processor in a reserved area in the memory. This information is required to enable the processor to resume the program it was executing. It suspends the current program it is executing.

Step 4: The processor sends an interrupt acknowledge signal to the interrupting I/O interface and jumps to another program already stored in the memory to service the interrupt.

Step 5: The interrupt servicing program carries out the required data transfer from or to the specified I/O device. The last instruction in the interrupt servicing program restores the contents of all the processor registers including the program counter which was stored in the memory by the suspended program.

Step 6: The suspended program is resumed.

In practice, a processor should handle a variety of interrupts from many I/O devices. The order of importance or priority of these interrupts will differ. Besides interrupts to transfer data from or to devices, other interrupts are also generated in a computer. An example is the occurrence of an emergency condition such as a power failure. When a sensor detects an impending power failure, it sends an interrupt signal to the processor. The processor initiates a power failure service routine which stores the content of all important registers in the memory so that the program may be resumed when the power is restored. Interrupts caused by events outside the processor such as those from I/O devices, power failure, low voltage, etc. are called *external interrupts*.

There is another class of interrupts known as *internal interrupts* or *traps* which occurs when there is a mistake in a user's program. Common mistakes that lead to traps are attempts to divide by zero, accumulator overflow or underflow, and an illegal operation code. When such an error is detected by the processor, it interrupts a user's program and branches to a trap routine which usually prints out the value of the program counter and other registers when the trap occurred along with a message giving the possible reason for the trap. The processor may continue executing the program if the error is not serious. If the mistake is serious and continuing the program is meaningless, then the program is aborted.

Another type of internal interrupt is caused if the hardware of a computer develops a fault. When the error-detecting circuitry detects a fault, the processor is informed of the location and nature of the fault. The processor then jumps to a fault servicing routine which determines if it is a correctable fault (such as when error correcting codes are used), carries out the correction, and resumes the user's program. If it is a non-correctable fault, the operation is stopped after printing an appropriate message.

Interrupts are also generated by the real-time hardware clock in a computer. Such a clock regulates the allocation of processor time to users. Such interrupts are necessary to ration out time to users and to throw out programs stuck in endless loops.

Internal interrupts are usually given high priority and resolved before attending to external interrupts.

Multiple external interrupts from I/O devices may be handled in several ways. In the simplest method, when an interrupt occurs, an interrupt servicing routine interrogates each I/O interface in turn, normally starting with the device that has the highest priority. After finding out which device interrupted it, it jumps to the I/O device handling program appropriate to that device. This method is called *programmed device polling.* While a device handling program is being run, the interrupt line is disabled so that during this time no further interruptions can take place. This solution is a software solution. It is inexpensive but slow.

The most sophisticated method uses special hardware. In this method, the processor has an interrupt register which has one bit corresponding to each source that can interrupt the processor. Each interrupting source sets its *private* bit in this register. In Figure 8.7, we illustrate such a register for four sources. The processor has a register called an *interrupt masking register* which has one bit corresponding to each interrupting source. The bits in this register may be set by a programmer. When an interrupt is received, the bit corresponding to the interrupting source is set to 1. If a particular interrupt i is to be ignored, the corresponding bit in the mask register is set to 0 by the programmer (see Figure 8.7). The corresponding bits of the interrupt register and the mask register are ANDed, resulting in bits $M1$, $M2$, $M3$, and $M4$. If more than one

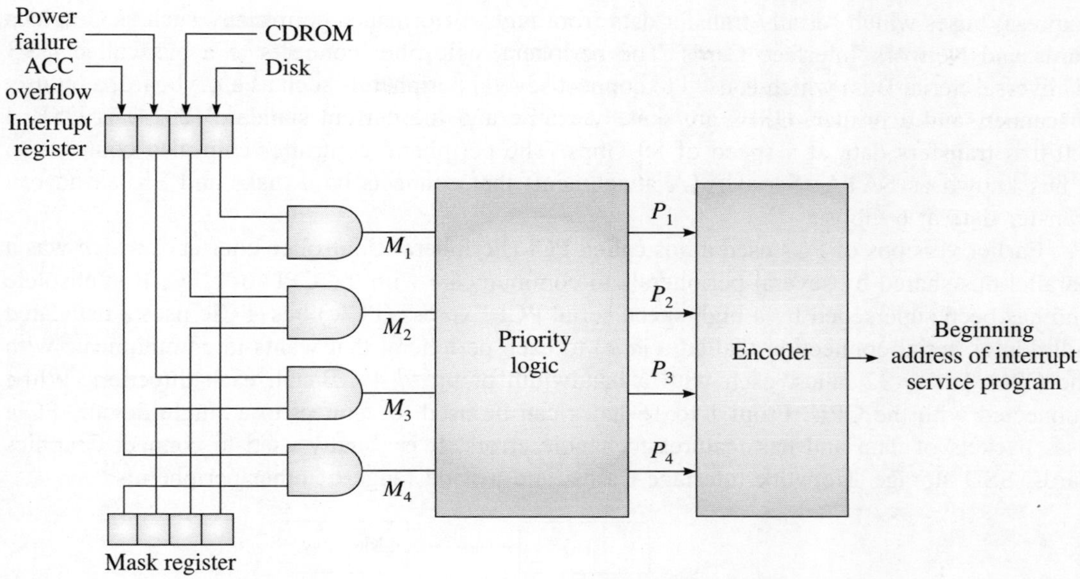

Figure 8.7 Priority interrupt logic.

an interrupt is set and admitted by the mask register, a priority logic circuit enables only the highest priority interrupt line. These lines $P1$, $P2$, $P3$, and $P4$ are fed to an encoder which gives the beginning address of the interrupt servicing program of the interrupting device.

8.5 BUS ARCHITECTURE OF PERSONAL COMPUTERS

So far, we have presented the major ideas used in managing the communication between I/O devices and the processor and between the processor and the main memory. We will now see how these ideas are used in a Personal Computer.

Physically a PC has a large printed circuit board called the *motherboard*. The motherboard has the CPU chip, various support chips, memory chips, and slots to which extra memory can be connected. Over the past two decades, the number of transistors that could be integrated into a chip has increased enormously. Modern CPU chips used in PCs have multiple processors, integrated cache memory, and memory controller. Some chips also have integrated graphics. Besides these, CPU chips have logic to connect them to an external peripheral controller, called Platform Controller Hub (PCH) chipset. The peripheral controller chip manages the orderly transfer of data between various input/output units such as a keyboard, printer, disk drives, and the main memory of the computer. Figure 8.8 is a logical diagram of a modern Personal Computer (2024) such as the one using the Intel Core i3/i5/i7/i9 series of processors and its connection to peripherals. The CPU-Memory Bus is connected to a peripheral controller chip (Typically Intel C256 Platform Controller Hub - PCH series in 2024) to control the orderly transfer of data from a variety of peripherals ranging from slow devices such as keyboard and mouse to fast devices such as Solid-State Disks (SSD) and Graphics Processor. The peripheral controller incorporates a switch to connect one of many PCIe (Peripheral Connect Interface

Express) buses which serially transfer data from high-performance peripherals such as Graphics cards and Network Interface Cards. The peripheral controller connects to a bus called USB (Universal Serial Bus) which is used to connect several peripherals such as a keyboard, a mouse, a scanner, and a printer. USBs are quite versatile and the current standard (2024) is USB 4 2.0 that transfers data at a speed of 80 Gbps. The peripheral controller chip also connects to a bus known as SATA (Serial ATA attachment) that connects hard disks and SSDs and can transfer data at 6 Gbps.

Earlier versions of PCs used a bus called PCI (Peripheral Controller Interface) which was a parallel bus shared by several peripherals to communicate with the CPU of a PC. It is obsolete and has been superseded by a high-speed serial PCI Express (PCIe) bus. PCIe uses a dedicated full-duplex serial connection (called a lane) to each peripheral that wants to communicate with the CPU. Up to 32 lanes, each with a bandwidth of up to 4 GB/s in each direction can be connected with the CPU. From 1 to 16 lanes can be used to connect to a single device. PCIe uses packets of data and has features to handle errors. It is usually used to connect Graphics cards, SSD storage, Network Interface Cards, and a wide range of other peripherals.

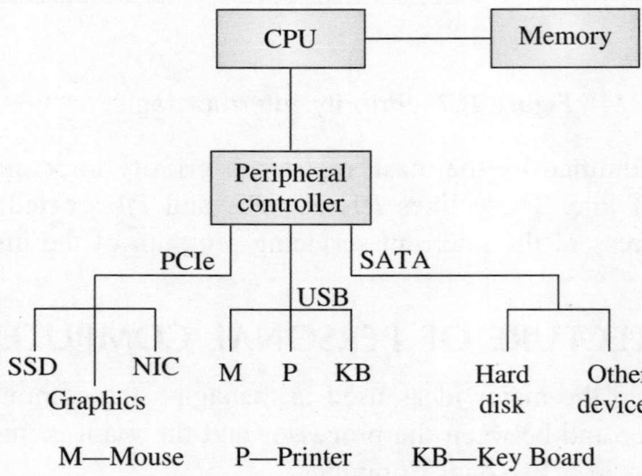

Figure 8.8 Bus architecture of recent (2024) PCs.

We pointed out earlier in this section that a Universal Serial Bus is attached to the peripheral controller to connect peripherals to and from which data is transmitted serially, that is, one bit after another. It is a versatile bus that is widely used and continuously improved. The primary goals of USB standards, as set when it was introduced in 1996, were the following:

1. Allow users to connect a new device with a standard cable to a standard socket while a computer is processing. PC should recognize the device and allocate an appropriate address to it. This is called *hot plugging*.
2. The I/O devices should get power from the computer through the USB cable. The current standard allows up to 240 watts.
3. Up to 127 devices should be connectable.
4. It should support the real-time operation of peripherals such as telephones.
5. The interface to USB should be inexpensive.
6. The current standard USB4 version 2.0, standardized in 2022, supports a data transfer rate of 80 Gbps.

The USB cable has four wires: two for data, one for ground, and one for power (+5 V). The USB cable hub is connected to the peripheral controller and a serial port is brought out to the back of the PC cabinet. A device connected to a PC via USB can have some more USB ports. This allows more devices to be connected to the PC. This is called *daisy chaining*. The USB wire is thin (only four wires inside the sheath) and is connected with a standard plug.

8.6 MULTIPROGRAMMING

In Section 8.3, we discussed that by introducing a DMA interface with some processing capability, a processor can delegate I/O transfer responsibility to the DMA and proceed with program execution. If during program execution, some data is required and it has not yet been transferred to the memory by the DMA interface, then the processor has to wait. To eliminate this waiting time, programmers should estimate accurately when data will be needed. This is difficult and impractical. If, on the other hand, two independent programs are stored in the memory, when one program is suspended due to lack of data, the other may be started by the processor. When the input required by the suspended program is sent by the DMA interface to the memory, the processor may be interrupted and the original program resumed after suspending the second program. This method prevents the processor from being idle due to the non-availability of data. This method of utilizing the processor's resources is known as *multiprogramming*. This is illustrated in Figure 8.9. Remember that the processor executes only one program at a time.

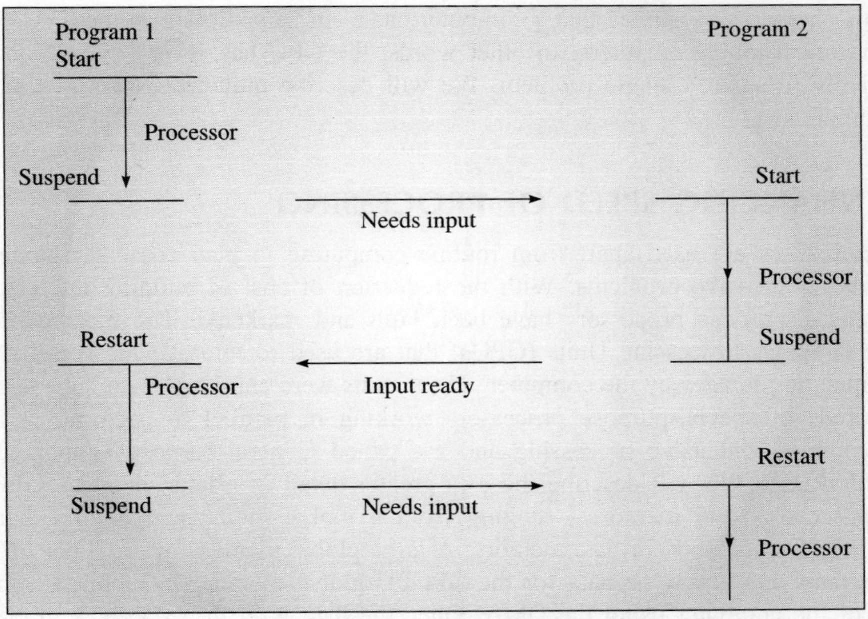

Figure 8.9 Illustration of multiprogramming.

We observe that multiprogramming overlaps the working of the processor and the I/O devices. For multiprogramming to be effective, it is necessary that when one of the programs is waiting for data from the I/O device, the other must have the required data to keep the processor busy. If both programs need data from the I/O devices simultaneously, the processor will be idle again. As the speed mismatch between the I/O devices and the processor is very large, the processor must be able to work simultaneously on many programs (about four to eight) to keep it always busy. With many programs waiting for execution in the processor, the probability of the processor being suspended due to lack of input data is very small.

To implement multiprogramming, a computer requires many special hardware and software features. First, the main memory of the computer should be large enough to accommodate all the programs that are multiprogrammed. When a program is suspended, all information required to restart it should be saved in the memory. Besides this, it is necessary to prevent one program from overwriting the memory locations occupied by another program. To do this, one may allocate specific locations in the main memory to each program and protect them with a 'lock'. A program can write in these locations only if it has a 'key' which fits the protection 'lock'. This is usually a hardware feature and is called *a memory allocation and protection* feature.

To perform all the above functions, namely, scheduling programs, attending to interrupts, storing information regarding suspended programs to enable them to be restarted, attending to I/O errors, etc., it is necessary to write a program called a *supervisor* or *executive.* The supervisor has to permanently reside in the main memory in a reserved area and it should receive top priority. The supervisor is a part of what is known as the *operating system* of a computer. We will discuss this again in Chapter 10.

In this chapter we assumed that a computer has a single processor in the CPU. All modern computers are parallel computers. In other words, the CPU has several processors that work cooperatively to solve a single problem. We will describe multiprocessors in Chapter 11 on microcomputers.

8.7 ENHANCING SPEED OF PROCESSING

Recent computers are used apart from routine computing to play computer games and also solve numeric-intensive problems. With the reduction of cost of building integrated circuits, several special-purpose processors have been built and marketed. The most popular among them are Graphics Processing Units (GPUs) that are used to improve the speed of rendering and manipulating images by the computer. These units were enhanced with huge extra memory and hundreds of special-purpose processors working in parallel to perform, in addition to graphics, numeric-intensive processing and are called General-Purpose Graphics Processing Units (GPGPUs). (We will describe these in greater detail in a later chapter). GPGPUs have several processors and memories ranging from a global memory, memory shared by the processors and processors' private memory. A large global memory of the order of a few GBs store programs and data. The data for the GPGPU global memory is supplied from the main memory of the computer using the DMA. Once the data is in the GPGPU's global memory, distributing it has to be managed by GPGPU's circuitry. This is done by what is known as a Tensor Memory Access (TMA) unit in the GPGPU. The term tensor indicates that the data type handled by GPGPU are mostly multi-dimensional arrays. TMA transfers data asynchronously between GPGPU's global memory and other memories without disturbing the processing units in a way similar to DMA.

SUMMARY

1. Computer architecture is concerned with designing and coordinating the operation of different units in a computer system, namely, the I/O units, the main memory, and the processor, to use the computer system optimally. Optimal use implies that all the units are kept busy while executing programs.
2. The processor of a computer is about 30 times faster than the main memory and the memory is about 1000 times faster than the I/O units. The challenge in computer design is to find hardware and software solutions to keep all the units of the computer simultaneously active and perform useful tasks.
3. The individual units of a computer are interconnected with *buses.* A set of wires that carries a group of bits in parallel and has an associated control scheme is known as a *bus.*
4. In one scheme, the I/O units are connected to the processor using a device address bus, a data bus, and a control bus. In this case, data to and from the memory is sent via a processor register to the I/O units. As the I/O units are 1000 times slower than the processor, this forces the processor to wait.
5. In another scheme, the I/O units are connected to the memory via a DMA logic interface using a data bus and a memory address bus. The processor is also connected to the I/O device via a memory address bus, an I/O device address bus, and a control bus. When an I/O command is sent to a device, data is directly transferred I/O unit to the memory via DMA without using any processor register, thereby not forcing the processor to wait.
6. In a unibus system, the I/O units, the processor and the memory share a common system bus. This allows the I/O devices to be addressed in the same way as memory addresses. As the processor, the memory, and the I/O devices share one bus, the transfer of data can take place at any given time only between two of the three units.
7. To alleviate the speed mismatch between the processor and the main memory, a cache memory is interposed between the main memory and the processor. A cache is a small, fast memory. As most programs are sequential, most references to the main memory will be restricted to small contiguous words. This locality of memory reference is used in designing a cache. The part of the program currently being executed is automatically brought to the cache by the hardware. Thus, most of the required instructions will be in the cache and the effective speed of the memory will be increased. Besides a cache to store instructions (called an instruction cache), another cache is provided to store the data to be processed by the instructions. This is called a *data cache*. Data to be processed are also normally stored in contiguous locations in the main memory.
8. In all recent computers, the cache memory is organized into two levels. Level 1 cache (instruction and data) is within the processor chip and is of size 32–128 KB. Level 2 cache is outside the chip and uses SRAM and its size is between 256 KB and 2 MB. These sizes are almost doubling every 18 months.
9. Data from the I/O devices may be transferred to the main memory via a processor register using program-controlled interrupt data transfer. In this scheme, an I/O command is issued by the processor well before data is needed. When the data is assembled by the

I/O interface logic, it sends an interrupt signal to the processor. The processor suspends the current task it is executing, receives the data, and puts it in the memory.

10. In DMA transfer, an interrupt is sent by the I/O interface to the processor when data is ready to be transferred. The processor yields a memory cycle and the data and address buses to the DMA interface to enable it to transfer the data to memory. DMA transfer of data is faster and more convenient to use than program-controlled transfer.
11. As there are many I/O devices in a system, there could be several interrupts. A system should be established to recognize the interrupting source and take appropriate action based on the device's priority. A combined software-hardware solution is normally used.
12. A trap is an internal interrupt generated by mistakes in a user's program, such as an attempt to divide by 0. Unrecoverable hardware errors also lead to traps.
13. Early PCs had a single system bus called ISA (Industry Standard Architecture) bus to which the processor, the memory, and the I/O interfaces were connected. This bus had 16 data lines and 24 address lines and operated at a maximum speed of 16 MB/s, which was too slow when faster Intel processors became available.
14. A serial bus called the Peripheral Component Interconnect Express (PCIe) bus has been standardized for connecting high-speed peripherals to PCs. The PC has an internal processor to memory bus to which a Peripheral Controller Chip is connected. This Chip connects various peripherals to the CPU using several PCIe buses, Universal Serial Buses (UBS), and SATA. PCIes connect fast peripherals such as graphic cards, SSDs, and Network Interface Cards. SATA is used to connect Disk drives. Universal Serial Bus (USB) is connected to the Peripheral Controller chip so that slower, cheaper peripherals can be connected easily to a PC without having to go through a complex installation procedure, thus enabling hot plug-and-play.
15. Multiprogramming is an architectural solution using both software and hardware to solve the problem of processor—I/O speed mismatch. In this method, several programs are simultaneously kept in the main memory. They are scheduled so that when one program is busy performing I/O, another program uses the processor. Thus, both the I/O device and the processor are kept simultaneously active. A good mix of I/O-intensive and processor-intensive programs is needed to implement this idea successfully. Besides this, a large physical main memory, a large disk and a protected memory area for the multiprogramming supervisor are essential.
16. With the reduction in cost of integrated circuits, special purpose processors to perform numeric-intensive operations called General Purpose Graphics Processing Units (GPGPU) assist CPUs. GPGPUs use Tensor Memory Access (TMA) internally to asynchronously distribute data from its global memory to other memories without disturbing its processors.

REVIEW QUESTIONS

8.1 What is the nature of the speed mismatch between different units of a computer?

8.2 Which is the fastest unit in a computer and which is the slowest? What is the order of magnitude of the difference in speed between them?

8.3 Define a 'bus'.

8.4 What buses are used to connect I/O devices to the processor?

8.5 What are the functions of each of the buses used to connect I/O devices to the processor?

8.6 What buses are used to connect the memory of a computer to the processor?

8.7 What bus systems are used to interconnect I/O devices to the memory?

8.8 What is a DMA? What is its function?

8.9 What is a 'unibus system'? What are the advantages and disadvantages of using a unibus system?

8.10 Give the detailed steps used in memory–processor communication.

8.11 What is a 'cache memory'?

8.12 What important idea makes the use of a cache memory effective?

8.13 Explain how a cache memory reduces the time taken to access a word stored in the main memory.

8.14 What are Level 1 and Level 2 cache memories? What are their typical sizes?

8.15 Why are caches organized in two levels?

8.16 What is a cache line? What is the typical size of a cache line?

8.17 What is an I/O device controller? Explain its functions.

8.18 What is I/O device interface logic? Explain its functions.

8.19 Give the algorithm used in program-controlled I/O transfer.

8.20 If data is to be written from the main memory to an output device, how will it be done by a program-controlled transfer via a processor register?

8.21 What is an interrupt signal? Explain how a processor can take advantage of an interrupt signal to reduce its waiting period to read input data.

8.22 Explain how data is read into the main memory from an input device using DMA interface logic.

8.23 What is cycle stealing?

8.24 How is data written on an output device using a DMA interface?

8.25 What is the advantage of DMA data transfer as opposed to program-controlled data transfer?

8.26 What is an interrupt service routine?

8.27 Explain how a processor services an interrupt.

8.28 What is the difference between an external and an internal interrupt?

8.29 What is a trap? What are the different trap conditions which may occur in a computer?

8.30 Explain how multiple interrupts are handled by a software routine.

8.31 What is programmed device polling? When is it used?

8.32 Explain how multiple interrupts can be handled by special hardware. How is the priority of different interrupts dealt with in this method?

8.33 How is device interrupt priority handled in software interrupt servicing?

8.34 What bus was used in early PCs (such as 80486)? What was this bus called?

8.35 Did early PCs (from 80286 to 80486) have a single bus or two buses?

8.36 What is bus arbitration? When is it used?

8.37 Give a block diagram of modern PCs using a Peripheral Controller Chip.

8.38 What is a PCIe bus? Is it an industry-standard bus?

8.39 What is a USB? What is it used for? What are its advantages?

8.40 What is plug and play? Which bus supports it?

8.41 What is multiprogramming? What are the objectives of multiprogramming?

8.42 What special hardware features are needed to support multiprogramming in a computer system?

8.43 What conditions should be satisfied to meet the objectives of multiprogramming?

8.44 What is the function of a multiprogramming supervisor?

8.45 What is a GPU? How is it used in a computer.

8.46 What is a GPGPU and what is its function?

8.47 What is TMA? Where is it used and why?

8.48 What is the difference between DMA and TMA?

9 Programming Languages

LEARNING GOALS

After reading this chapter, you should be able to:

- Explain what programming languages are and why we need them.
- Differentiate between low and high level languages.
- Explain why syntax and semantic rules are needed for programming languages.
- Explain the basic ideas used in translating high level languages to machine language.
- Describe some popular high level languages, the distinction between them and where they are applied.

Programs, namely, the list of instructions to be executed by a computer, are known as the *software* of a computer. The electronic circuits used to build a computer that executes the software are known as the *computer's hardware*. To take an analogy, a TV set is hardware; the program you watch on a TV is software. It is immediately evident that hardware is necessary but software is vital. What is the use of a TV set if the programs you watch on it are not good? Another important point brought out by this analogy is that hardware is a one-time investment. In contrast, software is often a continuing expense as you pay a monthly subscription to the program provider or even if you pay once you often have to update the software on the system and pay for the updates.

We saw in Chapter 1 that computer software may be classified into two broad categories: *application* and *system software*. Programming language translators are examples of system software. A word processor is an application software. In this chapter, we will discuss the evolution of programming languages and associated translators. In the next chapter, we will discuss important system software known as *operating systems*.

9.1 WHY PROGRAMMING LANGUAGES?

In Chapter 5, we examined the logical structure of the processing unit of computers. We explained in detail the structure of a hypothetical computer we called HYPCOM. An instruction for HYPCOM consisted of an operation code that specified the operation to be performed and an operand address which specified the address in memory where the operand would be stored. A sequence of such machine instructions called a *machine language program,* was used to solve problems.

To write a machine language program, a programmer has to remember all the operation codes of the computer and know what each code does and how it affects various registers in the processor. She has to keep track of all the operands and know exactly where they are stored in the memory. Writing a machine language program requires meticulous attention to detail and deep knowledge of the internal structure of the computer. Writing long machine language programs and testing them takes a lot of time. Thus, it is necessary to look at better methods of writing programs for a computer.

The main purpose of using computers is to solve problems that would otherwise be difficult to solve. It must thus be possible for a computer user to concentrate on designing good algorithms for solving problems rather than be concerned with the details of the internal structure of the computer. This situation is analogous to that which confronts the user of a car. From a car owner's point of view, it is meant to take her from one place to another. If she has to know all about how the car's engine works before she can drive it, she will think twice before buying a car. Driving must be made as simple as possible with minimum knowledge of how the engine works so that it would be easy for anyone to drive and fulfill the objective of owning a car. A general understanding of how the car's engine works is useful if a person wants to be a good driver and reduce the wear and tear of the car and petrol consumption. It is, however, not essential for a driver to be a good mechanic. Similarly, it is desirable, but not necessary, for a programmer to know in detail how a computer works.

Computer programming languages are developed with the primary objective of facilitating a large number of people to use computers without the need to know in detail the internal structure of the computer. Languages are matched to the type of operations to be performed and the type of data used by algorithms for various applications. Languages are also designed to be *machine-independent.* In other words, the structure of a programming language should not depend upon the internal structure of a specified computer. Ideally, one should be able to execute a program on any computer regardless of who manufactured it or what model it is. In brief, *programming languages* are precise and concise notation to express algorithms computers execute.

9.2 ASSEMBLY LANGUAGE

The first step in the evolution of programming languages was the development of what is known as an *assembly language.* In an assembly language, mnemonics represent operation codes, and strings of characters are used to represent addresses. We give in Table 9.1 a machine language program and the corresponding assembly language program. Observe from this table that there is a one-to-one correspondence between the assembly language program

Table 9.1 An assembly program and its machine language equivalent

Assembly code		*Machine code*	
Operation	*Operand address*	*Operation*	*Operand address*
READ	K	A	200
READ	L	A	201
READ	M	A	202
READ	N	A	203
CLA	K	1	200
ADD	L	2	201
ADD	M	2	202
ADD	N	2	203
STO	W	6	204
PRT	W	B	204
HLT		F	

and the equivalent machine language program. As an assembly language is designed mainly to replace each machine code with an understandable mnemonic and each address with a simple alphanumeric string, it matches a particular computer's processor structure. It is thus *machine-dependent.* An assembly language programmer must know all the details of a computer's logical structure to write a program. It therefore suffers from many of the disadvantages of machine language.

To execute an assembly language program on a computer, it should be translated into its equivalent machine language program. This is necessary because the computer's circuitry is designed to execute only the machine's operation codes. The mnemonic operation codes should be converted to absolute numeric operation codes. The symbolic addresses of operands used in assembly language should also be converted to absolute numeric addresses. The translator that does this is known as an *assembler* (see Figure 9.1). The input to an assembler is the assembly language program, known as the *source program.* Its output is the equivalent machine language program known as the *object program.* The assembler is a system program that is supplied by the computer manufacturer. It is written by system programmers with great care.

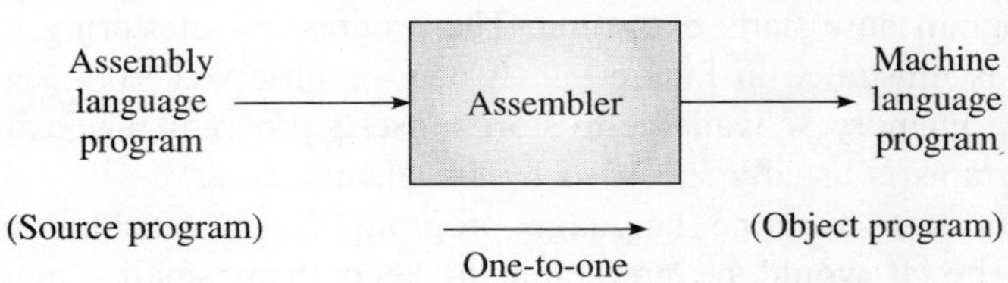

Figure 9.1 Block diagram of an assembler.

The main advantage of using an assembly language for programming is the efficiency of the machine language program resulting from it. As all hardware features available in the processor of the computer, such as registers, stacks, etc., are available to the assembly language programmer, he has great flexibility in writing programs well matched to that computer.

The main disadvantages of an assembly language are:

(i) It is machine-dependent. Thus, programs written for one model of a computer cannot be executed on another model. In other words, it is *not portable* from one machine to another.
(ii) An assembly language programmer must be an expert who knows all about the logical structure of the computer for which the program is written.
(iii) Writing assembly language programs is difficult and time-consuming.

The trend is thus to avoid using an assembly language. It is used only when efficiency or cost is of paramount importance or when there is a need to control input/output devices. Efficiency is important, for instance, if a command to control an aircraft is to be given within a specified time. In cost-sensitive applications, for example, when a microprocessor-based controller is used as a consumer item such as a washing machine, the program is stored in Read Only Memory (ROM) and the size of the ROM determines the cost. The control program has to be concise and writing the program in Assembly Language ensures that the object code requires minimal storage.

9.2.1 Executing Assembly Language Program

To execute a machine language program, it should be stored in the computer's memory. The program is read into the main memory by another program called a *loader* already stored in the memory. The loader, or Initial Program Load (IPL), is usually stored in a ROM and is automatically moved to the main memory by the computer's hardware when it is switched on.

The loader program should be kept small. Thus, a procedure is used whereby the first few instructions of the loader load the rest. This is called *bootstrap loading*.

To execute an assembly language program, we must first store the loader. The loader then reads the assembler from a secondary memory (such as a disk) and stores it in the main memory. The assembler would be written in machine language and can thus be stored directly in memory. The assembler now reads each instruction of the assembly language, translates it into a machine language statement, and stores it in the main memory. When the entire assembly language is translated and stored, control is passed to the first instruction of the assembled user program. This program now starts execution. The progression of storing various programs in the main memory is illustrated in Figure 9.2. It may be observed from Figure 9.2 that only a portion of the main memory is available to store a user's program. The available free memory for the user's programs is usually specified by the manufacturer.

The assembler is a machine language program. Since machine language programs are difficult to write, it would be preferable to keep them small. One method would be to define an assembly language with minimal features and write an assembler for this language. A higher-level assembly language may then be defined (e.g., one that allows expressions for addresses). A program in this higher-level assembly language may be translated by a program written in the rudimentary assembly language for which a translator

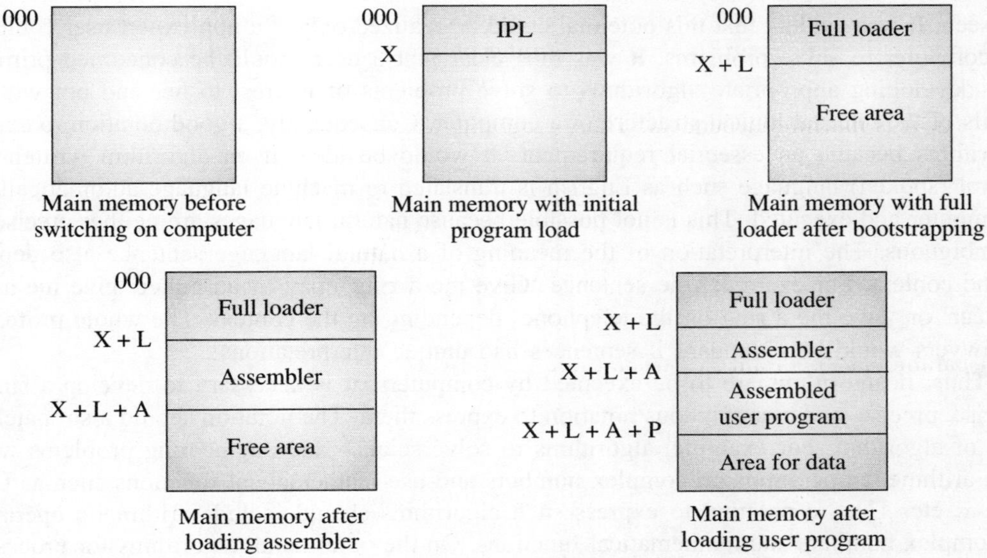

Figure 9.2 Illustration of memory allocation for loader and assembler.

already exists. This is a powerful method and is called *the bootstrap method*, which is illustrated in Figure 9.3.

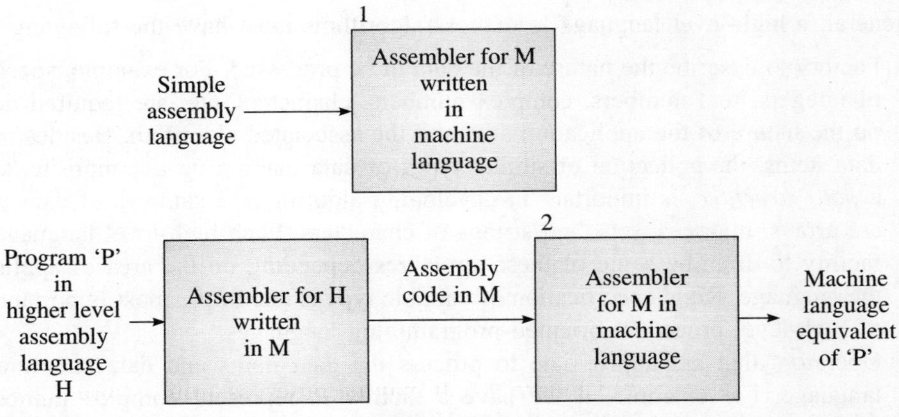

Figure 9.3 Bootstrap method of writing translators (boxes 1 and 2 are identical).

9.3 HIGHER-LEVEL PROGRAMMING LANGUAGES

During the evolution of computers, till about 1955, computers were slow and had a small memory. Thus, programming efficiency was essential and assembly language was dominant. The use of computers was also limited to a small group of scientists. With technology improvements, computers were designed with larger memory capacity, higher speed, and improved reliability. The tremendous potential of computer applications in diverse areas was foreseen. It was evident that this potential could be realized only if a non-expert user could use the computer to solve problems. It was thus clear that a user should be concerned primarily with developing appropriate algorithms to solve problems of interest to her and not with the details of the internal logical structure of a computer. Consequently, a good notation to express algorithms became an essential requirement. It would be ideal if an algorithm written in a natural (spoken) language such as English is translated to machine language automatically by a computer and executed. This is not possible because natural languages are neither precise nor unambiguous. The interpretation of the meaning of a natural language sentence also depends on the context. For example, the sentence 'Give me a ring' may mean either 'give me a ring to wear' or 'give me a ring on the telephone' depending on the context. The whole profession of lawyers would be redundant if sentences had unique interpretations!

Thus, if algorithms are to be executed by computers, it is necessary to develop a simple, concise, precise, and unambiguous notation to express them. The notation should also match the type of algorithm. For example, algorithms to solve science and engineering problems would have arithmetic operations on complex numbers and use mathematical functions such as tan x, cosh x, etc. Thus, a notation to express such algorithms should include arithmetic operations on complex numbers and mathematical functions. On the other hand, algorithms for processing business data would have operations to be performed on massive amounts of organized data known as files. The arithmetic to be performed would be simple. The notation in this case must facilitate describing files and instructions to process files.

Such notations used to express algorithms are known as *high-level procedure-oriented programming languages.*

In general, a high-level language to express algorithms must have the following features:

(i) Facility to describe the nature of the data to be processed. For example, specifications of integers, real numbers, complex numbers, characters, etc. are required depending on the nature of the application area and the associated algorithm. Besides individual data items, the collection of similar types of data making up a composite, known as a *data structure,* is important in developing algorithms. Examples of data structures are arrays, matrices, sets, and strings of characters. Each high-level language has the facility to describe some of these structures depending on the area of application of the language. Rigid specification of variable type is one of the most important features of high-level procedure-oriented programming languages.

(ii) Operators that are appropriate to process the data items and data structures in the language. For example, if we have a facility to represent complex numbers, then complex addition, subtraction, multiplication and division operations would be useful.

(iii) A set of characters using which symbols in the language are constructed. These symbols have a precise meaning in the context of the language. For example, the symbol ** represents the exponentiation operation in FORTRAN. Thus, A**B would mean raising A to the power B.

(iv) Facility to perform an alternate set of statements based on the result of testing a condition. Repeated execution of groups of statements is also necessary in many algorithms. Thus, a high-level language should provide statements to alter the flow of control in algorithms. For example, a common statement found in a high-level language is:

```
if A > B then X:= Y + Z else X:= P + Q;
```

This means: 'compare the numbers stored in A and B. If the number stored in A is larger than that stored in B, then add the number stored in Y to that stored in Z and store it in X, otherwise add the number stored in P to that stored in Q and store it in X'.

Repeating a group of instructions, for example, is:

```
     I:= 0; N:=0;
repeat
     I:= I + 1;
     SUM:= SUM + N;
     N:= N + 5;
until   (I = 10);
```

(v) A set of words, each with a precise and unambiguous meaning and a role to play in creating the program. For example, the keywords READ, WRITE, DO have specific meanings in the context of a programming language.

(vi) A set of *syntax rules* which precisely specify the combination of words and operators permissible in the language. For example, a language may specify that A * B is a legal combination, whereas A*/B may be illegal. The syntax rules are rules of grammar valid for the language. These rules are derived systematically and their number is kept small to enable users to memorize them.

(vii) A set of *semantic rules* which assign a single, precise, and unambiguous meaning to each legal syntactic structure in the language. For example, the statement: 'C = B/D' may mean in a particular high-level language: 'Divide the number stored in B by the one stored in D and store the result in C'.

A syntactically correct statement is not necessarily semantically meaningful. In a natural language (English), for instance, the sentences

'Ram plays football'

'Football plays Ram'

are both syntactically correct. The second sentence, however, is semantically meaningless. Similarly, the statement C = B/D would be semantically incorrect if D happens to be zero. In high-level languages for computers, there should be no semantic ambiguity. Each syntactically correct structure should have one and only one semantic interpretation. This is in contrast with natural languages.

(viii) The syntax and semantic rules of the language, besides being concise and precise, should aid in understanding the program. An understandable program is self-documenting and thus easily maintainable. One chooses keywords in the language which have meanings similar to their meanings in English usage.

Besides this, the facility to intersperse the program with comments (which are ignored by the translator of the program) should be provided to aid program understanding.

High-level languages are designed independent of the structure of a specific computer. This facilitates executing a program written in such a language on different computers. Associated with each high-level language is an elaborate computer program which translates it into the machine language of the computer in which it is to be executed. Figure 9.4 explains various terms used in high-level language translation. Figure 9.5 illustrates how machine independence is achieved by using different translators to translate a high-level language program into machine languages of different computers.

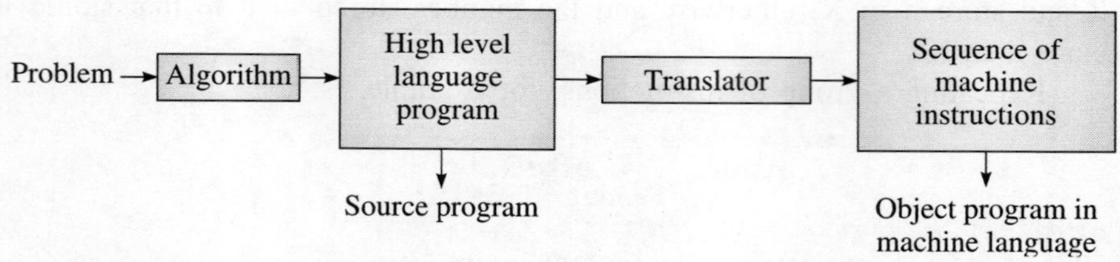

Figure 9.4 Terminologies used in high level language translation.

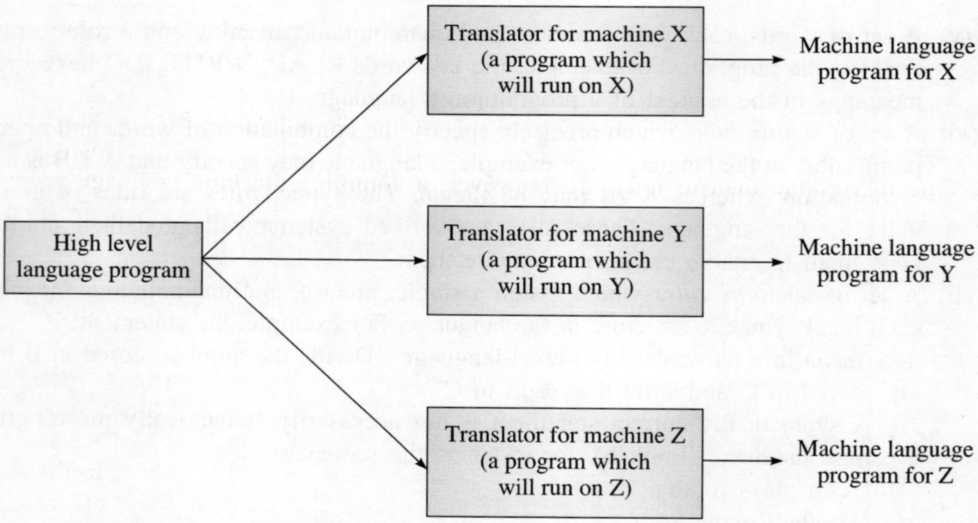

Figure 9.5 Machine independence of high level language.

In Table 9.2, we illustrate a small program written in a high-level language called BASIC and the equivalent machine language program of HYPCOM. Observe that one high-level language statement is translated into *many* machine language statements. This is *a one-to-many translation*. The terminology, high-level language, is due to this. An assembly language is a low-level language as its translation to machine language is one-to-one. It is possible to translate a high-level language to one at a lower level, but the reverse is not always possible.

There are two approaches to writing language translators. One method is to take one statement of a high-level language at a time and translate it into a machine instruction which is immediately executed. This is called an *interpreter*. Interpreters are easy to write and do not require large memory space in the computer. The main disadvantage of interpreters is that they need more time to execute programs on a computer.

Table 9.2 A basic program and its HYPCOM machine language equivalent

Basic program	*Machine language*
10 READ K, L, M, N	A 200 A 201 A 202 A 203
20 LET W = K + L + M + N	1 200 2 201 2 202 2 203 6 204
30 PRINT W	B 204
40 END	F

The other approach to translation is to store the high-level language program, scan it, and translate the whole program into an equivalent machine language program. Such a translator is known as a *compiler*. A compiler is a complex program compared to an interpreter. It takes more time to compile than to interpret. However, a compiled machine language program is short and runs much faster than an interpreted program.

The difference between an interpreter and a compiler may be understood with the help of the following analogy. Suppose we want to translate a speech from Russian to English. There are two approaches one can use. The translator can listen to a sentence in Russian and immediately translate it into English. Alternatively, the translator can hear the whole passage in Russian and then give the equivalent English passage. If the speaker repeats the same sentence six times, then, in the first case, the equivalent English sentence will also be repeated six times. In the second case, the translation will be more concise as the English equivalent of a whole passage will be given without repeating the same sentence six times. A person who can translate an entire passage has to be a better translator and must remember more information than one who translates sentence by sentence. An interpreter is similar to sentence-by-sentence translation, whereas a compiler is similar to the translation of the whole passage.

High-level languages which have the power to express a general class of algorithms are known as *procedure-oriented languages.* These languages express in detail the procedure used to solve a problem. In other words, a programmer details *how* to solve a problem. Another class of high-level languages is called *problem-oriented languages.* These languages are designed to solve a narrower class of problems. A user of such a language need not give in detail the procedure used to solve the problem. Ready-made procedures are preprogrammed. The user merely presents the input data to the program in a flexible 'language'. For example, a problem-oriented language called STRESS (STRuctural Equation System Solver) accepts a description of a set of equations to be solved in a simple format of the type:

```
NODE 5 IS AT X = 25.5, Y = 20.7, Z = 10.5
     BEAM BETWEEN NODES 5 AND 15
. . . . . . . . . . . . . . . . . . . .
. . . . . . . . . . . . . . . . . . . .
```

It then generates the equations to be solved, invokes the built-in algebraic equation solution program and solves the problem. The user need not specify how to solve the problem. He merely has to state *the* problem is to be solved using the appropriate language.

Recent popular problem-oriented languages are MATLAB and MATHEMATICA. MATLAB is popular among scientists and engineers for solving a wide class of problems modelled by differential equations and matrices. MATHEMATICA is used to simplify complex algebraic expressions and find expressions resulting from indefinite integration and similar symbol manipulation problems.

9.4 COMPILING A HIGH-LEVEL LANGUAGE PROGRAM

In this section, we will discuss briefly the steps used to compile a high-level language program to an executable machine language program. Broadly, the compilation process consists of two steps. The first step is the analysis of the source program and the second is the synthesis of the object program in the machine language of the specified machine (Figure 9.6). The analysis step uses a precise description of the source programming language. A source language is described using *lexical rules, syntax rules, and semantic rules.*

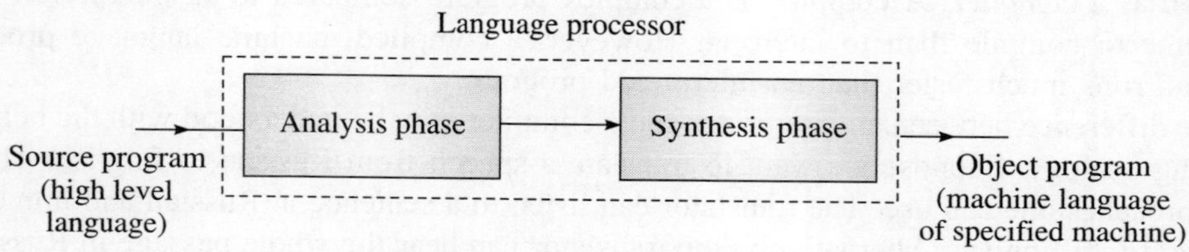

Figure 9.6 Block diagram of a language processor.

Lexical rules specify the valid syntactic elements or words of the language. *Syntax rules* specify how the valid syntactic elements are combined to form statements of the language. *Semantic rules* assign meanings to valid statements of the language.

Consider, for example, the following statement in a high-level language:

```
principal:=principal*(1+rate/100);
```

The syntactic elements of the statement are:

```
principal, := , *, ( , 1, +, rate, /, 100) and ;
```

The syntactic elements principal and rate are called *identifiers*. The symbols :=, +, and / are *operators*. The numbers 1 and 100 are *integer constants* and the symbol ; is called a *delimiter*. Each syntactic element is defined using the syntax rules of the language. The syntax rules are given using the notation called *Backus–Naur Form*, abbreviated BNF in honour of Backus and Naur who invented this notation to describe computer languages. Each syntactic unit is given a name and shown as <name>. For example, the syntactic unit digit is defined as:

```
<digit> → 0|1|2|3|4|5|6|7|8|9|
```

The arrow → represents 'defined as' and the vertical bar | represents 'or'. The above definition is thus read as: <digit> is defined as 0 or 1 or 2 or 3 or 4 or 5 or 6 or 7 or 8 or 9. We define a letter as:

```
<letter> → a|b|c ...... x|y|z
```

In other words, a <letter> is any one of the lowercase (or small) English letters. These characters are combined to form a syntactic unit called <identifier>, which is defined as:

```
<identifier> := <letter> | <identifier><letter>|<identifier><digit>.
```

Observe that the above definition is defined in terms of itself. This is called a *recursive definition.* Using this rule, the following are valid identifiers:

```
p, pr, pr2, principal
```

As p is a <letter> it is an <identifier>. pr is an <identifier> namely, p followed by a <letter> r. Following this argument, pr followed by a <digit>, namely, 2 is also an <identifier>. The reader can verify that principal is a valid identifier as it conforms to these rules. On the other hand, the following are not valid identifiers as they violate syntax rules.

```
2p, 2 + p, p - 2, ? x, x; y
```

Some other rules are:

```
<a.o> → + | - | * |/
```

where <a.o> is abbreviation for <arithmetic operator>

<delimiters> →) | (| ;

<assignment operator> → :=

Having defined the 'words' of the language, we next define how 'sentences' of the language are formed using syntax rules. Some of the rules are given below:

```
<a.e>→<identifier><a.o><identifier>where<a.e>is abbreviation
```

for arithmetic expression.

```
<a.e> → <(a.e)>
<a.e> → <a.e> <a.o> <a.e>
```

An arithmetic statement <a.s> is defined as:

<a.s> → <identifier> := < a.e>. Using the above rule and the rules given earlier defining <a.e>, it can be verified that

```
principal := principal * (1 + rate/100)
```

is a syntactically correct arithmetic statement. Next, we have to assign meanings to syntactically correct units. In the above example, the semantic interpretation of the computation is as follows:

Compute the value of the expression on the right-hand side of := and replace the value stored in the variable name principal by this value. The rules on how to compute the arithmetic expression should also be specified as semantic rules.

The steps used to translate a high-level language source program to executable code are given in Figure 9.7. The first block in Figure 9.7 is a lexical analyzer (or scanner). It reads successive lines of a program and breaks them into individual lexical items, namely, identifier, operator, delimiter, etc., and attaches a type tag to each. Besides this, it constructs a *symbol table* for each identifier and finds the internal representation of each constant. The symbol table is used later to allocate memory to each variable.

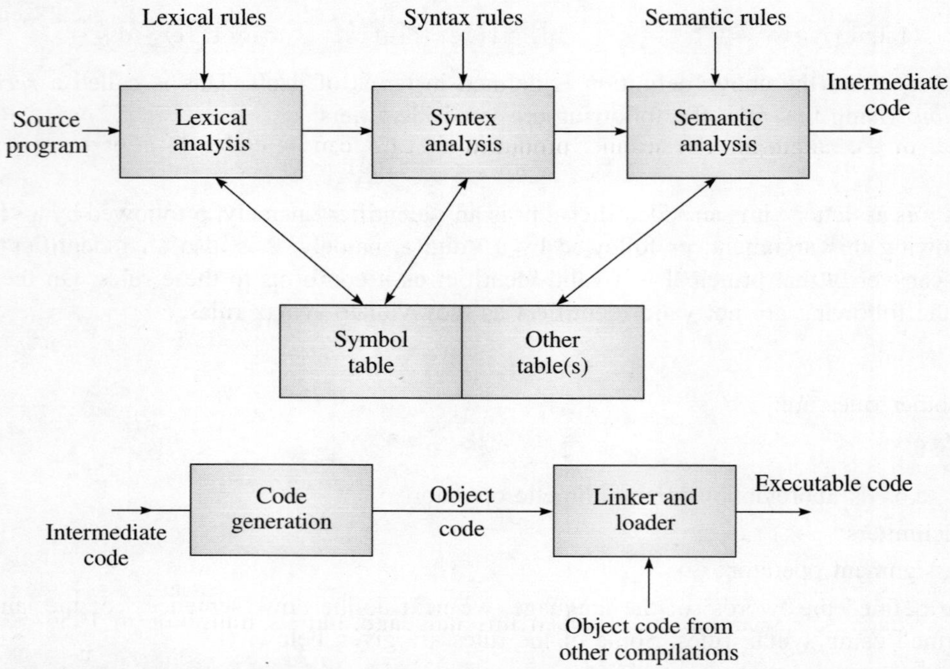

Figure 9.7 Steps in the translation of high level language to machine language.

The second stage of translation is called *syntax analysis* or *parsing*. In this phase, expressions, statements, declarations, etc. are identified by using the results of lexical analysis. Syntax analysis is aided by using techniques based on the formal grammar of the programming language.

In the semantic analysis phase, the syntactic units recognized by the syntax analyzer are processed. An intermediate representation of the final machine language code is produced. This phase bridges the analysis and synthesis phases of translation (see Figure 9.6).

The last phase of translation is *code generation*. Several optimizations to reduce the length of the machine language program are carried out during this phase. The output of the code generator is the machine language program of the specified computer. If a subprogram library is used or if some subroutines are separately translated and compiled, a final linking and loading step is needed to produce the complete machine language program ready for execution. If subroutines are separately compiled, the addresses of the resulting machine language instructions will not be their final addresses when all the routines are placed together in the main memory. The linker's job is to find the correct locations of the final executable program. The loader will then place them in the memory at their right addresses.

9.4.1 Tools to Build Compilers

We saw that the analysis step of all high-level language translators has three distinct phases: lexical analysis, syntax analysis, and semantic analysis. The output of the analysis phase is an intermediate representation (see Figure 9.7). As the analysis method is well understood and applies to several language processors, tools have been developed to automatically generate programs for scanning the source code to identify syntactic units, parsing the programs, and generating the intermediate code. Two popular tools are called LEX (Lexical Analyzer) and YACC (Yet Another Compiler Compiler). LEX accepts an input specification of strings representing lexical units of a high-level language and semantic actions necessary to build the intermediate code and generates a scanner. YACC generates a parser of the language given the grammar of the language. The scanner produced by LEX can be called by a parser generated by YACC. LEX and YACC normally generate C code which is machine-independent. The code generators for specific computers are written using the intermediate code as input. Some tools have also been developed to obtain code generators if formal specifications of the processors of the target computers are given but are not as popular as LEX and YACC.

9.5 SOME HIGH-LEVEL LANGUAGES

In this section, we will briefly describe some popular high-level languages and the areas where they are applied.

FORTRAN

FORTRAN stands for *FOR*mula *TRAN*slation. This language is the oldest high-level programming language. In a pioneering effort, John Backus and his team at IBM (International Business Machine Corporation) developed this language and its translator in 1956–57. The language was designed to solve scientific and engineering problems and is currently a popular language among scientists and engineers using high-performance computers. With the evolution of better computers and with the increasing maturity of users, FORTRAN has also evolved. The first version which was extensively used in the late 1950s and early 1960s was known as FORTRAN II. The next popular version was FORTRAN IV. This version was standardized by the American National Standards Institute (ANSI) in 1966. In 1977, an updated version of FORTRAN IV incorporating widely adopted good features and improvements was announced and standardized by ANSI. This version is known as FORTRAN 77.

Later a version of FORTRAN known as Fortran 90 was standardized to supersede FORTRAN 77. (Observe that the earlier notation that used all capital letters, namely, FORTRAN was replaced by Fortran). Special features incorporated in Fortran 90 include recursion, pointers so that lists can be defined, and modules (similar to objects). Besides this, Fortran 90 has features to store and manipulate characters, operations for vector operands, and better constructs for expressing program loops. Fortran 95 which superseded Fortran 90 incorporated features to write programs for parallel computers. In 2003, Fortran was upgraded to include all aspects of Object-Oriented programming. It allowed interoperability with C. The latest version of Fortran to appear was in 2023 and it supports concurrent programming. Fortran is being continuously upgraded by a dedicated group of scientists and engineers.

As the new versions of Fortran compilers are expensive whereas C compilers are free, Fortran is losing users even though Fortran is more readable than C, and developing programs for applications in science and engineering is easier with Fortran.

The *computational instructions* in Fortran resemble ordinary algebra. For example, X = (A + B + C)/(D + E) is a computational instruction. *Control* and *input/output* instructions resemble English imperative statements. For example, IF (A . GT . B) GO TO 10 is a control instruction. READ*, A, B, and WRITE (3, 35) X, Y, Z are input and output instructions. Storage instructions resemble English declarative sentences. For example, NUMBER = PREVNO is interpreted to mean 'store in a memory location with the name NUMBER, the content of the memory location with the name PREVNO'.

Given below is a Fortran 90 program to calculate the average height of boys in a class. (In all the programs, we assume that at least one data item is read.) A statement following ! is a comment to help one understand the program.

```
!PROGRAM TO FIND AVERAGE HEIGHT OF BOYS IN A CLASS
!roll_no = 0 SIGNALS END OF STUDENT DATA
PROGRAM average_height
     IMPLICIT NONE
     INTEGER:: total_boys = 0, roll_no
     REAL:: height, total_boy_height = 0, av_boy_height
     DO
        READ *, roll_no, height
        IF (roll_no = = 0) EXIT! EXIT FROM DO LOOP
            total_boy_height = total_boy_height + height
            total_boys = total_boys + 1
            CYCLE ! RETURN TO FIRST STATEMENT FOLLOWING DO
     ENDDO
     av_boy_height = total_boy_height/REAL (total_boys)
     PRINT *, "Total boys =", total_boys,
     "Average height of boys =", av_boy_height
END PROGRAM average_height
```

As we pointed out, Fortran has continuously evolved with advances in computer technology.

C language

C was developed by Dennis Ritchie in 1972 at the Bell Telephone Laboratories in the USA. C was designed to have the advantages of a high-level language, namely, machine independence. At the same time, it is concise, providing only the bare essentials required in a language so that a translator can translate it into an efficient machine language code. The first major use of C was to write an operating system known as UNIX. C is popular due to its efficiency and its connection with UNIX. Many ready-made programs used by UNIX which are written in C can be easily borrowed by a C programmer in writing application programs.

C is powerful as it allows users to access addresses in memory where variables are stored. These addresses are known as pointers. The access to pointers and the operations that can be performed with pointers distinguish C from other high-level languages such as Fortran. Fortran 90 provides pointers but restricts their use. C has minimal restrictions on the use of pointers.

C has been standardized by ANSI. The main disadvantages of C, particularly for a beginner, are its conciseness and extensive use of pointers. Concise programs may be written to carry out complex computations. This is a disadvantage as it is difficult to read a C program and understand what it does particularly when pointers are used extensively.

Despite these deficiencies, why has C become popular? The reasons are:

1. It is flexible and can be used to program different applications.
2. It is efficient as the object code it produces is concise. This is because C is closer to machine language semantics.
3. C compilers are widely available and are free.
4. It is reasonably easy to port applications written in C to diverse computers.

A C program which finds the average height of students in a class is given below:

```
/* Program to find average height */
# include <stdio.h>
main ( )
    { int number = 0;
    float sum, height, average;
    sum = 0;
    while (scanf (“%d”, & height)!= EOF)
        { sum += height;
        ++ number;
        } /* end of while */
average = sum/float(number);
printf (“average height=%f\n”);
} /* end of main */
```

C++ language

Languages such as FORTRAN, and C are purely algorithmic. These languages provide a methodology to break up a large job into several tasks and program the tasks independently as functions or subroutines. These functions or subroutines are then combined to form a program. The general idea is to simplify debugging a program and reuse the procedures in other programs that may need them. Over the years, it was realized that this was not sufficient to enable reuse of programs. Subroutines and functions are too rigid as they require a specific data type to be used and data to be passed to them in a rigid order. As the cost of programming continually increased, it was realized that building programs using a library of reusable ‘components’ was imperative. This led to the emergence of the so-called *object-oriented languages*. In these languages, the concept of subroutines/functions is extended to that of an *object*. An object models a complex real-world or abstract object. A real-world object, for example, is a student, whereas an abstract object is a course taken by a student. In an Object- Oriented Program (OOP), an object is modelled by a collection of data structures and a set of procedures that can be performed on this data. A program consists of a collection of objects, each object providing a service when it is invoked and all the objects cooperating to get the job done. Objects are invoked by sending messages to them and these objects return messages when they complete the jobs assigned to them. One of the concepts of object-oriented programming is *encapsulation*. Encapsulation bundles data (attributes) and methods that operate on the data into a single object.

It restricts direct access to some of the components of the object. This protects the integrity of data. The internal state of an object can be modified only by its methods.

The action performed in response to a message can vary depending on the data type of parameters. This is called *polymorphism*. Objects form a class hierarchy with superclass (parent) and subclass (child) relationships. An object can use procedures and data defined on objects in its superclass through *inheritance*.

The advantages of OOP accrue only when a large software project is undertaken—also known as 'programming in the large'. The methodology of OOP enables a programmer to remain close to the conceptual higher-level model of the real-world problem. One of the earliest OOP languages which was developed was Smalltalk. It, however, did not become popular. An object-oriented version of C called C++ is currently the most popular OOP language. C++ was designed by B. Stroustrup in 1983 at the Bell Telephone Laboratories. It was designed as an extension of C and its popularity is mostly due to the popularity of C.

C#

C# (Pronounced C- sharp) is a C++ version released by Microsoft for computers using the MS Windows operating system. It is widely used as it provides better run-time checks compared to C++. It is simple to learn. It provides automatic memory management. It restricts the use of pointers.

Java

Java was developed in 1991 by a group led by James Gosling at Sun Microsystems (now closed down). It was originally designed for embedded computers used in consumer devices. Machine independence and efficiency of the compiled code were the primary goals. These features were found very relevant with the advent of the Internet and the need to execute programs on diverse computers. Java is made machine-independent by defining a Java *virtual machine* for which a Java compiler is written. By a virtual machine, we mean a non-existent machine. In other words, it is a hypothetical machine that can be simulated by software similar to the one we used to simulate HYPCOM in Chapter 8. The Java code compiled for the Java virtual machine called the *Java byte code* is then executed on any machine by an interpreter which generates machine code from the Java byte code for that specific machine. This technique makes it easy to port Java language to any machine quickly (see Figure 9.8).

Java is an object-oriented language. Its syntax rules are simple. It has built-in security features. It is used extensively in enterprise software development, big data processing, scientific computing, and web development.

Language extensions for parallel computing

From early this century parallel computers have proliferated. There are two broad classes of parallel computers. They are *message passing parallel computers* and *shared memory parallel computers*. In message passing parallel computers a set of computers cooperatively solve a problem by interchanging messages among processes running in them using send and receive primitive operations. A send primitive is of the type: *Send (destination processor address,*

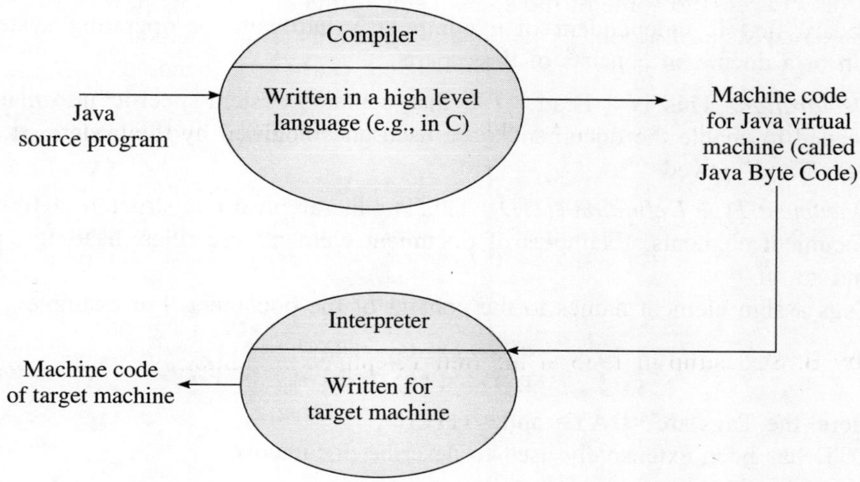

Figure 9.8 Illustration of portability of Java.

variable name, size) where size is the number of bytes to be sent. A receive primitive is of the type: *Receive (source processor address, variable name, size).* These primitives are added to languages such as C and Fortran. The syntax and semantics of message passing primitives have been standardized as Message Passing Interface (MPI). (http://www.mpi-forum.org).

In shared memory parallel computers two statements are added to a programming language to enable creation of processes and for waiting for them to complete. A *fork* primitive of a Process X creates a process Y and uses a *join* primitive when it needs the results from Y to continue. Besides these a primitive *lock* < *VN* > prevents processes from writing in a shared variable *VN* until it encounters an *unlock* <*VN*> that allows processes to resume writing in it.

A portable standard known as Open MP (openmp.org) has been designed that provides a set of compiler directives and runtime library routines to express parallelism in shared-memory programs. They are used to ease programming shared memory parallel computers using Fortran, C or C++.

Nowadays General-Purpose Graphics Processing Units (GPGPU) incorporate numerous tiny processors that work in parallel to speed up computation. They are used as add-on processors to CPUs. They are programmed using CUDA a parallel programming extension to Fortran and C.

Markup languages

The World Wide Web, an Internet application, is universally used. Websites are developed on the World Wide Web by many organizations to publicize their activities. Websites contain a group of related documents called web pages. Web pages should be visually appealing and are normally linked to other web pages. Markup languages are designed to create visually appealing web pages.

By markup, we mean a symbol added to a document that gives special meaning to the document. A markup language is used to describe the content and structure of a document. A markup language called Standard Generalized Markup Language (SGML) is an international open standard that is independent of a computer's hardware or operating system. SGML description of a document consists of three parts:

1. *Declaration:* This is a header file that contains system-specific information that is needed to enable the document to be used and modified by the system on which it is stored and viewed.
2. *Document Type Definition (DTD):* This is a hierarchical tree structure definition for the document elements. Examples of document elements are titles, headings, paragraphs, and so on.

   Tags assign element names to the content of the document. For example:

   ```
   <DAY> Friday </DAY>
   <TITLE> Displaying Textual Data </TITLE>
   ```

   Here, the Tags are <DAY> and <TITLE>.

   DTD has been extensively used to describe documents.
3. *Document instance:* This is the actual document with added tags in the correct order as determined by SGML specification.

   Even though SGML is the original attempt to formalize the description of documents, other languages based on its ideas have become more popular and are widely used. They are HTML and XML. HTML is primarily used to format documents stored as web pages on the World Wide Web. XML is a successor of HTML. HTML's main purpose is to properly format web pages and provide facilities to link them, while XML's aim is not only to format documents but also to exchange them among cooperating businesses by using meaningful Tags.

Scripting languages

C and Java are also known as *systems programming languages*. For example, C has been used to write the UNIX operating system. System programming languages use strong typing, that is, each variable must be declared as a particular type—real, integer, pointer, etc. Typing is used both for easy readability and for enabling more efficient compilation and error detection. Another class of languages that is gaining wide acceptance is called *scripting languages*. Scripting languages are interpreted. Each source code line is interpreted and executed. They provide high-level abstraction and thereby simplify programming. Their syntax is concise and readable and enhances readability and maintenance. Many scripting languages allow dynamic typing at run time. They are ideal for rapid prototyping. They are less efficient compared to compiled programming languages. Many scripting languages assume that a collection of useful programs, each performing a task, already exists. It has facilities to combine or glue these components to perform a complex task.

Some widely used scripting languages are Python, JavaScript, Bash, Ruby, Perl, and PHP.

One of the earliest scripting languages is *UNIX Shell*. In the UNIX shell, filter programs read a stream of bytes from an input and write a stream of bytes to an output. Any two programs can be connected by attaching the output of one program to the input of the other. The following shell commands stack three filters to count the number of lines in a text that contains the word 'language'.

```
select | grep language | wc
```

The program select reads the given text currently on the display and places the text on its output; the program grep reads this and outputs the lines containing the word 'language'; the program wc counts the number of lines output by grep. Each of these programs select, grep and wc are independent programs that could be combined with other programs in many ways.

Python

Python is a popular scripting language. It was developed by Guido Van Rossum, a Dutch computer scientist, with partial financial support from the US Defence Advanced Research Project Agency (DARPA) in late 1999. It aimed to create a programming language for everybody; easy to learn, write readable code, and versatile. It met its design aims and is currently widely used. Its syntax is English-like with significant indentation. It has a comprehensive standard library permitting gluing them to create complex programs. Some key features of Python are dynamic typing, automatic memory management, cross-platform compatibility, and extensibility with modules written in C or C++. It is commonly used for Web development, data analysis, scientific computing, and scripts for file management and system administration. It is an interpreted language and its source code is open and free.

JavaScript

JavaScript is a scripting language that is extensively used for Web development. It was introduced in 1995 by Netscape, a browser developer. It has evolved over the years and currently over 90% of all websites use it.

JavaScript is an interpreted scripting language primarily used to enhance web pages by making them interactive and dynamic. It runs on the user's web browser. This allows JavaScript programs to respond to actions by users in real time. JavaScript programs are often used to enhance the features of browsers such as incorporating ad blockers.

In Table 9.3, we compare some of the languages.

Table 9.3 Comparison of languages

	Assembly	*System programming (e.g., C)*	*Scripting (e.g., PERL)*
No. of machine instructions per one statement of language	1	5 Compiled	100 Interpreted
Specification of data types	None	Strong	Weak
Applications	Time-critical, cost critical	Web development, gluing components, rapid prototyping	Web development, gluing components, prototyping pprrapidprototyping

Non-procedural languages

In Procedural languages (also known as imperative languages), each statement causes the values stored in one or more memory locations to change. Program design consists of writing a sequence of statements that transform the 'state' of the memory from an initial state to a final state, which is the solution to the problem. In non-procedural languages, on the other hand, variables are not synonymous with locations in memory. They are treated as arguments of functions. One class of non-procedural languages is known as *applicative* or *functional languages.* These functional languages solve a problem by applying functions to the initial variables in specific ways to get the answer. The syntax of such languages is similar to

$$(f_{n-1}\ (f_{n-2}\ ....f_1\ (\text{data}))......)$$

where f_{n-1}, f_{n-2}, etc. are the successive function applications that transform their arguments. LISP, SCHEME, and ML are some languages that support this model. LISP has been widely used to program Artificial Intelligence applications.

Another non-procedural class of languages is called *rule-based languages* or *logic programming languages.* A logic program is expressed as a set of atomic sentences (known as facts) and Horn clauses (*if-then* rules). A query is then posed. During program execution, the system finds out if the answer to the query is *true* or *false* for the given facts and rules. PROLOG is the best-known logic programming language and has been extensively used in Artificial Intelligence applications.

Publishing languages

The simplest publishing language is word processors used with Personal Computers. Other text processing languages such as LATEX accept a set of commands and produce an output program in postscript page description language. This file named .ps file is compiled by a processor usually incorporated in a laser printer. Other popular languages used in publishing are InDesign designed by Adobe Systems, LaTeX, and Scribus available as free software.

Figure 9.9 gives a classification of programming languages.

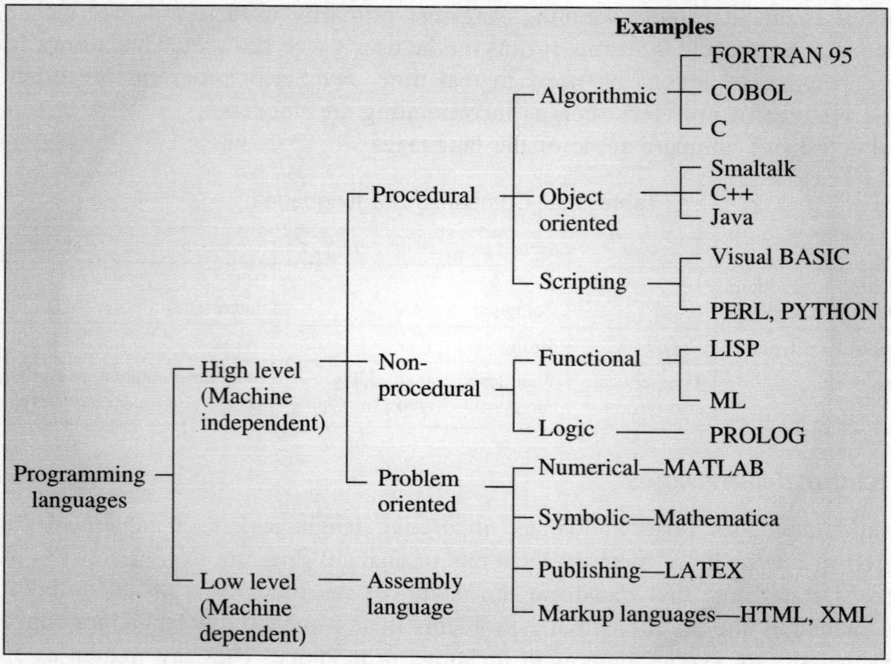

Figure 9.9 Classification of programming language.

10 Operating Systems

LEARNING GOALS

After reading this chapter, you should be able to:

- Describe the major functions of a system program known as an Operating System (OS).
- Explain why we need an OS in computers.
- Describe how OS evolved from a simple control program to batch OS, multiprogramming OS, and time-sharing OS as the storage capacity and CPU speed of computers improved and users' demands also changed.
- Explain how virtual memory is implemented and how an OS manages memory.
- Outline the structure of a simple OS intended for PCs.
- Explain how the OS for PCs improved as PCs became more powerful.
- Describe the overall objective and structure of a popular OS called UNIX and its variant LINUX.

In this chapter, we will first discuss the need for a system program called an *operating system*. We will then look at the evolution of operating systems (abbreviated OSs) during the last six decades and discuss their features.

10.1 WHY DO WE NEED AN OPERATING SYSTEM?

We saw in the previous chapter that high-level languages were developed to enable computer users to concentrate on designing appropriate algorithms for solving problems instead of being concerned with the details of a computer's internal structure. Operating systems were also developed with a similar objective. When a program written in a high-level language is executed by a computer, the following steps are followed:

(i) The compiler that translates the program is loaded into the memory.
(ii) The source program is read and loaded in the memory.
(iii) The source program is compiled into the object program. While compiling if any syntax errors are detected in the program, appropriate messages are displayed or printed.
(iv) During compilation, machine language routines for reading and writing data the program requires are brought from a library of routines stored in a secondary store and linked to the object program. The resulting program is stored in the secondary memory (usually a disk).
(v) The compiler may now be removed from the main memory as its job is over and the space is available for the data and the compiled object program. The object program is now executed. If any errors are detected during execution, the contents of various registers in the CPU at that time are communicated to the user to aid him in correcting the program.

If a computer system supports many languages, it will have many compilers. Therefore, the appropriate compiler should be selected and loaded in Step 1. The input-output routines for different devices should include monitoring their status and detecting errors. Experts program these with great care to relieve users of this chore. As all programs need these routines, they are kept in secondary storage with appropriate identification for easy retrieval.

In effect, a computer system must provide, besides the hardware and high-level language translators, many other routines that enable a user to use the system effectively. An *operating system* provides these routines. The computer user does not merely interact with the physical hardware of the machine. She interacts with hardware + operating system + compilers + application programs. In Figure 10.1, we have illustrated this fact. Thus, a user of a modern computer system uses a *virtual* (or non-existent) *machine* with features that include, besides those provided by its hardware, several, functions provided by an operating system.

An operating system (abbreviated as OS) may thus be defined *as a set of system programs that control and coordinate the operations of a computer system to provide an intuitively simple, high-level abstraction of its hardware to a user hiding all low-level details.* It also allocates a computer's resources to users efficiently when requested. Some of the major functions of a modern operating system are:

- Ease of interaction between humans and computers. This is known as *the human-computer interface*, which may be a Graphic User Interface (GUI) or command lines.
- Start the operation of a computer automatically when power is turned on.
- Load users' programs along with the appropriate compiler.
- Control input and output devices and programs.
- Control execution of programs.
- Schedule processes.
- Manage inter-process communication.
- Manage the use of various memory levels, namely, the caches, the main memory, and the disk.

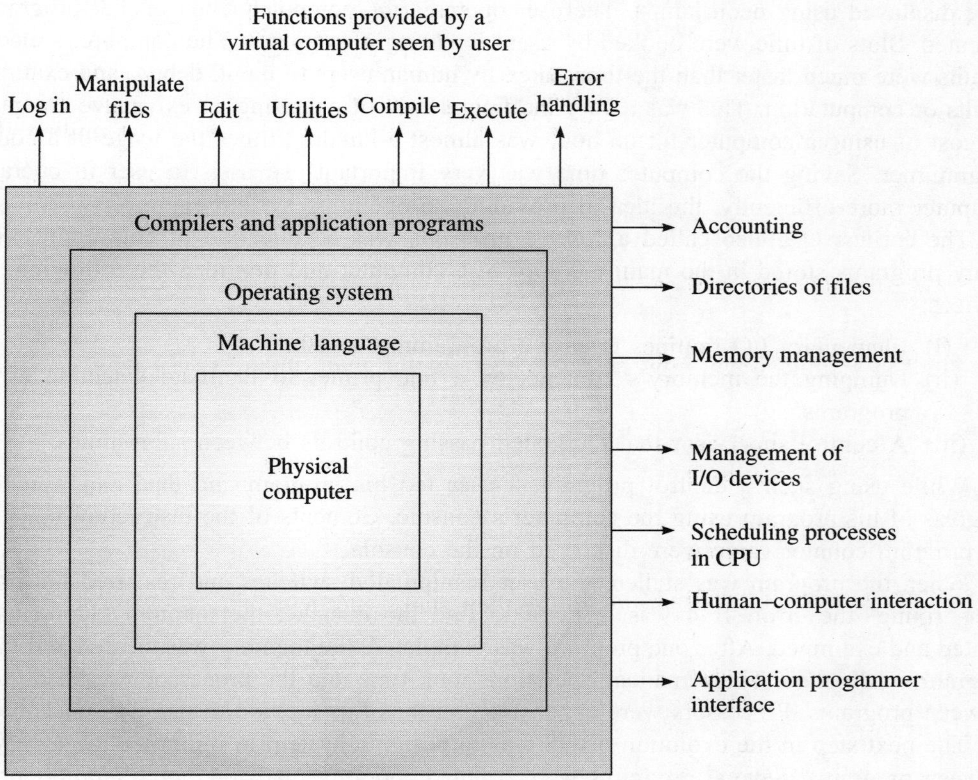

Figure 10.1 Illustration of user's virtual machine.

- Manage and manipulate files, that is, manage opening, writing, editing, and closing named files.
- Maintain directories of users' files and facility to search directories.
- Provide security to users' programs and data files.
- Account for the usage of the computer's resources.
- Allow application programs to use some of the low-level services of the OS, such as device drivers, and function calls, through Application Programmer Interface (API).
- Optimize the utilization of hardware resources of a computer.

Every OS has a *kernel* or a *nucleus* that permanently resides in the main memory of the computer to perform some of the basic functions of the OS and to access other portions of the OS only when they are needed. The remaining parts of an OS are normally stored in a disk ready to be loaded into the main memory when required and ordered by the kernel.

10.2 BATCH OPERATING SYSTEM

When computers were first designed, during the early 1950s, they primarily had machine language and I/O using card readers or paper tape readers. There were switches on the front panel of a computer that could be operated by the user. The contents of important registers were displayed using neon lamps. The user operated the computer when his/her program was executed. Slots of time were booked by users for using a computer. The computer's electronic circuits were much faster than the time taken by human users to input, debug, and examine the results of computation. This was a very inefficient way of operating an expensive computer as the cost of using a computer for an hour was almost a hundred times the wage of a computer programmer. Saving the computer time was very important. To assist a user in operating a computer more efficiently, the idea of providing an operating system emerged.

The earliest OS, also called a *control program,* was a collection of commonly required utility programs stored in the main memory of a computer and provided the following simple services:

(i) Elementary I/O routines to ease a programmer's task.
(ii) Dumping the memory's contents on a line printer to facilitate detecting errors in programs.
(iii) A control supervisor that facilitated passing controls between subroutines.

While using such a control program, a user fed his program and data and watched the progress of his program using the computer's console. Contents of the instruction register and the program counter value were displayed on the console.

When the program was stalled, the user manipulated switches and restarted the program after 'fixing' the error. If it was difficult to find the mistake, the memory's contents were printed and examined. After one program was completed, the memory was cleared and the next program was loaded. These manual operations took time and the processor was made to wait between programs. Processors were expensive and thus this method of use was uneconomical.

The next step in the evolution of OS was to design a system to minimize the time wasted between programs. Several programs were batched and kept ready. A *batch monitor* program was written which facilitated the transition from one program in the batch to the next without manual intervention. The algorithm of a batch monitor was as follows:

```
Repeat
    begin
        Read a program;
        Compile the program;
        if no errors are found during compilation
            then execute the object code and take the next program
            else give an error message and take the next program;
    end
Until no programs are left in the input queue.
```

Each program was identified by a distinctive 'program-begin' statement and a 'program-end' statement. The batch monitor used these statements to separate one program from the next.

In a *batch operating system*, whenever a computer accepts a batch of programs for processing, some means should be available to separate the programs in a batch, provide a program with the appropriate compiler, detect errors during compilation or execution, and provide the I/O routines required by it. For this purpose, each program has, besides the program itself, a set of Job Control Language (JCL) instructions that inform the batch operating system about the identity and the requirements of the job.

10.3 MULTIPROGRAMMING OPERATING SYSTEM

In a batch OS, programs are executed sequentially one after another. If one program requires only half the available memory, the other half is not utilized. Further, when a program requires I/O, the CPU will be idle. As I/O is slow, processor time is often wasted. To solve this problem, an OS that used multiprogramming emerged in the early 1960s. In a multiprogrammed OS, programs belonging to several users are stored in the computer's main memory and scheduled to maximize the utilization of resources, such as the processor and the main memory. To enable an OS to do this effectively, several innovations in computer architecture were introduced. The specific features of interest in designing multiprogrammed OS are:

- DMA (Section 8.1)
- Interrupts (Section 8.4)
- Base register to allow program relocation in memory (Section 5.5)

We will now see how these hardware features are used by the multiprogrammed OS to optimize the use of resources in a computer system.

Let us take a computer in which we want to run three programs J1, J2, and J3. All these programs will require input and output. In Figure 10.2a, we give a time chart of running these three programs J1, J2, and J3. If they are run sequentially, one after another, the total time to complete J1, J2, and J3 is 27 units. Out of this, the processor is used only for 12 units of time, whereas I/O takes 15 units of time.

In a multiprogrammed OS (see Section 8.6 on multiprogramming), we keep all three jobs J1, J2, and J3 ready in the main memory. We schedule jobs by picking J1 first which needs minimum I/O time to run. As soon as J1's I/O is over, J2's I/O can be scheduled and overlapped with J1's processing. Taking care that the I/O and processing of two jobs go on simultaneously, we arrive at Figure 10.2b. Observe that by overlapping the scheduling of the I/O and processing of these three jobs, the completion time of J1, J2, and J3 has reduced to 16 units from 27 units and the processor idle time from 15 units to 4 units. In this example, we have taken I/O times to be quite small (to enable drawing of the figures), even though in practice it is much larger. I/O is at least 1000 times slower than processing. In practice, several programs with the necessary data ready to be allocated CPU will be kept in the main memory and scheduled. To design a multiprogrammed OS, we have to find answers to several important questions. They are:

1. Among several programs waiting to be allocated CPU time in the main memory, which should be selected and assigned CPU time? This is called *processor allocation*.
2. How does an OS allocate sufficient space in the main memory for programs? How does an OS ensure that a program stored in the main memory does not overwrite other programs sharing the main memory? How does an OS ensure that the main memory space is efficiently utilized? This is called *memory management*.
3. How does an OS select a program from among several programs waiting in the secondary memory to be allocated space in the main memory so that it can be executed? What other resources does a program require which should be allocated to it? This is called *scheduling* and *resource allocation*.

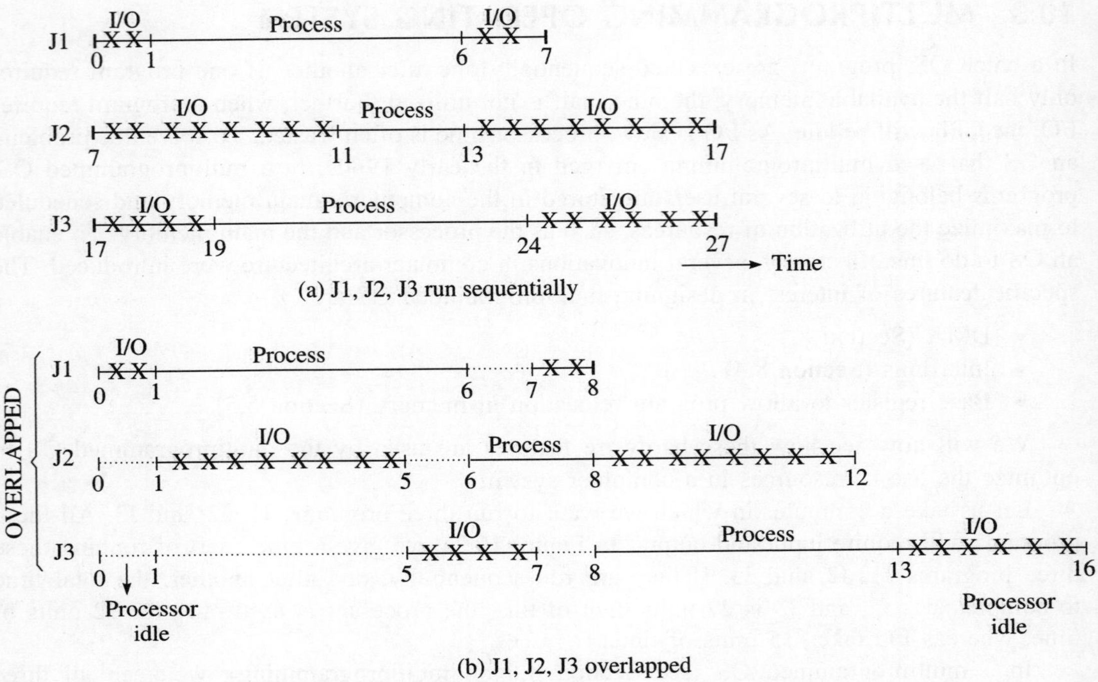

Figure 10.2 Scheduling jobs in multiprogramming.

We will now discuss these aspects of a multiprogrammed OS in what follows:

Process states

Before we begin, we explain the difference between a *program* and a *process*. A program is a set of instructions stored in the main memory as static text. When the program is allocated CPU time and permitted to start execution, it becomes a process. In contrast to a program, a process is dynamic. It executes instructions, reads and writes data, and may overwrite data in memory.

In a multiprogrammed system, several selected programs will reside in the main memory and several on a disk (see Figure 10.3). Programs called *monitor* and *scheduler* are part of the OS which permanently reside in the main memory. I/O programs to read/write to external devices are also normally stored in the main memory. Many programs are stored in the disk and are read from the disk and placed in the main memory for execution as and when required.

A program in the main memory may be in one of three states. They are:

1. It is ready for execution but is waiting to be allocated CPU time. This is called the READY state.
2. It is selected by the scheduler of the OS, has moved to the CPU, and starts executing. It is called the RUNNING state.
3. It may require to read from an input device or to write on an output device and thus cannot execute further. It is called the BLOCKED state.

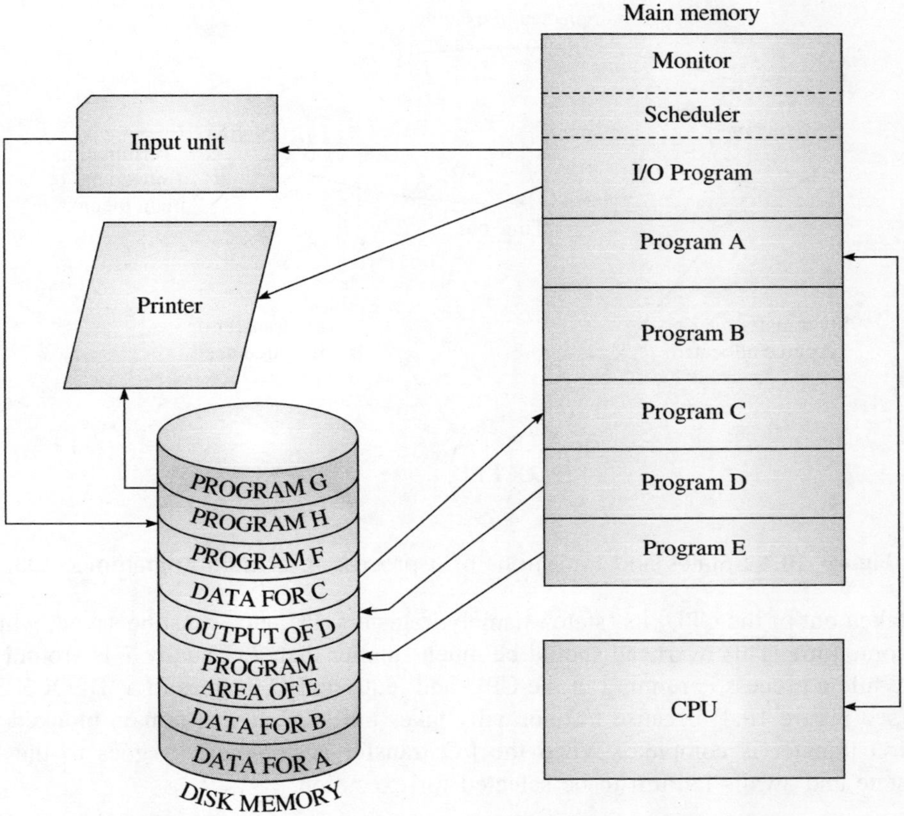

Figure 10.3 Illustration of a multiprogrammed operating system.

In Figure 10.4, we illustrate how a processor transitions between these states. Normally execution proceeds in the following steps.

1. A program with the data necessary to execute it waits in the main memory ready to run as soon as it gets CPU allocated. It is now in a READY state. When does it get its turn to run? It is a design issue. It may get to use the CPU because it is waiting for a long time or has high priority (it may be an OS Job). Usually, to ensure fairness, the programs stored in the main memory are queued up and a first-in, first-out policy is often used.
2. When a program is at the top of the queue, it is selected to execute in the CPU and goes to the 'RUNNING' state. The major policy decision now is how long this process should be allowed to run. To ensure that a long-running process does not monopolize the CPU and that a process stuck in a loop due to an error does not run indefinitely, a fixed time T is allocated to a process. As soon as this time is over, it is taken out of the CPU and sent to the main memory. In Figure 10.4, it is shown as 'time out'. This fixed time T should not be too small because each time a process is

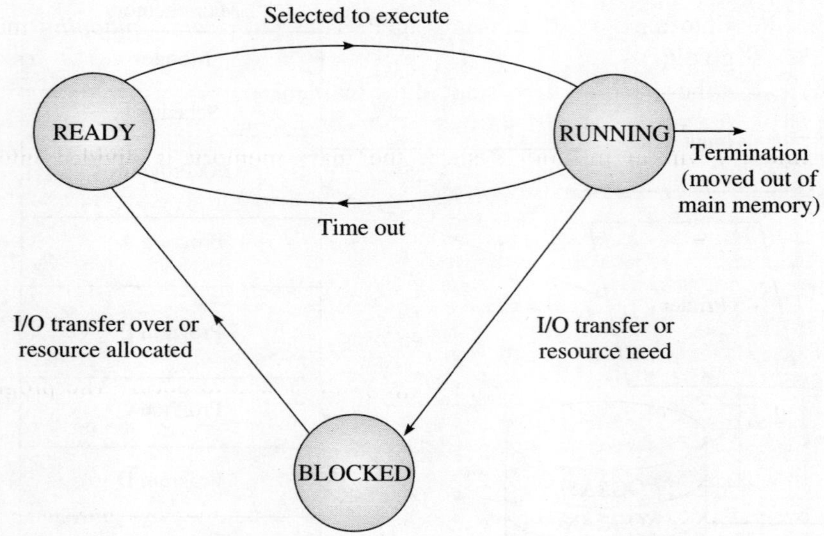

Figure 10.4 States and transitions of a process in a multiprogrammed OS.

taken out of the CPU, its 'state', namely, registers, PC, etc., must be saved, which takes some time. This overhead should be much smaller than *T*. Usually *T* is around 200 ms.

3. While a process is running in the CPU and requests I/O, it goes to a 'BLOCKED' state (see Figure 10.4) because I/O normally takes too long. It will remain blocked until the I/O transfer is complete. When the I/O transfer is complete, it goes to the READY state and awaits its turn to be selected for execution.

The task of selecting a program to run and monitor its progress is performed by a scheduler which is part of the OS.

Virtual memory

One may loosely describe a *virtual memory* as a hierarchy of two memory systems. One is a low-cost, high-capacity, low-speed system and the other is a high-cost, low-capacity, high-speed system. The two memory systems are managed by the OS in such a way that it appears to a user as a single, large, directly addressable, and fast main memory. There are two main reasons why virtual memory is used. They are:

1. To allow users to have the convenience of using a large addressable memory space without worrying about the size limitations of a physical main memory.
2. To permit, in a multiprogrammed OS, efficient sharing of the main memory space among different users.

To understand virtual memory systems, we must distinguish between the symbolic address appearing in a program, called the *logical address space* L, and the set of actual addresses available in the main memory, called the *physical address space* P. L is usually larger than P and hence the term virtual memory. During the execution of a program, each logical address *l* in L is translated into a physical address *p* in P. Thus, an *address-mapping* mechanism is needed which will give $f(l) \rightarrow p$.

If it is found that the specified item is not in the main memory, the execution of the program is suspended while the relevant item is transferred to the main memory from the disk memory.

To implement a virtual memory system, the main memory is divided into fixed-size contiguous areas called *page frames*. Programs are also divided into slices of the same size called *pages*.

At any given time, the processor uses the logical address to retrieve an item from the memory. A *page address table* is maintained by the OS which has information on which pages of each program are in the main memory at a given time. Before retrieving a word, the algorithm checks the page address table to see if the required word is on a page in the main memory. If it is not in the main memory, a *page fault* is said to occur. The program is then suspended till the required page is brought to the main memory from the disk memory. The page address table is simultaneously updated. In a multiprogrammed OS, the processor will switch to another program while a page is swapped from the disk to the main memory. Page swapping is an I/O operation between the disk and the main memory and is independently controlled by a DMA channel.

An algorithm called a *demand paging* algorithm is used to swap programs between the main memory and the disk memory and is given below:

Algorithm for demand paging

```
Step 1:  Compute the physical address l of the next word to be retrieved by the program;
Step 2:  Look up the page address table to see if l is in the main memory M;
Step 3:  if l is in M
         then
         begin
             Fetch the required word from the main memory; Decode the fetched word and
             execute the instruction;
             go to Step 1
         end
         else Suspend normal execution of the program and continue with the next step;
Step 4:  if there is a free page frame in M
         then go to Step 5
         else
         begin
             Select a page frame F in M to be replaced and mark it as free.
             if F is altered
             then Transfer page frame F to the disk
             else go to Step 5
         end;
Step 5:  Transfer page containing l from the disk to free page frame F in M;
Step 6:  Update the page address table and go to Step 1.
```

A base register is used for dynamic memory management in such a system. The OS adds the content of the base register, which is a *page address,* to every memory address generated by a program, thereby translating it to the right page. The OS maintains a page address table for each program.

Memory management

In a multiprogrammed system, several programs are stored in the main memory. Figure 10.5 gives a snapshot of the main memory.

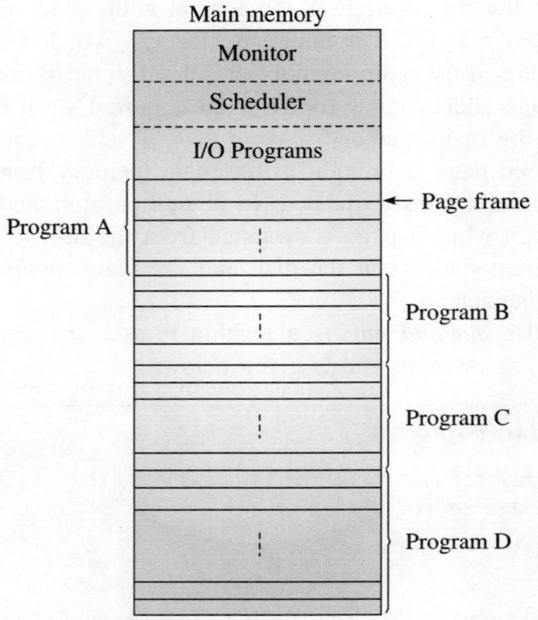

Figure 10.5 Paging of programs in main memory.

Some essential parts of the OS and some frequently used I/O programs are kept permanently in the main memory. These will occupy some page frames. Page sizes are normally about 512 bytes. Thus, a main memory of 4 GB will have 8192K page frames. Out of these, several programs may be allocated a few thousand pages each. The number of pages allocated to each program may be different. As the size of a program may be much larger than the number of pages allocated to it in the main memory, only a part of it will be in the main memory and the rest will be in the disk store. Thus, the memory management system of the OS has to perform the following two tasks:

1. Given the address *a* of an instruction of, say, a process B in RUNNING state (see Figure 10.4), transform that address to a page number and location in the page number.
2. Find out whether this page has been allocated a page frame in the main memory. If yes, find the page frame address and its location in the memory and execute it. If no, decide which page of B has to be moved to the disk from the main memory to accommodate this page. As this procedure will take some time (as the disk access is slow), B will be blocked. Thus, control is handed over to the OS scheduler.

The first task is straightforward as the formula for finding page numbers and location is simple. If the page size is p, the page number of address a is:

page number = a div p, where div gives integer quotient

location = a mod p, where mod gives remainder after division

The second task is to find whether this page is in the memory. To expedite these tasks, the OS maintains one table for each program currently in the main memory. This table has the entries given in Table 10.1.

Table 10.1 Page table entries for program B

Page No.	*Is it in memory?*	*Page frame*	*Information on page usage*
X	Yes	Y	xxx
U	No	Nil	–
Q	Yes	Z	yyy

In the example of Figure 10.5, there are four programs resident in the main memory and thus there will be four tables maintained by the OS. This table has to be referred for each address of the program to be executed. If it is kept in the main memory, two accesses to the main memory would be required for an instruction to be executed. This can slow down a process. Thus, this table is kept in a small fast memory that is a part of the CPU.

If the page to be executed is not in the main memory, the OS has to choose a page frame of B, the currently running process, to take out of the memory to accommodate the page containing the instruction to be executed. As examples, we describe three policies which can be used to make this choice:

1. *LRU policy*: Remove from the memory the least recently used page. The logic is that if a page is not used recently, it may not be used again soon. (Remember that most programs are sequential with locality of memory access).
2. *First-in, first-out policy*: Remove the page that came in first, that is, has been resident for a long time in the main memory. The logic of this policy is that the page that came in first has been in the main memory for a long time and may not be needed anymore.
3. *Working set policy*: In this policy, for a specified window of time T, a table of recently used pages is kept (this window moves in real-time). If a page is not in this window, it is removed from the main memory to accommodate a new page. This new page is now a part of the working set. The logic of this policy is again the locality of reference to instructions and data by most programs. Thus, pages in the working set are most likely to be referred to again soon.

The fourth column in Table 10.1 has the information used to implement one of the above three policies chosen by the OS.

Process scheduling

An important responsibility of an OS is to select one program from among the many programs waiting in the main memory to be executed and allot CPU time to it. All programs in a ready state are candidates to be scheduled to run on the CPU. There are several policies one may use for this. Two of them are as follows:

1. *Round Robin:* In this policy, a quantum of about 100 ms is allocated to each ready program. When it exhausts its allocated time, the next program in the queue is given CPU time. After all the waiting programs run on the CPU, the first program in the queue is scheduled again.
2. *Priority scheduling:* Each program is given a priority weight. The programs are allocated to the CPU based on their priority. A danger in this method is that a low-priority program may never be serviced. Thus, a parameter for assigning priority is how long the program has been waiting to be serviced. In general, priority given to a program would be a function of its resource need, available resources, the length of time it is waiting, and the urgency to process it. For example, a program to read a disk is more urgent than that needed to read from a keyboard. In this method, each program specifies the resources it needs. A programmer may specify it using a command language (to be discussed later) which will be interpreted by the OS. The OS assigns priority based on the resources requested and those available.

Resource-based scheduling can be static or dynamic. In static scheduling, all the resources needed are reserved for the quantum of time a process needs it and only then the process is scheduled. In dynamic scheduling, resources are allocated when they are free. One problem which may arise in dynamic scheduling is a *deadlock.* A process B may hold a resource X which is needed by another process C. Process C may hold a resource Y needed by B. This situation blocks both processes. (It is similar to a traffic jam at a railway level crossing where some vehicles overtake a queue and occupy the wrong lane. On both sides of the level crossing, this may happen and no vehicle can proceed as both lanes are blocked.) There are several methods to prevent a deadlock. We will not discuss these. Those interested should read the books on OS mentioned in the references.

10.4 TIME SHARING OPERATING SYSTEM

If a computer is used in batch mode, a user submits his job along with several other users, and all the jobs are put in a job queue and fed to the computer. Many jobs in the queue are kept in the computer's memory and a multiprogramming OS is invoked which schedules the execution of individual jobs, with the main objective of keeping all computer's units busy. Using this method, the total number of jobs the computer processes in a given period is maximized. This is known as maximizing the computer's *throughput.* An individual user, on the other hand, would like to minimize the time elapsed between submission of his job and getting the results. This time is known as the *turnaround* time. If the user can use the computer to execute only his job and no other jobs (as is done when you use a PC), the turnaround time will be minimal. It is very desirable for a programmer to observe the effect of changes in his program on the results during program development. A multiprogrammed batch system will not allow such an interaction with an individual programmer because it aims to increase the throughput of a computer system. *Time sharing operating systems* were designed in the mid-1960s to give a fast turnaround to an individual user while catering to many users. The main motivation for this was the decline of computer hardware cost, whereas the cost, of programmers who develop software was increasing. Programs were also becoming larger and more difficult to debug. Interactive computer use with a time shared OS expedited debugging and saved programmers' time.

It is not economically feasible to allow a single user to use a large expensive computer (such as a mainframe or a supercomputer) interactively as his speed of thinking and typing is much slower than the processing speed of a computer. Thus, a computer would be idle most of the time if only a single user used it interactively. It is, therefore, necessary to allow a large number of users, each using the computer interactively, to time share it. A time sharing operating system provides this facility. In a time sharing system, many video terminals are attached to a computer. Each user has a terminal available to him. A user can initiate a program from his terminal and interact with the computer during its execution. Typically, a user enters a program from a terminal and corrects any data entry errors. The program is then stored as a file on disk. The user then compiles his program by invoking a compiler through a command from the terminal. If any syntax errors are found in the program by the compiler, they are displayed on the video screen. The user corrects his program using an editing system and recompiles it from the terminal. When all the syntax errors are corrected, the program is submitted to the processor for execution. The requisite data is fed from the terminal during program execution. The data may also be stored in a disk and fed to the program when needed. Errors encountered during the execution of the program are displayed on the terminal. If no errors are found, the answers may be displayed on the terminal or stored on a disk.

In a time shared computer, around 50 terminals are connected to a large computer, and all the terminals are simultaneously provided access to the computer's resources. The time sharing operating system allocates about 20 ms to each terminal during which a program belonging to this terminal's user is executed. In 20 ms, about $(20 \times 10^{-3})/10^{-7}) = 200{,}000$ instructions can be carried out by a processor whose speed is 10 million instructions per second. If 50 terminals are working simultaneously and if 20 ms is allocated to each terminal, a given terminal will get the processor's attention once in every 20×50 ms = 1 s. As human reaction time is a few seconds, a terminal user will not notice any delay in carrying out his commands and may feel that the machine is working solely for him! As the total memory available in a computer is limited, it is impossible to keep the entire programs of all the users of a time sharing system simultaneously in the main memory. The time sharing operating system would keep only that portion of a program that is being executed currently in the main memory. The remaining part is kept in disk storage. As and when a segment of a program is to be executed, it is brought to the main memory from the disk, and the inactive segment is sent to the disk. Transferring programs from the main memory to the disk storage and back is known as *swapping*.

Multiprogramming is necessary in a time sharing system because several programs are kept in the disk memory. Thus, one may view a time sharing OS as a multiprogramming OS with a job scheduling algorithm to aid simultaneous interactive use of a large computer by many users.

In this and previous sections, we described batch OS, multiprogramming OS, and time sharing OS. These systems evolved primarily between the mid-1950s and mid-1970s. They were used in computers which are known as mainframe computers. Nowadays mainframe computers which are capable of handling tens of thousands of data records such as payroll processing, tax calculations, and computations for large banks are primarily used by big corporations, financial institutions, and airlines. Airlines and railways have large volumes of transactions to process. Their computers have to simultaneously cater to several customers' requests for service (such as railway reservations). Time sharing OS with fast response is appropriate for these transaction processing applications. Batch processing with multiprogramming OS is primarily used for processing large volumes of data. The number of mainframes manufactured today is small. International Business Machines (IBM) is the primary manufacturer of mainframe computers (IBM z17 in 2025). It uses an operating system called Linux which we describe later in this chapter.

A less expensive alternative to mainframes is called *a server*. Servers use the same architecture as PCs but with much larger configurations. In other words, they have large main memory of around 256 GB, large disks of around 2 TB, and high-speed CPUs with clock speeds exceeding 5 GHz. These servers are connected to low-cost PCs with smaller configurations called *clients* and to diskless computers with very little computing power that provide a graphical user interface like PCs, known as *thin clients*. These clients are used as intelligent terminals and can use the computing power and files stored in the server. Multiprogramming/time sharing OSs are executed on the servers. Servers are primarily used for transaction processing. They are also used to host web pages of large organizations as they will be accessed by clients from all over the world. Currently, popular OSs for servers are Unix and Linux, and Microsoft's Windows Server 2022. Microsoft Server OS is also used by servers in Microsoft's Cloud named Azure. (See Section 17.4 on Cloud Computing).

Multitasking

Currently, desktop and laptop computers dominate the market and millions of people own them. With the improvement in technology PCs now (2025) have over 32 GB memory, disks of over 1 TB, and CPUs with multi-processors running at 5 GHz clock. They are used for applications such as word processing, surfing the World Wide Web, playing games, accessing databases, and running spreadsheet programs. A single user uses the computer in a time-shared mode. In other words, slices of CPU time are allocated to programs just as in a time-shared OS. The computer is used to perform several tasks seemingly simultaneously. Music from an Internet radio station may be playing in the background while word processing. This is called *multitasking*. In multitasking, the CPU is time shared by several programs of a single user. The operating systems of PCs, nowadays, are multitasking OSs.

10.5 ONLINE AND REAL-TIME SYSTEMS

A time shared operating system allows a user to interact with a computer and it facilitates program development. The *response time* of a good time shared computer system to users' requests is 1 or 2 seconds. Delays in response are irritating to a user but are not catastrophic. Users' files are available 'online' on a disk and may be retrieved quickly. Several users' programs are stored in the system in their protected areas on the disk.

Another mode of use of a time shared system is to have one application program and one database (shared by this application program) stored in a large capacity disk. Many users can simultaneously use this application program. Time sharing is useful in implementing an airline or railway reservation system where several users simultaneously access the computer to make reservations. In such a system, the response time should be very short because a customer's ticket should be reserved while he waits. A small delay, however, would not be disastrous. Access to the system should be serialized when two users simultaneously try to reserve the last available seat. This is called concurrency control. Files should be updated immediately after a transaction is completed. As soon as a seat is reserved for a flight, the available seats should be reduced by one. Such systems are called *online transaction processing systems*.

There are applications in which a computer is expected to control the operation of a physical system. For example, a satellite in orbit is normally controlled by a computer. The position, velocity, acceleration, and spin information of the satellite are fed to the control computer which is programmed to compute the orbit and give instructions to the rocket motors of the satellite to correct the orbit. In such an application, the operation is in *real-time*; that is, the control has to be exercised during the actual functioning of the system. Any delay beyond that specified for control would be disastrous. Real-time operating systems have to work within strict time limits for critical jobs. Critical jobs are locked in memory and receive the highest priority.

Real-time systems should be highly reliable, without downtime, and incorporate fault-tolerant design. Any failure of a system that controls a space vehicle in motion may result in a fatal accident. In such cases, duplicate systems are used so that if one system fails, the other will take over.

10.6 OTHER FACILITIES PROVIDED BY OPERATING SYSTEMS

I/O handling

Operating systems have an important job of handling I/O. The major problems in handling I/O devices are:

- I/O device characteristics vary enormously. For example, a printer is a slow device, whereas a disk is a fast device.
- I/O devices are manufactured by a large number of different manufacturers and have properties specified by the manufacturer and they are not uniform.
- New types of I/O devices appear regularly and an OS has to handle a new device as and when it is introduced in the market.
- OS has to initiate the I/O operation and end it when the job of the I/O device is over.

To alleviate the problem of handling a variety of devices, another program called a *device driver* is usually supplied by device manufacturers. Device drivers have two parts: a logical layer to interact with the OS and a physical layer that issues device-specific commands. The logical layer is loadable to the kernel of the OS and is loaded as necessary. Users' commands may be as simple as reading from a device, writing using a device, starting a device, stopping a device, etc. These are transformed into appropriate system calls by the I/O module of the OS suitable for the device, relieving the user from dealing with the low-level details of the device.

I/O requests are handled by the OS as follows:

- It checks whether the request is legitimate for the process.
- It initiates the transfer of data by executing an OS program appropriate for the device command.
- The process requesting I/O is blocked as I/O is slow. The scheduler of the OS assigns CPU to the next ready process in the queue.

OS is also responsible for handling interrupts. It has to perform the following tasks:

- Determine the source of the interrupt
- Save the state of the interrupting process
- Monitor I/O activity
- Resume the interrupted process when I/O is complete by restoring its state

The entire interrupt handling and I/O transfer operation is invisible to the system's user. Thus, users are relieved of dealing with all low-level details.

File system

One of the important facilities a computer provides to its users is the filing of their programs and data. A *file* may be defined as a collection of records about an object. Examples are a program to sort a set of records, data about a group of students in a class, a chapter in a book, and a set of emails received from an individual. Files can be of various types. They may be binary executable files (i.e., compiled programs ready to execute), ASCII files (such as word-processed files), or pictures, audio, video, etc. Normally most OSs allow users to name a file and also to indicate the nature of the file. For example, programl.exe may be an executable file. The part following the dot, namely, exe, indicates to the OS that it is an executable file whereas chapter2.docx would be a Word file, mypicture.jpg a picture file, and myprogram.c a C program source code. The part following the dot is called the file extension and tells the OS how to treat the file.

A file system in an OS typically has facilities to:

- Create a file by giving it a name
- Access a file using its name
- Delete a file
- Manage storage of files in the secondary memory
- Protect files from unauthorized access
- Protect loss or corruption of a file due to hardware or software failures
- Maintain a directory of names of files and their corresponding location in a secondary storage

In a multiuser system, each user will have a *directory*. To enable users' independence in naming files, files are arranged as a two-level directory as shown in Table 10.2.

Observe that each user may use the same name without any clash, as the locations of his/her file are different and the directory gives the file's location on the disk. Usually, besides the name and location, miscellaneous useful information, such as the date of creation of the file, its size, access rights, the date of last update, etc., is kept in the directory for each file.

Table 10.2 Two-level file directory

Master Directory Entries

User 1 Location in disk

⋮

User *n* Location in disk

User 1 directory
myprogram.c–location
mypictures.jpg–location
⋮

User 2 directory

…

User *n* directory
myprogram.c
mypictures.jpg
⋮

Normally OS also provides facilities to back up users' files on a different storage medium to recover the files in case of accidental corruption. Both incremental backup, that is, storing only changes, and full backup, which is storing entire files periodically, are provided.

OS command language

Normally a user is expected to tell the OS what to do. Typically, a user would specify the following:

- Operations to be performed. For example, copy a file XYZ in another file PQR, execute myprogram.c, and delete file ABC.
- The source and destination I/O units from where files are to be accessed. For example, copy file xyz from the disk to a pen drive, and print file ABC on a laser printer.
- Resource needs. For example, print 100 pages of file xyz. If a user does not know the resource needs, the OS will assume a default value.
- Give a username and password to use the computer. The username is also used to bill computer use.

The OS command language is interpreted by a command interpreter. Most current command languages (e.g., oPen drivef Unix OS) are quite easy unlike earlier command languages (called Job Control Language) with mainframe computers. In GUI-based OS, the command language is simplified to use icons and mouse clicks.

10.7 PERSONAL COMPUTER OPERATING SYSTEM

The advent of Personal Computers (PCs) brought about a revolution in computer use. The main mode of PC use (as its name implies) is by a single user. PCs' OS was originally designed as a single-user, single-task operating system, that is, it is assumed, that only one user uses the machine and runs only one program at a time.

The early operating system of PCs consisted of two parts. One part called BIOS (Basic Input Output System) was stored in a ROM (Read Only Memory). The other part called DOS (Disk Operating System) was stored in a hard disk. MS-DOS (Microsoft Disk Operating System) was widely used in IBM PCs and clones.

In MS-DOS, when power is turned on, BIOS takes control. It does what is known as a power-on-self-test. The test sees whether the memory is all right and all other relevant units function. Having done this, it reads from the disk a small portion of the OS known as the *boot* and loads it into the main memory. The boot program then 'pulls' the rest of the OS from the disk and stores it in the main memory. This is known as *booting the system*. Other programs contained in BIOS are as follows:

- System configuration analysis
- Time-of-day
- I/O support programs for
  - — keyboard
  - — disk
  - — pen drive
  - — printer
  - — display

One of the main features of BIOS is that it provides hardware-independent access to the physical devices of a PC, ensuring that programs are simple and portable to other PCs.

BIOS provides basic low-level services, whereas DOS provides many user-level services. The major services available in DOS are:

- File management which allows users to create, edit, read, write, and delete files.
- Directory management allows users to create, change, search, and delete directories.
- Memory management which allows users to allocate and deallocate memory.
- Command interpreter which interprets commands issued by the user and executes DOS functions, utility programs, or application programs.
- Executive functions that provide programs to load and execute user programs, retrieve error codes, and correct and re-run programs.
- Utility programs that do housekeeping chores such as COPY, ERASE, DIR, etc.

The interfaces and levels of functionality of MS-DOS are not well separated (Figure 10.6). Application programs can access I/O routines to write directly on the disk, display unit, etc. which allows programs to corrupt users' systems without their knowledge.

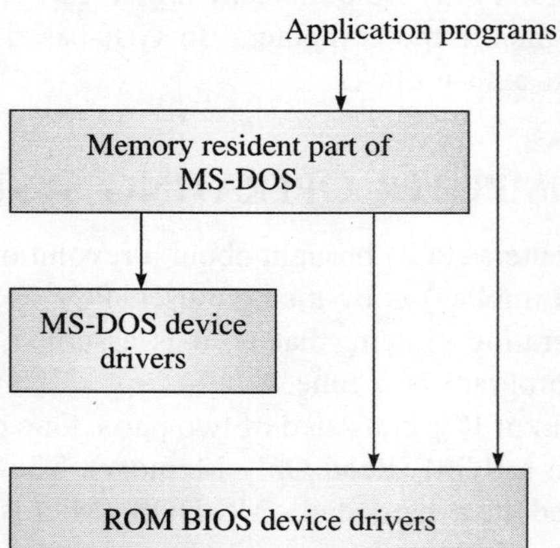

Figure 10.6 Structure of MS-DOS operating system.

Earlier versions of MS-DOS were written for smaller IBM systems which used Intel 8088 microprocessor. They limited program addressability to 640 KB. Furthermore, MS-DOS did not allow two programs stored in memory to run concurrently protected from one another.

Currently, microprocessors have become very powerful. They use fast processors and have main memories of 16 GB and a hard disk of 1 TB. Owing to its limitations, MS-DOS cannot use this power. Better OSs were written. The important ones were MS Windows released in 1985, Windows 95 released in 1995, Windows XP released in 2001, Windows 7 released in 2009, and recently Windows 11 in 2021. All these were released by Microsoft and are proprietary. Another popular OS used by PCs is Linux, an OS similar to Unix, which we will describe in Section 10.9. Apple's PCs use a Unix-based OS called macOS.

A major release of Microsoft was Windows 95. Windows 95 provided an easier way for a user to work with a PC using a Graphical User Interface. Instead of typing commands, a user can point to a graphical icon on the monitor and click a mouse button. It provided a taskbar and a desktop metaphor on the screen. Icons representing files, folders, and trash bin were available to users. For example, to delete a file, a user moved it to a trash bin appearing on the screen and clicked a button on the mouse. File names could be long (up to 255 characters). MS Windows 95 allowed multitasking.

The latest Microsoft OS is named Windows 11 and was introduced in 2021. It has the following features:

- An improved taskbar and new icons.
- Hot plug and play. In other words, new input/output devices can be connected to the computer while it is working.
- Personalized widgets such as a clock, calendar, weather, news, etc. can be quickly accessed.
- Multitasking has been improved.
- Virtual desktops could be created for different projects.
- Improved biometric security for logging in.
- Microsoft Teams – a video conferencing system can be accessed using an icon on the taskbar.
- It supports touch gestures and voice typing.
- It integrates AI tools such as Windows Copilot.

The main drawback of Windows 11 is the need for a modern multi-core high-performance PC with a system clock of at least 1 GHz, 4 GB RAM, 64 GB available storage, secure booting, a better graphics card, and a good Internet connection.

The other popular Personal Computer OS is macOS used by Apple's Mac series of computers. Various versions of macOS are used in Apple desktops and laptops. Apple iPhones use iOS. All of them are based on the Unix OS which we discuss in what follows. The major advantage of macOS is its security. Whereas Microsoft's OSs are prone to virus attacks and need anti-virus software, macOS has better built-in protection against virus attacks. macOS also has a user-friendly graphical user interface.

10.8 UNIX OPERATING SYSTEM

Unix is a *multiuser, time sharing operating system* that was written in 1973 by Ken Thompson and Dennis Ritchie at the Bell Telephone Laboratories, USA. It was not conceived as a commercial system but was written for the convenience of a group of programmers at Bell Laboratories. It was written for a small PDP-7 computer manufactured by Digital Equipment Corporation (DEC). Unlike other operating systems in the 1970s, Unix was written in a high-level language C, which was revolutionary. By writing the OS in C, both storage and running time increased by 30–40% but as events have shown, this loss in efficiency did not affect the spread of Unix as an OS because computer systems became larger, faster, and cheaper every year. Unix became a very popular OS and has been implemented on numerous models of computers. The varieties of Unix systems implemented use the general philosophy advocated by Unix designers but differ in implementation details. The version of Unix implemented by IBM on their workstations is called AIX, and Hewlett Packard's version of Unix is known as HP-UX. A version available in the open domain (by open domain we mean that the source code is available free of cost and can be copied from a computer connected to the Internet) is called *Linux* and is popular. One may wonder why Unix is popular. The major reasons for its popularity are as follows:

- Unix is written in C, a high-level language, and is thus portable to a range of computer systems.
- The interface provided to users is simple and powerful. It provides most of the services that a user normally wants.
- The file system used by Unix is hierarchical which allows efficient implementation and easy maintenance.
- Unix considers all files to be a continuous sequence of characters, known as a *byte stream.* Application programs thus have the flexibility to format the files as per their requirements.
- Unix treats peripheral devices as if they are files. They are given file names, and thus programs can access peripheral devices with the same syntax as they use when accessing regular files. Thus, Unix provides a simple, consistent interface to peripheral devices.
- Unix is a multiuser, multiprogrammed, time-shared OS. Individual users can execute several processes simultaneously. Processes can communicate among themselves. It can also be time shared by several users.
- Unix supports a scripting language (see Chapter 9) called *shell* which allows complex jobs to be performed using several built-in programs provided by Unix. The output of a shell command can be fed as input to another shell command, without the need to store the output in a file, by a mechanism known as a *pipe*.
- Unix assumes no knowledge of a machine's architecture from a user. Thus, programs written using Unix can be run on several architectures.
- Unix can support any programming language with a compiler or an interpreter, provided it has an interface that maps user requests for OS services to the standard set of requests used by Unix.

As we can see from the above, the philosophy of the design of Unix emphasizes uniformity and simplicity.

10.8.1 Unix System Layers

The Unix OS can be thought of as a layered system. The innermost core is called the *kernel.* The kernel is a set of programs that perform various primitive operations requested by user processes. The following services are provided by the Unix kernel:

- Controlling the creation, suspension, and termination of processes. Kernel also controls Inter-process communication.
- Scheduling processes on the CPU. In a time-shared mode, the CPU is shared by several processes. Thus, to be fair, each process is given a time slice. When the time slice expires, the process is suspended and one of the waiting processes is scheduled. The suspended process is scheduled again when its turn comes.
- The main memory is allocated to an executing process as requested by the process. If sufficient memory is not available, a waiting process is written on a disk, and memory occupied by it is temporarily allocated to the executing process. Processes may have private and public address space. Kernel protects the private address space from accidental tampering.
- It manages users' files by providing them space in secondary storage, protecting them from illegal access, and ensuring efficient storage and retrieval.
- It provides processes-controlled access to peripheral devices, such as terminals, disk drives, and network devices.

All these services are provided by hiding all low-level details from user processes.

The next layer has programs supported by the OS. The most interesting of these is called *shell*, which is a command interpreter.

Shell provides a large number of useful commands. Users can create a series of shell commands and store them in a file. This file can be made an executable file and when invoked will act as a new shell command. Unix also provides a very interesting idea called a *pipe.* A pipe is a way to send the output of one program as the input of another program without storing the output of the first program in a temporary file. A *pipeline* is a connection of two or more programs through pipes.

There are large families of Unix shell programs that read an input, perform a single transformation, and write an output. For example, there is a command called *grep* which searches a file for lines that match a given pattern and outputs them. A command *sort* sorts a file as specified. A command that accepts its standard input processes it, and sends the result to its standard output is called a *filter*. Apart from filters provided by the system, a user can create a filter by combining shell commands.

The outermost layer of Unix has language compilers for C, Fortran 90, etc. A unique feature of the language compilers in Unix is that they provide a common object code format which allows easy mixing of high-level languages.

Unix has some good text-processing programs. Many utilities, such as calendars, games, and graphics, are available. In Figure 10.7, we show the structure of the layers in Unix.

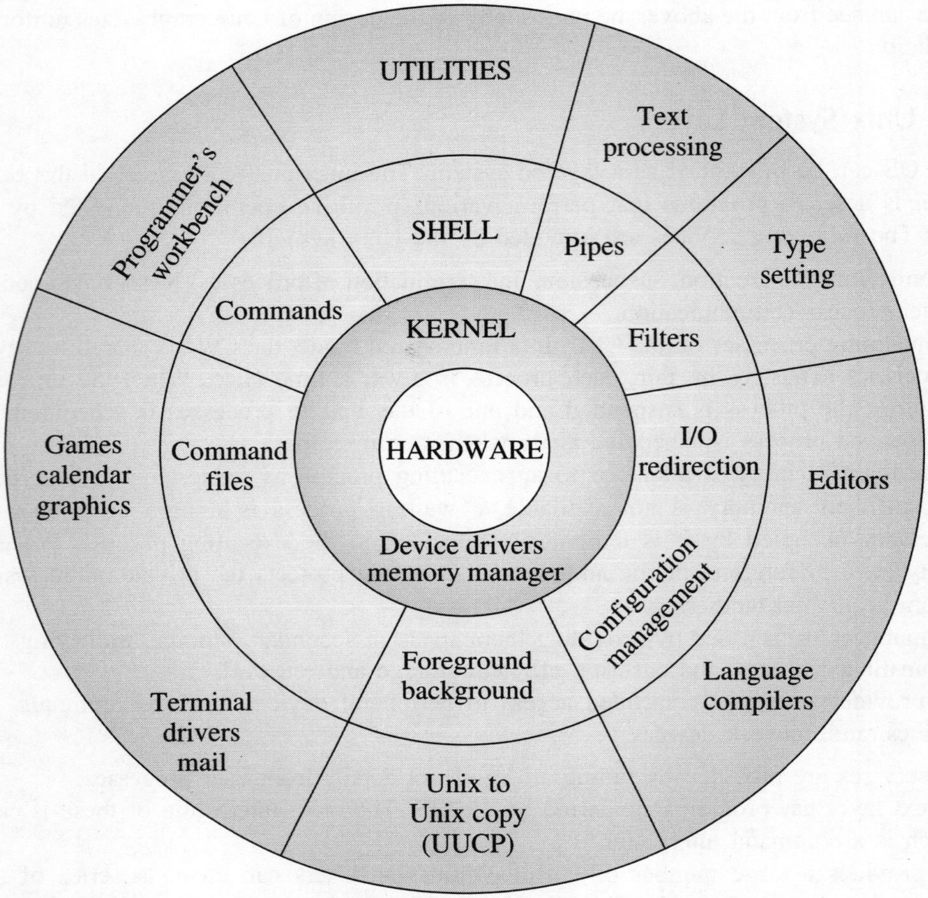

Figure 10.7 Layers of Unix operating system.

Execution of user processes on Unix systems is divided into two modes known as *user mode* and *kernel mode*. When a user process requests services provided by the Unix kernel, the execution mode changes from the user mode to the kernel mode. In the user mode, the user process can access its instructions and data and not those belonging to the kernel. The kernel process can, however, access the addresses of user processes. Kernel also controls inter-process communications. Furthermore, some special hardware instructions can be executed only in kernel mode. It should be remembered that the kernel runs on behalf of a user process and does not function independently. Processing interrupts and exceptions and management of memory are all delegated to the kernel. Control of kernel mode is available only to a *root account*. The root account is managed by a *super user* who can use any Unix command without restriction. The super user should be assumed to be the system administrator.

10.9 LINUX OPERATING SYSTEM

Linus Torvalds while he was a student at the University of Helsinki in Finland obtained a copy of GNU, a Unix-like operating system, developed by Richard Stallman and his group at MIT. He found that the system did not include a kernel. He wrote a kernel for GNU using an Intel 80386-based PC in 1991, integrated it with GNU, and called it Linux. He released the Linux source code written in C as a free operating system. It was a well-written OS and soon became popular. Whereas Unix was proprietary and vendors charged a licence fee, Linux was free. As its source code was available groups could modify and improve it. The primary differences between Unix and Linux are:

1. Unix kernel is monolithic and difficult to modify. Linux has loadable kernel modules which allow users to add or remove kernel functionality dynamically.
2. Linux has a huge community support as it is open-source and free. This provides enhanced security.
3. Linux manages files better compared to Unix. Linux kernel provides a Virtual File System layer that supports multiple file types seamlessly.
4. Device management is more flexible in Linux as its kernel is modular.
5. Process and memory management is more flexible in Linux compared to Unix.

Its flexibility and open source have made Linux very popular. Several groups improved Linux over the past decades. The most popular versions of Linux are Debian, Ubuntu, Fedora, Mint, and Open SUSE. Red Hat, a company, released a cleaned-up, priced version of Linux with excellent documentation, educational material, and support to customers. IBM acquired Red Hat in 2019 for $39 billion! It is estimated that Linux and its versions have over 3 million users. It is used in tiny Raspberry Pi computers, Personal Computers, and in the most expensive supercomputer Frontier.

10.10 ANDROID OPERATING SYSTEM

Android operating system was developed by Google in 2008 for smart mobile phones and hand-held tablet computers with touch screens. It is an open-source operating system based on the Linux kernel. The architecture of Android is modular with several layers. Its key features include a customizable interface, multitasking, pre-loaded Gmail, Google Drive, Google Maps, and Google Assistant. It provides Google Play Store which hosts millions of Apps many of which are user-developed and free. It has excellent security and scans apps for malware. It is upgraded frequently for enhanced security and improvements. It supports several natural languages. It has features to assist users with disabilities.

Android, besides its use in smartphones, has also been adapted to wearable devices such as smartwatches, smart TVs, automobiles, and smart home appliances.

10.11 OPERATING SYSTEM UPGRADES AND UPDATES

As mentioned in the pervious chapter unlike hardware, software is often subscription based and there can be several upgrades and updates to software during the lifetime of a computer even when there is no change in the hardware. The operating system too undergoes updates and upgrades frequently. The updates to an operating system may involve fixing bugs, improving security, and upgrading the system to provide new features and better performance.

These updates and upgrades of operating systems are performed by a software known as a *Package Manager* which is an important component of operating systems. The package manager helps in simplifying software installation by automating updating and deleting programs, and resolving dependencies. It provides access to a centralized repository of vetted applications, ensuring consistency, stability, and security across the system. The usability and life of an OS is dictated by the package manager, therefore there is a growing focus on its security, with tools integrating vulnerability scanning and support to streamline software deployment on modern systems. Additionally, there is a trend towards AI-driven package managers for more reliable and efficient package management solutions that can be applied in the cloud as will be discussed in chapter 17 on cloud computing. Examples of Package managers (2024) are APT (Advanced Package Tool) used in Linux variants such as Ubuntu, YUM (Yellowdog Updater Modified) used by Red Hat version of Unix, Homebrew used by macOS, and WinGet used by MSWindows.

SUMMARY

1. An Operating System (OS) of a computer is a set of system programs that provide several facilities to a user to allow easy computer use. Among the facilities provided are (a) programs to control input/output devices, (b) programs to select appropriate translators requested by a user, (c) allocation of resources of a computer, (d) programs to manage user files, and (e) a good interface for human-computer interaction.
2. To reduce the time wasted between jobs when several jobs are to be processed by a computer, and to reduce the manual operations of loading each job, in early mainframe computers, a batch monitor system was used. In a batch monitor jobs were batched and fed to the computer. The monitor loaded the appropriate compiler for each job in the batch, compiled the program, kept track of error messages, and facilitated a smooth transition from job to job. Batch monitors were a primitive OS used in the 1970s.
3. To alleviate the speed mismatch between I/O devices and the CPU in a high-speed computer, a batch operating system spooled all programs and the results in a secondary memory (disk). The spooling was done by a slower, inexpensive computer. The faster computer took the programs from the disk, computed the results, and stored the results in a disk. The I/O computer printed the results from this secondary memory.
4. A multiprogrammed operating system keeps in a computer's memory a set of jobs belonging to different users, schedules them on the CPU, provides I/O facilities requested by each user, and optimizes the use of the computer's resources. The primary objective of a multiprogramming operating system is to maximize the number of programs executed by a computer in a specified period and keep all the units of the computer simultaneously busy. In other words, it maximizes the throughput of a computer.
5. A multiprogrammed OS is designed to use several architectural features, including DMA, interrupts, and virtual memory. The major functions of a multiprogrammed OS

include memory management, process scheduling, I/O handling and support for file systems, and an OS command language.

6. Virtual memory is a hierarchy of two memory systems: a main memory of size S1 and a secondary, slower, and cheaper memory of a much larger size S2. The two systems are managed by a software system such that it appears to a user that a main memory of size S1 + S2 and speed nearly equal to that of the main memory is available.
7. Virtual memory is implemented by dividing the logical memory space into a group of *page frames*. Programs are also divided into small pieces, each requiring one *page*. A demand paging algorithm is used to place a page required by a user automatically in the main memory from the secondary disk memory.
8. A time shared operating system allows several users to use a computer simultaneously. The primary objective of a time shared operating system is to provide a fast response to each computer user. Programmer productivity is considerably improved through access to a time shared computer. A multitasking system is a time shared system that executes several programs of a single user.
9. An on-line system has files that are updated as soon as a transaction is completed. Response time should be short, but a delay would not be fatal. Airline reservation systems fall into this category.
10. A real-time system is used in the control of physical systems. The response time of such systems should match the needs of the physical system. A delay in response may lead to fatal failures.
11. Personal Computers are now widely used. The majority of early PC users used a single user OS called MS-DOS along with a Basic Input Output System (BIOS). BIOS was stored in a ROM supplied by the hardware vendor. BIOS provided the device drivers and initial program to load MS-DOS into the main memory. MS-DOS provided services such as editing, file management and other utility programs.
12. MS-DOS was superseded by MS-Windows, Windows 95, and in 2021 by Windows 11. They are improved OS for more powerful PCs with a large memory (16 GB) and disk (2 TB). This new generation of Microsoft OS provides a good Graphical User Interface (GUI) which simplifies the use of computers. It also allows multitasking, namely many programs can be stored in the memory and executed in a time-shared mode by the CPU. A user can see the progress of computation in multiple windows.
13. Multiprogramming and Time Sharing OS originally designed for mainframe computers are now used on large PCs called servers which have several smaller PCs called clients connected to them.
14. Unix is a very popular multiuser, time shared OS implemented in a large class of machines from PCs to supercomputers. It is popular as it provides a very simple yet powerful command interpreter. Unix is written in C, thus making it portable. Unix is organized as a layered OS. The innermost part is called the kernel. It provides low-level services such as device drivers and memory management. The next level is called the shell and is a command interpreter. The outermost level provides miscellaneous services. The user interacts with the kernel using commands and utilities.
15. An open-source free version of Unix is Linux. It has improved many of the features of Unix. Several versions of Linux are available. Linux is used from PCs to supercomputers.

16. The Android operating system was developed by Google for smartphones and tablet computers with touch screens. It is based on the Linux kernel and integrates many Google apps such as Gmail, Google Search, and Google Maps. It has several apps distributed by the Google Play store.
17. A Package Manager is an important part of operating systems. It automates updating, schedules updating, manages dependency, and has access to centralized repositories.

REVIEW QUESTIONS

10.1 What is the operating system of a computer?

10.2 Why is an operating system required for a computer?

10.3 What facilities are provided by an operating system to a user?

10.4 What do you understand by the term 'users' virtual machine'?

10.5 What do you understand by the term batch operating system?

10.6 What facilities are provided by a batch operating system?

10.7 What do you understand by the term multiprogramming?

10.8 Why is multiprogramming used in a computer?

10.9 What special hardware features are required in a computer to implement multiprogramming?

10.10 What do you understand by the term 'throughput' of a computer system?

10.11 What do you understand by the term 'turnaround time'?

10.12 Briefly describe various functions of a multiprogrammed OS.

10.13 Define 'virtual memory'.

10.14 What is the objective of introducing a virtual memory feature in a computer?

10.15 What is the difference between logical address space and physical address space of a computer's main memory?

10.16 What do you understand by the term 'page frames'?

10.17 What is a 'page' of a program?

10.18 What is 'demand paging'?

10.19 Explain how a demand paging algorithm works.

10.20 In what way is a base register useful in implementing a virtual memory system?

10.21 What is a 'page address table'? How is it used in implementing a virtual memory system?

10.22 How are virtual memory and paging used in memory management of multiprogrammed OS?

10.23 What is an OS command language?

10.24 What do you understand by the term 'time sharing operating system'?

10.25 Why is a time sharing operating system used?

10.26 What hardware facilities are required to implement time sharing in a computer system?

10.27 Are time sharing and multiprogramming mutually exclusive?

10.28 What do you understand by the term response time of a time sharing system?

10.29 What is an online transaction processing system? What are its special requirements? Give an example of an online transaction processing system.

10.30 What is a real-time system? Give an example of a real-time system.

10.31 What are the differences between a real-time system and an online transaction processing system?

10.32 Is an online transaction processing system a time shared system? If your answer is yes, explain why it is so.

10.33 What are the functions of a BIOS in PCs?

10.34 Why is BIOS stored in a ROM?

10.35 What are the functions of MS-DOS?

10.36 How is MS-DOS loaded into main memory?

10.37 What do you understand by booting?

10.38 What does the boot sector in a DOS disk contain?

10.39 Is MS-DOS a multiuser OS?

10.40 How does MS Windows 95 differ from MS-DOS?

10.41 What facilities are provided by MS Windows 95?

10.42 What is the latest MS Windows OS? What facilities does it provide?

10.43 What are the differences between multiprogramming, time sharing, and multitasking?

10.44 Why has Unix become a popular OS?

10.45 Is Unix a multiuser OS?

10.46 What are the functions of the kernel of Unix?

10.47 What is a shell in Unix?

10.48 What do you understand by shell programming?

10.49 What facilities are provided by the outermost layer of Unix OS?

10.50 What do you understand by Unix pipes?

10.51 What do you understand by a Unix filter?

10.52 Give the features of the Linux OS.

10.53 Why has Linux become a popular OS?

10.54 Distinguish between a real-time system and an online system.

10.55 Give an example of a real-time system.

10.56 Why is response time critical in a real-time system?

10.57 What is the most important requirement of an online system?

10.58 Is UNIX a multitasking OS?

10.59 Who developed the Android OS?

10.60 What are the major facilities provided by the Android OS?

10.61 What is a packet manager of an operating system? Describe its functions.

11 Microcomputers

LEARNING GOALS

After reading this chapter, you should be able to:

- Outline the important parts of a microcomputer and its architecture.
- Explain how data is input and output from a microcomputer.
- Describe the evolution of various generations of microprocessors.
- Outline the important features of RISC processors.
- Analyze the structure of two important special-purpose microprocessors, namely, Digital Signal Processors (DSPs) and microcontrollers used in embedded systems.
- Describe smart cards and their applications.

In the previous chapters, we described the logical organization of computers and the software systems necessary to use a computer. In this chapter, we will take an example of a specific 'real-life' computer. We have chosen to discuss microcomputers first as they have ushered in a revolution in computer usage by making computers inexpensive and widely available. All computers manufactured nowadays from laptop computers to supercomputers use microcomputers as their CPU. Microcomputers have advanced to an extent that the architectural features once available only in expensive mainframe computers are now available in microcomputers which cost a few thousand rupees.

The first microprocessor chip, which is the main component of a microcomputer, was invented by Ted Hoff, Masatoshi Shima, Stan Mazor, and Federico Faggin at Intel, a semiconductor manufacturer in the USA, in 1970 and it became a commercial product in 1971. It used a 4-bit data path, sixteen 4-bit registers, a 4-bit adder, and 45 instructions, with a 740 KHz clock and did not have a built-in memory. Since then, microprocessor technology has progressed rapidly. Now (2025) microcomputers with 64-bit wide data paths, 5 GHz clock, built-in cache memory of around 1MB, and around 16 processors working in parallel and integrated graphics processor are available to users. There are also a multitude of manufacturers with a bewildering array of products. It would be counterproductive to concentrate on a specific processor in an introductory discussion.

We will thus give a general picture of the structure of microprocessors.

11.1 IDEAL MICROCOMPUTER

An ideal microcomputer is a self-contained computer fabricated as an *integrated circuit* (IC) on a single silicon chip. A microcomputer (Figure 11.1) has N input lines and M output lines. Within the microcomputer, a program is stored to process the data presented to it through the N input lines. The data processed by the program is put on the M output lines which may be connected to displays, actuators, printers, digital to analog converters, or any of a host of output devices. Both the input and the output are constrained to be binary digits. The outputs at any instant are thus dependent on the complete history of past inputs and the stored program.

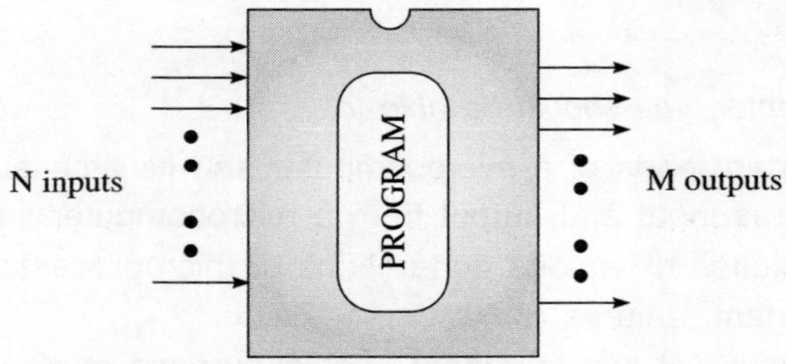

Figure 11.1 An ideal microcomputer.

11.2 ACTUAL MICROCOMPUTER

Even though an ideal microcomputer would have enough memory to store a program, in actual practice (with the current state-of-the-art), sufficient storage cannot be provided within a single IC chip for the entire program and data. However, instruction and data caches are integrated into the chip. Besides this, technology constrains the number of input and output lines. A typical microcomputer would thus consist of the following units (Figure 11.2):

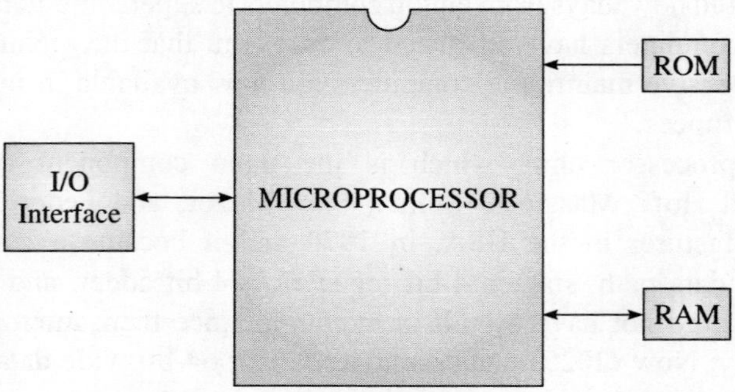

Figure 11.2 A typical microcomputer.

1. A microprocessor has on a single IC chip several processing units called *cores.* Each core is an independent processor. The number of cores in a modern microprocessor (2025) ranges between 4 and 64. Most commonly used microprocessors have 4 to 8 cores. Each core can execute one task in a multitasking system. The cores can also cooperatively execute a single complex task.
2. Random Access Memory (RAM) is used normally to store programs and data.
3. A Read Only Memory (ROM) is used normally to store invariant programs.
4. Input/output (I/O) interface units.
5. Power supply and clock circuits.

11.2.1 Processor

The processor is a single Very Large-Scale Integrated Circuit (VLSI) chip called the *microprocessor*. This chip contains many processing cores. Each core has the following units:

- An instruction register and a decoder
- An arithmetic logic unit (ALU)
- Several registers to store and manipulate data
- Control and timing circuits
- Cache memory called L1 and L2 caches.

The microprocessor is connected to the other units in the system using an *address bus,* a *data bus,* and a *control bus.* The functions of the various units are as follows:

(i) *Instruction register and decoder*: The instruction register holds the instruction read from the memory by the core. The decoder sends the control signals appropriate to the decoded instruction to the ALU.

(ii) *Arithmetic logic unit*: ALU has circuits to perform the basic arithmetic operations (add, subtract), logical operations (and, or, complement, exclusive or), register operations (clear, shift, load, move, etc.), memory operations (store, read), program sequencing control operations (such as jump, conditional jump, and jump to subroutine) and input/ output operations.
In addition, it usually has two registers known as an accumulator and a temporary register. It also has a *status register* that typically has bits that are set to 1 to indicate the results of the ALU operation. The status bits are:
- Negative result
- Zero result
- Overflow of result
- Carry
- Parity
- Interrupt mask bits to enable interrupts from I/O devices

Figure 11.3 gives the structure of a microprocessor core and its connections.

(iii) *Working registers*: The time required to retrieve data from registers and to store the results in them is at least ten times shorter than that needed to retrieve and store data in the L1 cache memory. Thus, some working registers are provided in the core to temporarily store intermediate results obtained during computation. Besides these, there are two other registers known as PC (Program Counter) and SP (Stack Pointer).

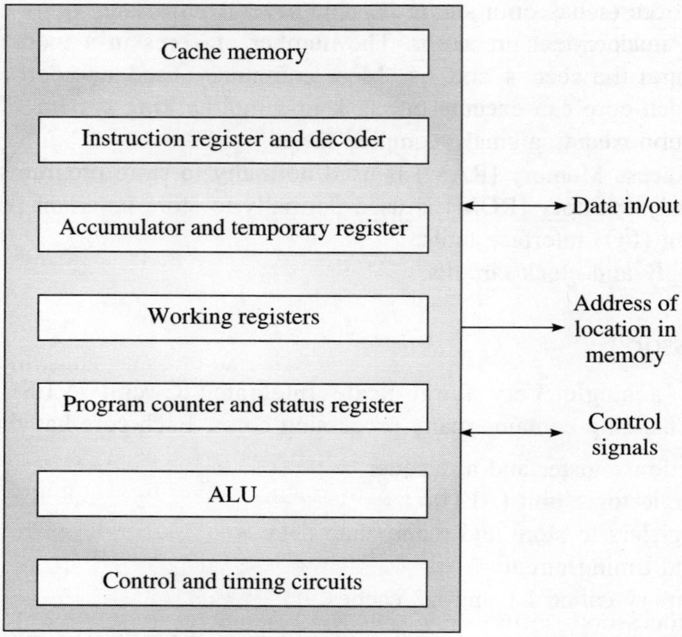

Figure 11.3 The internal structure of a microprocessor core.

The PC register holds the address of the instruction to be executed next. A *stack* is a memory in which data is stored and retrieved from a location called the top of the stack. As data is received, it is pushed into the stack. Thus, the data which is stored last is retrieved first. It is, therefore, known as a last-in, first-out (LIFO) memory. In microcomputers, a stack is simulated by using a part of the main memory (RAM) of the computer which may be visualized as a consecutive sequence of words. Only one of these words may be accessed at a time, which is the one at the top of the stack. To simplify operations using a stack, the core has a stack pointer register that stores the address of the top of the stack. An operation PUSH (R1, SP) takes the contents of register R1 and stores it in the main memory at the address given by SP, which is the address of the top of the stack. An operation POP (R2, SP) takes the contents of the main memory from the address given by SP (which is the top of the stack) and places it in register R2.

A stack is useful in many applications. When a program is interrupted and the control has to jump to an interrupt service routine, a stack is used to temporarily store the contents of specified registers and the address to which the control should return after servicing the interrupt. When a program calls a subroutine, the return address is normally stored in the stack. In higher-level language compilers, a stack is used to assist in evaluating arithmetic expressions.

(iv) The number of working registers in the processor core is small as they should be addressable. As was pointed out, the main memory is much slower than the processor. To alleviate this speed mismatch two caches called L1 and L2 are used in each processor core (see Section 8.2). The L1 cache is closest to the processor and takes around 4 clock cycles to read/write. Its size varies between 32 KB to 512 KB depending on the chip model. It is divided into instruction and data cache of equal size. The next level of cache memory is called L2 cache and is also divided into an instruction cache and a data cache. The size of the L2 cache is between 256 KB and 4 MB. It is slower than L1 cache. As the number of transistors in a chip doubles every 18 months, the sizes of L1 and L2 caches continuously increase.

11.2.2 Data Bus

One of the important constraints in fabricating a microcomputer on an IC chip is the limit on the number of pins that can be used to connect it to external circuits. Thus, the number of pins allocated for input and output lines is limited. Usually, the number of input lines equals the number of output lines. The number of input/output lines is known as the *data path width* or the *word length* of the microprocessor. The lines which carry the data are collectively known as the *data bus.* Data bus width or word length is one of the most common parameters that characterize a microprocessor. In 64-bit processors, the data bus width is 64. Figure 11.4 illustrates a shorthand notation that we will use to indicate the bus width. With 64 input and 64 output lines, one would need 128 pins on the microprocessor. To economize further on the pins, many microprocessors use the same pins for both input and output. This is possible if input and output are not done simultaneously. Physically the mode of data transfer—input or output—is indicated by a control output. When the control output is 1, the mode is input mode and switches inside the microprocessor will route the signals as input, otherwise the direction of data transmission will be reversed. This is shown in Figure 11.5. Such a data bus is known as a *bidirectional data bus.*

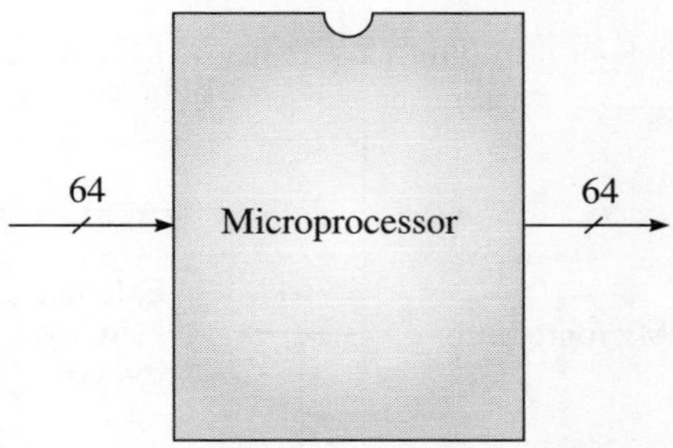

Figure 11.4 Notation to indicate bus widths.

11.2.3 Address Bus

In the ideal microcomputer (Figure 11.1), we have shown program memory within the chip. As pointed out earlier, technology does not permit fabricating a large memory within a chip. Thus, one is constrained to use a memory external to the chip. If we want to address 4 GB of memory, we need 32 addressing bits. These bits are transmitted via 32 lines which constitute the *address bus* of the microprocessor. Modern microprocessors (2025) use 64 address bits. Some microprocessors time-share data bus as part of the address bus. Figure 11.6 illustrates

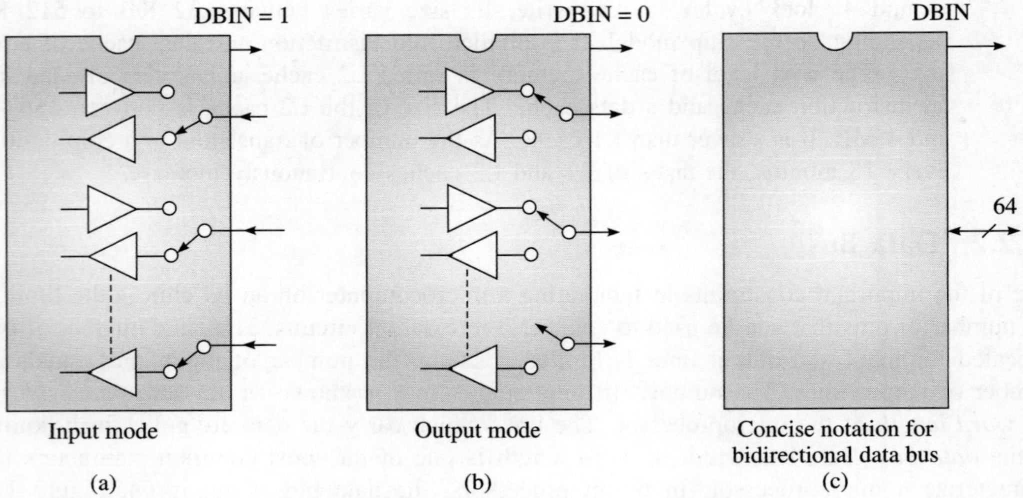

Figure 11.5 Bidirectional data bus.

the use of the address bus. Observe that data may be written into or read from memory using the bidirectional data bus. In Figure 11.6, we have assumed separate address and data buses. Many microprocessors use a single 64-bit bus as both data and address bus. In one cycle an address is sent to memory. In a subsequent cycle, the data is read or written using the same bus. With 64 lines for an address bus, one can address 2^{64} = 16 Exabytes memory, an enormous value enough for the foreseeable future! The main memory of modern microprocessors is of the order of 64 GB.

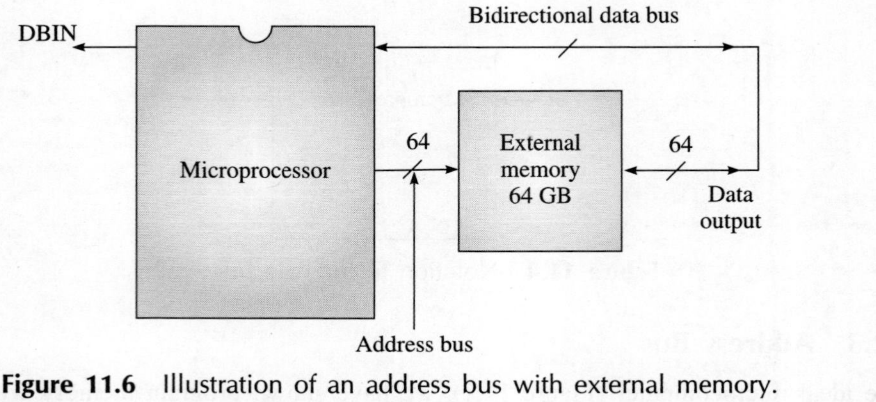

Figure 11.6 Illustration of an address bus with external memory.

11.2.4 Control Bus

In addition to data and address buses, microprocessors also require a set of control lines. We have already encountered one such control output line which indicates whether the data bus is in input or output mode. Control lines are required to synchronize the operation of the microprocessor with that of the external circuitry such as peripheral devices.

As an example of a control input line, consider the operation of a peripheral device. If a peripheral device is to transfer some data to the memory without going through the processor, it may be achieved by logically disconnecting the address and data buses from the processor and handing them over to the peripheral device for its use. Such a transfer of information is known as DMA (Direct Memory Access) transfer. A microprocessor does this by using a control input signal known as HOLD. This signal places the address and data buses in a so-called *tristate* condition which effectively disconnects them from the microprocessor (see Figures 11.7 and 11.8). Once the address and data buses are disconnected in response to the HOLD signal on the control input line, the microprocessor acknowledges this by putting on a HOLDACK control output line a 1. The external peripheral device waits till it receives this HOLDACK = 1 signal before it takes control of the data and address buses for data transfer to memory. Observe in Figure 11.8 the position of the address line and data line switches. They are both disconnected from the microprocessor chip. This communication protocol of sending a request and waiting till it is acknowledged before acting is called *handshaking protocol*.

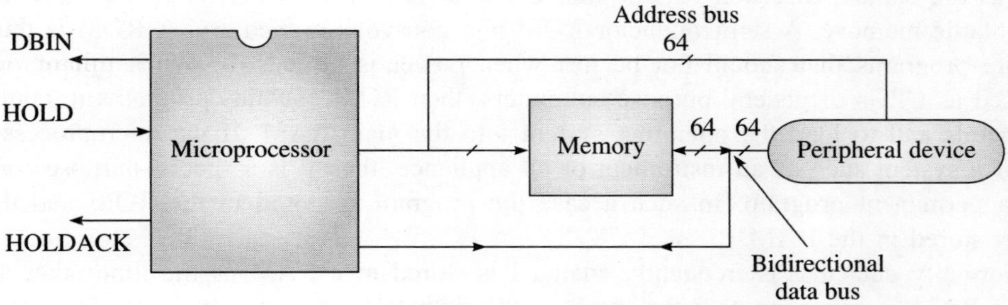

Figure 11.7 Illustration of DMA transfer.

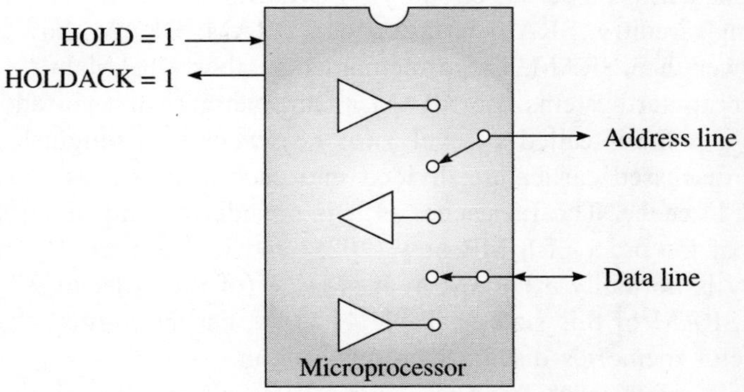

Figure 11.8 Illustration of tristate condition of data and address lines.

We may now consolidate all the buses and obtain the picture of a microprocessor shown in Figure 11.9. Besides data, address, and control buses, a microprocessor also has lines for power supply and ground connections.

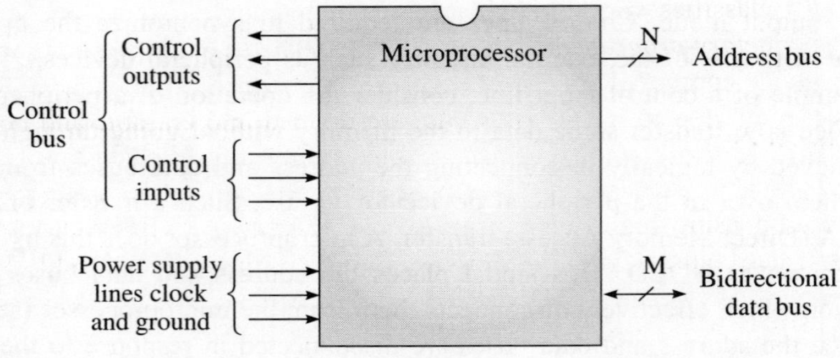

Figure 11.9 A generalized microprocessor.

11.3 MEMORY SYSTEMS FOR MICROCOMPUTERS

Two distinct types of memory may be used in a microcomputer. These are volatile memory and non-volatile memory. The data in volatile memory is lost when power is switched off, whereas the content of a non-volatile memory is stored permanently. A semiconductor RAM is a volatile memory. A semiconductor ROM is a non-volatile memory. A ROM is thus used to store programs that should not be lost when power is turned off. When microprocessors are used as CPUs of general-purpose computers, then ROM contains programs to control the peripherals and to load the operating system into the main RAM. If the microprocessor is a part of a system such as an instrument or an appliance, then it is a special-purpose controller with a permanent program. In such a case the program is stored in the ROM and the data read is stored in the RAM.

Normally data that is frequently changed is stored in a RAM as the time taken to read from a RAM is approximately the same as the time taken to write in it. RAM is classified as *dynamic RAM* (DRAM) or *static RAM* (SRAM). In a DRAM, the stored data has to be periodically refreshed using external circuitry. A SRAM, on the other hand, does not require any such refreshing circuitry. SRAM is faster than DRAM. DRAM, however, is cheaper and consumes less power than SRAM. Large memories are thus DRAMs.

Many microcomputer systems use SRAM as an external cache in addition to the caches in the chip. Such a cache is called a Level 3 (or L3) cache to distinguish it from the on-chip caches, which as discussed earlier are divided into caches known as Level 2 (or L2) cache and Level 1 (or L1) cache. The L3 cache, as it is outside the chip is larger than the L1 and L2 caches and is of the order of 8 MB now (2025) and will become larger in years to come. The main memory is normally a DRAM as it is large (of the order of 32 GB) and it will be expensive to use SRAM of this size. In Table 11.1, we list the normal sizes and applications of the semiconductor memories discussed in this section.

Table 11.1 Applications of semiconductor memories

Type	Normal size	Applications
SRAM	4 MB to 128 MB	External cache (L3 cache)
DRAM	2 GB to 32 GB	Main memory
ROM (User Programmed)	4 KB to 64 KB	Small permanent programs (e.g., BIOS)
ROM (Factory Programmed)	512 B to 2 KB	Tables, combinatorial circuits

Figure 11.10 classifies various RAM and ROM memory systems. ROM memories may be classified as *factory-programmed* or *user-programmed.* Factory-programmed ROMs are manufactured using appropriate masks. They are thus the most reliable and also the least expensive. User-programmed ROMs (PROMs) are divided into erasable and non-erasable. The non-erasable PROM is programmed using fuse links. Once a fuse link is burnt, it is permanent. Erasable programmable ROMs (EPROMs) can be erased and reprogrammed by a user. The contents are erased using high voltage pulses and is known as EEPROM. As discussed in Section 4.3.1, a new entrant to the EEPROM family is flash memory. Flash memory sizes are continuously increasing and their cost is also reducing. As flash memories up to 128 GB capacity are available, they are used as Solid State Disk (SSD) drives to store large programs and data.

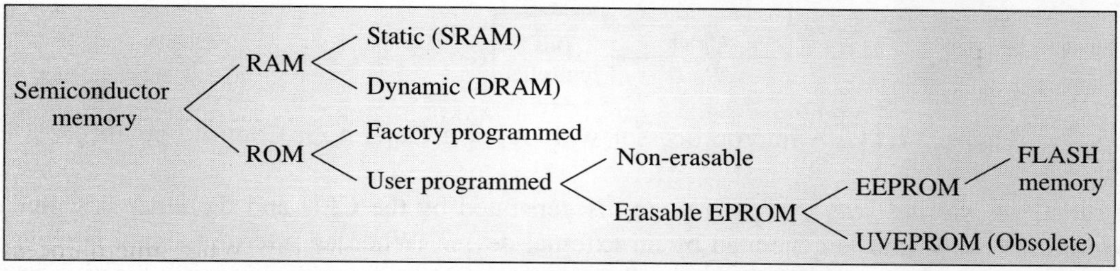

Figure 11.10 Types of semiconductor memories

11.4 MINIMUM MICROCOMPUTER CONFIGURATION

Along with a microprocessor chip, other support chips are required to configure a microcomputer system. At the very minimum, it is necessary to have the following chips:

(i) A voltage regulator chip. It is used along with a full-wave rectifier connected to the mains. This provides a power supply regulated to ±5%.
(ii) A clock signal, which is a square wave, is required to synchronize the operations of a microprocessor. A special clock chip is used along with an appropriate quartz crystal to generate this clock.
(iii) Integrated circuit chips to buffer and control the data flow from the memory to the processor and from the input/output devices to the processor.
(iv) Memory chips and associated controllers to interface them to the processor.

Figure 11.11 shows a microcomputer using support chips. The trend is to reduce the need for support chips and build all the required controllers within the processor.

11.4.1 Interrupts

Interrupt signals are used in a microcomputer when an error occurs while executing an instruction (e.g., an attempt to divide by zero) and needs immediate attention or when devices external to the microcomputer require attention (e.g., when some data to be fed to the microcomputer from a peripheral device is ready, or when data for a real-time process is to be acquired). The former

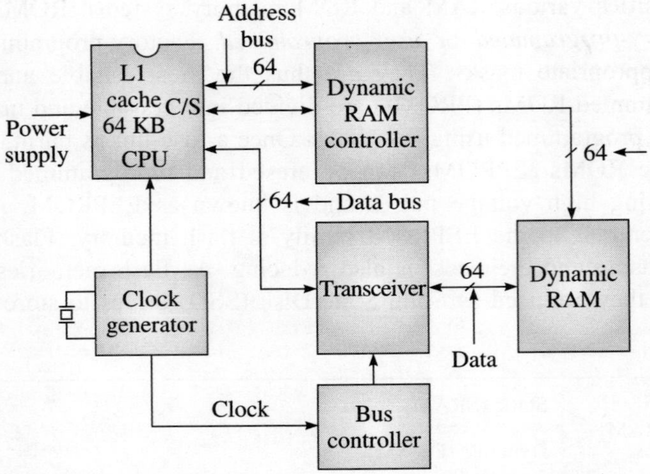

Figure 11.11 A microprocessor with support chips (C/S: Control Signal).

is called an *internal interrupt or trap* and is generated by the CPU and the latter is called an *external interrupt* and is generated by an external device. When an interrupt signal is received by a processor, the program running in the microcomputer jumps to a specific location in the main memory where an *interrupt service routine* is stored. In practice, there may be many devices requesting attention. Thus, a microcomputer has to discriminate between these requests and allocate priorities. The various methods usually available are categorized as follows.

Interrupts

Maskable	*Non-maskable*	*Fixed location*	*Vectored*
DI (disable interrupt) instruction can prevent the further interrupts till EI (enable interrupt) command is given	Cannot be disabled by software	Will always branch on interrupt to a fixed location in the memory	Will branch to different locations depending on signal at the interrupt port

Consider, for example, an IBM PC in which four classes of interrupts are possible. They are:

(i) CPU internal interrupts
(ii) Non-maskable interrupts
(iii) External interrupts
(iv) Single-step interrupts

These interrupts have a priority determined by the CPU. Internal interrupts, namely, divide error, overflow, and program interrupt, have the highest priority. The next priority is for non-maskable interrupts. This is followed by an external device (maskable) interrupts and finally internally programmed single-step interrupts (see Figure 11.12).

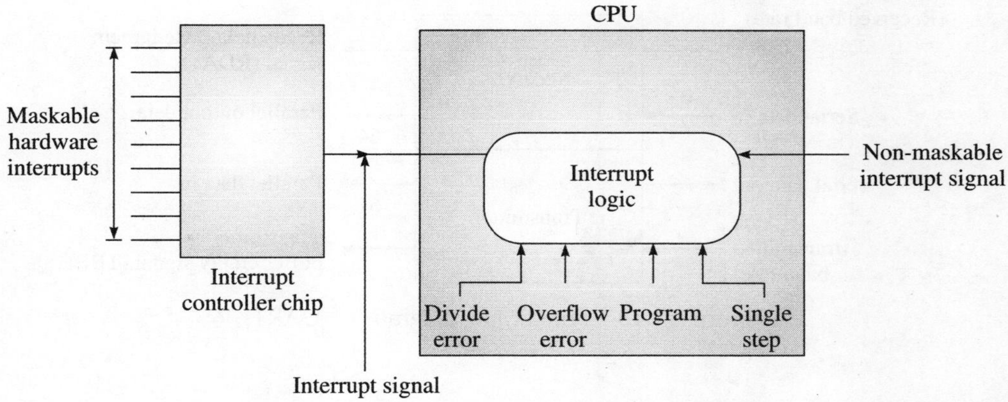

Figure 11.12 Interrupt sources of IBM PC.

The CPU recognizes an interrupt when appropriate interrupt signals are sensed by the CPU chip. When an interrupt is recognized, the CPU transfers control to a new program location. Locations 000 (hex) to 3FF (hex) (total of 1024 locations) are dedicated to storing up to 256 4-byte interrupt vectors. Each vector is the starting address of interrupt routines stored elsewhere in the main memory.

When an interrupt occurs, the CPU completes its current instruction and then services the interrupt based on its priority. The delay between the recognition of an interrupt by the CPU and the execution of the interrupt service routine varies between 50 and 60 clock cycles. The delay includes the time taken to save CPU status and register contents. When an interrupt is being serviced, other interrupts can occur. They are serviced based on their priority. A higher priority interrupt cannot be interrupted by a lower priority interrupt.

11.4.2 Parallel to Serial and Serial to Parallel Conversion

In the minimal microcomputer configuration presented in Section 11.4, we assumed that all I/O ports will send and receive 64 bits in parallel. In practice, there are many situations in which data can be transmitted only serially as a sequence of bits. In particular, when data is sent or received from a remote location through a communication line, only serial data transmission is economical. Most peripheral devices such as video terminals and teletypes accept and transmit bits serially. As serial to parallel and parallel to serial conversion is frequently needed, a special IC chip called UART (Universal Asynchronous Receiver Transmitter) is available. Figure 11.13 illustrates the function of a UART. Logically, UART may be divided into a receiver part and a transmitter part. The receiver receives a series of bits at a predetermined bit rate (bits per second). A clock at a frequency equal to the bit rate synchronizes the received bits. A UART assembles 64 serial bits and puts them out as a parallel set of 64 bits. When the bits are assembled and ready for transmission, a ready bit (RDA) is put out on an output port.

The transmitter part of UART accepts 64 bits in parallel, serializes them, synchronizes them with another clock of appropriate speed, and transmits the bits serially. As soon as the 64 bits are serialized, and the buffer in UART is emptied, a signal TBE (Transmitter Buffer Empty) is set to 1 by UART. The TBE and RDA signals may be used as interrupt signals to a microprocessor.

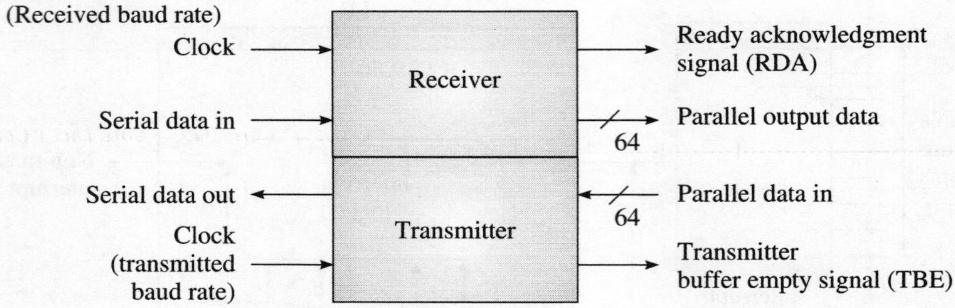

Figure 11.13 Functional diagram of UART.

11.4.3 Direct Memory Access

The fastest way an external device can store and retrieve data from the main memory (RAM) is by taking over the data and address buses from the microprocessor and using them to transfer data. This is known as direct memory access. In the simplest method, the DMA sends a bus request signal to the microprocessor. This is acknowledged by the microprocessor after it completes the current machine cycle by (i) disconnecting itself from the address and data buses (by placing the bus buffers in a tristate condition) and (ii) sending an acknowledge signal after yielding the buses to the DMA chip. In Section 8.3 we have already discussed how a DMA controller functions and we will not repeat it here.

11.5 EVOLUTION OF MICROCOMPUTERS

Ever since the introduction of microprocessors, integrated circuit technology has improved rapidly. Early microprocessors had only a 4-bit data path and could address only small memories. Now microprocessors are available with 64-bit data paths and can address up to 64 GB memory. The specifications of some popular microprocessors and the year they were introduced are given in Table 11.2. It is clear from this table that both clock speed and the number of transistors in the microprocessor have continuously increased in the last three decades. In late 2011, Intel introduced Core i7-3930K processor which uses a 3.2 GHz clock. Observe that the clock speed has not increased. However, the chip has multiple processors called multi-cores. Core i7-3930K has six cores that can work in parallel, increasing the processor's throughput. It can carry out 12 instructions in parallel. This is achieved by a technique called *multithreading* which uses available multiple processors effectively. It has three levels of cache memory called LI, L2, and L3. It has 6 × 32 KB data and 6 × 32 KB instruction L1 caches, 6 × 256 KB L2 cache, and 12 MB shared L3 cache in the chip. There are 2.27 billion transistors in the chip. Its throughput is 1,250,000 times compared to 8008. In October 2023 Intel released a slew of microprocessors. One of them is the Core i9-14900 high-end microprocessor. It has 24 cores, 32 threads, 80 KB L1 cache/core, 2 MB L2 cache/core, and 36 MB shared L3 cache. (See Table 11.2 for other data). In effect, microprocessors today are as powerful as supercomputers of the 1990s. Today all computers from PCs to supercomputers use microprocessors as their basic building block.

Table 11.2 Evolution of microprocessors

	MICROPROCESSOR							
	8008	8080	8086	68020	Power PC 603	*Pentium 4 Core Duo*	*Pentium Core Duo*	*Pentium Core i9-14900*
Year of introduction	1972	1973	1978	1984	1993	2001	2008	2023
Data path width (in bits)	8	8	16	32	64	64	64	64
Internal register width (bits)	8	8	16	32	64	64	64	64
Number of internal registers		8	14	16	64	32	32	?
Directly addressable memory (bytes)	16 K	64 K	1 M	4 G	4 G	4G	4 G	192 G
Estimate of throughput	1	10	100	1000	5000	200,000	800,000	8,000,000
Clock speed (MHz)	0.75	3	5	16	80	1300 1300	3300	6000
Manufacturer	Intel	Intel	Intel	Motorola	IBM	Intel	Intel	Intel
No. of transistors in chip (in 1000 s)	4	6	29	120	1600	8000	160,000	40,000,000

11.6 REDUCED INSTRUCTION SET COMPUTERS

In the evolution of CPU architecture, early machines had small instruction sets as complex hardware was expensive and difficult to build. With the advent of integrated circuits, it became simpler to fabricate complex hardware which was reliable and inexpensive. Most programming was done by using high-level languages such as FORTRAN and COBOL. A primary concern of CPU architects was to provide instructions in the CPU to make it easy to translate high-level language programs to machine language programs and to ensure that the machine language programs run efficiently. To achieve this, a large number of instructions were introduced. For example, many computers had over 100–200 instructions. Besides this, as the main memory was expensive, designers tried to pack more instructions in the memory by introducing variable length instructions, such as half-word, one and half-word, etc. For example, an operand in an immediate instruction needs fewer bits and can be designed as a half-word instruction. A variety of addressing modes were also provided. Computers with numerous instructions, complex addressing modes, and variable-length instructions are now called *Complex Instruction Set Computers* (CISC). The Intel family of microprocessors we discussed in the last section is CISC.

In the early 1980s, CPU designers saw that using too many instructions was counterproductive as the frequency of use of some of the instructions was very small. Furthermore, it was felt that if a small number of instructions with uniform length are used, decoding and execution become simple and fast. If the instructions are designed in such a way that they retrieve operands stored in registers in the CPU rather than from the main memory, it will speed up computation. These ideas have been used in designing *Reduced Instruction Set Computers* (RISC).

The general philosophy of designing instruction sets and the CPU structure of RISC includes the following:

1. Reduce the number of instructions and make them of equal length.
2. Reduce addressing modes. These make decoding instructions easy. The decoding circuits can be integrated as part of the CPU chip. This will enable instructions to be decoded fast.

3. Reduce references to the memory to retrieve operands. This is achieved by increasing the general-purpose registers in the CPU. Operands and intermediate results are stored in these registers. Usually, 32–256 registers are provided in the CPU of RISC machines. Only two instructions refer to the memory. They are to load an operand from the memory into a register in the CPU and store a result from the CPU register to a location in memory. Thus, RISC architecture computers are sometimes called *Load–store architecture* computers.
4. When an instruction is to be executed, the following steps are carried out:
   (i) Fetch an instruction from the memory
   (ii) Decode the instruction to determine what is to be done
   (iii) Fetch the operand from a register
   (iv) Execute the instruction
   (v) Store the result in a register

If the operands and the results are stored in the CPU and the decoding circuit is simple, then each of the above steps takes about the same time. This allows the overlapping of various stages of instruction fetching and execution as shown in Figure 11.14 when a sequence of instructions is retrieved from the memory. This is called *pipelining*. One instruction can thus be executed in one CPU clock cycle. One of the distinguishing features of the RISC architecture is *a single-cycle execution* of most instructions.

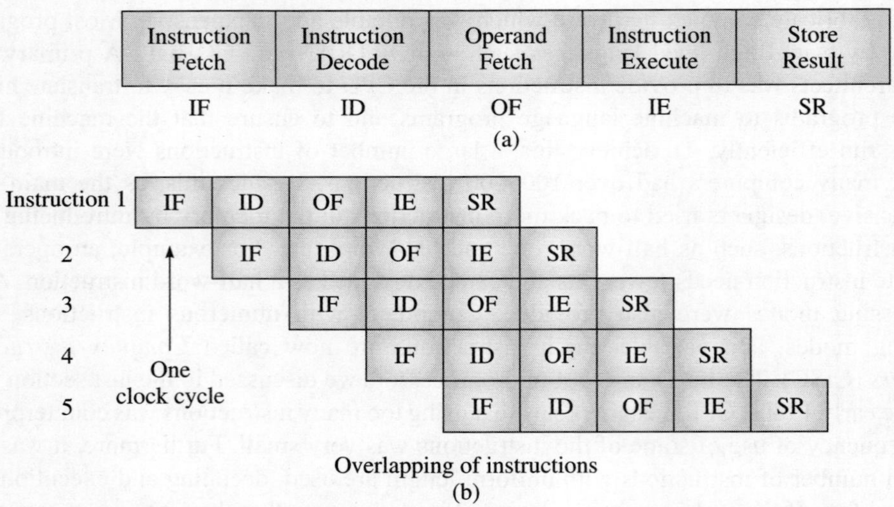

Figure 11.14 Instruction pipelining in RISC machines.

The pipelined execution given above is upset if there is a branch instruction. Details of RISC CPU design are outside the scope of this book and the interested student can refer to the book by Rajaraman and Radhakrishnan [6] given in the references of this chapter at the end of this book.

Recently, RISC machines have been further improved, leading to CPUs which are known as *superscalar RISC.* The term superscalar means that in one CPU clock cycle, more than one instruction can be carried out. This is achieved by having multiple arithmetic execution units on a CPU chip so that two or more instructions can be executed simultaneously.

11.7 SPECIAL PURPOSE MICROPROCESSORS

We have discussed so far general-purpose microprocessors. With the lowering of the cost of designing and fabricating very large-scale integrated circuits, special-purpose microprocessors for specialized applications, particularly in consumer products such as washing machines, mobile phones, CD players, televisions, and automobiles, are growing. In this section, we will describe two important classes of microprocessors Digital Signal Processors (DSPs) and microcontrollers.

11.7.1 Digital Signal Processors

Digital signal processors are special-purpose microprocessors optimized to process real-time audio and video signals. In other words, the input is a stream of bits that arrive in real-time and have to be processed as they come and output as a stream of bits. As they are widely used in cost-sensitive consumer products, such as mobile phones, their cost must be much lower than that of a general-purpose microprocessor such as Pentium. Compared to the cost of general-purpose microprocessors which are in the range of hundreds of dollars, the cost of DSPs is in the range of tens of dollars. In Figure 11.15, we show how a DSP is connected to external input/output. The input signal to DSP is analog; that is, it is a continuously varying signal such as speech, music, video, or an electrocardiogram. A typical analog signal is shown in Figure 11.16 as a function of time. This signal can be represented as a sum of sine waves (using Fourier analysis) as given in Eq. (11.1).

$$h(t) = V_1 \sin 2pf_1t + V_2 \sin 2pf_2t + \cdots + V_n \sin 2pf_nt \tag{11.1}$$

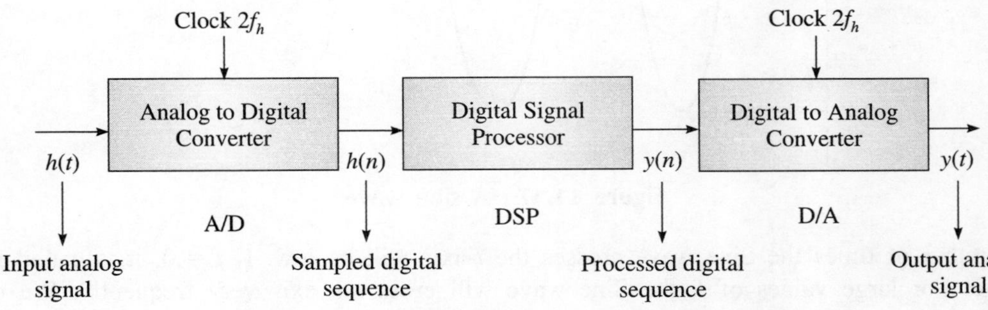

Figure 11.15 Connecting DSP to analog input.

In order to understand this representation, it is necessary to understand the characteristics of a Sine wave signal. A Sine wave signal is shown in Figure 11.17. The amplitude of the signal is defined as V and its frequency is defined as f. The amplitude of an electrical signal is measured in volts and its frequency in hertz (abbreviated Hz). If the frequency is low,

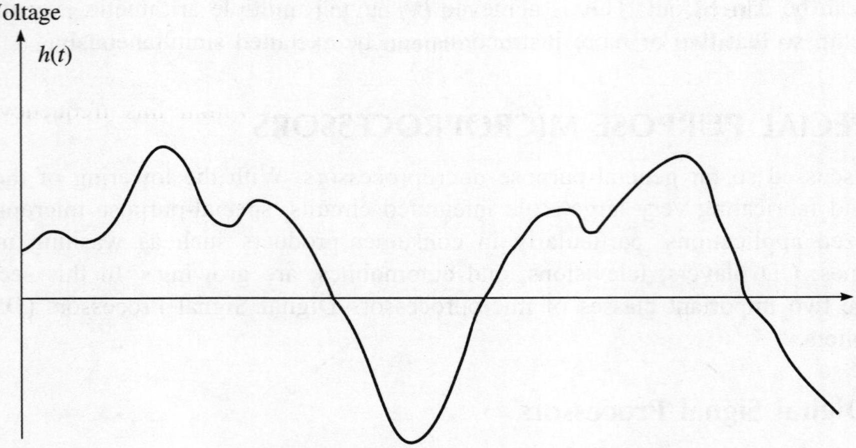

Figure 11.16 An analog signal.

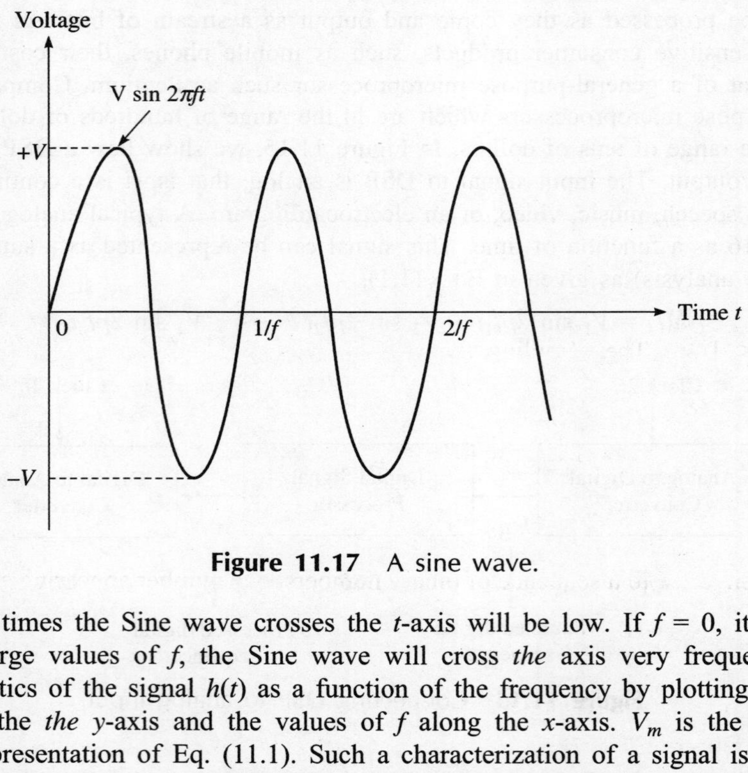

Figure 11.17 A sine wave.

the number of times the Sine wave crosses the t-axis will be low. If $f = 0$, it is called DC voltage. For large values of f, the Sine wave will cross *the* axis very frequently. We can plot characteristics of the signal $h(t)$ as a function of the frequency by plotting the values of $(V/V_m)^2$ along the *the* y-axis and the values of f along the x-axis. V_m is the highest value of V in the representation of Eq. (11.1). Such a characterization of a signal is known as its frequency domain or power spectrum representation. In Figure 11.18, we give the spectrum of $h(t)$. In the frequency domain, the analog signal is characterized by its spectrum. From the spectrum, we can find the bandwidth of the signal. Observe that $V(f)$ is zero when $f = 0$ for our sample signal and zero for $f > f_m$. $V(f)$ is flat over a range of values of f. The lowest frequency where $(Vf/V_m)^2$ is 50% of the value in the 'flat' portion of the curve is called its low cut-off frequency f_l. The highest frequency where $(Vf/V_m)^2$ is again 50% of the value in the flat portion of the curve is called the high cut-off frequency f_h of the signal. The difference between these two frequencies is known as the *bandwidth* of the signal. The physical significance of the bandwidth is that most of the energy in the signal is within this frequency range.

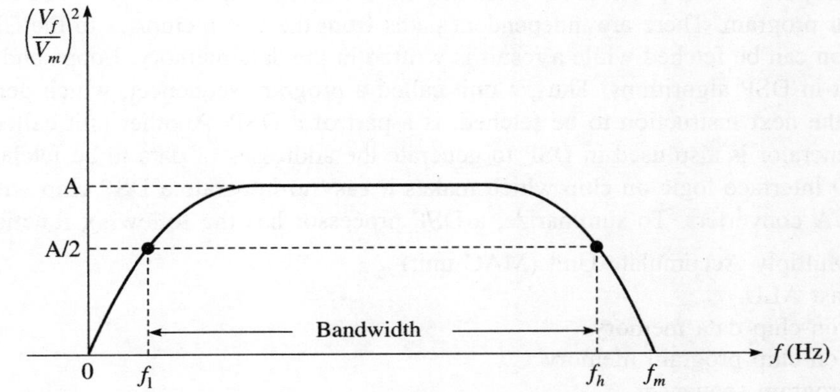

Figure 11.18 Frequency domain representation of an analog signal.

The analog signal $h(t)$ is converted to a digital equivalent before it is fed to the DSP. How do we represent an analog signal by its digital equivalent? It is done by taking samples of the analog signal at times t_1, $t_1 + t$, $t_1 + 2t$, $t_1 + 3t$, ..., $t_1 + nt$ and representing the amplitudes $x_1, x_2, x_3, \ldots, x_n$ by their binary values. The two questions which arise are: What should be the value of t and how many bits should be used to represent the amplitudes $x_1, x_2, \ldots, x_n$? The value of t is found using the *sampling theorem* proved by Nyquist. This theorem states that if the high cut-off frequency of an analog signal is f_h, then the samples should be taken at intervals $t < 1/2f_h$. The sampling theorem guarantees that if a sample is taken slightly more than once every $(1/2f_h)$ seconds, no peaks of the signal $h(t)$ will be missed and all the information contained in the original continuous signal will be preserved in the samples. The number of bits used to store $x_1, x_2, x_3, \ldots, x_n$ will depend on the precision with which we want to represent the amplitudes of the samples. If we use n bits, $2n$ amplitude levels can be represented. If $n = 12$, $2^{12} = 4096$ levels can be represented. 4096 levels represent a precision of 1/4096 = 0.024%, which is adequate for most practical purposes. Observe that an analog signal can be converted to a sequence of binary numbers, one number appearing every t seconds. This sequence of numbers is what is input to a DSP. If $f_{max} = 20$ kHz, then $t < 1/(40 \times 10^3)$ = 24 μs. If the DSP is required to process the input in real-time, then it should process each sample of 12 bits appearing every 24 μs. This is equivalent to a processing rate of $12/24 \times 10^{-6}$ bits/s = 500 Kbps for a single-channel audio. For video signals, the processing rate will be at least 1000 times higher. It is thus necessary for a DSP to have fast processing capability.

Most DSP applications such as speech synthesis and signal filtering multiply digitized sample values and accumulate the products as shown in Eq. (11.2).

$$y_n = \sum_{k=1}^{m} x_k h_{n-k} \tag{11.2}$$

for $n = 1, 2, \ldots, p$ with m between 8 and 16.

Thus, a fast multiply and accumulate unit, called MAC, is an important unit of a DSP that distinguishes it from general-purpose microprocessors. The ALU of a DSP is also made fast so that it can carry out each operation in 1 clock cycle. The ALU and MAC of DSP are dual ported; that is, there are two paths—one to write and one to read and they can be used simultaneously in 1 clock cycle. DSPs normally have two on-chip memories—one for data and the other for program. There are independent paths from the two memories to the CPU so that an instruction can be fetched while a result is written in the data memory. Loops and branching are frequent in DSP algorithms. Thus, a unit called a program sequencer, which generates the address of the next instruction to be fetched, is a part of a DSP. Another unit called the Data Address Generator is also used in DSP to generate the addresses of data to be fetched. A DSP also has I/O interface logic on chip which makes it easy to integrate a DSP chip with external A/D and D/A converters. To summarize, a DSP processor has the following functional units:

- A Multiply Accumulate Unit (MAC unit)
- A fast ALU
- An on-chip data memory
- An on-chip program memory
- A program sequencer
- A data address generator
- On-chip I/O interface logic

Figure 11.19 is a block diagram of a typical DSP chip. In this figure, we have shown only the essential parts of the chip. Observe that the chip has separate instruction and data memory. Such an architecture is known as *Harvard architecture* as opposed to *Von Neumann's*

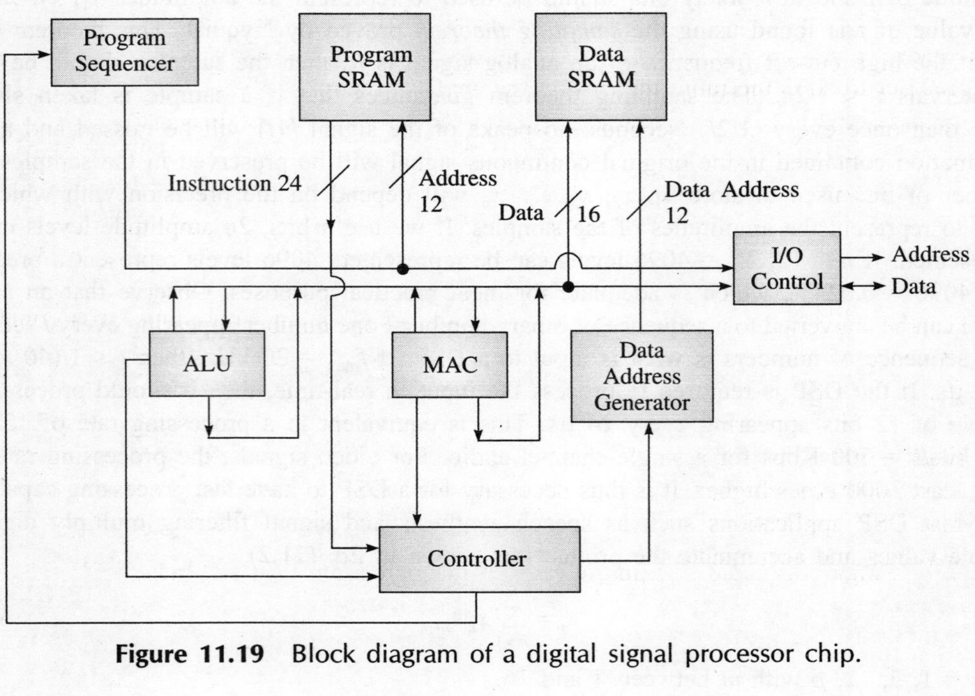

Figure 11.19 Block diagram of a digital signal processor chip.

architecture of general-purpose computers in which the same memory is used to store both data and programs.

Texas Instruments manufactures a range of DSPs. An example is TMS320C6416. Its specifications are available on their website TI.com.

11.7.2 General Purpose Graphics Processing Unit (GPGPU)

To relieve the microprocessor used as a CPU of personal computers from performing graphics operations that were becoming popular in 1990s for playing games a special-purpose microprocessor was designed. It was called a Graphics Processing Unit (GPU). It was used on an add-on card to the main processor board. (It is described in detail in Chapter 15). In the early 2000s the GPUs which originally had fixed processing pipeline were made programmable to support interesting rendering techniques used mainly in gaming. These GPUs began to be repurposed for general compute intense tasks by users as it used several simple processors that worked in parallel executing a single program on multiple data streams. This style of computing is called single program multiple data (SIMD) parallel programming. To enable general-purpose computing on these improved GPUs, NVIDIA a graphics processor design company, introduced Compute Unified Device Architecture (CUDA) in 2006. CUDA assisted in the transition of GPUs from specialized graphics processors to general-purpose compute devices that are used extensively for compute intense tasks. They were called General Purpose Graphics Processing Unit (GPGPU).

The GPGPUs are designed for parallel processing capabilities using the SIMD model programming. The GPGPU processor is closely aligned with RISC principles as it emphasizes on simplicity, efficiency and parallelism. It also incorporates some elements of CISC design to deal with large amounts of complex data types (multi-dimensional array computations) making it effective for applications like scientific computing, machine learning and data analysis.

Another trend is the rapid increase in the applications of Artificial Intelligence in problem solving using computers. Current AI systems extensively use neural networks (we will describe neural networks in detail in Chapter 18) for solving problems. Training neural networks is computing intensive. In particular training neural networks use matrix multiplications extensively with 8 and 16-bit operands. They also require fast access to memory. Specialized integrated circuits called *Neural Processing Units* have been designed that incorporate fast matrix multiplication with 8 and 16-bit floating point operands, parallel computing, and fast local memory. They are used as add-on processors to the main CPU chips. It is conjectured that in due-course as AI gains popularity, these chips will be integrated in the CPU chip along with GPGPUs.

11.7.3 Microcontrollers

Microcontrollers are special-purpose microprocessors whose architecture is tuned to cater to control applications. Many consumer products such as washing machines, VCRs, microwave ovens, and high-end audio systems have built-in microcontrollers to obey commands from a remote control or are programmed to follow a cycle through some states based on the occurrence of some events. For instance, a washing machine senses the level of water in the wash tub and when it reaches a preset level, starts the wash cycle. A timer is set by a user for a specified time and a timer starts. When the specified time is over, the controller automatically opens a drain valve to drain out the soapy water. A sensor determines the empty state and the controller opens the water inlet valve to let in water for the rinse cycle. A timer set by the user determines the duration of this cycle, after which the drain valve is again opened by the controller to drain out the water. When water is drained, a sensor sends a signal to the controller to start the spin cycle. After a preset time, the spinner stops. A beeper is activated by the controller to indicate to the user that washing is over. We summarize the actions initiated by the washing machine controller in Table 11.3.

Table 11.3 Washing machine control

Event	*Action*
Start pressed	Open inlet valve
	Fill tub
Tub full	Close inlet valve
	Start wash cycle
Wash time over	Open outlet valve
Tub empty	Close outlet valve
	Open inlet valve
Tub full	Close inlet valve
	Start rinse cycle
Rinse time over	Open outlet valve
Tub empty	Start spin cycle to dry clothes
Spin time over	Close outlet valve
	Activate beeper

Observe that the system follows a specific sequence determined by various events and by sensing a timer. A microcontroller is ideally suited to control the washing machine as it has features to support such sequential control applications.

The basic characteristics of a microcontroller as opposed to a general-purpose microprocessor are as follows:

- It has a built-in ROM within the chip to store the control program. The ROM size was of the order of 4 KB in early processors. Now (2025) some processors have 1 MB ROM.
- It has a relatively small built-in SRAM for temporary data storage. The SRAM size was of the order of 128 bytes in early processors. Now (2025) some processors have built-in 64 KB SRAM.
- The CPU uses 8/16 bit instructions so that the limited program memory (ROM) is effectively used.
- Many microcontrollers have a Boolean coprocessor along with the CPU to simplify implementing Boolean expressions occurring often in control applications.
- Microcontrollers have built-in counters and timers which can be set by users.
- They have built-in I/O ports, control, and A/D converters for easy interaction with external devices.

Nowadays microcontrollers incorporate a Control Area Network (CAN) interface so that several microcontrollers can be networked to control a system cooperatively.

As can be seen, with very few external circuits, the microcontroller can carry out its function effectively. The cost of a microcontroller is a fraction of the cost of a general-purpose microprocessor. In Figure 11.20, we give a block diagram of a typical microcontroller chip.

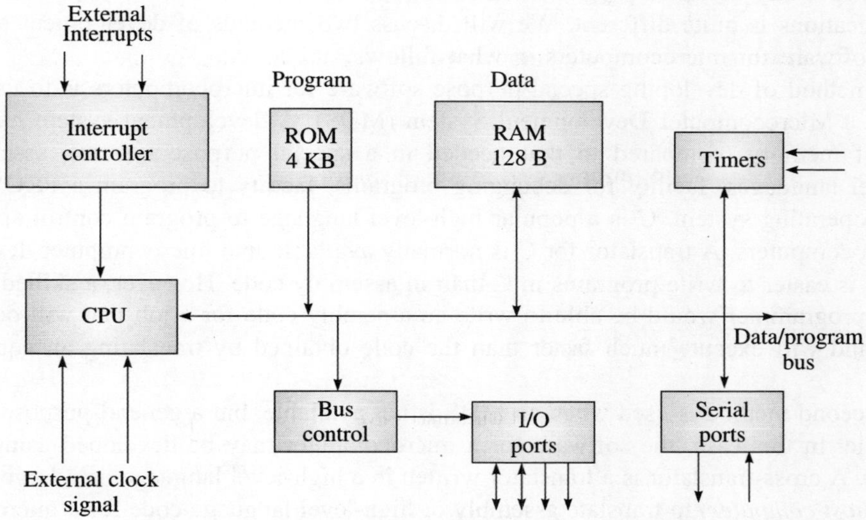

Figure 11.20 Internal architecture of a single-chip microcontroller.

For a long time, a popular microcontroller was Intel's model 8051 (now obsolete). The low-cost model had 128 bytes of SRAM and 4 KB of ROM for the program. The programs in microcontrollers are usually factory-programmed for specific applications. Models with flash memory are normally used to build a prototype in the laboratory for testing the program. Low power versions are also being manufactured which are used in portable systems. A low-cost 8-bit model is Atmega 328 PB. It has a clock of 16 MHz, 32 KB ROM, 2 KB SRAM, 1 KB EEPROM, and built-in A/D and D/A converters. It costs around $1 to 3 depending on the quantity purchased. A popular microcontroller released in 2023 is Ardunio R4 Minima which uses a 32-bit ARM Cortex-M4F core at 48 MHz, 256 KB ROM, 32 KB SRAM, and 8 KB EEPROM. A popular low-cost microcontroller board designed by a company named Raspberry Pi is Pico with a dual-core Arm Cortex-M0+ processor with 133 MHz clock, 264 KB on-chip SRAM, 2 MB on-board ROM and 2.4 GHz 802.11n WiFi connection.

Development systems with the necessary software are available for different models of microcontrollers. Such systems create bug-free application programs before the microcontroller is incorporated into a product such as a washing machine.

11.8 SPECIAL PURPOSE MICROCOMPUTER SOFTWARE

There are two different classes of microcomputer applications. One class is their use in general-purpose computers. In this case, high-level languages such as FORTRAN, C, and C++ are available. Besides this, suitable operating systems such as MS Windows and Linux are used.

The other class of use is in special purpose applications, such as controllers of motors, lifts, traffic lights, data loggers, data processors in sophisticated instruments, communications controllers such as a small telephone exchange, etc. Only small 8-bit microcomputers such as Intel's 8085 or microcontrollers are used in such applications as cost is an important criterion in consumer products. In these applications, the available memory is small, and only one dedicated, specially designed program will run all the time. The software design philosophy in such applications is quite different. We will discuss two methods of development of special-purpose software for microcomputers in what follows.

One method of developing special-purpose software for microcomputers is to use what is known as a Microcomputer Development System (MDS). A development system has a larger amount of memory (compared to that needed in a special purpose system), assembly and high- level languages, facility for debugging programs, facility to program a PROM and an adequate operating system. C is a popular high-level language to program control applications with microcomputers. A translator for C is normally available in a microcomputer development system. It is easier to write programs in C than in assembly code. However, a skilled assembly language programmer would be able to write an assembly code for a job that will occupy less memory and will execute much faster than the code obtained by translating an equivalent C program.

The second method is used when an MDS is not available, but a general-purpose computer is available. In this case, the software for a microcomputer may be developed using a *cross-translator*. A cross-translator is a translator written in a high-level language on a large computer (called a *host computer*) to translate assembly or high-level language code for a microcomputer to produce machine code for that microcomputer. The concept of a cross-translator is shown in Figure 11.21. The main advantages of a cross-translator are:

(i) A cross-translator is easier to develop because one can use all the resources of a large computer to develop it.
(ii) It is usually written in a high-level language such as C which expedites its development.
(iii) It may be designed to produce the machine code for a variety of microcomputers/ microcontrollers.

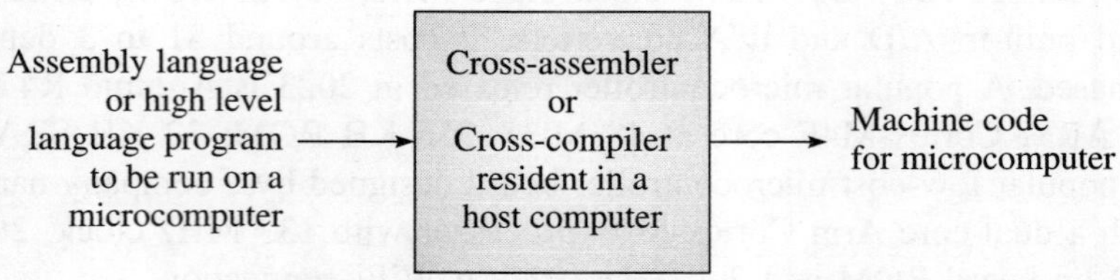

Figure 11.21 Illustration of a cross-translator.

The main disadvantages of a cross-translator are:

(i) The machine code may not be efficient.
(ii) As the machine code is produced on another machine, it is necessary to run it on the microcomputer for which it is intended before it can be authenticated.

11.9 SPECIAL PURPOSE APPLICATIONS OF MICROCOMPUTERS

11.9.1 Microcomputer as a Furnace Input Feed Controller

The versatility of a microcomputer stems from the fact that by changing the program stored in it, we can use it for a variety of jobs. As a specific example of a microcomputer application, consider the design of a controller for adjusting the input feeds to a furnace in a foundry that melts scrap iron. As the composition of the scrap is variable from batch to batch, it is necessary to control the quality of the molten metal in real time to reduce rejections of castings. Quality may be measured in real time by means of a spectrum analyzer. The output of the spectrum analyzer is converted to a binary digital form and fed as an input to a microcomputer. The computer, using a stored program based on metallurgical theory, determines the amount of silica, carbon, and manganese that need to be added to meet the specifications of the output iron. These outputs are communicated to operate feeders for silica, carbon, and manganese. Load cells measure the weights of the materials added and stop the feeders when appropriate quantities of materials are added to the furnace. The system is shown in Figure 11.22. Observe that this is a closed loop system that works in 'real-time'.

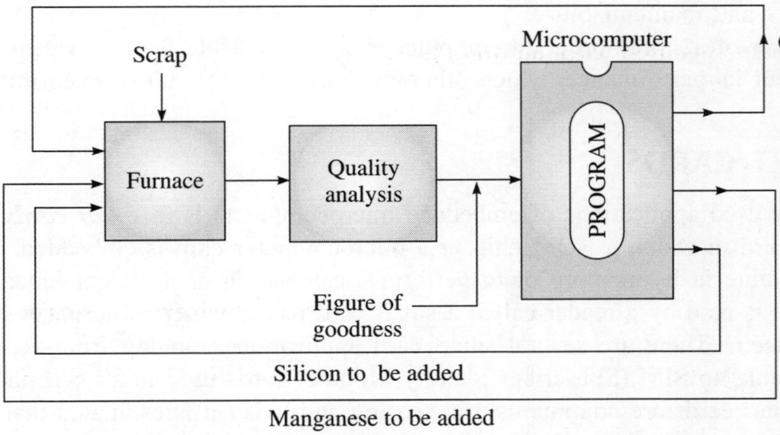

Figure 11.22 A microcomputer application.

11.9.2 Other Applications

Application areas of microcomputers and microcontrollers are limited only by the imagination of users. More than 80% of the current applications are in the replacement of hard-wired transistor circuitry. They are used in data collection terminals, office equipment, business machines, calculators, point-of-sale terminals, and data communications equipment. The programmability and flexibility of microcomputers make them popular in all types of instruments, including those for electronics labs, medicine, and physical analysis. Even areas where electronics was not used previously find microcomputers quite useful. These include control of traffic lights, as well as appliances such as washing machines and microwave ovens. They are also used to assist handicapped persons, in automobiles, and in entertainment electronics like TV games.

Compared to the number of general-purpose microcomputers used in PCs/workstations, the number of special-purpose microcomputers/controllers used in applications is at least 1000 times more. Every smartphone has at least one digital signal processor/microprocessor. A typical high-end car uses between 50 and 100 microprocessors.

There are several reasons for microcomputers becoming so popular. The most important reason is that they provide a good substitute for hard-wired logic and are programmable and flexible. It has been shown that a ROM can replace a large number of standard logic gates and a single 16-Kbit ROM is equivalent in logic power to 100 or more small-scale integrated circuits. Nowadays any system that uses a microcomputer to control its operation is called 'intelligent' as it is programmable, providing flexibility to the system. The following advantages of microcomputer-based systems are worth mentioning:

(i) Designing with ROMs and programming microcomputers is simple compared to designing with logic gates and hardware troubleshooting. This simplicity brings down the development time and leads to a host of associated benefits.

(ii) Their flexibility makes it possible to adapt quickly to market needs and changes required by users.

(iii) The smaller number of components in a microcomputer-based system increases its reliability and maintainability.

(iv) The power of a stored-program computer makes it possible for the system to collect data about its performance, which otherwise might be difficult or even impossible.

11.10 SMART CARDS

One of the widely used applications of embedded microcomputers is in *smart cards*. A smart card is a plastic card in which a ROM chip or a microcomputer chip is embedded. It is used either to store a value in its memory or to perform a calculation or a logical function on its inputs. Smart card is read by a reader called a smart card reader which is normally connected to a computer system. There are several smart card applications, ranging from secure credit cards issued by banks to SIM (Subscriber Identity Module) cards used in all cell phones. The applications of smart cards are continuously increasing and today it is estimated that there are over 6 billion smart cards used worldwide. A major reason for the proliferation of smart cards is the personalization, tamper-proof storage, and security of data exchange between smart cards and computers.

There are two major types of smart cards—contact cards and contactless cards. Contact cards have gold-plated terminals which make electrical contacts with connectors that read the contents of the smart card. SIM cards are contact cards. Contactless cards have an embedded antenna that, when taken near a coupler unit, transfers data wirelessly from the card to the reader. This is useful in applications such as access control of vehicles to a parking area or a toll road.

11.10.1 Memory Cards

Another classification of smart cards is a memory card or a microprocessor card. Memory card normally stores data that can be read and new data can be written. The memory may be segmented to allow some parts to be 'read-only' with no writing possible. The normal size of memory for segmented/protected memory cards is between 3 and 64 Kbits. These cards have built-in logic to control the access to specified memory segments. Usually, passwords (called Personal Identification Numbers) are used to control access. These cards are sometimes called *intelligent memory* cards. (The memory size continuously increases with advances in integrated circuit technology. The reader is advised to search the web for the current manufacturer's data sheets.)

Another type of memory card is called a *stored value memory* card. The size of this card is between 256 bits and 1M bits. It has a password key and hard-coded logic at the point of manufacture. A typical application of such a card is a prepaid SIM card used in a mobile phone. This card has data in cells that get cleared as units of telephone call time are used up, and when all the calls are used up, the phone is cut off. Additional money may be paid and the vendor will write this in the memory (commonly known as top-up). Some card types do not allow rewriting data in the memory. They are called single-use cards and are thrown away after use.

11.10.2 Microprocessor-based Smart Cards

These smart cards have data processing capability built into them. They organize and control files in their memory with a special purpose OS called Card Operating System (COS). COS controls access to the on-card memory which allows multiple applications of the card. The applications can be customized by appropriate programming and executing the programs with the built-in microprocessor. With this technology, many applications can be combined into one card for a user. For example, a consumer may be able to use one multipurpose card to debit an account, use a toll road, have his/her health data stored, etc. These cards range in power from an 8-bit processor with 128 KB of user memory to 32-bit high-performance processor with 1 MB user memory and a math coprocessor to expedite operations such as encryption. As the available memory is limited, the application programs are developed on a host computer, converted to machine code of the smart card's microprocessor, and downloaded into its memory. In Table 11.4, we summarize our discussion.

Table 11.4 Smart card types

Memory cards	*Microprocessor cards*
Segmented memory (3–64 Kbits)	8-bit low-end processor and OS,
	1–128 KB memory.
	16-bit medium performance,
	from 8 KB to 1 MB memory.
Stored value memory (256 to 1M bits)	32-bit high performance,
	32 KB memory, maths coprocessor.

Standards for Smart Cards have evolved which specify their size, thickness, and other physical characteristics. These standards also give electrical and logical standards. The standards are ISO 7816:1 to 6.

A smart card is normally read by a smart card reader. There are a large variety of readers in the market. They read the data stored in the smart card and transfer it to a PC for further processing. The transfer to a PC may be via a serial port, USB port, parallel port, etc.

More sophisticated smart card readers have processing power and are called terminals. The terminals have an OS to control reading or writing from or to a smart card and support many other functions such as debiting the value of a purchase from a stored credit limit, printing the current transaction, etc. Typical terminals are those found with shopkeepers who read credit cards and get the transaction approved.

11.11 RADIO FREQUENCY IDENTIFICATION

Another rapidly increasing application of embedded memories and microprocessors is in *Radio Frequency Identification (RFID)*. RFIDs have become popular in the last few years. They identify objects such as items on the shelves of a supermarket, books in a library, vehicles passing through a toll gate, animals in reserve forests, etc. RFID system consists of two parts (see Figure 11.23). One is called an RFID tag, a microchip memory that permanently stores the unique identification code of the object and other important data (usually up to 2 KB). This microchip memory is embedded in a plastic sheet and is coupled to a small antenna coil. The data stored in this tag is read by an RFID reader with an antenna that transmits electromagnetic waves. These waves are picked up by the antenna coil embedded in the RFID tag and a voltage is induced. This voltage is used to read the content of the microchip memory in the RFID tag and transmitted electromagnetically by the antenna coil in the RFID tag to the reader's antenna. Observe that in this method of reading, there is no physical contact between the RFID reader and the tag in which the data is stored. The RFID tags described above are called *passive tags* as they do not have an internal power source. They get the power they need by electromagnetic induction from the RFID reader. Highway tolls are collected automatically from RFID tags (called FASTag in India) stuck on the windshield of vehicles.

There is another type of tag called *active tags*. Besides memory, they have a small processor and a built-in battery to provide power for reading the memory and processing. These are called smart RFID cards.

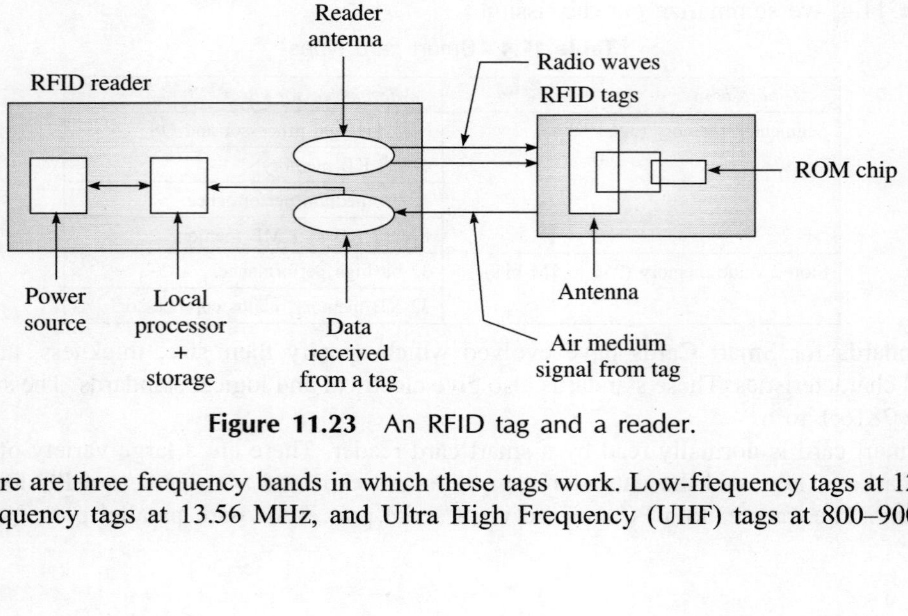

Figure 11.23 An RFID tag and a reader.

There are three frequency bands in which these tags work. Low-frequency tags at 125 kHz, high-frequency tags at 13.56 MHz, and Ultra High Frequency (UHF) tags at 800–900 MHz.

Low-frequency tags are cheap but have a short range (a few cm). High-frequency tags (13.56 MHz) are most popular as they have a range of up to 1 m, their cost is reasonable and they are ideal for tracking items. UHF tags are expensive but have higher reading speeds. They are used for toll collection of moving vehicles. These tags are normally *active*.

The main advantages of RFID tags are as follows:

- No physical contact is required to read them. (Contrast this with bar codes and bar code readers.)
- They can be read even if some obstacles are in the way.
- Many RFID tags can be read simultaneously.
- The speed of reading is high.

SUMMARY

1. An ideal microcomputer is a self-contained computer fabricated on an integrated circuit chip. It accepts data from N inputs, processes these using a stored program, and gives M outputs.
2. An actual microcomputer consists of a microprocessor chip which contains the arithmetic logic and control circuits, a ROM chip to store program, a RAM chip to store program and data, a power supply chip, and several interface chips to connect peripheral devices to the microprocessor.
3. One of the main limitations of fabricating a microcomputer on a chip is the limited number of pins allowed on it. This constrains the data path width, the addressing capacity, and the number of control lines. Sometimes the same set of lines is used at different times for different purposes. Advances in semiconductor fabrication, however, are making this constraint less important. General-purpose microprocessors such as Intel's Pentium had 273 pins, and microprocessors with over 1000 pins are now available.
4. A data bus is used to send and receive data in a microprocessor; an address bus is used to specify the address in memory from which data or instructions are to be sent or received; a control bus is used to send/receive signals to coordinate the functioning of the processor with the input/output devices and memory.
5. Interrupts are used in microcomputers whenever an error occurs during processing such as register overflow or when an external device wants data to be sent to or received. An interrupt halts the currently running program in the microprocessor and activates another program to service the appropriate I/O device.
6. A UART chip is used to serialize parallel data from a microcomputer and send it on a communication line. Similarly, serial data from a communication line is reformatted as a parallel set of bits and sent on the data bus.
7. A DMA chip transfers data from a peripheral device to the memory without using CPU resources.
8. Microprocessors have evolved in 30 years from small 8-bit systems which could address 16 KB memory to 64-bit systems with the capacity to address 64 GB memory. Current microprocessors incorporate multiple processors (called cores) in the chip and have a large built-in cache memory system. All computers nowadays use microprocessors as building blocks.

9. In the 1970s, the trend was to introduce numerous instructions, a variety of addressing modes, and variable-length instructions to build powerful CPUs. Such processors are known as Complex Instruction Set Computers (CISC).
10. In the 1980s, with the advancement in integrated circuit technology, memory became cheap and the art of writing compilers to translate high-level languages to machine language matured. This led to a newer CPU architecture called RISC (Reduced Instruction Set Computers). RISC has numerous registers in the CPU and has only two instructions that reference the main memory. They are to load a register from the main memory and store the contents of a register in the main memory. RISC uses simple addressing modes and has uniform instruction length. The total number of instructions is also small. This simplifies instruction decoding and allows instructions to be carried out fast (one instruction per clock cycle).
11. With the lowering of the cost of digital VLSI chips, newer special-purpose microprocessors have emerged. These are Digital Signal Processors and Microcontrollers.
12. Digital Signal Processors accept continuously varying signals in real-time, digitize them with Analog to Digital Converters, process them, and reconvert them to analog form for output using Digital to Analog Converters.
13. Special features of DSPs are fast ALU and Multiply Accumulate unit, separate on-chip data and program memory, and I/O controllers. Their main uses are speech synthesis, video signal processing, mobile phones, CD players, and many high-quality consumer entertainment electronics systems.
14. When users started using PCs to play games rich in graphics designers built specialized microprocessors called Graphics Processing Units (GPU). They were used to assist CPUs to perform graphics. Soon they became powerful and users started using them as General Purpose Graphics Processors (GPGPU) that, in addition to graphics, were used for numeric-intensive computing.
15. With Artificial Intelligence applications becoming integral part of computing special integrated circuits useful in training neural networks are emerging. These are called Neural Processing Units (NPU). They are currently used as add-on chip to CPU chip.
16. Microcontrollers are special-purpose microprocessors whose architecture is tuned to cater to control applications. They have built-in ROM for storing programs and RAM for storing data. Besides these, they have built-in I/O controllers and timers. The architecture is well suited to design programmed controllers for products such as washing machines, VCRs, automobiles, etc. Programmed controllers are much more flexible and versatile compared to hard-wired digital electronic systems. Many products incorporating microcontrollers are advertised as 'intelligent systems'.
17. Microcomputer applications fall into two distinct classes. One class is their use as general-purpose computers and the other class is their use as special-purpose systems. A Microcomputer Development System (MDS) is used to program. special-purpose applications. An MDS usually has a large memory, high-level language translators, and a PROM programmer.
18. If an MDS is not available, then special-purpose applications are programmed using a larger general-purpose computer. A cross-translator may be implemented in a large

computer that accepts a high-level language program intended for a microcomputer and produces a machine language program corresponding to it.

19. All general-purpose computers, from laptop computers to high-performance parallel computers, use microprocessors as their CPU. The latest microprocessors have a clock of 3 GHz and can carry out several billion operations per second.
20. Special-purpose applications of microcomputers are data entry units, office equipment, data communication equipment, controllers of lifts, traffic lights, washing machines, etc. They are extensively used to replace large relay controllers and transistor digital circuits.
21. A widely used application of microcomputers is in smart cards. Smart cards are plastic cards with either an integrated circuit memory alone or memory with an embedded microprocessor.
22. Smart cards are extensively used in applications such as credit cards, SIM (Subscriber Identity Module) cards, access cards, and multifunction cards. Cards with microprocessors use 8–32-bit microprocessors and have memory up to 256 KB. They also incorporate a small OS.
23. RFID (Radio Frequency Identification) system for objects has a tag with a small ROM and an antenna. The ROM is used to store the unique identification codes of an object. An RFID reader sends electromagnetic waves to the tag whose contents are transmitted wirelessly to the reader.

REVIEW QUESTIONS

11.1 Define an ideal microcomputer.

11.2 What is the difference between an ideal microcomputer and an actual microcomputer?

11.3 What are the main constraints in realizing an ideal microcomputer?

11.4 What is a microprocessor?

11.5 Describe the logical structure of a typical microprocessor.

11.6 What is the purpose of the data bus of a microprocessor?

11.7 Why is the width of the data bus an important parameter in microprocessors?

11.8 Define the word length of a microprocessor.

11.9 What is the purpose of the address bus in a microprocessor?

11.10 What is the maximum size of memory that can be addressed with an address bus width of 20 bits?

11.11 What is the purpose of a control bus in a microcomputer?

11.12 What do you understand by the term tristate condition?

11.13 What is the use of a ROM in a microcomputer?

11.14 Is ROM used to store programs or data?

11.15 Is ROM a volatile or non-volatile memory?

11.16 What is the difference between a RAM and a ROM?

11.17 What is a PROM?

11.18 What is the main use of a PROM?

11.19 What is an EPROM?

11.20 What is the main use of an EPROM?

11.21 Give a block diagram of a microcomputer.

11.22 What are the 'support chips' in a microcomputer?

11.23 Define an interrupt.

11.24 Why are interrupts used in a microcomputer?

11.25 What is an interrupt service routine?

11.26 What is a UART?

11.27 What is the main function of a UART?

11.28 What do you understand by the term 'baud rate'?

11.29 What is DMA?

11.30 How does a DMA chip cooperate with a microprocessor to transfer data from an I/O device to memory?

11.31 Among the microprocessors listed in Table 11.2, which is closest to the ideal microprocessor?

11.32 What is the significant difference between INTEL 80386 and Core i7 microcomputers?

11.33 What do you understand by the term RISC architecture?

11.34 Enumerate the important characteristics of a RISC CPU.

11.35 What are the main differences between a RISC CPU and a CISC CPU?

11.36 What do you understand by the term superscalar RISC?

11.37 Give the significant differences between a general-purpose microprocessor and a digital signal processor.

11.38 What are the applications of DSP?

11.39 How many samples per second of an analog signal (with the highest frequency of 20 kHz) should be taken for converting it to its digital equivalent?

11.40 The required precision in A/D conversion is 0.05%. How many bits per sample of the analog signal should be taken?

11.41 What is the function of the MAC unit in a DSP?

11.42 What is GPU? What are its uses.

11.43 What do you understand by the term SPMD style of programming? Where is it relevant?

11.44 What is a GPGPU? How is it used?

11.45 Give the significant differences between a general-purpose microprocessor and a microcontroller.

11.46 What are the applications of a microcontroller?

11.47 Can a microprocessor be used in place of a microcontroller in applications? Justify your answer.

11.48 What is a Microcomputer Development System?

11.49 What facilities does MDS provide for microcomputer program development?

11.50 What is a cross-translator?

11.51 Why are cross-translators used in program development for microcomputers?

11.52 Why are microcomputers preferred over hard-wired logic in control applications?

11.53 What are smart cards? What are the different types of smart cards?

11.54 What are the different applications of smart memory cards?

11.55 What are the applications of smart microprocessor-based cards?

11.56 What is the typical memory size of a memory-only card?

11.57 What is the memory size of a high-end smart card with a microprocessor?

11.58 What is an RFID system? How does it function?

11.59 Enumerate some of the applications of RFID system.

11.60 What are the frequencies used by RFID tags?

11.61 What is the distinction between an active and a passive RFID tag?

12 Computer Generations and Classification

LEARNING GOALS

After reading this chapter, you should be able to:

- Classify computers into various generations.
- Classify computers as mobile devices, tablet, laptop, desktop, workstation, server, mainframe, and supercomputer.
- Describe the characteristics of parallel computers.

In this chapter, we will present a historical perspective on the development of computers. The term 'computer generation' is widely used, particularly by computer manufacturer sales personnel. It is most often used regarding computer hardware. We will take a broader view and examine developments in software and applications besides hardware. The classification into generations is subjective. There are no objective criteria. We have used our judgment and milestone events to determine the break-points.

In the second part of the chapter, we will explain the commonly used classification of computers as Tablet computers, Laptop computers, Personal computers, Servers, Mainframes, Distributed computers, Parallel computers, and High-performance or Supercomputers.

12.1 FIRST GENERATION OF COMPUTERS

The first electronic computer was built in 1946 by a team led by J. Presper Eckert and John Mauchly at the University of Pennsylvania in the USA. This computer called the Electronic Numerical Integrator and Calculator (ENIAC), used vacuum tubes as switching devices. It was programmed using plug boards that interconnected arithmetic units and was designed primarily to calculate artillery firing tables using the trajectories of shells and bombs. ENIAC took about 200 μs to add two ten-digit numbers and about 2800 μs to multiply them.

A breakthrough occurred in the logical design of computers when the concept of a *stored program* was proposed by John Von Neumann in 1946. His idea was to store machine instructions in the memory of the computer along with data. These instructions could be modified as required by other instructions. This allowed easy implementation of program loops. In the second avatar of ENIAC, its function tables were re-purposed as a small memory to store programs in 1948. The first electronic computer that could be programmed to solve complex problems using a stored program was commissioned at Cambridge University, UK, under the leadership of Maurice Wilkes in 1949. This computer called EDSAC (Electronic Delay Storage Automatic Calculator) used mercury delay lines for storage.

Commercial production of stored program electronic computers began in the early 1950s. One of the first commercial computers was UNIVAC I designed by Eckert and Mauchly and manufactured by the Univac division of Remington Rand Corporation and delivered in 1951. This computer used vacuum tubes. As vacuum tubes used filaments as a source of electrons, they had a limited life. Each tube consumed about half a watt of power. Computers typically used about ten thousand tubes. Power dissipation was very high. As a large number of tubes, each with a limited life were used in fabricating these computers, their mean time between failures was low—of the order of a few hours. Several innovations such as improving the cathode design and reducing the voltage used to power the filaments improved the reliability of computers using vacuum tubes. These innovations increased their mean time between failures to about a week.

During this period, computers were programmed using machine language. Assembly language was invented in the early 1950s. Initially, ENIAC and EDSAC were used to solve problems in science and engineering. UNIVAC I was built with the support of the US Census Bureau to tabulate the US census data and was used for commercial data processing. The concept of an operating system had not yet emerged. During this period, one had to be a good electronics engineer, understand the logical structure of a computer in great detail, and also know how to program an application to use a computer. It was somewhat like the early days of cars when one had to be a good mechanic to drive a car!

12.2 SECOND GENERATION

The invention of transistors by John Bardeen, Walter Brattain, and William Shockley at the Bell Telephone Laboratories in 1947 revolutionized electronics. Transistors made of the germanium semiconductor material were highly reliable compared to tubes since transistors had no filament to burn. They occupied less space and used only a tenth of the power required by tubes. They could also switch from a 0 to a 1 state in a few microseconds, about a tenth of the time needed by tubes. Thus, switching circuits for computers made with transistors were about ten times more reliable, ten times faster, dissipated one-tenth the power, occupied about one-tenth the space, and were ten times cheaper than those using tubes. Computer manufacturers thus replaced tubes with transistors. The second generation computers emerged around 1955 using transistors instead of vacuum tubes in computers. The first widely used transistorized computer was IBM 1401 released in 1959. Over 12,000 IBM 1401s were sold worldwide. The second generation lasted till 1965.

Another major invention by Jay Forrester at MIT in 1952 was *magnetic cores* for building memories. Magnetic cores are tiny rings (0.05 cm diameter) made of ferrite that can be magnetized in clockwise or anticlockwise directions. The two directions are used to represent a 0 and a 1. Magnetic cores were used to construct large random access memories. Memory capacity in the second generation was about 100 KB. Magnetic disk storage was also developed during this period.

The higher reliability of computers and large memory availability led to the design of high-level languages. FORTRAN, COBOL, Algol, and SNOBOL were developed during this generation. With higher-speed CPUs and the advent of magnetic tape and disk storage, operating systems were developed. Good batch operating systems, particularly the ones on IBM 7000 series computers, emerged during the second generation.

Commercial applications rapidly developed during this period and dominated computer use by the mid-1960s. More than 80% of installed computers were used in business and industry. All systems were batch-oriented. Payroll, inventory control, marketing, production planning, and general ledger systems were developed. Several operations research applications such as Linear Programming, Critical Path Methods (CPM), and Simulation became popular. Engineering applications in systems design and process control increased rapidly.

New computing professions such as systems analysts and programmers emerged during the second generation. Academic programmes in computer science were also initiated during the mid-1960s.

12.3 THIRD GENERATION

The third generation began in 1965 with the replacement of transistors by Integrated Circuits (ICs). Integrated circuits were invented independently by Jack Kilby at Texas Instruments and Robert Noyce at Fairchild Semiconductors. Circuits consisting of transistors, resistors, and capacitors were grown on a single chip of silicon eliminating wired interconnection between components in ICs. They started with small-scale integrated circuits with about 10 transistors per chip. Soon the technology developed into medium-scale integrated circuits with 100 transistors per chip. The switching speed of transistors went up by a factor of 10, reliability increased by a factor of 10, power dissipation reduced by a factor of 10, and the size of transistor switches was also reduced by a factor of 10. The effect of this development was the emergence of extremely powerful CPUs that could carry out 1 million instructions per second. Several new architectural ideas, such as virtual memory, interrupts, DMA, and base registers, became part of commercial computers and were extensively used.

Magnetic core memories improved rapidly. The size of the main memories reached about 4 MB. Magnetic disk technology also improved and 100 MB drives became feasible.

The combination of high-capacity main memory, powerful CPU, and large disk memory led to the emergence of time-shared operating systems that increased programmer productivity.

Many important online systems became feasible. In particular, dynamic production control systems, airline reservation systems, interactive query systems, and real-time closed-loop process control systems were implemented. Integrated database management systems emerged.

High-level languages improved. FORTRAN IV and optimizing FORTRAN compilers were developed. COBOL 68 was standardized by the American National Standards Institute. IBM introduced PL/1, combining the features of FORTRAN and COBOL. PL/1 was used to write operating systems and application programs.

The third generation ended around 1972 with the fabrication of a computer's entire CPU on a single IC, called a microprocessor. Intel 8008, an 8-bit processor on one chip revolutionized the design of computers. The improvements in computer design during the period 1965–1972 were substantial.

12.4 FOURTH GENERATION

12.4.1 First Decade (1973–1985)

The fourth generation may be identified by the advent of the microprocessor chip. Medium-scale integrated circuits progressed to Large and Very Large Scale Integrated (VLSI) circuits that packed around 100,000 transistors in a chip. Magnetic core memories were replaced by semiconductor memories. Semiconductor memory sizes of 16 MB with a cycle time of 200 ns were in common use. Computer technology grew in two directions with the emergence of the microprocessor. One was the emergence of powerful personal computers and the other was the emergence of time-shared minicomputers. Computer prices came down so rapidly that professionals owned computers to use in their offices and homes. Hard disks provided a low-cost, high-capacity secondary memory.

A development that was to have a major impact on the history of computing was the decision of IBM to enter the Personal Computer market. IBM's decision to make the architecture of IBM Personal Computer (IBM PC) open and use a non-proprietary processor (Intel 8008) had far-reaching consequences. Another concurrent decision by IBM was to outsource the development of the Operating System of the IBM PC to Microsoft, a software company founded by Paul Allen and Bill Gates. Microsoft negotiated with IBM a non-exclusive agreement permitting it to license the OS to anyone. Microsoft first developed a very small OS called MS-DOS (Microsoft Disk Operating Systems) which was a successor of a system called CP/M (Control Program for Microcomputers) designed by Gary Kildall in 1974.

The open architecture of IBM PC allowed many small companies to make PCs, conforming to IBM's design, using off-the-shelf Intel microprocessors. These were called IBM clones. All IBM clone manufacturers licensed their OS from Microsoft. This had a far-reaching consequence on the proliferation of IBM PCs, the dominance of Microsoft as an OS vendor, and the emergence of several application software developers who could design applications using MS-DOS (which was becoming a de facto standard) for IBM PCs and their clones. Numerous applications such as word processors, spreadsheets, and database management systems for PCs emerged. IBM PC soon became a common office machine on everyone's desk replacing typewriters.

Another development was the decentralization of computer organization. Individual microprocessor controls for terminals and peripheral devices allowed the CPU to concentrate on processing the main program. Networks of computers and distributed computer systems were developed. Disk memories became very large (1 GB/drive). Concurrent programming languages were designed to program distributed systems and real-time systems. The most ambitious language of this type was ADA. Another important development was interactive graphic devices and language interfaces to graphic systems. The emergence of graphics hardware gave great impetus to computer-aided engineering design and computer games.

The fourth generation saw the coming of age of UNIX OS and time-shared interactive systems. These systems became user-friendly and highly reliable. The effective cost of computing came down and computers began to be used widely.

12.4.2 Second Phase (1986–2000)

The second phase of the fourth generation has seen a relentless increase in the speed of microprocessors and the main memory size. The speed of microprocessors and the size of the main memory and hard disk went up by a factor of 4 every 3 years. Many of the features originally found in the CPUs of large expensive mainframe computers of the first decade of the fourth generation became part of the microprocessor architecture in the 1990s. Thus, the mainframe computer of the early 1980s died in the mid-1990s. The alpha microprocessor chip designed by DEC in 1994 packed 9.3 million transistors in a single integrated circuit, was driven by a 300 MHz clock, and could carry out a billion operations per second. It had a built-in 64-bit floating point arithmetic unit used 64-bit data and 64-bit address buses. It had a built-in cache memory of 64 KB and 32 registers to store temporary operands. Apart from this IBM, Apple computers, and Motorola cooperated in designing a microprocessor called Power PC 600 series. Intel designed a powerful chip in the 1990s called Pentium (1993) which sold in large numbers. The original Pentium was followed by Pentium with MMX (Multimedia Extension) and Pentium II with a clock speed of 466 MHz and a Celeron processor with a 300 MHz clock. In 2000, Intel introduced a 64-bit processor called IA-64 or Itanium.

Microprocessors such as Pentium and Power PC are being used as the CPUs of Personal Computers, portable laptops, and hand-held computers. Desktop workstations and powerful servers for numeric computing, as well as file services, used RISC microprocessors such as Alpha, MIPS, and SUN SPARC.

The area of hard disk storage also saw vast improvements. 1 GB disk on workstations became common in 1994. For larger disks of 100 GB capacity, RAID technology (Redundant Array of Inexpensive Disks) was used. Optical disks also emerged as mass storage, particularly for read-only files.

Optical storage sizes were of the order of 650 MB on a 5.25″ disk. New optical disks known as Digital Versatile Disk ROMs (DVDROMs) with a maximum storage capacity of around 17 GB emerged around 1998. Writable CDs were developed around the same time. The availability of optical disks at low cost saw the development of multimedia applications. Multimedia workstations were widely used.

Computer Networks came of age. The networks became very powerful with the advent of fibre optic Local Area Networks which could transmit 100 MB/s to 1 GB/s. Many mainframes were replaced by powerful workstations connected by a fibre optic network. Another major event during this phase was the rapid increase in the number of computers connected to the

Internet. This led to the emergence of the World Wide Web which eased information retrieval. The Internet also brought out the need to execute programs on a variety of computers. This led to the emergence of a new object-oriented language called Java. Applications written in Java, called Java applets, could be glued with JavaScript to create large programs.

In the area of languages, the C language became popular. This was followed by a new method of design called the object-oriented design. The primary objectives of object-oriented design were to generalize programs and to reuse objects. The C++ language emerged as the most popular object-oriented language. One also saw a trend towards the design of specification-oriented languages. PROLOG was designed for logic-oriented specification language and Haskell, ML, etc. as functional languages. With the emergence of distributed computers connected by networks, considerable effort has gone into programming distributed systems. Various parallel computers were built, but no commonly accepted standard parallel programming language emerged.

12.5 FIFTH GENERATION COMPUTERS (2001–2022)

It was thought in the early 1990s that a new generation computer would emerge which will have an architecture radically different from the Von Neumann architecture. The goal was to have a computer which will allow specification-oriented programming and incorporate artificial intelligence features. Initiatives were taken in the mid-1980s by various countries led by Japan and followed by the UK, Europe, USA, and India. However, there was no revolutionary architectural change. The major outcome of these efforts was the emergence of a variety of parallel computer architectures using several hundreds to thousands of processors. This initiative also attempted to build Artificial Intelligence computers such as LISP and Prolog computers without success.

Meanwhile, the relentless increase in the number of transistors that could be placed in a single chip went on. This led to changes in processor architecture. Primarily the idea was to use several processors called "cores" on a chip with shared on-chip memory to implement parallelism. In other words, the programmers' model of a processor did not change. However,compilers improved to extract as much parallelism as possible from sequential programs and schedule parallel operations on several cores on the chip. IBM released the Power 4 dual-core microprocessor in 2001. It was followed by Intel releasing the Pentium dual-core processor in 2005 and AMD releasing the Opteron 800 dual-core in 2005. The fifth generation may be characterized by the emergence of multi-core microprocessors and extensive use of parallelism in computing. Several parallel computers entered the market. Desktop computers made by HP and Apple became versatile and powerful. Complete high-performance computers mounted on a single printed circuit board called "blade servers" emerged. Several blades were assembled on racks and interconnected. Many racks were assembled to configure what is known as Warehouse Scale Computers that became workhorses of cloud computers.

Another important development was the emergence of specialized graphics processing units used as co-processors in computers. A leading manufacturer, NVIDIA, introduced the GeForce 256 GPU. GeForce used the huge inherent parallelism in image processing and image generation. They were introduced initially for use in computer games as games became sophisticated and the market for gaming computers became huge. It was soon realized that graphics processors could enhance the speed of high-performance computers when used as co-processors. The speed of high-performance computers increased enormously using graphics co-processors and an ExaFLOPS (10^{18} Floating Point Operations per Second on 64-bit operands) computer named Cray HPE Frontier was released in 2022.

Processor architecture called Very Large Instruction Word (VLIW) with an instruction size of 128–256 bits that could execute several instructions in parallel emerged. Intel's new generation processor Itanium used this idea. This architecture, however, did not become popular as writing compilers for these processors was difficult. Intel discontinued Itanium.

The other important development was the rapid improvements in communication technology. The combination of computing and communication technologies and the increase in bandwidth of networks led to revolutionary changes. An important consequence of this is the emergence of the Internet. The Internet and the World Wide Web an application using the Internet infrastructure changed the style of computing and spawned several new applications such as e-commerce and web design languages. Large computer installations named Warehouse-Scale computers that used banks of computer blades (a single-board self-contained computer) emerged. These were used to provide on-demand computing services to users over the Internet, known as Cloud Computing (described in Chapter 17).

Another significant trend is mobility which meets the user's demand for any time–any place access to data and processing. This is being met by the emergence of WiFi (Wireless High-fidelity) that connects computers wirelessly to the Internet. Wireless-enabled processor chips (e.g., Centrino of Intel) which are used in laptop and hand-held computers emerged. Mobile devices are battery-operated and thus it is important to design microcomputers for these devices whose power consumption is low. A microprocessor family called ARM processors emerged and are widely used. Concurrently, efficient OS for mobile devices such as smartphones emerged. Among them, Apple computer's OS iOS, and Google's Android are the most significant ones. The other major trend is the demand for multimedia, allowing users to use simple graphical user interfaces, listen to good-quality audio, and watch videos on their desktop and mobile computers.

In Table 12.1, we summarize and compare various generations of computers.

12.6 MOORE'S LAW

In 1965, Gordon E. Moore (one of the founders of Fairchild Semiconductors, USA) predicted, based on data available then that the density of transistors in integrated circuits would double at regular intervals of around 2 years. Based on the experience from 1972 to date, it has been found that his prediction has been surprisingly accurate. The observation of Moore is called 'Moore's law'. In Figure 12.1, we have plotted the number of transistors per chip in microprocessors along the *y*-axis and years along the *x*-axis. Observe that the *y*-axis uses a logarithmic scale and the *x*-axis uses a linear scale. Observe that in 1972 the number of transistors in Intel 8008 was 3500 and it is over 10^{10} in 2024. Table 12.2 gives the number of transistors in Intel microprocessors from 1972 to 2024.

Table 12.1 Computer generations—a comparison

Generation	*Years*	*Switching device*	*Storage device*	*Switching time*	*Typical computers*	*Software*	*Applications*
First	1949–55	Vacuum tubes	Acoustic delay lines and later magnetic drum. 1 KB memory	0.1–1 ms	UNIVAC I IBM 650	Machine and assembly languages. Simple monitors	Mostly scientific. Later simple business systems
Second	1956–65	Transistors	Magnetic core main memory, tapes and disk peripheral memory. 100 KB main memory	1–10 µs	IBM 1401 CDC 3600 IBM 7090	High level languages. FORTRAN, COBOL, Algol, Batch operating systems	Extensive business applications. Engineering design optimization, scientific research
Third	1966–75	Integrated Circuits (IC)	High speed magnetic cores. Large disks (100 MB). 1 MB main memory	0.1–1 µs	IBM 360 IBM 370 DG NOVA mini	FORTRAN IV, COBOL 68, PL/1. Time shared operating system	Database management systems. On-line systems
Fourth—First phase	1975–84	Large-scale integrated circuits. Microprocessors (LSI)	Semiconductor memory. Winchester disk. 10 MB main memory. 1000 MB disks	10–100 ns	IBM PC VAX 11/780	FORTRAN 77, Pascal, ADA, COBOL-74, Concurrent Pascal	Personal computers. Distributed systems. Integrated CAD/CAM real-time control. Graphics oriented systems
Fourth—Second phase	1985–2000	Very large-scale integrated circuits. Over 100 million transistors per chip	Semiconductor memory. 1 GB main memory. 100 GB disk	1–10 ns	SUN Micros SG Indigo IBM RS/6000 Intel IPSC/860	C, C++, JAVA, PROLOG, Haskell FORTRAN 90/95	Simulation, Visualization, Parallel computing, Virtual reality, Multimedia
Fifth generation	2001-2022	Multi-core processors Graphics processors Billion transistors per chip	8 GB main memory SSD 500 GB 4 TB disk	0.5 to 5 ns	Apple iPad IBM Blue Gene IBM QS22 Blade	C, C++, Python, JavaScript, C#	Web applications, Gaming, Cloud computing

* MTBF — Mean time between failures of the processor.

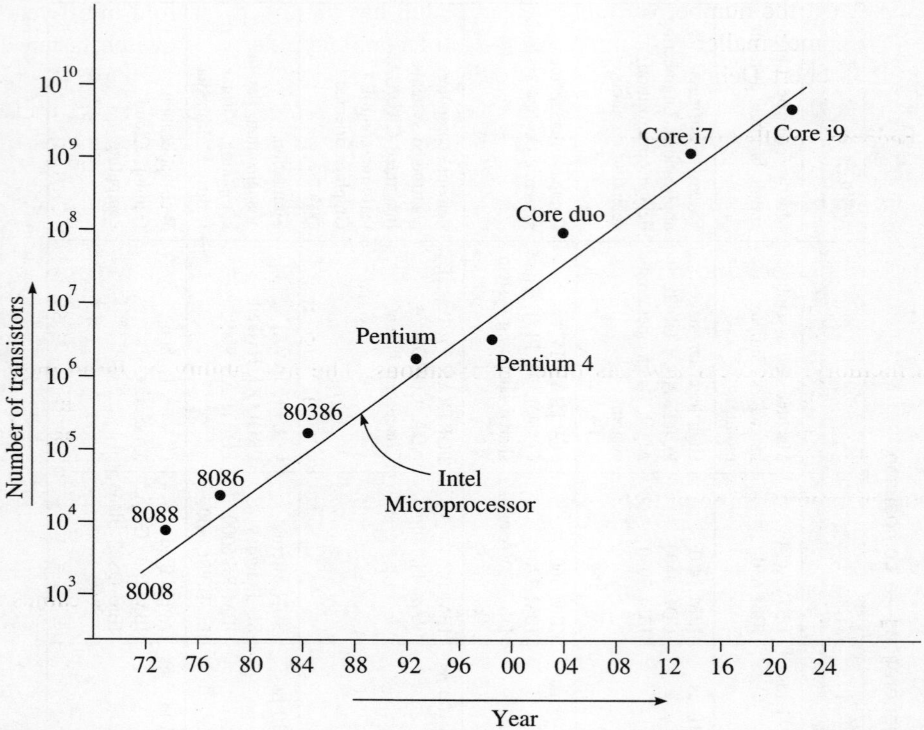

Figure 12.1 Moore's law showing the growth of the number of transistors in Intel microprocessors from 1972 to 2024.

Table 12.2 Number of transistors in Intel microprocessors and clock speed

Year	*Chip name*	*Number of Transistors*	*Clock Speed*
1972	8008	3500	500 KHz
1974	8080	8000	2 MHz
1978	8086	29,000	5 MHz
1982	80286	134,000	6 MHz
1985	80386	275,000	16 MHz
1989	80486	1.2×10^6	25 MHz
1993	Pentium	3.3×10^6	60 MHz
1997	Pentium II	7.5×10^6	230 MHz
2000	Pentium IV	42×10^6	1.4 GHz
2006	Core 2 Duo	140×10^6	2.8 GHz
2010	Core i7	550×10^6	2.66 GHz
2015	Core i7-6950X	1.4×10^9	2.66 GHz
2020	Xeon W3175X	8.6×10^9	3 GHz
2024	Core i9-14900K	10^{10}	3.4 GHz

Observe that the number of transistors in a chip has increased 10^7-fold in 50 years. When transistors become smaller with improvements in technology, they also switch faster. This was observed by Robert Dennard of IBM in 1974 and is called "Dennard scaling". Thus, higher-frequency clocks could be used in microprocessors over the years. However, as transistors in a chip become smaller the leakage current between their sources and sinks increases, which increases the power they dissipate, heating the chip rapidly affecting its performance. The current generation microprocessors are 64-bit processors with clocks in the range of 3 GHz. Beyond this clock speed, the heat generated becomes very high and requires special cooling methods. Thus, increasing clock speed is not a solution to get faster computing. Chip manufacturers have instead placed multiple processors on a chip that work in parallel to increase computing speed. These are called *multi-core processors*. Currently, up to 20 cores are integrated into a chip that share a memory. Moore's law has other implications. The availability of large memory and fast processors has increased the size and complexity of systems and applications software. It has been observed that software developers have always consumed the increased hardware capability faster than the growth in hardware. This has kept up the demand for hardware.

Another interesting point to be noted is the increase in disk capacity. In 1984, disk capacity in PCs was around 20 MB, whereas it is 32 TB today (2025)—a 1.6-million-fold increase in 40 years, again doubling every 20 months which is similar to Moore's law. Another significant event during the past 5 years is the doubling of the bandwidth of fibre optic cables every 9 months. These improvements in the capability of computers have come about with hardly any price increase. The price of computers has been coming down!

Moore's law implies that in the foreseeable future, we will be getting more powerful computers at a reasonable cost. It will be up to our ingenuity to use this increased power of computers effectively. Several applications such as understanding natural language, replying to natural language queries in natural language, image and speech generation, and recognition, called Artificial Intelligence (AI) applications, which require a large amount of memory and computing power—will be extensively used.

12.7 CLASSIFICATION OF COMPUTERS

Until recently computers were classified as microcomputers, minicomputers, supermini computers, mainframes, and supercomputers. Technology, however, has changed and this classification is no longer relevant. Today all computers use microprocessors as their CPU. Thus, classification is possible only through their mode of use. Based on their mode of use we classify computers as Tablets, Laptop PCs, Desktop PCs, Servers, Mainframes, and Supercomputers. Another classification of several inter-connected computers cooperatively solving problems is: distributed computers and parallel computers.

Tablets/Smartphones

With miniaturization and high-density packing of transistors on a chip, computers with capabilities nearly that of PCs which weigh around 350 g and can be held in one's palm have emerged. They have a touch-sensitive screen (8–10″) on which a virtual QWERTY keyboard can be displayed. Besides this, icons are displayed to invoke applications using one's finger.

Tablets also have a Wi-Fi connection to the Internet and can access a browser using which all Internet applications can be used. An open-source OS called Android developed by Google is used universally on most Smartphones and Tablet computers. Apple Computers manufactures a Tablet computer called iPad which is very popular due to its excellent graphical user interface and the availability of a large number of user-developed applications called Apps. Besides this, Apple sells from its App Store many useful Apps, music, videos, and books. Apple uses a proprietary OS called iOS. Numerous application programs written by individuals and groups are available on other manufacturers' Tablets. Many of these are free. The availability of Apps, mobility, and multiple uses, such as a mobile phone, camera, audio recorder, and radio, have increased the popularity of Tablets.

While tablets became popular, users demanded a mobile phone that has, in addition to its phone function, access to the Internet and applications such as search engines, navigation aids such as Google Maps coupled with Global Positioning System, and apps available on tablets. This led to the development of Smartphones with as much computing power as many tablets. The main difference between Tablet computers and Smartphones is the small screen size of Smartphones as these phones are required to be carried in one's pocket. Some popular Smartphones are Apple's iPhone, Samsung Galaxy, Motorola Moto, and several Chinese Smartphones.

Laptop PCs

Laptop PCs are portable computers weighing around 2 kg. They have a keyboard, 12 to 15" flat screen liquid crystal colour display, and an Intel or AMD processor. They normally use Microsoft's Windows OS or an open-source OS called Linux. A popular set of applications is MS-office which has a word processor, spreadsheet program, presentation program, and a database management system. Several manufacturers market a variety of models. Apple Computer has a popular Laptop computer called Apple iMac. It uses an Apple proprietary microprocessor called M2 Pro and an OS called MacOS and has developed office productivity programs such as a word processor, spreadsheet program, etc. Laptop computers come with a hard disk (around 1 TB), 16 GB of main memory, and several USB ports that can be used for pen drives, external disks, etc. They run with rechargeable batteries and are thus designed to conserve energy by using power-efficient chips. Laptops are connected to the Internet using wireless connectivity called Wi-Fi. The most common use of Laptop computers is for word processing, spreadsheets, PowerPoint presentations, database management, and accessing the Internet using a browser.

Desktop Computers (PCs)

The most popular PCs used in offices are desktop machines. Desktop PCs nowadays (2025) use either Intel Core i5 or AMD's Ryzen 57600 processor that has 4 to 6 cores running at 3 GHz, main memory size between 8 and 16 GB, and secondary memory of about 1 TB SSD. Several manufacturers such as HP, Lenovo, and Dell have competing models. The latest Microsoft OS, Windows 11, is usually sold along with the hardware. An open-source Linux-based OS is also popular. Microsoft Office 365, a cloud-based suite of programs that includes a word processor, a spreadsheet program, PowerPoint software, and a database system is available on subscription. Free open-source software such as Libre Office and Apache Open Office is also available. Besides these several browsers such as Chrome and Firefox are available as free downloads from the Web. Apple Computers market PCs known as Apple iMac. Macs use Apple's proprietary M2 chip with 10 cores and a 16-core GPU. Apple uses a proprietary OS which is designed for simplicity of use. Apple also provides a suite of application programs.

Servers

Servers are high-end computers used for specific purposes, such as high-performance numerical computing (called compute server), web page hosting, e-mail service, database storing, and printing. Computer servers have high-performance processors such as Intel Xeon 40 cores or AMD EPYC, 128 cores running at 3GHz, with 32 GB to 12 TB main memory, 1 TB to 20 TB hard disk, 256 GB to 2 TB SSD, several USB ports, Ethernet connection to clients, and several high-speed printers. Servers are normally connected to a computer network (Chapter 13) with several desktop PCs that access servers for specialized services.

Thin clients

An alternative to desktop PCs to access servers connected to a computer network is a *thin client*. The emergence of thin clients is motivated by several reasons. They are:

- Desktop PCs rapidly become obsolete.
- They consume too much power.
- Desktop PC needs an OS and software such as MS Office.
- Each PC needs virus protection and a UPS.

A thin client is an intelligent terminal with a low-power processor with a slow clock (500 Mhz), to access servers connected to a network. It has relatively small main memory (2 GB), no disk, and a lightweight OS to provide on its screen the same graphical user interface as a desktop PC.

An icon on its screen may be selected to run the required software centralized in a server. The results are sent back to the thin client. The main advantages of thin clients are:

- They are cheaper than desktop PCs and do not become obsolete.
- System administration is simpler as only servers are to be attended to.
- Software cost is lower as thin clients do not have powerful OS, virus protection and
- application software.

The main disadvantage of thin clients is that they depend on a communication system to access servers. If the communication system fails, or the server fails, they are useless as they do not have any computing power and cannot be used independently.

Mainframe computers

Organizations such as banks and insurance companies process a large number of transactions online. They require computers with large disks to store several terabytes of data and transfer data from disk to main memory at several hundred megabytes/second. The processing power needed from such computers is several hundred million transactions per second. These computers are much bigger and faster than servers and hundreds of times more expensive. These types of computers are called *mainframes*. Mainframes have proprietary OSs that are very reliable and provide extensive services such as user accounting, file security, and control. Two prominent manufacturers of mainframes are IBM and Hitachi. Mainframes are normally used by large organizations such as banks, insurance companies, airlines, and railways. The number of mainframe users has reduced as many organizations are rewriting their systems to use networks of powerful workstations. An example mainframe in 2025 is z 17. It uses an IBM proprietary processor Telum II - 8 core with a 5.5 GHz clock, 64TB main memory with 360 MB on-chip caches, and a 20 TB disk. It uses IBM's z/OS or Linux.

Supercomputers

Supercomputers or High-performance computers are the fastest computers available at any given time and are normally used to solve problems that require intensive numerical computations. Examples of such problems are numerical weather prediction, designing supersonic aircraft, design of drugs, and modelling complex molecules. All these problems require around 10^{20} calculations on 64-bit floating point operands. These problems require about 3 hours on a computer that can carry out several trillion floating point calculations per second with 64-bit operands. Such a computer is classified as a supercomputer today. Today (2025) computers that can carry out 10^{15} floating point operations per second on 64-bit floating point numbers are called supercomputers. Supercomputers are built by interconnecting several high-performance processors and programming them to work cooperatively to solve problems. Recently, applications of supercomputers have expanded beyond scientific computing. They are now used to analyze large commercial databases, produce animated movies, and play games such as chess.

Besides arithmetic speed, a computer to be classified as a supercomputer should have a large main memory of around 100 TB and a secondary memory of 1000 Peta Bytes. The speed of transfer of data from the secondary memory to the main memory should be at least a tenth of the memory to CPU data transfer speed. All supercomputers use parallelism to achieve their speed. In Section 12.9, we discuss the organization of parallel computers. The world's fastest computer, Cray HPE Fronter, was built in 2022. Its speed is 1.102 ExaFLOPS. It has 47 PB main memory, 700 PB disk, consumes 21 megawatts of power, and costs $600 million.

12.8 DISTRIBUTED COMPUTER SYSTEM

A configuration of computers in which a large number of computers are interconnected by a communication network is called a distributed computer system. A common use of distributed computers is in *client-server computing*. In this mode, servers provide several specialized services. For example, there may be a high-performance computer in the network for solving numeric intensive programs, another with high-speed printers, a third with plotters, and a fourth with a 1 PB disk to store big files. A user with a PC, connected to the network of computers may do some local computing, debugging, etc., and may then requisition the services of a computer in the distributed computer system for storing files, providing language translators, and carrying out intensive numeric computing. The PC requisitioning services is called the *client* and the computer providing the services is known as a *server*.

Sometimes there are problems requiring either large storage or high-speed processing which cannot be solved using a single computer in a network. In such a case, it may be possible to get a set of computers connected to the network to cooperate and solve the problem. In distributed computer systems, often many computers are not fully utilized; either they are idle because no one is presently logged on or the user may be doing tasks such as editing or word processing which do not fully use the available computing power. In such a case, a user requiring more CPU resources than what he has in his computer can steal CPU cycles from idle processors to do his job. Software systems have been designed to use idle CPU resources.

The communication network connecting the computers in a distributed system is normally a Local Area Network (discussed in Chapter 13). For applications discussed above, such a communication network is adequate.

12.9 PARALLEL COMPUTERS

A set of computers connected by a high-speed communication network and programmed in such a way that they cooperate to solve *a single large problem* is called a *Parallel Computer.* There are two major types of parallel computers. One of them is called a *shared memory parallel computer.* In this case, several processing elements are connected to a common main memory by a communication network (see Figure 12.2). A program for this computer uses computers to cooperatively to solve a problem. The processes are allocated to different processors and they read and modify data accessible to them in memory. Programming such a computer is relatively easy provided the problem can be broken up into parts that can be solved concurrently. The main problem with this architecture is that it is not scalable beyond about 16 processors as they share a common memory. This memory is accessed via a single communication network which gets saturated when many processors try to read or write from memory. Today (2025) a single microprocessor has several cores or processors sharing memory and is a parallel computer.

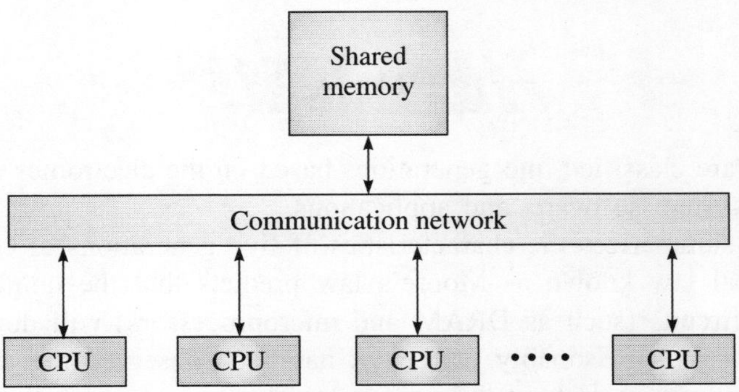

Figure 12.2 A shared memory parallel computer.

The other type of parallel computer is called a *distributed memory computer*. In this type, several processors, each with an independent memory, are interconnected by a communication network. A program is divided into many parts and each computer works independently. Whenever processors need to exchange data to continue with computation, they send messages to one another via the communication network. Such computers are also known as *message-*

passing parallel computers. Distributed memory parallel computers are scalable to over 4000 processors as each computer works reasonably independently and multiple communication paths are there to exchange messages. A popular interconnection network is called a *hypercube* (see Figure 12.3).

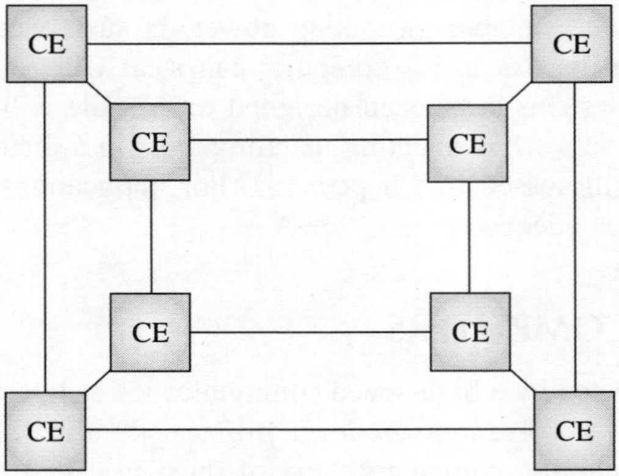

Figure 12.3 A distributed memory parallel computer (CE is a computing element with a CPU and memory).

Another trend in building parallel computers is to use off-the-shelf high-performance PCs and interconnect them using a standard connection such as a high-speed Ethernet. Ethernet speed of 10 Gbps is now available. Using a Linux distributed programming environment, these computers work in parallel to solve compute-intensive tasks. Using these ideas, powerful low-cost distributed memory parallel computers, called Beowulf clusters have been built in many laboratories. Some clusters with a speed of 10 GFLOPS have been built using commodity off-the-shelf processors.

SUMMARY

1. Computers are classified into generations based on the electronics technology used, the associated system software, and applications.
2. Table 12.1 summarizes the characteristics of five generations of computers.
3. An empirical law known as Moore's law predicts that the number of transistors in integrated circuits (such as DRAM and microprocessors) will double almost every 2 years. The law is reasonably correct. It has been observed that the capacity of hard disks also increases at about the same rate. The cost of computers, however, is going down. The implication is that the cost of computers has remained constant while their performance has doubled every 2 years. Thus, computers have been employed in a larger number of very complex applications and are widely used. Software has become very complex as applications have become complex.
4. Computers may be classified based on their mode of use and the way individual computers are interconnected.

5. Based on the nature of use, computers are classified as Mobile Smartphones, Mobile Tablet computers, Laptop computers, Desktop Personal computers, Thin Clients, Servers, Mainframes, or Supercomputers. Smartphones, Tablets, and Laptop computers are portable and can be wirelessly connected to the Internet. Personal computers are low-cost computers used for word processing, small database maintenance, and executing small programs. Servers provide specialized services such as e-mail, database, printing, and numeric intensive computing to a set of desktop PCs connected to them via a network. Thin clients are cheaper alternatives to PCs to access servers. Mainframes are used for massive transaction processing. Supercomputers are primarily used for intensive numerical computation.
6. Based on interconnections, computers are also classified as distributed computers or parallel computers.
7. Distributed computers consist of several servers and PCs interconnected by a communication network. A common mode of use of a distributed computer is in a client-server configuration. In this mode, specialized services such as large disk resources, numeric intensive computing, and printing are provided by servers that are used by clients in the network. Clients would use multiple servers to solve problems.
8. A set of computers connected by a high-speed communication network and programmed in such a way that they cooperate to solve a single large problem is called a parallel computer.
9. There are two types of parallel computers: one is called a shared memory parallel computer and the other distributed memory parallel computer. In a shared memory computer, several CPUs share a common main memory. These machines are easy to program but are not scalable. In distributed memory parallel computers, many independent computers are connected by a high-speed network. A problem is broken up into parts and allocated to the computers in the system. These computers cooperatively solve the problem by computing locally and by exchanging messages among them. Distributed memory parallel computers are also known as message-passing parallel computers. They are scalable up to about 64,000 computers.

REVIEW QUESTIONS

12.1 Who built the first electronic computer and what was it called?

12.2 When was the first electronic computer built?

12.3 Who invented the concept of the stored program?

12.4 Which was the first stored program computer and where was it built?

12.5 Which was the first commercially produced computer?

12.6 What switching device was used in the first generation computers?

12.7 What type of memory was used in the first generation computers?

12.8 What languages were available in the first generation computers?

12.9 What new switching device led to the emergence of second-generation computers?

12.10 What is the main difference in characteristics between the first and the second generation computers?

12.11 What was the main memory technology used in the second generation computers?

12.12 What important developments in software took place during the second generation of computers?

12.13 What was the important peripheral memory device invented in the second generation computers?

12.14 What type of operating system was used with the second generation computers?

12.15 What main technological change ushered in the third generation of computers?

12.16 What are the advantages of integrated circuits compared to transistors?

12.17 What was the main memory technology in the third generation computers?

12.18 What improvements in peripheral memory took place during the third-generation computers?

12.19 What was the most significant development in software in the third-generation computers?

12.20 What technological change ushered in the fourth generation of computers?

12.21 What development in computer architecture took place during the first decade of the fourth generation?

12.22 What significant developments in software took place during the first decade of the fourth generation?

12.23 Answer Question 12.21 for the second phase of the fourth generation.

12.24 Answer Question 12.22 for the second phase of the fourth generation.

12.25 What major new applications were undertaken during the first decade of the fourth generation?

12.26 What technological change ushered in the fifth generation of computers?

12.27 What significant developments in software took place during the fifth generation of computing?

12.28 What is Moore's law?

12.29 What are the implications of Moore's law in the development of computer technology?

12.30 What are the special features of Tablet computers?

12.31 What are the main parameters used to classify computers?

12.32 What is a Laptop computer?

12.33 What is a Personal Computer?

12.34 What hardware facilities are normally available in a Personal Computer?

12.35 What is a Server?

12.36 In what way is a Server different from a Personal Computer?

12.37 What are the important applications of Servers?

12.38 What is a mainframe computer?

12.39 When are mainframes useful?

12.40 What do you understand by the term supercomputers?

12.41 What are the applications of supercomputers?

12.42 What do you understand by a distributed computer?

12.43 What is client-server computing?

12.44 What is a parallel computer?

12.45 How is a parallel computer different from a distributed computer?

12.46 Why do we need parallel computers?

12.47 What are the two types of parallel computers called?

12.48 What are the main differences between them?

12.49 Which type of parallel computer is scalable?

12.50 What is a thin client? Compare it with a desktop PC.

13 Computer Networks

LEARNING GOALS

After reading this chapter, you should be able to:

- Describe what are computer networks and classify them.
- Explain the advantages of networking computers.
- Explain the need for standard protocols or rules for orderly communication between computers connected to a network.
- Explain how computers are connected as a Local Area Network.
- Explain what is the Internet and how it is implemented and used.

Early computers were used as 'stand-alone' systems in organizations. With the widespread use of computers, it was realized that the value and utility of a computer increases if it is connected to other computers. For example, by connecting your home computer to the Internet, you can access a huge amount of information stored on numerous computers worldwide. You can also correspond with all your friends by email. The utility of email increases enormously when all the computers connected to the Internet have this facility. It would also be advantageous to interconnect computers within an organization. Advances in computer technology have made these interconnections possible. Nowadays it is rare to find an isolated computer. All computers have built-in hardware, called a *Network Interface Card* (NIC), to connect them to a communication system. In this chapter, we will describe in detail how computers are connected to form networks and how networks are connected to form Internetworks, also known as the Internet.

13.1 NEED FOR COMPUTER COMMUNICATION NETWORKS

We describe the need for network computers in what follows.

- An employee of an organization who has a Personal Computer (PC) at home would use it for most of his or her work and connect it through communication lines to a powerful computer called a *server* situated in the organization for executing larger programs and accessing special library programs and data resident in it. A variety of servers are maintained by big organizations. One of them would normally be a high-performance computer, another would store large databases, a third would provide specialized printing, and a fourth one may archive data files.
- Another important remote PC application is for information retrieval. Some information sites store large amounts of data on patents, technical reports, journal articles, etc. in an organized fashion and make it available to anyone via the Internet. A user requiring specific information, say on patents in a specified area, can connect his PC through cable, mobile wireless network, or a telephone line to an Internet Service Provider (ISP) and retrieve the required information from the information server using appropriate keywords in a search engine.
- Local Area Networks (LANs) are used to interconnect many computers within an organization to share files, share programs, and decentralize specialized functions. Another reason for creating a LAN is to share the use of expensive peripherals such as fast printers, large disks, graphics workstations, etc. LANs are also useful in a laboratory environment where every sophisticated instrument has a built-in microprocessor. These instruments may be interconnected to a general-purpose computer with powerful I/O and storage devices. The general-purpose computer enables analyzing the outputs of the instruments. Besides this, data gathered and processed by all the instruments may be correlated and analyzed.
- Local area networks are also used in factories for controlling plants and processes. Individual small computers would be normally installed to monitor and control critical processes in the plant. These computers may be interconnected and connected to another computer that performs supervisory functions. Such a network provides an integrated control of the plant.

The communication lines interconnecting the computers in a LAN are short. They are also localized to 'private' areas and do not use a public data network. As distances are small, and fast communication between computers connected to a LAN is desirable, high-speed communication lines that can transmit around ten million to ten billion bits per second (abbreviated bps) are used in LANs.

Wide area computer networks are mainly used to connect several widely dispersed computers. The main objective of such an interconnection is to allow network users to access specialized library programs, databases, languages, and special facilities available on any of the computers in the network. For example, it would not be possible for many organizations to install a supercomputer which may cost 15 million dollars. If a supercomputer is connected to a network, many organizations can access it from their locations. This will enable the organizations to use their local computer for most purposes and utilize the supercomputer only for those problems that require its speed and memory capacity.

There are following two types of wide area networks:

1. *Wide area networks of organizations:* For example, an organization may have branches located in several cities in a country or even in many countries. Each location would

have a LAN. It is essential to exchange information among the branches and to update a central database. In such a case, the LANs are interconnected to form a wide area network. One way of interconnecting LANs is by using private leased communication lines. The advantage of this is the security of the organization's data. This is an expensive solution. However, some organizations such as banks require security. Some other organizations have special requirements and maintain their private networks. Three such networks are as follows:

(i) A wide area network maintained by the Indian Railways for railway reservations. Using this network, passengers can book tickets on most major trains anywhere in India. Indian Airlines also maintains a network for airline reservations.

(ii) World airlines interconnect their network of computers which are used primarily for passenger reservations. Such inter-networking is essential because a passenger may fly by many airlines during international travel and the reservation status of each airline would be required. Thus, the database containing the reservation status of individual airlines must be accessible via the network to all the cooperating airlines. Two international networks of this type are the Amadeus network and the Sabre network.

(iii) International banks cooperate and have a banking network SWIFT to reconcile their accounts and for electronic fund transfers.

2. *Internet*: The Internet is a worldwide network of computer networks that uses a standard communication protocol. The computer networks in organizations and the computers in homes are interconnected in each country using broad-band data networks maintained by several companies. The country networks are interconnected by undersea broadband cables spanning the world. We describe the Internet in great detail later in Section 13.6.

13.2 COMMUNICATION PROTOCOLS

When several computers and terminal equipment are to be connected to form an integrated system, a well-understood standard method of communication and physical interconnection should be established. This becomes particularly critical when computers supplied by different vendors are to be connected since each vendor has its proprietary standard. If computers in several countries are to be connected, yet another problem arises due to the need to use communication systems belonging to different nations that have their own telecommunication regulations. Commonly agreed rules followed to interconnect and communicate between computers are known as *protocols*.

A universally used standard method of connecting user terminals to computers is the Universal Serial Bus (USB) standard described in Section 8.5.

The interconnection protocol for computer-to-computer communication is much more complex. It should define, besides the physical characteristics such as voltage levels and speeds of the physical medium used to interconnect computers, the following:

1. How to begin and terminate a session between two computers.
2. How the messages in a session are to be framed.
3. How errors in the transmission of messages are to be detected.

4. How messages are to be retransmitted when errors are detected.
5. How to find which message block was sent by which computer and to whom.
6. How the dialogue proceeds on the communication line.

An interconnection protocol for computer-to-computer communication as recommended by the International Standards Organization (ISO) is a useful reference standard. It is an approach based on defining several distinct layers, each addressing an aspect of the linking. This is known as the ISO model for *open systems interconnection* (OSI). The OSI model has seven layers as shown in Figure 13.1. Each layer has a specific independent function. The primary objective of defining standards based on layers is to allow independent design and improvement of each layer. As long as the interfaces between layers are clearly defined, the internal functioning of a layer is of no concern to other layers. When two computers are interconnected, then only the communication protocols between corresponding layers need to be specified. These protocols will remain the same even if improvements due to changes in technology take place in the other layers. For example, one may change the physical medium from coaxial cables to optical fibres to increase the speed. This should not affect the network and transport layer protocols. The standardization achieved by each of the layers is explained in what follows:

(i) *Physical layer:* This layer defines the electrical and mechanical aspects of interfacing computers to a physical medium for transmitting data and also how physical links are set up, maintained, and disconnected.

(ii) *Data link layer:* This layer establishes an error-free communications path between computers over the physical channel. It gives the standard for framing messages, checking the integrity of received messages, accessing and using the channels, and sequencing the transmitted data.

(iii) *Network control layer*: This determines the setting up of a logical path, in other words, routes between computers in a network, message addressing to computers, and controlling message flow between computer nodes.

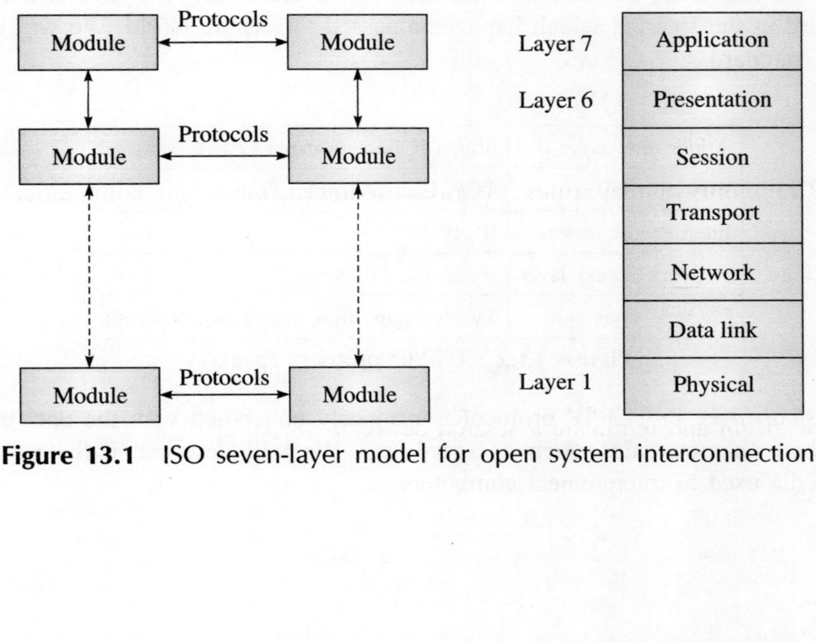

Figure 13.1 ISO seven-layer model for open system interconnection.

(iv) *Transport layer*: Once a path is established between computers, it provides control standards for a communication session so that applications may exchange data reliably and sequentially, independent of which systems communicate with one another, or their location in the network and how the connection is terminated.

(v) *Session control layer*: This establishes and controls system-dependent aspects of communications sessions between specific computers in the network and bridges the gap between the services provided by the transport layer and the logical functions running under the operating system of a particular computer in the network.

(vi) *Presentation layer*: This layer provides facilities to convert encoded transmitted data into forms that may be understood by the application layer. It handles encryption, compression, and syntax conversion.

(vii) *Application/user layer*: This layer provides services that directly support users such as file transfers, email, web browsing, remote file access, and remote login.

We reiterate that the main advantage of the layered approach is that each layer can be improved and modified independently. With changes in communication technology and standards, easy adaptation is important. One standard that defines the bottom three layers of ISO is the CCITT X.25 protocol that has been integrated into the network architecture by many vendors.

The ISO seven-layer OSI standard was originally intended for adoption by manufacturers of computer network subsystems and systems. It did not happen. It has, however, become a good reference model to describe protocols.

The protocol that has been adopted universally is called Transmission Control Protocol/ Internet Protocol (TCP/IP). This evolved from an experimental packet switched network called ARPANET funded by the Advanced Research Projects Agency (USA). This protocol is also a layered architecture consisting of five layers as shown in Figure 13.2 and roughly corresponds to the bottom four layers and the top layer of the OSI standard. The application layer in the TCP/IP protocol subsumes the functions the top two layers of the ISO model. It is now used as the standard in the Internet which has encompassed the whole world. We will now briefly describe this standard.

Application layer	http, ftp, domain name system, smtp
Transport layer	TCP, User Datagram Protocol
Internetwork layer	IP, IPv6
Network access layer	IEEE 802.11, etc.
Physical layer	Twisted pair, fibre optics, wireless, etc.

Figure 13.2 TCP/IP protocol layers.

The *physical layer* in TCP/IP protocol is primarily concerned with the data transmission media and their characteristics, such as speed, etc. We will describe in the next chapter a variety of media used to interconnect computers.

The layer above it is the *network access layer*. This depends upon the type of local network and is concerned with the orderly exchange of data between computers connected to the local area network. The local network may, for example, use a protocol called the Ethernet protocol. In general, the local network may have its own set of rules for communication which need not concern the sending/receiving messages between two different networks. Thus, this is taken as a separate layer.

The next layer called *the Internetwork layer* has a role only if data are to be exchanged between computers connected to different networks. In general, several networks may be connected by a *router*. A router is a special-purpose computer whose primary job is to relay data received from a source network to a destination network.

The protocol used by this layer is called the Internet Protocol (IP). The Internet Protocol routes data across multiple networks. This protocol is implemented in all the computers that are to be connected to the Internet and also in all the routers.

The layer above this is called the *transport layer*. Its primary function is to ensure that data is received reliably by the receiver from the sender. The Transmission Control Protocol (TCP) is the standard currently used for this. TCP ensures that all data sent by the sender application are received by the intended receiver in the right order. This protocol is independent of the specific application.

The topmost layer is the *application layer*. It contains the logic to support various user applications such as web browsing, mail transfer, file transfer, remote login, etc. The session layer of OSI is subsumed in the application layer.

Later in the chapter, we will describe in detail the top four layers of the TCP/IP protocol and how the various functionalities such as encryption, authentication and compression of the OSI model are accommodated.

13.3 LOCAL AREA NETWORKS

When computers located within a small geographical area such as an office or a university campus (within a radius of 10 km) are interconnected, we call it a Local Area Network (LAN).

Four important aspects characterize different types of LANs. They are as follows:

1. Topology of the networks; that is how the individual computers are interconnected.
2. The type of transmission medium used to interconnect the individual computers.
3. The protocol used to access the physical medium by a computer connected to a LAN. This is called *Media Access Control* (*MAC*). This corresponds to the Data Link layer of the OSI model and the Network Access layer of the TCP/IP protocol model.
4. How smaller LANs called subnetworks are interconnected to form a network encompassing the whole organization which may have thousands of computers.

Two topologies are available to form LANs. They are a *bus* (see Figure 13.3) and a *switched interconnection* (Figure 13.5). Historically the bus topology was the first one to be used. It is now obsolete and has been superseded by the switched interconnection. We briefly describe the bus connection for historical reasons.

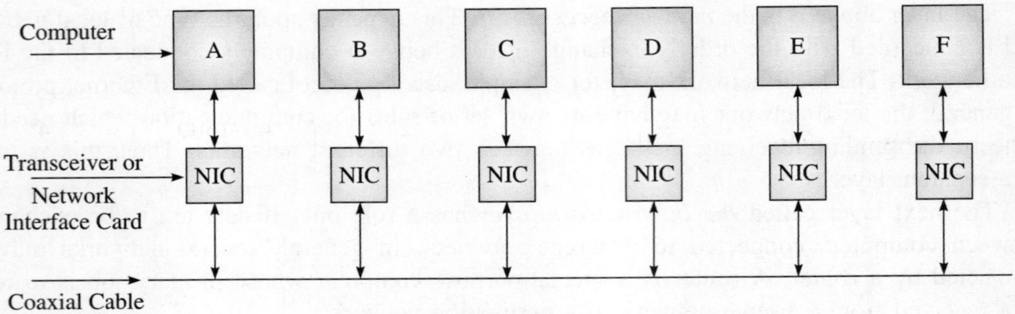

Figure 13.3 An Ethernet LAN.

13.3.1 Ethernet Local Area Network—Bus Topology

Ethernet LAN was invented by Robert Metcalfe and David Boggs while they were working at Xerox PARC in 1975. They connected several desktop computers named Alto to a cable as shown in Figure 13.3 and designed the *Ethernet protocol* for communication between the computers within a small geographical area. This was later refined and standardized as IEEE standard 802. The original standard was for interconnection of computers using a *bus*. The physical layer was specified as a shielded coaxial cable supporting a data rate of 10 Mbps. Ethernet has advanced much beyond the earlier standard.

The data link layer defines controlling access to the network (called media access control or MAC for short) and how data packets are transmitted between computers connected to the network. Every NIC attached to a computer has a unique address called its MAC address assigned by the manufacturer to enable it to communicate with NICs attached to other computers. The MAC address is a 48-bit address. Referring to Figure 13.3, we observe that all computers are connected to the bus and each computer communicates with the bus via a full duplex (i.e., it can send and receive data at the same time) NIC which is a combined transmitter and receiver. Each computer delegates the task of sending/receiving data as a set of unmodulated bits to NIC. Modulation is not necessary as the maximum length of the cable is small. Transmission of bits on the cable without modulation is known as *base-band transmission*. Data exchange between NICs proceeded using a protocol called *Carrier Sense Multiple Access* with *Collision Detection* (CSMA/CD). It is called Multiple Access as any of the NICs can try to send data on the bus or receive data from the bus. Multiple access would lead to the collision of data sent to the cable by two computers and collision has to be detected and appropriate action taken by the protocol. It is an ingenious protocol but no more relevant and we will not describe it.

In the Ethernet literature, a data packet is called an *Ethernet frame*. It consists of 7 bytes for clock synchronization, followed by 1 byte start of frame indicator. This is followed by the MAC address of the destination NIC, the MAC address of the source NIC, the data to be transmitted, and check bits (Figure 13.4). An Ethernet frame sent by a NIC is monitored while it is in transit by all other NICs on the bus and the NIC to which it is addressed receives the frame and stores it. Other NICs ignore it. It is possible to *broadcast* a frame to all NICs. A frame can also be *multicast*. In this case, the frame is sent to a subset of NICs.

Preamble	SOF	Destination address	Source address	Frame type	Data packet	Check bits
7 bytes	1 byte	6 bytes	6 bytes	2 bytes	46–1500 bytes	4 bytes

Figure 13.4 The format of an Ethernet frame.

The length of the data packet is between 46 and 1500 bytes. It depends on the bus length and the number of NICs connected to the bus. Ethernet using a bus was the most popular Local Area Network for several decades. The bus structure has limitations as adding and removing computers to a bus is not easy. A bus, however, is inexpensive. As the number of computers connected to the bus increases, the collision probability increases which can slow down the network.

13.3.2 Switched Ethernet LAN

During the last decade integrated circuit technology has grown rapidly and their cost has decreased. A special-purpose computer called a switch is used nowadays to interconnect computers in a LAN. This is called a switched LAN. The bus-based Ethernet LAN has become obsolete and replaced by a switched *Ethernet* LAN.

A switched Ethernet LAN logically follows the same principle for media access as a bus-based Ethernet. The topology is shown in Figure 13.5. The physical transmission medium is an unshielded twisted pair of copper wires normally used in telephone networks.

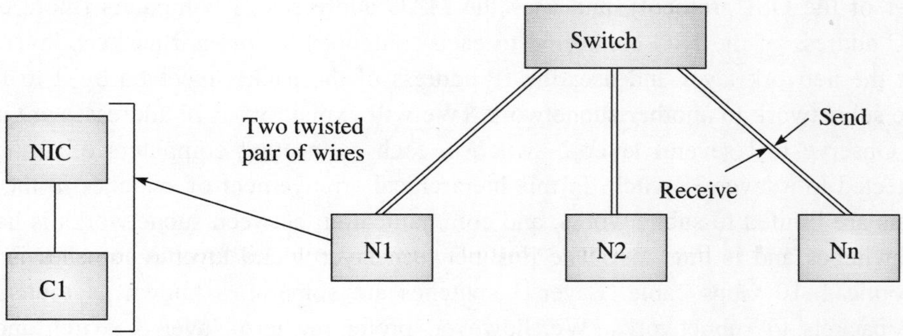

Figure 13.5 Ethernet using an unshielded twisted pair of wires and a switch.

In this topology, each computer (remember that each computer has built-in NIC) is connected to a switch using a twisted pair of wires (see Figure 13.5). The switch is a small special-purpose computer that receives an Ethernet frame, inspects the MAC address of the destination computer, and sends it to that computer via the port to which it is connected.

For example, if computer N1 sends a frame addressed to computer N4 to the switch, the switch will send the frame directly to N4. If at the same time, another computer N2 sends a frame addressed to computer N5 to the switch, it will also be sent directly to N5 by the switch. Thus, multiple frames can be simultaneously sent by the switch. The switch has sufficient storage to store the frames and forward them to the destination addresses. It acts as a post office. The number of computers that can be connected to a switch depends on its capacity, namely, its memory size, addressing capability, and speed. Inexpensive switches can normally handle up to 32 computers. The number of computers that can be connected to a switch is, however, limited by a problem that occurs when one of the computers broadcasts a frame to all the other computers. The frame has to be sent simultaneously to all the computers connected to the switch and this causes a jam. If several broadcasts take place in succession, the entire network will suffer. In switched Ethernet CSMA/CD protocol is not used as the switch examines the MAC address of each frame and sends it to an appropriate destination. However, the frame format is identical to the CSMA/CD-based Ethernet standard.

13.3.3 Tree Network for Large LANs

If an organization has several hundred PCs and other devices such as printers (all of which have built-in NICs) to be connected to a LAN, the system is arranged as several subnetworks, each with around 32 computers. They are all formed as a tree network as shown in Figure 13.6. At the lowest level of the tree (Layer 1) there are several switched LANs. These subnetworks are connected by what are known as *layer 2 switches* (see Figure 13.6) at the next level of the tree. The subnetworks in layer 2 are connected to a group of layer 3 switches as shown in Figure 13.6. Whereas a layer 2 switch works in the MAC layer (i.e., the data link layer of the OSI protocol), and uses the MAC addresses of computers (more accurately the MAC address of the NIC connected to each computer) to forward packets, layer 3 switch works at the network layer and uses the IP address of the packet received by it to forward it from one subnetwork to another subnetwork. (We will explain what IP addresses are in Section 13.5.1.) Observe that several layer 2 switches, each connecting computers of a subnetwork, are connected to a layer 3 switch. In this hierarchical arrangement of switches in the network, broadcasts are limited to subnetworks, and communication between subnetworks is handled by layer 2 switches and is thus fast. The link between layer 2 and layer 3 switches is normally a fibre optic 1–10 Gbps cable. Layer 3 switches are sometimes known as routers as they route IP packets to subnetworks. We, however, prefer the term layer 3 switch and use the term *router* for devices that route messages between WANs of multiple organizations spread all across the world, finding the best path for the message to travel. We will describe routers later in this chapter.

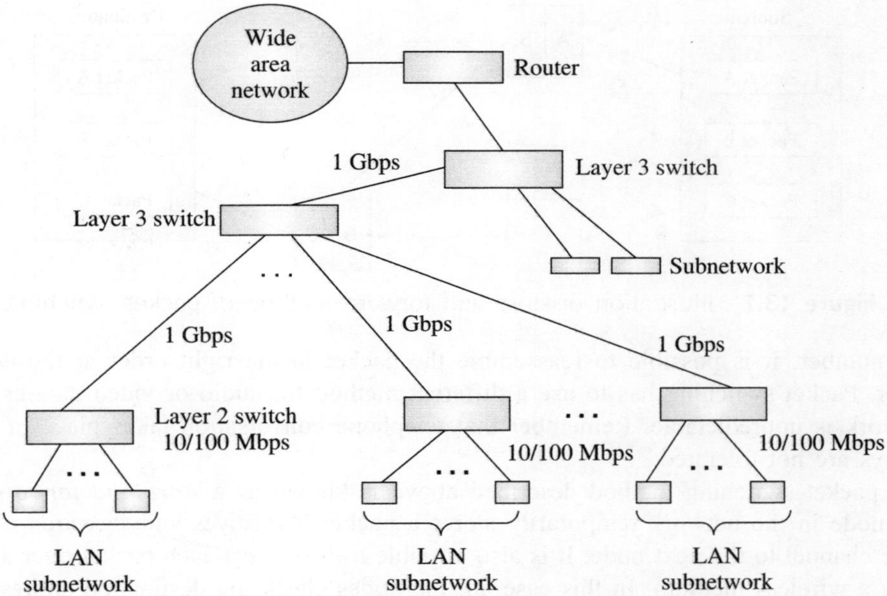

Figure 13.6 Typical configuration of a large LAN in a big organization.

13.4 USING PUBLIC DATA NETWORK TO CONNECT COMPUTERS

When computers are connected to a Public Data Network (PDN) maintained by several companies, such as BSNL, Airtel, or Jio in India, a method called *packet switching* is used. Data networks are normally a network of cables spanning a geographical area with segments interconnected by special-purpose computers called routers. In packet switching a block of data to be communicated from one computer to another is formatted by the computer as a group of packets called *IP packets*. An IP packet contains, besides the block of data to be sent (of the order of 1500 bytes), bits for synchronization, control information, message number, number of the current and last packet, destination and source addresses (called IP addresses which are different from MAC addresses), acknowledgement, and error checking bytes. In what follows we will use the term packet and IP packet synonymously. The packet is sent on the transmission line and when it reaches a *router* in the network, the destination address of the packet is examined and it is routed to the next router based on an available free communication channel. The actual path taken by the packet to its destination is dynamic as the path is established while it travels. When a packet reaches a router, the communication channel on which it came is released for use by another packet. As communication channels are used only when packets are transmitted, this method uses the channels very efficiently. This method is suitable for computer-to-computer data communication which occurs in bursts. Figure 13.7 illustrates a packet switching system. In this figure, the data to be sent from the source to the destination is broken up into three packets A, B, C. Observe that each packet takes a different route but all of them combine at the destination. As each packet has a destination address and

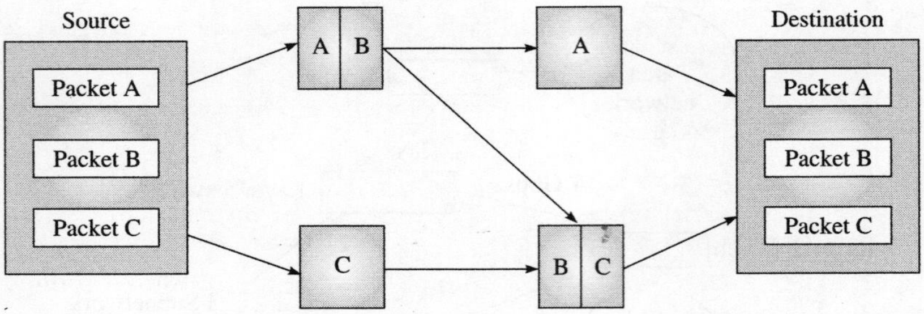

Figure 13.7 Illustration of store and forward method of packet switching.

a serial number, it is possible to reassemble the packet in the right order at the destination computer. Packet switching has to use a different method for audio or video data as delay on the network is unpredictable. Remember that telephone conversation takes place in real time and delays are not tolerated.

The packet switching method described above is known as a *store and forward* method as each node in the network temporarily stores a packet it receives and forwards it using an available channel to the next node. It is also possible to *broadcast* each packet over a medium, normally a wireless medium. In this case, all the nodes check the destination address of each packet as they pass by and accept only those addressed to them (see Figure 13.8). This approach eliminates routing delays inherent in store and forward systems. In this scheme, however, all nodes must be connected to the channel. As all computers share a medium, there could be a collision if two computers broadcast messages at the same time. In wireless broadcast medium, a protocol called CSMA/CA (Carrier Sense Multiple Access with Collision Avoidance) is used. In this protocol, a computer connected to the medium listens to the medium and checks whether any message is being transmitted on the medium. If the computer detects any message and the message is not addressed to it, it waits for a random period and sends a message when the medium is free. Else it continues to wait for another random period before it broadcasts the message. Normally after the first waiting period, it would get a chance to transmit the message. By experimentation it has been found that this protocol works and all computers get a fair chance to use the broadcast channel. This protocol is used in Wi-Fi.

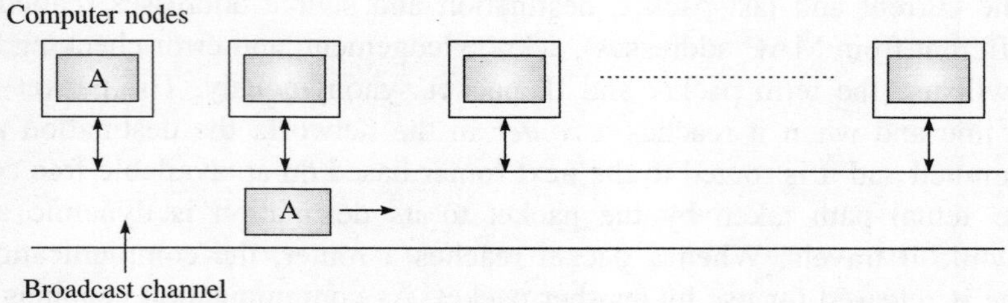

Figure 13.8 Packet switching with packet broadcast.

Message switching is a variation of packet switching. In this case, all message packets are received and stored by a central message router connected to all the computers. This central message router then routes messages to their addresses. This method is used when message delays are not critical. Figure 13.9 illustrates message switching.

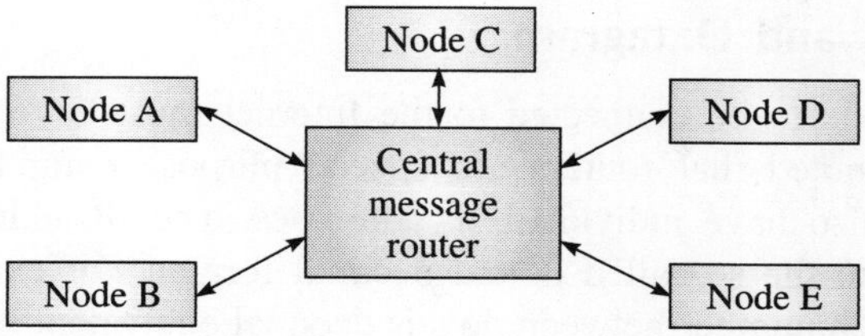

Figure 13.9 Message switching with a central message router.

Historically when the Internet was first introduced Public Switched Telephone Networks (PSTN) were in wide use. They are now replaced by data networks and cellular mobile systems.

13.5 INTERCONNECTING NETWORKS

We examined Local Area Networks in Section 13.3. LANs connect machines in a small geographical area (around a 10 km radius) and can operate up to a speed of 10 Gbps (gigabits per second).

Networks which connect machines in larger geographic areas are known as Metropolitan Area Networks (MANs) and Wide Area Networks (WANs). MANs operate over an area of around 100 km radius at a speed up to 156 Mbps depending on the technology used such as Internet or leased lines. Wide Area Networks, also known as *long haul networks*, operate over the entire world with speeds up to 156 Mbps. The speed figures are indicative of the order of magnitude and should not be taken literally as speeds continue to increase with improvements in technology.

To build a large network, smaller networks are interconnected. We already saw in Section 13.3 how small networks connected using layer 2 switches can be interconnected using layer 3 switches (Section 13.3.3) to form large networks which have hundreds of computers, normally belonging to one organization. If networks belonging to several organizations which are widely dispersed have to be interconnected creating an Internetwork, they are connected using Data Networks which incorporate *routers* described in the previous section. Routers steer traffic through multiple networks and ensure that the least congested route is taken. Traffic within a LAN is not disturbed by a router. Unlike layer 2 switches, routers are known to the destination computers so that they can send messages to routers to find out about frames sent by the source computers. Routers have features for error correction and congestion control.

When larger networks are built interconnecting smaller networks, one should have as the main goal *interoperability*. By interoperability we mean the ability of software and hardware of multiple machines from multiple vendors to communicate and operate together meaningfully. This is achieved to a great extent by a worldwide computer network known as the *Internet*. The Internet is a collection of interconnected packet switched networks using a protocol called Transmission Control Protocol/Internet Protocol.

When this protocol is used, the technology used by individual networks is irrelevant. The individual networks may be broadcast Ethernet, switched Ethernet, or any other technology. It is, however, essential for all these networks to use TCP/IP protocol for communicating with one another. In the subsequent sections, we will describe the TCP/IP protocol in greater detail.

13.5.1 IP Address and Datagram

Every computer which is to be connected to the Internet must have an address called its IP address. It should be noted that routers are special purpose computers which interconnect networks. They must also have individual IP addresses. The IP address is currently 4 bytes long and is expressed in the so-called dotted decimal format. For example, an IP address is: 134.16.79.48, where each number between dots is decimal equivalent of a byte. The assignment of IP addresses follows a systematic process to ease routing of messages between networks. Each *Internet Service Provider* (ISP) who manages a group of users is assigned a set of IP addresses by an international agency. ISPs, in turn, assign a subset of addresses to each organization from this set. Data to be transmitted can be of various sizes, ranging from a few hundred bytes to large files. Each computer must have software called TCP software which splits up the data to be sent into a set of what are known as *datagram* (each about 1000 bytes).

13.5.2 Operation of TCP/IP

We will explain the operation of TCP/IP protocol using Figure 13.10 showing the four layers of the Internet protocol. Assume that an application C running in computer X wants to send a data to an application B running in computer Y. The application C running in X hands over the data to the transport layer TCP with instructions to deliver it to the application B in Y. Each application has a unique identity known to TCP of both X and Y. TCP examines the data and if it is very long, it is broken into smaller segments called a datagram. Each datagram should

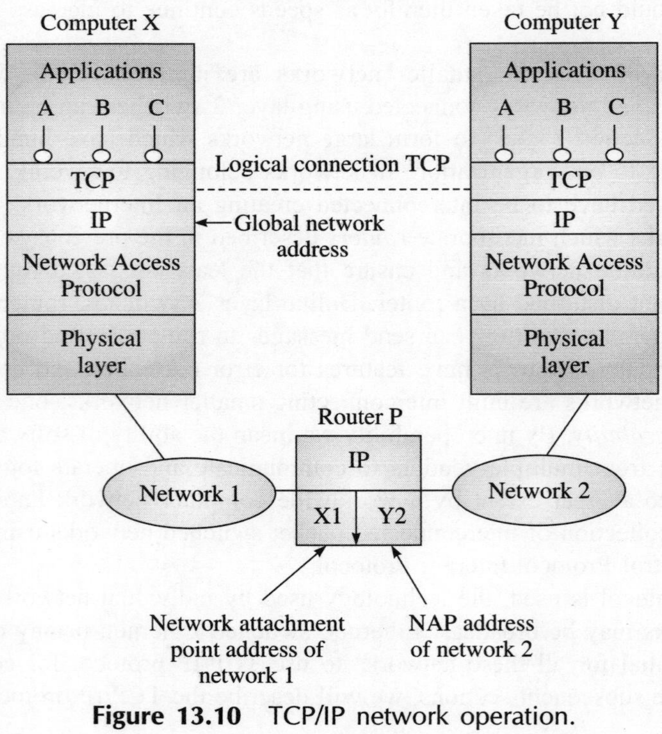

Figure 13.10 TCP/IP network operation.

not be more that 1 KB. To each datagram, TCP appends control information known as a *TCP header*. This control information is needed by computer Y which will receive the datagram and interpret it. This information includes the following:

(i) The application B to which the data is intended. It is called the destination port.
(ii) Serial number of the datagram. This will enable the recipient to put the datagram in correct order if it is received out of order.
(iii) Check sum of data in each datagram to find if any error occurred during transmission.

TCP hands over these data segments to the Internetwork layer, namely, the IP layer of X, instructing it to hand them over to computer Y. IP need not know to which application in Y the data segments are to be handed over. IP now hands over the data segments to the network access layer along with control information called an *IP header*. The IP header contains the following data (see Figure 13.11):

(i) Control bits which include the length of data, error check bits, etc.
(ii) Serial number of the datagram
(iii) Source address (i.e., the IP address of X)
(iv) Destination address (i.e., the IP address of Y)

The IP header is appended to the data segments handed over by the TCP layer. The resulting data packet is called *IP packet.* (see Figure 13.11).

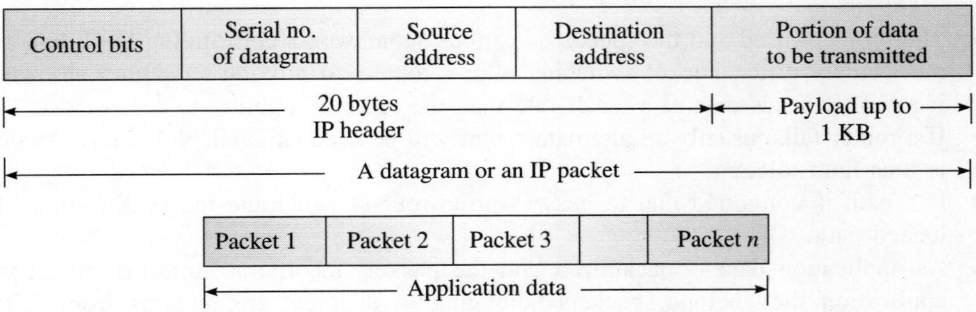

Figure 13.11 Application data broken into IP packets.

The network access layer appends its own header (called the MAC address) which is needed to transport the IP packet to the destination network to which computer Y is attached. This header includes information such as the priority of the packet and destination network address.

The network access layer hands over the packet to the physical layer which by examining the destination address finds that it is to be sent to another network. The packet is thus sent to Router P which is connected to destination network (see Figure 13.10). The router removes the MAC address and examines the address in the IP header. This header has the destination address. Using this address, the router determines to which subnetwork the packet should be forwarded. While forwarding the packet, the router appends the network access point address of network 2 so that the packet reaches the network to which the computer Y is attached.

When the packet reaches computer Y, the reverse process occurs. The received packet is moved up from the bottom to the top layer. As it moves up the layers, each layer strips the header corresponding to that layer. Finally, the data sent by application C running in X reaches the intended recipient, namely, application B in computer Y.

In the above explanation, we have shown only one router connecting the two networks. In practice there will be many intermediate routers connecting a source network to a destination network as shown in Figure 13.7. As explained earlier, a long message sent from a source to a destination is broken into a number of packets and each packet may take a different route to reach the destination. In order to route packets, routers build and maintain routing tables and discover the best route for a packet to travel from the source to the destination. Routing tables have IP addresses of other routers connected to it to enable routing. Routers are special purpose computers which perform many functions besides routing. They detect errors in packets, translate IP to MAC address and prioritize packets among other functions. A detailed discussion on routers is outside the scope of this book and interested readers should read a textbook on computer networks given in the references at the end of the book.

13.5.3 Packet Switching with TCP/IP

We saw in the last section how data to be sent by an application C in computer X reaches an application B in computer Y. We saw that TCP breaks up a large file into a number of smaller packets. Each packet is handled by the IP layer as though it is an independent unit. Thus, each packet can travel along different paths to reach the destination. The reasons why packet switching is used are as follows:

- The protocol used and the speeds of various subnetworks constituting the Internetwork may widely differ. Packet switching allows routers to provide temporary storage area if a sender sends data at a faster rate than the receiver's ability to receive data.
- If a router fails, usually an alternate router will be used (if available). Packet switching is thus fault tolerant.
- If a path is congested due to heavy traffic, routers will route the traffic via a lightly loaded path.
- As application data is packetized and the packets incorporate information on which application they belong, packets belonging to different applications from different computers can be sent along the same path. Paths can thus be fully utilized.

The Internet Protocol is said to be 'connectionless best effort' delivery protocol. It is called connectionless as no specific path is reserved for the entire duration of transfer of data of an application. Different packets may take different routes to reach the destination. It is called 'best effort' as IP does not guarantee delivery of all packets. Some packets may be lost due to insufficient storage in the memory of routers. As the protocol is connectionless, packets need not be delivered in the same order as they are sent. Applications, however, demand delivery of *all* packets and in the *correct* sequence. This requirement is ensured by the TCP protocol. TCP protocol has to be implemented in all computers connected to the Internet. TCP ensures that lost packets are retransmitted and all the packets are delivered to the application in the correct sequence. The TCP software ensures this in the following ways:

(i) *Lost packet recovery*: When a packet is received by the intended receiver, it is expected to send an acknowledgement to the sender. If the sender does not receive an acknowledgement within an estimated time *T*, it is assumed by the sender that the packet has been lost and the sender sends a duplicate packet. Meanwhile if the receiver gets the original packet sent by the sender, the receiver discards the duplicate using the serial number of the packet to identify the packet.

(ii) *Reordering packets*: Packets sent by the sender may not be received by the receiver in the serial order in which they were sent. This is due to the fact that the packets may take different paths to reach the destination. It is the job of the TCP software at the receiver's computer to reorder the received packets according to their serial numbers and to deliver the data in the correct serial order to the application.

Adaptive flow control

We stated (in the paragraph on lost packet recovery) above that a receiver waits for an estimated time *T* before sending an acknowledgement to the sender as the packet travel time in the network is variable. It is not a good idea to fix *T* permanently. If there is too much traffic in the network, the delay in packet receipt may be high and if it is light, it will be low. It will also vary. Thus, *T* should be adaptively changed to account for traffic condition. Too small a value of *T* will cause the receiver to send a retransmission request to the sender in a slow network, leading to unnecessary retransmission and worsening the congestion. Thus, TCP calculates an average time of receiving a packet periodically and adaptively adjusts *T* to a value which will prevent unnecessary retransmission of packets.

Thus, TCP and IP protocols together cooperate to deliver data reliably from a sender to a receiver using the Internet.

13.5.4 Internet and Intranet

We saw that any computer in the world can be connected to any other computer using a public switched telephone network. When a computer uses the TCP/IP protocol and has an IP address assigned by an ISP, it is said to belong to the Internet, an international network of computers. There are many problems with the Internet. One of them is lack of security. Vandals known as 'hackers' are known to have logged on to computers breaching password security (by exploiting weaknesses in the operating system of certain computers) and stolen or erased files. The other is slowing down of the entire network due to very heavy traffic as the number of computers connected to the Internet is increasing very rapidly. The strength of the Internet is its protocol which has proven to be robust. Many other services available on the Internet such as email, file transfer, remote log-in, and World Wide Web are found to be very useful. Many organizations thus felt that all the computers in their organization can be connected by a private network using the same protocol as used by the Internet, namely, TCP/IP. In many large organizations, this will be a wide area network. Such a network is called an *intranet*. Observe that intranet is private to the organization.

13.6 INTERNET SECURITY

The Internet uses a public data network which is accessible to a large number of persons. Thus, it is not difficult for determined vandals (often called hackers) to obtain unauthorized access to computers connected to the Internet. To prevent unauthorized access to an organization's intranet by any user of the Internet, a barrier called a *firewall* is erected between the router leading to the Intranet from the Internet. (see Figure 13.12). The primary purpose of a firewall is to examine each packet arriving from the Internet addressed to a computer in the Intranet and decide whether to pass it on. Packets originating from unknown sources, if suspicious, are blocked. Firewall software can be implemented in the router leading to the network (see Figure 13.12) or in a dedicated security server. There are the following three major types of firewalls:

1. *Packet filter firewalls* which block suspicious incoming packets from unknown IP addresses. They also disallow access to undesirable IP addresses from a computer connected to the intranet. Normally access to most computers in the intranet of an organization except perhaps its web server will be prevented by firewall software.
2. *Application firewalls* filter viruses, unwanted email and application programs (called applets) which are not authorized. As this firewall software does an extensive checking, it would adversely affect the speed of communications via the Internet.
3. *Proxy firewalls* prevent outsiders from seeing the IP addresses of computers in the intranet. Only the IP address of the firewall (also called proxy server) is visible to outsiders. All incoming traffic will be only to the proxy server. It will then forward the transaction to the intended recipient in the organization's intranet. A member of an organization's Intranet can access the Internet via a proxy server. The proxy server will remove the IP address of the source and substitute its own before sending the packet out. Thus, proxy, as the name implies, will act on behalf of all computers connected to the organization's intranet.

All firewall software systems implement a large number of decision rules which are needed to accept or reject incoming/outgoing packets.

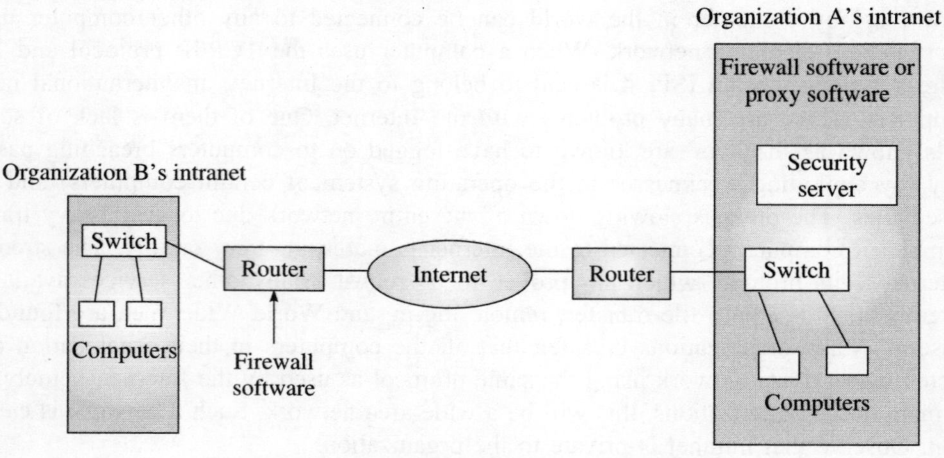

Figure 13.12 Use of firewalls in Internet.

13.6.1 Extranets and Virtual Private Networks

We saw in Section 13.5.4 that an organizational intranet is private to an organization to ensure security and uses TCP/IP protocol for communication. The organizational network is a private network. If an organization is spread out with divisions and branches in many cities in a country or even in many countries, there are two alternatives to build the intranet. One is to lease communication lines for the exclusive use of the organization and its constituents and build a world-wide Intranet. This is the most secure method of communication but is expensive as leasing lines for the exclusive use of one organization is costly. The other alternative is to use the Internet. We saw that Internet is not secure. As a first line of defence, each of the networks which are geographically far apart should have a firewall to prevent unauthorized access. This is not sufficient as a determined spy can monitor communications between branches and download confidential data. Stronger security is thus needed when the Internet is used. A reasonably secure method that uses the Internet is called a Virtual Private Network (VPN). VPN is a secure network operated on a public network infrastructure (normally the Internet). Security of transactions on the Internet may be ensured by using a protocol called the Internet Protocol Security Architecture (IPSEC). This protocol adds an additional security layer to the TCP/IP protocol. This layer is created by encapsulating an original IP packet in a new IP packet. This encapsulation is performed in IPSEC compliant routers at the boundary of networks in different locations or by IPSEC compliant servers. The encapsulation process encrypts the data within the IP packet as well as the IP address using a secret key and attaches another unencrypted IP header to the encrypted packet (see Figure 13.13). This is called IP *encapsulation*. This secure packet can be decoded only by IPSEC compliant routers or servers. Messages sent using IPSEC protocol on the Internet between two IPSEC compliant routers/servers is known as *tunneling*. When the Internet uses tunneling, it is called a virtual private network (see Figure 13.14).

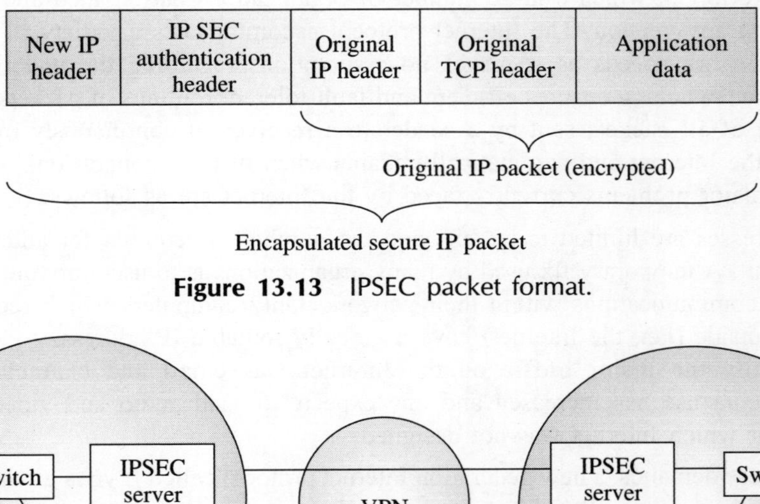

Figure 13.13 IPSEC packet format.

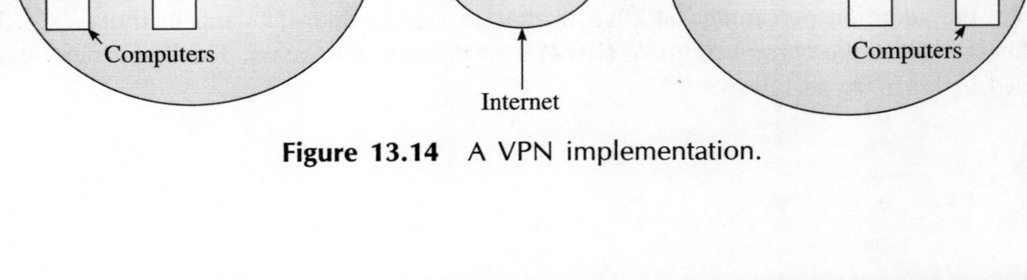

Figure 13.14 A VPN implementation.

An intranet is within an organization. Most organizations cannot work in isolation. They have to cooperate with their business partners. For example, a manufacturer has to closely work with suppliers and distributors. Sometimes it may even be useful to allow a supplier to look at the production schedule and database of parts of a manufacturer to enable it to supply parts just in time without the manufacturer building up a large inventory. When intranets of a group of cooperating organizations are interconnected using TCP/IP protocol, it is called an *Extranet*. Owing to security reasons, the intranets of cooperating organizations are interconnected using VPNs.

13.7 THE FUTURE OF INTERNET TECHNOLOGY

From humble beginning in the late 1960s, today the Internet spans the whole world with more than 18 billion devices (including mobile phones, household appliances etc.) connected to it and it is increasing every month. The remarkable achievement of the Internet technology is that it has been able to accommodate exponential growth (i.e., doubling each year) of the number of computers connected to it. Also, the speed of computers has been doubling every 18 months, and there are a variety of computers connected to the Internet. Individual LANs in an organization may use one of a variety of interconnections and local protocols for communication. The physical connection between computers may range from fast gigabit fibre optics to slower wireless. In spite of this variety of technologies and speeds, the Internet still works effectively. The reason for this is the universal adoption of TCP/IP as the standard protocol which has proved very robust in spite of rapid changes in technology. TCP/IP protocol emerged as a result of cooperative effort in which a large number of organizations participated and experimented before accepting any version. The Internet protocol accommodates a variety of hardware and a variety of network speeds as it makes no assumptions regarding the underlying network hardware. Packet switching ensures efficient and fault-tolerant routings of packets. TCP ensures reliable receipt of all packets sent by a sender to a receiver. It continuously monitors traffic conditions on the Internet and automatically adapts when there is congestion.

The only major problems currently faced by the Internet are as follows:

1. IP addresses are limited to 32 bits and the number of requests for addresses exceeds this limit. A temporary fix used by many organizations is to use a private address space for all communications within their network. Only computers which require visibility from outside (i.e., the Internet) have a globally routable IP address.
2. Originally the major traffic on the Internet was email and character files. Now multimedia use has increased and one expects to send audio and video files in real time for which Internet was not designed.

To meet these demands, a new generation Internet protocol called IPv6 is gradually replacing IPv4, the current protocol. IPv6 has now been adopted as a standard but implementation is slow as many existing hardware has to be upgraded and systems have to be redesigned. For example, the adoption percentage of IPv6 in the USA is around 45% and in India 78%. IPv6 will slowly replace the current protocol (IPv4) over the next few years. The major new features proposed in IPv6 are as follows:

1. 128-bit addresses for source and destination in place of 32 bits the current address size. This address size will allow a huge increase in the number of devices which can be connected to the Internet.
2. The packet length can go up to 64 KB. This will allow easy transfer of multimedia data, particularly voice.
3. The protocol has a feature to specify the kind of data being transmitted and will permit real-time multimedia data to be given priority in transmission.
4. The proposed protocol incorporates IPSEC as part of its specification for all data sent over the Internet.

Thus, it is clear that Internet has come to stay and will continue to grow in the coming years. With increasing use of wireless and mobile systems, even ordinary household systems such as refrigerators, and home air conditioning systems are being connected to the Internet and controlled remotely.

SUMMARY

1. Access to a computer may be provided from a remote location by connecting a terminal to the computer via a telecommunication line.
2. A Local Area Network (LAN) is an interconnection of computers and terminals located near one another (within a 10 km radius) via a fast communication link.
3. Computers in a LAN are used to share data files, computing resources, and peripherals.
4. An interconnection of widely dispersed computers via a public telecommunication system is known as a wide area computer network.
5. Computer networks located in different organizations, cities, or countries may be interconnected. This is called Internetworking.
6. Internetworking is useful if we can ensure interoperability, that is, allow diverse hardware and software of different computers to work cooperatively.
7. A computer network allows users to share library programs, databases, language compilers, and special facilities such as an expensive supercomputer.
8. Common agreed rules followed to interconnect and communicate between computers in a network are known as protocols.
9. A protocol defines how a session between two computers is begun and terminated, how messages are framed, how errors are detected and communicated, identifies source and destination computers, and how communication between computers proceeds.
10. The International Standards Organization has suggested a protocol. This is a layered approach in which each layer addresses one aspect of the communication problem. This approach allows each layer to be independently developed and improved. This protocol has seven layers.
11. A protocol which has five layers in contrast to ISO's seven-layer protocol is called TCP/ IP protocol. This has become the de facto standard for interconnecting computer networks worldwide.
12. Ethernet is a very popular LAN. Early Ethernets used a multidrop coaxial cable or unshielded twisted pair of wires to interconnect computers and communicate at

10 Mbps. It used a protocol called CSMA/CD (Carrier Sense Multiple Access with Collision Detection) to communicate between computers. The data packet defined by the Ethernet protocol is called an Ethernet frame and is shown in Figure 13.4.

13. With the reduction in cost of integrated circuits, cable-connected Ethernets are now obsolete. Computers are interconnected by a special-purpose computer called a switch. A switch forwards data from one computer to another using their MAC addresses. It does not use the CSMA/CD protocol. It uses the data packet format defined by the Ethernet protocol.
14. Switches will permit simultaneous message transfer between independent pairs of computers connected to it.
15. Large LANs with hundreds of computers are designed as a tree network. Switched Ethernets are connected by layer 2 switches. Layer 3 switches are used to connect subnetworks of a large LAN and route messages between subnetworks using the IP address of computers connected to subnetworks.
16. Computers in a wide geographical area are connected by a high bandwidth data network maintained by telecommunication service providers. Data is exchanged by these computers using packet switching. In packet switching, blocks of messages to be transmitted between computers are broken into packets each with a source and a destination address, error detection bits, and control bits. A computer wishing to send data to another computer places the packet on the communication channel. Packets are routed through the network using the address information. It is economical to use packet switching because most computer-to-computer communications are usually in bursts.
17. In message switching, packets to be sent from one computer to another are sent to a central computer. The central computer stores and forwards the messages to the appropriate destination addresses.
18. A Wide Area Network interconnects multiple networks belonging to organizations which may be spread all over a country. They are interconnected using public data networks rented by telecommunication companies such as Bharat Sanchar Nigam Ltd. (BSNL), Airtel, Jio, etc.
19. Each organizational network is connected to a public data network using Routers. Routers are special-purpose communication computers which act as a post office receiving and sending data to various computers connected to the WAN.
20. Besides a router, each organizational network has a computer called a firewall computer which protects the organization's network from intrusion by unauthorized persons.
21. Internet is a worldwide network whose constituents are millions of smaller networks. In other words, it is a network of networks.
22. Individual networks connected to the Internet need not be identical. Each network may use its own internal set of rules to communicate and work at any speed.
23. All computers connected to the Internet and wanting to use it for sending/receiving data must follow a common set of rules for communication called a protocol. The protocol used by the Internet is called TCP/IP (Transmission Control Protocol/Internet Protocol).
24. Internet Protocol requires a unique address called IP address to be assigned to each device such as PCs and routers on the Internet.

25. IP address is 32 bits long (4 bytes). It is expressed in a dotted decimal form such as 134.16.79.50, where each number separated by a dot is the decimal equivalent of a byte.
26. IP addresses are assigned by Internet Service Providers (called ISPs) who facilitate connecting individuals and organizations to the Internet.
27. Files of data to be transmitted via the Internet are broken into packets, with 1K bytes of data in each packet. Each packet has a serial number, IP address of the sender and the receiver, and error control bits.
28. Packets are dispatched by a sender to a receiver. Each packet travels independently from a source to a specified destination.
29. This method of transmitting/receiving data between sender/receiver connected to the Internet is known as packet switching.
30. Packet switching improves utilization of communication networks and also provides fault tolerance.
31. In packet switching, each packet may follow a different route to reach a receiver from a sender and may experience different delays. Thus, they may not reach the receiver in the correct serial order. It may also happen that some packets are lost due to failure of routers or congestion in the network.
32. Ensuring reliable receipt of all packets and rearranging received packets in the correct serial order is performed by the Transmission Control Protocol (TCP) of the TCP/IP protocol suite.
33. When computers belonging to one organization are connected using TCP/IP protocol and implement applications such as email and web browsers, it is called an intranet.
34. When intranets belonging to cooperating organizations are connected by secure private leased lines, it is called an extranet.
35. Leased lines are expensive. A cheaper alternative is called a Virtual Private Network (VPN). It encapsulates encrypted IP packets in secure envelopes. The method of interchanging messages on VPN uses a protocol called tunneling.
36. TCP/IP is a very robust protocol and has been able to keep the Internet operational without a major breakdown in spite of the exponential growth of computers connected to it.
37. The Internet is growing so fast that the 32 bits provided for address in the current version of the Internet protocol IPv4 is insufficient. Thus, a new protocol IPv6 has been standardized that has a 128-bit address. IPv6 also has a provision to prioritize data packets and has built-in security.

REVIEW QUESTIONS

13.1 What is the purpose of using a remote interactive terminal connected to a computer?

13.2 What is a local area network?

13.3 What are the objectives of a local area network?

13.4 What is a computer network?

13.5 What are the objectives of a computer network?

13.6 What is Internetworking? Why is it useful?

13.7 Give some examples of computer networks and their applications.

13.8 What is the ISO model for open systems interconnection?

13.9 Why is a layered approach to protocol design adopted by ISO?

13.10 What are the various layers and their functions in the ISO proposal?

13.11 What are the layers in the TCP/IP protocol and the functions of each layer?

13.12 What information is there in an Ethernet frame?

13.13 What is an Ethernet switch?

13.14 What is a layer 3 switch? When is it used?

13.15 What is packet switching?

13.16 Why is packet switching useful in digital data communication between computers?

13.17 Explain how the packet switching method is implemented.

13.18 What is message switching?

13.19 What is the difference between packet switching and message switching?

13.20 What is a router? When is a router used?

13.21 What do you understand by interoperability? Why is interoperability essential in the Internet?

13.22 What do you understand by TCP/IP?

13.23 How is communication between computers established on the Internet?

13.24 What is the protocol used by computers connected to the Internet?

13.25 What is an IP address? Why is it needed?

13.26 What is the format of an IP packet? What is the maximum size of the payload in a packet?

13.27 Why is data to be communicated between computers connected to the Internet packetized? Do all packets follow identical paths from source to destination?

13.28 What is an IP datagram? Does IP guarantee the delivery of packets to the intended recipient or is it the best effort?

13.29 What is the function of TCP? Is TCP essential in the Internet? Why?

13.30 How does TCP recover lost packets? How does it sequence packets in the right order? How does TCP control congestion on the Internet?

13.31 What types of firewalls are available to protect organizations' intranet from intruders?

13.32 What is an Intranet? What is an extranet?

13.33 Can extranet be implemented using the Internet? If yes, what are the problems of doing so?

13.34 Can the extranet be implemented using leased private lines? If yes, what are the problems of doing so?

13.35 What is a Virtual Private Network? When is it used?

13.36 How is a Virtual Private Network implemented using an Internet infrastructure?

13.37 What is the current IP version used in the Internet? What are its advantages and disadvantages?

13.38 Compare IPv4 and IPv6 protocols. How does the IPv6 protocol ensure flexibility of the Internet?

14 Voice and Data Communications

LEARNING GOALS

After reading this chapter, you should be able to:

- Explain the characteristics of communication channels that connect computers.
- Differentiate between voice and data communications.
- Describe how communication channels can be shared among several users by multiplexing.
- Describe the characteristics of physical communication media such as unshielded twisted pair, coaxial cables, fibre optic cables, microwave, and satellite links.
- Explain the basics of public switched telephone networks and their use in computer-to-computer communication using modems.
- Describe how ADSL and cable modems connect client computers to the internet service providers' services.
- Explain the basics of the 4G and the 5G mobile communication systems.
- Describe how the Wi-Fi and Bluetooth wireless systems function.

In the previous chapter, we explained why computers are interconnected and the advantages of computer networks. We also described how computers situated all over the world are interconnected to form the Internet and the protocol used to ensure orderly communication. In this chapter, we will explain the infrastructure needed to interconnect computers.

14.1 CHARACTERISTICS OF COMMUNICATION CHANNELS

To enable computers to communicate, we need communication channels to connect them. In this and subsequent sections, we will examine the types of communication channels, their characteristics, and methods used to transmit data using them. We will use the term channel as a synonym for communication channel in what follows.

By a communication channel, we mean a medium through which signals are transmitted. Signals are mostly electrical. However, optical and acoustic communication channels also exist. Optical channels such as fibre optics transmit light signals. Sound signals are carried by air, water, and metal wires. Signals transmitted may be classified as analog or digital. An *analog channel* transmits continuously time-varying signals such as sine waves. A *digital channel,* on the contrary, transmits binary digits represented by voltage pulses. For example, a +5 V pulse to represent a 1 and a –5 V pulse a 0. An example of a digital channels is optical fibres. Digital signals are transmitted on buses in computers. (We described analog and digital signals in the context of Digital Signal Processing in Chapter 11. Some of that material is repeated to make this chapter self-contained.)

Analog signals are continuously varying voltages of the type shown in Figure 14.1. These signals may be represented as a sum of sine waves. A sine wave is specified by the expression $V \sin 2\pi ft$. Thus, an arbitrary analog signal $h(t)$ may be represented by the following equation:

$$h(t) = V_1 \sin 2\pi f_1 t + V_2 \sin 2\pi f_2 t + \dots + V_n \sin 2\pi f_n t \qquad (14.1)$$

To describe the characteristics of an analog channel (which transmits analog signals), it is necessary to understand the characteristics of a sine wave signal. A sine wave signal $V \sin 2\pi f_t$ is shown in Figure 14.2. The *amplitude* of the sine wave is defined as V and its *frequency* is defined as f. The amplitude of electrical signals is measured in volts and their frequency in hertz (in honour of Heinrich Hertz who first generated electromagnetic waves), abbreviated as Hz. Sine wave signals may be generated in a laboratory with an *oscillator*. The amplitude and the frequency of signals an oscillator generates can be varied. For low frequencies, the number of times a sine wave crosses the time axis (Figure 14.2) will be small. In the limit when $f = 0$, the signal is said to be a direct current (DC) signal. For high frequencies, the number of times a sine wave crosses the time axis will be very large.

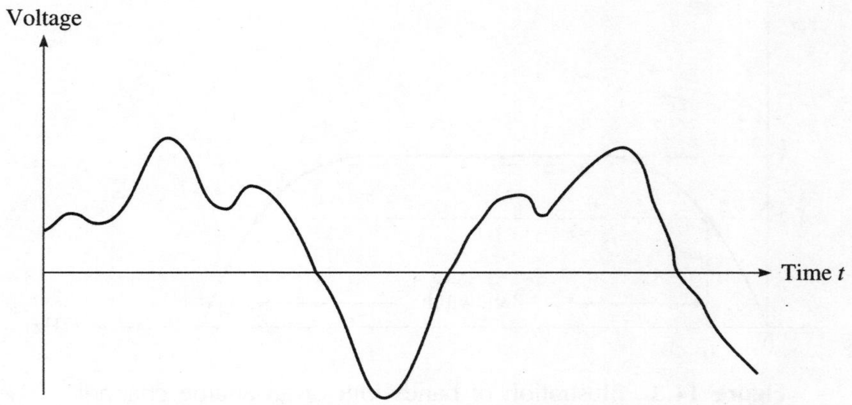

Figure 14.1 An analog signal.

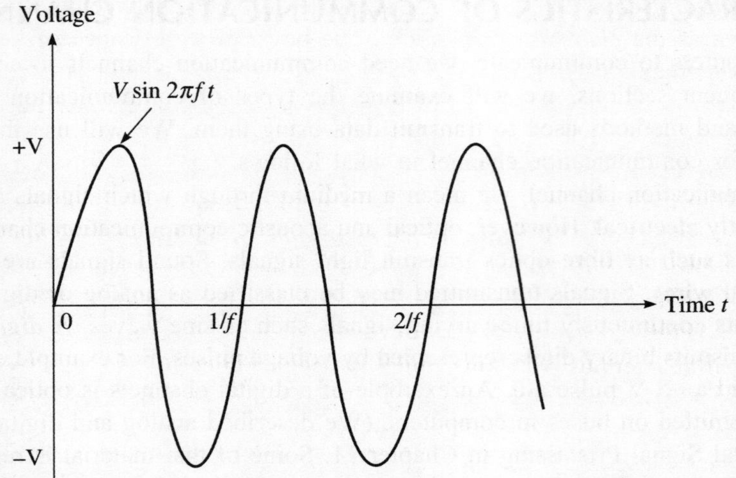

Figure 14.2 A sine wave.

The capacity of an analog channel is specified by its *bandwidth.* We may measure the bandwidth of an analog channel by connecting an oscillator at one end of the channel and sending a sine wave of amplitude V_s through it. The amplitude of the sine wave received at the other end of the channel V_r is measured. The frequency of the sine wave is varied and at each frequency, V_r, and V_s are measured. The ratio (V_r^2/V_s^2) is plotted as shown in Figure 14.3. As may be seen from Figure 14.3, the ratio V_r^2/V_s^2 of the channel at low frequencies is small and it increases and remains constant over a range of frequencies and again decreases at very high frequencies. The lowest frequency where V_r^2/V_s^2 reaches 50% of the value in the 'flat' portion of the curve (Figure 14.3) is called the *low cut-off frequency* f_l of the channel. The the highest frequency where V_r^2/V_s^2 again becomes 50% of the value in the flat portion of the curve is

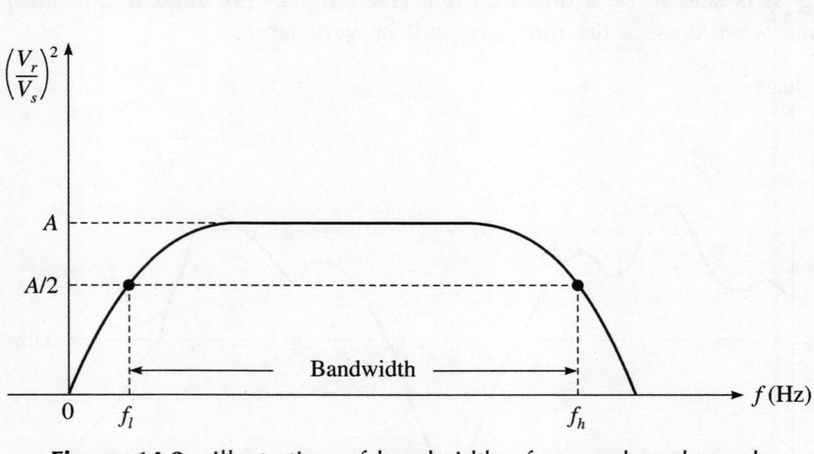

Figure 14.3 Illustration of bandwidth of an analog channel.

called the *high cut-off frequency* f_h of the channel. The difference between these two frequencies ($f_h - f_l$) is known as the *channel's bandwidth.* The physical significance of bandwidth is that sine waves in the frequency range f_l to f_h would be transmitted without considerable loss of power. The range of frequencies of human speech signals lies between 300 and 3300 Hz. Thus, the value of f_l of telephone lines used for voice communication would be about 300 Hz and f_h about 3300 Hz. The human voice will be transmitted by such lines without loss. Such lines are known as *voice-grade communication channels.* A speech signal transmitted on such a channel in its original form is known as the *baseband signal.* Baseband transmission is used for communication over short distances, such as from a telephone exchange to a subscriber's premises, as the signal attenuation is not high and inexpensive wires are used. Baseband communication is not used for long-distance communication as it is necessary to amplify and reshape the signal at intervals of 1 km, which is uneconomical.

The larger the bandwidth of a channel, the higher its capacity to carry information. For example, the bandwidth of coaxial cables used for inter-city trunk telephone calls (STD calls) is about 300 MHz. Such channels transmit several conversations simultaneously using a *carrier modulation* scheme. In carrier modulation, an analog signal is *modulated* or carried by a higher frequency called a *carrier* frequency and transmitted at the new frequency. For example, if $V \cos 2\pi ft$ is the original signal and $V_c \sin 2\pi f_c t$ is a carrier frequency signal, then the *amplitude-modulated* signal is (see Figure 14.4)

$$(V_c + V \cos 2\pi ft) \sin 2\pi f_c t \tag{14.2}$$

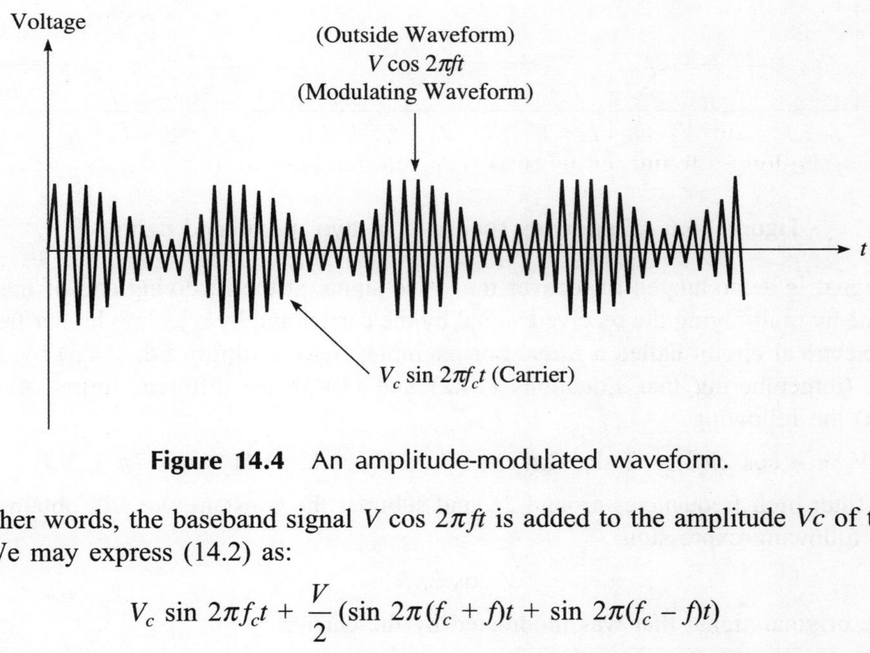

Figure 14.4 An amplitude-modulated waveform.

In other words, the baseband signal $V \cos 2\pi ft$ is added to the amplitude Vc of the carrier signal. We may express (14.2) as:

$$V_c \sin 2\pi f_c t + \frac{V}{2}(\sin 2\pi(f_c + f)t + \sin 2\pi(f_c - f)t) \tag{14.3}$$

The carrier's frequency is shifted to ($f_c + f$) and ($f_c - f$). The frequencies in the amplitude-modulated signal are $f_c - f$, f_c, and $f_c + f$. If a voice signal in the frequency range from f_l to f_h amplitude modulates a carrier f_{cl}, the range of modulated signal frequencies and amplitude would be as shown in Figure 14.5. If another voice signal modulates another carrier f_{c2}, this modulated signal will be in the frequency range from $(f_{c2} - f_h)$ to $(f_{c2} + f_h)$ as shown in Figure 14.6. If the channel bandwidth is large, then by using a large number of carrier frequencies and modulation, the channel may carry many voice signals.

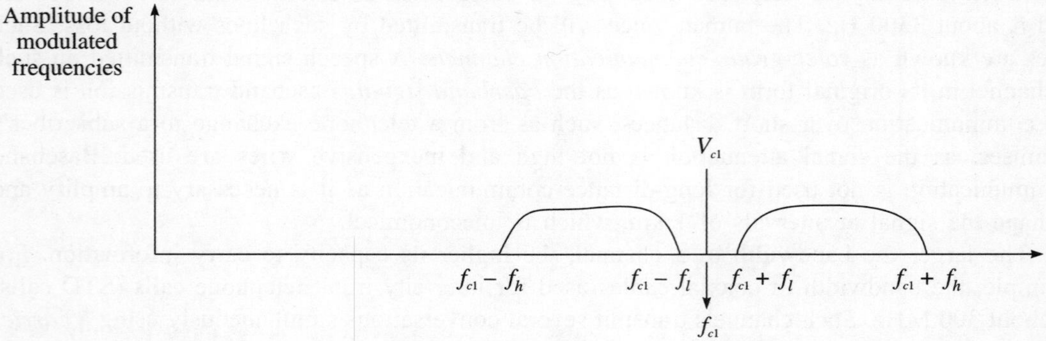

Figure 14.5 Frequency spectrum of a modulated carrier.

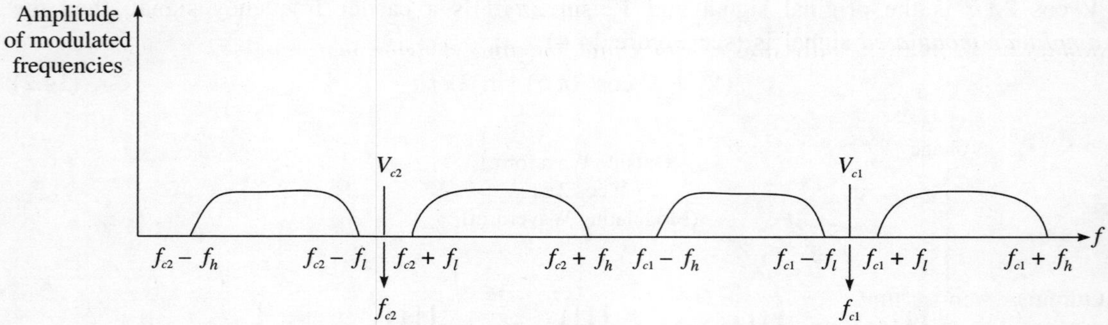

Figure 14.6 Frequency spectrum of two modulated carriers.

The signal is demodulated to recover the voice signal at the receiving end of the channel. This is done by multiplying the received signal by the carrier and by rejecting higher frequencies using an electrical circuit called a *filter*. For example, if we multiply Eq. (14.3) by 2 sin $2f_ct$, we obtain (remembering that Equations (14.2) and (14.3) are different forms of the same expression) the following:

$$(V_c + V \cos 2\pi ft) \times 2 \sin^2 2\pi f_c t = (V_c + V \cos 2\pi ft)\,(1 - \cos 2\pi \times 2f_c t) \qquad (14.4)$$

If we filter high frequencies around $2f_c$ and subtract the constant, we will obtain from Eq. (14.4) the following expression:

$$V \cos 2\pi ft \qquad (14.5)$$

This is the original signal that was modulated by the carrier.

To summarize, we saw that an analog channel carries continuously varying signals. The channel's bandwidth specifies the range of frequencies that the channel can faithfully transmit. The higher the bandwidth of a channel, the larger its capacity to carry information. To use the larger bandwidth available in some channels, several carrier frequencies may be used to modulate voice signals, translating them to different bands in the frequency spectrum before they are transmitted. The signals are recovered at the receiving end by demodulating them with the respective carrier frequencies. Thus, when we make an STD telephone call, our conversation in the frequency range of 300–3000 Hz would get shifted around a carrier of about 50 kHz and will be transmitted on the line in the range of 47–53 kHz. At the receiving station, the signal will be demodulated with the 50 kHz carrier and transmitted to the telephone instrument as a voice signal in the range of 300–3000 Hz. The same cable will also carry several other subscribers' conversations using carriers of 60, 70, 80, 90, 100 kHz, etc., depending on the available bandwidth of the cable.

14.2 ALLOCATION OF COMMUNICATION CHANNEL

A communication channel is an expensive resource. In computer communication, except for short communication lines, a channel is shared, for economic reasons, by many computers. A channel is shared to maximize the channel capacity. The method of dividing a channel into many sub-channels so that several independent signals may be transmitted on it is known as *multiplexing*. There are three basic methods of multiplexing channels. They are *space division multiplexing, frequency division multiplexing,* and *time division multiplexing*.

14.2.1 Space Division Multiplexing

In space division multiplexing (SDM) many independent signals are carried in the same physical space. An example is many fibre optical cables bundled in a sheath carrying independent signals. Another example is a multi-core fibre optics cable that carries multiple signals. In mobile communication space division multiplexing is used in MIMO (Multiple Input Multiple Output) antennas that carry many signals between pairs of antennas of a sender and a receiver.

14.2.2 Frequency Division Multiplexing

Frequency Division Multiplexing (FDM) is the technique used to divide the bandwidth available in a physical medium into several smaller independent logical channels, each with a small bandwidth. Using several carrier frequencies, each of which is modulated by an independent voice signal (discussed in Section 14.1), is frequency division multiplexing.

Another example of FDM is the way different bands in the wireless spectrum are allocated among users. Jio 5G operates around 3.5 GHz and Wi-Fi uses a band around 2.4GHz.

In a bounded medium such as a telephone cable, the cable is connected between exchanges of main cities. Transmission of signals along a telephone cable may be termed 'guided transmission'. In this case, a cable has a bandwidth of about 200 kHz. Each telephone conversation would need a bandwidth of 3000 Hz. We can transmit 10 different speech signals simultaneously on this channel by using a FDM scheme. We pick 10 carrier signals of 50, 60, 70, …, 140 kHz to modulate 10 different speech signals. These are transmitted over the cable and at the receiving telephone exchange, they are demodulated using the respective carriers, filtered, and routed to the appropriate telephone instruments (see Figure 14.7).

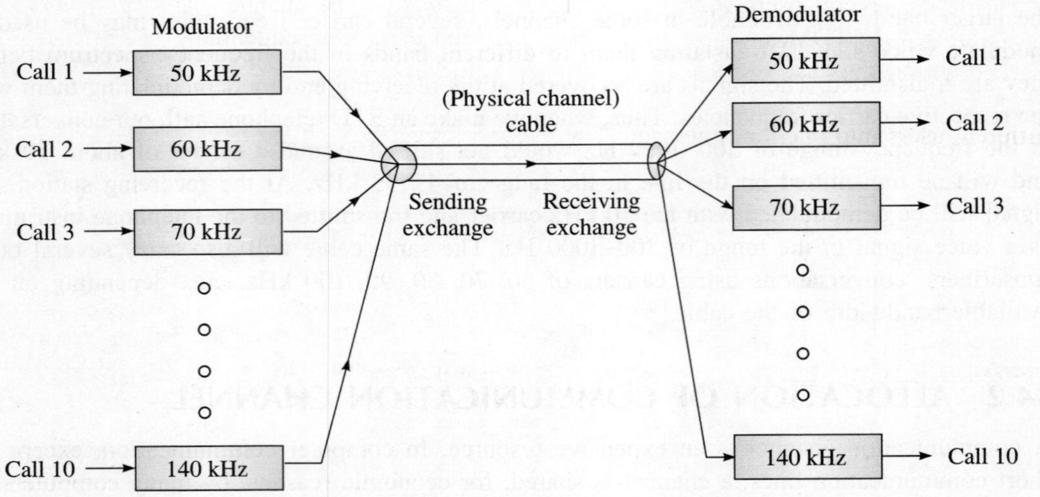

Figure 14.7 Illustration of frequency division multiplexing.

We will now examine FDM's characteristics. The first important characteristic of FDM is that the signals to be transmitted must be analog signals. For digital signals to use FDM, they must be converted to analog form. We will see how this is done later in this chapter.

The second important characteristic of FDM is that all the signals in the physical channel travel *simultaneously*. The third characteristic is that the *physical* channel is split into several *logical channels*. Each logical channel is distinct and carries an independent signal. The available bandwidth of the physical channel is efficiently utilized. Finally, we need a modulator at the sending end and a demodulator at the receiving end for each logical channel. In the above method of transmitting messages, the communication from a sender to a receiver is one way. This is called *half-duplex* communications. For telephone conversation, we need two-way communication—from the sender to the receiver and back from the receiver to the sender. This is called *full duplex* communication. There are two ways of achieving full duplex communication. One is to use two physical channels, one from a sender to a receiver and the other from the receiver to the sender. In this case, the same set of frequencies can be used for transmitting and receiving. A modulator and a demodulator are required at each end. A modulator-demodulator pair is known as a *modem*.

Another way of obtaining full duplex communication using a single physical cable is to use two different sets of carrier signals—one set for sending messages from senders to receivers and the other set for messages from receivers to senders. In this case also, modems are needed at each end.

14.2.3 Time Division Multiplexing

Time Division Multiplexing (TDM) is another popular method of effectively utilizing a physical channel's capacity. Each channel user is allotted several small time intervals during which the user may transmit a message. Thus, the total time available in the channel is divided into several slices and each user is allocated time slices.

In FDM several users send messages simultaneously. The channel bandwidth is divided and allocated. In TDM, on the other hand, users send messages sequentially one after another. Each user can thus use the full channel bandwidth during the period he controls the channel. The channel capacity is fully utilized in TDM by interleaving several messages belonging to different users into one long message. The messages sent through the physical channel must be separated at the receiving end. Individual chunks of messages users send should be reassembled into a full message (see Figure 14.8).

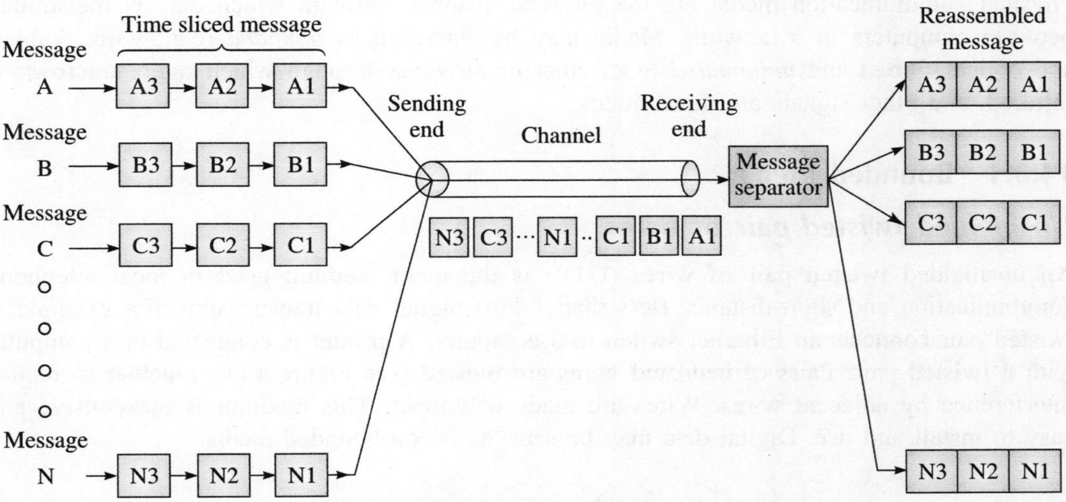

Figure 14.8 Illustration of time division multiplexing.

TDM may be used to multiplex digital or analog signals. For digital data communications, it is more convenient to transmit data directly in digital form, and thus TDM is more appropriate. Besides this, communication between computers takes place in short fast bursts. Each burst would need the full channel bandwidth and in TDM this bandwidth is available.

Another aspect of channel allocation that we should consider is how long the channel is allocated and how much data may be transmitted during this time. In TDM, a time slice is allocated and the amount of data that can be transmitted during this time slice is a function of the channel bandwidth. Suppose the channel bandwidth for digital data is 1 Mbps and the allocated time slice is 100 ms. Then a *packet* of 100,000 bits may be transmitted during the allocated time. Observe that the channel is 'switched' between different users quickly and frequently. For example, if there are 10 users of the 1 Mbps channel and each user gets a 100 ms slice, the user will get the channel to send the next packet after a second. A reallocation of time slice may be made as necessary to ensure an equitable use of the channel.

In contrast, in voice transmission using an FDM telephone channel, once a circuit is allocated to a sender and he is connected to the intended receiver of his message, he can have exclusive use of the logical channel as long as he wishes.

Frequency and time division multiplexing may be combined. In this case, a channel can use a certain frequency band for a specified time. This allows several users to use the system in a time-sharing, frequency-sharing mode.

The main disadvantage of this scheme is that the sender and the receiver should know the exact frequency band and the exact time of transmission to allow uninterrupted communication. Two senders will interfere if they select the same frequency simultaneously. If the frequency change is fast enough, the interference may be small and will not affect the receiver.

14.3 PHYSICAL COMMUNICATION MEDIA

Physical communication media are the physical channels through which data is transmitted between computers in a network. Media may be classified as *bounded* (e.g., wires, cables, and optical fibres) and *unbounded* (e.g., ether or airwaves through which radio, microwave, infrared, and other signals are transmitted).

14.3.1 Bounded Media

Unshielded twisted pair of wires

An unshielded twisted pair of wires (UTP) is the main medium used in local telephone communication and short-distance (less than 1 km) digital data transmission. For example, a twisted pair connects an Ethernet switch to a computer. A printer is connected to a computer with a twisted pair. Pairs of insulated wires are twisted (see Figure 14.9) together to reduce interference by adjacent wires. Wires are made of copper. This medium is inexpensive and easy to install and use. Digital data may be sent 'as is' on bounded media.

Figure 14.9 An unshielded twisted pair of wires.

The Electrical Industries Association has standardized the specifications of UTP, including the diameter of the wires, the distance between twists, the type of insulation, and the type of connectors to connect them to equipment. Five categories of UTP cables are specified. They are called Category 3, Category 4, Category 5, Category 6, and Category 7, and abbreviated, respectively, as Cat 3, Cat 4, Cat 5, Cat 6, and Cat 7 UTP cables based on the bandwidth of signals they can support.

Coaxial cables

Coaxial cables offer much higher bandwidths and noise immunity. They are widely used for long-distance data transmission. Coaxial cables consist of a central copper wire surrounded by a Teflon or PVC insulation, over which a sleeve of copper mesh or extruded aluminum is placed. The metal sleeve is covered by an outer shield of thick PVC material (see Figure 14.10). The signal is carried by the inner copper wire. The signal is electrically shielded by the outer metal sleeve. Coaxial cables have a very high bandwidth. A 3/8 in. cable can carry digital signals at very high rates of 500 Mbps. Long-distance cables need a repeater every 1 km to amplify and reshape signals. With the advent of optical fibre cables, copper coaxial cables are being replaced by them for long-distance communication as they need fewer repeaters and are cheaper.

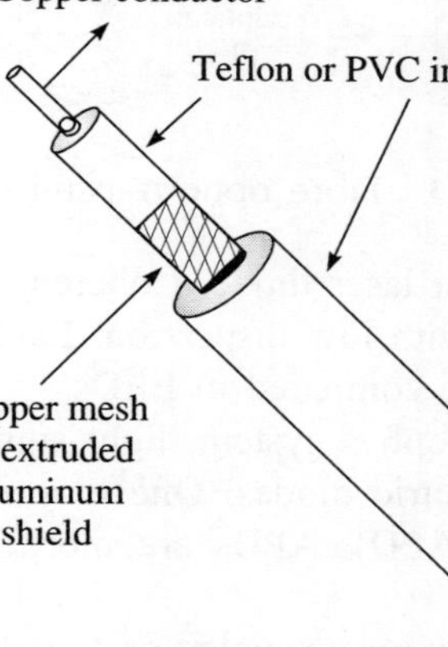

Figure 14.10 A coaxial cable.

Optical fibre

Physically an *optical fibre* consists of a glass core, a plastic or glass cladding, and a protective coating. The core diameter is between 8 and 200 mm. The refractive index of the cladding is less than that of the core. If the core has a single refractive index, then there is an abrupt change in the index between the core and the cladding. Such a fibre is called a *step-index fibre*. When the refractive index of the core changes gradually, the fibre is known as *graded index fibre*.

When a light beam is generated by a Light Emitting Diode (LED) or Injection Laser Diode (ILD) placed at the input end of an optical fibre cable, it propagates along the glass fibre by *total internal reflection*. Total internal reflection takes place as the refractive index of the glass core is greater than that of the cladding material. Thus, light is propagated along an optical fibre as a set of guided light waves called the *modes* of the optical fibre. Depending on the fibre's geometry and refractive index variations, either several modes propagate or a single mode propagates. The first one is called *multimode fibre* and the second is a *single-mode fibre*. Single-mode propagation requires a small core dimension (1.5–5 mm diameter), whereas multimode propagation requires a larger core dimension (50–200 mm diameter) as only with a larger core diameter the refractive index can be graded. Both single-mode step index and multimode-graded index fibre cables are used. The most popular graded index multimode fibre is specified as 62.5 mm/125 mm. The inner core is 62.5 mm and the outer cladding is 125 mm. Single-mode fibre has lower losses and higher bandwidth, whereas multimode-graded index fibre has higher losses and lower bandwidth. The single-mode fibre is less expensive compared to multimode fibre. For long distances, single-mode fibre is used and for shorter distances, multimode fibre is used. It is difficult to have tappings on a single-mode fibre to connect computers, and thus it is not used in local area networks. Tappings, on the other hand, are possible in multimode fibres.

In fibre optic communications, electrical signals are transformed into light pulses by a modulator, transmitted over the fibre as light waves, detected, and converted back to electrical signals by photoelectric diodes (Figure 14.11).

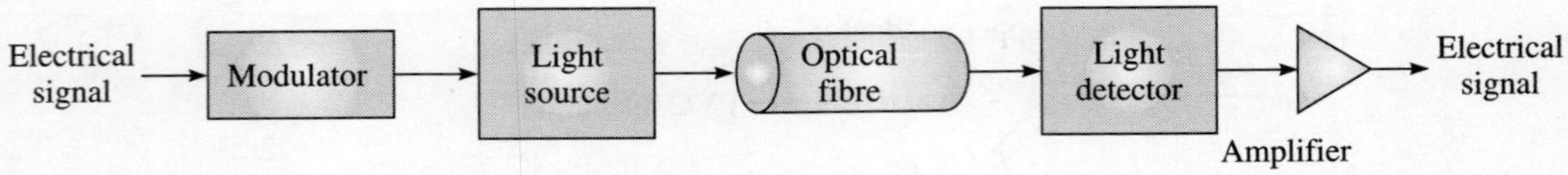

Figure 14.11 Fibre optic transmission.

The light source used is LED or a laser diode. Coherent monochromatic light is needed to transmit light over long distances with low dispersion. Lasers provide this, whereas LEDs do not. Lasers are, however, expensive compared to LEDs.

At the receiving end of the fibre optics system, light signals are detected and converted back to electrical signals by photoelectric diodes. One may use PIN diodes (*P Insulated N* channel) or Avalanche photodiodes (APD). APDs are more sensitive and effective but are expensive compared to PIN diodes.

Optical fibres may be used to communicate analog or digital signals. In analog transmission, the light intensity is continuously varied, whereas in digital transmission the light source is turned *on* or *off*. The most common use of optical fibres is for digital data transmission.

The speed of data that can be transmitted by a fibre cable depends on the quality of the fibre and is specified by the notation OC-x, where x is a variable. For example, OC-1 = 51.84 Mbps. OC-n is n times OC-1 speed. Current fibre optics cables are OC-192 with a speed of 9953.28 Mbps (almost 10 Gbps) and OC-384 with a speed of about 20 Gbps. The capacity of an optical fibre to carry data may be increased by using what is known as *Wave Division Multiplex* (*WDM*). In this case, several signals at different wavelengths are propagated along a multimode fibre. (Remember that the wavelength λ is related to the frequency f by the formula $f\lambda = c$, where c is the speed of light.) The term WDM is normally used for optical signals, whereas the term frequency division multiplex is used for radio frequency signals.

Optical fibres have several advantages. They are as follows:

(i) Each fibre can carry many independent channels, each using a different wavelength of light (*wavelength division multiplex*). Up to 80 channels are deployed in commercial systems. Each channel has a bandwidth of around 40 Gbps.
(ii) Data carried by optical fibres are not affected by electromagnetic interference.
(iii) Data carried by optical fibres are more secure as they cannot be tapped easily.
(iv) Optical fibres are lightweight and are not corroded.
(v) Data carried by optical fibres have lower attenuation. Repeaters are needed only at intervals of tens of kilometres for multimode fibre and hundreds of kilometres for single-mode fibre.

The major disadvantages of fibres are as follows:

(i) It is difficult to align and join two fibres in the field without special equipment.
(ii) They are fragile and cannot have sharp bends.

14.3.2 Unbounded Media

Wireless media are called unbounded. The signals are radiated into the atmosphere and picked up by the device(s) to which they are sent. There are several varieties of wireless communications which may be classified as shown in Figure 14.12.

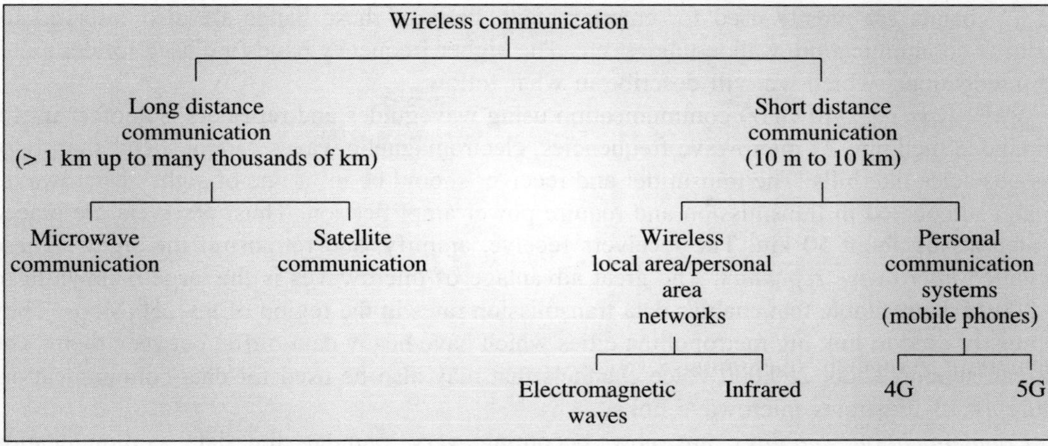

Figure 14.12 Variety of wireless communications.

Wireless transmission depends on the propagation of electromagnetic waves. James Clerk Maxwell predicted their existence in 1865 and Heinrich Hertz experimentally created electromagnetic waves in 1887. Electromagnetic waves travel at the speed of light, that is, $c = 3 \times 10^8$ m/s (light is also an electromagnetic wave). The frequency varies from 10^4 to 10^{24} Hz. In Table 14.1, we show the spectrum and their application in each frequency band.

Table 14.1 Frequency bands used by various applications

Frequency range	*Application*	*Frequency range*	*Application*
500 kHz to 30 MHz	AM Radio	800 MHz to 8 GHz	Mobile phones
80–110 MHz	FM Radio	2.4, 5, 6 GHz	Wireless LAN
100 MHz to 1 GHz	TV	1–100 THz	Infrared
500 MHz to 40 GHz	Microwave	10^{14} to 5×10^{14} Hz	Visible light
1–50 GHz	Satellite communication	5×10^{14} to 3×10^{16} Hz	Ultraviolet

The frequency f, the speed c, and the wavelength λ of electromagnetic waves are related by the formula

$$\lambda f = c$$

Thus, if $f = 1$ GHz, then wavelength λ is

$$\lambda = 3 \times \frac{10^8}{10^9} = 3 \times 10^{-1} \text{ m} = 30 \text{ cm}$$

The size of the antennas required to radiate electromagnetic waves is less than $\lambda/4$. Thus, a mobile phone operating in the 3 GHz band will have an antenna size of less than 2.5 cm.

The electromagnetic spectrum is a scarce resource and is controlled by Governments that license spectrum bandwidth for various uses. International agreements also exist to share the spectrum between countries and limit the radiated electromagnetic energy. The AM, FM, and TV bands are mostly used for entertainment. Parts of these bands are also reserved for maritime communication, walkie-talkies, etc. The higher frequency bands are used for computer communications, which we will describe in what follows.

Microwave (0.5–40 GHz) communication using waveguides and repeaters is another useful unbounded medium. At microwave frequencies, electromagnetic waves cannot 'bend' sharply or pass obstacles like hills. The transmitter and receiver should be in 'a line of sight'. Microwaves are also attenuated in transmission and require power amplification. Thus, receivers are placed at intervals of about 50 km. The receivers receive, amplify, and retransmit the signal. These are called *microwave repeaters*. The great advantage of microwaves is the large bandwidth of 40–200 MHz available that enables data transmission rates in the region of 90–250 Mbps. They are mostly used to link big metropolitan cities which have heavy data traffic between them. The link can support about 250,000 voice channels that may also be used for data communication. Figure 14.13 illustrates microwave links.

Communication satellites are now becoming very popular for data communication between computers. Communication satellites are now launched either by rockets or by space shuttles and parked in a *geostationary* orbit at 36,000 km above the equator. The speed of the satellite in this orbit equals the speed of rotation of the Earth, and thus the satellite is stationary relative to Earth. The Indian national satellite (INSAT) is launched periodically by the Indian Space Research Organization (ISRO) and is parked to be accessible anywhere in India, including the islands of Andaman, Nicobar, and Lakshadweep.

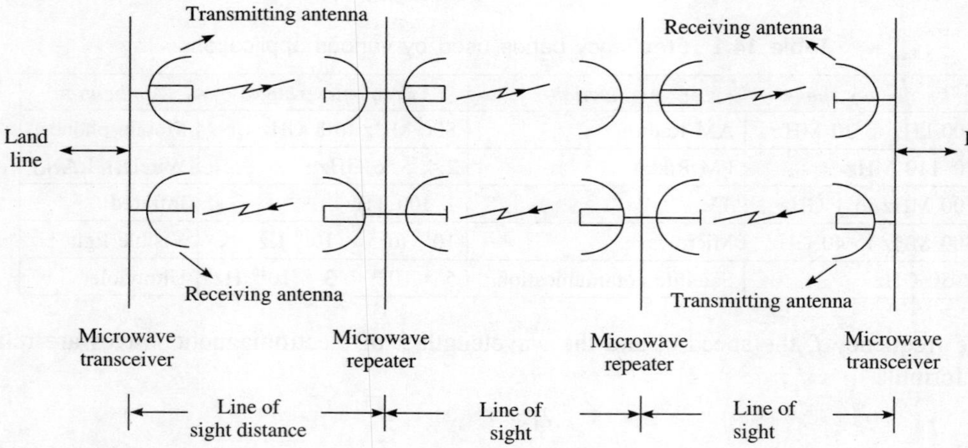

Figure 14.13 Microwave relay.

A communication satellite is essentially a microwave relay station in the sky. Microwave signal at 6 GHz is beamed to it from a transmitter on the earth. It is received by the satellite as a feeble signal due to 36,000 km of travel. It is amplified and retransmitted to the earth at 4 GHz by a *transponder* mounted on the satellite. The retransmission frequency is different as otherwise, the powerful retransmission signal will interfere with the weak incoming signal. The main advantage of the satellite is that it is a single microwave relay station visible from anywhere in a country. Thus, transmission and reception can be between any two randomly chosen places. The bandwidth of signals which can be handled by a transponder varies between

25 Mhz and 72 MHz depending on several factors including modulation method, atmospheric conditions, noise etc. A 72 MHz transponder would give a data transmission speed of several hundred Mbps.

A satellite has many transponders, thus providing enormous communication capability at costs that favourably compete with microwave links on Earth. Figure 14.14 shows a satellite communication link.

The interesting features of a satellite communication link are as follows:

(i) There is a 240 ms propagation delay between the sending of data from one terminal or computer and its reception in another computer or terminal. This is due to the distance of the satellite from the earth station.

(ii) The transmission and reception costs are independent of the distance between computers.

(iii) Very high bandwidth is available if a user has an antenna in his premises or a radio link to an earth station. The cost of receive–transmit ground stations has considerably reduced and now one may install a 'private receiving/transmitting station' for about ₹10 lakhs. The cost of rooftop antennas and receivers of satellite broadcast signals is very low, a few thousand rupees. This has popularized satellite TV broadcasts.

(iv) A signal sent from a satellite is broadcast to all receivers within the satellite's range. Thus, special security precautions such as encryption (i.e., scrambling the signals) would be necessary.

(v) A transmitting station can receive back its transmission and check whether the transponder has transmitted the data correctly. If an error is detected, the data will be retransmitted.

(vi) Recently higher frequencies for uplink (i.e., earth station to satellite) and downlink (satellite to earth station) are being used. The band 4 GHz–6 GHz is called the C-Band. The higher frequency band in the range of 12–14 GHz is called the *Ku* band. The use of *Ku* band transmission is, however, affected more by atmospheric disturbances, particularly during the monsoons.

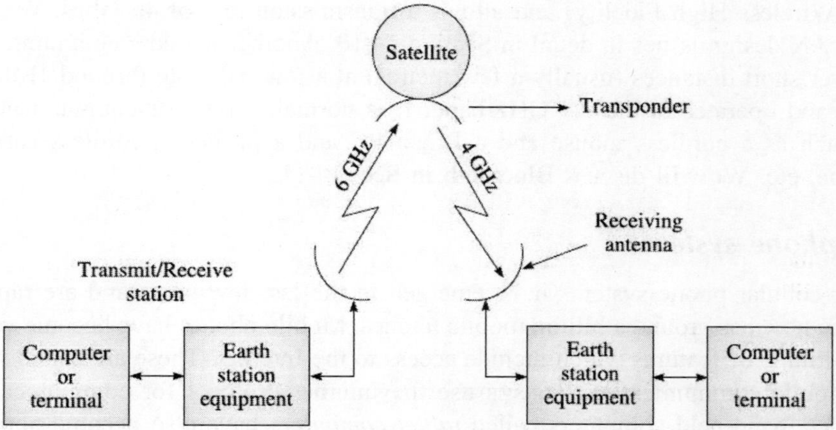

Figure 14.14 Illustration of satellite communication.

(vii) When a satellite system is to service a large number of users, it is desirable to reduce the cost of the earth stations to be located at each user's site. This can be done provided the transponders in the satellite are improved and provide higher power output. Recently, systems of this type have been built with Very Small Aperture Terminals (VSATs) at users' sites. The aperture refers to the diameter of the dish antenna which is about 1–2 m. Smaller antennas and lower power transmitters and receivers at users' sites make VSATs affordable.

A new entrant to satellite communication is Low Earth Orbiting Satellites or LEO. These are constellations of thousands of satellites orbiting earth at a distance of between 200 and 2000 km. LEOs have become feasible as the cost of launching satellites is now (2025) much cheaper. LEOs being much closer to Earth reduces the latency of communications to around 30 ms as compared to 240 ms of geostationary satellites. The energy needed to communicate with users on the earth is also much lower as they are closer. Constellations also cover the whole world. Many companies are planning to provide Internet services and mobile communication services using LEOs. Currently (2025) operational systems are Starlink which has around 6900 satellites orbiting the Earth at a distance of around 500 km and OneWeb with around 600 satellites orbiting the Earth at a distance of around 1000 km. An advantage of LEOs is their coverage of remote locations not accessible to mobile phone and other communication networks.

Wireless local area network

Wireless local area networks are now becoming popular. They use the 2.4, 5, and 6 GHz wireless frequency band (known as a free band as no licensing from the Government is needed to use this band). The wireless power that can be transmitted is restricted to less than a watt. It is primarily used to communicate between a fixed transceiver and one or more mobile computers. This has been standardized by IEEE and is called IEEE 802.11 series of standards. There is another frequency band used for short-range wireless which is also unlicensed. It is the 915 MHz band used for cordless telephones, microphones, etc.

IEEE 802.11be is the latest standard introduced in 2024 for wireless LANs. This is called Wi-Fi 7 (Wireless High Fidelity) and allows a transmission rate of 46 Gbps. We will discuss wireless LAN design issues in detail in Section 14.10. Another wireless communication system for use over short distances (usually a few metres) at a low data rate (around 1Mbps) is called *Bluetooth* and operates in the 2.4 GHz band. It is normally used for communicating between devices such as a cordless mouse and a PC, a PC and a printer, a cordless earphone and a smartphone, etc. We will discuss Bluetooth in Sec. 14.11.

Mobile phone systems

Mobile or cellular phone systems have emerged in the last few years and are rapidly gaining users. India now has around a billion mobile phones. Mobile phones have become very powerful with a multitude of features which include access to the Internet. These are called *smartphones*. Current mobile communication systems use the Internet Protocol for communication Besides smartphones, hand-held computers called *tablet computers* have also become popular and use the communication system used by mobile phones. These mobile devices have the advantage of being able to transmit both voice (analog) and high-speed digital data. Currently, 4G and 5G mobile communication systems are used in India. Different operators use several frequency bands each ranging from 700 MHz to 2500 MHz for 4G and 700 MHz to 26 GHz for 5G. In India 5G operators use frequency in the range 3300 to 3500 MHz Different bands are used depending on the type of use. The area of operation of a mobile communication system is divided into hexagonal cells. In this frequency band operators normally use 5 MHz to 20 MHz to run their service. The area covered can range from a few hundred metres to 5 km depending on the communication speed. The frequency used to transmit data/voice from mobile handsets is different from that used for receiving data/voice so that there is no interference between outgoing and incoming signals from and to the handset. We will describe the technology of mobile communication systems later in this chapter.

Infrared technology

For short-distance line-of-sight communication infrared light (IR) can be used to transmit data. The most common IR device used is the hand-held remote control of devices such as TV, VCRs, Audio Systems, air-conditioners, etc. IR is in the wavelength range of 800–900 nm and allows high-speed data communication up to around 50 Mbps over a few metres in experimental systems. Commercial systems available now have 10 Mbps speed. The most common use is thus in Local Networks. A portable computer with an IR communication interface can communicate with a stationary computer a few metres away, provided there are no walls or similar obstructions in the line-of-sight path. The main advantage of IR is that it has a restricted range, and thus the same frequency can be used in adjacent rooms without interference.

IR-based products to interconnect computers are marketed by IBM and other vendors. It is used only in special applications.

The use of infrared bands does not require any licensing. Unlike wireless, it is secure as infrared cannot be picked up outside the room in which it is deployed.

In Table 14.2, we summarize the bandwidth available from various physical media we have discussed in this section.

Table 14.2 Frequency band of various physical media

Medium	*Copper UTP*	*Coaxial cable*	*Microwave links*	*Satellite links*	*Fibre optic cables*	*Wireless LAN*	*Mobile phones*
Frequency band	0–100 MHz	100 KHz to 750 MHz	500 MHz to 20 GHz	1 GHz to 50 GHz	100 THz to 1000 THz	2.4, 5, 6 GHz unlicensed bands	700 MHz to 26 GHz 5G, to 2.5 GHz4G

14.4 PUBLIC SWITCHED TELEPHONE NETWORKS

In the last section, we described several technologies used in communication systems. In this and subsequent sections, we will describe how these technologies are used to build systems. The telephone networks maintained by local telephone companies such as BSNL in India are called Public Switched Telephone Networks (PSTN). These systems have been in existence for almost a century and were designed primarily to cater to audio conversations between customers spread all over the world. The use of PSTN is declining but will take a while to disappear as it is secure and connects nooks and corners of India. Current estimates (2024) of the number of landline telephones in India is 31 million and, in the USA, it is 85 million. The general structure of PSTN is shown in Figure 14.15.

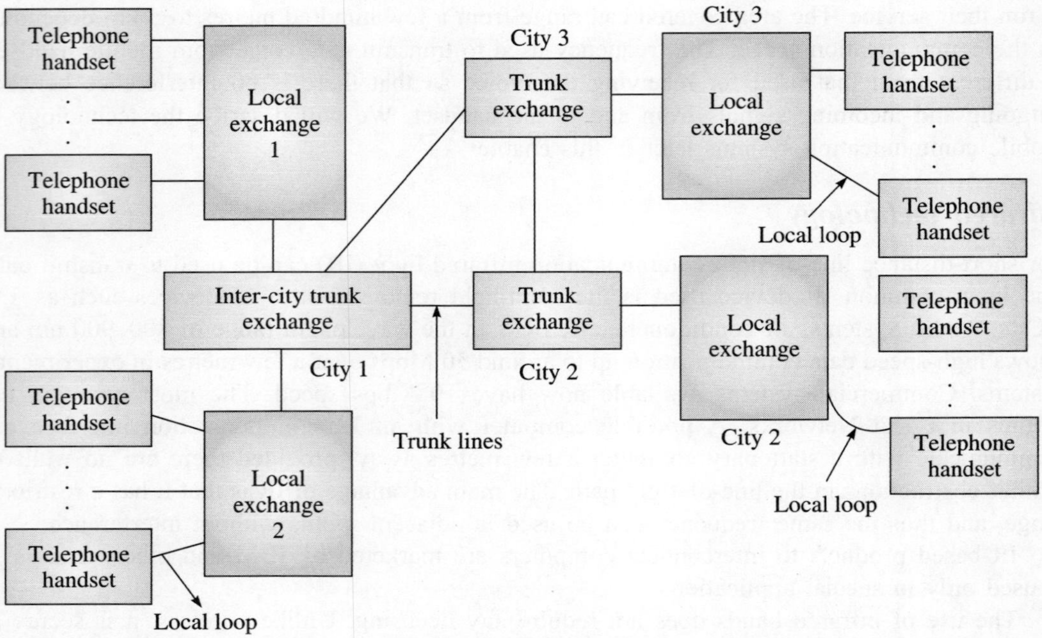

Figure 14.15 Structure of a public switched telephone network.

The subscribers' telephones are connected to a local telephone exchange which recognizes the called number and routes it to an appropriate local exchange in the city if it is a local call. If it is an STD or an ISD call, the local exchange connects the call to an inter-city trunk exchange. The trunk exchanges of different cities are interconnected by high-capacity lines called trunk lines (coaxial cables, microwave links, or fibre optic cables) which can transmit several thousand conversations. The telephone handset at a customer's premises is normally connected to the local exchange by twisted pair copper wires (usually Cat 3 twisted pairs) and is called a local loop. As of now most local and trunk exchanges are digital and trunk lines are also very reliable. The only unreliable part is the local loop which normally extends to about 1–2 km (called the last mile problem).

14.4.1 Digital Communication on the Local Loop with Modems

Home computers are connected to the Internet, by Internet Service Providers (ISPs). There are two popular methods. ISPs in most big cities run fibre optic cables or coaxial cables from their centres to homes. These cables are connected to routers at homes and offices. The routers are connected to Ethernets and Wi-Fi. The other method is to use the telephone landlines at homes that are connected to the local telephone exchange using the local loop. The exchange is, in turn, connected to an Internet Service Provider (ISP). The percentage of users relying on landline telephone lines for Internet access has rapidly declined as it is slow. However, it is used in small towns. The local loop is designed to transmit telephone conversations. It is called a voice grade line and is designed to transmit analog signals of bandwidth around 3 kHz. If a digital signal as shown in Figure 14.16 is sent on this line, it gets severely distorted as shown at the bottom of the figure. Thus, it is converted to an analog signal before transmission. This is done by a *modulator*. The analog signal travels over the telephone network as any other voice call and reaches the ISP's server as an analog signal. ISP may be in a different part of the city connected to a different exchange. ISP's telephone number is thus dialed to connect to it. The analog signal received by the ISP's computer is converted back to a digital signal by a *demodulator* to permit processing. The processed digital data is modulated by the ISP to an analog signal and returned via the telephone network to the user's computer, where the analog signal is demodulated to a digital signal for display. Thus, we need a *modulator-demodulator* pair at both ends of the telephone line. This equipment is called a *modem*. Figure 14.17 illustrates the use of modems. There are two main reasons for using modems. They allow higher transmission speed on a given analog line, and they reduce the effects of noise and distortion.

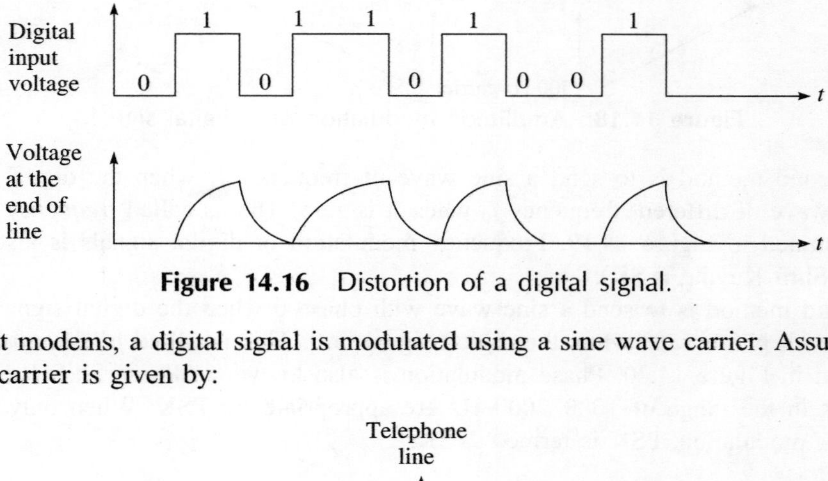

Figure 14.16 Distortion of a digital signal.

In most modems, a digital signal is modulated using a sine wave carrier. Assume that the sine wave carrier is given by:

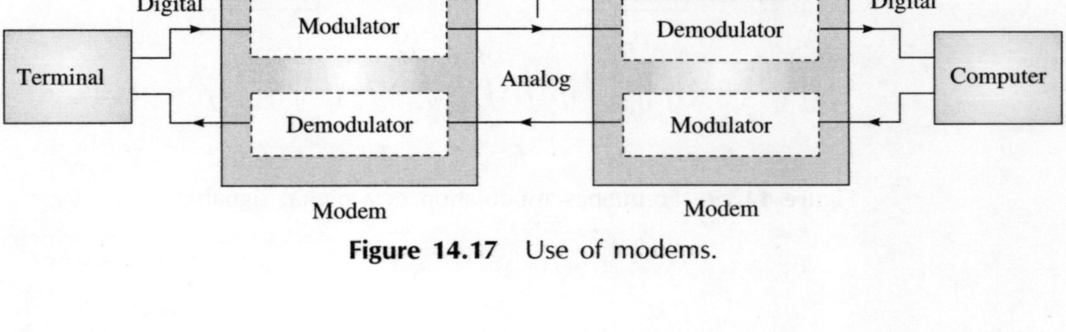

Figure 14.17 Use of modems.

$$v(t) = V_c \sin(2\pi f_c t + \phi)$$

where

$v(t)$ = instantaneous amplitude of the carrier voltage at time t
Vc = the maximum amplitude of the carrier
fc = the carrier frequency
ϕ = the phase

There are three ways of modulating the sine wave carrier by a digital signal. The first method is to modulate the amplitude of the carrier with the digital signal as shown in Figure 14.18. Observe that when the digital bit is 1, the carrier is transmitted and when the bit is 0, it is not transmitted. Another amplitude modulation method would be to use amplitude A for 1 and another amplitude B for 0.

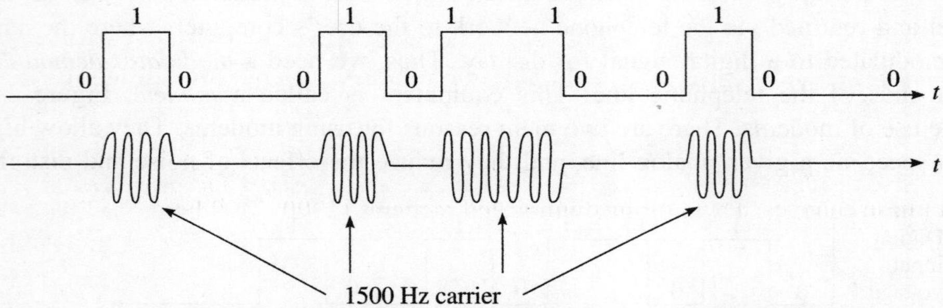

Figure 14.18 Amplitude modulation of a digital signal.

The second method is to send a sine wave of frequency f_1 when the digital signal is 1 and a sine wave of different frequency f_0 when it is zero. This is called *frequency modulation* and is illustrated in Figure 14.19. Frequency modulation of digital signals is also known as Frequency Shift Keying (FSK).

The third method is to send a sine wave with phase 0 when the digital signal is 1 and a sine wave with phase 180° when the digital signal is 0. This is called *phase modulation* and is illustrated in Figure 14.20. Phase modulation is also known as Phase Shift Keying (PSK). Frequencies in the range of 1000–2000 Hz are appropriate for PSK. When only two phases are used for modulation, PSK is termed 2PSK.

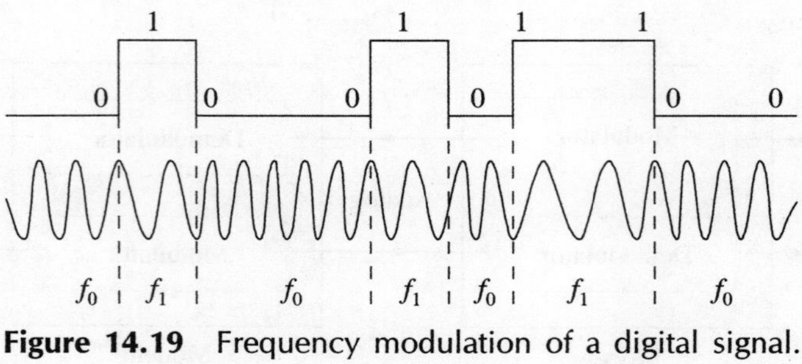

Figure 14.19 Frequency modulation of a digital signal.

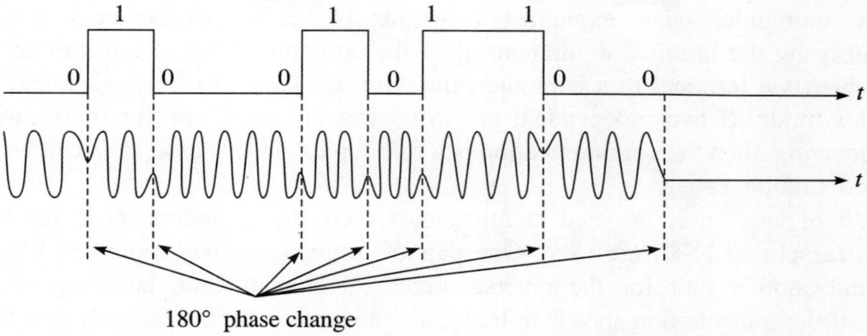

Figure 14.20 Phase modulation of a digital signal.

Amplitude-modulated signals are sensitive to impulse noises picked up by the transmission line. Impulse noises arise due to electrical sparks near the transmission line. Frequency and phase-modulated signals, on the other hand, are not sensitive to large impulse noise. In these modulation schemes, an amplitude limiter is used, as the binary information is detected by the frequency or the phase values and not by the amplitude. Frequency modulation modems (FSK modems) are easier to design because discrimination between two frequencies is simpler than detection of phase changes. Thus, for medium-speed modems (1200–2400 bps), the FSK scheme is preferred. For higher speed transmission of 9600 bps phase modulation is more reliable. We described PSK with two phases, a phase of 0 to represent binary 0 and a phase of π to represent 1. We can use four phases $\pi/4$, $3\pi/4$, $5\pi/4$, and $7\pi/4$ to represent 00, 01, 11, and 10, respectively, of the input bit string. The carrier frequency is not changed. With this encoding, the transmission speed in bits per second can be doubled as 2 bits are sent for each phase change. Note that a single frequency is used, thereby conserving bandwidth. This modulation is known as 4 PSK as four phases are used. It is also known as Quadrature Phase Shift Keying (QPSK). Instead of four phases, we can use eight phases to represent groups of 3 bits, but detecting phase difference becomes more difficult. 8 PSK is combined with amplitude modulation (two levels) to represent groups of 4 bits, giving high-speed modems.

Another modulation scheme called Quadrature Modulation uses a Sine wave $Vc \sin(2f_c t)$ to represent a binary 1 and a Cosine wave $V_c \cos(2\pi f_c t)$ to represent a 0. It can be combined with amplitude modulation by using two amplitudes V_c and $2V_c$ for each wave to represent 00, 01, 10, and 11. This is called Quadrature Amplitude Modulation (QAM). Two amplitudes and two phases for the Sine and Cosine waves are used for modulation to represent strings of 4 bits. It is called 16 QAM and is used in Wi-Fi, cable modems, and mobile communication systems.

Modems have been standardized by CCITT (Consultative Committee for International Telephone and Telegraph). A recent modem standard is V.32bis, which has a speed of 14.4 Kbps on leased lines. In this modem, groups of 7 bits are coded using amplitude and phase. Recent modems called V.92 incorporate arithmetic error correction (using redundant codes) and data compression. They are capable of working at 56.6 Kbps on ordinary voice-grade telephone lines.

14.4.2 Half Duplex and Full Duplex Transmission

Terminal equipment such as modems may be designed to either transmit data on a transmission line or receive data from the line, but not both simultaneously. Such a system is called *half duplex* communication as explained in Section 14.2.2. If data can be sent and received simultaneously by the terminal equipment, then the communication is *full duplex.* If one pair of wires connects a terminal to a computer, the wire can send or receive data and operates in a half-duplex mode. If two independent pairs of wires are used, one for transmitting and the other for receiving, then the communication is a full duplex. In this case, data can be transmitted and received simultaneously.

One pair of wires may be used in full-duplex mode by a modem, provided four distinct frequencies (assuming FSK) are used. One pair of frequencies may represent 1 and 0 in one direction and another pair for the reverse direction. This method, however, requires large bandwidths if the transmission speeds in both directions are to be the same. If data transmission in one direction is slow, a lower bandwidth is sufficient. Typically, 4-wire full duplex modems are used on public telephone lines. 4 or 8 PSK using two frequencies can also be used for full-duplex communication on a pair of wires. Some recent modems standardized by CCITT (e.g., V.92) use this method and work at 56.6 Kbps. Much faster modems are now available. We will describe them in Sec. 14.4.4.

14.4.3 Asynchronous and Synchronous Transmission

Data may be sent on a transmission line in one of two modes. These are called *asynchronous* transmission mode and *synchronous* mode. In asynchronous transmission, data is transmitted character by character. At the beginning of a character, a start signal is sent. The nature of the start signal is standardized and is 'understood' by the receiving end equipment, which prepares to receive the coded character. The start signal is followed by the bits of the coded character. If ASCII code is used, the seven coded bits and a parity bit are sent. Following the character code is the stop signal (Figure 14.21).

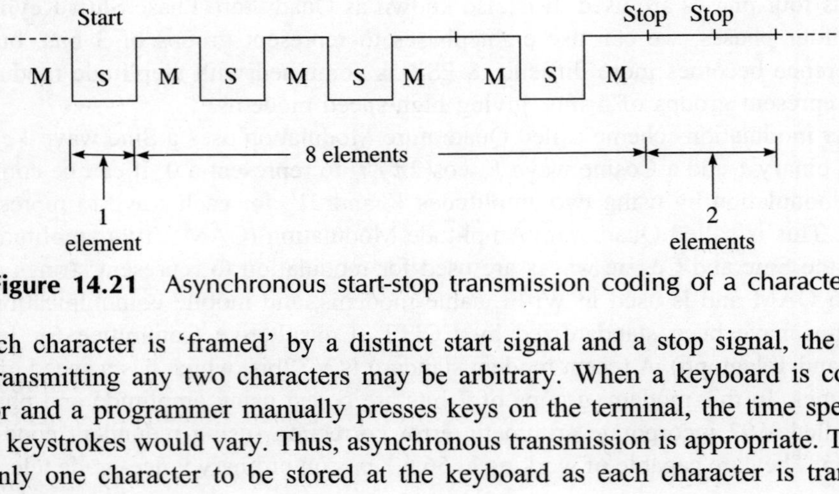

Figure 14.21 Asynchronous start-stop transmission coding of a character.

As each character is 'framed' by a distinct start signal and a stop signal, the time taken between transmitting any two characters may be arbitrary. When a keyboard is connected to a processor and a programmer manually presses keys on the terminal, the time spent between successive keystrokes would vary. Thus, asynchronous transmission is appropriate. This method requires only one character to be stored at the keyboard as each character is transmitted as soon as it is keyed in.

The main disadvantage of asynchronous transmission is that the transmission line connecting a remote terminal and a computer is idle during the time intervals between transmitting characters. If the lines are short, this is not bad because line cost would be low and idle time not expensive. The advantage of asynchronous transmission is that it does not require any local storage at the terminal or the remote computer and is thus cheaper to implement.

In synchronous data transmission, blocks of about 100 characters are sent at high speed on the transmission line connecting a sender and a receiver. This mode is particularly suitable for computer-to-computer communication. A distinctive synchronization pattern is sent at the beginning of a data block. This is used by the receiving device to set its clock in synchronism with the sending end clock. The synchronization pattern is followed by codes to identify the sender, the receiver, and the characters of the message. The number of characters in the message may be variable with an upper bound, which depends on the quality of the transmission line. The message is terminated by an end-of-message character followed by a check character to aid detection of any transmission error. The format of a data block for synchronous transmission is shown in Figure 14.22.

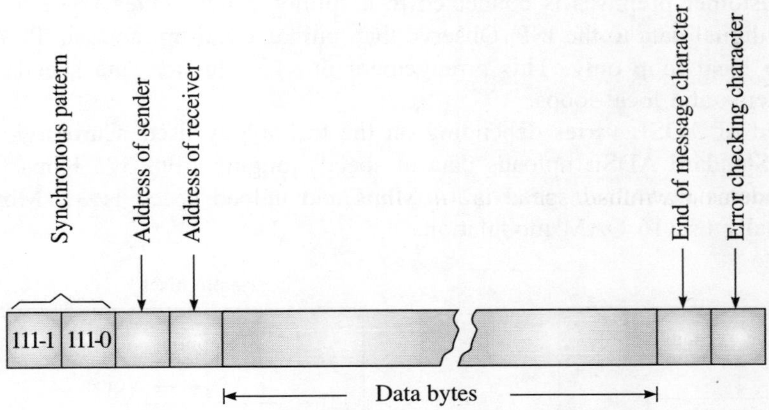

Figure 14.22 Typical format of a data block for synchronous communication.

The main advantage of synchronous transmission is the efficient utilization of the transmission line. The period between blocks is kept small and the block itself is sent at nearly the maximum line speed. The main disadvantage of synchronous transmission is the need for local buffer storage at the two ends of the communication line to assemble blocks and the need for accurately synchronizing the clocks at both ends.

14.4.4 Asymmetric Digital Subscriber Lines

The maximum speed available if modems are used to connect computers to ISPs using a telephone line is only 56.6 Kbps. The Cat 3 copper twisted pair local loop in a telephone system can transmit digital signals at much higher speeds in the Mbps range. The reason why telephone lines have a bandwidth of 3 kHz is because human voice signals have a bandwidth of 3 kHz and telephone companies installed filters to limit the bandwidth of the line. This is done to prevent phone conversations from being corrupted by noise at frequencies higher than the audio frequencies. With the demand for higher data speed for accessing the Internet to download multimedia data, telephone companies have responded with a technology called Asymmetric Digital Subscriber Lines (ADSL). The primary objectives of ADSL are as follows:

- It must work with existing Cat 3 UTP copper local loops.
- It must not affect the voice telephone service to the customers.
- It must give a data speed of tens of Mbps for downloading data from the Internet. The upload speed may be lower as most customers download a larger quantity of data than they upload.
- It must be on always, that is, it is not a dial-up line and the charges should either be a flat monthly rate or a monthly rate plus a charge for the volume of data transmitted.

An ADSL modem arrangement is shown in Figure 14.23. A device called a splitter is installed both at the telephone exchange and at the customer's premises. The splitter is a filter that separates the data to be transmitted or received by the computer from the voice used in telephone conversations. At the customer's premises, an ADSL modem is connected between the NIC of a computer and the splitter (see Figure 14.23). At the exchange end, the telephone line from a customer premises is connected to a splitter which routes voice to the telephone exchange and digital data to the ISP. Observe that, unlike a dial-up modem, the ADSL modem is used in the local loop only. This arrangement provides higher data speeds with existing telephone systems and local loops.

The speed of ADSL varies depending on the technology used. Currently, there are two technologies. Standard ADSL uploads data at speeds ranging from 375 Kbps to 3072 Kbps. ADSL 2+ modems download speed is 14 Mbps and upload speed is 3.5 Mbps. ADSL 2+ modems normally use 16 QAM modulation.

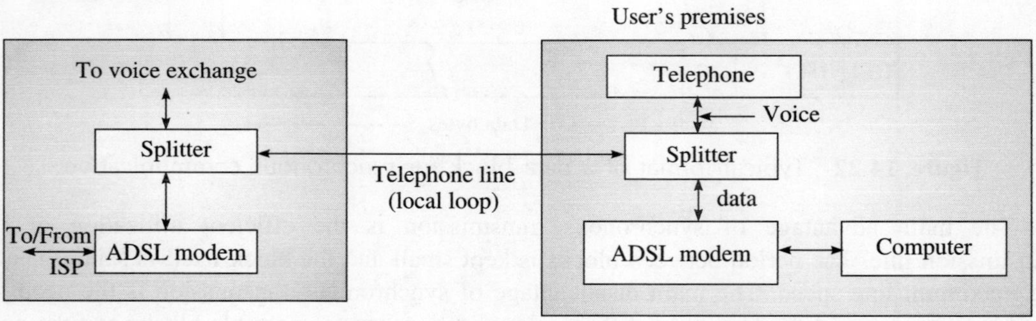

Figure 14.23 Asynchronous digital subscriber line.

14.5 CABLE MODEMS

The penetration of cable TV in India is quite high, particularly in small towns. Furthermore, the potential bandwidth available on coaxial cables provided by cable operators is quite high. A rough configuration of cable TV networks in urban areas of India is shown in Figure 14.24. One or more major operators have a group of antennas to receive several satellite channels. They, in turn, have franchisers in several localities to whom they send the programmes via fibre optic cables. The fibre cables terminate at the 'head-end' premises of the franchisers. The franchisers run coaxial cables (over treetops, terraces, etc.) to individual homes. These networks have potentially a large bandwidth (around 750 MHz), and thus several cable operators are providing broadband Internet connectivity to homes that is on always; that is, it is 24-hour service with no per minute usage charge for using the cable connection. The main problems to be solved are:

1. The cables are meant for one-way downloading of programs and are not designed to support two-way communication needed for Internet users.
2. As most franchisers in India string the cables carelessly and the connectors are of poor quality, special precautions are to be taken to alleviate noise.
3. The head-end operator and franchisers require uninterrupted power which is often not available and the entire cable network becomes non-functional.
4. A single cable is shared by a large number of houses (around 100). Thus, the available bandwidth has to be shared.

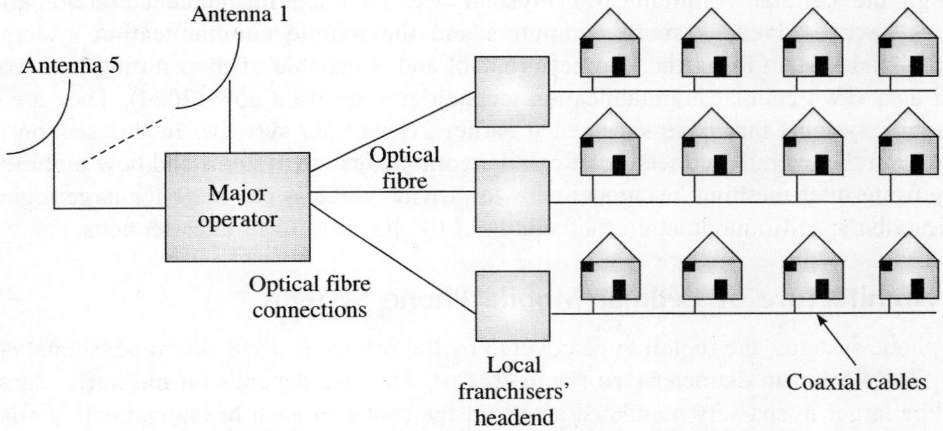

Figure 14.24 Configuration of cable TV network.

To provide two-way communications and alleviate noise, a *cable modem* should be installed at each subscriber's premises. An appropriate system is also needed at the head end. The bandwidth available on a coaxial cable and its allocation is shown in Figure 14.25.

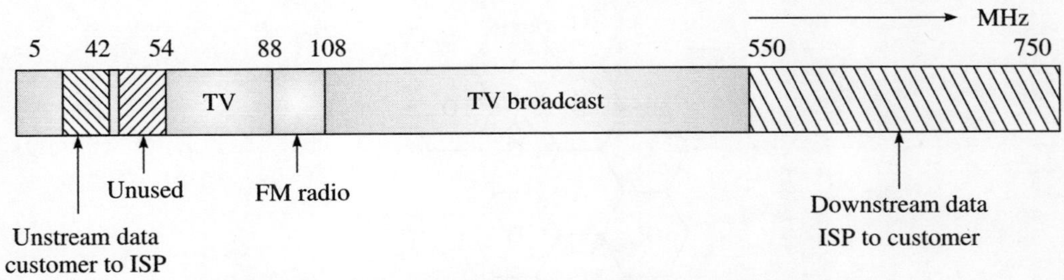

Figure 14.25 Allocation of bandwidth in TV cable.

Cable modem specifications have not been standardized by IEEE or ISO and thus differ between manufacturers. One design uses QPSK for upstream traffic (home to ISP), giving approximately 9 Mbps rate. As the cable is shared by many users, each user is allocated time for 1 packet of 8 bytes each for upstream. Downstream uses QAM (quadrature phase and amplitude modulation) called QAM-64. It provides 27 Mbps per user and allocates 184 bytes packets per user.

14.6 CELLULAR COMMUNICATION SYSTEMS

In Section 14.4, we saw how the PSTN system primarily intended for voice communication has evolved to allow digital communication. Another important development that has taken place during the last decades is the emergence of a cellular or mobile communication system, which is a wireless system. The primary objective of a mobile communication system is to allow customers to use mobile phones that connect to other mobile phone users anywhere anytime. Even though the cellular communication system was intended for voice communication, smartphones have evolved as small computers and the mobile communication system is currently a digital system using the Internet Protocol and is capable of transmitting both voice and digital data. Two cellular communication technologies are used now (2024). They are 4G and 5G mobile systems that have superseded earlier 2G and 3G systems. In this section, we will first explain the overall architecture of cellular communication systems and how mobility is ensured by using inter-meshing hexagonal cells to provide wireless coverage for large regions. We will describe specific modulation methods used by 4G and 5G in later sections.

14.6.1 Architecture of Cellular Mobile Phone Systems

In mobile phone systems, the region to be covered by the service is divided into hexagonal cells that are typically 5 km in diameter (see Figure 14.26). The size depends on the traffic density and would be larger in sparsely populated areas. At the centre of each hexagonal cell is a *base transceiver station* (BS) which sends and receives data to or from the mobile phones within its range. The cell shape is hexagonal as the distance between the centres of neighbouring hexagons is constant. This property is useful to ensure easy handoff, that is, transfer of control of a

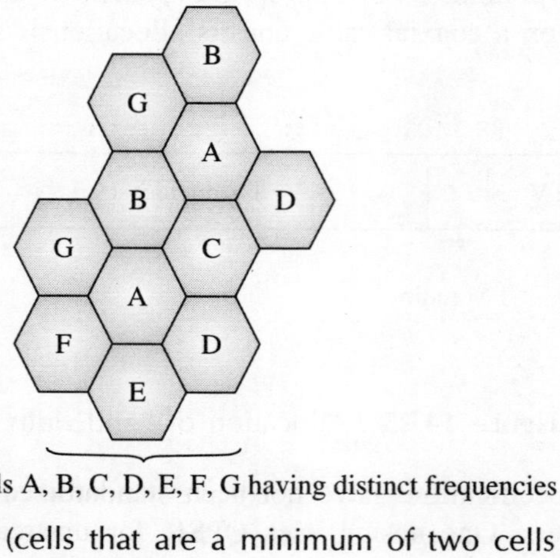

Figure 14.26 Cellular structure (cells that are a minimum of two cells away use the same frequencies).

mobile phone from one cell to an appropriate adjacent cell when the user of the mobile phone moves from one location to another. The base station has several antennas, a controller, and a set of transceivers, one transceiver for each channel assigned to that cell. All the Base Stations (known as enodeB in 4G and gnodeB in 5G) in mobile systems are connected to an Evolved Packet Core (EPC) unit usually by a high-speed transport network (typically fibre optic cables or microwave links). All information transported is based on packet communication including interactive voice calls and video conferencing and nonreal-time data transfers such as files. For compatibility with the Internet all packet communication is carried over the IP protocol stack.

The architecture of a mobile communication system is shown in Figure 4.27. In this figure the landline connecting PSTN and EPC has a packet voice gateway (not explicitly shown). This gateway packetizes voice signal which flows via the Internet to EPC. (Landlines and PSTNs are gradually disappearing)

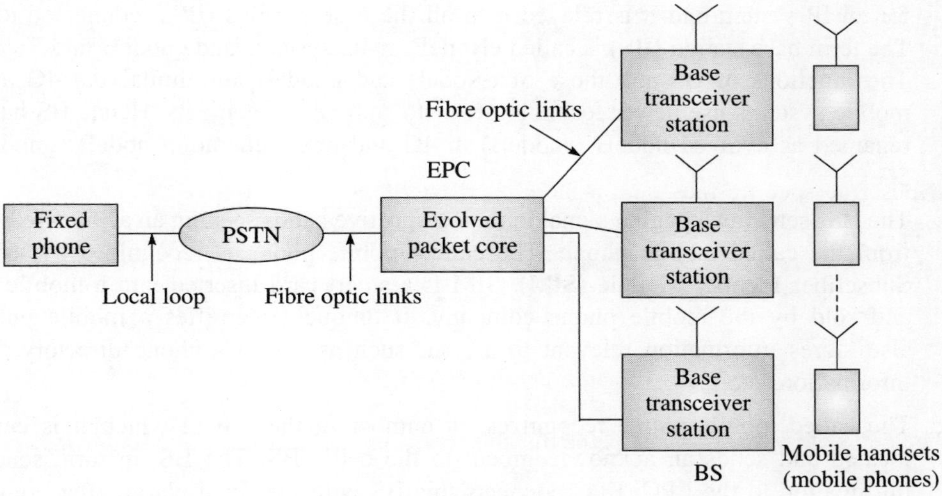

Figure 14.27 Architecture of mobile communication system.

The major functions of the Evolved Packet Core are to:

(i) Connect a fixed phone which may be circuit switched to an IP-based mobile phone.

(ii) Connect two mobile phones while they move without interruption and manage the session.

(iii) Ensure end-to-end IP connectivity to various applications including Internet access.

(iv) Monitor the calls in progress, charge for use, and ensure Quality of Service.

(v) Ensure security of communications.

EPCs are all digital as the current mobile communication systems are packet switched, use IP, and are integrated with IP networks.

Before describing how a mobile phone and a fixed phone are connected, as well as how two mobile phones are connected, we will have to understand how channels are allocated to mobile phones when they want to communicate. The most expensive resource in a mobile phone system is the electromagnetic spectrum allocated to mobile phone companies. Bands of frequencies are auctioned to cell phone companies by the government which has to be used judiciously by the companies to support as many mobile subscribers as possible.

As mobile phones have limited power (due to their small size and the need to conserve battery life), their transmission has a limited range and thus the sizes of cells are small (a few km and smaller in crowded areas). Thus, a sub-band of frequencies allocated to a cell can be reused in other cells not in their immediate vicinity. This frequency reuse is an important feature of the cellular communication system. We will now explain how a connection between two phones is established in a cellular system. There are two cases we consider. One is connecting a fixed to a mobile phone and vice versa. The other is connecting two mobile phones. The following steps are followed in the first case.

***Case 1:* Calling a mobile phone from a fixed phone**

Step 1: A fixed phone calls a mobile phone. The voice signal is converted to packets suitable for an IP system and it is relayed it to all the base stations (BSs) connected to EPC. The term base station (BS) is called eNodeB in 4G systems and gnodeB in 5G systems. The functions of BS and those of eNodeB and gnodeB are similar but 4G and 5G mobile systems use newer technologies with some enhancements. Hence BS has been renamed as evolved nodeB (enodeB) in 4G and next generation nodeB (gnodeB) in 5G.

Step 2: The BSs send out a paging signal in their respective bands seeking an acknowledgement from the called mobile phone. The called mobile phone is recognized by using its Subscriber Identity Module (SIM). SIM is a smart card inserted into a mobile phone and sold by the mobile phone company. It uniquely identifies a mobile phone. It also stores information relevant to a user, such as a user's phone directory, billing information, etc.

Step 3: The called mobile phone recognizes its number in the cell in which it is currently located and sends an acknowledgment to the cell's BS. The BS, in turn, sends this information to the EPC. EPC connects this BS with the fixed phone after converting audio packets to a circuit switched mode appropriate for PSTN. It also allocates a free channel to BS to communicate with the mobile phone.

Step 4: If the mobile phone moves away from the cell whose BS established the connection, it picks up a new signal from the BS into whose domain it has shifted. This BS now allocates a channel to the mobile phone and connects it to the EPC. This is called handoff from one BS to another.

The above procedure is for a call from a fixed phone to a mobile phone. If a mobile phone wants to call a fixed phone, it connects with the BS whose signal is strongest and this is connected to the EPC. The EPC assigns a channel to the mobile phone if it finds that the fixed phone is free to receive a call. It converts the audio packets to signals suitable for landline. Else it sends a busy tone. If the mobile phone moves during a call, the procedure explained in Step 4 above is followed.

***Case 2:* Calling a mobile phone from another mobile phone**

The EPC manages the transmission of voice packets between mobile phones as the system is IP-based. The steps followed for making calls from one mobile phone to another mobile phone are as follows:

Step 1: A mobile phone subscriber who wants to call another mobile phone subscriber turns on the phone. It senses wireless signals available on various frequencies and picks the strongest one. It then selects the BS sending this signal as its base.

Step 2: The selected BS forwards the called mobile number to the EPC. The EPC relays this to all the Base Stations. These BSs send paging signals in their respective bands seeking an acknowledgment from the called mobile number.

Step 3: If the mobile number called is ON, it picks up the paging signal and sends an acknowledgment to the BS in whose cell it is currently located.

Step 4: The BS sends this information to the EPC which connects the BSs of the two mobiles so that conversation can proceed. If in Step 3 no acknowledgment is received by any BS owing to the called mobile being switched off, busy, or out of range, this information is sent to the EPC which relays this information to the calling mobile via its BS.

Step 5: If any one or both mobile phones move from their current cells, a procedure similar to that described in Step 4 of the previous procedure, namely, a fixed phone calling a mobile phone, is followed. All the above steps take place fast and once a connection is established, it is maintained regardless of any movement of the mobile phones and without any obvious disruption of the ongoing conversation.

14.7 OVERVIEW OF 4G—LTE TECHNOLOGY

The early mobile technologies used by mobile communication systems were called 2G and 3G. They used communication systems known as GSM and CDMA which are now obsolete. A group of standards organizations called the 3rd Generation Partnership Project (3GPP) evolved a new standard for mobile communication called Long Term Evolution (LTE). It is often called a 4G mobile system although it does not meet all the specifications set by the International Telecommunication Union.

The electromagnetic spectrum is a scarce resource. It is controlled by the government and bandwidth in the spectrum is auctioned. The bands for 4G range from 600 MHz to 2.6 GHz. This range is divided into around 25 bands of varying widths. Usually, operators buy one or more bands, usually 20 MHz bandwidth.

The key technologies used by 4G - LTE are:

1. It is a fully digital system and uses the TCP/IP protocol for communicating multimedia data. It uses the IPv6 standard that has a large IP address space.
2. It uses Orthogonal Frequency Division Multiplexing (OFDM) for wireless data transmission. This method divides the radio spectrum into multiple sub-carriers that optimize transmission under varying conditions. We will describe OFDM in the next section.
3. Its Transmitters and Receivers use multiple antennas to improve signal strength and data transmission reliability. Multiple antennas and receivers use multiple independent

paths to send and receive signals thereby improving signal strength and reliability. This is called Multiple Input Multiple Output (MIMO).

4. It combines different frequency bands within an allocated band to increase the overall speed. This technique is called Carrier Aggregation.

The key features of 4G - LTE are:

1. Theoretically, it is designed to allow users to download data at speeds up to 300 Mbps and upload data at speeds up to 75 Mbps. In practice, however, the speeds are more realistically about 150 Mbps download and 40 Mbps upload.
2. Theoretically, it is expected to have a latency of 10ms but in practice, it is around 50 to 100 ms.
3. It supports a flexible bandwidth option from 1.4 MHz to 20 MHz depending on environmental conditions to modulate data and transmit it.

14.8 ORTHOGONAL FREQUENCY DIVISION MULTIPLEX (OFDM)

4G mobile communication systems use Orthogonal Frequency Division Multiplexing to modulate digital data for transmission. OFDM simultaneously transmits multiple data streams over closely spaced subcarriers. It significantly enhances data throughput and uses the radio spectrum efficiently. It also alleviates interference of transmitted data travelling along several paths from the transmitter to the receiver.

The following steps are used in OFDM by the transmitter to send a stream of bits.

Transmitter end

1. The incoming serial data stream is converted into a set of parallel data streams.
2. Each parallel data stream is modulated by around 1000 orthogonal subcarriers each of bandwidth around 15 KHz using 16 QAM or 16 PSK scheme. The modulation scheme may be chosen dynamically based on the communication channel conditions. We have explained 16 QAM and PSK in Sec. 14.4.1.
3. The quadrature-modulated signal of each subcarrier is combined and converted into one serial time-domain signal by Inverse Fast Fourier Transform (IFFT).
4. In wireless transmission, the radiated electromagnetic signal arrives from the transmitter to the receiver along different paths including reflections from obstructions. The signals along various paths are not uniform. Some fade more than others. This is called the multipath fading problem. This would lead to inter-symbol interference. To mitigate this a copy of the last part of the time domain signal called a cyclic prefix is added to its beginning. This is also called guard interval.
5. This time signal is appropriately transformed for transmission as a radio signal on the communication channel.

Receiver end

1. The transmitted radio signal is sensed by the receiver and demodulated.
2. The cyclic prefix is removed from the received signal.

3. The time domain signal is converted to the frequency domain using Fast Fourier Transform (FFT). The subcarrier of each user is separated.
4. The modulated data of each subcarrier is demodulated and the original parallel bit streams are recovered.
5. The parallel data streams are serialized to obtain the original bit stream with which we started.

The primary advantages of OFDM are:

1. It efficiently uses the available bandwidth by employing orthogonal subcarriers.
2. The problem arising from multipath propagation delays is alleviated by using a lower symbol rate per subcarrier.
3. It allows the employment of different modulation schemes by different subcarriers based on the conditions of the communication channels.
4. It vastly increased the number of bits/second that can be transmitted over a given bandwidth.

OFDM is used widely in several systems besides LTE-4G. It is the standard in Wi-Fi. It is also used in digital TV transmission and ADSL modems.

14.9 5G MOBILE COMMUNICATION SYSTEM

5G mobile communication has been allotted three frequency bands. The low band is from 600 MHz to 1 GHz, the mid band is 1 to 6 GHz, and the high band is from 24 GHz to 40 GHz. In India and many countries 5G operators have bought 5G bands in the low and mid bands in 2023. In the 25 GHz band, the wavelength of wireless data is a few mm. It is difficult and expensive to design systems in this short wavelength. Most of the features quoted for 5G are available only at this high-frequency band. In the midband (around 3 GHz) 5G systems have better data download speed and lower latency than 4G systems. Operators normally buy 20 MHz to 100 MHz in the midband.

The ideal 5G system using the 25 GHz band has the following features:

1. Data download speed up to 20 Gbps and upload speed 10 Gbps.
2. Low latency up to 1 ms.
3. Supports up to a million devices per square km.
4. High speed mobility up to 500 km/h
5. Low energy consumption.

The fast speed and low latency are necessary for playing interactive games and to design Virtual Reality systems. 5G supporting a large number of devices is necessary to design the Internet of Things (IoT). The high speed and low latency are also very useful for controlling driverless vehicles using mobile devices.

In 5G systems using the midband (around 3 GHz) the download speed is between 700 Mbps and 1 Gbps and the upload speed is between 100 Mbps and 300 Mbps. The latency is between 5 ms and 20 ms.

The technology of the 5G system is similar to the 4G system. The major differences are:

1. 5G uses Orthogonal Frequency Division Multiple Access (OFDMA) which is a refined version of OFDM. It supports multiple users by dynamically allocating subcarriers

to different users depending on their needs. The network efficiency is improved by allowing simultaneous data transmission from multiple devices.

2. The MIMO used in 5G uses arrays of dozens of antennas. Massive MIMO use increases the capacity and throughput as it enables simultaneous connections to several users without compromising performance.
3. 5G incorporates Multi-user MIMO (MU-MIMO). This allows beamforming, which directs signals towards specific users. This improves signal quality and reduces interference.

14.10 WIRELESS LAN

In the previous sections, we described cellular wireless communication systems that transmit data wirelessly between mobile phones. Even though mobile communication systems were originally designed for voice communication 4G and 5G systems are all digital and are used to communicate between smartphones spread over a large geographical area. In other words, it is a Wide Area Network (WAN). The question that arises is whether the wireless technology used in a WAN could be used in a LAN. The answer is yes. The cellular radio technology used by mobile phones has been adapted to communicate between mobile laptop computers and stationary Local Networks. This is called Wi-Fi. The major difference is that in a local network, we do not require the elaborate infrastructure consisting of Base Stations, EPS, etc. used in a cellular network as the distance between a mobile computer and a fixed network with which it communicates is not more than a few hundred metres.

To wirelessly communicate between a mobile computer and a fixed LAN, the mobile computer should have a transceiver (a combination of a wireless transmitter and receiver) and the LAN must have a wireless hot spot with a transceiver to transmit and receive data from the mobile computer (see Figure 14.28).

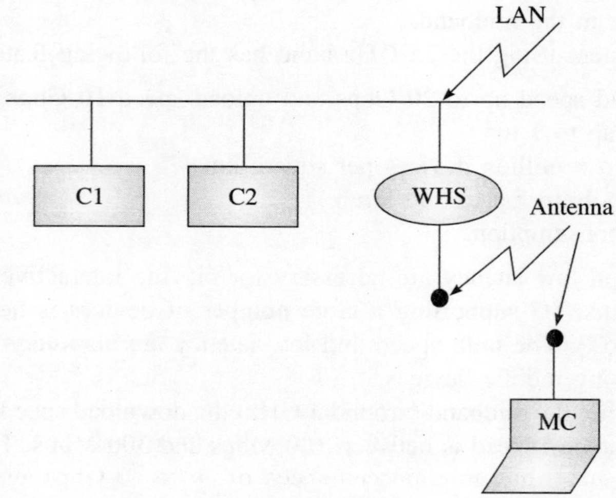

Figure 14.28 Mobile computer and wireless hot spots. C1, C2, fixed computers; WHS, wireless hot spot; MC, mobile computer.

The system used for wireless communication in a local area is called Wi-Fi. Wi-Fi is a brand name adopted by a consortium of around half a dozen companies that standardized their wireless systems based on the IEEE 802.11 series of standards in 1997. The modulation scheme used by early Wi-Fi systems was OFDM (see Section 14.8). The input signal is transmitted (at a low power level) using several subcarriers. OFDM alleviates problems of multipath transmission due to reflection from walls and other objects. It is currently succeeded by OFDMA for high-speed Wi-Fi systems.

There are currently four standards for Wi-Fi; IEEE 802.11n (Wi-Fi 4), IEEE 802.11ac (Wi-Fi 5), IEEE 802.11ax (Wi-Fi 6), a variation of IEEE 802.11 ax (Wi-Fi 6E). IEEE 802.11be (Wi-Fi 7) was released in 2024. IEEE 802.11 family of standards use a carrier in the unlicensed 2.4, 5, and 6 GHz bands and transmit data at rates up to 46 Gbps.

Normally a wireless modem/router in a fixed spot (called wireless hot spot) is available at airports, hotels, etc. that are connected to ISPs to access the Internet. This hot spot may be accessed from a mobile device with a built-in wireless transceiver. Laptop computers, tablet computers, and smartphones have built-in wireless transceivers and can access these hot spots. This is one of the most common uses of Wi-Fi. All these devices share a common broadcast medium to communicate with the modem/router. As explained in Sec 13.4 they use the CSMA/CA protocol for communication. Desktop computers, laptops, and smartphones at home are connected nowadays to a Wi-Fi modem cum router which allows them to connect to an ISP.

In Table 14.3, the five IEEE wireless data transmission standards are compared.

Table 14.3 Chart Comparing IEEE Wi-Fi standards

	802.11n	802.11ac	802.11ax	802.11ax	802.11be
Maximum data rate (Gbps)	0.6	3.5	9.6	9.6	46
RF band (GHz)	2.4, 5	5	2.4, 5	2.4, 5, 6	2.4, 5, 6
Modulation	OFDM	OFDM	OFDMA	OFDMA	OFDMA
Name	Wi-Fi 4	Wi-Fi 5	Wi-Fi 6 0	Wi-Fi	Wi-Fi 7

Recently another wireless system called WiGig was adopted by the industry and standardized by IEEE as IEEE 802.11ad. It is used for wireless transmission of massive amounts of data between devices in one room with no obstacles between them. The line-of-sight distance allowed between them is 1–10 m. It operates in the license-free 60 GHz band. The mid-frequency of this band is 60.48 GHz with a bandwidth of 2.16 GHz. This is a microwave frequency, and thus a specially designed beam-forming directional antenna is required to transmit data. It is normally used to transfer massive amounts of data such as HDTV video from a device to a computer. It is also used in gaming and Virtual Reality. The modulation method is OFDM. The data transmission rate varies between 700 Mbps to 7 Gbps.

A successor to IEEE 802.11ad is IEEE 802.11ay. It is also a line-of-sight system using the 60 GHz band. It has a longer range from 300 to 500 metres. It uses a MU MIMO antenna system to form a beam. It has an enhanced speed of up to 40 Gbps and low latency.

14.11 PERSONAL AREA NETWORK—BLUETOOTH

In the previous section, we described Wireless Local Area Networks. The range of such networks is a few hundred metres. If there is a shorter connection of a few metres, for example, connecting a mouse to a desktop or a laptop computer or connecting a headphone to a smartphone without wires, a different standard is used. As the distance between devices to be connected is small, such networks are called Personal Area Networks. The most popular standard for such networks is called Bluetooth. It was originally suggested by a Swedish company Ericsson in 1994. Later around 400 companies joined Ericsson to develop and improve the standard. The name Bluetooth is unusual. It was named after a Danish king Harald Blatand who united several countries in Scandinavia; the standard similarly united several competing specifications. His surname Blatand roughly translates to Bluetooth. This standard was later modified as the IEEE 802.15.1-2005 standard. The standard is envisaged as a wireless replacement of cables to connect portable and fixed electronic devices. The standard specifies three ranges: 100 m (long range, high power (100 mW), 10 m (ordinary range, normal power (2.5 mW), and 10 cm (short range, low power (1 mW). Bluetooth operates in the unlicensed ISM (2.4 GHz) band. It is particularly effective for short distances (1 or 2 m) and noisy environments in which many other devices operate. It uses Frequency Hopping Spread Spectrum technology (FHSS) as the modulation scheme for wireless transmission. FHSS switches the carrier frequency over a wide band in a random sequence known only to the sender and the receiver. This method enhances security and avoids interference from other signals by hopping to a new frequency after transmitting or receiving a data packet. Bluetooth uses 79 hops, starting at 2.402 GHz with a displacement of 1 MHz between hops and ending at 2.480 GHz. The duration of each hop is 625 ms. The payload of each packet is specified as 2745 bits. Devices using the same Bluetooth channel are said to be part of a piconet that has one master and one or more slaves. The master starts transmission in a time slot and the next slot is used by a slave. Other slaves transmit in odd-numbered time slots. The digital signals are modulated using FSK. Early versions allowed a data rate of about 720 Kbps but later versions have enhanced data rates of 3 Mbps.

SUMMARY

1. Communication channels required to interconnect computers may be classified as analog channels or digital channels. Analog channels are designed to transmit continuously varying signals, whereas digital channels transmit two levels of voltages.
2. An analog channel is characterized by its bandwidth. The bandwidth specifies the range of frequencies of sinusoidal waves which the channel can transmit without attenuation. The larger the bandwidth, the higher is its capacity to carry information.
3. The bandwidth available in a channel may be utilized to send several independent signals. This is called multiplexing. Three types of multiplexing are commonly used. They are Space Division Multiplexing (SDM), Frequency Division Multiplexing (FDM), and Time Division Multiplexing (TDM).
4. In Space Division Multiplexing (SDM), several signals are sent sharing a space. An example is using multiple antenna pairs to send/receive wireless signals.

5. In Frequency Division Multiplexing (FDM), the bandwidth of a channel is shared by a number of independent signals. This is done by modulating these independent signals (e.g., telephone conversations) by several high frequency carrier signals.
6. In Time Division Multiplexing (TDM), each user is given a specific time slot during which he/she can use the entire bandwidth of the channel.
7. The capacity of a channel to carry digital signals is specified by the maximum number of bits per second (bps) that can be reliably transmitted via the channel.
8. Physical communication media may be classified as bounded or unbounded media. Twisted pair of wires, coaxial cables, and fibre optic cables are examples of bounded media. Radio, microwave, and satellite communication are examples of unbounded media.
9. An unshielded twisted pair of wires (called UTP) is an inexpensive medium used in voice-grade telephone lines. Cat 5 UTP may be used for the transmission of signals up to 100 Mbps.
10. Coaxial cables have a wide bandwidth of the order of 500 MHz. They are used in long-distance telephony and in cable TV.
11. Fibre optic cables are plastic or glass fibres and provide high-quality transmission of signals at very high rates, up to 1 Gbps.
12. Wireless media are called unbounded. Figure 14.12 shows the classification of a variety of media and Table 14.2 specifies the frequency bands used in various applications.
13. Microwaves are used for wide bandwidth and line-of-sight communication. Rates of transmission up to 250 Mbps are possible with this medium.
14. Communication satellites are microwave relay stations in the sky. Transponders on the satellite are used to receive, amplify, and retransmit signals sent from an earth station. The main advantage of a communication satellite is its wide coverage of a large area, and it may be used from inaccessible locations. A transponder has very large capacity and can transmit data at speeds up to hundreds of Mbps.
15. Computers separated by a few metres (in the same room with no intervening obstacles) can communicate using infrared light (1000–3000 MHz) at a speed of around 50 Mbps.
16. To communicate between computers located a few kilometres apart, voice-grade public telephone lines may be used. Digital signals are modulated and converted into sine waves by a modulator and transmitted on a transmission line. The received signals are converted to digital signals by a demodulator. As the computers at the two ends of the line have to both send and receive signals, a modulator-demodulator pair known as modem is used at both ends.
17. Currently, modems called V.92 have been made using phase shift keying, error correction, and data compression. They are capable of a speed of 56.6 Kbps on ordinary telephone lines.
18. A communication channel that allows a computer to receive data or send data but not both simultaneously is called a half-duplex channel. A channel that allows a computer to receive and send data simultaneously is called a full duplex channel.
19. When data are sent character by character and each character is framed by independent start and stop signals, the transmission is called asynchronous.

20. In synchronous transmission, blocks of about 100 characters are sent at high speed. A distinct synchronizing pattern is sent at the beginning of each block.

21. The telephone lines laid by PSTN are UTP cables and are capable of transmitting digital signals up to 14 Mbps with appropriate technology. A technology called Asynchronous Digital Subscriber Line (ADSL) is introduced by PSTNs. It uses two devices called a splitter, which separates voice signals from digital data, and an ADSL modem, which acts as an interface between the splitter and a user's computer. In an ADSL modem, the data upload speed to an ISP is lower than the data download speed. DSL modems are symmetric and their data upload and download speeds are the same.

22. The widespread availability of cable TV makes TV coaxial cable an attractive communication medium to connect a user's PC with an ISP. TV cable uses a broadcast mode, whereas duplex communication is needed with an ISP. This is achieved by using a cable modem at the user's premises. The cable modem uses frequencies outside the TV broadcast band for duplex communication.

23. Wireless communication is now becoming very important as it provides anytime, anywhere connection to both computers and telephones.

24. Wireless communication also uses the three types of multiplexing that we described earlier. This allows the precious wireless spectrum to be used optimally.

25. Wireless communication channels can transmit only analog data. Thus, digital data is modulated before transmission. Frequency Shift Keying (FSK) used in modems is modified to utilize the available bandwidth efficiently. The modulation methods used are 16 QAM and PSK.

26. Currently, mobile phones have become very popular. The number of mobile phones has overtaken fixed phones. Mobile phones are capable of providing voice communication and also digital messaging service.

27. Two major systems for mobile communication are currently in use. They are called 4G -LTE and 5G.

28. 4G LTE mobile communication is a fully digital system. Data is communicated using the Internet Protocol. It uses the Orthogonal Frequency Division Multiplexing for modulation. It is capable of data download speed of up to 150 Mbps and upload speed up to 40 bps. It's latency is between 50 and 100 ms. It uses the 600 MHz to 2.6 GHz band.

29. Orthogonal Frequency Division Multiplexing is used to modulate digital data for transmission in 4G mobile and Wi-Fi wireless systems. OFDM simultaneously transmits multiple data streams over closely spaced subcarriers. It significantly enhances data throughput and uses the radio spectrum efficiently. It also alleviates interference of transmitted data travelling along multiple paths from the transmitter to the receiver.

30. 5G mobile communication has been allotted three frequency bands. The low band is from 600 MHz to 1 GHz, the mid band 1 to 6 GHz, and the high band is from 24 GHz to 40 GHz. In India and many countries 5G operators have bought 5G bands in the low and mid bands in 2023. In the 25 GHz band, the wavelength of wireless data is a few mm. It is difficult and expensive to design systems in this short wavelength. Most of the features quoted for 5G are available only at this high frequency band.

31. 5G uses Orthogonal Frequency Division Multiple Access (OFDMA) which is a refined version of OFDM. It supports multiple users by dynamically allocating subcarriers to different users depending on their need. The overall network efficiency is improved by allowing simultaneous transmission of data from multiple devices. The MIMO used in 5G uses arrays of dozens of antennas. Use of massive MIMO increases the capacity and throughput as it enables simultaneous connections to several users without compromising performance.

32. In 5G systems using the midband (around 3 GHz) the download speed is between 700 Mbps and 1 Gbps and the upload speed is between 100 Mbps and 300 Mbps. The latency is between 5ms to 20 ms.

33. Wireless communication may be used to communicate between LANs and mobile laptop or tablet computers. A wireless transceiver called a wireless hot spot is connected to the LAN. The mobile computer also has a built-in transceiver. The wireless transmission uses the unlicensed 2.4, 5, or 6 GHz band. IEEE has standardized the wireless transmission protocols as IEEE 802.11 series of protocols. In Table 14.3, we summarize the characteristics of these standards.

34. For transferring a huge amount of data over short distance (line of sight) by wireless transmission, a standard called WiGig (IEEE 802.11ad) is available. This standard uses the 60 GHz unlicensed band. Using this standard, data can be transferred at a maximum rate of 7 Gbps.

35. For transmitting data by wireless over short distances such as from a keyboard to a computer or from a headphone to a smart mobile phone, a technology called Bluetooth is used. Bluetooth uses the 2.4 GHz band and low power. It uses frequency hopping spread spectrum technology and can transfer data at a maximum speed of 3 Mbps.

REVIEW QUESTIONS

14.1 What do you understand by the terms analog channel and digital channel?

14.2 How is the capacity of an analog channel specified?

14.3 Define the terms low cut-off frequency, high cut-off frequency, and bandwidth of an analog channel.

14.4 What are the characteristics of a voice-grade telephone line?

14.5 What do you understand by the terms baseband transmission and carrier modulated transmission?

14.6 Describe how a signal is amplitude-modulated and demodulated.

14.7 Why is modulation used in signal transmission?

14.8 How do you specify the capacity of a digital channel?

14.9 Why are channels multiplexed for signal transmission?

14.10 What is space division multiplexing?

14.11 What is Frequency Division Multiplexing (FDM)?

14.12 Give an example of FDM.

14.13 How are voice signals frequency division multiplexed in a wideband channel?

14.14 Describe the characteristics of FDM transmission via a channel.

14.15 What is a modem?

14.16 What is Phase Shift Keying (PSK)?

14.17 What is Quadrature PSK?

14.18 What is 8 PSK and how is it useful in designing high-speed modems?

14.19 What is 16 QAM and how is it useful in designing high-speed modems?

14.20 What is Time Division Multiplexing (TDM)?

14.21 Can TDM be used for digital channels?

14.22 Explain the operation of a TDM channel.

14.23 Explain the differences between FDM and TDM.

14.24 What is a bounded communication medium?

14.25 What is an unbounded communication medium?

14.26 What is a twisted pair? What is the maximum speed of Cat 3 and Cat 5 UTP?

14.27 What is a coaxial cable? What is the typical bandwidth of a coaxial cable?

14.28 What is the capacity of typical coaxial cables for digital transmission?

14.29 What is a fibre optic cable? What is the bandwidth of a typical fibre optic cable?

14.30 What is the typical digital speed of a fibre optic cable?

14.31 How is data transmitted via a fibre optic cable?

14.32 Give some examples of unbounded media.

14.33 What are the frequency bands used by various applications of wireless media?

14.34 What types of wireless systems are used for long-distance communication?

14.35 What are the advantages and disadvantages of infrared wireless communication?

14.36 Explain how microwaves can be used for computer-to-computer communication.

14.37 What are the advantages and disadvantages of using microwave communication?

14.38 Explain how communication satellites may be used for communication.

14.39 What are the advantages of using a communication satellite?

14.40 What is a transponder?

14.41 What is the typical bandwidth available per satellite transponder?

14.42 How many and at what speeds can digital signals be normally transmitted via a satellite?

14.43 When are public telephone lines used to connect a terminal to a computer?

14.44 What is the normal speed of transmission of voice signals on a telephone line?

14.45 Why are modems necessary when telephone lines are used for digital data communication?

14.46 What are the modulation methods used to modulate digital data?

14.47 Explain the term frequency shift keying.

14.48 What do you understand by the terms half-duplex transmission and full-duplex transmission?

14.49 Is full duplex transmission essential for computer-to-computer communication?

14.50 What is asynchronous transmission?

14.51 What are the advantages of asynchronous transmission?

14.52 What is synchronous transmission?

14.53 What are the advantages of synchronous transmission?

14.54 What is ADSL? What are the primary objectives of ADSL?

14.55 Explain how ADSL improves the speed of digital communication in a PSTN.

14.56 What is a cable modem? What are the advantages of using a cable modem? What are the disadvantages?

14.57 What are the multiplexing methods available in wireless communication?

14.58 Give an example of space division multiplexing in wireless.

14.59 Describe frequency division multiplexing in wireless. Give an example.

14.60 What is time division multiplexing in wireless communication? Can it be combined with frequency division multiplexing?

14.61 What cellular communication technologies are used in India?

14.62 Why should digital data be modulated using systems such as 16 QAM in wireless communication?

14.63 What are the various modulation methods used in wireless communication?

14.64 What is PSK? How is it different from FSK?

14.65 What is the general architecture of a cellular telephone system?

14.66 What is EPC? What is a Base Station? What are their functions?

14.67 How is communication established between a mobile phone and a fixed phone and vice versa?

14.68 How is communication established between two mobile phones?

14.69 What is cellular structure in a mobile phone system? Why are hexagonal cells used?

14.70 What is frequency reuse in mobile phones? Explain how it is done.

14.71 What multiplexing method is used in 4G - LTE? What are the up and downlink speeds of 4G -LTE?

14.72 What are the frequency bands allocated to the 4G mobile communication system?

14.73 What is the bandwidth usually purchased by 4G mobile operators?

14.74 Explain how OFDM works.

14.75 Briefly explain why multiple carriers are used in OFDM.

14.76 Explain why quadrature amplitude modulation is used in OFDM.

14.77 Explain how the 5G mobile communication system functions.

14.78 What are the advantages of the 5G compared to the 4G -LTE? What are its disadvantages?

14.79 What are the uplink and downlink speeds of the 5G mobile system?

14.80 What is the latency of the 5G system?

14.81 What are the frequency bands allocated for the 5G? What is the most commonly used band in 2023?

14.82 What is MIMO? Why is it used in the 4G and the 5G?

14.83 Compare the 4G and the 5G systems' features.

14.84 What is Wi-Fi? When is it used? Does it use unlicensed or licensed wireless frequency?

14.85 What are the differences between IEEE 802.11n, IEEE 802.11ac, IEEE 802.11ax, and IEEE 802.11be standards?

14.86 What wireless modulation technique is used by the IEEE 802.11ac standard?

14.87 What is WiGig? When is it used? What are its advantages and disadvantages?

14.88 What wireless frequency band does WiGig use? What are the advantages and disadvantages of using this wireless band? Is it an unlicensed band?

14.89 What is Bluetooth? When is it used? How does it compare with Wi-Fi?

14.90 What modulation technique is used by Bluetooth? What is the advantage of using this?

14.91 What frequency band is used by Bluetooth? Is it a licensed band? What is the speed at which data can be sent when Bluetooth is used?

14.92 How can a mobile communication system be used to connect mobile computers? A smartphone or a mobile computer may use either a Wi-Fi connection or a mobile communication network to access the Internet. Compare and contrast the two systems. What criteria would you use for comparison?

14.93 It is stated that the 4G and the 5G systems use the Internet Protocol. What does this statement imply?

15 Advanced Input/Output Interfaces

LEARNING GOALS

After reading this chapter, you should be able to:

- Identify Graphical User Interfaces (GUI) and list their advantages.
- Define the difference between Vector and Raster Graphics.
- Describe accelerated graphics and distinguish between fixed rendering pipeline and programmable rendering pipeline in computer graphics.
- Describe various input/output devices, including 3D displays, head mounted displays, accelerometers, haptic devices, and other recent trends in human computer interfaces.

We described various input/output devices in Chapter 3. These devices are essential for us to interact with computers. The computing power and memory capacity of computers are continuously improving as discussed in Chapter 12 and this enables alternative ways in which we interact with computers. For example, with multi-touch interfaces, it is possible to define gesture-based interaction, where placing two fingers on the screen and pulling them together means zoom out, and moving them apart means zoom in. This gesture is known as the pinch gesture. Also, it is possible to flip through pages displayed on a screen, much like turning pages of a book in real life. These interactions feel like magic compared to what was possible in the early days of computers. In this chapter, we discuss the recent improvements in the input-output interfaces to computers and the trends in human-computer interaction.

15.1 GRAPHICAL USER INTERFACE

The data on early computers were primarily text and numbers, and therefore the keyboard was the most suitable input device. The interface to the programs in these computers included text commands consisting of a short sequence of characters or words. This interface to computers is known as the *Command Line Interface* (*CLI*). As computers became more powerful, several commands were defined with many parametric options to execute complex tasks. Using the command line approach to interact with a computer requires the users to memorize several commands and learn to use them by providing the right options and parameters. Typing commands becomes error-prone when the number of commands, options, and parameters increases.

Graphical User Interface (*GUI*) was designed to enable a user to access programs on a computer through image objects called *icons* that are linked to the programs. The most commonly available GUI design consists of the window, icon, menu, and pointing device usually called WIMP elements. It presents the user with icons that can trigger various commands available on the system. The computer mouse device described in Chapter 3 is the most commonly used pointing device in this paradigm of user interface.

The Xerox Star Workstation was the first system to introduce a GUI–based operating system commercially in 1981; it was followed by the Apple Lisa system in 1983. Early GUIs used different keys and key sequences to trigger different programs on the computer; for example, F3 was used to activate the help function in some systems. The Common User Access (CUA) is a standard defined and published in 1987 by IBM to make the keys used to interface with the operating system and computer programs more uniform.

Today's common GUIs include Microsoft Windows, Mac OS X, and Linux's X Window System. These Operating Systems (OSs) typically provide both GUI and CLI–based methods for interaction with the computer programs available on the system.

GUIs are visually rich in detail nowadays because of the availability of more computing power. They use visually detailed icons, shadings for window borders, several buttons, checkboxes, and menus for options. The technology required to render graphics on a screen is significantly different from the rendering of text. In the following three sections, we describe techniques in computer graphics that support the creation of rich visuals on the display units of computers.

15.2 VECTOR GRAPHICS

The subject of computer graphics developed due to the need to display graphics for user interfaces and the application of computers to generate graphs and pictures for illustrations. Early computer graphics were mostly two-dimensional, and the display device used was the Cathode Ray Tube (CRT). The CRT supported programming commands to control the cathode ray gun to move from point to point on the screen and turn it on and off. *Vector graphics* was, therefore, used to render non-text information on the screen.

Vector graphics create an image by directly drawing the lines to compose it. The main advantages of vector graphics are:

- Lines are smooth
- It accurately transforms the mathematical equations used to model the lines
- It is easy to resize

Some disadvantages of vector graphics are:

- It is slow when several elements have to be drawn (can start to flicker)
- It is difficult to create filled polygons of arbitrary shape

Vector graphics is the preferred technology for rendering fonts and schematic line drawings due to its advantages. It is still used despite the widespread use of raster graphics technology. *Scalable Vector Graphics* (SVG) is a commonly used standard for vector graphics that is defined by the World Wide Web Consortium (W3C). SVG is completely independent of the device resolution and applies to both printers and display monitors. The SVG format consists of text commands that describe the straight lines and curved lines and other attributes like colour of lines that define the drawing.

15.3 RASTER GRAPHICS

Raster graphics represents an image as a two-dimensional array of picture element (pixel) values. Rendering an image involves displaying the value of the pixels on the screen. It is a discretized representation of images, and it is defined by the size of the two-dimensional array representing the image, called the resolution of the image. Raster graphics cannot be scaled up arbitrarily as the information at each pixel is not available when the size of the array representing the image is increased from the original resolution. This property is unlike vector graphics, where the equations of the lines representing the drawing can be re-evaluated to give the values at each pixel for various image sizes. However, raster graphics is advantageous to represent images where the regions are filled with continuous tone values such as photographs and photo-realistic images. Figure 15.1 illustrates vector graphics and raster graphics.

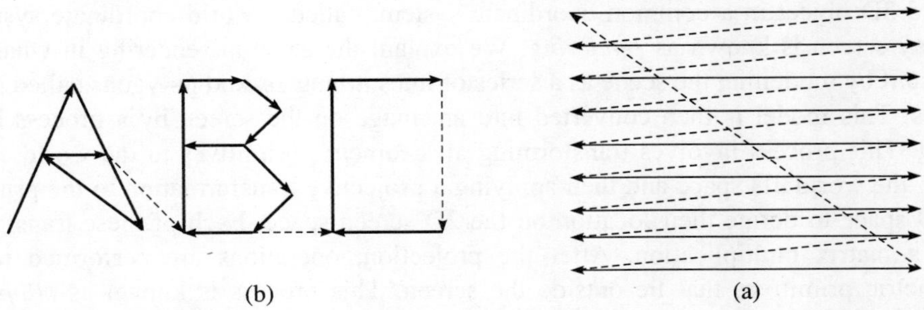

Figure 15.1 (a) A vector drawing of letters ABC, where the pixels along the solid arrows are repeatedly set. (b) Raster graphics involve the repeated setting of all pixels on the screen from top left to bottom right. The dotted lines indicate a move to operation where a repositioning action occurs during drawing without setting pixels on the screen.

The main advantages of raster graphics are:

- Representing filled polygons and colour variation in filled areas is easy
- It takes constant time to redraw any number of elements on the screen (no flicker)

The main disadvantages of raster graphics are:

- It produces jagged edges while converting lines to pixels
- It is a discretized version of a model, and therefore not easy to resize

When working on a computer with GUI, we often open several windows; use some windows to write documents and others to make presentations, draw diagrams, watch videos, and play computer games. We expect all these windows to respond immediately to our actions. This requires the Central Processing Unit (CPU) to be very powerful, especially since graphics operations are computationally intensive.

15.4 ACCELERATED GRAPHICS WITH GPU

The *Graphics Processing Unit* (GPU) was designed to reduce the computational load on the CPU. When a GPU is configured to support a CPU in a computer, they together form a heterogeneous co-processor computing model. The CPU executes the main logic of the program while GPU executes all graphics functions that are typically computationally intensive. Since the CPU and GPU process the program in parallel, the user experiences faster system performance

15.4.1 Rendering Pipeline

Suppose we want to display an image of a teapot on a display screen. A teapot is a three-dimensional object but a display screen is two-dimensional. The teapot looks different depending on the angle from which one views it. The texture of the teapot and its shadow depends on the light source illuminating it. This should also be realistically shown by a graphic system. Finally, a mapping of the 3D scene to a 2D screen is required for display. The process of displaying a real-world 3D object in a common coordinate system, called a world coordinate system, on a 2D display screen is known as *rendering*. We explain the steps in rendering in what follows.

We start by modelling the scene as a series of lines, triangles, and polygons called geometric primitives. This model is then converted into an image on the screen by a process known as rendering. This process involves transforming all geometric primitives to the world coordinate system in the world 3D space and then applying a projective transformation to the primitives in world 3D space to define their location on the 2D screen space. Each of these transformations requires a matrix multiplication. After the projection, operations are performed to discard the geometric primitives that lie outside the screen. This process is known as *clipping*. This is followed by the rasterization process that takes the vector specification of the projected geometries that are visible on the screen and converts them into pixel values in a memory array called a *frame buffer* that is displayed on the computer's display unit. Since all the geometric primitives defining the graphics environment have to undergo these transformations using matrix multiplications and other repetitive operations, a specialized processor that performs these operations in hardware was designed as the GPU to support the CPU. The GPU also supports *texture mapping* and lighting. Texture mapping is the technique of creating a realistic appearance of an image. Hardware support for texturing is used during rasterization; it involves looking up the memory that stores the texture image and applying it to evaluate the pixel value. Lighting is the part of the rendering process that computes light interaction with the geometric primitives that model the scene. Parameters for the lighting computation are evaluated in the world 3D space and passed on to the rasterization stage, where these values together with texture values, if present, are used to evaluate the colour of the pixels. Lighting is essential to convey the idea of shapes with subtle variations in shading to the human eye. Since rendering involves a definite sequence of transformations and computations that every geometric primitive has to undergo, it is called a rendering pipeline and is parallelized in a GPU. Figure 15.2 illustrates the graphics rendering pipeline.

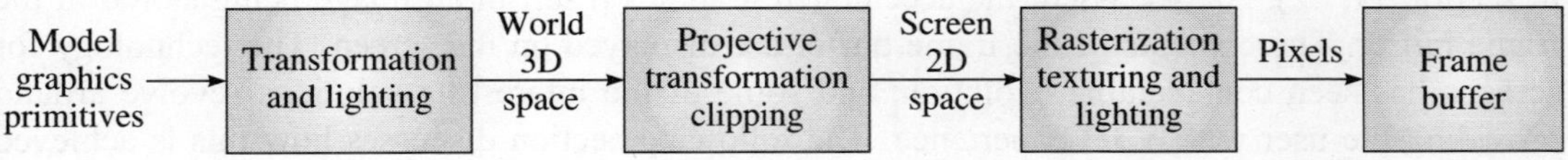

Figure 15.2 Rendering pipeline.

As graphics programs are used across several applications, including GUIs, gaming, scientific visualization, graph drawing, presentation software like PowerPoint, etc., standard libraries have been developed that implement graphics algorithms so that they need not be rewritten in the context of each application. There are mainly two graphics, libraries OpenGL (open source standard) and DirectX (by Microsoft), that are commonly used and the functions defined in them can be accessed by well-defined Application Programming Interfaces (APIs). When a GPU is present in a computer system, most of the operations specified in these libraries are offloaded from the CPU to the GPU. The other available libraries include OpenGL- ES (Embedded System), which is a subset of the OpenGL library that works well on mobile devices that typically have less computing power, and WebGL, which is a JavaScript-based library that can be executed in a browser environment.

15.4.2 Programmable Rendering Pipeline

When the computing power of computers increased, it became possible to perform computations that allowed some detailed graphics in the form of more polygons used to model the environment and more compute-intensive techniques to define detailed light interaction with the surface to generate shading on the surface. Since these operations have to be performed repeatedly, it was meaningful to implement them on the graphics card. However, different applications could have completely different kinds of processing for the vertices and surface shading. Therefore, an approach that supported a programmable rendering pipeline was developed. Figure 15.3 illustrates a programmable graphics pipeline.

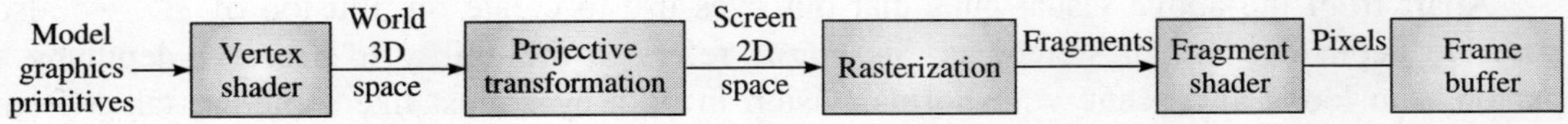

Figure 15.3 Programmable rendering pipeline.

As can be seen, the pipeline is very similar to the fixed rendering pipeline illustrated in Figure 15.2, except that the initial transformation and lighting segment has been replaced by *Vertex Shader* and the texturing and lighting that occurred along with rasterization have now moved out and occur in a segment called *Fragment Shader*. A fragment is a pixel with additional information that allows effective texturing and lighting. The 'Shaders' are the programmable part of the rendering pipeline. They consist of small programs that are compiled and placed into the memory of graphics cards to be executed on the data passing through the pipeline at a specified stage. The 'shaders' got their name because earlier they were primarily used to shade the model being rendered; however, they have evolved and one can program them to do any operations. Sometimes these programs do not relate to graphics and then one is said to be doing general-purpose computing on the GPU, namely, GPGPU computations (as mentioned in section 11.7.2). As discussed, the accelerated graphics result in an image being stored in the frame buffer. The contents of the frame buffer are displayed on the screen. The technology for screens has seen considerable evolution, and some of the interesting solutions revolve around providing the user with a 3D experience. The following section discusses how this is achieved in modern display technologies.

15.5 STEREO DISPLAY UNITS

In the last section, we saw how 3D objects can be rendered on a 2D screen. In this section, we will explore how an illusion of 3D shapes may be created on a 2D screen by various visual cues that exploit the way images are viewed by our eyes and processed by our brain. These techniques have been well explored by artists in paintings. They include the following:

- *Overlapping or occlusion of objects in a scene:* Objects are perceived to be in front of the objects whose visibility they block.
- *Linear perspective:* This is how parallel lines appear to converge at a distance. One observes this at once when one looks down railway tracks.
- *Visual angle subtended by an object of known size:* This follows from the idea of perspective and the fact that distant objects tend to look smaller. For example, if a person appears a certain size in an image, we automatically assume the approximate distance of the person based on the size on the screen.
- *Vertical position:* Objects that are higher in a scene are assumed to be more distant.
- *Haze, desaturation, and a shift to bluishness:* Objects that appear less clear, dull in colour, and have a bluish tint are perceived to be at a greater distance than similar objects when they exhibit clear bright colours.
- *Change in size of textured pattern detail:* Smaller texture patterns are assumed to be more distant.

Apart from the above visual cues that our eyes use to create the illusion of 3D, we also perceive depth because of stereopsis. *Stereopsis* refers to the ability to perceive depth by a person who looks at a scene with normal vision in both eyes. Just like a picture taken from a camera kept in two different positions is different, the image seen in each of our eyes is slightly different because of the difference in position. This difference in images seen in each of our eyes is known as binocular disparity. Our brain can interpret this disparity into depth information about objects in the scene. One can become aware of this ability of our brain by closing one eye and trying to make a finger from the left hand meet a finger from the right hand. One will notice that more effort is needed when one closes one eye, and the fingers are not aligned as well as they are aligned if both eyes are open.

This concept of depth perception is exploited to create the illusion of depth with some of the recent technologies. The depth perceived by this approach is much more immersive than the other techniques mentioned above.

When display units are used to create the 3D effect by exploiting stereopsis, the typical way one does it is by creating two images of the same scene with optical disparity. This is done by placing the virtual camera in two positions, approximately separated horizontally by the average distance between eyes, and rendering the scene. The two images are projected or displayed on a screen using technology that supports easy separation of the images meant for each eye. Different kinds of glasses called viewers are used to make one eye see one of the images, while the other eye sees the other image. In this way, natural binocular disparity is mimicked, and the result is one perceives 3D just like in the real world. The viewers can be passive or active. Passive viewers apply constant filtering for each eye, and there is no need for synchronization with the display. Active viewers have controls in them that communicate with the display device to synchronize them and make sure that the filters to each eye are applied correctly.

Passive polarization system

Here, the projector uses separate polarization filters to project the two images, and the viewer is such that it allows only one of the polarized images to reach each eye, thus creating a disparity between images seen by each eye, leading to the appearance of 3D.

Passive colour anaglyph system

Here, each image is passed through a different coloured filter and rendered superimposed on each other on a screen. Typically, red and cyan coloured filters are used. If they are printed, then complementary colours are used to print on white paper. Coloured glasses have to be used to view these images. These glasses separate the images for each eye. Many alternative uses of colour to code the images for each eye are prevalent; they are patented by various companies.

Active shutter systems

These systems require the two images, one for each eye, to be projected or displayed alternately at a high frequency. Ideally above 60 Hz and less than 120 Hz refresh rate are considered to give a flicker-free experience. One views these images through liquid crystal glasses that alternately block the light to each eye when a voltage is applied to it. The glasses synchronize with the projection system or screen through a wired or wireless signal and expose each eye to one of the images, creating the 3D experience.

15.6 OTHER VISUAL DISPLAYS

The previous section described stereo display units that use a screen similar to a display unit in front of a person. In this section, we present alternate forms where the device is significantly different from a display unit.

15.6.1 Head-Mounted Displays

Head Mounted Display (HMD) has been well explored in the context of creating immersive virtual reality experiences. It typically has the form of a helmet which houses two small screens near the eyes that are magnified through lenses and viewed by the eyes. The effect of stereo 3D can be easily reproduced in them by directing the binocularly disparate images to the screens of each of the eyes. The glasses can also be used to create an augmented reality experience, where the actual physical world is projected onto the screen and is augmented by rendering virtual objects using graphics. These systems require technology that senses viewing direction to update the view to mimic the change in view due to turning of the head. Various technologies are used to implement HMDs. With the constant improvement in technology and the ability to make smaller devices, in recent times HMDs have taken the form of devices that nearly look like normal eyeglasses. They also integrate several sensors into the system, including voice command through a microphone, accelerometer, gyroscope, magnetometer, ambient light sensor, proximity sensor, etc. We describe these input devices later in the chapter. All these sensors help to create an interface to computer information that is natural and intuitive.

15.6.2 3D Projection Systems

All the above systems create a 3D experience on screens, and so there is a screen space in which the images are rendered. Unlike the previously described systems, 3D projection systems create an object with light projections that occupy a space in the real world environment. Note that these technologies are mainly applicable to creating 3D objects that are rendered into the real world rather than creating immersive 3D virtual worlds. Some examples of such technology include volumetric displays, holographic displays, and integral images.

Volumetric displays

These techniques create a projection of points of light in a volume. These points of light that occupy 3D space are called volume elements or *voxels* and are analogous to pixels in 2D space. The voxels may be rendered in multi-planar displays, which as the name implies consist of a stack of display planes, onto which slices of the 3D model are rendered. In some cases, an illusion of multiple planes is created by rotating a display very rapidly and displaying on it the slices of the model from an appropriate angle. Apart from the above technologies which have some form of volumetric screens, there is an alternative technology where the infrared laser is focused in space according to the shape being rendered, and the focus causes small bubbles of plasma to form which emit light in the visible spectrum, thereby creating a visual of the volume object.

Holographic displays

Holographic technology exploits motion parallax, accommodation, and convergence to create the illusion of depth apart from binocular disparity. Motion parallax is the depth hint we get from relative changes in the occlusion of objects when we move. Accommodation is the ability of the muscles in our eyes to bring objects in the near field of vision into focus by changing the focal length of the lens. We can make inferences about the depth of objects in the near field of vision based on the sensation of accommodation of the eye. Convergence is the sensation of our eyes pointing inwards to watch objects in close range; it works as a depth cue for objects that are within 10 m in front of our eyes. The advantage of holograms is that there is no need for special glasses to view the 3D object.

Integral imaging

Integral imaging technology uses an array of microscopic lenses in front of an image to present different views of an object depending on the angle of viewing. It is sometimes referred to as a *multiscopic 3D display*, as it supports viewing an object from several angles and not just two separate viewpoints as in stereoscopic displays. This technology reproduces the detailed light interaction with an object from various viewing angles; the light interaction model is called the 4D light field.

15.7 INPUT DEVICES FOR INTERACTION

Early computers mainly required programs to be entered into the system; therefore, keyboards were the main and best interface to computers. However, the applications of computers have changed greatly and the trend is to have interfaces to computers that are more natural and smarter. For example, it is normal to encounter responsive screens nowadays on smartphones that always show a picture the right way up, independent of the direction in which you hold the device. We now expect a speech interface to systems, and the trend is to make such interfaces mimic a conversation that one would have with another person. In this section, we describe some common input devices that are often found in devices and their applications.

15.7.1 Accelerometers

Accelerometers are sensors that can detect the magnitude and direction of acceleration of a device. Under normal conditions, on earth's surface, the accelerometer detects the direction of acceleration due to gravity (g) and it can also measure the magnitude of acceleration. The accelerometers may be multi-axial and they can detect the magnitude and direction of application of g on a device as a vector quantity that can be used to infer the orientation of the device. This ability to sense orientation is exploited to maintain the correct side up on mobile devices, independent of the direction in which they are held.

Another innovative use of accelerometers is found in gaming. A three-axis accelerometer is used in gaming input devices, such as the Wii remote controller manufactured by the Nintendo gaming company. Using this system of three-axis accelerometers, the exact direction and speed with which the Wii remote was moved is estimated and transmitted to the game to react accordingly. Nintendo sports games such as tennis and golf have exploited this ability of the Wii remote to make the ball react to the action of the user and have successfully created very engaging experiences.

15.7.2 Gesture Recognition

Gestures are any bodily motion that is performed to express thoughts and emotions. It is a natural way in which humans communicate. The trend towards more natural interfaces, therefore, is to explore ways in which gesturing can be used to interact with computers. We describe next some technologies which enable interaction with computers using gestures.

Wired gloves

These come under the category of wearable computers. As the name suggests, these gloves have sensors that transmit the relative orientation of the palm and fingers. The sensors used in the glove may be accelerometers, fibre optic cables, or optic markers. We have already described the accelerometer in the previous section. In optic fibres, the fibres are made to run along the back of the palm; they are flexible and bend when the fingers are bent while gesturing. The light is transmitted along these fibres and the loss in light owing to bending when the fingers are moved is used to determine the position of the palm. Optic markers are passive technology, that is, they do not require any power input for functioning. They are light reflectors that are placed at the key position of the palm. A camera is used to record the position of the markers and a model for the palm is used to reconstruct the gesture based on key joint locations obtained from the camera. The output of these sensors is interpreted by a program and gestures are recognized, which are used by a computer to trigger a suitable reaction. The advantage of a glove is that sometimes it can also be used for output by embedding haptic devices in it. We present more details about haptic technology in Section 15.9.1.

Controller-based gestures

Sometimes certain actions performed with the device by a user are grouped and interpreted as a gesture. For example, pointing to a single location with a mouse is an action while a sequence of positions of the mouse is interpreted as a stroke, and strokes may be mapped to the motion of the hand. For example, moving a mouse at the corner of a page to make a stroke would invoke page-reading software to interpret the stroke as a page-turning gesture and go to the next page of the document. In some cases, an animation of a page being turned is displayed to the user.

The motion of the Wii remote is also interpreted as a gesture in some forms of interpretation of the signals. In this case, rather than monitoring the sensor at a single instance, a sequence of sensor values over a period of time are interpreted together into a gesture.

Touch screens that enable multi-touch have interesting intuitive gestures that enable interaction with data displayed on the screen. One can easily drag and drop objects, examine them by zooming in with the pinch gesture as described at the beginning of this chapter, and in some cases discard objects with a fast stroke called a flick. The operation associated with a gesture can vary from system to system, and sometimes a user can select the action performed by a gesture. The latter is known as the customizable design of the user interface.

15.7.3 Digital Cameras with Computer Vision Technologies

One of the important ways in which people get inputs about their environment is through the sense of sight/vision. The developments in digital camera technology, described in detail in Chapter 16 have made it easy and inexpensive to input images in real time to a computer. There has also been significant development in the area of computer vision, which is the technology of interpreting the images into meaningful information about the environment. Therefore, it is possible for a computer to get inputs from its environment in much the same way as people, using cameras and computer vision. We describe some of the approaches that have been developed for interfacing to computers using these technologies.

Single camera approaches

Here, as the name indicates, a single camera's input is used to make inferences about the environment. Various computer vision algorithms that infer shape from shading are used to interpret the image. Often a sequence of images is used as better results are obtained by analyzing the temporal information present in these images to resolve possible ambiguities. Since gestures can be obtained from a sequence of images, these systems are suitable for gesture-based interaction.

Multiple cameras and depth

As explained in the context of stereoscopy, it is possible to infer depth information from the disparity in images taken by two cameras from different locations. This idea is exploited in the multiple-camera approaches. The limitations of camera images as the input for depth estimation are as follows:

- Attributes of the cameras, namely, focal length and the distance between camera locations, should be accurately calibrated.
- Scene should be well lit; it is difficult to identify shapes in low lighting environments.

Depth aware cameras

These cameras overcome the limitation of normal cameras that require the scene to be well-lit. Depth-aware cameras project light into the environment and infer depth from the light reflected. Since the device projects light into the environment, it has a limited range in which it can infer the depth information. An example of this kind of technology is the Kinect technology used with the Xbox gaming console. It uses an infrared projector and a CMOS sensor to infer the depth information in an environment. The outputs of these cameras are images, just like the regular digital cameras; however, the value at each pixel in these images represents the distance from the camera (or depth) rather than colour. Knowing the depth of an environment is very useful for the reconstruction of a 3D model of the environment in the computer for understanding the environment.

15.8 SPEECH AND AUDIO INTERFACE

One of the most natural ways of communication between people is through speech. People have been communicating with speech alone on phones for several years with ease even though there is no supporting visual feedback. Therefore, speech and audio interface to a computer is natural and can serve as an independent communication channel without the need for support from outputs such as display devices.

Processing of speech signals is a computationally intensive task, and therefore speech inputs to a computer were not explored till efficient speech processing algorithms were developed.

However, speech and audio interfaces to computers are now commonplace. Systems that use audio input and speech output for interaction are said to have a Voice User Interface (VUI) which is analogous to the Graphical User Interface (GUI) discussed in the Section 15.1.

Several design approaches may be adopted while building a VUI and computers may be used to a varying extent to achieve desirable user experience. For example, pre-recorded audio messages may be played to a user based on his or her selection of input. The pre-recorded messages may be spoken by humans, stored on the computer, and played back or they can be text-to-speech conversion synthesized by a computer in real-time in response to the input. The input itself may be selected by entering it on a keyboard or number pad if it is a phone, or it can be speech, which has to be recognized and interpreted by the computer. The technology and challenges in the latter case are discussed in Chapter 14. Some examples of speech input are the iPhone app Siri, the Google app for searching on Android mobiles, and voice-activated dialing.

The design of VUI is not easy; one has to pay attention to small details while doing it as the expectations of users are high when they are interacting with a machine in a natural mode. If the machine makes mistakes, it quickly leads to frustration. The right amount of support for using the system has to be provided and the speech should be clear and unambiguous so that the user does not lose interest because of repeatedly having to listen to the same message to understand it.

15.9 TACTILE INTERFACES

Touch is one of the important senses of a person that enables him/her to know the roughness and smoothness of texture, hold objects and move them around, carve and sculpt artwork, etc. Tactile interfaces enable this kind of interaction with virtual objects. The technology used to enable tactile interfaces is known as haptic technology. We describe this technology and its evolution in the following section.

15.9.1 Haptic Technology

Haptic technology gives output as forces, vibration, and motion that is detectable to the users' touch. These devices provide the user with a feeling of a physical object in the real world that they can manipulate. To do this, the haptic devices have force sensors that measure the force applied by a user. A simulator computes the reactive force that the system should apply back based on the material and shape of the object being simulated and applies the computed force back on the user.

Haptic technology has been extensively explored in the context of virtual reality, as any attempt at creating an alternative reality has to engage all the senses. Since addressing the problem of creating virtual reality systems began in the 1970s, various technologies have been applied to achieve tactile feedback, depending on the technological advances of that period. There are four generations of haptic technology, which are discussed next.

First generation

Early *touch feedback systems* used electromagnetic technologies such as vibratory motors. This technology is found in the vibrating alert of the present-day cell phone. It was mainly a proof of concept that it was possible to give an output from a computer to the tactile sensation of a user. It had limited applicability as the output was very coarse and could not be easily controlled and contained spatially.

Second generation

The haptic devices of this generation consist of arrays of sensors that react to touch. The reaction is restricted to the location of touch, rather than the whole device vibrating. The intensity, duration, and frequency of activation of each point of output can be varied to create a haptic interface to virtual objects. User studies have shown that the frequency of haptic stimuli has to be below 150 Hz; higher frequencies in the range of 250–300 Hz, which is the range of the first-generation technology, is often considered unpleasant and not favoured for extended use. The second-generation technologies are electroactive polymers, piezoelectric, electrostatic, and subsonic audio wave surface actuation. These technologies can achieve low-frequency stimuli. The response time of these technologies is in the range of 5–15 ms, making them better than the first-generation technology which had a 35–60 ms response time. The fast response time is critical to avoid lag in the user experience when one is synchronizing a haptic and visual experience.

Third generations

When we sense textures of objects by touching, we have a detailed experience of a stimulus that varies depending on whether the texture is rough or smooth. For example, we can sense the difference between silk and cotton cloth. This kind of experience requires detailed control of the stimulus signal at each point on a surface. Two technologies of the third generation, audio haptics, and electrostatic haptics, enable this kind of detailed simulation of materials through customizable effects that they can create with low latency control chips. We know that when we touch objects, the sensation of the object is converted to electric signals that traverse our nerves and are interpreted in our brains as the texture and feel of the object. In this technology, a very weak oscillating electric field is applied to the user's finger to create a sensation of friction and thus the sensation of texture. The electric field can be controlled by the waveform, amplitude, and frequency; by varying these parameters, the sensation of various textures can be created.

Fourth generation

In the real world, the sensation of the object is different, depending on how hard we press on the surface. This effect of haptic technologies which was not captured in the previous generations was enabled in the fourth generation technology. Therefore, not only does this technology deliver a stimulus, but it also senses the intensity of pressure applied and modifies the response accordingly.

Future generation

More recently techniques are being explored to eliminate the physical devices for providing tactile feedback of virtual objects, instead, ultrasound waves are used to create tactile sensations. This technology is called "Ultra Haptics".

15.10 BRAIN COMPUTER INTERFACE (BCI)

Brain Computer Interface (BCI), often called a mind-machine interface (MMI) or direct neural interface, or brain-machine interface (BMI), was originally developed to assist people with disability which impaired the use of their regular faculties to interact with computers. These interfaces to computers are primarily focused on assisting, augmenting, or repairing human cognitive or sensory-motor functions by sensing the electric signals in the brain.

There are two types of BCI: one is invasive where the compute device or part of it is directly inserted into the brain to sense and transmit control signals, and the other is placed on the surface of the head. This approach is more challenging, as it requires the advanced technology to isolate the weak brain signals that are available on the surface of the head. We describe each of these technologies in detail next.

Invasive BCI

The early research on BCI conducted in the mid-1990s involved developing neuroprosthetic devices to help repair damaged sight. The technology consisted of an array of BCI electrodes that are implanted in the visual cortex. The implant induces the sensation of perception of light (phosphenes) based on signals that it receives from a camera mounted on glasses worn by the person with the implant. The initial versions of the devices were large and not portable, but recent implants are portable. It should, however, be noted that they do not restore vision; they give only visual clues of brightness with phosphenes spread out in the visual field.

BCI has also been applied to motor neuroprosthetic devices. Here, the goal is to help individuals with paralysis. Paralysis is caused by damage to the nervous system that causes it to no longer generate the control signals required to control certain parts of the body. In this case, a brain implantation is used that produces signals to simulate movement.

The other case when BCI is applied is in the context of amputees where the signals that are generated by their nervous system are used to control an artificial limb. Initial techniques achieved such control by tapping into the brain directly for the signals. However, more recent technology attempts to tap the signals in the brain by placing electrodes on the surface of the skull. Once the electrodes are able to tap the signals, they can be used to control a robotic arm; therefore, the arm moves in response to their thought of moving it. Recent research has shown that it is possible to control a robotic prosthetic limb with many degrees of freedom by using direct connections to an array of neurons in the part of the brain that controls motion.

One such technology is Neuralink which uses a coin size device with 1024 electrodes implanted into the brain through robotic surgery, to enable directly tapping the neural signals and using them to communicate with digital devices. The device is powered by a wirelessly rechargeable battery and can record neural activity with high precision and transmit it wirelessly to external devices. These signals can be used in various ways, for example, restoring mobility in paralyzed individuals, or for thought-based control of computers.

Partially invasive BCI

In partially invasive BCI, the implants are not directly in the brain, but rather inside the skull and outside the grey matter. They bypass the signal attenuation and distortion by the skull due to their location within the skull, and as they are not inserted into the brain tissues, they do not cause scar tissues, which happen in the case of invasive approaches.

The partially invasive technology is known as electrocorticography (ECoG), and it measures the electrical activity of the brain. It was first tried out on humans in 2004; because of its location within the skull, the signal-to-noise ratio is better than the non-invasive techniques described next. Also, a larger number of signals in a wider frequency range can be measured by this technique. This makes it easier to derive control signals from the signals in the brain, and therefore it is found that the people using this system require less training than that for non-invasive techniques and higher levels of control can be achieved by the system. Scientists have shown that a teenage boy was able to play a computer game using a ECoG implant.

Non-invasive BCI

These devices are easier to wear compared to the invasive and partially invasive devices. However, they suffer from poor signal inputs from the brain as the skill dampens signals and scatters them, and this makes it difficult to separate the signals and estimate the origin of each signal. The most commonly studied non-invasive technology is electroencephalography (EEG). As the signals to this system are weak and distorted, people need intensive training to use the system. The training is time-consuming and challenging as people should learn to control the signals produced in the brain so that they can be detected and isolated for use to control devices. Just like in invasive BCI techniques, in this case also one of the main applications of this interface is prosthesis control for people with paralysis or disabilities.

Most applications of BCI have mainly been limited to research and application to improve the quality of life for people with disabilities or illnesses. However, recently BCI has gained attention because it is being explored in the context of gaming. An area of gaming called *Neurogaming* has been invented, which uses non-invasive BCI for gamers to interact with a gaming console. If these applications of BCI are commercially successful, one may find more wide-scale use of BCIs. However, before that, some ethical issues around mind reading, mind control, and privacy will have to be resolved.

15.11 EVOLVING USER EXPERIENCE (UX)

This chapter presented many advanced modes of input and output to the computers. Using all these state-of-the-art technologies together does not ensure the effective use of a computer. When using these technologies, they should be brought together in various permutations and combinations to create a coherent user interface to the computer that is intuitive and allows seamless interaction. The objective is to create an engaging user experience that makes it easy to accomplish tasks with a computer.

Since users have different preferences, it is not possible to create a single user interface for the computer and expect that all users will find it equally engaging. Therefore, an important step in addressing this issue involves creating digital doubles of users that capture their abilities, interests, and preferences and use this information to customize the user interface to create a more engaging experience tailored to each user. A digital double can be defined as a virtual representation of real people created using advanced technologies, that enable creating personalized and adaptive user experiences. A simple example of a digital double is a predictive keyboard that suggests the next word a user will type based on the sequence of words typed by the user.

SUMMARY

1. The increase in computing power and memory capacity of computers enabled the development of novel ways of interacting with computers that are easy, for example, the multi-touch interface of the pinch gesture that allows zooming in or out of content displayed on the screen.
2. The keyboard is most suitable for text input to the computer. The Command Line Interface (CLI) consists of a short sequence of characters or words that cause the execution of various programs on the computer. When the number of commands, options, and parameters is large, the process of typing commands becomes error prone.
3. Graphical User Interface uses icons to link to programs and users access the programs by selecting the icons with a pointing device like the mouse. The most commonly used GUI is the window, icon, menu, and pointing device (WIMP) paradigm of GUI.
4. Vector graphics makes use of mathematical representation of lines and curves to draw the elements that compose an image. The resulting images are easy to resize and the lines in them are smooth.
5. Raster graphics represents the image as a two-dimensional array of picture elements called pixels. It is a discretized representation of images; raster graphics is good for representing filled areas.
6. Graphics requires considerable computing resources; a Graphics Processing Unit (GPU) is used to reduce this computational load on the CPU.
7. A fixed rendering pipeline is implemented in hardware on the GPU; the stages of the pipeline include the processes of transformation, projection, clipping, rasterization, texturing, and lighting.
8. A programmable rendering pipeline makes the fixed rendering pipeline flexible by introducing the vertex shader and fragment shader. These 'shaders' are small programs that are compiled and placed in the memory of the graphics cards to execute on the data passing through the pipeline.
9. Stereo display units make use of stereopsis to create the appearance of 3D. Stereopsis refers to the ability to perceive depth by a person who looks at a scene with normal vision in both eyes.
10. Technologies used in creating 3D displays include passive polarization, passive colour anaglyph systems, and active shutter systems.
11. Head-mounted displays (HMDs) are used to create immersive virtual reality experiences. They bring together technologies such as voice command through microphones, accelerometers, gyroscopes, magnetometers, ambient light sensors, proximity sensors, etc. to create an engaging experience.
12. The 3D projection systems are used to render a 3D object into the real world; some of the technologies that enable this are volumetric displays, holographic displays, and integral imaging.

13. Accelerometers are sensors that detect the magnitude and direction of acceleration of a device. They are commonly used in mobile devices to maintain the correct side of the screen up.
14. Gestures are any bodily motion that is performed to express thoughts and emotions. It is a natural way in which humans communicate. Gesture recognition approaches enable more natural human-computer interaction. Technologies that support gesture-based interaction include wired gloves, controller-based gestures, and computer vision-based techniques.
15. Voice User Interface (VUI) enables interaction with computers using speech and audio. The technology of speech recognition and automatic text-to-speech conversion plays an important role in voice user interfaces.
16. Tactile interfaces allow users to interact with the computer using a touch interface. Haptic technologies enable touch feedback. They have evolved through four generations of successive refinement, and it is possible to create the sensation of various detailed textures with the latest technologies.
17. Brain Computer Interface (BCI), often called Mind-Machine Interface (MMI), or direct neural interface, or Brain-Machine Interface (BMI), assists people with disabilities or illnesses that impair their ability to interact with computers. These interfaces to computers are primarily focused on assisting, augmenting, or repairing human cognitive or sensory-motor functions by trapping into the electric signals in the brain.
18. BCI can be invasive, that is, have electrodes embedded in the brain tissues, partially invasive, where the electrodes are on the surface of the brain, or non-invasive, where the electrodes are present on the surface of the head. Recently, the non-invasive technology has been employed in gaming.

REVIEW QUESTIONS

15.1 What is CLI? When is it preferable to use CLI?

15.2 What is GUI? Give an example. What is the advantage of GUI?

15.3 Name the system that had the first GUI.

15.4 What is a GPU and why is it needed?

15.5 What is Vector graphics? When is it useful?

15.6 What is SVG?

15.7 What is Raster graphics? What are its advantages?

15.8 Compare Vector and Raster graphics and give examples for each.

15.9 What is a rendering pipeline? What are the kinds of rendering pipelines?

15.10 What is the difference between a fixed rendering pipeline and a programmable rendering pipeline?

15.11 What is a 'Shader'? Name the shaders present in a programmable graphics pipeline.

15.12 Describe the visual cues that are rendered into an image to create an impression of depth.

15.13 What is stereopsis?

15.14 What is binocular optic disparity?

15.15 Describe the technologies used to create 3D displays.

15.16 What is the difference between active and passive stereo displays?

15.17 What is an HMD? When is it used? What technologies are used to create an experience with an HMD?

15.18 Describe 3D projection systems. When are they used?

15.19 What are accelerometers? Give three applications of accelerometers.

15.20 What is gesture recognition-based computer interaction? How is it different from the point- and select-based approach to interaction with computers?

15.21 Give examples of technologies that enable gesture-based human-computer interfaces.

15.22 What is VUI? What are the challenges faced during the design of a VUI?

15.23 Describe tactile interfaces and the evolution of haptic technology over four generations.

15.24 What is BCI? What are the kinds of BCI that are currently being developed for interaction with computers?

16 Multimedia Data Acquisition and Processing

LEARNING GOALS

After reading this chapter, you should be able to:

- Describe how images are acquired, why they should be compressed, how they are compressed, and the file formats of image data.
- Explain how videos are acquired, why they should be compressed, and video compression standards.
- Describe how audio data are acquired, why they should be compressed, and audio compression standards.
- Explain how audio and video are generated, processed, and stored.

Computers are widely used to process multimedia data, namely, images or pictures, audio, and video. In this chapter, we will first explain how images can be acquired and processed by a computer (we will use the terms image and picture interchangeably depending on the context). We will also describe several standard formats used to store images. Numeric, text, and image data are essentially static, that is, time is not a variable. Audio and video, on the other hand, are time-dependent. To process and store these in computers, a large storage space is needed. Early generations of computers did not have hardware facilities to either store or process audio and video data. With cheaper memories (both primary and secondary) and the availability of powerful processors, it became feasible for computers to handle multimedia data. By *multimedia,* we mean primarily a combination of image, audio, and video data. The capability to process and store these data types has led to many new innovative applications of computers. In this chapter, we will describe how pictures and video, namely, moving pictures, are acquired and stored in a computer. The main difference between a picture and a video is the need to repeat pictures at least 30 times per second to enable us to see movement. The number of times a picture is repeated in video depends on the persistence of our vision. In a moving picture, each picture frame is slightly different from the previous one and this change is what is perceived as motion. As the number of pictures to be stored per second is 30, the storage needed to store video is massive. Furthermore, if the video is to be sent via a communication channel, the channel bandwidth must be very high. Video data must therefore be compressed. In this chapter, we will discuss how images, video and audio data are acquired, compressed, and stored. Video and audio may be combined in applications such as computer-generated animation with sound.

16.1 IMAGE ACQUISITION AND STORAGE

There are two major devices available to acquire images. They are *flatbed scanners* that acquire documents, drawings, and photographs, and *digital cameras* used to photograph people, scenery, and documents. Often cameras built-in to smartphones are used instead of stand-alone digital cameras. We briefly described how flatbed scanners work in Sec.3.2.5. In Sec 16.1.1 we describe in greater detail how flatbed scanners work to make this chapter self-contained.

16.1.1 A Flatbed Scanner

A flatbed scanner has the following parts:

1. An optical system consisting of a light beam, lens, and mirrors.
2. An array of CCDs (Charge Coupled Devices) that sense light and give an electrical output depending on the intensity of the light.
3. An electronic circuit that converts the electrical output given by the array of CCDs to a set of bits that are stored in a computer's memory.

The scanner has a flat glass surface over which the document to be scanned is placed with the printed side facing the glass just as in a photocopying machine. The paper is now pressed down with a cover.

A light source focuses light on an entire line as a thin beam. This is called a scan line. Light is reflected from the paper along the scan line. Wherever there is a dark spot (corresponding to a printed character), no light is reflected and wherever there is no print, that is, it is white, bright light is reflected. The reflected light is gathered by a row of CCDs. The CCDs store 0s for dark spots which do not reflect light, and 1 for white spots which reflect light. In many scanners, 600 CCDs per inch are arranged along a row, giving a resolution of 600 bits per inch. After gathering bits from one scan line, the motor moves the light source to the next scan line and gathers bits corresponding to this line. The process continues till the entire page is scanned from top to bottom. The number of scan lines in the vertical or Y direction is determined by the mechanical precision of the motor moving the light beam. It is usually double the horizontal resolution. Thus, if the horizontal resolution is 600 bits per inch, there will be 1200 scan lines per inch in the vertical direction. It usually takes between 30 and 90 seconds to scan a full page.

Each reflected light beam picked up by the CCD array is called a picture element, abbreviated *pixel*. Thus, a scanner with 600 CCDs per inch in the X direction and 1200 scan lines per inch in the Y direction will store 600 × 1200 = 720,000 pixels per square inch.

16.1.2 Acquiring Monochrome Pictures

Two-tone or black-and-white pictures such as freehand drawings, cartoons, printed text, and handwritten documents are acquired using a scanner. As the image data is black and white, 2 bits are used to store a pixel (picture element). A drawing in A4 (8.25″ × 11.7″) size paper will need (720,000 × 6.25 × 9.7) = 5.44 MB storage, assuming 1″ margins all around.

In two-tone, that is, black and white pictures, each scan point is represented by 1 bit, a 1 for white and a 0 for black. Unlike cartoons, handwritten documents, etc., where only black and white are relevant, a monochrome photograph will have various shades of grey. Besides pictures, X-rays and shaded pencil drawings also have several shades of grey. If 2 bits are used per pixel, then 2 × 2 = 4 shades of grey can be represented (see Figure 16.1). With 4 bits, we can represent 2 × 2 × 2 × 2 = 16 shades of grey.

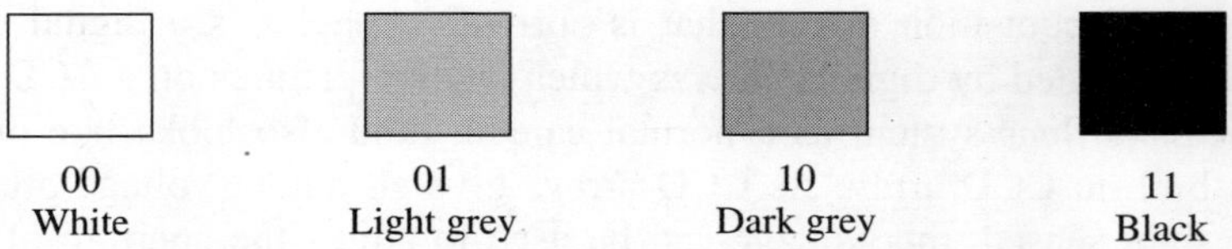

Figure 16.1 Multi-tone with 4 grey levels.

The CCD array in a scanner can sense intensities of reflected light and convert the intensities to equivalent bit strings. The number of intensity levels that can be sensed by a CCD of a scanner determines its capability to represent grey levels. A good scanner uses 8 bits for each pixel, which gives 2^8 = 256 grey levels. This is sufficient for most practical applications. The storage requirement for storing greyscale images is eight times larger than that required for black and white scanners as 1 byte rather than 1 bit is used per pixel. A 7″ × 9″ size picture will thus need 600 × 1200 × 7 × 9 × 8 bits = 45.36 MB storage.

16.1.3 Acquiring Colour Pictures

Most scanners available today scan black and white and coloured pictures. Red, Green, and Blue are the primary colours and our eyes perceive different colours by adding these primary colours in proportions. Thus, the principle used in colour scanning is to measure the intensity of Red, Green, and Blue colours (called RGB) in the light reflected by a picture element. The RGB components in reflected light are found by rapidly rotating a disk with R, G, and B filters (see Figure 16.2) and picking up R, G, and B components separately. The intensity of each of these is measured by a CCD to 8 significant bits (in most scanners). If R, G, and B are combined, we have 24 bits to represent different colours. Thus, 2^{24} = 16 million colours can be displayed. All 1s represent white and all 0s black and each bit pattern is one colour. A 7″ × 9″ colour picture will require 136.08 MB of storage space.

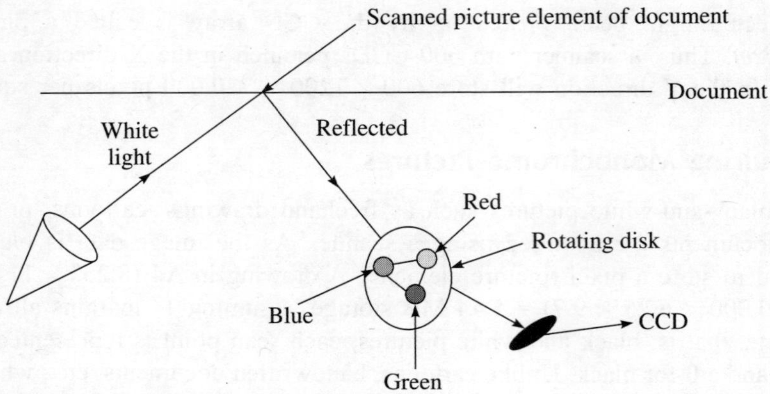

Figure 16.2 Finding RGB components in reflected light in a colour scanner.

16.2 IMAGE ACQUISITION WITH A DIGITAL CAMERA

An important image acquisition system that is currently popular is a digital camera. Flatbed scanners are supplemented by digital cameras which capture pictures on a CCD array. A digital camera uses the same lens system as a normal camera (and also looks like one) and focuses the image on a built-in CCD array. As CCD arrays give an output voltage proportional to the intensity of the light sensed, this voltage can be used to adjust the aperture of the shutter and get good pictures even with poor lighting. Automatic focusing is also a standard feature. Most smartphones nowadays have a built-in camera with most of the features of larger cameras and have become very popular for taking pictures of people, places, and documents. Both monochrome and colour pictures may be captured by digital cameras. Colour is usually the default mode.

To obtain colour images, a mosaic of red, blue, and green filters (see Figure 16.3) covering the entire CCD array is used. The red, green, and blue colours are sensed by CCDs which are covered, respectively, by red, blue, and green filters. To get the correct colour of the image at a pixel, the camera has software that interpolates or 'guesses' it by multiplying (using appropriate weights) the sensed intensities of red, green, and blue at the neighbouring pixels. The complexity of the software determines the quality of the resulting colour image. This picture can be viewed on a display in the camera. It can be downloaded and viewed on a computer's display or printed using a colour printer.

Figure 16.3 A mosaic of filters used to capture colour pictures with a CCD array in a digital camera.

The number of pixels in an image depends on the number of CCDs in the camera. Currently (2025) many cameras use 24 to 64 Megapixels. With an aspect ratio of 3:2, the cameras use 6000 × 4000 pixels for images. This resolution is adequate if the picture is to be viewed using a monitor on a PC or if the image is sent via the Internet to be viewed by a friend.

If 6000 × 4000 pixels are used, the storage needed for a colour image is 6000 × 4000 × 3 bytes as 8 bits represent each colour intensity. This is 72 MB storage.

A *flash memory* (see Chapter 11) card is used to store the images captured by a digital camera. Flash memory cards of 32 GB to 2 TB capacity are available in 2025. In a 32 GB flash memory, over 8000 low-quality JPEG compressed 6000 × 4000-pixel images or 2000 high-quality images can be stored. (JPEG compression is explained in the next section).

The most important advantages of a digital camera are:

- It is easy to use. The final picture stored in the memory can be viewed on the camera's display. Even novices can take good pictures.
- It uses a powerful processor to interpolate and compress images. The complexity of the algorithm used for this will determine the quality of images shot by the camera and consequently its cost.
- As the image acquired by a digital camera is a sequence of bytes, it can be transmitted using the Internet as soon as it is shot. Unlike a normal camera, there is no need to develop a film. This feature is useful, particularly for press photographers who can transmit the photographs from the locations where they are taken to the newspaper office instantly.
- Another advantage of a digital camera is the possibility of processing the picture using a computer. Processing is easy as the image is already stored digitally. One of the dangers of digital photographs is the ease with which they can be altered. You can put the face of a person with the body of another person by sticking two different digital images!

16.3 STORAGE FORMATS FOR PICTURES

Pictures are represented as a set of pixels. A pixel is coded by 1 bit for black and white images, 8 bits for monochrome pictures with 256 grey levels, and 24 bits for colour pictures. The representation of pictures by an equivalent array of bits is called a *bit map* representation. A file that stores the bit map representation of a picture is called a *bmp* file. Another standard method of storing digitized images is called tagged image file format (abbreviated *tiff* file). The tag refers to the information about the image stored in this format. The information is the image's height and width in pixels and a table of colours used (see Figure 16.4). The main problem with bmp and tiff files is their huge size. A scanned 7″ × 9″ picture will need 7 × 9 × 300 × 600 bits = 1.4175 MB if stored as a bit map. If 24 bits colour per pixel is used, the storage needed is 24 times, that is, 34.02 MB. This is huge. Thus, it is essential to compress an image file into one that requires a smaller number of bits without lowering the quality of the picture. The number of bits in pictures taken with a digital camera are much larger.

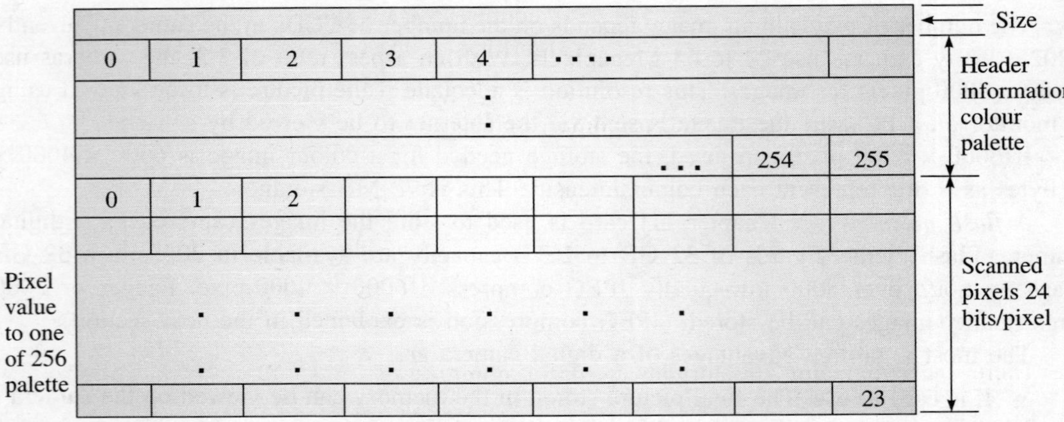

Figure 16.4 Tagged image file format. Observe that 24-bit colour is mapped to one out of 256 palettes of colours. The header gives data on the number of pixels in the rows and columns of an image.

There are many methods available to *compress image files*. The main idea used to compress a file is to use the processing power of a computer and perform several processing operations on the file which results in a file that uses less storage (see Figure 16.5). In other words, we spend processing time to save storage. Reducing the storage space is essential as storage requirements, particularly for colour pictures, are very high. It is cheaper to store a compressed file. If an image is to be transmitted using a communication line, it should be compressed and sent. This reduces the time and cost of communication. At the receiving end, the file is decompressed, that is, it is expanded, using processing power to view the original image or print it using a printer. Decompression also requires time. The decompressed image must be a truthful reproduction of the original image without distortion and colour change. Another important point to remember is that the time taken to compress an image file may be comparatively high, for example, it may take a minute to compress a file. Decompression time, however, has to be short. People get impatient if they have to wait for more than 10 seconds for a compressed image to be expanded for viewing.

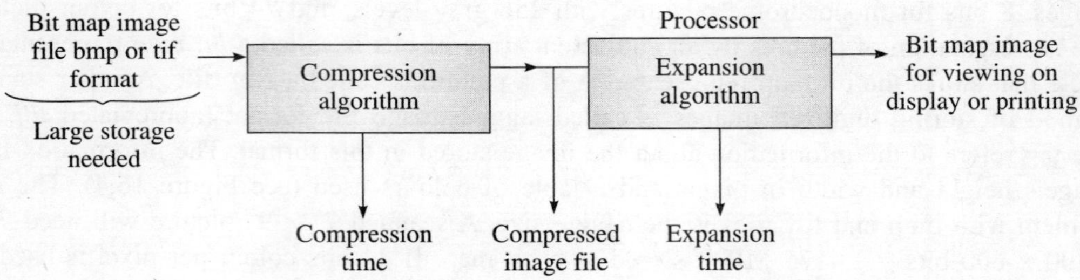

Figure 16.5 Compression and expansion of an image file.

The following are the advantages of compression:

1. Storage space is reduced.
2. It can be transmitted faster.

Many algorithms have been proposed to compress image files. The main criteria to be taken into account to compare compression algorithms and compressed files are:

- By what proportion does the image file get compressed?
- How much time does it take to compress the image file?
- How much time does it take to expand the compressed file and get back the image for viewing?
- Is the quality of the image lowered due to compression/expansion?
- What is the type of image for which it works well?
- Is the format of compressed files widely accepted so that such files can be exchanged among users? (Standardization is very important in this Internet age.)

There are two major file formats used for compressed image files. They are graphics interchange format (gif) and joint photographic experts group (jpeg) format.

Graphics Interchange Format (GIF)

This format is standardized for 256 colours (8 bits per pixel) of a maximum size of 65,535 × 65,535 pixels. It is widely used for World Wide Web images. The compression algorithm uses the statistical regularity of images to compress them. The algorithm used is called LZW compression. As a first step, 24 bits of colours per pixel given by a scanner is reduced to 8 bits per pixel. This group of 8 bits is used to look up in a table of 256 colours. One of the colours can be called transparent, which is usually the same as the background colour being used in the display. The reduction of 24 bits of colour to 8 bits compresses the image file by 67%. This colour reduction is not a great sacrifice from the point of view of quality as most PC monitors can display only 8 bits colour images. Only very expensive colour graphics workstations use 24 bits colour. One of the features of GIF that has made it popular is called *interlacing*. It first transmits every alternate line of an image during decompression so that a user sees a blurry image quickly, which is preferred by viewers who are normally impatient to see an image. The full image with all lines follows next and is of better quality. A compression ratio of 1:6 to 1:10 is achieved with GIF compression.

Graphics Interchange Format (GIF) is the preferred file format for monochrome greyscale images as such images use only 8 bits per pixel. The GIF compression method works very well if the picture is a line drawing, cartoon, handwritten text, or an X-ray which does not have the richness of colour and details of a colour photograph. This format is a preferred format for transmitting pictures on the World Wide Web as the compression provided by it is satisfactory for web applications and it is supported by all web browsers. The picture quality is quite sufficient for most display devices.

Joint Photographic Experts Group (JPEG) format

It is a compression method pronounced as the Jay-peg standard. It is a standard arrived at by an international group of experts and is very popular for compressing colour photographs with rich details. JPEG supports up to 24 bits colour per pixel and image sizes up to 65,535 × 65,535 pixels. The standard provides a range of quality factors that allow a user to sacrifice quality for higher compression of an image. Compression ratio is defined by specifying bits per pixel of a compressed image compared to the number in the original image. If 24 bits per pixel is used in an uncompressed image and 1 bit per pixel is used in the compressed image, the compression ratio is 1:24; in other words, the bit requirement to store the image is reduced 24-fold. Compression performance is best specified by stating the image quality (after the compression/decompression cycle) and the corresponding bits per pixel obtainable by the compression algorithm. For a set of colour pictures, it is stated in the literature that JPEG gives the results shown in Table 16.1.

TABLE 16.1 JPEG compression and quality for colour pictures using 24 bits per pixel

Compressed image quality	*Bits per pixel after compression*	*Average compression ratio*
Moderate quality image	0.25–0.5	1:64
Excellent quality image	0.75–1.5	1:21
Indistinguishable from original	1.5–2	1:14

The method of compression used by JPEG is said to be lossy as it throws away many bits in the picture that are not relevant to the quality of the image as seen by the human eye. These bits cannot be recovered. This works very well for pictures with rich detail but poorly for line drawings, colour cartoons, etc. For such pictures, GIF is better as its compression ratio is higher and the image quality is better. Unlike GIF which combines a compression algorithm and file format for compressed images, JPEG specifies only the compression algorithm. BMP or TIF files are compressed using the JPEG algorithm and the compressed file is stored using a file format known as JFIF (JPEG File Interchange Format). However, the file extension used for jpeg compressed files is .jpg. Another format is called TIFF 6.00, which is JPEG files stored using TIFF format. In Table 16.2, we summarize the discussions in this section.

TABLE 16.2 Image file formats

File format	*Applications*	*Advantages*	*Remarks*
Bit map (.bmp)	Uncompressed output of a scanner or camera	All information in image preserved	High storage. Should be compressed
Tagged file format (.tiff)	Exchanging image files	Widely used	Not usually compressed, but can be compressed
Graphical interchange format (.gif)	Exchanging compressed files. Most common in World Wide Web graphics. Good for line drawings, cartoons, monochrome images	Reasonable compression. Compression speed high. Lossless compression of 1:6 to 1:10	Limited colour palette. Widely supported
JPEG compression (.jpg), JPEG file format (.jfif)	Compressing colour pictures with rich detail	Can specify high compression for low quality and low compression for high quality. For overall compression, see Table 16.1	Complex compression algorithm. Should not be used for line drawing, cartoons, and monochrome images

16.4 CAPTURING A MOVING IMAGE WITH A VIDEO CAMERA

Digital video cameras are used to capture moving images. The principle of its working is similar to the digital still camera which we discussed in Section 16.2. Still image is captured using an exposure time much smaller than (1/30) of a second. Subsequent frames are obtained at a rate of 30 frames per second. These frames are compressed and stored in a flash memory in the camera. The frame size for an HD-ready video camera is 1280 × 720 pixels. Thus, one frame takes 1280 × 720 = 9,21,600 samples. As one frame takes (1/30) second to display, the number of samples to be taken per second is 921600 × 30 = 27648000. Each sample requires 1 byte for its representation and storage. Thus, we need to store 27.648 MB per second for monochrome video. If it is colour, each colour R, G, B requires 1 byte to represent it. Thus, the number of MB per second generated by a video colour camera is 82.944. If we take a video for 2 hours, the number of bytes generated is 2 × 60 × 60 × 82.944 MB ≅ 600 GB. This is very large and it is impractical to store this economically in the camera. We should thus compress this without degrading the quality. Currently, 1280 × 720 is considered low resolution and is being replaced by a standard known as Full HD progressive scan (also 1080p) which is 50 frames per second. The resolution in this standard is 1920 × 1080 pixels (an aspect ratio of 16:9). (This is the best High Definition camera standard evolved from HDTV.) The number of bytes required to store one colour frame in this standard is 1920 × 1080 × 3 ≅ 6 MB. As the repetition rate is 50 frames per second, 2 hours video will generate 6 × 2 × 60 × 60 × 50 = 2160 GB, which requires compression.

16.5 COMPRESSION OF VIDEO DATA

We saw in the last section the enormous amount of storage required to store digitized video. Apart from the storage required, the huge size of data leads to difficulty in the display and transmission of images. If the image is stored in a secondary memory, the bandwidth needed to display one colour picture frame using 1080p standard is (1920 × 1080 × 50 × 24) bits/s which is nearly 2.5 Gbps. If the picture is to be transmitted over a communication line from a video server to a display, around 2.5 Gbps bandwidth is needed from the communication line, which is expensive. Thus, we need compression of video for storage and transmission. We should, of course, expand it before it is displayed. In Section 16.3 we saw how still images can be compressed in various ways. One of them is the JPEG compression algorithm, which achieves compression by a factor of about 20. This compression is good for still pictures, but for video, we look for further possibilities of compression. As a group of pictures are transmitted one after another rapidly and there is very little variation between the pictures in a sequence, this fact should be exploited for compression. For example, in a scene where a bus is going on a road, most of the background, such as the sky, hills, etc., will not change; only a small part of the video corresponding to the moving bus will change from frame to frame. In such a case, only the changing part needs to be stored or transmitted for display. If the bus occupies (1/8) of the image area, then we need not store or transmit (7/8) th of the image in each frame. Only the first frame and the *changes* in subsequent frames need to be stored.

This is the main principle used in a compression algorithm standardized by an international committee known as the Motion Picture Experts Group (abbreviated MPEG, pronounced em-peg). In MPEG compression, a sequence of 12–20 frames constitute a package known as a group of pictures (GOP). This GOP is stored temporarily in the video camera and compressed by a local processor. The compressed images are stored in the camera's memory. The MPEG compression algorithm works as follows.

A JPEG-compressed frame is used to begin the process. This is called an I picture or intra-coded picture. It is a key picture that is used to compress subsequent frames. The I picture is divided into 'tiles' of 16 × 16 pixels. Corresponding tiles are taken in the next frame and the difference in pixel values of these tiles is calculated (see Figure 16.6). For most tiles, this difference will be very small as the background such as the sky or hills remains stationary. Only a small part of the picture will be different. The difference in pixel values will typically require very few bits; instead of storing 24 bits per pixel, the difference may be only 2–4 bits, thus reducing the number of bits stored by a factor of 12. When the difference in pixel values starts changing too much, we take another I-picture to begin the process again. The actual MPEG compression algorithm uses this idea but is in detail more complicated to get the maximum compression. If JPEG compression is used for I pictures and motion compression for a group of pictures, we get using MPEG2 a reduction of 100–150 in the bits stored for the video. Thus, a 2-hour video will require 20 GB storage instead of 2000 GB for the uncompressed video. It is possible to store 20 GB in a pen drive.

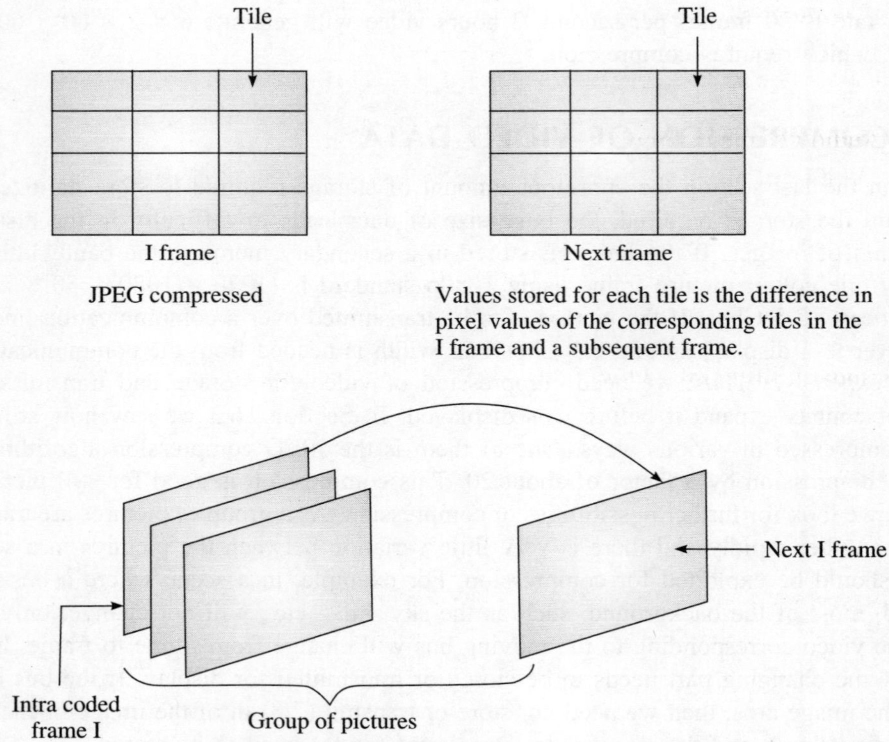

Figure 16.6 MPEG compression principles.

We saw that the bandwidth required for transmitting one compressed image frame within (1/50) of a second is 2.5 Gbps. After MPEG compression, the bandwidth needed will go down by a factor of 100–150. Thus, the bandwidth required to transmit compressed high-quality video will be around 20 Mbps, which is feasible with the current technology.

MPEG compressor is a complex piece of digital hardware that must have a memory to temporarily store a group of pictures and a fast processor to implement the compression algorithm. The hardware must be fast enough to compress the video in real-time, that is, while the video is being played. The decompressor also should have sufficient speed. With the improvement in PCs' speed, decompression can be performed by software running on a PC and pictures can be displayed on a display.

16.6 MPEG COMPRESSION STANDARD

Just like the JPEG standard gives the trade-off between the quality of the image and the amount of compression, MPEG's aim is also to provide flexibility allowing appropriate features based on application. The major features of the MPEG compression method are:

1. The compression method gives a 1–1.5 Mbps playback rate with acceptable quality of at least 320 × 240 pixels per frame.
2. It is possible to access any specified frame at random in the compressed video. The random access points are coded as I frames.
3. In addition to normal playback of the video, fast forward, and fast reverse to specified points is possible.
4. Audio/video synchronization is maintained.
5. Compression, decompression delays can be controlled.
6. Compressed video can be edited.
7. Low-cost processors and integrated circuit chips are available to compress the video in real-time.

MPEG is not a single standard but a series of standards. MPEG-1 is a standard used for video file transfer over the Internet. It is also used for TV-quality video. MPEG-2 supports 1080p standard. MPEG-4 addresses the problem of transmitting video on slow communication channels. It allows integrating animations with camera-captured video. Telephone lines with low speed are used in video-conferencing and applications using the World Wide Web. MPEG-2 is emerging as the *de-facto* standard for standard TV broadcasts on cables. MPEG-4 has a higher compression ratio of 200–300 and is used by satellite TV broadcasters.

16.7 ACQUIRING AND STORING AUDIO SIGNALS

There are many types of audio signals: speech, music, and noise. Each has its special characteristics. An important feature of audio is that it is a continuous function of time. In this section, we will describe how audio signals are acquired and converted to a digital form. This is essential to store and process audio signals using a computer. (In Section 11.7.1 we described how analog signals are converted to a sequence of bits by an analog-to-digital converter.)

Audio signals are acquired and stored using the system shown in Figure 16.7. Sound wave is converted to electrical signals by a microphone. This electrical signal is what is shown as an audio signal in Figure 11.15. This signal is fed to an appropriate A/D converter (See Sec.11.7.1). A large variety of A/D converters are available in the market. If we want to digitize telephone conversation, we use an A/D converter which gives 8 bits of digital output per sample and samples the input signal 6250 times per second (as the bandwidth of speech is 3 kHz). If the signal to be digitized is high fidelity audio, we use an A/D converter which uses 16-bit digital output for each sample and uses 44,100 samples per second as the bandwidth of good quality music is 22 kHz. The digitized audio file has a file extension .wav.

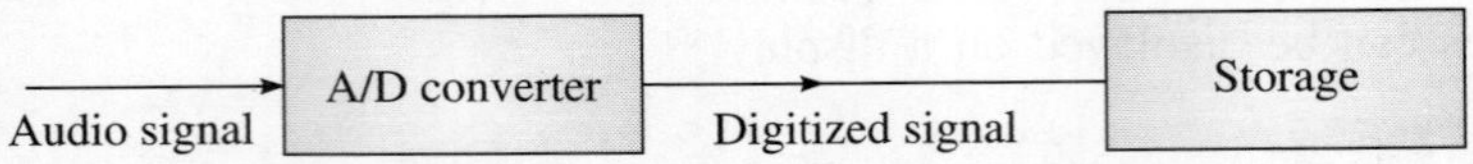

Figure 16.7 Digitizing audio signal.

The digital output of an A/D converter is stored in a memory. The type of memory used will depend on the type of input audio signal and the duration for which the values are to be stored. For a telephone message of 1 min duration, we need 6250 × 60 = 367 KB storage. This is small and we may store it in the main memory or the disk of a computer. For high-fidelity music, the memory needed to store 1 minute of music = 10.1 MB. Unlike telephone conversations, music lasts much longer. If we want to store 60 minutes of music, the storage needed is 60 × 10.1 MB = 606 MB. This may be stored in a pen drive.

We have discussed the need for an electronic circuit called A/D converter to digitize audio signals. Such a circuit is built into an electronic circuit called a *sound card*, which is nowadays built into the motherboards of PCs. To convert music on your (now obsolete) audio cassette tape to digital form, connect the audio out of the tape recorder to the audio input jack of your PC with an appropriate connector. You invoke a program on your PC to read the audio signal. This program will use the sound card, convert the input audio signal to digital form, and store it on the hard disk as a file. Such a file has a file extension .wav. It is called a *wave file*.

In multimedia PCs, good-quality loudspeakers are normally built-in. The digitized audio signal can be played back using the sound card. The card has an electronic circuit called a digital-to-analog converter (D/A converter) which reads the sequence of bits stored in a .wav file, converts it to a continuously varying analog signal, amplifies it, and feeds it to the loudspeakers. The volume control on the speakers can be used to adjust the loudness.

We emphasize that wave files are all digital, that is, a series of bits. A file name can be given to each song when you play the audio tape and store it on the PC. Using this file name, you can select this song from the disk and play it back whenever you need it.

Nowadays smartphones are most often used to store and play music. A built-in recorder in smartphones records live music or that from a player and stores it in its memory normally as a named .wav file. This can be played back using its file name.

CDs as common media for music are disappearing. They are now replaced by music streaming subscription services such as Spotify, Amazon Music, Apple Music, etc. Some Websites sell music. They are all digital and can be downloaded to your PC or smartphone. YouTube also has plenty of music that can be downloaded or streamed.

16.8 COMPRESSION OF AUDIO SIGNALS

We saw in the previous section that if we want to store 60 minutes of good-quality music in digital form, we need 606 MB of memory. If many hours of music are to be stored on a website, we should compress the digitized audio file without sacrificing the quality of the audio signal. The ideas used in audio compression are similar to that used to compress pictures. The standard compression method is called MP3. MP3 is the short form for Moving Pictures Experts Group—Version 2—Layer 3 audio compression standard. This method has been standardized by an international group of experts. This compression algorithm uses the characteristics of the human ear which, when two sounds are played, hears the louder sound rather than the softer sound. The softer sound need not be stored. The number of samples of audio signals may be reduced during periods when its frequency is low. Silent periods in music or speech need not be stored. MP3 compression uses these features of audio. MP3 algorithm reduces the storage requirement by a factor of 10–14. Thus, 60 minutes of music may be stored in 606/13 = 46.6 MB (taking 13 as the compression ratio). With this compression, 24 hours of music occupies only 1.12 GB. MP3 compression programs are widely available. Websites can store hundreds of hours of music economically in MP3 format. MP3 decompression programs are built as part of the OSs of modern PCs and smartphones using Android or iOS.

16.9 AUDIO SIGNAL PROCESSING

Audio signal processing may be classified as transforming, generating and recognizing audio signals. We will discuss these in what follows.

16.9.1 Transforming Audio Signals

The types of transformation or manipulation we would like to perform on audio signals are as follows:

- Remove noise such as a hissing sound found in old audio tapes or crackling sounds in old radio recordings. This operation is generally known as filtering noise. Sometimes it is called *digital re-mastering* of old analog records.
- Enhance lower frequencies in a recording called bass enhancement to improve the sound quality we hear.
- Adjust the amplitudes of various sound frequencies to enhance the sound quality.
- Produce special effects such as the 'concert hall effect' by simulating echoes. This is done by mixing the sound file with a slightly delayed file so that the composite file will sound as though the audio is heard in an auditorium.
- Blank out some parts of a recording that may not be necessary, such as long applause and speeches.
- Add a recording of what is known as 'canned laughter', that is, pre-recorded laughter of a group, to a recording of a joke. This is an example of audio editing.
- Create a new recording by cutting and pasting songs from several other audio files.

All the above types of transformation or processing may be done with a multimedia PC equipped with a *sound card* and loudspeakers. If the uncompressed audio file is stored with file extension .wav, an OS such as Windows has a program called a media player which provides a window display with control buttons similar to that of a CD player. Buttons are displayed for play, fast forward, rewind, pause, and stop all, as illustrated in Figure 16.8.

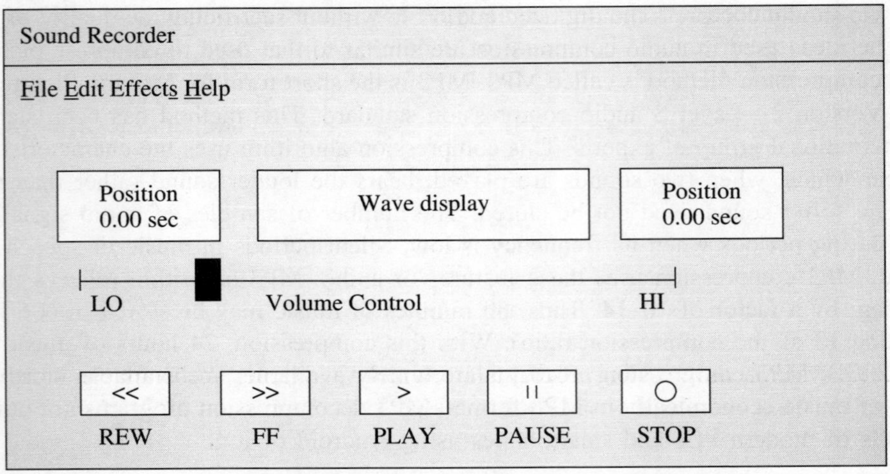

Figure 16.8 Media player window.

An audio file manipulation program is provided with the media player. This player has commands to cut and paste audio files, add special sound effects, blank out parts of the file, etc. By pressing the PLAY button, the audio file is played and as it advances, its position can be seen on the display. This facilitates the editing of the audio file. With the increasing speed of processors, files stored in MP3 compressed form may be expanded to .wav format continuously as they are read from the memory and manipulated/edited and played using the built-in speakers to assess the effects. The processed file may be compressed again to MP3 format for storage if needed.

16.9.2 Generation of Audio Signals

You would have heard people playing a music synthesizer such as a Casio keyboard. This electronic system can mimic the sounds of various musical instruments, such as violin, piano, flute, viola, and many other instruments. They can also combine them to simulate the effects of an orchestra. The basic idea used by these synthesizers is to have pure tones corresponding to the seven notes sa, ri, ga, ma, pa, da, and ni. There are seven identical notes in Western music known as doh, re, me, fa, soh, la, te, which are also called C, D, E, F, G, A, and B. Music is generated by combining these notes and their harmonics with different amplitudes and adding them. By varying the amplitudes of various notes, we can generate an enormous number of musical compositions. The synthesizers have electronic circuits to generate these notes, and their harmonics, adjust amplitudes, and add notes to modulate the sound. Note that selections and amplitude adjustments are done manually by keyboard players. A music synthesizer can be simulated by a PC with a sound card. PC can store the seven notes and their harmonics in digital form and a program can be written to combine them to generate music. Many modern composers mimic orchestras using computer-based simulation.

To be able to connect a music synthesizer to a PC and vice versa, the electronic musical instruments industry has standardized what is known as the Musical Instrument Digital Interface (MIDI). MIDI specification consists of the following two parts:

1. Hardware connection standard—cable type, connector, and output port type.
2. Instrument specification—beginning of a note, end of a note, basic frequencies, and sound volume. MIDI standard allows 10 octaves corresponding to 128 notes.

Programs are available to create a MIDI file on a PC and communicate it to electronic musical instruments that will play the music.

16.9.3 Generation of Speech from Text

Another audio generation system is known as a text-to-speech system. Given an ASCII-coded text, a computer should be able to speak it out. This is particularly useful for visually handicapped persons who cannot read web pages that may have time-varying information. Text-to-speech systems have a long history and currently, systems are available which do an excellent job, including what is known as *prosody.* Prosody means the stress and the tone used for words. For example, a question is spoken differently compared to a statement. A general block diagram of a text-to-speech system is given in Figure 16.9. It uses the idea of putting together the sounds of letters called *phones.* For example, c in cat and p in pat have two different phones.

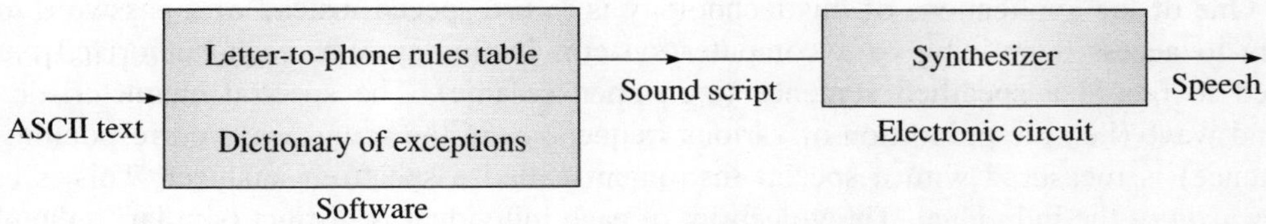

Figure 16.9 A text-to-speech system.

Given a word, one may attempt to put together individual phones to create that word sound. English is not a phonetic language, and thus such a simple idea does not always work. For example, k in the word knife is silent, unlike k in kite. A dictionary of exceptions is therefore needed. Once the individual letter sounds are generated, they are connected to form sounds for words. This is done by using *morph,* which is the smallest speech unit that carries a meaning. For example, war is a morph but not a warship. The synthesizer creates morphs and combines them to obtain speech. More sophisticated synthesizers introduce prosody and attempt to produce natural-sounding speech. The current state-of-the-art produces excellent text-to-speech systems which sound very natural. There are even versions that use British pronunciation of sentences that are different from American pronunciation.

16.9.4 Recognition of Audio Signals

An important recognition problem is speech recognition which we will briefly describe in this section. In Figure 16.10, we give an overview of problems related to the analysis and recognition of speech. A simple application of speech analysis is recognizing a speaker from his speech sample.

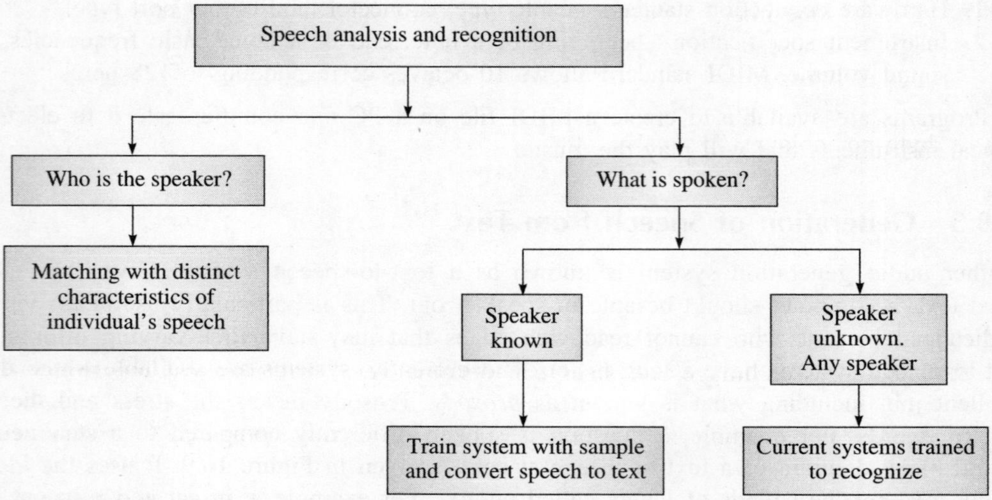

Figure 16.10 Overview of problems in speech analysis and recognition.

One of the applications of this technology is to use speech instead of a password to allow users to access a building or a computer system. In this system, each authorized person is asked to record a specified sentence (e.g., open sesame). The spectral characteristic of the sound wave (i.e., the proportion of various frequencies in the sound wave corresponding to the sentence) is measured with a special instrument called a spectrum analyzer. This is called a *voiceprint* of the individual. The voiceprint of each individual is distinct (similar to thumbprints of individuals which are distinct). This voiceprint is used to control access to a facility. Use of voiceprints is not foolproof. If there is too much background noise, recognition of a voiceprint may not be easy. Also, if the speaker's voice becomes hoarse due to his catching a cold, it may be rejected. If another person trains himself to mimic the speech of an authorized person, he can fool the system.

A more difficult problem is to recognize speech and convert it to text. As of now (2025) many speech-to-text systems are available and their performance is excellent. They have used large neural networks and machine learning to train them. Once trained they are able to convert speech to text. Many systems can even understand several accents and perform a reasonable job.

Another interesting development is natural language question-answering systems. Notable among them is Alexa, a system developed and marketed by Amazon. One can ask it a question in English and it gives a reasonable answer in English. For example, one can ask about the cricket score of a specific match and it searches the Internet and answers. It is even able to distinguish between different accents and reply reasonably accurately.

SUMMARY

1. Pictures and textual material are acquired using a scanner or a digital camera. Printed text, handwritten text, and black-and-white cartoons are stored as a bit map with 1-bit storage per pixel.

2. A multi-tone image is scanned with the same scanner, but each pixel is stored as a byte. A byte can represent 64 levels of grey.
3. A multicolour image uses three colours, red, green, and blue, in appropriate proportions to represent each pixel. A scanner codes a colour picture using 24 bits per pixel (one byte per colour). The value of the byte represents the intensity of the colour. When these three colours are combined, we get 16 million colours.
4. The representation of pictures by an equivalent array of bits is called a *bit map* representation. A file that stores the bit map representation of a picture is called a *bmp* file. Image files may be stored using several file formats. The simplest format stores the bit equivalents of pixels, with a header specifying the number of rows and columns in the pixel array. This is called a tiff file (tagged image file format).
5. Uncompressed image file sizes can become very large (several megabytes). Thus, image files are normally compressed before they are stored. When the image is to be displayed, it is expanded (decompressed).
6. There are two primary compression methods. They are called GIF (Graphical Interchange Format) and JPEG (Joint Photographic Experts Group).
7. The method used to compress images in GIF is called LZW compression. It uses the images' statistical property to reduce its storage requirement.
8. JPEG compression transforms an image to another form and throws away information which does not contribute significantly to the image's appearance. This is called lossy compression and works well for photographs.
9. Table 16.2 summarizes various image file formats, compression methods, and their advantages and disadvantages.
10. A digital camera uses the lens system of a normal film camera. Instead of a film, a CCD array senses the image. A mosaic of colour (Red, Blue, Green) filters capture colour pictures. JPEG compression is used to store the images in a flash memory.
11. A video camera acquires a moving picture by taking 30 images per second so that motion is captured.
12. For good quality images 24 Megapixel cameras store 6000 × 4000 pixels per frame. Each pixel needs 3-byte coding to represent colour.
13. A video standard called 1080p (evolved for high-definition TV) uses 1920 × 1080 pixels per frame and 50 frames per second. In this standard, a 2-hour video needs 2160 GB storage.
14. Besides the enormous storage, we need a high-speed readout to view the video. It is thus essential to compress the digital video data.
15. In video compression, each image frame is first compressed using JPEG compression.
16. In most videos, a large portion of the background image does not change; movement is limited to a small part of an image. This fact is exploited in video compression.
17. A group of pictures (around 20) are taken. A starting image is used as a reference for the group. The difference in pixel values of corresponding pixels in the group of images is much smaller than the number of bits used per pixel. This idea is used to encode other images in a group, thereby compressing the video. Compression by a factor of 100–150 has been achieved by using MPEG-2.

18. A set of standards called MPEG (MPEG-1, MPEG-2, MPEG-4) is used to compress videos using the general principle stated in point 16 of this summary. MPEG-1 is used for normal TV and computer display. MPEG-2 is used for video using 1080p standard, also known as High Definition Digital TV. MPEG-4 is used in World Wide Web applications that use low-speed data transmission paths. Satellite TV broadcasters use MPEG-4 in their systems.
19. Audio signal, unlike text and pictures, has time as an explicit variable. It is a continuous function of time. It is called an analog signal.
20. Audio signals are converted to a sequence of bits; that is, they are digitized because digitized audio provides noise tolerance and allows easy processing to enhance sound quality.
21. Audio signals are digitized by an electronic circuit known as an analog-to-digital (A/D) converter. Digitized audio signals are converted back to continuous audio signals by another electronic circuit known as a Digital to Analog (D/A) converter.
22. Currently available PCs and smartphones have features to convert audio signals to digital form and store them in a file with extension .wav. These files can also be played back and heard using built-in speakers.
23. As the number of bytes needed to store 60 minutes of music is around 600 MB, it is compressed before storage. Audio is compressed by a program to what is known as MP3 audio file format. MP3 is an industry-standard. MP3 compresses the number of bits in an audio file by a factor of 10 to 14.
24. Major audio processing applications are: modifying existing digitized audio files, generating or synthesizing audio files using primitive sound patterns, recognizing speakers from audio samples of their speech, and converting text-to-speech, and speech-to-text.
25. Audio data processing consists of modifying digitized sound files to remove noise, enhance sound quality, add special effects to existing sound files, edit audio files by cutting and pasting, etc. All these operations are possible with a multimedia PC with built-in tools to perform these tasks.
26. Computers may be used to synthesize music by combining pre-recorded samples of basic notes.
27. Manufacturers of electronic musical instruments (such as music keyboards) have standardized an interface to interconnect a set of electronic musical instruments and a computer. This standard is called Musical Instruments Digital Interface (MIDI). Computers can be connected to electronic musical instruments equipped with MIDI and send commands to the instrument to create music.
28. Programs are available to convert textual input to spoken output. The general idea is to combine sounds corresponding to each letter to create word sounds. This is done by using a set of rules evolved by experimentation.
29. Recognition of audio signals (particularly spoken sounds) may be classified into two broad categories: (i) Recognizing a speaker from a sample of his speech and (ii) converting spoken sentences to ASCII text. The conversion of speech to text can, in turn, be classified as speaker-dependent or speaker-independent.
30. Recognizing a speaker based on specific spoken sentence(s) analyses the speech sound

and creates a voice print that is distinct for each speaker.

31. Speaker-dependent text-to-speech system works after the system is trained by the speaker with his voice and pronunciation. Currently, such systems work quite effectively with a large vocabulary of over 20,000 words.

32. Speaker-independent speech recognition is now widely available and used.

REVIEW QUESTIONS

16.1 What is a scanner? Explain how it works.

16.2 What is the difference between two-tone images and multi-tone images? Which of the following are two-tone and which are multi-tone?
   (i) Black and white map of a country
   (ii) An X-ray picture
   (iii) Black and white cartoons
   (iv) A black and white photograph

16.3 How many bytes are needed to store 100 black-and-white scanned pictures of size 3″ × 4½″? Assume a scanner with a resolution of 300 × 600 and 256 grey tones.

16.4 A 24-bit colour scanner is used to scan a coloured map of India of size 12″ × 16″. As it is a map, a high-resolution scanner with 600 × 1200 resolution is used. What is the storage needed if the map is stored in a .bmp file?

16.5 What is a .tif file? In what way is it different from .bmp file? Explain the file format used in .tif files.

16.6 What is image compression? Why do we compress image files? Why should decompression time be shorter than compression time?

16.7 What are the criteria that must be examined for comparing image compression algorithms?

16.8 What is .gif compressed image format? What method of compression is used in gif compression? Approximately how much compression is achievable with this compression?

16.9 What is jpeg compression? Where is it used? What is the primary advantage of jpeg compression?

16.10 Which compression method allows trading of compression ratio with quality?

16.11 What is a digital camera? How does it acquire images?

16.12 Does a digital camera use any compression algorithm to compress and store images? If yes, what compressed file format does it use?

16.13 What are the advantages of using a digital camera? Do digital cameras give negatives like usual optical cameras? What are the disadvantages of digital cameras?

16.14 What is the difference between still images and video? Why does digitized video require a large storage space to be stored?

16.15 How much storage does a 640 × 480-pixel monochrome image video of duration 2-hour need? How much is the storage if it is a colour video? How much storage is needed if 1080p standard is used?

16.16 Why is it necessary to compress digital video data? Briefly explain the principle of the method used for MPEG2 compression.

16.17 What is an I frame? What are the basic requirements to be met by a frame to be picked as an I frame?

16.18 Which is the most cost-effective compression method? Justify your answer.

16.19 What is the compression ratio achieved using MPEG2 file format?

16.20 Explain the difference between acquiring monochrome video and acquiring colour video.

16.21 Explain how a video is acquired using a digital video camera.

16.22 What are the major objectives of the MPEG compression method? What are the series of MPEG standards and what is each one intended for?

16.23 An English colour movie of a 2-hour duration is to be digitized and stored in a Pendrive. How much storage is needed in the Pendrive?

16.24 What is audio? Enumerate different types of audio signals.

16.25 Distinguish between graphics and audio.

16.26 Why are audio signals digitized?

16.27 What are the advantages of digital processing of audio data?

16.28 What are the steps used in converting an audio signal to its digital equivalent?

16.29 What is MP3 compression? Why is MP3 compression used? How is MP3 compression done?

16.30 How are audio signals digitized and compressed using a PC? What file extension is used to represent audio files on a PC?

16.31 Assume you have a music library with 50 tapes, each of 45 minutes in duration. If this audio library is digitized and compressed to MP3 format, how big a pendrive is needed to store it?

16.32 What are the operations normally performed on audio files? Which of these operations can be performed with a PC or a smartphone?

16.33 What do you understand by the term music synthesis? How can music be synthesized using a PC?

16.34 What is MIDI? Where is it used?

16.35 What is a text-to-speech system? What are its applications?

16.36 What is speech recognition? What are its applications?

16.37 What is a speaker-independent speech recognizer? Is it feasible in practice? What are its possible applications?

17 Emerging Computing Environments

LEARNING GOALS

After reading this chapter, you should be able to:

- Identify the technology trends that are influencing the computing environment of computer users.
- Describe various methods of computing that have emerged and use computers connected to the Internet to solve problems cooperatively.
- Compare peer to peer, volunteer, grid, and cloud computing and describe their features.

In Chapter 13, we discussed computer networks. We described how local area networks in organizations enhance the utility of individual computers and the productivity of organizations. We also described how a worldwide network of computers, namely, the Internet, can be built using the TCP/IP protocol for communication among computers. We described how several new services, such as email, file transfer, remote login, and the World Wide Web, are built using the Internet.

Several developments have taken place since the early days of the Internet. The availability of a worldwide infrastructure of computing and communications, the low cost of using this infrastructure, and improved security of usage have spawned numerous novel applications. The most important among these are:

- E-commerce
- Digital library and information search engines
- Multimedia services using IP such as Voice over IP and Internet television
- Web 2.0 applications, namely, Blogs, Facebook, YouTube, and Twitter
- 4 G and 5 G mobile communication that use the Internet Protocol to communicate.

Several other emerging applications depend on using the collective computing power of numerous individual computers connected to the Internet.

The computing environment available to users is changing rapidly. The next generation will see a transformation in the manner computers are used today. The objective of this chapter is to discuss how the availability of a worldwide computing infrastructure is changing the computing environment for the users.

17.1 CURRENT COMPUTING SCENARIO

We will briefly examine the current computing scenario. Nowadays every bank clerk, office worker, salesperson, and those involved in similar jobs have to access a desktop/laptop computer for their routine activities. Most desktop/laptop computers use processors with 3 GHz clock, have 32 GB of main memory and 200 GB to 1 TB disk drives. They also have common software such as Office, browsers, and antivirus and are connected to the Internet. Every 24 months the computing power doubles and every 18 months the secondary storage size (disk and pen drives) doubles at no extra cost. The OS and applications become more complex, using most of the hardware resources.

There are several other problems in the current scenario:

- Most desktops do not use their full capacity, namely, CPU power and disk space, as they are not required for routine jobs.
- Most desktops are not utilized 24 hours a day, 7 days a week. Utilization of 50% is considered good. On the average, less than 25% of the capacity is used.
- Desktops become obsolete usually in 3 years and have to be replaced (obsolescence is planned as no spare parts for repair are available).
- Specialized application programs such as accounting, engineering design, and database management are expensive and have complex licensing rules. Even routine software such as for office applications has to be bought or licensed for each desktop. The cumulative cost of the software for an organization with hundreds of desktops is very high.
- Most large organizations have hundreds of desktops and several servers that need continuous troubleshooting and assistance to users, thereby wasting an enormous amount of organization's time. This cost is hidden.
- Organizations invest large amounts to create, maintain, and continuously update their computing infrastructure. Computing is not the core activity of most organizations.

Thus, they would prefer to avoid this expense if there is a good alternative. On the positive side, we have the following developments:

- The Internet has become all-pervasive. All desktops are connected to a LAN and the LAN to the Internet using Wi-Fi.
- The communication speeds are doubling almost every 9 months with no increase in cost. Due to this, most local networks have a bandwidth of 100 Mbps to 1 Gbps. The Internet service providers provide broadband connection to the Internet at high speeds of 1 to 100 Mbps from homes and speeds of 1 to 10 Gbps from organizations. Mobile bandwidths are also increasing and mobile Internet connections are becoming

less expensive. Higher bandwidth implies that when a user accesses a server from a desktop, he/she will not know whether the server is in his/her organization or is with a service provider who is a few thousand kilometres away. The difference in response time will not be perceptible. This has spawned several new computing environments, most of them using computers connected to the Internet.

17.2 PEER TO PEER COMPUTING

One of the earliest methods of using computers connected to a local area network was and continues to be, the client-server model. We discussed this in Section 12.8. In this model, several desktop computers connected to a local area network can access one or more powerful servers for specialized services such as computing, printing, database access, etc. A client-server model has an unequal relationship, a client requesting a service and a server providing it. Another model which succeeded the client-server model is called a *peer to peer (P2P)* computing model. The dictionary meaning of 'peer group' as applied to people is a group of persons of equal merit, rank, etc. In other words, two peers have a symmetric relationship. As applied to computers connected to a network, any computer can act as a client or a server depending on the problem to be solved; there is no distinction. Thus, peers may provide or use the services of other peers. The system is decentralized and each computer has equal power. The network is robust and resistant to single-point failure.

A major problem in the P2P model is peer discovery. How does one find peers to work with? One method would be to broadcast a request. This is not very practical on the Internet. Another possibility is to send a message to a server that has a directory of peers and resources available, that is IP addresses of PCs which are in a peer group and resources they can offer. A new member may then send a request to join the group which may be accepted when some criteria are met by the requester. In a file-sharing situation, a new member should be able to offer some files of interest to other peers. A centralized server model may create a bottleneck at the server. One more method assumes that a computer desiring to join a peer group has the address of at least one group member. This member would have a directory of other members of the group. Thus, a new member can join the group if it is allowed based on a set of membership criteria that may be available to all peers. The new group member would then store the directory and other peers would update their respective directories. Peers currently logged on to the Internet can be found by IP multicast.

One of the first popular applications of the P2P model was a service called *Napster* designed by Shawn Fanning in 1999. In this service, a peer group of computers had an agreed protocol, whereby any PC belonging to the group could access music files stored in any other PC in the group and download them on their PC. This allowed the peers to exchange music files. To facilitate this exchange, Napster dedicated a server that kept a directory of music files available with each member. The music industry filed a case against Napster alleging copyright infringement. A court in the USA ordered Napster to close down in 2001.

Another active and widely used P2P file-sharing protocol is called BitTorrent which enables sharing of files distributed in computers connected to the Internet. It was created in 2001 by Bram Cohen. A large file such as a widely used open-source software is divided into small pieces and distributed among a group of cooperating peers. A website hosts a tracker that keeps a file with the addresses of all the peers that have previously downloaded the file. A person requiring the file can access several peers having it and download pieces from them using much less bandwidth and assemble them locally. This copy now becomes a part of the peer group and its address is stored by the tracker. This site becomes a new member of the peer group allowing another peer to download the file. This peer to peer (P2P) file sharing is much faster. BitTorrent has been widely used to download large video files such as movies. The use of BitTorrent to download copyrighted material is illegal.

Recently a technology known as Blockchain has emerged. It is a distributed ledger that records transactions across multiple computers of a P2P network to ensure the security, transparency, and immutability of data in the ledger. Each node in the P2P network stores a complete copy of the blockchain. New blocks can be added to the blockchain only if it satisfies a previously agreed consensus rule. No file in the Blockchain can be changed unilaterally as this change will be known to all the peers. Observe that blockchain is decentralized and distributed and not subject to centralized control. An example of a Blockchain is Bitcoin.

17.3 VOLUNTEER COMPUTING

This idea of a group of volunteers sharing files was extended to sharing computing resources. In this model members belonging to a group would allow the use of idle CPU time in their computers by other members. This model known as *Volunteer Computing* led to two useful and important worldwide cooperative efforts in which computers connected to the Internet are shared. The two projects are named SETI@home and Folding@home. SETI@home has as its objective, finding whether there is any other intelligent civilization in our universe. Electromagnetic waves are received at all times from space. The idea is to find if there is any regularity in these waves indicating non-random 'intelligent communication' that may be sent by another civilization. A program was written by a group of scientists to analyze these waves to detect any signals of significance. As the amount of data is enormous (several petabytes), the time taken to analyze it on even a supercomputer would be too large and too expensive. Besides, the project has a long period. Thus, the SETI@home project requested all those with Internet connection at home to donate CPU time from their machines when they are idle. The SETI@home project distributed a program to each of the volunteers along with a chunk of data to analyze. All these programs were executed in parallel using the idle CPU times of participants (also called *scavenging CPU cycles* whenever a CPU is not busy) and the results were sent to a server for inspection. The number of volunteers was quite large (over 300,000) and the resulting computing power was around 528 teraflops. The project stopped in March 2020.

Another current project is on protein folding. Protein folding programs predict how a sequence of amino acids will fold into their 3D shapes to fight diseases, build tissues, and transport nutrients and are compute-intensive. In this project also several volunteers donate time on their idle computers connected to the Internet. Folding@home is still active (2025). The total computing power used by the project is 45 petaflops. Both these problems are known as *single program multiple data* parallel programs. In other words, all computers in the volunteer group execute identical programs on different data sets.

As no communication is needed among volunteers and the volunteers work independently, the speed that one can get in solving a problem is almost linear. In other words, if the CPU speed of the ith computer is s_i and there are n computers in the volunteer group, the effective speed available for solving the problem in parallel is the sum of s_i for $i = 1$ to n.

As several such projects were initiated, the University of California, Berkeley, developed a software suite Berkeley Open Infrastructure for Network Computing (BOINC) (www.boinc.berkeley.edu) and invited volunteers to install it on their computers to donate free CPU cycles. This suite allows universities, for example, to create a virtual supercomputer by cooperatively using several thousand PCs located throughout a campus. It also allows many projects to run on computer time donated by the volunteers. As of 2025, BOINC has been installed in over 133,000 computers with a total nominal speed of 20 Petaflops.

The idea of Volunteer computing and the possibility of using numerous computers connected to the Internet to solve problems cooperatively led to the next development.

17.4 GRID COMPUTING

We stated at the beginning of this chapter that the bandwidth of communication networks has been doubling every 9 months with no increase in cost. A major consequence is that the distance between a client and a server is irrelevant. In other words, computing resources may be spread across the world in several organizations, and if the organizations decide to cooperate, a member of an organization will be able to use the computer of a cooperating organization whenever the member needs it, provided it is not busy. Even if it is busy, the member may be able to reserve it for later use. Organizations may cooperate and share not only computers but also scientific instruments, databases, and specialized software. The interconnected resources of cooperating organizations constitute what is known as a *computing grid.* The idea of grid computing was proposed by Ian Foster and his coworkers around 2000 and has spawned several projects worldwide. A project called *Globus* was started as a cooperative effort of several organizations to make the idea of grid computing a reality. Globus has developed standard tools to implement grid computing systems.

The Globus project (www.globus.org) defined a computer grid as: "an infrastructure that enables the integrated, collaborative use of high-end computers, networks, databases and scientific instruments owned and managed by multiple organizations". It was later refined to emphasize the fact that there is no centralized control. The definition added: "a system that coordinates resources that are not subject to centralized control using standards, open general-purpose protocols, and interfaces to deliver a non-trivial quality of service".

Comparing these two definitions, we observe that both of them emphasize the fact that resources are owned and operated by independent organizations, not subject to centralized control and that the resources may be combined to deliver a requested service. The first definition emphasizes the collaborative use of computing and other facilities. The second definition emphasizes, in addition, the use of open standards and protocols, as well as the importance of ensuring a specified Quality of Service (QoS). Several important aspects related to grid computing which we may infer from these definitions are as follows:

- Remote facilities are used by an organization only when such facilities are not locally available.
- Remote facilities are owned by other organizations which will have their policies for use. There is no centralized control.

- Open (i.e., nonproprietary) standards and protocols are to be used to allow cooperation among grid members.
- While using remote facilities, an organization should not compromise its security and that of the host.
- There must be some mechanisms to discover what facilities are available in a grid, where they are available, and policies on their use such as charging, priority, etc.
- As the grid belongs to a 'virtual organization', namely, separate organizations with agreed policies on collaboration, there must also be a policy defining QoS. QoS may include a specified time by which the requested resource should be provided and its availability for a specified time.
- Computers belonging to member organizations of the grid may be configured to work cooperatively (in parallel) to solve a single large computing-intensive problem.

To support a grid infrastructure, the software components must perform several functions. The important ones are as follows:

1. Authenticate a user and determine his/her access rights to resources and limits on their use.
2. Interpret the user's request for resources and forward it in an appropriate form to a resource manager. Quote the cost of resources requested where appropriate.
3. Log diagnostic messages and forward them to the user.
4. Provide a time estimate for job completion. This is one of the QoS parameters.
5. Send results to the user when the job is complete.
6. Maintain a directory of resources and the cost for their use.
7. Schedule users' jobs and monitor the progress of each job.
8. Encrypt data being sent to the grid and provide security of jobs.
9. Guard against threats such as viruses, worms, etc.
10. Ensure security of users' data and the data resident in the grid infrastructure.

These software components are normally organized as a layered architecture. Each layer depends on the services provided by the lower layers. Each layer, in turn, supports several components which cooperate to provide the necessary service. The layered architecture is shown in Table 17.1.

Table 17.1 Layered grid architecture

Layer name	*Components in layer*
Application layer	Scientific and engineering applications, collaborative computing environment, collaborative databases, software environment
Collective layer	Directory of available services, Brokering (resource management, selection, aggregation), Resource discovery, diagnostics, monitoring
Resource and connectivity layer	Secure resource allocation, Quality of service monitoring and provision, User authentication, calculating and collecting usage costs, encryption, etc.
Physical layer	Computers, storage media, instruments, networks, databases, OS, software libraries

The collective layer in this layered architecture performs functions 1, 2, 3, 4, 5. The resource and connectivity layer performs functions 6 to 10. The application layer specifies the applications appropriate for the grid infrastructure and the software environment available. The physical layer is a collection of various resources which are parts of the grid and system software.

The software requirements to support a grid infrastructure are so huge that it is impractical for a single organization to develop it. Several organizations including computer industry participants developed an open source Globus toolkit consisting of a large suite of programs. They are all standards-based and the components are designed to create appropriate software environment to use the grid. There is also a global open grid forum (www.ogf.org) which meets to evolve standards.

We will now examine how the grid infrastructure is invoked by a user and how it carries out a user's request. The steps are as follows:

1. A user develops a distributed program using appropriate tools available in the application layer software.
2. A user specifies the data resources needed and QoS requirement and submits the task to a broker (the broker is part of the collective layer). The broker has access to the resource directory, equivalent resources, availability, and cost.
3. Using the above data, the broker finds the optimal set of resources which can be scheduled to carry out the user's request, meeting user's QoS requirement.
4. Before scheduling a user's job, the broker estimates the cost and verifies the customer's capacity to pay based on its available credit. The broker may send the cost estimate to the user and get the user's concurrence before proceeding further.
5. If the user agrees, the broker schedules the job on the identified resources. It monitors the job's progress and notifies the user in case of any problem.
6. When the job is completed, the results and the cost of running the job are sent to the user.

17.4.1 Enterprise Grid

The grid computing environment we described so far assumes that several organizations cooperate to form a virtual organization. Large enterprises often have computing facilities distributed in different locations. A multinational enterprise may, for instance, have computing facilities at branches spread in several countries. Each branch would have a local view. From an enterprise point of view, it is desirable to have a global view and optimize the configuration and the use of all the computers, particularly high-performance servers located in the branches. The research done by the grid computer group and the availability of Globus software tools has motivated large enterprises to examine the creation of an *enterprise grid*. An enterprise grid would interconnect all computers and other resources, particularly databases, to create a computing fabric accessible to all the members of the enterprise. Several advantages accrue to an enterprise when it uses grid architecture. Some of them are as follows:

- Savings which arise due to reducing the idle time of computers. Idle computers in one location may be used from other locations
- Access to high-performance computing to all from their desktop.
- Improvement in reliability and QoS.

- Reduced hardware and software costs, reduced operational costs, and improvement in the productivity of resources.
- Better utilization of the enterprise's intranet.

Other benefits that accrue when an enterprise grid is used are as follows:

- It promotes collaboration between employees and the formation of (virtual) teams spread across the enterprise.
- Provides easy seamless secure access to the remote instruments and sensors besides software and hardware.
- In case of system failure at one location, the grid allows migration of applications to other locations of the enterprise so that there is minimal disruption.
- Overall enterprise grid infrastructure benefits the enterprises by enabling innovations and making better business decisions as an enterprise view is now possible. It also reduces the overall cost of computing infrastructure.
- Several vendors have cooperated to establish the enterprise grid alliance (www.ega.org). The objectives of this alliance are to adopt and deploy grid standards, including interoperability. They work closely with the Globus consortium.

There are also examples of enterprises collaborating with Universities to solve difficult problems. One often-cited industrial global grid project is a distributed aircraft maintenance environment (www.wrgrid.org.uk/leaflets/DAME.pdf). In this project, the Rolls Royce aircraft engine design group collaborated with several UK Universities to implement a decision support system for maintenance applications. The system used a huge amount of data which was logged by temperature sensors, noise sensors, and other relevant sensors in real-time from thousands of aircraft and analyzed them using a computing grid to detect problems and suggest solutions to reduce downtime of aircraft and to avert accidents.

Another emerging trend is creating Customer Data Platform (CDP) by enterprises that uses an enterprise grid environment. A CDP is a centralized system that collects, unifies, manages, and stores securely data about its customers. The data is collected from diverse sources such as the customers' websites, mentions in social media, and customer relationship management systems.

There are several such projects in the anvil and enterprise grids will be deployed widely soon.

17.5 CLOUD COMPUTING

One may define *cloud computing* as a method of computing in which a customer uses a set of services hosted by service providers over the Internet. The set of services includes computing infrastructure such as compute servers and storage servers, program development environment, and ready-to-use software systems. The term cloud computing is a metaphor for the Internet [which is often depicted as enclosed by a diffuse cloud in diagrams (see Figure 17.1)] over which the services are provided.

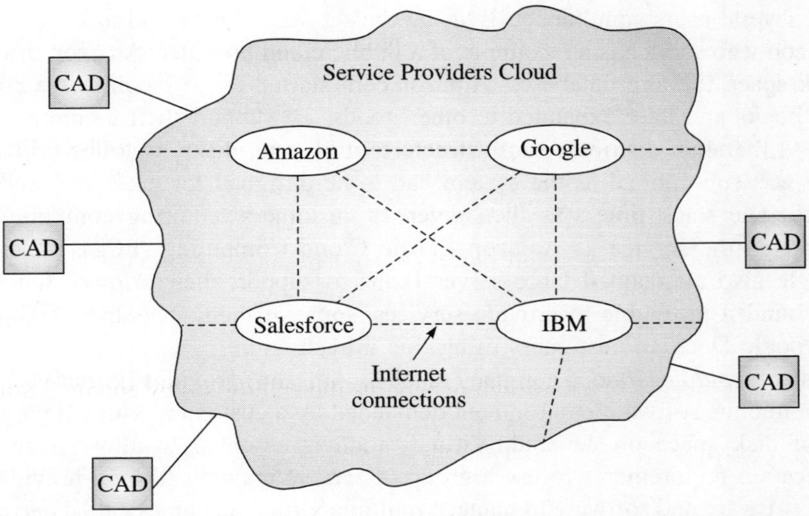

Figure 17.1 Cloud computing showing some vendors providing cloud computing services. CAD (Cloud Access Device): Desktop/Laptop/Thin client with Browser.

A cloud computing service has seven distinct characteristics:

1. The service is hosted on the Internet. It is sold by a service provider on demand to customers without human intervention.
2. A customer has the flexibility to use any one or several services, namely, computing infrastructure, compute servers with program development environment, or software for any contracted period.
3. The service is fully managed by the provider and the customer does not have to invest in any infrastructure except in a device to access the Internet. The access device may be a desktop, a laptop, a thin client, or a mobile device, depending on the service required. The service may be accessed from any place and at any time by a customer.
4. The service is elastic. In other words, a customer can increase or decrease the demand for disk space, server capacity, communication bandwidth, or any other service available from a provider. From a customer's point of view, the resources are unlimited. The customer pays only for the resources used.
5. The computing resources of a provider are geographically distributed and pooled. Several users use the resources simultaneously.
6. The system is adaptive. In other words, the load on the systems is automatically balanced to optimize the use of resources. A user is permitted to monitor and control resource usage to minimize cost.
7. The service provider normally signs a Service Level Agreement (SLA) with customers assuring a specified QoS.

17.5.1 Cloud Types

A cloud is normally classified as a *public cloud*, a *private cloud*, a *hybrid cloud*, or a *community cloud*. A public cloud sells services to anyone willing to pay the charges. At any given time, there may be several users simultaneously using the service. This is said to be a *multi-tenanted* service. Amazon web service is an example of a public cloud provider. Amazon provides server time and disk space to store databases. Amazon.com started as an e-commerce company that initially sold books and later expanded to other goods. To support their e-commerce business, Amazon had to maintain distributed infrastructure of servers, disks, etc. The utilization of the infrastructure was sub-optimal as the system had to be designed for peak load and it was idle at other times. The slack time was then given to customers requiring computing resources. Amazon marketed the service as Amazon Elastic Cloud Computing (EC2). Other companies such as Google also maintained large server farms to support their primary function (search engine) and found it profitable to provide services, some of them free such as Gmail, Google Drive, and Google Docs, to customers using this infrastructure.

In the case of a *public cloud*, a company (such as Amazon) provides (virtual) servers, that is, servers that mimic the software environment demanded by a customer, with unique IP addresses and blocks of disk space on demand. Virtualization is essential to allow many users with varying application requirements to use a group of servers maintained by a provider. Complex virtualization software and software to manage multiple virtual machines called a *hypervisor*, are installed on the provider's servers. Customers use the provider's API (Application Programmer Interface) to start, access, configure their virtual servers and disk space, and terminate use. More resources are brought online by the vendor whenever a customer requires them. This kind of service where the primary resources sold are servers and storage is called *Infrastructure as a Service* (IaaS).

A *private cloud* is a proprietary network and computing infrastructure which is provided to a single customer. The infrastructure may be owned by the customer or it may be owned by a provider to whom the service is outsourced.

A *hybrid cloud* is a combination of a private cloud and a public cloud. An organization may normally run all its applications on a private cloud and when there is an unforeseen increase in the demand for some services, it may migrate some of these to a public cloud provider. This is called *cloud bursting* in the literature.

A *community cloud* is one in which a set of cooperating institutions with similar requirements may request a provider to create a cloud infrastructure for their exclusive use.

17.5.2 Cloud Services

There are three major types of cloud services. They are called *Infrastructure as a Service* (IaaS), *Platform as a Service* (PaaS), and *Software as a Service* (SaaS). In IaaS, a provider maintains compute servers, storage servers, and communication infrastructure. Customers may deploy and execute their own systems and application software.

We may define PaaS as software and product development tools hosted on the provider's infrastructure. For example, PaaS providers would cater to customers' requests for a program development environment such as .NET of Microsoft, or a Unix programming environment.

In SaaS, a provider supplies software product(s) installed on its hardware infrastructure and interacts with the customer through a front-end portal. As both software and hardware are provided by the vendor, a customer may use the service from anywhere. Gmail is a free SaaS. The application software can be used by several users simultaneously. This is called multi-tenanted. In general, SaaS (not only cloud SaaS) is a system whereby a vendor licenses software application to a customer either hosted on vendor's website or downloaded to a customer's computer on demand for a fixed period. For example, Salesforce.com provides a widely used SaaS to manage all the software requirements of companies' marketing groups.

17.5.3 Advantages of Cloud Computing

The primary advantages of cloud computing are:

- An enterprise need not invest huge amounts to buy, maintain, and upgrade expensive computers.
- As and when more resources, such as more powerful servers or disk space, are needed, a cloud service provider may be requested to provide them. This flexibility is of great value to small and medium enterprises and also to entrepreneurs starting a software business.
- System administration is simplified.
- Several copies of commonly used software need not be licensed as payment is based on software used and time for which it is used.
- A large variety of software is available on the cloud.
- Quality of Service is assured based on Service Level Agreements with the service provider.
- The system is fault tolerant as the provider can shift the application running on a server to another server if the server being used fails.
- Organizations can automatically back up important data. This allows quick recovery if data is corrupted. Data archiving can be scheduled regularly.
- Disaster recovery will be easy if important applications are run simultaneously on servers in different geographic areas.

17.5.4 Risks in Using Cloud Computing

The primary risks of using cloud computing are:

- Managers of enterprises are afraid of storing sensitive data on disks with a provider due to security concerns even though the data is encrypted. They are also afraid of losing data due to hardware malfunction. To mitigate this concern, a backup copy should be normally kept with the enterprise.
- Failure of communication links to the cloud from an enterprise would seriously disrupt an enterprise's function. To mitigate this, duplicate communication links to the cloud should be maintained.
- Failure of servers of a provider will disrupt an enterprise. Thus, service level agreements to ensure a specified QoS should be assured by the provider.
- If the service of a cloud service provider deteriorates, managers will not be able to go to another provider as there are no standards for interoperability or data portability in the cloud.
- If a provider's servers are in a foreign country and the data of a customer are corrupted or stolen, complex legal problems will arise to get appropriate compensation.

- There is a threat of clandestine snooping of sensitive data transmitted on the Internet by some foreign intelligence agencies that use very powerful computers to decode encrypted data.
- Cloud computing is provided by several vendors. A customer signs a contract with one or more of these vendors. If a customer is dissatisfied with a vendor, it is difficult to migrate applications to another vendor as there is no standardization and thus no interoperability. There is no service provided by a group of cooperating vendors.

17.5.5 Applications Appropriate for Cloud Computing

A major reservation many organizations have about shifting all their applications to a cloud provider is due to concerns about security, even though this is not as serious as it is made out to be. Security breaches are most often due to improper controls within the organization. As cloud providers' sole business is selling data processing services, they employ very good professionals and follow best practices to ensure security. Organizations, as of now, are cautious about handing over all their data processing to an outsider. Some of the applications appropriate for outsourcing to a cloud computing service provider are as follows:

1. Routine data processing jobs such as payroll processing, order processing, sales analysis, etc.
2. Hosting websites of organizations. The number of persons who may log in to the websites of organizations is unpredictable. There may be surges in demand which can be easily accommodated by a cloud provider as the provider can provide more servers and bandwidth to access the servers as the demand increases.
3. High-performance computing or specialized software that may be required occasionally and not available in the organization. Such resources may be obtained from a provider on demand.
4. Parallel computing, particularly tasks in which a program is executed in a large number of processors concurrently with multiple data sets to speed up computation. The example SETI@home described in Section 17.2 used computers belonging to several individuals, each executing the same program on different data sets. This is called a Single Program Multiple Data (SPMD) parallel computing model. This model is eminently suitable for execution on a cloud infrastructure as a cloud provider has thousands of processors available on demand. This model is used, for example, by search engines to find the URLs of websites in which a specified set of keywords occurs. A table of URLs and the keywords occurring in each URL may be created. This table may be split into, say, 1000 sets. Each set may be given to a computer with a program to determine whether the keywords occur in them and note the URLs where they are found. All the 1000 computers search simultaneously and find the URLs. The results are combined to report all the URLs where the specified keywords occur. This speeds up the search almost a thousand-fold. An open-source software suite called Hadoop MapReduce has been developed for writing applications on the cloud that process petabytes of data in parallel in a reliable fault-tolerant manner which in essence uses the above idea.
5. Seasonal demand such as processing results of an examination conducted during staff recruitment once or twice a year.

6. Archiving data to fulfill legal requirements which are not needed day to day. It is advisable to encrypt the data before storing it in a cloud provider's storage servers.

17.6 CONCLUSIONS

As of now (2025), cloud computing is provided by several vendors using the Internet. Each vendor owns a set of servers and operates them. There is no portability of programs or data from one vendor's facility to that of another. On the other hand, grid computing aims to create a virtual organization by interconnecting the resources of a group of cooperating organizations. It has interoperability standards and tools for program portability among the group members. It would be desirable to combine the basic idea of the grid, namely, cooperation and open standards, with that of the cloud, namely, vendors maintaining infrastructure and providing services (IaaS, SaaS and PaaS) as a pay for use service to customers. This will result in what we term a *cooperative cloud*. Such a cloud infrastructure is not yet widely available.

We conclude the chapter by comparing the emerging computing environments we have described in this chapter (see Table 17.2). As can be seen, these environments provide a user with a lot of flexibility.

Table 17.2 Comparison of computing environments

Computing environment	*Members*	*Resources available and service(s) provided*	*Charging policy*
Peer to peer Volunteer computing	Cooperating individuals	File sharing. Donate idle computing time to solve important scientific problems	Normally free
Grid computing	Cooperating organizations. Each independent. Pool resources on an availability basis. Services provided to members	Resources include computing, databases, and instruments. Services include the use of all resources by members on an availability basis. Scientific collaboration. Ensure QoS	Cooperative budgeting. Aim to recover cost. Non-profit virtual organization
Cloud computing	Service provider to customers	Computers, disk storage, application software, software development platforms. Services called IaaS, SaaS and PaaS. Ensure QoS	Individual vendors announce prices. Pay for resources used.

SUMMARY

1. The availability of the Internet, the low cost of using it, and improved security of usage of the Internet infrastructure have spawned several novel applications such as e-commerce, digital information services, social networking, etc. It has also created new computing environments for computer users. These new environments are based on the cooperation of several computers connected to the Internet.

2. The earliest method of cooperatively using computers connected to the Internet is peer to peer (P2P) computing. In P2P computing, there is no client-server relationship among computers connected to a network. A computer can be a client or a server, depending on the circumstances.
3. Peers can share files. Napster was one of the first file sharing programs that shared music files. BitTorrent is a popular P2P system used to share large files. P2P computing is the backbone of Blockchains, a distributed system of ledgers.
4. Volunteer Computing is a system that allows a group of users to donate idle CPU cycles on their computers to solve a compute-intensive program cooperatively. Berkeley Open Infrastructure for Network Computing (BOINC) (www.boinc.berkeley.edu) is installed by volunteers to enable donating idle computing cycles.
5. A computing grid may be defined as an infrastructure that enables the integrated collaborative use of high-end computers, networks, databases, and scientific instruments owned and managed by multiple organizations. The resources are not subjected to centralized control but are coordinated using open general-purpose protocols and interfaces and are expected to provide users of the grid with a reasonable Quality of Service (QoS).
6. A set of standardized software tools and components to design grids has been developed by a consortium of organizations. It is called *the Globus toolkit*.
7. A four-layered architecture is proposed to support a grid. The higher layers use the services provided by the lower layers. Layers may be independently designed. Table 17.1 shows this architecture.
8. Software required to support the functions of a grid includes authenticating a user, interpreting users' requests, providing diagnostics, maintaining a directory of resources, scheduling jobs, providing job and data security, and ensuring a specified Quality of Service (QoS).
9. Large enterprises with computers and databases spread across several branches found that it is advantageous to interconnect those using the ideas of grid computing. This is called an enterprise grid.
10. Cloud computing is a method of computing in which a customer uses a set of services hosted by service providers over the Internet. The services include computing and disk space, namely, infrastructure (Infrastructure as a Service—IaaS), integrated application development tools (Platform as a Service—PaaS), and application software (Software as a Service—SaaS).
11. Payment for services is based on the facilities used. Facilities available in a cloud would normally expand or contract as demanded by a customer.
12. There are four types of cloud: private cloud, public cloud, hybrid cloud, and community cloud.
13. A major concern of organizations in using cloud infrastructure is the security of their data and programs. Good encryption methods are available and should be used to encrypt data and programs while using a grid infrastructure.
14. An important advantage of a cloud infrastructure is its elasticity. As demand increases, servers are provided by the cloud vendor. Payment is only for the hardware and software facilities used.

15. High performance computers, specialized software, and massive parallel computing facilities are nowadays available on the cloud.
16. A comparison of P2P file sharing, volunteer computing, grid computing, and cloud computing is given in Table 17.2.

REVIEW QUESTIONS

17.1 What are the drawbacks of the current computing scenario? Do users fully utilize the power of today's desktop PCs?

17.2 What problems do organizations face while using a large number of desktop computers?

17.3 What are the rates of increase in speed of computing, size of disk storage, and communication bandwidth as of now? What is the main implication of this?

17.4 The distance between a client and server is 100 m. The speed of the communication network connecting them is 800 Mbps. How much time will it take to transfer 1 MB of data from client to server? If the distance between a client and server is 100 km and the network speed remains the same, how much time will be required to transfer 1 MB data from client to server?

17.5 Define peer to peer computing. What are the primary applications of peer to peer computing?

17.6 What do you understand by the term single program, multiple data parallel computing? How is this model used in volunteer computing?

17.7 What is the primary objective of the SETI@home project? How is volunteer computing used in this project?

17.8 In P2P computing, how are peers discovered by a new member who wants to join a peer group?

17.9 Explain how the Napster file-sharing program is used in P2P computing. What types of files are most commonly shared in Napster?

17.10 Explain how BitTorrent file sharing program is used in P2P computing. What types of files are most commonly shared using BitTorrent?

17.11 What is the role of P2P computing in Blockchains?

17.12 Define grid computing. We gave two definitions of grid computing in the text. Combine them and formulate a new definition.

17.13 Can a grid environment be used to cooperatively use several computers to solve a problem? If yes, suggest ways of achieving this.

17.14 What functions should be provided by the software system in a grid computing environment?

17.15 Why is grid software architecture specified as layers? Give the components in each layer and explain their functions.

17.16 Explain how a grid environment is invoked by a user and how it carries out a user's request for service.

17.17 What is an enterprise grid? In what way is it different from an academic grid?

17.18 What are the advantages that accrue to enterprises when they use an enterprise grid?

17.19 Define cloud computing. What are its distinct characteristics?

17.20 Define IaaS, SaaS, and PaaS.

17.21 Describe different types of clouds and their unique characteristics.

17.22 List the advantages of using cloud computing.

17.23 What are the risks of using cloud computing?

17.24 What applications are appropriate for outsourcing to a cloud computing provider?

17.25 What are the major differences between cloud computing and grid computing?

17.26 What are the major differences between community cloud and grid computing?

17.27 What are the major differences between private cloud and a public cloud?

17.28 Compare and contrast enterprise grid and private cloud.

18 Basics of Artificial Intelligence

LEARNING GOALS

After reading this chapter, you should be able to:

- Define Artificial Intelligence (AI)
- Explain the difference between symbolic AI and connectionist AI
- Explain the core ideas of machine learning and different types of machine learning
- Explain the main ideas in designing Expert Systems
- Explain Artificial Neural Networks (ANN) and how they learn
- Explain the basics of Natural Language Processing
- Explain the basics of Computer Vision
- Explain the basics of Robotics
- Enumerate some applications of AI
- Discuss ethical and social concerns on the applications of AI

Speculation about designing a machine simulating a human brain is as old as humanity. In each era of history, scientists and philosophers tried to use the then-prevalent mechanisms to mimic a brain and its functions. Therefore, having a historic context to the evolution of the area of artificial intelligence is insightful.

In 1943 Warren McCullough, a neurophysiologist, and Walter Pitts, a mathematical prodigy, collaborated to model the operation of a brain using a neural net. They formally established that the neural net could be employed for computation. Alan Turing wrote a paper, Computing Machinery and Intelligence, in 1950 in which he asked: "Can machines think?" and argued that trying to answer such a question may lead to absurd conclusions. Instead, he designed an imitation game between a woman, a man, and an interrogator in which the interrogator had to decide who the man was and who the woman was based on the answers to questions posed by the interrogator. The imitation game has been modified as the Turing Test, in which a computer replaces the woman. The interrogator asks the man or the computer a number of questions without knowing to whom the question is sent. At the end of the interrogation, if the interrogator cannot decide which answers the computer gave and which the man, then one may conclude that the machine exhibits intelligent behaviour. Passing the unrestricted Turing Test involves the computer understanding language and having a vast knowledge repository, including cultural nuances. It is speculated that no machine can pass the test suggested by Turing even though some currently available chatbots such as ChatGPT can converse naturally on a variety of subjects.

Another stream of work was related to the fundamental limitation on what is computable by machines based again on Turing's seminal research during 1936-37 in which he described an abstract machine called the *Turing machine* that, in principle, can compute anything that a computer can and showed that there exist some problems that are not computable.

In 1956, John McCarthy of Dartmouth College, Marvin Minsky of MIT, Nathaniel Rochester of IBM, and Claude Shannon of Bell Labs requested the Rockefeller Foundation to fund a 2-month, 10-man study of Artificial Intelligence based on the conjecture that every aspect of learning or any other feature of intelligence can in principle be so precisely described that a machine can be made to simulate it. They stated that an attempt will be made to find how to make machines use language, form abstractions and concepts, solve kinds of problems now reserved for humans, and improve themselves. This was the first time the term "Artificial Intelligence" was used. The proposal was approved and research in Artificial Intelligence (AI) began. The term Artificial Intelligence was used to describe a set of diverse topics stated in the proposal, including game playing by computers, natural language understanding by computers, neural networks, computational complexity, and self-improvement or learning by computers.

18.1 WHAT IS ARTIFICIAL INTELLIGENCE?

Artificial Intelligence is a sub-field of computer science that attempts to create computer programs (called agents) that mimic human intelligence to solve problems. Human intelligence when solving problems includes the ability to learn, understand, and speak languages, reason, interpret data (that may be text, numbers, images or videos, 3D environment) and build models to simulate and predict situations in the environment and act autonomously. Therefore, AI solutions implement algorithms and agents that exhibit similar behaviour to various extents for example they may reason, learn languages, navigate environments, and act autonomously.

18.2 CONNECTIONIST AND SYMBOLIC AI

Two different approaches to implement AI evolved in the mid-1950s. One was to write programs that simulate how humans solve problems using their knowledge and logical reasoning. It is based on the idea that humans manipulate symbols and use rules to solve real-world problems. This is called *Symbolic AI* or Good Old Fashioned AI (GOFAI).

Symbolic AI

In symbolic AI knowledge is represented using symbols such as logical expressions, word statements, and numbers. Emphasis is placed on how knowledge is structured and organized. A set of inference rules, including inductive and deductive inference, are used to manipulate the symbols and derive new knowledge.

The major problems tackled using symbolic AI were:

(i) Computers playing board games such as Checkers and Chess with humans.
(ii) Designing Expert Systems that gave advice similar to humans in selected domains such as diagnosing faults in systems, diagnosing diseases given symptoms and medical history, and prospecting for minerals and oil based on geological features of an area.
(iii) Natural language processing using grammar rules.
(iv) Proving theorems in mathematics.

The major advantages of symbolic AI are explainability and knowledge representation. In other words, the system explains the reasoning used to arrive at a solution that gives confidence to a user. It provides a well-defined method of representing knowledge. The symbolic AI systems can be modified and improved based on new knowledge that augments a system.

The major drawbacks of symbolic AI are the difficulty of acquiring knowledge from experts and the difficulty of representing and including commonsense knowledge which is extensive. It is often not scalable when the knowledge becomes vast. Many real-world problems need the problem solver to combine diverse methods requiring experience and expertise.

Despite its drawbacks, symbolic AI is valuable as it is based on knowledge representation, uses logical reasoning, and is explainable.

Connectionist AI

Whereas symbolic AI mimics how humans solve problems using logical reasoning, *connectionist AI* attempts to model the human brain and solve problems like a brain does using its intricate connections of neurons. Neurons are simulated using a mathematical model. An interconnected network of layers of neurons, called an Artificial Neural Network (ANN), is used to solve AI problems. These ANNs learn to solve problems using data without being explicitly programmed. They extract complex patterns from data. These ANNs enable computers to understand, interpret, and generate human language. They recognize speech, recognize and interpret handwriting, recognize faces, play games, give expert advice, interpret medical images, answer questions, translate from one natural language to another, drive vehicles, and perform similar tasks, once thought to be only possible for humans. ANNs can learn from huge data and solve problems that could not be solved by using symbolic AI. ANNs could solve AI problems only after huge quantities of computer readable data from the Internet and very fast computers became available around 2012.

The drawbacks of ANNs are that their inner workings are opaque and one cannot understand how they arrived at a solution. (There is ongoing research on designing explainable ANNs. It is in a nascent state). They require huge amounts of reliable data relevant to the problem to be solved which are often unavailable. The computing power necessary to train ANNs is enormous and training consumes massive energy. Another drawback is the non-robustness of solutions given by ANNs. In other words, a small perturbation of input data presented to an ANN sometimes leads to an incorrect solution. Researchers are attempting to alleviate these drawbacks in ANNs .

There are numerous applications of ANNs. Some examples are: image processing, natural language processing, voice assistants, chatbots, video processing, robotics, and predicting weather as well as financial trends.

18.3 SYMBOLIC AI

In this section we describe in detail the implementation of artificial intelligence as algorithms that make use of a representation of knowledge and achieve intelligent behaviour by using techniques that interpret this knowledge and interact with users.

18.3.1 Expert Systems

An expert system is a computer program that mimics the decision-making ability of human experts in specific domains. It has four components. They are: a *knowledge base* that contains domain-specific facts and rules. This knowledge is acquired from experts in the field by the expert system designers through extensive interaction extracting both facts and some rules of thumb known to the experts based on their experience. An *inference engine* that applies logical reasoning to the knowledge base to reach conclusions or deduce new facts. A well-designed *user interface* for expert system users. This interface is used to ask questions and seek explanations on how the expert system came to a conclusion. An *explanation engine* that gives a logical explanation to a user on how the expert system came to a conclusion.

An expert system design is vitally dependent on the knowledge base. The knowledge base grows and some knowledge becomes obsolete. Thus an expert system should be flexible and accommodate changes. Extracting relevant knowledge from experts requires an inquisitive mind and general knowledge. A profession of *knowledge engineers* able to extract knowledge from experts and codify it arose.

The first expert system was designed by Edward Feigenbaum during 1964-68 at Stanford University. It was called DENDRAL that predicted the structure of organic molecules from their mass spectra. The knowledge was extracted from a group of post-doctoral students working in Professor Carl Djerassi's laboratory at Stanford. It performed well. The next successful expert system called MYCIN was developed by Edward Shortliffe over a period of five years. It was used by doctors to identify bacteria causing severe infections and recommend an appropriate antibiotic and dosage. It had 600 rules and an explanation module.

We give below a very simple example that illustrates how an expert system is designed.

Example: Designing an Expert System to diagnose faults in a washing machine.

Step 1: Create a knowledge base consisting of if-then-else rules for a set of common faults

Fault 1: The machine does not start

Rules: If the washing machine is switched on and does not start then
    If the plug is loose.
        Plug it in properly and start.
    Else
        Check if the door of the machine is closed properly and close
    Else
        Check if the circuit breaker has tripped.
        If it has tripped reset the circuit breaker and start
        Else
            Call the electrician to check the circuit.

Fault 2: The drum does not spin when switched on

If the washing machine is turned on and power is OK and the drum does not spin then
if the load exceeds the limit then reduce the load and start
Else
    Check if the load is unbalanced and balance it by redistributing clothes
Else
    Check if the drive belt is loose or broken
    If loose tighten and start
    Else
        Call the technician to replace the belt.
    If the drive belt is OK
        The drive motor is faulty. Call technician.

Fault 3: Water not filling the tub

If the washing machine is not filling water
    Check if the tap is open.
If not open, open it fully.
Else
    Check if the inlet pipe is twisted or a weight is placed on it.
    If yes untwist the pipe or remove the weight
    Else
        Check if your overhead tank is empty fill it
    Else
        Call the technician to check the water inlet valve of the machine.

Fault 4: Machine makes excessive noise when turned on.

If there is a foreign object remove it
Else
    If the machine is placed on an uneven surface properly place it on a level surface
Else
    Check if a bearing is worn and call a technician.

Add more rules for other common faults and update rules periodically.

Step 2: Design a user interface

User input: "My washing machine does not start."

Expert System Response:

1. Is the power chord plugged in properly and switch is ON?
2. Is the door of the washing machine closed properly?
3. Has the circuit breaker tripped?

User Input: " My washing machine drum is not rotating"

Expert System Response:

1. Is it overloaded?
2. Is the load improperly distributed?
3. Is the drive belt loose or broken?

The other user inputs and responses are designed using a similar principle of formulating questions based on the if-then-else rules.

The very simple example above is to provide basic ideas used in Expert Systems design. Real systems have hundreds of rules in their knowledge base. They are formulated by a knowledge engineer through long question-answering sessions with experts in the appropriate subjects.

18.3.2 Computer Programs that Play Board Games

Board games such as checkers and chess are complex, the rules are clear, a winning position is well-defined, it requires strategic thinking ahead of several moves, and it is challenging to write programs that could play as well as humans. Early AI researchers thus chose board games and wrote computer programs that could play as well as humans and even beat them, exhibiting intelligence. Learning about game-playing algorithms is important as they demonstrate how computers make decisions in a well-defined situation. These principles are applicable in solving real-world problems such as financial modelling, medical diagnosis, and problems that use decision trees.

We will explore in what follows the key concepts in game playing. All possible moves and outcomes of a game are represented by a structure known as a *game tree*. The game tree consists of a set of nodes. Each node represents the game's current state. Branches that connect nodes represent moves in the game. A move transitions a game from one state to another. The tree leaves represent the outcome, namely, win, lose, or draw. An algorithm known as *Minimax* is often used to decide a player's move in a game tree in a two-person game. This algorithm assumes that both players use an optimal strategy to maximize their chance of winning while minimizing that of the opponent. The algorithm evaluates all possible moves up to a certain depth in the game tree. The algorithm chooses the move with the highest score for the maximizing player and assumes that the opponent will try to minimize this score. In other words, the maximizing player tries to get the highest score while the minimizing player tries to reduce the maximizing player's score. For example, in the game tic-tac-toe, the algorithm evaluates all possible moves, predicts the opponent's response, and chooses the best possible winning move at each game state. A method known as alpha-beta pruning makes the minimax method more efficient by not exploring the branches of the game tree that do not influence the outcome of the game. Assume alpha represents the best score that the maximizing player can guarantee and beta the best score the minimizing player can guarantee. The branches whose score is outside the alpha-beta range are pruned.

Chess is a very complex game and writing computer programs to play chess with humans was a challenge. Claude Shannon, known for his seminal research in information theory, took up this challenge. He estimated that there are around 10^{120} chess games, and it is impossible to find the best move in a game analytically. In 1949, he described two types of heuristic tree-search algorithms to play chess, called Type A and Type B. Type A is a brute force search that evaluates all legal moves by a player up to a reasonable depth (around 4) in the game tree. Type B drastically reduces the number of moves by eliminating many unpromising moves using alpha-beta pruning. Shannon's algorithm traverses the game tree depth-first. Since then, most chess-playing programs have used Shannon's idea, and their variations are based on better heuristics and examining patterns of pieces on a chess board to make an appropriate move.

The final triumph of computer chess was the contest between Gary Kasparov, the world chess champion, and the IBM Deep Blue computer. IBM Deep Blue was a parallel high-performance computer with hardware enhancements to play chess and could evaluate 200 million chess positions per second. A team of IBM researchers wrote a chess-playing program primarily based on Shannon's type A method and challenged Kasparov to play. Their program could recognize the positions of various pieces on a chess board, look 20 moves ahead, and learn from past games. Kasparov won the first match 4-2 in 1996. The software team tweaked the program, and Kasparov played a rematch in May 1997. Deep Blue won 3.5 to 2.5 and established the AI program's supremacy in chess.

Since Deep Blue's historic win, there has been considerable progress in computer chess-playing programs. Today, programs on PCs can play at a grandmaster's level. Chess players, including those within the world's top 10, routinely play against computers to hone their skills.

With the advent of neural networks and deep learning algorithms, game-playing programs learn to play games by playing a huge number of simulated games without using game trees and evaluation functions.

18.4 CONNECTIONIST AI

As we pointed out earlier, McCullough and Pitts modelled the human brain as an interconnected network of billions of neurons. They formally established that a network of neurons could compute. Connectionist AI, also known as Artificial Neural Networks (ANNs), involves creating interconnected computational models of neurons, where knowledge is distributed and represented across the connections. ANNs normally consist of several layers of interconnected neurons. The connections between neurons have weights that determine the strength of signals transmitted between neurons. ANNs learn by adaptively altering the weights using training data presented to them. There are many learning algorithms among which are backpropagation which calculates the error gradient and minimizes the error by adjusting the weights, reinforcement learning which uses rewards and penalties based on performance, and deep learning which uses numerous hidden layers of neurons that derive representations of data presented to it.

In this section, we will describe how human brains are simulated using a computational model of neurons and how these neurons are interconnected in different ways to make specialized ANNs. We explain how these ANNs can be trained using machine learning algorithms and applied to solve a variety of problems such as recognize objects in images, understand speech, generate text, etc.

18.4.1 Mathematical Models of Neurons

A human brain has a collection of around 100 billion brain cells called neurons (Figure 18.1).

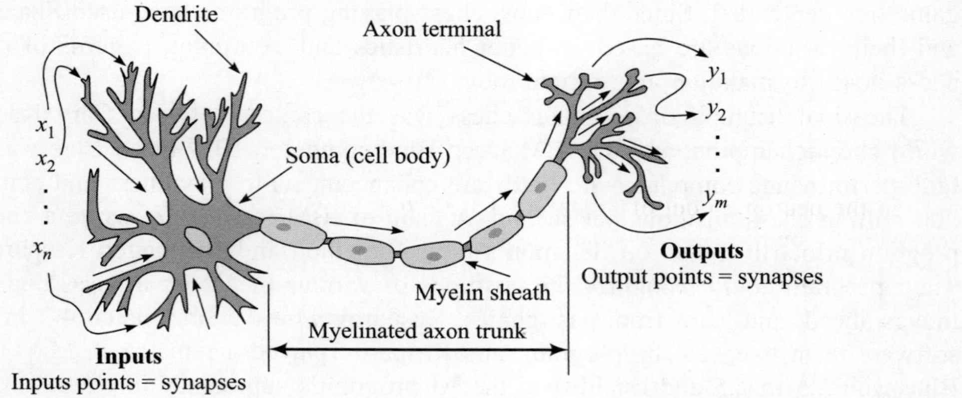

Figure 18.1 Model of a Neuron (Figure courtesy of Wikipedia)

Neurons accept numerous inputs $x_1, x_2, \ldots, x_n$ that send signals $y_1, y_2, \ldots, y_n$ to other neurons using synapses. External stimuli from organs (smell, touch, sight, sound, etc.) are accepted by dendrites that create electrical impulses that are processed by soma and travel through the network of neurons via axons. The neurons decide whether to send the impulses to other neurons to take necessary action or to ignore them. An approximate mathematical model of a neuron is given in Figure 18.2.

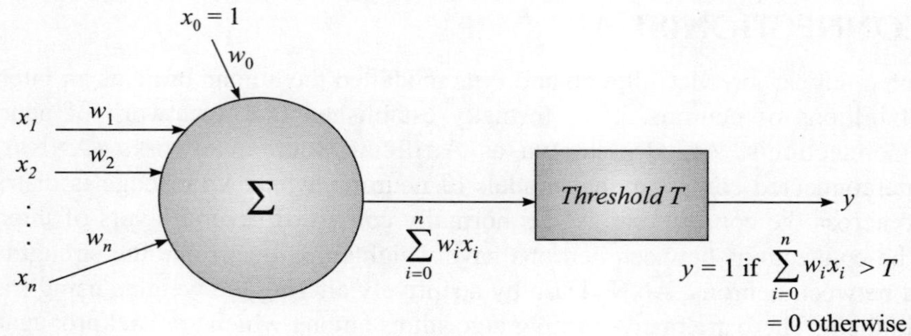

Figure 18.2 A simple mathematical model of a neuron. T is the threshold.

In this model of a neuron the neuron fires, that is gives an output signal *y*, when the sum of the weighted inputs exceeds a threshold T as shown in Figure 18.2. Over a period researchers gave better models of neurons using more sophisticated functions for the threshold. One such model is shown in Figure 18.3.

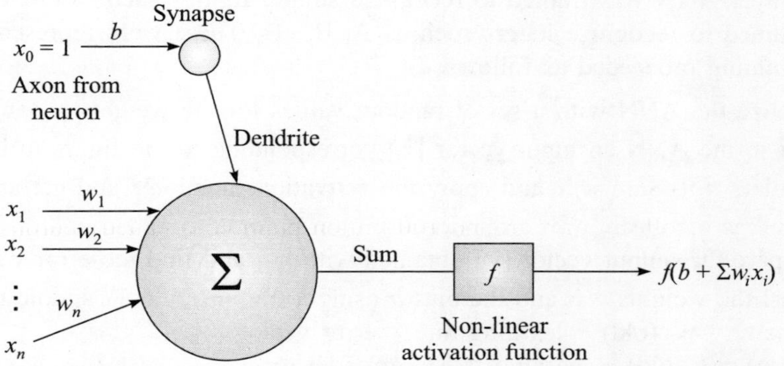

Figure 18.3 A more sophisticated model of a neuron. The activation function *f* is a nonlinear function.

In the neuron model of Figure 18.3 if $f\ (\ b + \Sigma w_i y_i) > T$ (a pre-set threshold) the neuron fires and the output is 1, else it is 0. This is a more realistic model. In this model *b* is called bias and *f* is the activation function. The bias as well as the weights are adjustable. They are modified during the training phase of neural networks which is a complex interconnection of many neurons. Some popular activation functions are:

1. Binary step function where $f(x) = 0$ for $x < 0$ and $f(x) = 1$ for x
2. Linear function $f(x) = x$
3. Sigmoid function $f(x) = 1/(1+ \exp(-x))$
4. Tanh function $f(x) = (\exp(x) - \exp(-x))/(\exp(x) + \exp(-x))$
5. Rectified Linear Unit (ReLU) $f(x) = 0$ for $x < 0$ and $f(x) = x$ for $x > 0$.

As we pointed out, our brain is a complex network of billions of neurons. The mathematical models of the brain are simple interconnections of several thousand neurons using diverse interconnection patterns that we will discuss in later sections. Models are chosen for various interconnections of neurons based on how realistically they mimic biological functions and also on computational complexity in training neural networks using those models.

Perceptron

The model of a neuron given in Figure 18.2 was used in 1957 as the basis to build an artificial neuron using electronic tubes by Frank Rosenblatt, a psychologist. The input to an artificial neuron is a set of bits x_i that are multiplied by a set of numbers called weights w_i. There is one input x_0 called a bias input that is set to 1. (Nowadays neurons are simulated by software rather than hardware).

If $\sum_{i=0}^{n} w_i x_i$ is greater than a threshold T, the neuron fires and gives an output 1 else a 0. He built a machine called a *Perceptron* by using a network of 500 artificial neurons first and increased it to 1000 neurons later. It was called an Artificial Neural Network (ANN). A Perceptron has an input layer, a set of weights that multiply these inputs and feed them to a single layer of artificial neurons, and outputs of this layer (See Figure 18.4). Only a single layer of neurons was used as building with electronic tubes was expensive.

A single-layer ANN was trained to recognize simple figures such as circles and squares. It was also trained to recognize letters such as A, B, etc. These were represented by vectors of bits. The training proceeded as follows:

Step 1: Initialize the ANN with a set of random values for the weights w_{ij} and bias b.

Step 2: Input to the ANN an input vector $[x_i]$ corresponding to the figure to be recognized.

Step 3: Calculate b + Sum $w_{ij}x_i$ and apply the activation function f and get an output vector $[y_i]$.

Step 4: Compare the output vector $[y_i]$ obtained with $[x_i]$ and find the error vector $[y_i] - [x_i]$.

Step 5: Adjust the weights w_{ij}s and the bias b using a training rule. A simple training rule is:
w_{ij} (new) = w_{ij} (old) + learning rate × error vector × $[x_i]$
b (new) = b (old) + learning rate × error vector
Remark: Set learning rate between 0.01 and 1.

Step 6: Repeat steps 2 to 5 until the error vector is less than a preset small value. (If the error vector does not become less than a specified small value after a preset number of trials it means that the perceptron is unable to recognize the input).

Observe that ANN uses supervised learning. In other words, it is trained to learn input patterns such as a circle or a square. The data given is labelled. For example, the letter A it learns to recognize is labelled. The learning rate is based on the increments to be used to adjust the weights and bias. This learning rule can be shown to converge in most cases.

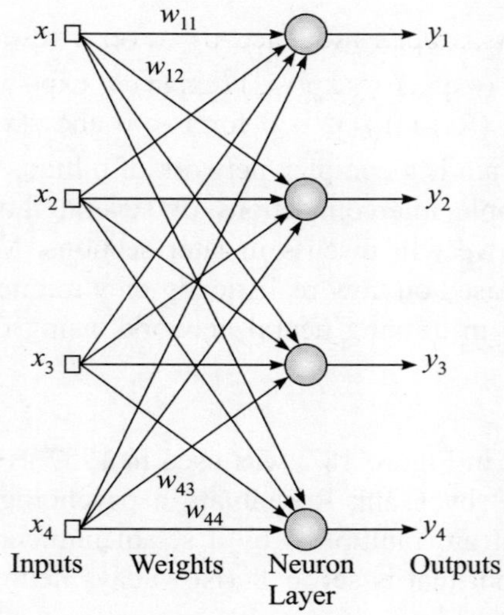

Figure 18.4 A simple model of a single-layer ANN. Each circle is a neuron as shown in Figure 18.3.

We have given only a simple training rule. Researchers have explored different training rules, activation functions, and error functions such as mean square error and rules that guarantee convergence when some conditions are met.

As we pointed out the Perceptron was successful in simple classification. In other words, it can separate a square from a circle and the letter A from B.

As building electronic circuits was costly and using software to simulate ANNs was very slow with computers in the 1950s Rosenblatt built only an ANN with a single layer of artificial neurons. Perceptron was oversold, particularly by the popular press, who called it a "brain", and implied that it could solve many difficult recognition problems.

Marvin Minsky and Seymour Papert wrote a book titled "Perceptron" in 1969 and showed that a single-layer Perceptron had serious limitations. They formulated a theory describing how a Perceptron learnt and showed that a Perceptron could classify only linearly separable data, that is, data that can be divided into two classes by a straight line or a hyperplane. The book dampened research in Artificial Neural Networks (ANN) for almost a decade.

18.4.2 Multi-layered Artificial Neural Networks

Multi-layered ANNs were explored to overcome the deficiency of Perceptron. A sample multi-layered ANN is shown in Figure 18.5. In practice, multi-layered neural networks have tens of thousands of neurons per layer and hundreds of hidden layers. Multi-layered neural nets (also known as deep neural nets) do not have the limitation of Perceptron. Training deep neural networks is more time-consuming. It became feasible with the increase in the speed of computers. A major advance was made by Hinton and his coworkers who invented an algorithm called the backpropagation algorithm to train multi-layered neural nets in 1986. The basic idea has been modified by several researchers and it is applicable to various types of multi-layered neural networks. It has been found quite robust and is widely used for a variety of ANNs.

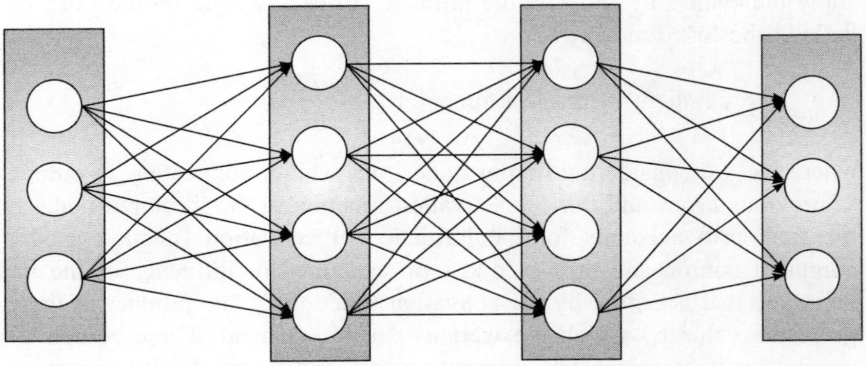

Figure 18.5 A multi-layered artificial neural network

The training of the multilayer ANN involves computing and updating the weights of the neuron models across the layers. Initially the output for each input for the current value of weights is computed, this output is compared with the target output, the difference is treated as error. This error is used to change the weights suitably so that the output with the new weights is closer to the target output. From the previous description it is seen that an important aspect of training the multilayered ANN is to propagate the error seen at the output back to the hidden layers and adjust the weights accordingly. Hence the name backpropagation.

Backpropagation algorithm to train a multi-layered artificial neural network

Step 1: Initialize the ANN with a set of random values for the weights w_{ij} and bias b and an activation function f. Commonly used activation functions are Sigmoid or ReLU.

Step 2: Input to the ANN an input vector $[x_i]$ corresponding to the object to be recognized.

Step 3: For each neuron in a hidden layer calculate b + Sum $w_{ij}x_i$ and apply the activation function f.

Step 4: Perform Step 3 for all the hidden layers. Obtain the result vector $[y_i]$ of the output layer.

Step 5: Subtract the output vector $[y_i]$ from the desired output $[d_i]$ and find the error vector. Calculate the mean square error by calculating (Sum $([d_i] - [y_i])^2)/2$ for all i. Call this loss function L.

Step 6: This is a key step of the algorithm as backpropagation is performed in the computations in this step. The goal is to find by how much the weights should be modified such that the output is closer to the target output for each of the training examples. We intuitively know that we have to change the weight of each connection based on how much it influences the output error, therefore we have to consider the partial differential of the output error with respect to the weights. But the output is arrived at by passing the sum of the weights through an activation function. Therefore we apply the chain rule and find the influence of each weight on the Loss. In Step 5 we defined the loss function L.

$$\text{Gradient of the loss function } L = \frac{\partial L}{\partial w_{ij}} = \frac{\partial L}{\partial f_j}\frac{\partial f_j}{\partial w_{ij}}$$

where we are considering output node j, w_{ij} weight connecting j^{th} output to i^{th} node of previous layer, and f_j is the activation function of the jth output node. In the above the first term accounts for the influence of activation function used to compute output of neuron and then second term accounts for influence of the weight w_{ij} on the value that is output by the activation function f_j. The product of these two terms gives the value by which the weights can be changed. These computations can be geometrically interpreted as computing the gradient of the loss function. Therefore the backpropagation algorithm is considered to be a gradient decent algorithm, where one is moving along the gradient of the error surface computed by L so as to reach a minimum point in the error function.

While we know the error directly at the output layer during the training process, it is more complicated at the hidden layers as we do not have the target output value. However we can propagate the error computed at the output nodes by continuing the partial derivatives with respect to the activation function and weights as above and using the chain rule to multiply the values. This is the computation that achieves the backpropagation of error from the output through the hidden layers during training.

Step 7: Update the weights and biases using the gradient as follows:
w_{ij} (new) = w_{ij} (old) – learning rate × gradient of the loss function L
b_i (new) = b_i (old) – learning rate × gradient of the loss function L
(The learning rate is < 1 (around 0.1) and is adjusted experimentally.)

Step 8: Repeat Steps 3 to 7 until $L < e$, a preset error, or a specified number of steps have been performed.

We have used mean squared error as the function to be minimized for training in the above algorithm. This is appropriate for regression tasks. Another measure called cross entropy is used for tasks such as image classification. Cross entropy is based on the difference between the probability distribution of the recognized object and that of the correct object.

18.4.3 Classification of Artificial Neural Networks Based on Connectivity

There are many types of neural networks each specialized for tasks such as image recognition, speech recognition, natural language processing, image generation, machine translation, weather prediction, drug discovery, and creating synthetic data. They primarily differ based on characteristics such as specialised layers for specific tasks such as image processing, feedback between layers, incorporating memory, and multiple competing networks. We will describe five important neural networks and their areas of application.

Convolutional Neural Network

A Convolutional Neural Network (CNN) is a deep neural network with three types of neuron layers besides the input and output layers. They are a set of convolutional layers, max-pooling layers, and dense layers. It is primarily used to recognize images and videos. The convolutional layers filter the input image to extract features, the pooling layers reduce the number of extracted features to decrease the number of computations, and the dense layer is a fully connected neural network that makes the final predictions. This network is trained using the backpropagation algorithm.

As stated earlier CNN is primarily used to classify and recognize images. For example, recognizing faces, recognizing fingerprints, and object recognition such as separating automobiles from trucks. It is also used for videos. It can process sequences of images and recognize actions such as walking, jumping, and running. It can track objects within videos such as a moving train, and identify unusual activities.

The major strength of CNN is its capacity to learn features such as corners, textures, and edges in images. The recognition is not affected even if an image is slightly rotated.

Recurrent Neural Networks

Recurrent Neural Networks (RNN) have an input layer to which data to be processed is fed, hidden layers that process the inputs, and an output layer that gives the results. The distinct feature of RNNs is the neurons in the hidden layers. These neurons' outputs are connected back to their inputs. This feedback loop acts as a memory allowing the network to retain information from previous inputs.

The memory in RNNs is useful in stock market prediction, weather forecasting, and other time-dependent data. Besides these applications, it is also used in natural language processing tasks such as text summarization, machine translation, sentiment analysis (i.e. emotional tone in text), speech recognition, and text generation. It is also used to track objects in a video.

RNNs are also trained using the backpropagation algorithm. One of the problems during training RNNs is what is known as a vanishing or exploding gradient. In other words, while computing gradients during training, the gradient can become too small or too large due to the feedback loops. RNNs also cannot recognize long-term dependencies.

Long Short-term Memory (LSTM) Neural Networks

LSTMs are specialized RNNs which incorporate memory cells in the hidden layers. These can store data for a long time. This is useful in capturing long-term dependencies. It also uses gates that determine what data should be stored, which should be deleted or forgotten, and which should be used to compute the current output.

LSTMs are used in time series analysis such as stock market prediction, weather forecasting, natural language processing, text generation, speech recognition, generating descriptions of images, video analysis such as object tracking, and action recognition.

The primary advantage of LSTMs is their capability to capture long-term dependencies that regular RNNs cannot. The gates in these networks mitigate the problem of vanishing and exploding gradients when using the backpropagation algorithm.

Generative Adversarial Networks (GANs)

GANs are a pair of neural networks that generate synthetic data of diverse types, such as images, videos, audio, and text indistinguishable from real-life data. GANs are two neural networks. One is called a *Generator* which is fed a random noise input that is transformed into synthetic data such as an image or a text. Another neural network called a *Discriminator* takes as input the generated data and outputs a probability score which indicates whether the input is real or fake. Both the generator and the discriminator are initialized with random weights. The generator creates synthetic data that tries to fool the discriminator into believing that it is real. The discriminator on the other hand tries to distinguish the data generated by the generator from real data. The two neural nets are trained simultaneously competing with one another. While the generator learns to generate more realistic data, the discriminator learns to detect fake data. This adversarial training of the two neural networks is continued until the discriminator cannot detect the synthesized data of the generator and declares it as real.

There are numerous applications of GANs. They can generate realistic images from scratch such as images of animals, people, and imaginary scenes. These are used by entertainment industries. They can transform images such as redrawing sketches into realistic images. GANs can enhance the resolution of images such as medical images and satellite images. They can generate synthetic training data. They can generate images from word descriptions. They can generate videos such as animation and special effects used in movies. They can detect anomalies in data sets that are useful in security and medical diagnosis. They can synthesize novel art, music, and literature. While GANs are powerful they are difficult to train and the generator may not produce large data sets.

They require huge computing resources. GANs also lead to ethical concerns if used to create deepfakes (namely doctored images) and spread fake news.

Transformer Neural Networks

Transformer Neural Networks are made up of several types of neural networks each fulfilling a specified function. The network's first layer called the *embedding layer* is not a traditional neural network. It is used to represent words as vectors in an N-dimensional vector space where N is very large. Words with similar meanings are near one another in this vector space. This conversion facilitates the input sequence to be processed by neural networks. The next layer is called an *encoder* which has an identical set of layers each with two sub-layers. It determines the importance of different words in an input sequence of words. This is the core idea of a transformer network. A fully connected feedforward neural network is applied separately to each position which captures long-range dependency. Thus the encoder's function is to understand and represent input data and capture long-range dependencies. The encoder is followed by a *decoder* which has multiple identical neuron layers with each layer having three sub-layers. The decoder generates the output sequence one word after another based on the encoded input and the previously generated words. The decoder output is fed to a fully connected neural network using a softmax activation function that determines the probability of a word being the next word in the output sequence of words.

Transformer networks are very good at understanding context and relationships within sequences of data. This feature is very useful in natural language processing where the meanings of words depend very much on the words surrounding them. Thus they are used in text generation, summarization, and question answering. They are also used in image classification and generation, speech recognition, music generation, and drug discovery. They capture long-range dependencies and can be pre-trained with a small corpus of data.

18.4.4 Machine Learning

Machine learning is the capability of computers to learn how to solve a problem given a set of sample inputs and outputs. There are three models of machine learning. They are *supervised learning, unsupervised learning, and reinforcement learning.*

Supervised Learning

In supervised learning a computer is given a set of input values and the corresponding output values. For example, if a computer is given a table that gives the price of a house as a function of its floor area, number of rooms, number of bathrooms, PIN code of its address, year built, and its distance from the nearest metro station it would create a model (or learn) based on which it will predict the price of a house for sale given these values. The following formal definition of machine learning was given by Tom Mitchell in 1997.

"A computer program is said to learn from experience E with respect to some task T and some performance measure P, if its performance on T, as measured by P, improves with experience E".

In the example of house price prediction, the table of values of prices is E, T is the task of predicting the price of a house for sale in the market, the performance measure is the error in the predicted value. The larger the table of house prices, the machine learning algorithm is expected to give a better prediction. In the above example one may model the data by using a formula:

House price = *f* (area, rooms, baths, pin, year, dist.) and fits a function *f* using the table of values given using a curve fitting formula. Normally statistical regression method is used. The computer program learns *f* using the sample values given and uses it for prediction.

There are also other modelling methods known as decision tree regression, support vector regression, random forest regression, and neural network regression.

Machine learning is quite general and not restricted to the numerical example given above. It has three steps. The first step is collecting data relevant to the problem. The data may include numbers, text, images, and videos. The data must be reliable and should be properly organized. The second step is training. During this step, an algorithm analyses the data, identifies patterns, and builds an appropriate model. Model building is crucial and one may have to iterate and refine the model. The third step is to evaluate the accuracy of the model and its reliability in prediction.

The machine learning example we have described is called *Supervised Learning*. In supervised learning, the inputs and the corresponding outputs are given. This is also known as learning from labelled data. For example, a machine learning algorithm to classify emails as relevant or spam is given a set of emails labelled spam and relevant that enables the algorithm to classify newly arriving emails appropriately.

Unsupervised Learning

In these algorithms, the model classifies or clusters the given data set into distinct sets based on similarity in characteristics with no data labelling. For example, given a set of viewers of movies on television over a period, the algorithm would cluster groups of viewers with similar movie tastes. Unsupervised learning is also used to detect outliers (i.e., abnormal data) that deviate from normal such as fraudulent data or abnormal machine function.

Reinforcement Learning

In this model of learning, the learning algorithm learns by trial and error. It rewards a good action and penalizes a bad action. For example, in a game playing program, a move that improves the probability of winning is given a positive score while one that reduces the winning probability is given a negative score.

There are several applications of machine learning. Some examples are: credit rating of customers by banks, fraud detection, trading suggestions in stock markets, route optimization for travellers, movie recommendations, dynamic pricing of products, medical diagnosis, drug discovery, and designing autonomous vehicles.

The primary challenges in machine learning are: the quality and quantity of data needed for training, adequate computing power, bias in training due to poor data, and explainability of the predictions.

Machine learning algorithms are available in both symbolic AI and connectionist AI. Nowadays machine learning algorithms based on varieties of ANNs have become popular because plenty of data is available from the Internet and computers are becoming very fast with huge memory and their cost is steadily decreasing.

18.5 APPLICATION DOMAINS OF AI

In this section we describe key domains in which we find extensive use of AI. They can be broadly thought of as AI that processes text data (Natural Language Processing), AI that interprets image and video data (computer vision) and AI that interacts with the real world (Robotics).

18.5.1 Natural Language Processing

Natural language processing (NLP) is concerned with endowing computers with the ability to understand, interpret, and generate human language. This is a challenging area of computer science and attempts to understand and process natural languages started as early as the 1950s. NLP is challenging due to ambiguity inherent in natural languages with the same word having different meanings based on the context. For example: "Give me a ring" can mean phone me or give me a ring to wear. The sentence "I saw her duck" can mean that I saw her bend down or she showed me a duck. There are also idioms whose literal meaning is quite different from common usage. For example, the idiom "He let the cat out of the bag" means that he revealed a secret, not its literal meaning. The rules of grammar are complex and difficult for even humans to completely master. Early symbolic AI used large dictionaries and formulated numerous rules to generate meaningful sentences and translate one language to another. These attempts were unsuccessful due to ambiguity in natural languages, context dependency, idiomatic usage, and the general complexity of human languages. Later attempts used machine learning for NLP by statistically analysing huge natural language samples. These methods were better than rule-based methods but still not very successful. The current approach to NLP is using a variety of deep neural networks to process natural languages. They are successful. They use a very large corpus of machine-readable natural language data from sources such as Wikipedia. Coupled with the availability of very powerful computing resources (such as graphics processing chips repurposed to solve large sets of simultaneous algebraic equations) at a reasonable cost, it is now possible to train huge neural networks with thousands of neurons in each layer and few hundred layers to process natural languages. Many real-life applications of NLP are now routine. Recently Transformer Neural Networks have been extensively used and they have revolutionized NLP.

Applications of NLP

There are several applications of NLP. They are:

1. *Machine translation:* Translating one natural language to another such as English to German, Hindi to English. Early attempts in the 1950s and 60s failed miserably. Modern systems such as Google Translate use deep neural networks and perform well.
2. *Chatbots:* Chatbots are computer programs that can converse with humans in a natural language. They have a long history starting with a Chatbot called Eliza implemented by Weizenbaum in 1966 that mimicked the conversation of a patient with a psychiatrist. Continuous improvements in human-computer conversation culminated in recent chatbots that use deep neural networks. Notable are Alexa designed by Amazon and Google Assistant. They answer a variety of questions posed by users. They understand the intent of the questioner, extract relevant keywords, recognize the context of the question, carry on an intelligent conversation, and obey the requests of users. For example, Alexa can play a music track requested by a user from a music library maintained by Amazon, tell a user the time of day, and a day's weather forecast, and set an alarm. Chatbots are used by many companies to answer routine questions from customers, assist users with routine fault detection in gadgets, and assist in repair.
3. *Sentiment Analysis:* Sentiment analysis is the process of detecting the emotional tone in a sentence. This is useful in detecting customer satisfaction in his/her feedback. Market surveys use it to detect customer preferences. It is also useful in machine translation.
4. *Text Extraction and Summarization:* It is the process of extracting from a document the key ideas and generating a good summary. It is useful to create summaries of long documents such as legal papers and long speeches. There are two types of summarization. A simple method is to highlight important sentences and create a summary. The other is to write an abstract understanding the essence of the document which is more difficult.
5. *Speech-to-Text Conversion*: Understanding spoken language is a challenge as accents differ. After extensive research and experiments, AI-based systems are now available that can take dictation and produce a Word document – a task normally performed by stenographers. They are not yet as good as humans but can produce text after training that can be edited. Some good speech-to-text systems are Dragon by a company named Nuance which is 97% correct, Apple Dictation by Apple Computers which is 96% correct, and Windows 11 speech recognition which is 96% accurate.

Natural Language Processing by Deep Neural Networks

The use of Deep Neural Networks has revolutionized NLP. We will not delve into the details of the methods used as there are a variety of tools and techniques. These are outside the scope of this book. In brief, the following procedure is used. The words in a sentence are converted into multi-dimensional vectors. This is called word embedding. Word2Vec by Google and GloVe by Stanford University are two early systems that performed this operation. Newer improved vector embedding methods such as BERT by Google appear periodically. In a vector representation of a natural language, words with similar meanings are near one another. Tools known as doc2vec convert sentences to a vector representation. A corpus of natural language data such as a collection of Wikipedia articles are vectorized and used to train appropriate neural networks such as Recurrent Neural Networks, Convolutional Neural Networks, LSTM Neural Nets, or Transformer Neural Networks depending on the type of task to be performed on the textual data. These networks capture the sequential and contextual features of sentences in a language. Once these networks are trained they are capable of performing several NLP tasks such as text summarization and question answering.

Challenges in Natural Language Processing

Considerable progress has been made in NLP. Yet some problems remain. The problem of ambiguity and multiple meanings of words based on context is not yet fully resolved. The training of deep neural networks for NLP requires large, good-quality databases. It is not available in many languages. There are issues of copyright when some publicly available data such as those from magazines and newspapers are used to train neural networks. The training requires considerable computing resources and can be expensive. Attempts to alleviate these problems are currently being explored. Neural network-based solutions are currently not explainable. Attempts are afoot to develop explainable AI. There are also ethical concerns when private databases such as patients' medical data are used. There are concerns about some AI systems giving incorrect answers to queries. Such errors are difficult to detect. Synthesizing fake images or speeches from samples of images and speeches by cyber crooks using AI is also a serious problem.

18.5.2 Computer Vision

Computer Vision is concerned with *acquiring images* and videos using devices such as cameras and other sensors. These images or videos are often noisy, distorted, and may include irrelevant details. They are *pre-processed* using techniques such as filtering, normalization, and resizing to prepare them for further analysis. The pre-processed images or videos are used to *extract features* such as edges, textures, shapes, or patterns. The next step is *recognizing* and locating specified objects such as faces, cars, animals, or scenes in videos, classifying them based on pre-defined specifications, and dividing or segmenting the images and videos based on specified criteria. It is also concerned with cleaning blurred images and *generating images* based on a natural language description of an image. One of the goals of computer vision is to understand the contents of an image or a scene and act based on this understanding. For example, a computer vision system used by a self-driving car would detect a pedestrian crossing a road and stop the car. The main challenges faced by computer vision systems are the difficulty in analysing and detecting objects from images acquired under poor or variable lighting conditions, partially hidden or overlapping objects, and cluttered backgrounds. Currently, most of the image processing and recognition tasks are performed using deep neural networks. A challenge is to train these networks with a large corpus of relevant data.

Applications of Computer Vision

There are a large number of applications of computer vision due to its versatility. We enumerate some of them in what follows.

1. *Security and Surveillance:* Facial recognition technology is used to control access to restricted areas, verify identity, and in law enforcement. Closed Circuit Television (CCTV) cameras have now become common. Images captured by them are used to track persons based on face recognition and track suspicious activities in real-time by computer vision systems and alert security staff. Fingerprint recognition by neural nets have now become standard.
2. *Healthcare:* Computer vision systems are used extensively in medical diagnosis and treatment. X-rays, MRI scans, and CT scans are analysed by computer vision systems to detect fractures, cancers, and neurological abnormalities. Images of the retina are analysed for conditions such as diabetic retinopathy. Vision systems are used to guide surgeons by enhancing images of organs during surgical procedures. Without computer vision systems robot-aided surgery would not be possible.
3. *Agriculture:* Computer vision is used to analyse images acquired by drones of fields. The images are used to detect diseases and take appropriate action. Crop health and condition can be assessed to control irrigation, spraying insecticides, and fertilisers.
4. *Autonomous Vehicles:* Self-driving vehicles depend on computer vision to read road signs, sense signals, detect obstacles on the road, and continuously monitor the surroundings.
5. *Entertainment and Gaming:* Images and videos of imaginary persons, animals, and video sequences are generated by computer vision systems. Augmented reality and Virtual reality systems depend on computer vision to create an immersive experience for users.
6. *Retail shops and E-commerce:* Besides surveillance in retail stores to detect thefts, a new trend is to use a vision system to allow customers to pick up merchandise and walk out. The system identifies items picked up and put in a shopping cart, adds up their prices based on the recognition of items, adds up the cost, and charges it to the RFID-enabled credit card of the customer as he/she walks out of the store. This futuristic system is currently being tested by retailers such as Amazon. In E-commerce, one can upload images of products and search for similar products. Videos can also be generated to illustrate the functioning of some products.

Performing Computer Vision Tasks with Deep Neural Networks

A detailed discussion of image and video processing, the basic tasks in computer vision, is outside the scope of this book. We briefly enumerate the type of processing tasks in computer vision and the type of deep neural networks used for these tasks.

Image processing tasks are:

1. *Image Recognition and Classification:* The main tasks are identifying and separating scenes in images into categories. The most appropriate deep neural network for this task is a Convolutional Neural Network (CNN) which uses filters to scan the image and find simple features such as edges. These filters are organized in layers and each layer finds other simple features. They are combined to find more complex features. This hierarchy allows the CNN to learn to recognize features, step-by-step, from simple to complex.
2. *Object Detection:* The main task is locating specific objects in an image and placing them within boundaries. For example, a task may be to identify a car in an image. CNN is again the most appropriate deep neural network for this task.
3. *Image Segmentation*: The main task in image segmentation is to partition an image into multiple regions. For example, in object detection, we ask "Is there a car in this image" whereas in segmentation we ask " How many cars are there in this image and where are they located and give me the pixels of all the cars". The deep neural network used in this case is called a Fully Convolutional Neural Network. The main difference between this neural network and CNN is that the last layer in this network is also a convolutional layer rather than a fully connected layer as in CNN.
4. *Image Generation:* The task is generating a new image from scratch or modifying an existing image. Generative Adversarial Neural Networks are used for these tasks.
5. *Image Enhancement:* The task is to improve the quality of the image by removing noise, increasing contrast, focusing blurred images, and colouring images. CNNs and autoencoders are commonly used for these tasks.

Video Processing

The applications in this domain include the aspect of time variability of data. Therefore RNNs and LSTMs are suitable for video data.

1. *Video Classification:* This is concerned with the categorization of videos based on what they contain and the action scenes in them. For example, a dance video or a car race video. Recurrent Neural Networks (RNN) and LSTMs are appropriate for this task.
2. *Video Summarization:* Capturing the most important parts of a video and filtering out irrelevant scenes. RNNs are normally used for this task. Another type of task would be to pick dance sequences from a video. This is also performed by RNNs.
3. *Video Generation:* Creating a synthetic video is a task done by GAN neural networks.
4. *Video Enhancement:* It is to reconstruct old faded videos with scratches. RNNs are appropriate for these tasks.

18.5.3 Robotics

From ancient times Robots captured humans' imagination. Karl Capek, a Czech science fiction writer coined the name robot in a play he wrote in 1920. In this play, a fictional corporation developed a cheap humanoid machine called a *robot* (derived from the Czech word robota—forced labour) to perform miscellaneous tasks ordered by humans. This play added the word robot to English. The Oxford English dictionary defines a robot as "a machine capable of carrying out a complex series of actions automatically, especially one programmable by a computer". Robotics is the science of designing robots. It is an interdisciplinary field that integrates mechanical engineering to design robots' physical structure, electrical engineering to select appropriate sensors and actuators, automatic control systems to control their movement, computer vision to sense the environment in which they operate, natural language processing to understand and obey orders given to them, and AI to control their behaviour.

Applications of Robots

There are several types of robots for a variety of applications. They are listed in what follows.

1. *Industrial robots* are used in factories to assemble components, weld, paint, and transport materials. They are used to sort and pack items.
2. *Service robots* perform tasks such as vacuum cleaning, cleaning windows in tall buildings, and performing some household tasks such as even cooking. Restaurants in some countries employ robots to serve customers and clean tables.
3. *Healthcare robots* are used to perform complex surgeries assisted by computer vision systems. Some hospital carts carrying medicines and supplies are controlled by robots to deliver items to programmed destinations. Robot-assisted prosthetic limbs help disabled persons.
4. *Exploration and Surveillance* robots are used to explore and collect data from inaccessible places such as volcanos, ocean beds, and objects in outer space such as the moon, and Mars. Examples are the Mars rover and the Dante volcano explorer. Drones (autonomous flying objects controlled by robots) are currently used for many tasks such as delivery of medicines, fighting forest fires, surveillance of crops, and reconnaissance in warfare.
5. *Agriculture robots* are used for planting, watering, and harvesting crops. Drones are used to survey crops to detect diseases and spray them with appropriate medicines and insecticides.
6. *Autonomous navigation* systems such as self-driving vehicles use robotics extensively. They are also used to deliver items using drones.
7. *Humanoid* robots are built to resemble humans to provide companionship and perform simple tasks requested by humans. An interesting robot called Aibo by Sony is in the shape of a dog and performs many tasks ordered by its owner.

Robot Tasks and Appropriate Neural Networks

1. *Grasping and Manipulation* is concerned with picking, transporting, placing, and manipulating objects. For example, a robotic arm in a factory. Deep Reinforcement Learning and Generative Adversarial Neural Networks (GAN) are used to train

robots to grasp objects and place them in appropriate positions. Robot's ability to handle diverse objects is enabled by GAN's ability to synthesise data.

2. *Motion Planning and Control* is concerned with planning a path, avoiding obstacles, and moving precisely along the path. For example, a robot in a warehouse is taught to go to appropriate shelves and place items in them avoiding obstacles in the path. Motion planning and obstacle avoidance are taught by Reinforcement Learning algorithms.
3. *Autonomous Navigation* such as drones flying and carrying objects to be delivered. This task requires path planning and obstacle avoidance. This is performed by using LIDARs (LIght Detection And Ranging) and/or cameras whose output data is processed by Convolutional Neural Networks.
4. *Object detection, recognition, and tracking* are tasks required to be performed by several types of robots. An example is a self-driving car that is required to read road signs, read traffic lights, and detect pedestrians and other vehicles. Besides sensors such as LIDARs, and cameras, neural networks are used to do several recognition tasks. In addition, Simultaneous Localization and Mapping (SLAM) algorithms use sensor data to create and update a map of the environment while tracking the vehicle's position within it. This ensures that a car knows where it is and where it needs to go. The most appropriate neural networks for this task are Convolutional Neural Networks (CNN) which are used in image and video processing. CNNs are excellent for extracting features from visual data. This is used to identify objects, interpret scenes, and navigate. Besides these, autonomous cars also require complex control systems for steering, braking, and similar driving tasks,
5. *Human-robot interaction* is required in companion robots. These robots have to understand and respond to human gestures and behaviour. Multimodal neural networks that combine many types of neural networks are required for this complex job. CNNs are used for analysing visual data. Recurrent Neural Networks are needed for temporal data analysis. If oral commands are to be obeyed LSTM and Transformer networks are needed.

18.6 GENERATIVE ARTIFICIAL INTELLIGENCE

Generative AI creates new content such as text, images, audio, and video by learning patterns and structures from a large corpus of data available in computer-readable form. The text generation systems use Large Language Models (LLM). They are trained on billions of sentences from web content such as Wikipedia, computer-readable books, and articles. After a learning period, they can generate text by predicting the next word based on context. They use a Transformer Neural Network and use the so-called self-attention mechanism for context awareness. It is estimated that the deep neural networks used by these systems have around 100 layers of neurons, 1000 neurons per layer, and around a billion weights per layer. As the models become more "intelligent" the number of parameters in the neural networks including weights and biases may be several trillion. They are then fine-tuned by human feedback. They are used to answer questions, create new material such as poems, and even write computer programs from specifications. It is revolutionizing computer applications. It is a groundbreaking development that has led to anxiety among humans as seemingly human activities such as writing poetry, writing computer programs, and creating a work of art are now performed by AI-assisted programs.

There are several Generative AI systems available on the Internet. Both free-to-use and subscription-based systems are available. The earliest Generative AI system was ChatGPT where GPT stands for Generative Pre-trained Transformer released in November 2022 by Open AI in the USA. It is a revolutionary system and soon had millions of users. It gives human-like answers to a wide range of questions. DALL.E, another generative AI system (that uses a diffusion transformer neural network) draws pictures from a natural language description of the pictures. These were followed by Bard (renamed Gemini) by Google, and several others like LLaMA by Meta (Facebook), Claude by Anthropic, and Mistral by a French company Mistral AI. In December 2024 DeepSeek V.3 developed by the Chinese company Hangzhou DeepSeek Artificial Intelligence Basic Technology Research Co., Ltd., was released and it is reported that it cost only $6 million to develop and its performance matches that of ChatGPT, Gemini, and several other Generative AI systems. The basic Generative AI models such as ChatGPT, Gemini, and DeepSeek are free to use whereas their professional versions are subscription-based.

Tasks Performed by Generative AI

Text Generation: Generates text indistinguishable from human-generated text. It also writes poetry and essays based on requests. It can converse fluently. It can also write simple computer programs. Given below is a request for a poem and two samples written by ChatGPT.

My request: Write a couplet on Generative AI in the style of Ogden Nash.

Poem generated by ChatGPT:

AI writes with lightning speed, so spry,
Yet still can't tell a joke that's dry!

My request: Write a couplet on Generative AI in the style of Tennyson.

Poem generated by ChatGPT:

From code and thought, new worlds are born in light,
A dream of man, now shaped in silicon's might.

Image Generation: These systems generate images from natural language descriptions. Examples are DALL.E by Open AI and Stable Diffusion by Stability AI. Given below is a request for an image and the response by DALL.E.

My request to DALL.E: Draw a painting of a monkey riding a cycle in the style of Hussain

DALL.E's response:

M.F. Husain's style is known for its bold strokes, vibrant colors, and abstract yet expressive forms. While I can't create an exact replica of his work, I can generate an image inspired by his artistic approach, featuring a monkey riding a cycle with dynamic brushstrokes and a vivid color palette. Let me generate that for you.

I wasn't able to generate the image because the request didn't follow our content policy. However, I can still create an abstract painting of a monkey riding a cycle using a bold and colorful style inspired by modern expressionism. Let me know if you'd like me to proceed with that!

My response: Yes

DALL.E's answer:

Here is the abstract painting of a monkey riding a bicycle, inspired by modern expressionism. Let me know if you'd like any modifications!

Audio Generation: Generative AI tools are available to generate an audio output given a natural language request or MIDI-based commands (See Sec.16.9.2). There are several systems available in the market. Some of them are: MuseNet by OpenAI which uses MIDI input, Jukebox by OpenAI which accepts natural language input like "a modern Jazz piece with guitar and drums", WaveNet by Google DeepMind which enhances existing soundtracks with MIDI commands, and MusicLM by Google which accepts natural language input. There are around ten companies in the business of music generation such as AIVA, Amper Music, Sounddraw, etc.

Most of these systems use deep neural nets with transformer architecture, autoregressive CNNs, and generative neural networks.

Video Generation: Generative AI tools to generate video clips from natural language descriptions, or images have been designed by many companies. There are also tools to improve existing videos. Some of them are *Runway Gen-2* by Runway ML which generates a video from a natural language request such as "create a video clip of two cars racing and overtaking a motorcycle". It also takes an image and a request for an animation based on it. A video may also be uploaded and modified based on natural language commands. *Lumiere* by Google converts a natural language request to a video. It can also convert an image to a video. *Meta Make-A-Video* by Meta(Facebook) generates a video from a natural language request. There are several others such as Stability AI, Synthesia, and DeepMind Transformer.

They use deep neural networks of various types. The types of neural networks are: Transformer neural nets, diffusion models, GANs, and Variational Auto Encoders (VAE).

18.7 ARTIFICIAL GENERAL INTELLIGENCE

All the AI tools we have described so far in this chapter excel at specific tasks. For example, a chess-playing program can play chess at a champion's level but cannot play other board games as well. Machine learning uses massive amounts of data and computing power to learn languages and translate one language to another. The same system cannot generate music without being taught separately to do the task. Large Language models produce nice essays based on requests but do not "understand" what they generate. They often generate incorrect or misleading answers to questions. They seem creative when they generate a poem but it is done mechanically without any emotional attachment. This is known as narrow AI or task-specific AI.

Researchers have been aiming to produce a machine with human-like intelligence that is able to understand, learn, and apply knowledge in a wide area on a level comparable to the versatility of humans. Humans can learn new tasks, design innovative gadgets, improvise music, create new compositions, draw pictures, create new styles in painting, write fiction, and perform many other tasks. The features required of a machine capable of *Artificial General Intelligence* (AGI) are to be able to transfer knowledge, skills, and ideas learnt from one domain to an unrelated domain that humans can. Solve novel problems requiring intuition, creativity, and logical reasoning, Learn continuously and autonomously new methods of problem-solving and adapt to changing environments, have autonomy and perform tasks without human guidance or intervention. There is also a school of thought that requires AGI to be conscious similar to human consciousness. This feature is debated as we ourselves do not have a precise idea of human consciousness. Companies such as OpenAI are pursuing research projects to endow computers with AGI. As a first step researchers in AGI are taking tiny steps in *transfer learning*, that is repurpose a model trained on one task as the starting point for a model on a second, related task. Essentially, it allows a model to leverage previously learned knowledge to perform in related domains. Fortunately, currently, we are nowhere near endowing computers with AGI. Whether it will be achieved at all is uncertain due to the complexity of the human brain which is currently not fully understood.

18.8 ETHICAL AND SOCIAL ISSUES IN AI

Ethical Issues

There are several ethical issues related to Generative AI. An important concern is regarding whether generative AI systems generate responses that are fair and unbiased. As the responses are based on the data used to train the system, any bias such as gender-based or culture-based in the data would be reflected in the responses. It is thus essential to be cautious about the selection of training data. Some facial recognition systems exhibit racial bias that may result in unfair treatment of certain groups of people. If medical records, personal data, and criminal records are carelessly used without anonymisation people's privacy will be lost. This is a serious ethical concern. Some cities have a large number of closed-circuit cameras whose output is stored in databases and used to track crimes and in city planning. The data can also be used as a surveillance tool to track the activities of people for political purposes by governments impinging on the privacy of individuals which is unethical. Appropriate laws are required to prevent misuse. The non-explainable nature of several existing deep neural network-based systems is a serious concern when they perform harmful actions. For example, ethical problems would arise when an AI-driven medical care system prescribes a treatment plan that may result in unexpected side reactions or worsening of a patient's condition even though it was effective for some patients. Fixing responsibility in such cases is difficult. An ethical problem would arise if an AI-controlled self-driving vehicle causes an accident particularly because many of these systems cannot explain the reason for the accident and rectify the system. Another concern is the huge amount of power used to train generative AI systems. It is estimated that ChatGPT 4 took 60 Gigawatt hours of power to train. Answering each question consumes 3 watt hours of power. The daily power consumption of ChatGPT to run its service is estimated to be around 3 million kWh. This is the estimated power used by 500,000 houses in a city such as Mumbai per day. The huge power consumption will worsen global warming. It is estimated that ChatGPT 4 cost $100 million to train and use 2500 NVIDIA A100 GPUs. The training cost has been reduced to $6 million in the case of DeepSeek with improved algorithms. The main point is that poorer countries would find it difficult to design their own generative AI systems suitable for their requirements. The inequality between the rich and the poor will become worse. On the positive side many deep learning algorithms such as LLaMA and DeepSeek are now open source and innovative methods of using less powerful computers for training deep neural networks are emerging.

Social Issues

A major social problem with the advent of generative AI is its impact on employment. Many routine jobs performed by unskilled labour may be performed by AI-based systems. Already robots are employed widely in factories to perform routine tasks such as picking and placing items, mounting car wheels and screwing them, painting, and similar tasks. Robots also perform many warehouse tasks such as picking items from shelves, packing them in appropriate boxes, sealing boxes, and sticking address labels. As robots become more intelligent they may perform more complex routine jobs. This may lead to unemployment of persons with low skills. However, robots cannot perform some tasks such as plumbing repair tasks that would require dexterity, accessing hard-to-reach places, and trouble-shooting as the task progresses and unexpected problems arise. In other words, problem-solving skills in non-routine situations are still a human preserve. Our education systems should evolve to teach new skills that require problem-solving abilities in non-routine and unexpected situations.

Whereas robots impact the work of blue-collar workers, generative AI's impact will be felt more by white-collar workers. White collar workers are those performing desk jobs such as answering customers' questions, translating from one language to another, lawyers' clerks, developers of low-level software systems, and administrative support staff may lose their jobs as the productivity of workers will improve. In other words, a smaller number of people will be necessary. However, as companies' profits increase they may expand and employ more better trained persons. Generative AI's capability to generate music, paintings, and videos is more of a threat to those who are less talented. However, these tools could be used to enhance their productivity and will be an impetus for more innovative work. The art of asking the right questions to generative systems and guiding them step-by-step to enhance creativity will be a new skill people have to learn. Looking back at history new technologies disrupted the existing status of professions but created new professions requiring new skills. For example, the advent of PCs eliminated typists' and typesetters' jobs but created the profession of Desk-Top Publishing (DTP) operators whose work is more interesting and paid more. One should not fear new technology but learn to adapt and continue to learn new skills. In the long run, new technologies lead to new opportunities that require re-skilling and improving our lives.

SUMMARY

1. Artificial Intelligence (AI) is a sub-field of computer science that attempts to create computer programs that mimic human intelligence to solve problems. These programs can reason, learn, and act autonomously.
2. There are two different approaches to solving problems using AI: the symbolic approach and the connectionist approach. In the symbolic approach, knowledge is represented using logic symbols, word statements, and numbers. Inductive and deductive inference rules are formulated and applied to the knowledge base to solve problems. Early AI programs used symbolic AI to play games, solve problems in algebra and calculus, and prove theorems.
3. Symbolic AI's progress was slow and could not solve many complex problems due to the difficulty in acquiring and representing knowledge, particularly commonsense knowledge. Symbolic AI methods, however, used logical reasoning and were explainable.
4. Connectionist AI attempts to simulate the structure of the human brain which is a complex interconnection of neurons. It uses mathematical models of neurons and several complex interconnected networks of layers of neurons called Artificial Neural Networks (ANN).
5. ANNs excel at identifying patterns and relationships from large databases that are used to train them. The computing power required to train them is enormous. They are good at generalization and modelling and solve problems that could not be solved by symbolic AI.
6. Currently, the drawbacks of ANNs are their opaque inner workings and the need for huge amounts of reliable and unbiased data to train them.
7. The earliest AI programs were symbolic and were designed to play checkers and chess. Claude Shannon described two types of chess-playing algorithms based on heuristic search of game trees, called Type A and Type B search. Type A is brute force search for the best move by exploring up to a depth of 4 of the search tree.

In Type B search heuristics are used to prune many unpromising moves. Progress was slow until computers became very fast and parallel. Symbolic AI's triumph was beating the world champion chess player Gary Kasparov by IBM's Deep Blue computer (that used primarily Shannon's type A method) in 1977.

8. Machine learning is the capability of computers to learn how to solve problems given a set of sample inputs and outputs.

9. In supervised learning a set of inputs and corresponding outputs are given. The computer discovers a model that best fits the data. This model can predict the outputs for a new set of inputs.

10. In unsupervised learning an algorithm classifies or clusters input data into sets based on similarity.

11. In reinforcement learning an algorithm learns to fit a model by trial and error. The algorithm rewards a good prediction and penalizes a bad prediction.

12. An expert system is a computer program that mimics the decision-making ability of human experts in specific domains. It has a knowledge base containing domain-specific facts and rules, an inference engine that applies logical reasoning to the knowledge base to reach a conclusion or deduce new facts, a user interface for users to query the system, and an explanation engine through which a user can ask how the expert system arrived at an answer to the question.

13. Expert systems have been used for over thirty years from the 1980s in medical diagnosis, fault detection and repair of complex systems, geological exploration, and many other applications. Their popularity waned as designing a knowledge base was expensive and it was difficult to codify commonsense knowledge.

14. The human brain has around 100 billion neurons. Each neuron accepts numerous inputs and sends signals to other neurons. These collectively make decisions and solve problems.

15. A neuron is modelled using a set of inputs $x_1, x_2, x_3, \ldots, x_n,$ a set of arcs emanating from these inputs with weights $w_1, w_2, w_3, \ldots, w_n$, and a bias input b. The output of a neuron y is modelled by the equation: $y = b + \sum_{i=1}^{n} w_i x_i$. This output is fed to an activation function f. The neuron fires, in other words, its output is 1 if $f\left(b + \sum_{i=1}^{n} w_i x_i\right) > T$, a preset threshold, else it is 0.

16. Several activation functions f are used in different models of neurons. Two popular functions are: $f(x) = 0$ for $x < 0$ and $f(x) = x$ for x called ReLU, and $f(x) = 1/(1+ \exp(-x))$ called Sigmoid function.

17. A single layer of neurons forming an artificial neural network (ANN) was built using vacuum tubes by Rosenblatt in 1957. This neural net called a Perceptron was trained to recognize simple figures such as squares and circles.

18. The algorithm to train a Perceptron assigned random biases and weights to the neurons' arcs. The outputs of the neurons y_is were computed after applying an activation function with the desired outputs to find an error vector. The biases and weights were adjusted systematically using a simple training rule until the error vector was nearly 0.

19. The Perceptron recognized simple patterns. Minsky and Papert showed that the Perceptron had serious limitations and could recognize only linearly separable data. This dampened enthusiasm about ANNs and research in this area.

20. Research in ANNs resumed when researchers showed that multi-layered neural networks were powerful and did not have the deficiency of single-layer neural nets. However, multi-layered ANNs could be explored only when computers became fast with large memories and plenty of machine-readable data became available with the advent of the Internet.

21. Hinton and his co-workers invented the backpropagation algorithm, a major advance in the training of multi-layered neural nets (also called deep neural nets). Over time, the backpropagation algorithm has been found to be very robust and useful for training a variety of deep neural nets.

22. The backpropagation algorithm first calculates the loss function which is the difference between a neural network's actual output and the desired output. The algorithm then calculates the error gradient of this loss function with respect to the biases and weights. It does this by propagating the error signals backward through the network one layer after another. These gradients are used to update the weights and biases iteratively until the loss is minimum based on a preset criterion.

23. There are various neural network configurations tuned for different applications. They differ in the type of feedback between layers, the introduction of memory between layers, and having competing networks within one configuration.

24. There are five important types of ANNs. They are Convolutional Neural Networks (CNN) which has three types of layers besides the input and output layers. CNNs are used primarily in applications related to images and videos. Recurrent Neural Networks (RNN) incorporate feedback loops in neurons in the hidden layers. The feedback endows memory to the neural network. RNNs are used in natural language processing tasks. Long Short-term Memory Neural Networks (LSTM) incorporate memory cells in the hidden layers which capture long-term dependencies. They are used in stock market prediction, weather forecasting, and time series analysis. Generative Adversarial Neural Networks (GAN) consist of a pair of neural networks called the generator and the discriminator. They synthesize realistic speech, audio, images, and videos. Transformer Neural Networks consist of several types of neural networks each fulfilling a specific function. They are used in text generation and summarization, question answering, drug discovery, music generation, and image and video processing. Transformer Networks capture long-range dependencies and can be pre-trained with a small corpus of data.

25. One of the major applications of ANNs is Natural Language Processing (NLP). NLP is concerned with the ability of a computer to understand, interpret, and generate human language. Early attempts in NLP using symbolic AI and machine learning did not succeed due to ambiguity, idiomatic usage, and context dependency inherent in natural languages. ANNs have successfully overcome some of these problems by training with a huge corpus of natural language data from sources such as Wikipedia, newspapers, books, and similar material. NLP applications are: translation of one language to another, the ability to converse and answer questions in natural language, text summarization, and speech-to-text conversion.

26. Computer vision is concerned with acquiring images, videos, preprocessing them, and extracting features such as edges, textures, shapes, patterns, locating specified objects such as faces, and classifying them based on specified criteria. Computer vision systems also generate images and video from natural language descriptions. Current computer vision systems use deep neural networks to perform many tasks. Among the applications of computer vision are surveillance to aid security systems, analysis of medical images for diagnosis of abnormal features, analysis of images of plants in fields for detecting diseases, entertainment, playing games, providing vision to autonomous vehicles to enable them to drive, and e-commerce.

27. Robotics is the science of designing robots. It is an interdisciplinary field that integrates mechanical engineering to design robots' physical structure, electrical engineering to select appropriate sensors and actuators, automatic control systems to control their movement, computer vision to sense the environment in which they operate, natural language processing to understand and obey orders given to them, and AI to control their behaviour.

28. Robots may be classified as industrial robots used in assembly lines, service robots that perform services such as vacuum cleaning floors and window cleaning, health care robots that assist surgeons in performing complex surgeries, exploration robots such as the Mars rover, autonomous robot-controlled drones used to deliver items to remote locations and in warfare, and humanoid robots that resemble human beings and perform simple tasks requested by its owner and provide companionship. Robots are trained by a variety of ANNs to perform their tasks.

29. Generative AI creates new content such as text, images, audio, and video by learning patterns and structures from a large corpus of data available in computer-readable form. The text generation systems use large language models (LLM). They are trained on billions of sentences from web content such as Wikipedia, computer-readable books, and articles. After a learning period, they can generate text by predicting the next word based on context. They use a Transformer Neural Network and use the so-called self-attention mechanism for context awareness.

30. There are several generative AI systems in common use. Some of them are ChatGPT (developed by a company named OpenAI) which answers a variety of questions, writes poetry, essays, computer programs, solves mathematical problems, and summarizes. Similar competing systems are Gemini by Google, LLaMA by Meta, Claude by Anthropic, Mistral from France, and DeepSeek from China.

31. Systems are also available that generate images and video from word descriptions. DALL.E by OpenAI generates images from word descriptions. Some other systems are MusicLM by Google which generates music from word descriptions and Meta Make-A-Video by Meta (Facebook) which generates videos from word descriptions. Most of these systems are transformer neural networks, autoregressive convolutional neural networks, and generational adversarial neural networks.

32. Artificial General Intelligence (AGI) is the ability to transfer knowledge, skills, and ideas learnt from one domain to an unrelated domain that humans can. AGI systems can solve novel problems that require intuition, creativity, and logical reasoning. AGI systems learn continuously and autonomously new problem-solving methods and adapt to changing environments, have autonomy, and perform tasks without human guidance or intervention. There is also a school of thought that requires AGI to be conscious similar to human consciousness. This feature is debated as we do not have a precise idea of human consciousness. Companies such as OpenAI are pursuing research projects to endow computers with AGI. Fortunately, currently, we are nowhere near endowing computers with AGI. Whether it will be achieved at all is uncertain due to the complexity of the human brain which is currently not fully understood.

33. An ethical concern in generative AI systems is whether they generate fair and unbiased responses as they are based on the data used to train the system. Any bias such as gender-based or culture-based in the data would be reflected in the responses. It is thus essential to be cautious about the selection of training data. Indiscriminate data gathering by surveillance systems would impinge on the privacy of individuals. If AI-based medical systems prescribe treatment with adverse effects, it is difficult to fix responsibility. A similar situation would arise when AI-driven cars cause an accident.

34. Current AI systems consume enormous power that would worsen global warming.

35. A major social concern with the advent of powerful AI systems is their impact on employment. Many existing classes of jobs requiring low skill levels may be taken over by AI systems requiring people to be re-trained with higher skills. History shows that new technologies disrupt the status quo but lead to better productivity and prosperity in the long run.

REVIEW QUESTIONS

18.1 Describe the Turing Test. What is the goal of this test.

18.2 Define the term Artificial Intelligence (AI). Who coined this term and when?

18.3 What are the two approaches to solve AI problems?

18.4 Describe some problems that were solved using symbolic AI.

18.5 What are the main differences between symbolic AI and connectionist AI?

18.6 Describe the primary methods used to solve problems using symbolic AI.

18.7 Describe the primary method used to solve problems using connectionist AI.

18.8 What are the drawbacks of symbolic AI methods?

18.9 What are the drawbacks of connectionist AI methods?

18.10 Describe how computers are used to play board games such as Checkers and Chess.

18.11 What are the heuristics described by Claude Shannon to design computer algorithms to play Chess?

18.12 Define machine learning.

18.13 What is supervised learning? Give an example of supervised learning.

18.14 What is unsupervised learning? Give an example of unsupervised learning.

18.15 What is reinforcement learning? Give an example of reinforcement learning.

18.16 What are the challenges of machine learning?

18.17 What is an Expert System?

18.18 What are the components of an Expert System? Describe the functions of these.

18.19 What is a knowledge base? How is it developed?

18.20 Develop a basic Expert System to diagnose faults in a PC.

18.21 Give a model of a neuron and describe its parts.

18.22 Give a mathematical model of a neuron.

18.23 What is a bias in a neuron model?

18.24 What is an activation function of a neuron? Give some sample activation functions.

18.25 What is the purpose of a threshold in a neuron model?

18.26 What is a Perceptron?

18.27 Give an algorithm to train a Perceptron to recognize simple figures.

18.28 What is the main drawback of a Perceptron?

18.29 What is a multi-layered ANN? What are its features?

18.30 Describe the backpropagation algorithm to train a multi-layered ANN.

18.31 Does a backpropagation algorithm always converge?

18.32 What is a Convolutional Neural Network? What are its applications?

18.33 What is a Recurrent Neural Network? What are its applications?

18.34 What is a Long Short-term Memory Neural Network? What are its applications?

18.35 What is a Generative Adversarial Neural Network? What are its applications?

18.36 What is a Transformer Neural Network? What are its applications?

18.37 What is Natural Language Processing (NLP)?

18.38 What are the challenges in Natural Language Processing?

18.39 Enumerate the applications of NLP.

18.40 What types of ANNs are used to solve NLP problems?

18.41 Describe in brief how NLP problems are solved using ANNs.

18.42 Define computer vision.

18.43 What are some applications of computer vision?

18.44 Enumerate image processing tasks.

18.45 Enumerate video processing tasks.

18.46 What types of ANNs are used for image and video processing?

18.47 What is Robotics?

18.48 What are different types of robots and their functions?

18.49 What type of ANNs are used to train robots?

18.50 Describe the tasks performed by a robot controlling a self-driving car.

18.51 What is Generative AI?

18.52 What is a Large Language Model?

18.53 Enumerate generative AI systems available to users on the Internet.

18.54 Use ChatGPT to write a program in C to find the largest and the second largest number in a given set of 50 numbers. Test it to find if the program is correct.

18.55 Generate an image from a word description using DALL.E.

18.56 Define Artificial General Intelligence (AGI).

18.57 How is AGI different from Generative AI?

18.58 What are some of the ethical issues in using AI?

18.59 Is it ethical to use Generative AI to solve a homework problem in programming?

18.60 What are the social issues that have arisen with the proliferation of AI?

18.61 Discuss the impact of AI on employment.

18.62 What do you think would be the long-term impact of AI on society.

References

CHAPTER 1

1. D.E. Knuth, *The Art of Computer Programming—Fundamental Algorithms,* Vol. 1, Addison-Wesley, Reading, MA, 1969.
2. V. Rajaraman, *Computer Programming in FORTRAN 90/95,* PHI Learning, Delhi, 2009.
3. N. Wirth, *Systematic Programming—An Introduction*, Prentice Hall, Inc., Englewood Cliffs, NJ, 1976.
4. T.H. Cormen, C.E. Leiserson, R.L. Rivest, and C. Stein, *Introduction to Algorithms,* 2nd ed., MIT Press, Cambridge, MA, 2001.
5. D. Harel, *Algorithmics*, 2nd ed., Addison-Wesley, Reading, MA, 1992.

CHAPTER 2

1. V. Rajaraman and T. Radhakrishnan, *An Introduction to Digital Computer Design*, 5th ed., Prentice-Hall of India, New Delhi, 2008.
2. M.M. Mano and C.R. Kime, *Logic and Computer Design Fundamentals*, 4th ed., Pearson Education Asia, New Delhi, 2008.
3. V. Rajaraman, *Computer Oriented Numerical Methods*, 3rd ed., PHI Learning, Delhi, 2009.

CHAPTER 3

1. V. Rajaraman, *Introduction to Information Technology*, 2nd ed., PHI Learning, Delhi, 2013.
2. D.P. Curtin, K. Foley, H. Sen, and C.S. Morin, *Information Technology*, Tata McGraw-Hill, New Delhi, 1999.
3. D. Caganski and J.A. Orr, *Information Technology*, Pearson Education Asia, New Delhi, 2002.

CHAPTER 4

1. W. Stallings, *Computer Organization and Architecture*, 7th ed., Pearson Education Asia, New Delhi, 2006.
2. V.P. Heuring, H.F. Jordan, and T.G. Venkatesh, *Computer Systems Design and Architecture*, Dorling Kindersley (India), New Delhi, 2008.
3. www.wikipedia.org for Flash Memory and Solid State Disks.

CHAPTER 5

1. W. Stallings, *Computer Organization and Architecture*, 7th ed., Pearson Education Asia, New Delhi, 2006.
2. V. Rajaraman and T. Radhakrishnan, *Essentials of Assembly Language Programming for the IBM PC*, Prentice-Hall of India, New Delhi, 2000.
3. V. Rajaraman and T. Radhakrishnan, *Digital Logic and Computer Organization*, PHI Learning, Delhi, 2009.

CHAPTER 6

1. V. Rajaraman and T. Radhakrishnan, *Introduction to Digital Computer Design,* 5th ed., Prentice-Hall of India, New Delhi, 2008.
2. V.C. Hamacher, Z.G. Vranesic, and S.G. Zaky, *Computer Organization*, 5th ed., McGraw-Hill, New Delhi, 2011.

CHAPTER 7

1. J.E. Whitesitt, *Boolean Algebra and Its Applications*, Addison-Wesley, Reading, MA, 1961.
2. R.S. Sandige, *Modern Digital Design,* McGraw-Hill, New York, 1990.

CHAPTER 8

1. V.P. Heuring, H.F. Jordan, and T.G. Venkatesh, *Computer Systems Design and Architecture*, Dorling Kindersley (India), New Delhi, 2008.
2. W. Stallings, *Computer Organization and Architecture*, 7th ed., Pearson Education Asia, New Delhi, 2006.
3. D.A. Patterson and J.C. Hennessy, *Computer Architecture—A Quantitative Approach,* 5th ed., Morgan Kaufmann, CA, 2012.

CHAPTER 9

1. T.W. Pratt and M.V. Zelkowitz, *Programming Languages*, 3rd ed., Prentice-Hall of India, New Delhi, 1996.
2. V. Rajaraman, *Computer Programming in Fortran 90 and 95*, Prentice-Hall of India, New Delhi, 1997.

3. V. Rajaraman and H.V. Sahasrabuddhe, *Computer Programming in COBOL*, Prentice-Hall of India, New Delhi, 1984.
4. V. Rajaraman, *Computer Programming in C*, Prentice-Hall of India, New Delhi, 1994.

CHAPTER 10

1. A. Silberschatz, P.B. Galvin, and G. Gagne, *Operating System Concepts*, 8th ed., Wiley India, New Delhi, 2012.
2. B.W. Kernighan and R. Pike, *The UNIX Programming Environment,* Prentice Hall, Englewood Cliffs, NJ, 1984.
3. W. Stalling, *Operating Systems*, 5th ed., Pearson Education Asia, New Delhi, 2006.
4. L. Goldschlager and A. Lister, *Computer Science—A Modern Introduction*, Prentice Hall International, London, 1982.
5. P.C.P. Bhatt, *An Introduction to Operating Systems*, 3rd ed., PHI Learning, New Delhi, 2010.

CHAPTER 11

1. J.L. Antonakos, *An Introduction to Intel Family of Microprocessor*, 3rd ed., Pearson Education Asia, New Delhi, 1999.
2. L.A. Leventhal, *Introduction to Microprocessors: Software, Hardware, Programming,* Prentice-Hall of India, New Delhi, 1982.
3. M.A. Mazidi, J.G. Mazidi, and R.D. McKinley, *The 8051 Microcontroller and Embedded Systems*, Dorling Kindersly (India), New Delhi, 2008.
4. www.aimglobal.org/technologies.rfid/what_is_rfid.htm
5. Communications of ACM, September 2005, Special Issue on RFID.
6. V. Rajaraman and T. Radhakrishnan, *Computer Organization and Architecture*, Prentice-Hall of India, New Delhi, 2007.

CHAPTER 12

1. C.G. Bell and A. Newell, *Computer Structures: Readings and Examples*, 2nd ed., McGraw-Hill, New York, 1980.
2. B. Randell (Ed.), *The Origins of Digital Computers: Selected Papers,* Springer, New York, 1973.
3. A.S. Tanenbaum and T.M. Austin, *Structured Computer Organization*, PHI Learning, Delhi, 2012.
4. V. Rajaraman, *Supercomputers,* Universities Press, Hyderabad, 1999.
5. V. Rajaraman, *Elements of Parallel Computers*, Prentice-Hall of India, New Delhi, 2006.

CHAPTER 13

1. D.E. Comer, *Internetworking with TCP/IP,* Vol. 1, Prentice-Hall of India, New Delhi, 1995.

2. J.F. Kurose and K.W. Ross, 5th ed., *Computer Networking*, Pearson Education Asia, New Delhi, 2012.
3. W. Stallings, *High Speed Networks and Internet*, Pearson Education Asia, New Delhi, 2002.
4. V. Rajaraman, *Introduction to Information Technology*, 2nd ed., PHI Learning, Delhi, 2013.

CHAPTER 14

1. T. Viswanathan, *Telecommunication Switching Systems and Networks,* Prentice-Hall of India, New Delhi, 1992.
2. A.S. Tanenbaum and D.J. Wetherall, *Computer Networks*, 5th ed., Pearson Education Asia, NewDelhi, 2011.
3. W. Stallings, *Wireless Communications and Networks*, 2nd ed., Pearson Education Asia, New Delhi, 2009.
4. W. Stallings, *Data and Computer Communications*, 8th ed., Pearson Education Asia, New Delhi, 2007.

CHAPTER 15

1. E.S. Angel, *Interactive Computer Graphics: A Top-down Approach with Open GL*, Addison-Wesley, Reading, MA, 2005.
2. J.A. Jacko (Eds.), *Human Computer Interaction Handbook Fundamentals, Evolving Technologies, and Emerging Applications*, 3rd ed., Taylor & Francis, Boca Raton, FL, 2012.
3. A. El Saddik, M. Orozco, M. Eid, and J. Cha, *Haptics Technologies: Bringing Touch to Multimedia*, Springer, Berlin, 2011.
4. B.Z. Allison, S. Dunne, R. Leeb, J.D.R. Millán, and A. Nijholt (Eds.), *Towards Practical Brain–Computer Interfaces—Bridging the Gap from Research to Real-World Applications*, Springer, Berlin, 2013.
5. E. Musk, *Neuralink: An Integrated Brain-Machine Interface Platform with Thousands of Channels*. J. Med. Internet Res. 2019.
6. F. Vainionpää, M. Kinnula, A. Kinnula, K. Kuutti, and S. Hosio, *HCI and Digital Twins—A Critical Look: A Literature Review*, *In*: Proceedings of the 25th International Academic Mindtrek Conference, ACM, New York, USA, 75–88, 2022.

CHAPTER 16

1. R. Steinmetz and K. Nehrstedt, *Multimedia: Computing, Communications and Applications*, Pearson Education Asia, New Delhi, 2001.
2. D.P. Mukherjee, *Fundamentals of Computer Graphics and Multimedia*, Prentice-Hall of India, New Delhi, 1999.
3. J.F.K. Burford (Ed.), *Multimedia Systems*, Pearson Education Asia, New Delhi, 2000.
4. V. Rajaraman, *Introduction to Information Technology,* 2nd ed., PHI Learning, Delhi, 2013.

CHAPTER 17

1. See www.wikipedia.org for definition, basics and references on peer to peer, grid and cloud computing.
2. F. Berman, G. Fox and A. Hey (Eds.), *Grid Computing: Making Global Infrastructure a Reality*, Wiley, New York, 2003.
3. R. Buyya and S. Venugopal, *A Gentle Introduction to Grid Computing and Technologies*, CSI Communications, Vol. 29, No. 1, July 2005, pp. 9–19.
4. V. Rajaraman, *Towards a Computing Utility*, Annals of Indian National Academy of Engineering, Vol. 3, December 2006, pp. 1–10.
5. K. Jamsa, *Cloud Computing,* Jones & Bartlett India, New Delhi, 2014.
6. V. Rajaraman, Cloud Computing, *Resonance*, Vol. 19, No. 3, March 2014, pp. 242–258.
7. U.A. Kini and S.M. Shetty, Peer-to-Peer Networking, *Resonance*, Vol. 6, No. 12, December 2001, pp. 69–79.

CHAPTER 18

1. S. Russell, and P. Norvig, *Artificial intelligence—A Modern Approach* by Prentice-Hall, Series in Artificial Intelligence, Englewood Cliffs, NJ, 2020.
2. W.S. McCulloch, and W. Pitts, *A Logical Calculus of the Ideas Immanent in Nervous Activity*, Bulletin of Mathematical Biophysics, 5: 115–133, 1943.
3. M. Minsky, and S. Papert, *Perceptrons: An Introduction to Computational Geometry*, The MIT Press, Cambridge MA, 1972.
4. D. Rumelhart, G. Hinton, and R. Williams, *Learning Representations by Back-propagating Errors*, Nature, 323: 533–536, 1986.
5. S. Hochreiter and J. Schmidhuber, *Long Short-Term Memory*, Neural Computation, 9(8): 1735–1780, 1997.
6. Y. LeCun, Y. Bengio, and G. Hinton, *Deep Learning*, Nature, 521: 436–444, 2015.
7. J. Schmidhuber, *Deep Learning in Neural Networks: An Overview,* Neural Networks, 61: 85–117, 2015.

Glossary

A

Accelerometer: A sensor that can detect the magnitude and the direction of acceleration of a device. It is used in hand-held displays to orient images in a desired direction.

Access time: Time required for retrieving a specified data from a computer's memory.

Accumulator: A register in a computer's processor where an arithmetic operation is performed and the result is stored.

Address: A unique identification of a location in memory.

Address bus: A set of wires used to transmit addresses. One wire is used for each bit in the address.

A/D converter: An electronic circuit which converts a continuously varying signal to a sequence of bit strings.

ADSL modem: *A*symmetric *D*igital *S*ubscriber *L*ine modem provides a broadband connection to an Internet service provider from the residences/offices by Public Switched Telephone Networks. Downloading data is faster than uploading data to the Internet when this modem is used.

Algorithm: A finite sequence of precise and unambiguous instructions to solve a problem.

ALU: *A*rithmetic *L*ogic *U*nit of a computer which is used to perform arithmetic and logic operations.

Amplitude modulation: A scheme in which the amplitude of a carrier signal (usually a high frequency signal) is varied depending on the amplitude of a modulating signal (normally a speech signal).

Analog channel: A communication path used for transmitting and receiving continuously varying electrical signals.

Android Operating System: An operating system designed using Linux kernel by Google for smart mobile phones and other mobile devices such as Tablets. It is freely available and updated regularly.

API: *A*pplication *P*rogrammer *I*nterface provide function calls, subroutines, or software interrupts to use lower-level functions of operating systems, device drivers, and other lower-level software programs.

Apps: Application programs developed mostly by users and made available to mobile computers/phones via the Internet. Many of them are free. The idea was popularized by Apple Computers.

Artificial Intelligence (AI): AI is a sub-field of computer science that attempts to create computer programs that mimic human intelligence to solve problems. These programs can reason, learn, and act autonomously.

Artificial General Intelligence (AGI): AGI is the ability to transfer knowledge, skills, and ideas learnt from one domain to an unrelated domain that humans can. AGI systems can solve novel problems that require intuition, creativity, and logical reasoning. AGI systems learn continuously and autonomously new problem-solving methods and adapt to changing environments, have autonomy, and perform tasks without human guidance or intervention.

Artificial Neural Network (ANN): ANN is a mathematical model of neurons interconnected to form a network that simulates the neurons in our brain. They can be trained to learn to recognize patterns by adjusting the weights of the interconnections using training data.

ASCII: *A*merican *S*tandard *C*ode for *I*nformation *I*nterchange. This code is a string of seven bits used to code characters.

Assembler: A program which translates an assembly language program to its machine language equivalent.

Assembly language: A low-level language for programming a computer in which mnemonics are used to code operations and alphanumeric symbols are used to represent addresses.

Asynchronous communication: Communication between units operating independently with their own independent clocks.

Audio signal processing: A number of operations such as low frequency enhancement, filtering noise, compressing, etc. performed on digitized audio signals.

B

Bandwidth: Defined for a communication channel. It is the range of frequencies over which signals are transmitted without attenuation.

Back Propagation Algorithm: A supervised training algorithm for multi-layered ANNs, where the difference between the output values and desired target values (called error) is propagated through the hidden layers and used to update weights.

Bar coding: Small vertical bars of varying thickness and spacing printed on packages, tags, etc., and read by optical readers and converted to a unique code stored in computers.

Base: The number of distinct symbols used to represent numbers in a system for enumeration.

Base address: An address to which the address in an instruction is added to find the absolute address in memory for storage or retrieval. Normally used for program relocation.

Baseband transmission: Transmission of data on a communication line without modulation.

Base register: A register which stores the base address.

Base station: A transceiver station at the centre of each hexagonal cell of a cellular mobile communication system. It sends/receives calls from mobile phones in its range. Base stations communicate with other Base stations via MTSO (Mobile Telecommunication Switching Office).

Batch operating system: A system program which facilitates the execution of programs belonging to several users organized as a batch without any manual intervention.

BCI (*B*rain *C*omputer *I*nterface): Brain Computer Interface (BCI), often called Mind-Machine Interface (MMI), or direct neural interface, or Brain-Machine Interface (BMI), assists people with disabilities or illnesses that impair their ability to interact with computers. These interfaces to computers are primarily focused on assisting, augmenting, or repairing human cognitive or sensory-motor functions by trapping into the electric signals in the brain.

Binary: One of two possibilities. A numerical system with base two.

Binary arithmetic: Performing addition, subtraction, multiplication, and division with binary operands.

Binary coded decimal: A representation of decimal digits which uses a unique string of 4 bits to represent each digit.

Binary operators: Operators, namely, AND, OR, NOT, whose operands are binary variables.

BIOS: *B*asic *I*nput *O*utput *S*ystem which resides in a ROM (Read Only Memory) of a PC (Personal Computer).

Bit: A binary digit which is either 0 or 1.

Bit Map (bmp) file: A representation of a picture by a sequence of pixels in which each pixel's value is converted to its binary equivalent.

Bluetooth: A standard for transmitting data wirelessly over a short distance, typically a metre.

BNF: Backus-Naur Form is a notation used to precisely define the syntax rules of a programming language.

Boolean algebra: Algebra to check the logical consistency of propositions which are either *true* or *false* and to simplify such propositions.

Boolean operators: AND, OR, NOT are Boolean operators defined for Boolean variables.

Boolean variable: A variable which can assume a value *true* or *false*.

Boolean functions: A function whose operands are Boolean variables and operators are Boolean operators. Boolean functions may be represented by truth tables and equivalent Boolean expressions.

Bootstrapping: A method by which a translator is written for a simple assembly language for a computer and this assembly language is used to write a more powerful assembly language which can, in turn, be used to translate a high-level language.

Bounded media: Physical media such as cables, wires, and optical fibre used to transmit signals.

Bus: A set of wires which carries a group of bits in parallel and has an associated control scheme.

Byte: A group of eight bits used to represent characters.

C

C: A high-level programming language whose features allow one to write efficient programs.

C++: An object-oriented version of C.

Cable modem: A modulator–demodulator (modem) used to connect a computer to a TV cable. TV cable can then be used as a broadband connection to an Internet service provider.

Cache line: A block of instructions/data fetched from the main memory for storage in a cache memory (usually of the order of 16–64 bytes).

Cache memory: A small high-speed memory which is used to temporarily store a portion of a program (instruction cache) or data (data cache) from the main memory. The processor retrieves instructions or data from the cache memory. Cache memory speeds up computation.

Canonical form of Boolean expressions: Standard forms used to represent Boolean expressions either as a sum of products or a product of sums.

Cartridge tape: Magnetic tape used to back up files from a hard disk. Standard used called LTO.

CAV (*Constant Angular Velocity*): Recording method used in magnetic hard disks. In this method, the angular velocity is the same for all tracks. Thus, tracks with smaller radius have a high linear velocity. The density of recording is higher in the innermost tracks.

CCD (*Charge Coupled Device*): An electronic device which converts light input to electric voltage whose value is proportional to the light intensity. Used in optical scanners and digital cameras.

CDROM (*Compact Disk Read Only Memory*): A shiny metal disk in which strings of bits are written along spiral tracks using a laser beam. The beam creates a tiny circular pit on the surface when a 1 is written and no pit is created for a 0. A 5.25 inch diameter CDROM stores around 650 MB. Once data is written on this disk, it cannot be erased. Versions of CDROM with read/write capabilities are called CDROM-R/W.

Cellular communication system: A wireless communication system used by mobile phones in which a geographical area is divided into hexagonal cells in such a way that the same wireless frequency can be used in different cells without interference, thereby conserving spectrum and catering to many subscribers.

Chatbot: An AI system that gives natural language answers to natural language questions.

Chat GPT: ChatGPT (developed by a company named OpenAI) is an AI system that answers a variety of questions, writes poetry, essays, computer programs, solves mathematical problems, and summarizes given text. Similar competing systems are Gemini by Google, LLaMa by Meta, Claude by Anthropic, Mistral from France, and DeepSeek from China.

Circuit switching: The method used to interconnect two computers (or more commonly telephones) in which the communication channel connecting them is exclusively allocated to them for the duration of interchange of data or speech signals.

CISC (*C*omplex *I*nstruction *S*et *C*omputer): A processor which has variable length instructions, several addressing modes, and a large number of instructions.

CLI (*C*ommand *L*ine *I*nterface): A line consisting of text, digits, and other key strokes to command a computer to perform desired operations.

Client–server computing: A method of using computers in which the required applications are grouped as services stored in servers. Client computers request services and servers provide them. This method is particularly suited for applications implemented on distributed computers.

Cloud computing: A method of computing in which a customer uses a set of services hosted by service providers on the Internet. Services include Infrastructure (computing, disk space) as a Service (IaaS), Software applications as a Service (SaaS), and integrated applications development tools—*P*latform as a *S*ervice (PaaS). Payment is based on services used.

Cloud computing types: Types are: (i) public cloud, which is available to any customer and the infrastructure is multi-tenanted, (ii) private cloud, which is operated for a single organization, and (iii) hybrid cloud, which is a combination of both.

Cloud storage: It is a storage service provided by a cloud computer operator on-demand on the Internet. Payment is based on the amount of storage reserved for a customer.

Coaxial Cable: Coaxial cables consist of a central copper wire surrounded by a Teflon or PVC insulation, over which a sleeve of copper mesh or extruded aluminum is placed. The metal sleeve is covered by an outer shield of thick PVC material. The signal is carried by the inner copper wire. The signal is electrically shielded by the outer metal sleeve. Coaxial cables have a very high bandwidth. A 3/8 in. cable can carry digital signals at very high rates of 500 Mbps.

COBOL: (*Co*mmon *B*usiness *O*riented *L*anguage). A high-level language used for business data processing.

Communication channel: A medium through which (electrical) signals are transmitted and received.

Communication protocol: Common agreed rules followed to interconnect and communicate between computers.

Compiler: A program which translates a high-level language such as C to instructions a computer can execute, called an object code. Normally one high level language instruction is translated to several machine instructions. The object code is executed after all the instructions of a high-level language are translated.

Computer: This is a machine which executes a program stored in its memory to process data fed to it and produces the required results.

Computer graphics: An application of computers concerned with the generation, manipulation and display of pictures with the aid of a computer. It mainly involves creating three dimensional models that rendered as images on the screen using specialized graphics hardware called Graphics Processing Unit (GPU).

Computer network: A group of geographically distributed computers which are interconnected using communication lines in such a way that any computer in the group may be accessed or used from any other computer in the group.

Computer Vision: Computer vision is concerned with applying a computer to interpret images it involves acquiring images, videos, preprocessing them, and extracting features such as edges, textures, shapes, patterns, locating specified objects such as faces, and classifying them based on specified criteria.

Connectionist AI: A type of AI that attempts to solve problems by simulating the structure of the human brain which is a complex interconnection of neurons. It uses mathematical models of neurons and several complex interconnected networks of layers of neurons called Artificial Neural Networks (ANN).

Control bus: A set of wires used to transmit signals to control the operation of various units of a computer.

Control program: A set of system programs to perform I/O operations, dumping memory on a printer to aid in error detection, and to supervise exchange of parameters between programs.

Convolutional Neural Network (CNN): A type of ANN which has three types of layers of neurons besides the input and output layers. CNNs are used primarily in applications related to images and videos.

CPU: *C*entral *P*rocessing *U*nit of a computer. It consists of circuits to perform arithmetic and logic and also has circuits to control and coordinate the functioning of the memory and I/O units of a computer (also known as Processor).

Cross-translator: A program to translate a source code of a computer *X* to an object code of another computer *Y*.

CSMA/CA: Carrier Sense Multiple Access/Collision Avoidance) is a network protocol used primarily in wireless networks, like Wi-Fi (IEEE 802.11), to manage how devices share the communication medium.

CSMA/CD: *C*arrier *S*ense *M*ultiple *A*ccess with *C*ollision *D*etection is a method used to access a shared communication medium by computers. It was a protocol used by a cable-connected Ethernet.

Cycle stealing: The method used to transfer data from the I/O units to the memory of a computer by suspending the memory to CPU data transfer for one memory cycle.

Cycle time: The time interval between the instant at which a read/write command is given to a memory and the instant when the next such instruction can be issued to the memory (also known as memory cycle time).

D

Data bus: A set of wires used to transmit data between units of a computer.

Data entry unit: A system with a keyboard to enter data and a storage medium to store the entered data.

Demand paging: A procedure used to transfer from the disk memory of a computer to the main memory a portion of a program (a page) to be executed.

De Morgan's theorem: A theorem in Boolean algebra which states how to complement a Boolean expression.

Destructive readout: A method of reading data from a memory in which the data stored in the memory cell is destroyed when read.

Device driver: A program supplied by device manufacturers to read/write data from the device to a computer's memory. The program is dependent on the operating system being used by the computer.

Digital to Analog (D/A) Converter: An electronic circuit which converts a sequence of bits to a continuously varying signal.

Digital channel: A communication medium through which data in binary (digital) form is transmitted.

Digital camera: A camera in which an array of charge coupled devices (one per pixel) is used instead of a film. CCD array senses light reflected by a scene, which is converted to electrical voltages. These voltages are converted to digits and stored in a memory in the camera.

Direct address: The address of an operand in main memory specified in an instruction.

Disk memory: A secondary or peripheral memory in which data is stored as magnetized spots on the surface of disks coated with the magnetic material.

Display unit: It is also called a monitor and consists of a video screen; it is used to display results obtained from a computer.

Distributed computers: Computers interconnected by a fast communication network.

DMA (*D*irect *M*emory *A*ccess): This is a method in which data from I/O devices to memory and vice versa is transmitted bypassing the central processing unit of a computer.

Dot matrix printer: A printer whose head consists of an array of pins which strike a black ribbon to print characters on paper.

DRAM (*D*ynamic *R*andom *A*ccess *M*emory): A random-access memory in which each storage cell is a capacitor. The memory is volatile and requires periodic refreshing.

DSP (*D*igital *S*ignal *P*rocessor): A microprocessor which is optimized to process real-time audio and video signals.

Duality principle: A principle which states that if a theorem in Boolean algebra is proved, a dual theorem in which 0s and 1s are interchanged and ANDs and ORs are interchanged is also true.

Duplex communication: A method of communication in which data can be sent in both directions, namely, sender to receiver and vice versa.

E

EEPROM: Electrically Erasable Programmable Read Only Memory in which data may be erased and written using electrical signals.

Effective address: The address in main memory, calculated by the CPU, which is used to retrieve data stored there.

E-ink display: A display which uses electrically charged black and white microcapsules which are organized by transparent electrodes to display characters. It is used by e-book readers.

Electronic mail: It is an application in which any user with an Internet connection can send/receive mail on his computer to/from any person in the world who has an electronic mail address.

Enterprise Grid: It is an interconnected computers and databases spread across several branches of an enterprise.

EPROM (*E*rasable *P*rogrammable *R*ead *O*nly *M*emory): A semiconductor memory in which data is semi-permanently stored. The data may be erased and new data written in it.

Error detecting codes: Binary codes of characters with added bits to enable detection of one or more errors when the data is read after it is transmitted on a communication medium.

Ethernet: A standard (IEEE 802) for local area network connection in which computers are connected using a switch. Data is broken into data packets of length between 74 and 1526 bytes and sent between computers. Originally Ethernet used a shared bus to connect computers in a Local Area Network.

Executive program: A system program used to monitor I/O devices and to allocate computer resources to user programs.

Expert System: It is a computer program that mimics the decision-making ability of human experts in specific domains. It has a knowledge base containing domain-specific facts and rules, an inference engine that applies logical reasoning to the knowledge base to reach a conclusion or deduce new facts, a user interface for users to query the system, and an explanation engine through which a user can ask how the expert system arrived at an answer to the question.

External interrupt: Interrupts generated from outside the CPU such as from I/O units.

Extranet: A network connection using the Internet protocol between cooperating member organizations.

F

FHSS (*F*requency *H*opping *S*pread *S*pectrum): A scheme in which a carrier frequency is spread by a pseudo random bit sequence. Used in Bluetooth wireless communication.

Fibre Optic Cable: A plastic or glass fibre cable that provide high-quality transmission of signals at very high rates, up to 1 Gbps.

Fifth generation computers: Computer designs which emerged in the late 1980s and were expected to be radically different from stored program computers to solve artificial intelligence problems. The attempts did not succeed commercially but led to the development of parallel computers, multi-core processors, and object-oriented languages.

Fifth generation mobile communication: See Mobile Communication 5 G.

File: A collection of data relating to objects such as students, documents, and programs. A file is identified by a file name.

Firewall: Software installed in a computer at the entry point of an organization's network to inspect data packets arriving/exiting the network and filter out suspicious/unauthorized packets.

First generation computers: Computers built between 1949 and 1955 which used vacuum tubes. Programming was in assembly language.

Flash memory: A non-volatile electronic memory which has high capacity (up to 1 TB) and is used as removable storage in digital cameras and in computers. These are also called memory sticks, pen drives, or memory disks.

Flat panel displays: Computer displays whose thickness is around 0.5–3 cm. They use liquid crystal or light emitting diode technology to display text and images.

Flatbed scanner: See scanner.

Flip-flop: An electronic circuit which can be placed in one out of two stable states. Each state may be used to represent a binary digit.

Floating point number: A number representation in which real numbers are expressed as a mantissa and an exponent. The mantissa is less than one with a non-zero leading digit. The exponent is a positive or negative integer. The mantissa is multiplied by the base of the number raised to a power equal to the exponent. For example, 44.86 in floating point representation is $0.4486E2 = 0.4486 \times 10^2$. Binary floating point numbers use binary mantissa with 1 as a leading bit and binary bit string as exponent.

Floating point arithmetic: Addition, subtraction, multiplication, and division of numbers represented using floating point representation.

Flow chart: A pictorial representation of a computational procedure. The symbols used in the picture are standardized by the ISO.

Fortran: *For*mula *Tran*slation; a high-level programming language used mostly for scientific and engineering applications. Continuously updated with new features. The latest Fortran standard in 2025 is Fortran 2023.

Fourth generation computers: Computers built between 1975 and 2004. They use large-scale integrated circuits, semiconductor memories, well-designed high-level languages and versatile operating systems.

Fourth generation mobile communication: See mobile communication 4G.

Frequency division multiplexing: A method in which a communication channel is shared by a number of independent messages. Each message is allocated a distinct range of frequencies.

FSK (*F*requency *S*hift *K*eying): A method of transforming digital signals 1 and 0 to two sine waves of different frequencies. This is done to transmit digital signals via an analog channel.

FTP (*F*ile *T*ransfer *P*rotocol): Rules used in a computer network to copy files from a remote computer to a requestor's computer.

Full adder: An adder which adds three binary digits and outputs a result bit and a carry bit.

Full duplex communication: A method of using a communication channel in which signals can be transmitted between a source and a destination in both directions simultaneously.

Functional Language (also known as Applicative language): A language in which a problem is solved by applying a sequence of functions to an input state to transform it to an output state.

G

Gesture recognition: Recognition by a computer of bodily motions used to express a thought or emotion.

Generative AI: It creates new content such as text, images, audio, and video by learning patterns and structures from a large corpus of data available in computer-readable form. The text generation systems use large language models (LLM). They are trained on billions of sentences from web content such as Wikipedia, computer-readable books, and articles. After a learning period, they can generate text by predicting the next word based on context. They use a Transformer Neural Network and use the so-called self-attention mechanism for context awareness.

Generational Adversarial Networks (GAN): An ANN that consists of a pair of neural networks called the generator and the discriminator. Used to synthesize realistic speech, audio, images, and videos.

GIF (*G*raphical *I*nterchange *F*ormat): A standard format for image files used to store and exchange images.

Giga: A word used to represent 1024 × 1024 × 1024 = $2^{30} \approx 10^9$. Abbreviated form G.

Globus Toolkit: A set of standardized software tools and components to design grids.

GPU (*G*raphics *P*rocessing *U*nit): A specialized processor that supports the graphics rendering pipeline in hardware. It optimizes graphics operations including projections, clipping, texture mapping and shading. The unit works along with the CPU of a computer.

GPGPU (General Purpose GPU): A GPU enhanced with huge extra memory and hundreds of special-purpose processors working in parallel to perform, in addition to graphics, numeric-intensive processing. They are used in High Performance Computers and to train ANNs.

GUI (*G*raphical *U*ser *I*nterface): An interface that enables a user to access programs on a computer through image objects called icons that are linked to the programs. A commonly used GUI consists of *W*indows, *I*con, *M*ouse, and *P*ointing device (WIMP).

Grid computing: An infrastructure that enables the integrated, collaborative use of high- end computers, networks, databases, and scientific instruments owned and managed by multiple cooperating organizations.

H

Half adder: An adder which adds two bits and gives the result bit and the overflow bit (if any).

Half duplex channel: A communication channel in which signals may be transmitted at a time in only one direction from a source to a destination or vice versa.

Haptic devices: Devices which make users detect mechanical forces, motion and vibration usually applied to the fingers of their hands.

Harvard architecture: A computer architecture in which there are separate memories to store instructions and data.

Head mounted display: A display in the form of a helmet that houses two small screens that are magnified by lenses for viewing near the eyes. It is used in virtual reality systems to create an immersive visual experience.

Hexadecimal system: A number system using 16 as base. The 16 symbols in this system are 0 to 9 and A, B, C, D, E, F.

High-level language: A high-level computer language is a programming language designed to be easy for humans to read, write, and understand. It is machine independent. A translator converts to an appropriate computer executable code. Some popular high-level languages are: Fortran, C, C++, and Python.

HTML (*H*ypertext *M*arkup *L*anguage): A language used to describe the format of web pages and hypertext links to other web pages in the World Wide Web.

Hub: An electronic switching circuit to which unshielded twisted pair wires from the NICs of computers are connected. It receives signals, reshapes and broadcasts them to all computers connected to it.

Hypertext: A document in which keywords are marked and pointers used to link it to other documents which have the same keywords.

I

IC (*I*ntegrated *C*ircuit): An electronic circuit fabricated on a single chip of silicon.

Image acquisition: Inputting both monochrome and colour pictures, converting them to digital form and storing them in computers.

Immediate addressing: An instruction in which the address part of an instruction is the operand and not the address of the operand.

Index register: A register in a CPU whose contents are added to the operand address specified in an instruction to find an effective address in memory from where the operand will be fetched. Normally used to perform operations on vectors.

Indirect address: An instruction in which the address part of an instruction gives the address where the address of the operand would be found.

Infrared communication: Communication using light signals in the infrared region. Used in both optical fibre and line of sight wireless communication.

Inkjet printer: A non-contact printer whose print head has nozzles through which ink is squirted on paper to print characters or draw pictures.

Input unit: A part of a computer used to feed programs and data.

Instruction: A command or order given to a computer. It normally consists of a code to indicate the operation to be performed and the address(es) in memory where the operand(s) would be found.

Instruction register: A register in the CPU which is used to store an instruction.

Interface logic: Electronic circuit used to interconnect I/O devices to a computer's CPU or memory.

Internal interrupt: Interrupt generated by an event in the CPU, such as division by 0 or wrong instruction code. It is also known as **trap**.

Internet: A worldwide network of computers connected using the TCP/IP protocol. Millions of individual computer networks are interconnected to form the Internet. Internet hosts the World Wide Web, provides electronic mail, telnet (remote login to computer), file transfer services and access to enormous amount of information and facilities to search for information.

Inter-operability: Ability of diverse computers from different vendors with different operating systems to cooperate in solving computational problems.

Interpreter: A translator which translates a statement of a high-level language to machine language and immediately executes it.

Interrupt service routine: A computer program stored in the computer which is invoked when an interrupt is sensed by a CPU. This program is usually used to transfer data from or to I/O devices to or from the main memory.

Interrupt signal: A signal generated by hardware or software and sent to the CPU indicating that an event requiring immediate attention has occurred such as when data from an input device is ready to be read or by an internal event such as an attempt to divide by 0.

Intranet: A computer network within an organization which uses the TCP/IP protocol used by the Internet and provides the same services as the Internet.

I/O controller: A unit which controls the operation of I/O units and facilitates orderly transfer of data between I/O units and the main memory of a computer.

I/O units: Input/output units of a computer.

IP address: Address assigned to each device (computer, smartphone, printer) connected to the Internet. In IPv4 protocol, 4 bytes long and is expressed in a dotted decimal format, for example, 144.16.79.48, where each number between dots is a decimal equivalent of a byte. It is being upgraded in IPv6 to 128-bit address.

IP packet/datagram: A data packet used by the Internet protocol in which data to be sent from one computer to another is broken into chunks of 1 KB or less and a prefix appended with the source and destination addresses, serial number of the data chunk, and control bits.

IPv4: Current protocol used by the Internet.

IPv6: Proposed Internet protocol. It will support 128-bit IP address, multimedia communication, and have built-in security.

ISA bus: *I*ndustry *S*tandard *A*rchitecture bus used to connect slow peripherals to a PC's CPU/Memory.

ISO protocol: A communication protocol to interconnect geographically dispersed computers. This protocol has been standardized by the International Standards Organization.

ISP (*I*nternet *S*ervice *P*rovider): An organization which provides facilities to its customers to connect to the Internet.

ISCII (*I*ndian *S*cript *C*ode for *I*nformation *I*nterchange): An 8-bit common code standardized by the Bureau of Indian Standards to represent characters of all Indian languages.

J

Java: An object-oriented language which is easily portable. It is normally used to program computers connected to the Internet.

JavaScript: It is a scripting language that is extensively used mainly for Web development. It was introduced in 1995 by Netscape, a browser developer. It has evolved over the years and currently over 90% of all websites use it.

Job control language: A special purpose language used by a computer's operating system to specify the resource requirements of programs fed to the computer. It is primarily used in batch operating systems.

JPEG file (jpg): A file format standardized by the Joint Photographic Experts Group to compress bit mapped image files. The file standard allows trade-off of compression ratio with fidelity of compressed images.

K

Kernel: A part of an operating system of a computer which permanently resides in the main memory and accesses other parts of the OS from the disk as needed.

Keyboard: An input used to manually enter data to a computer's memory.

Kilo: Used to represent 1024 = 2^{10} in computers. Abbreviated form K. As K is also used to represent 1000, some vendors use Ki to represent 2^{10} = 1024.

L

L1 cache: A cache memory which is fabricated as a part of a CPU chip. The access time is 3 to 4 CPU cycles. There are two L1 caches; a data cache and an instruction cache.

L2 cache: An on-chip memory slower than L1 cache. In recent microprocessors it is on-chip. There are two L2 caches; a data cache and an instruction cache.

L3 cache: A cache memory outside the CPU chip. It is usually an SRAM about 1000 times larger than a L2 cache memory. There are two L3 caches; a data cache and an instruction cache.

LAN: *L*ocal *A*rea *N*etwork is an interconnection (via a fast communication link) of many computers located within 10 km radius.

Laptop computers: A portable computer which weighs around 2 kg and runs all PC applications. It uses a liquid crystal display and a keyboard.

LEO: Low Earth Orbiting Satellite constellation orbiting between 200 Km and 2000 Km from the earth. They relay data received by them. Used for Internet communication.

Large Language Model (LLM): LLMs are advanced AI systems that utilize deep learning to understand and generate human-like text. They are trained using massive texts such as Wikipedia which enables them to recognize patterns and create coherent and contextually relevant responses.

Laser printer: A printer which uses a laser beam to trace the output data to be printed on a photoconductive drum which attracts a toner. The toner is transferred to paper that is in contact with the drum and prints the output data.

Latency time: The time taken for a record stored in a disk track (which is to be read) to come under the read/write head positioned over that track. Maximum latency time equals the time taken by a disk to rotate once. In general latency time is the delay between a user's action and the corresponding response. In networking, it specifically refers to the time it takes for data to travel from one point to another.

Layer 2 switch: A device used in LANs to interconnect computers. It supports multiple independent communications between pairs of computers connected to it. It works in the data link layer of the OSI protocol.

Layer 3 switch: A device used to connect independent subnetworks in an organization which intelligently localizes traffic within subnetworks and routes traffic between subnetworks.

LEX: A tool used to perform lexical analysis of a programming language.

Lexical rules: Rules to specify syntactic elements or words of a programming language.

Line matrix printers: A printer with print head consisting of pins which are moved electromechanically to strike a ribbon (usually black) placed between the print head and the paper. In line matrix printers, a comb of hammers prints a portion of pixels of a line by moving the comb back and forth slightly until all the pixels in a line are printed.

Linker: It is a system program which processes and combines a set of independently created object modules to produce a ready-to-execute object program.

Linux: A version of Unix Operating System whose source code is maintained by voluntary efforts and is available on the Internet free of cost.

LISP: A *List Processing* language. This high-level language is used to program applications in Artificial Intelligence such as theorem proving, game playing, etc.

Loader: It is a system program which accepts a linked object program produced by a linker and loads it in the memory ready for execution.

Logic circuit: An electronic circuit to realize Boolean expressions. It uses AND, OR, and NOT gates.

Long Short-term Memory Neural Network (LSTM): An ANN that incorporates memory cells in the hidden layers which capture long-term dependencies. LSTMs are used in stock market prediction, weather forecasting, and time series analysis.

LSI: A *Large-Scale Integrated* circuit. An electronic circuit with between 1000 and 10,000 logic gates fabricated on a silicon chip.

M

MAC address: A MAC (Media Access Control) address is a unique hardware identifier assigned to a network interface controller (NIC). It is used for communication within a local network, ensuring data packets are delivered to the correct device.

Machine independent language: A high-level programming language which is designed to be used with a variety of computers.

Machine language: A language which uses numeric codes to represent operations and numeric addresses of operands. Each model of a computer has a unique machine language.

Machine Learning: It is the capability of computers to learn how to solve problems given examples as input data. When the data set consists of only inputs it is called unsupervised learning and when the data set has both inputs and corresponding outputs it is supervised learning.

Machine readable form: Data which can be read by input devices connected to a computer.

Magnetic surface recording: Recording on a surface on which data is recorded as magnetic dipoles in one of two directions, one of them representing a 0 and the other a 1. Used by magnetic disks and magnetic tapes.

Magnetic tape: See cartridge tape.

Magneto-resistive head: Head used to read data recorded on magnetic surfaces. Data is read based on the change of resistance of the head when a magnetic dipole is taken near it.

Mainframe computers: Large computers used by organizations such as banks. They process hundreds of millions of transactions per second and have hundreds of terabytes of disks and very fast data transfer rate between the disks and the main memory. They can be accessed simultaneously by hundreds of terminals.

Markup language: Languages used to describe contents and structure of documents. An open standard is Standard Generalized Markup Language (SGML) from which Hypertext Markup Language (HTML) and Extensible Markup Language (XML) are derived.

MATHEMATICA: A problem-oriented language used to simplify complex algebraic expression symbolically. Also used for indefinite integration.

MATLAB: A problem-oriented language used by scientists and engineers to solve algebraic and differential equations.

MDS: A Microcomputer Development System intended to facilitate program development for a microcomputer.

Mega: Used to represent $1024 \times 1024 = 2^{20} \cong 10^6$. Abbreviated form M.

Memory: An organized collection of cells used to store data and programs in a computer.
Memory cell: A circuit which can store data. A binary memory cell stores a 0 or a 1.

Message Passing Parallel Computers: A collection of interconnected computers that cooperatively solve a problem by interchanging messages among processes running in them using send and receive primitive operations. A standard known as MPI (Message Passing Interface) is used to exchange messages.

Message switching: A method whereby messages to be transmitted between computers are all sent to a central computer, which gathers them and routes them to the appropriate destination(s).

MICR (*M*agnetic *I*nk *C*haracter *R*ecognition): Characters are printed with magnetic ink using special fonts (usually in cheques) which can be read and recognized by specially designed readers.

Microcomputer: A computer which is fabricated using a microprocessor and other integrated circuits, namely, a ROM, RAM, and I/O interface chips.

Microcontroller: An inexpensive special purpose microprocessor which is optimized for control applications. It has an in-built ROM to store control programs and also has built-in I/O controller.

Microprocessor: An integrated circuit which contains the CPU of a computer.

Microwave: Electromagnetic signals in the range 0.5–40 GHz transmitted using waveguides.

MIMO: MIMO (Multiple-Input Multiple-Output) is a wireless technology that uses multiple antennas at both the transmitter and receiver to enhance data throughput and reliability. It exploits multipath propagation, where signals bounce off objects, to create multiple data streams, thereby increasing capacity.

MIDI devices: *M*usical *I*nstrument *D*igital *I*nterface designed to read electronic signals from music synthesizers/instruments and store them as binary files in a standardized format.

Mobile Communication - 4G LTE: 4G LTE mobile communication is a fully digital cellular communication system. Data is communicated using the Internet Protocol. It uses the Orthogonal Frequency Division Multiplexing in the downlink and Single-Carrier Frequency Division Multiple Access (SC-FDMA) in the uplink. It is capable of data download speed of up to 150 Mbps and upload speed up to 40 Mbps. Its latency is between 50 and 100 ms. It uses the 600MHz to 2.6 GHz band.

Mobile Communication – 5G: It is a fully digital cellular communication system using the Internet Protocol. It uses the Orthogonal Frequency Division Multi Access for modulation. It uses advanced MIMO antennas. In 5G systems using the midband (around 3 GHz) the download speed is between 700 Mbps and 1 Gbps and the upload speed is between 100 Mbps and 300 Mbps. The latency is between 5ms to 20 ms.

Modem: *Mo*dulator–*dem*odulator units used to convert digital signals (to be communicated over an analog channel such as a telephone line) to sine waves at the sending end and convert the received sine waves back to digital signals at the receiving end.

Moore's law: A prediction that the number of transistors in a microprocessor will double every 24 months.

MOSFET (*M*etal *O*xide *S*ilicon *F*ield *E*ffect *T*ransistor): It's a type of transistor that uses an electric field to control the flow of current between the "source" and "drain" terminals. The control is achieved by applying a voltage to the "gate" terminal, which is insulated from the channel by a thin layer of oxide. It has several applications including use as an electronic switch and as a component of a memory.

Mouse: It is a small hand-held device with one or more buttons. Currently uses light emitting diodes to illuminate a flat surface on which it is moved. An optical sensor senses the relative motion of the mouse as it moves on a flat surface. This motion is processed by a special purpose integrated circuit chip which translates it to a movement of a pointer on the screen of the display unit of a computer.

MP3: A compression standard for digitized audio files. This standard is used by all music publishers and is an abbreviation of Motion Picture Experts Group—Version 2—Layer 3 standard.

MPEG compression: A compression standard for compressing digitized video streams standardized by *M*otion *P*icture *E*xperts *G*roup (MPEG). MPEG-2 is used for high quality video such as motion pictures. MPEG-4 is used for lower quality video and has a higher compression ratio.

MS-DOS: *M*icrosoft *D*isk *O*perating *S*ystem released in the 1980s by Microsoft Corporation for IBM compatible Personal Computers.

MSI: *M*edium *S*cale *I*ntegrated circuit. A circuit with over 12 and less than 100 logic gates fabricated on a single silicon chip.

MTSO: *M*obile *T*elecommunication *S*witching *O*ffice which establishes connection between fixed phones and mobile phones and between mobile phones using base stations of a mobile cellular network.

Multiplexing: A method in which a communication channel is shared by a number of messages or signals.

Multiprogramming operating system: An operating system in which a number of programs are kept in the main memory. These programs are executed using the CPU and I/O resources in such a way that all the units of the computer are kept simultaneously active.

Multitasking: Executing multiple programs residing in the main memory of a PC. Each task is allocated a time slice to use the CPU. All the tasks seem to be executing concurrently.

Multicore microcomputers: Microcomputers in which several CPUs are embedded and share an on-chip cache memory. These CPUs work in parallel. Quad core has four CPUs. The number of cores is increasing each year.

N

NAND gate: A gate which realizes a NOT of AND operation. It is a universal gate as any Boolean expression can be realized using only NAND gates.

Natural Language Processing (NLP): NLP is concerned with enabling a computer to understand, interpret, and generate human language. It focuses on algorithms that analyse both syntax and semantics of text data.

Network Interface Card (NIC): An electronic circuit used to connect a computer to a network. Its primary function is to enable the computer to communicate with other devices over a network, by converting digital data into network signals and vice versa.

Network topology: The structure of interconnection of nodes of a computer network.

Neuron: It is a nerve cell which is a fundamental unit of the nervous system. Neurons transmit electrical and chemical signals throughout the body. They are responsible for receiving sensory input, sending motor commands, and processing information within the brain and nervous system.

Neuron model: Neurons are modelled by a set of inputs $x_1, x_2, x_3, \ldots, x_n$, a set of arcs emanating from these inputs with weights $w_1, w_2, w_3, \ldots, w_n$, and a bias input b. The output of a neuron y is modelled by the equation: $y = b + \sum_{i=1}^{n} w_i x_i$. This output is fed to an activation function f. The neuron fires, in other words, its output is 1 if $f\left(b + \sum_{i=1}^{n} w_i x_i\right) > T$, a preset threshold, else it is 0.

Non-procedural language: Computer languages in which variables are treated as arguments of functions rather than as values stored in memory. Problems are solved by applying functions to transform variables.

NOR gate: A gate which realizes a NOT of OR operation. It is a universal gate as any Boolean expression can be realized using only NOR gates.

Normalized floating point number: A floating point number in which the most significant digit of the mantissa is non-zero.

Notebook computer: A Laptop Computer weighing less than 1 kilogram with touch screen interface.

O

Object: A programming model to represent a real-world object. All the necessary data structures and procedures needed to model an object are encapsulated in it. An object is invoked by sending a message to it requesting its services.

Object-Oriented Language: A programming language having facilities to model objects and methods to invoke objects.

Object program: The machine language program resulting from the translation of a program written in an assembly or a higher-level language.

OCR (*O*ptical *C*haracter *R*ecognition): Software used with scanners to convert scanned printed text (using standard fonts) to ASCII format.

OMR (*O*ptical *M*ark *R*eader): A reader which reads pre-printed forms in which areas are darkened manually.

On-line system: A computer system which has terminals connected to it and allows direct access to user files from terminals. The files are updated as soon as a transaction is completed.

Operating system: It is a set of system programs that control and coordinate the operations of a computer system with the goal of providing an intuitively simple, high-level abstraction of its hardware to a user hiding all unnecessary low-level details. It also allocates resources of a computer system to users efficiently when requested.

Operation code: A group of bits used to represent operations to be performed by a CPU.

Optical fibre: A glass fibre used to transmit electrical signals which are converted to light by light emitting diode. Light travels via the fibre using total internal reflection and is converted back to electrical signal.

Orthogonal Frequency Shift Multiplexing (OFDM): OFDM simultaneously transmits multiple data streams over closely spaced subcarriers. It significantly enhances data throughput and uses the radio spectrum efficiently. It also alleviates interference of transmitted data travelling along multiple paths from the transmitter to the receiver. It is used in 4G mobile communication and in WiFi.

OS command language: A set of commands to an operating system to specify the sequence of operations to be performed by it.

OSI: *O*pen *S*ystem *I*nterconnection is a seven-layer communication protocol standardized by the International Standards Organization for computer-to-computer communication.

Output unit: A unit of a computer used to print or display computed results.

Overflow: An overflow is said to occur if the result of an arithmetic operation is larger than the largest number which can be stored in a computer.

P

Packet switching: A procedure for communicating between computers in a network in which a block of data to be transmitted between two computers is divided into fixed size packets. Each packet is given source and destination addresses, bits for synchronization, error correction, and control bits and sent on the channel. The packets are routed along any available link using the source and destination addresses.

Page: A set of consecutive locations in memory treated as a block. Pages are moved from the main memory to a secondary memory and vice versa as commanded by the OS. A page replacement policy is used by an OS.

Parallel adder: An adder in which all the bits of the two operands to be added are added simultaneously.

Parallel computers: A set of computers connected together by a high-speed communication network or by a shared memory and programmed in such a way that they cooperate to solve a single large problem.

Parity bit: A bit appended to a string of bits to enable detection of errors.

PC (*P*ersonal *C*omputer): A small inexpensive self-contained desktop computer intended for an individual user. Most often used for email, word processing, searching for information, and small database applications.

PCB (*P*rinted *C*ircuit *B*oard): A phenol or glass epoxy board on which electronic components are mounted and interconnected by conducting copper strips bonded to the board.

PCIe Bus: *P*eripheral *C*omponent *I*nterconnect express bus standard used to connect high speed peripherals to PC's. PCIe uses a dedicated full-duplex serial connection (called a lane) to each peripheral that wants to communicate with the CPU. Up to 32 lanes, each with a bandwidth of up to 4 GB/s in each direction can be connected with the CPU.

Peer-to-peer computing: Computers connected to a network in which any computer can be treated as a client or server depending on application requirements. Mostly used for sharing files.

Perceptron: A single layer ANN built by Rosenblatt using electronic tubes that could recognize simple patterns such as squares and circles.

Peta: Used to represent $1024 \times 1024 \times 1024 \times 1024 \times 1024 = 2^{50}$, which is nearly a quadrillion (10^{15}).

Phase modulation: A method of modifying a sine wave carrier in which its phase is changed in accordance with the message to be transmitted. It is also called *P*hase *S*hift *K*eying (PSK).

Physical address space: Addresses in the main memory of a computer which are directly addressable and available for storing program and data.

Pixel: A picture element. It is used to represent one point in a picture or a scanned text.

Plotter: A device used to plot graphs.

Plug and play: Ability of a bus to allow a new I/O device to be connected to it while the computer is working. It is also called hot plug in.

Postulates of switching algebra: A set of equations in this algebra which are assumed to be true.

Precedence of Boolean operators: The order in which Boolean operators are to be carried out in a Boolean expression.

Printer: An output unit to print the results of computation. Line printers print one full line at a time. Character printers print one character at a time serially.

Publishing Language: Languages used to create documents ready to be printed. The simplest publishing languages are MSWord and LaTex. Professionals use InDesign by Adobe.

Problem oriented languages: High level languages designed to solve a narrow class of problems. The language does not describe the detailed algorithm to solve the problem but precisely states the problem and its data.

Procedure oriented languages: High level languages with the structure to describe in detail a general class of algorithms.

Process: A program in execution in a processor.

Processor: A unit of a computer which interprets instructions and executes them using arithmetic and logic circuits and controls the operation of all the other units of the computer (also known as CPU).

Program: An algorithm expressed using a precise notation (called a programming language) which can be executed by a computer.

Program controlled data transfer: A method of transferring data between I/O units and the main memory in which CPU participates.

Program counter: Also called an instruction counter. It is a register in the CPU which stores the address of the next instruction to be carried out by it.

Programming language: A precise notation (with precisely specified syntax and semantic rules) to express algorithms.

PSK (*P*hase *S*hift *K*eying): Another terminology used for phase modulation. In PSK, the phase of a sine wave carrier is 0 or *p* depending on whether a 0 or a 1 is to be transmitted. In NPSK, *N* values of phase of the carrier are used to represent *N* strings of bits (0, 0, …, 0) to (1, 1, …, 1).

PSTN (*P*ublic *S*witched *T*elephone *N*etwork): A network to connect telephones of customers which were designed primarily to carry audio signals. PSTNs are normally maintained in most countries by Government controlled companies.

Python: A popular scripting programming language. It is interpreted with easy to learn simple syntax rules.

Q

QAM (Quadrature Amplitude Modulation): Quadrature Amplitude Modulation (QAM) is a modulation technique that encodes data by varying both the amplitude and phase of a carrier wave. This allows for the transmission of more bits per symbol compared to simpler modulation methods, resulting in higher data rates.

QR Code: Two-dimensional codes (2D pattern of dark rectangles) called *Q*uick *R*esponse *C*ode used for storing URLs of websites and are read by digital cameras.

R

Radix: The number of distinct symbols used to represent numbers in a system for enumeration (same as base).

RAM (*R*andom *A*ccess *M*emory): A memory used as the main memory of a computer in which the time to retrieve stored data is independent of the address where it is stored.

Raster scan display: In this display, the image to be displayed is stored as a two-dimensional matrix of pixels. A pixel is usually several bits, and the number of bits depends on whether the display is a colour or monochrome display. The pixel storage is called a framebuffer or a refresh buffer. As scan lines move from left to right of a display device, the pixels are retrieved from the frame buffer and used to display the image.

Real-time system: A system in which a computer is used to control a physical system during its operation. The time taken to compute should match the needs of the physical system.

Record: A collection of related items of data treated as one unit.

Recursive definition: A definition which is defined in terms of itself. BNF definition of a high-level language, for example, is a recursive definition.

Recurrent Neural Networks (RNN): A type of ANN that incorporates feedback loops in the neurons in the hidden layers. The feedback endows memory to the neural network. RNNs are used in natural language processing tasks.

Register: A serially interconnected group of memory cells.

Remote login: The facility to login and use a remote computer in a network from a user's terminal.

Reinforcement Learning: In this method of machine learning an algorithm learns to fit a model by trial and error. The algorithm rewards a good prediction and penalizes a bad prediction.

Rendering pipeline: A sequence of operations performed by a GPU to display 3D objects on a 2D screen.

Response time: The time elapsed between entering a command and getting the result of computation (normally) on a terminal in a time-shared computer system.

RFID tag: *R*adio *F*requency *I*dentification tag. It is a device which is tagged to an item and stores its unique identification code. This code can be read remotely (up to a few metres) by a wireless reading device.

RISC (*R*educed *I*nstruction *S*et *C*omputer): A processor architecture which uses uniform instruction length, simple addressing mode, references to memory only to load and store operands, a small number of instructions to simplify control unit design, and pipelined instruction execution to enable at least one instruction to be executed in each clock cycle.

RLE: *R*un *L*ength *E*ncoding is a method used to compress data used often while storing data on a disk.

Robotics: It is the science of designing robots. It is an interdisciplinary field that integrates mechanical engineering to design robots' physical structure, electrical engineering to select appropriate sensors and actuators, automatic control systems to control their movement, computer vision to sense the environment in which they operate, natural language processing to understand and obey orders given to them, and AI to control their behaviour.

ROM (*R*ead *O*nly *M*emory): A memory in which data is permanently written. The data can be read quickly but not changed.

Router: It is a circuit which steers messages through multiple LANs and ensures that the least congested route is taken by messages.

RS 232-C standard: A standard defined by Electronics Industries Association (USA) which specifies the interface between computers, modems, and terminals.

S

Sampling theorem: A theorem which states that if an analog signal $s(t)$ has f_h as its highest frequency component, then a little more than $2f_h$ samples of $s(t)$ must be taken every second to preserve all the information contained in $s(t)$.

Satellite Communication: Communication using satellites. Satellites are used as microwave relay stations in the sky. Transponders on the satellite are used to receive, amplify, and retransmit signals sent from an earth station.

Scanner: A device to digitize and store monochrome and colour pictures drawn or printed (usually) on paper.

Scripting language: Language which has facilities to glue existing application programs called components to create more complex programs.

Second generation computers: Computers built during the period 1956–1965 which used transistors in CPU, magnetic core main memories, and high-level languages FORTRAN and COBOL for programming.

Seek time: The time required for a read/write head of a disk to move to the track where the record to be read or written is stored. The maximum seek time is the time taken for the head to move from the outermost track to the innermost track.

Semantic rules: Rules to assign meanings to valid statements of a language. These rules define what computations are to be carried out for each valid statement.

Serial access memory: A memory from which data is retrieved sequentially one bit after another.

Serial adder: An adder in which the bits of the operands are added one after another.

Servers: Computers which provide specific services such as high-speed computing, access to a database, or high-speed printing to several users called clients in a distributed computing system.

Shared Memory Parallel Computers: Several processors working cooperatively to solve problems sharing a common memory.

Shift register: A register in which the data stored may be shifted right or left or circularly.

Single-address computer: A computer in which a machine instruction specifies only one operand address.

Smart card: A plastic card in which a ROM or a microprocessor is embedded. The ROM is used to store a value which can be read by a smart card reader. The card with a processor can perform some elementary calculations and store the value in its ROM.

Smart Phone: A smartphone is a mobile phone with an operating system. It combines the functionality of a computer and a mobile phone. It allows users to access the internet, run a variety of applications, and perform various digital tasks in addition to traditional phone calls and text messages.

SMS/MMS: *S*hort *M*essaging *S*ervice (SMS) used to send messages up to 160 characters in Mobile communication. In *M*ultimedia *M*essaging *S*ervice (MMS) messages, pictures and sound can be sent.

Software: Programs for a computer.

Solid state disks (SSD): Emulation of magnetic disks using solid state flash memory. It has fast access time. Storage capacity of SSDs is increasing rapidly to several TBs.

Sound card: An electronic circuit mounted on a PCB which can be attached to a PC. It has A/D and D/A converters and a small processor to process audio files. Functionality of sound cards are now integrated in CPU mother boards.

Source program: A program written in a symbolic or high-level language.

Space division multiplex: It is a multiplexing technique that increases communication capacity by using distinct spatial paths or separations for signal transmission. This can be achieved through methods like multiple antennas (MIMO) in wireless systems or multi-core fibres in optical communications..

Speech input unit: A unit which will recognize spoken words and convert it to ASCII code (also called speech to text system). These units are classified as single word recognition or continuous speech recognition. A further classification is speaker dependent or speaker independent.

Speech output unit: A unit which will accept strings of ASCII characters and convert them into spoken words or sentences (also called text to speech system).

Speech Recognition: A system that understands spoken language. There are two types of systems; speaker dependent and speaker independent.

Spread spectrum: A modulation method in which the carrier frequency is spread over a large range using a pseudo-random bit string. It is used in secure wireless communication.

SRAM (*S*tatic *R*andom *A*ccess *M*emory): A RAM in which the storage cell is a flip-flop. It is normally faster than DRAM and does not require periodic memory refreshing.

SSI: *S*mall *S*cale *I*ntegrated circuit. An electronic circuit with less than 12 logic gates fabricated on a silicon chip.

Stack: A memory in which data that is stored last is on top and is retrieved first. It is also known as LIFO (last-in, first-out) store.

Stereo display unit: A unit which creates an illusion of seeing a 3D scene on a 2D screen.

Stereopsis: The ability to perceive depth due to binocular vision, that is, normal vision by two eyes separated by a distance which is processed by the brain to create depth perception.

Store and forward system: A system of computers and digital equipment in which messages or signals are sent to a central computer which receives and stores them and forwards them to the specified destinations.

Stored program computer: A computer where the program to solve a problem and the necessary data are stored in its memory.

Supercomputers: They are the fastest computers available at any given time and are normally used to solve problems requiring intensive numerical computation.

Superscalar processor: A processor in which multiple instructions are executed in one clock cycle.

Supervised Learning: It is a mode of machine learning in which a set of inputs and corresponding outputs are given. The computer discovers a model that best fits the data. This model can predict the outputs for a new set of inputs.

SVG (*S*calable *V*ector *G*raphics): A standard vector image format recommended by the World Wide Web consortium.

Switched Ethernet: Switched Ethernet is a form of Ethernet networking that uses network switches to connect devices within a local area network (LAN).

Symbol table: A table used by a programming language compiler to allocate memory to store variables.

Symbolic AI: In symbolic AI, knowledge is represented using logic symbols, word statements, and numbers. Inductive and deductive inference rules are formulated and applied to the knowledge base to solve problems.

Synchronous: The time elapsed between successive events is constant in synchronous systems. Events in such systems are controlled by a clock.

Syntax rules: Rules which specify how valid syntactic elements of a programming language can be combined into legal entities of the language.

System software: A set of programs written for a computer which provide the environment to facilitate the writing of application programs.

T

TCP/IP (*T*ransmission *C*ontrol *P*rotocol/*I*nternet *P*rotocol): A protocol used for reliable transfer of data packets between computers connected to the Internet.

Telnet: See Remote login.

Ten's complement: Ten's complement of a digit *x* is 10–*x*.

Tera: Used to represent $1024 \times 1024 \times 1024 \times 1024 = 2^{40} \approx 10^{12}$. Abbreviated form T.

Third generation computer: Computer built between 1966 and 1975 which used integrated circuits in CPU, high speed magnetic core main memories, and powerful high-level languages and saw the advent of time-sharing operating system.

Thin client: A terminal to access and execute programs on a server connected to a computer network. It has on its display the same graphical user interface as that in desktop PCs. It has no native OS.

Three D (3D) projection system: System which renders 3D images in space rather than on a screen.

Throughput: The number of jobs completed by a computer in a specified period.

TIFF (*T*agged *I*mage *F*ormat *F*ile): Called tiff files used to store images in a compressed form.

Time division multiplexing: A method of sharing a communication channel in which the channel is allocated to each signal successively for a specified period.

Time-sharing system: A computer system designed to allow many users to simultaneously use it.

Touch pad: A locator device used in laptop computers as a replacement for a mouse. It is operated by moving a finger over a capacitive coupled panel to point to a location on the screen.

Touch screen: A display screen with icons. When an icon is touched by a finger, capacitive coupling senses it and initiates an action by the computer attached to it.

Transformer Neural Network: An ANN that consists of several types of neural networks each fulfilling a specific function. They are used in text generation and summarization, question answering, drug discovery, music generation, and image and video processing. Transformer Networks capture long-range dependencies and can be pre-trained with a small corpus of data.

Transistor: A controlled electronic switch fabricated using a semiconductor.

Transponder: Device mounted on a communication satellite which receives, amplifies and retransmits signals received from earth stations.

Trap: An interrupt signal sent to the CPU when an event within a computer such as hardware error, arithmetic overflow, etc. occurs.

Truth table: A table which gives the input/output relationship of a logic circuit.

Turnaround time: The time elapsed between the submission of a program by a user to a computer and getting the results.

Two's complement: Used to represent negative binary numbers. 2's complement of a n-bit binary number x is $(2^n - x)$.

U

UART (*U*niversal *A*synchronous *R*eceiver *T*ransmitter): A device which converts serial data it receives to a parallel format and converts parallel data to serial form.

Underflow: Condition occurs when the result of an arithmetic operation is smaller than the smallest number which can be stored in the computer.

ULSI (Ultra Large Scale Integrated Circuit): An integrated circuit with over 100,000 logic gates fabricated on a single silicon chip.

Unibus: A single bus which interconnects I/O units, CPU, and memory of a computer.

Unicode: A 16-bit standard to represent characters.

UNIX: An operating system designed by AT&T Bell Telephone Laboratories (USA). It is a time-sharing OS written in C.

UNIX kernel: The innermost core of UNIX OS which performs various primitive operations requested by user processes.

UNIX pipe: A facility available in UNIX to feed a stream of bytes which are output of a program as input to another program.

UNIX shell: A command interpreter supported by the UNIX operating system.

Unsupervised Learning: In this method of machine learning an algorithm classifies or clusters input data into sets based on similarity.

URL (*U*niversal *R*esource *L*ocator): The unique address used to locate a web page.

Universal Serial Bus (USB): Universal Serial Bus (USB) is an industry-standard interface that enables communication and power transfer between computers and peripheral devices. Developed in the mid-1990s, USB aimed to simplify the connection of various devices to personal computers, replacing a multitude of specialized ports with a single, standardized connector.

UTF (*U*nicode *T*ransformation *F*ormat): Unicode format standardized by the World Wide Web consortium.

UTP (*U*nshielded *T*wisted *P*air): It is usually a pair of copper wires twisted together to provide noise-free communication between devices.

UVEPROM: *U*ltra *V*iolet *L*ight *E*rasable *P*rogrammable *R*ead *O*nly *M*emory.

V

Vector graphics: Composing an image by directly drawing line segments on a screen.

Venn diagram: A diagram used to illustrate the theorems of Boolean algebra.

Virtual machine: A computer as it is available to a user, which is not merely the hardware but also the hardware made usable by an appropriate operating system, high level languages, and application programs.

Virtual memory: A hierarchy of a fast main memory and a slower secondary memory (usually a disk) managed by a software system in such a way that a user has an effective addressable memory which equals the sum of the capacities of the two memories with an access time approaching that of the faster main memory.

VLSI (*V*ery *L*arge-*S*cale *I*ntegrated circuit): An electronic circuit with number of logic gates between 10,00 and 100,000 fabricated in a silicon chip.

Voice Interface Unit: Voice User Interface (VUI) enables interaction with computers using speech and audio.

Volatile memory: A memory in which the data stored is lost unless energy is continuously fed to it.

Volunteer Computing: Volunteer Computing is a system that allows a group of users to donate idle CPU cycles on their computers to solve a compute-intensive program cooperatively.

Voxel: Volume elements in 3D space, analogous to pixels in 2D space.

VPN (*V*irtual *P*rivate *N*etwork): A secure network operated using the Internet. Security is ensured by using a protocol called *I*nternet *P*rotocol *S*ecurity *A*rchitecture (IPSEC) which encrypts all transactions on the communication system connecting the organizations.

VSAT (*V*ery *S*mall *A*perture *T*erminal): An earth station which uses a very small diameter dish (1–2 m) antenna to transmit and receive digital data from satellites.

W

WAN: Wide Area Network is a network that connects computers in a geographically dispersed location.

Wave file: A file format used by Microsoft OS which converts analog signals to digital signals for storage in the computer.

Wi-Fi: Wireless broadband transceiver which provides to a customer reliable wireless connectivity to a backbone network and the Internet. There are 4 Wi-Fi standards. It uses CSMA/CA protocol for communication among devices sharing a common broadcast medium.

WiGig: A wireless standard (IEEE 802.11ad) used to communicate massive amounts of data between a computer and a device in line of sight (<10 m). It operates in the unlicenced 60 GHz band and transfers data at a maximum rate of 7 Gbps.

Windows Operating System: A series of multiuser, multitasking OS designed by Microsoft for PCs and servers. The latest is Windows 11 (2025).

Wireless LAN: A LAN in which a mobile computer such as a laptop computer can send or receive messages to or from a base station connected to it.

Word processor: A computer program which facilitates the creation of well-formatted, neat looking reports. Commonly used word processors are MS Word and LaTeX.

Working set: A table of page addresses recently allocated to the processor.

WWW (*W*orld *W*ide *W*eb): Information resource stored in a computer connected to the Internet which can be referenced by a hypertext link is called a web page. A collection of web pages is known as the World Wide Web.

Y

YACC: *Y*et *A*nother *C*ompiler *C*ompiler is a programming tool which generates the parser for a high-level language when the rules of syntax of the language are given.

Index